F L I G H T

V O L U M E   T W O

Ⓥ

Villard • New York

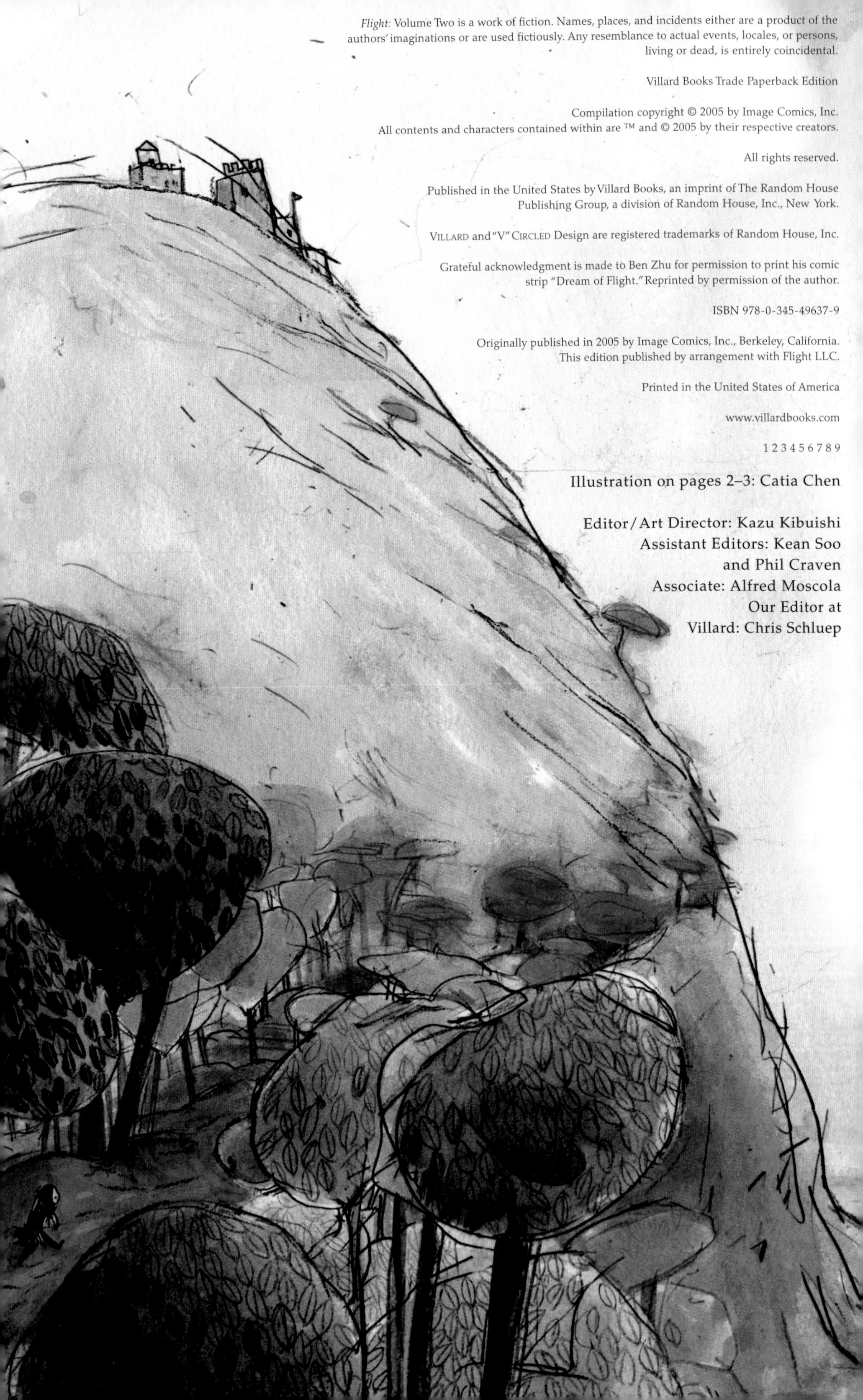

Villard Books Trade Paperback Edition

Published in the United States by Villard Books, an imprint of The Random House Publishing Group, a division of Random House, Inc., New York.

VILLARD and "V" CIRCLED Design are registered trademarks of Random House, Inc.

Grateful acknowledgment is made to Ben Zhu for permission to print his comic strip "Dream of Flight." Reprinted by permission of the author.

ISBN 978-0-345-49637-9

Originally published in 2005 by Image Comics, Inc., Berkeley, California.
This edition published by arrangement with Flight LLC.

Printed in the United States of America

www.villardbooks.com

1 2 3 4 5 6 7 8 9

Illustration on pages 2–3: Catia Chen

Editor / Art Director: Kazu Kibuishi
Assistant Editors: Kean Soo
and Phil Craven
Associate: Alfred Moscola
Our Editor at
Villard: Chris Schluep

CONTENTS

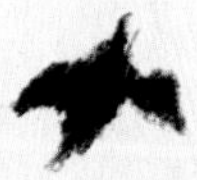

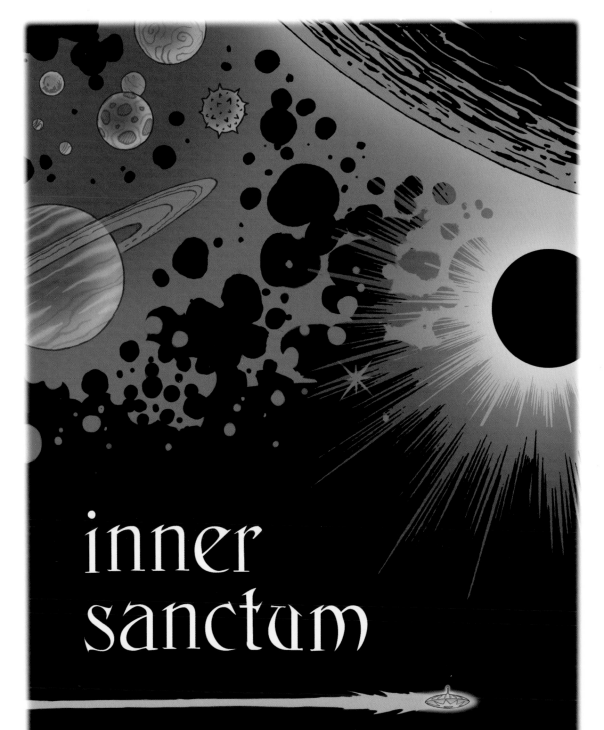

inner
sanctum

Michel Gagné

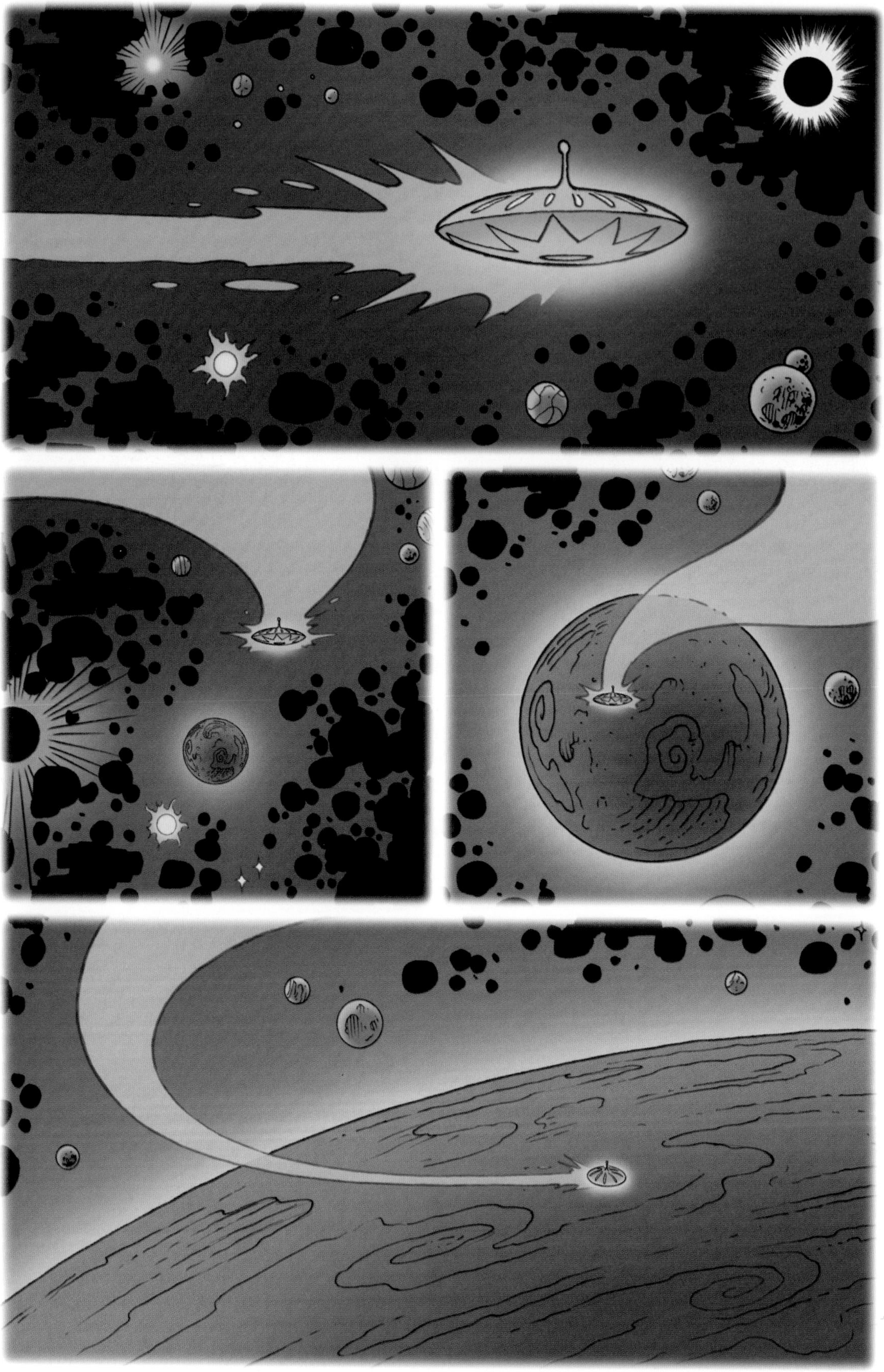

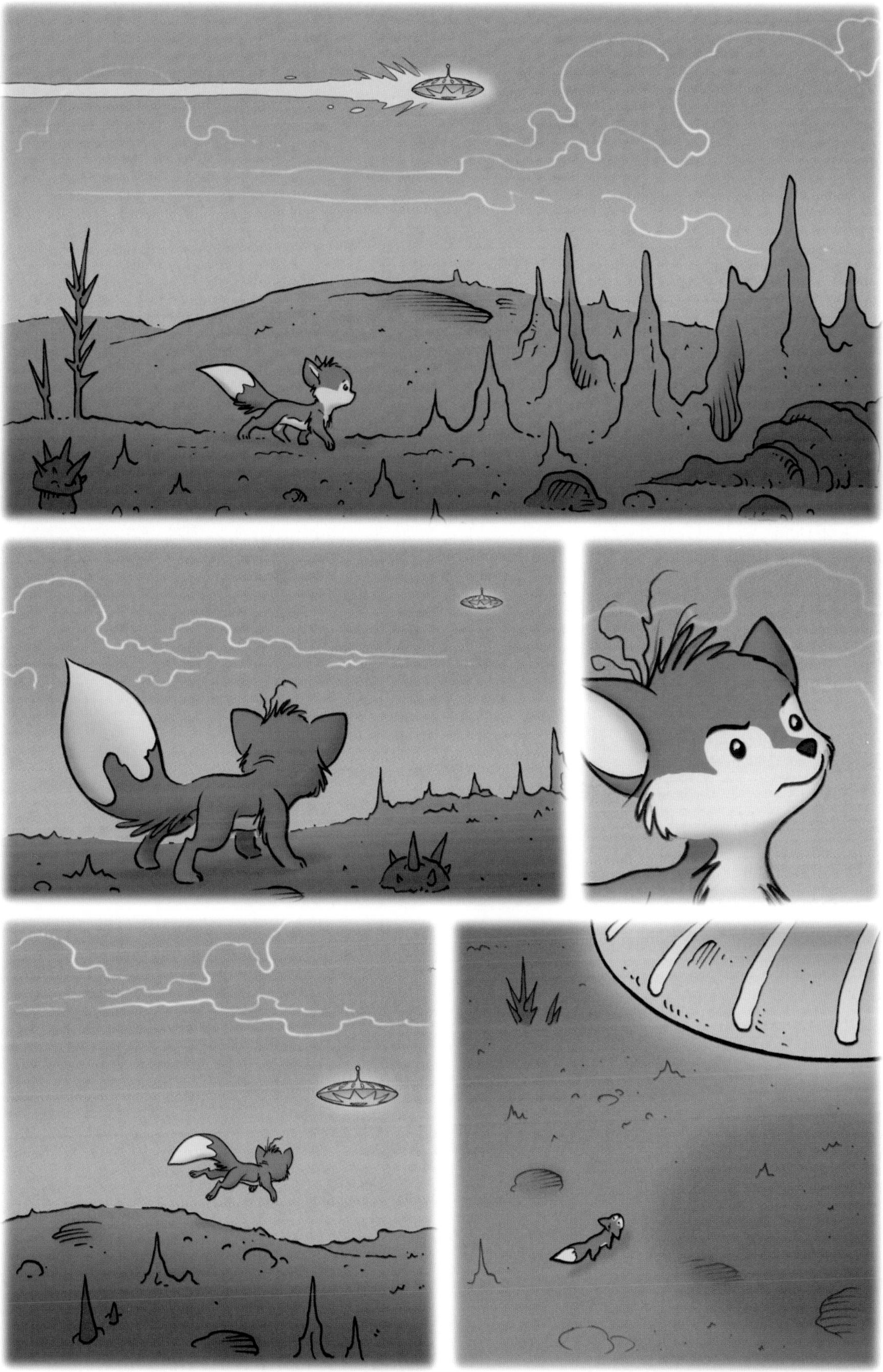

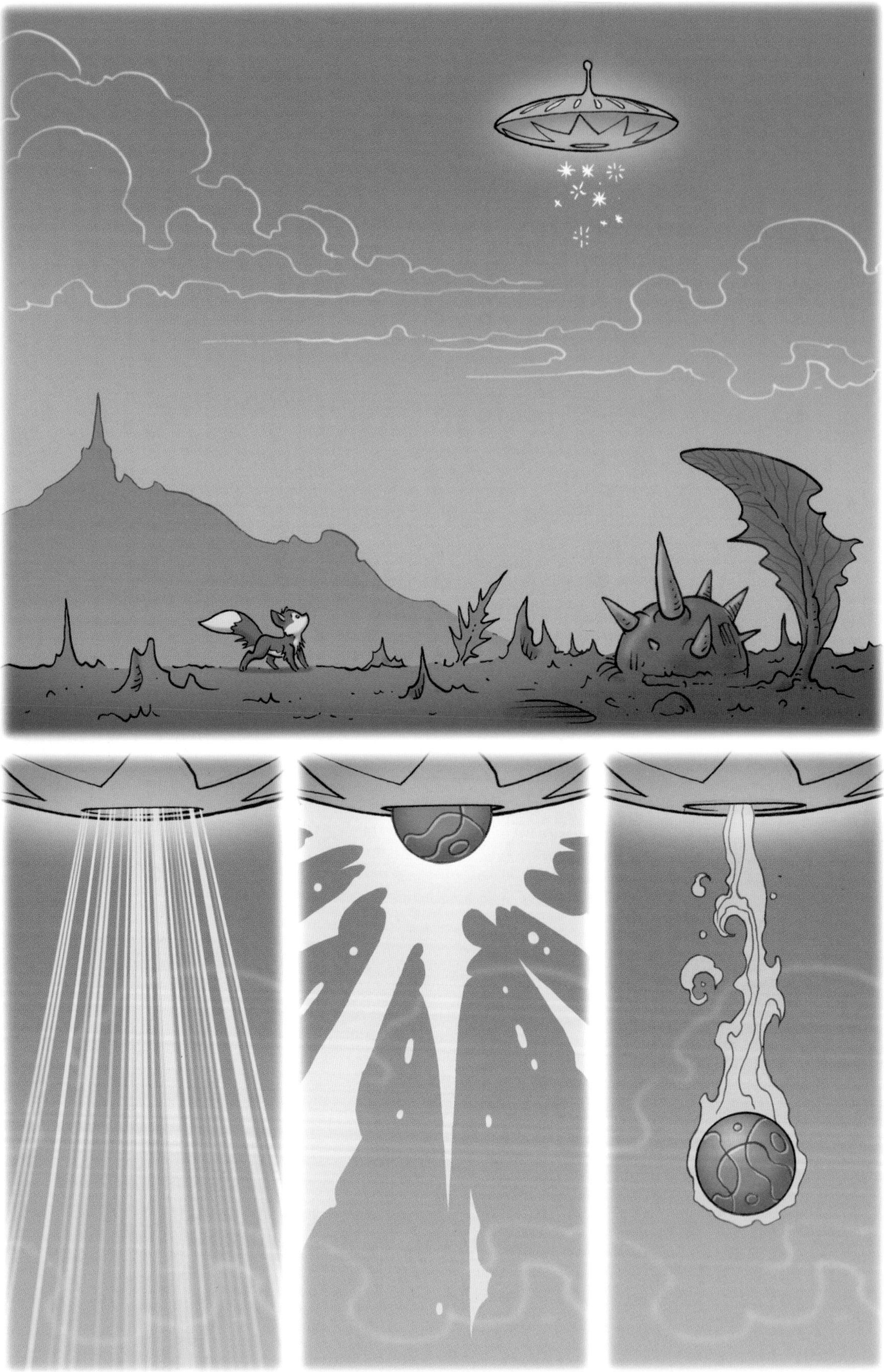

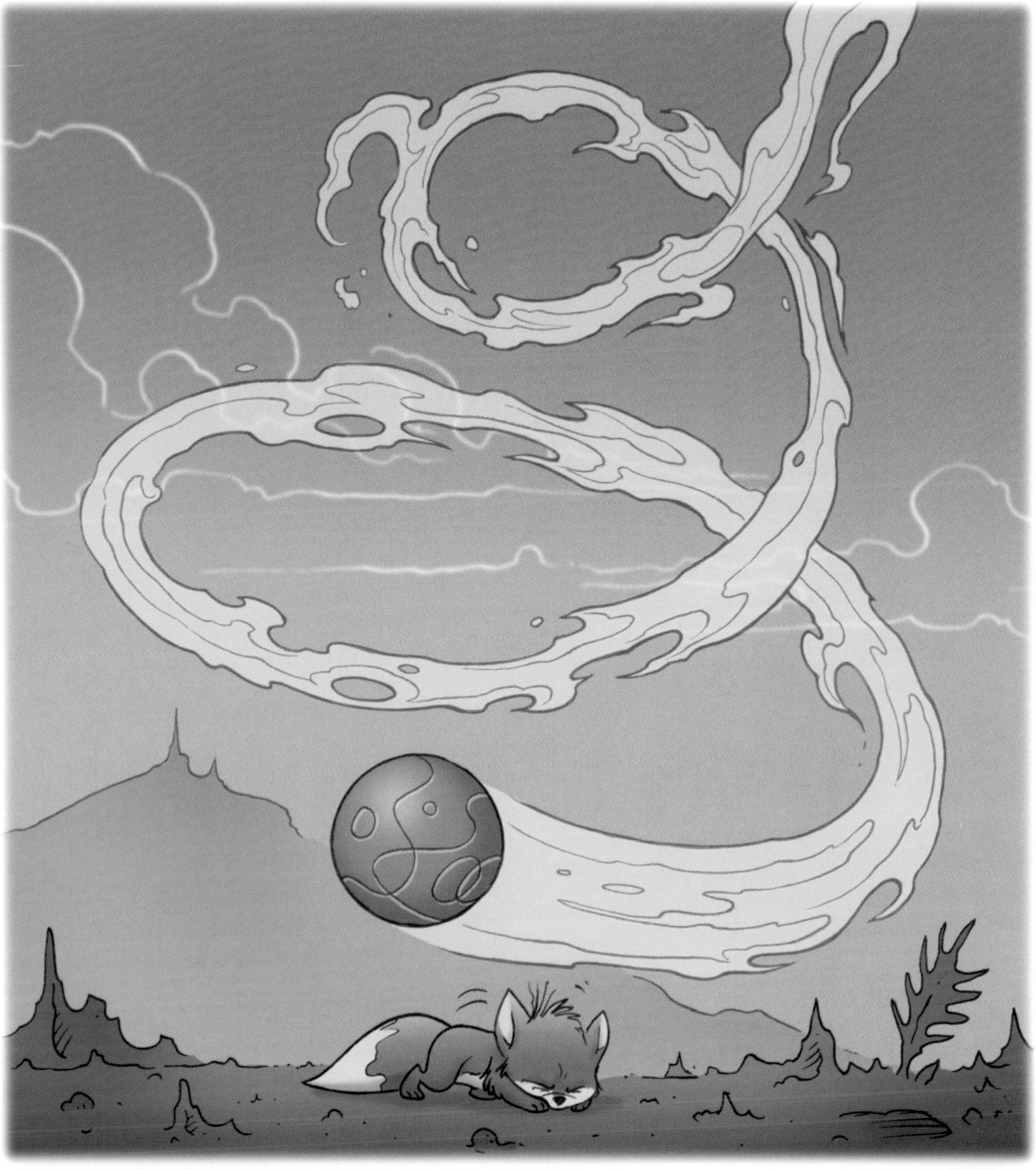

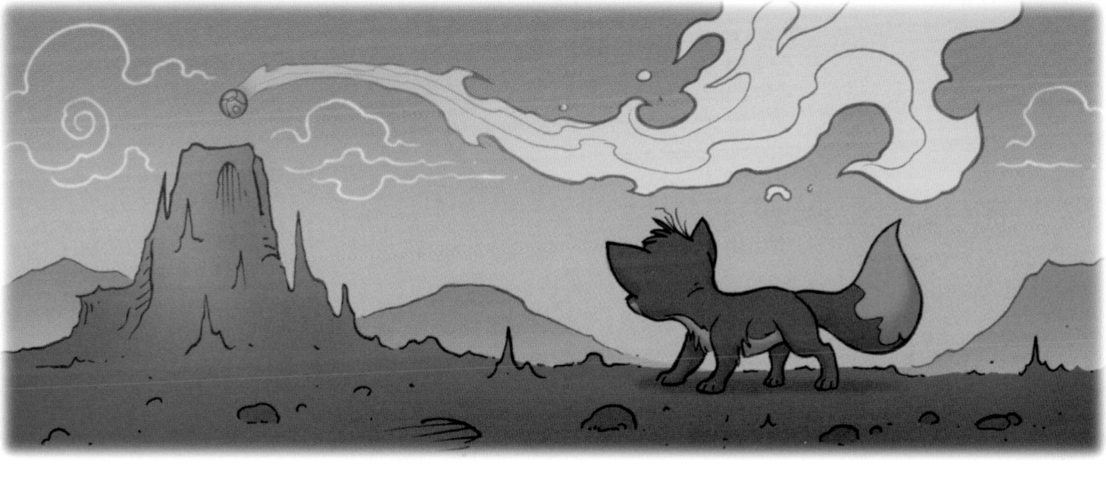

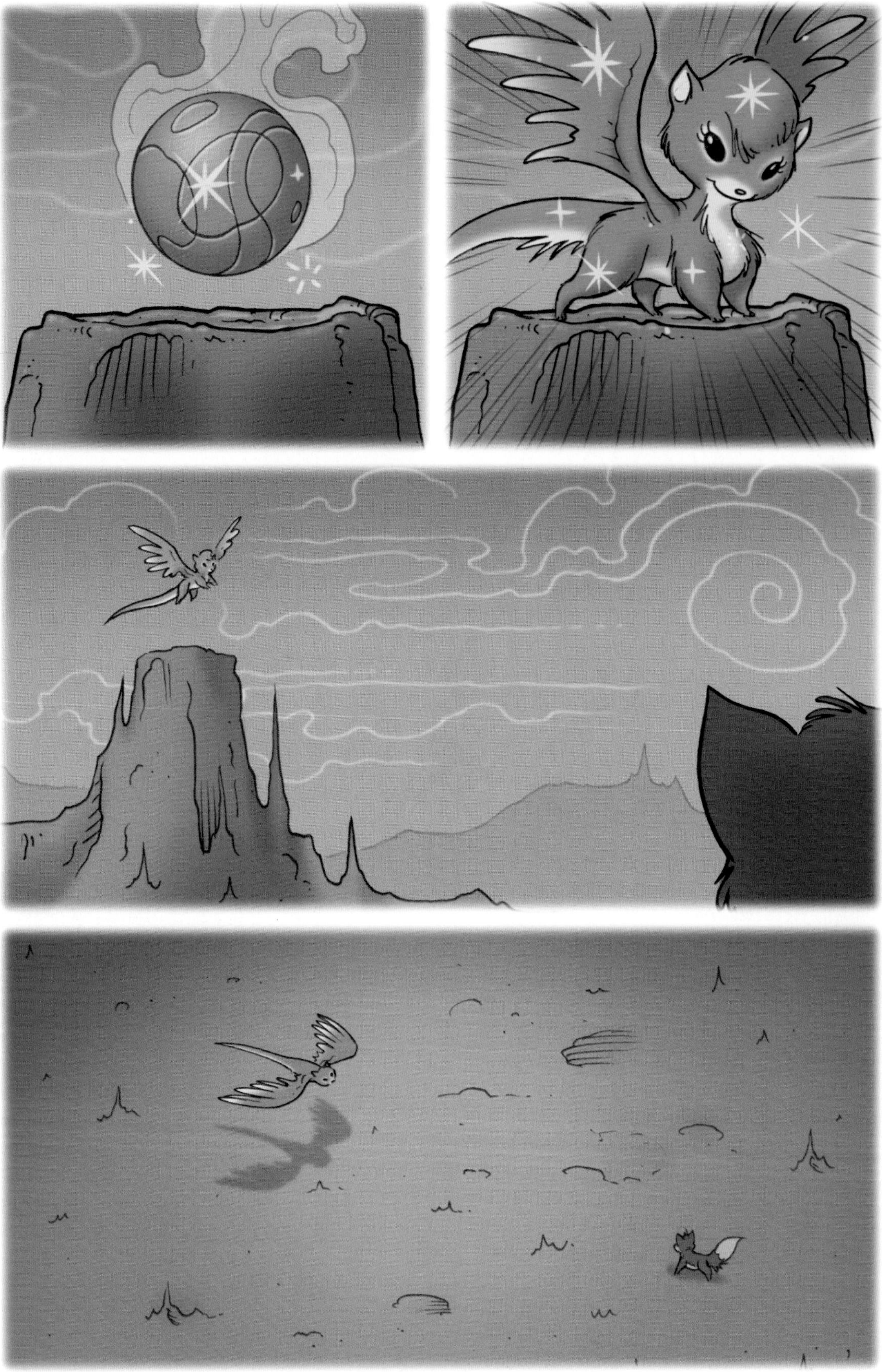

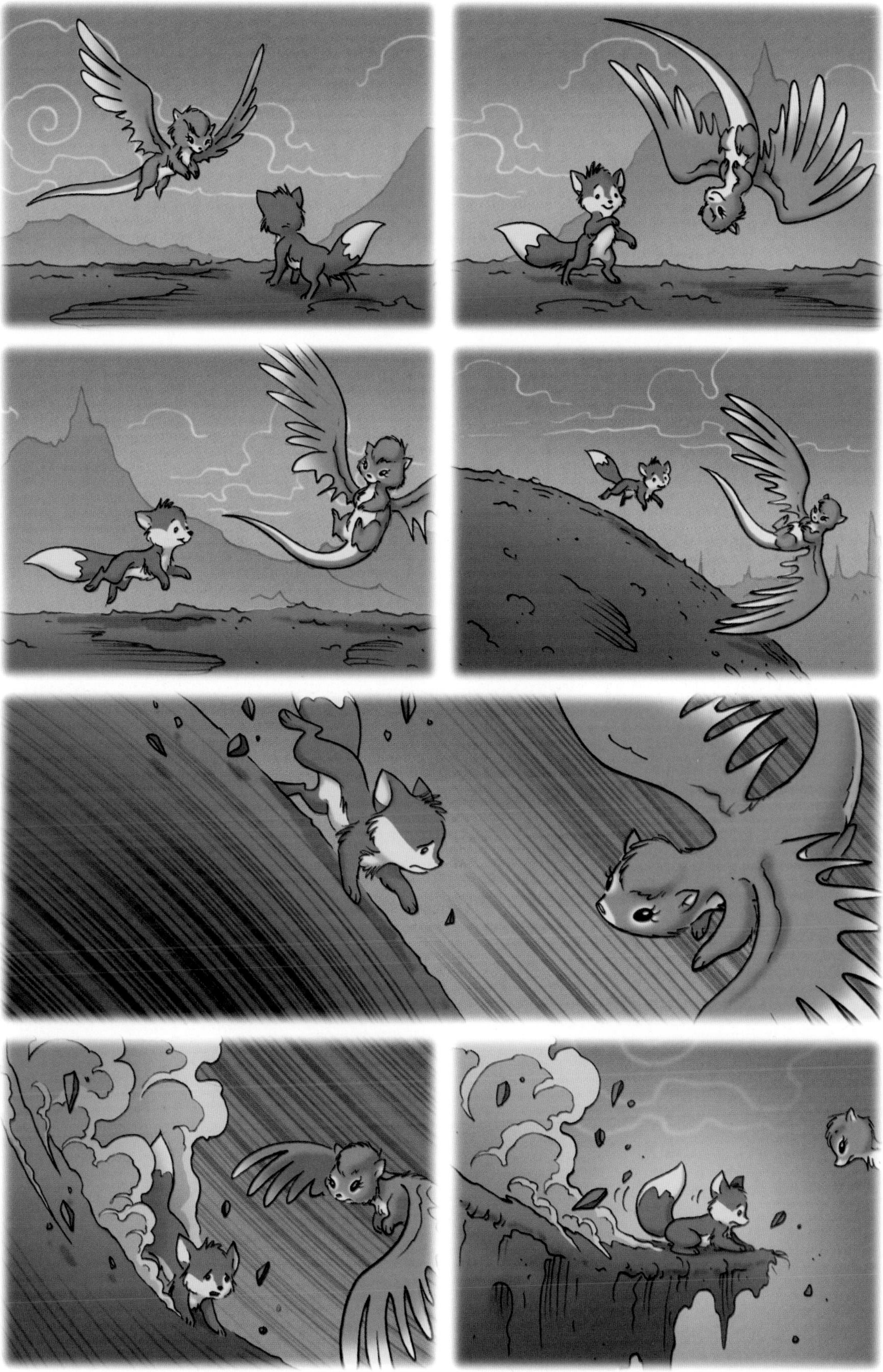

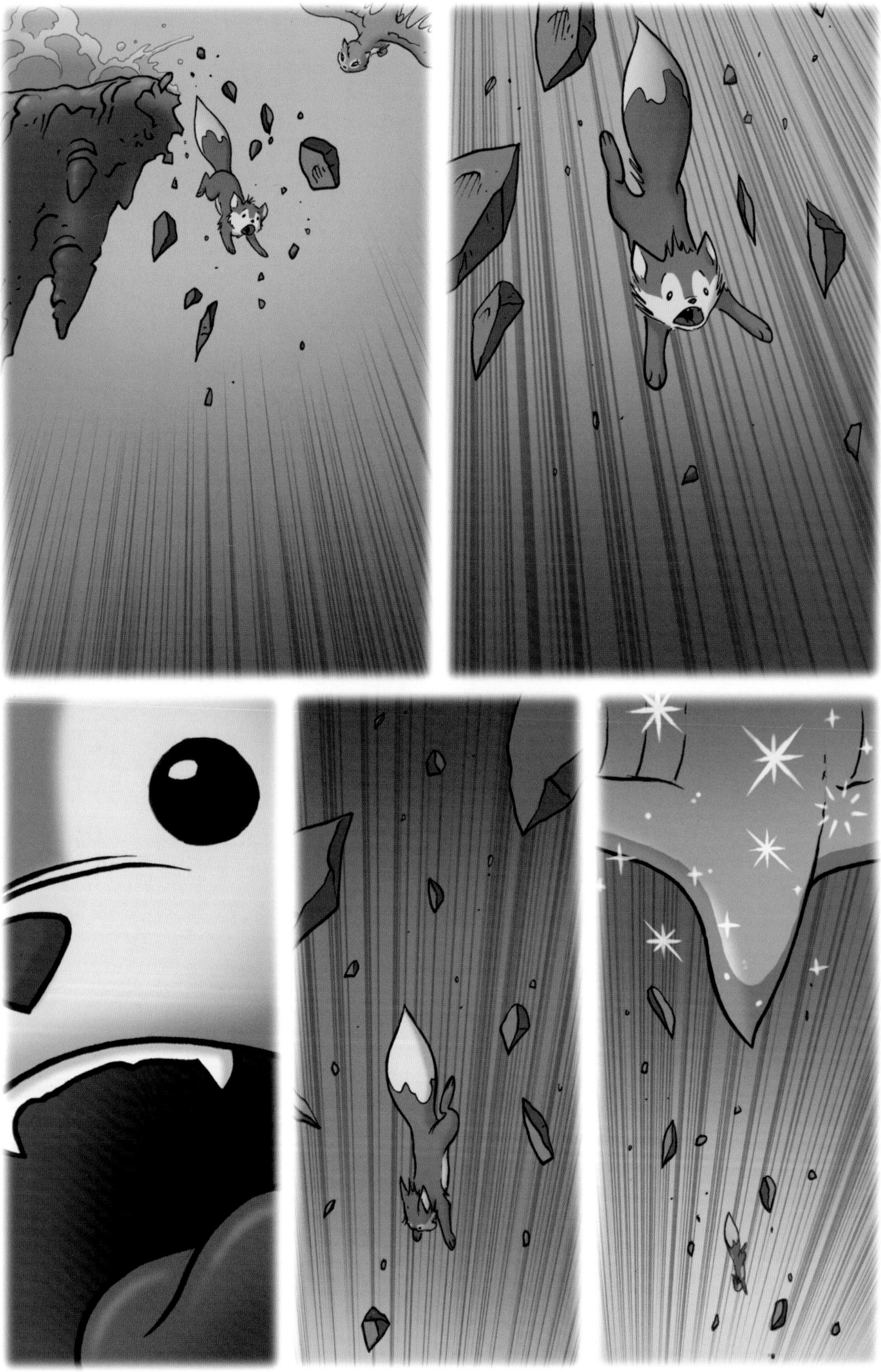

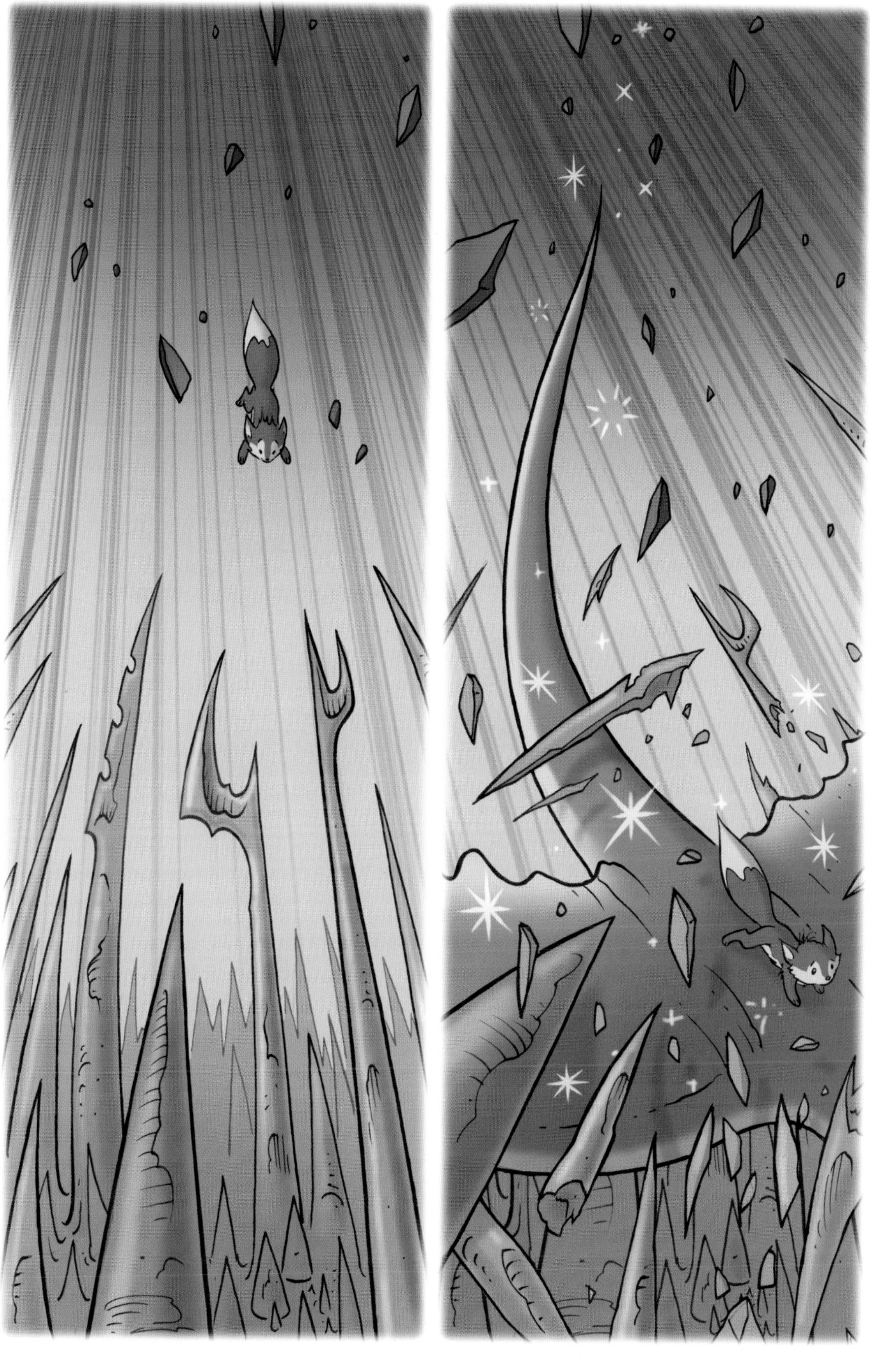

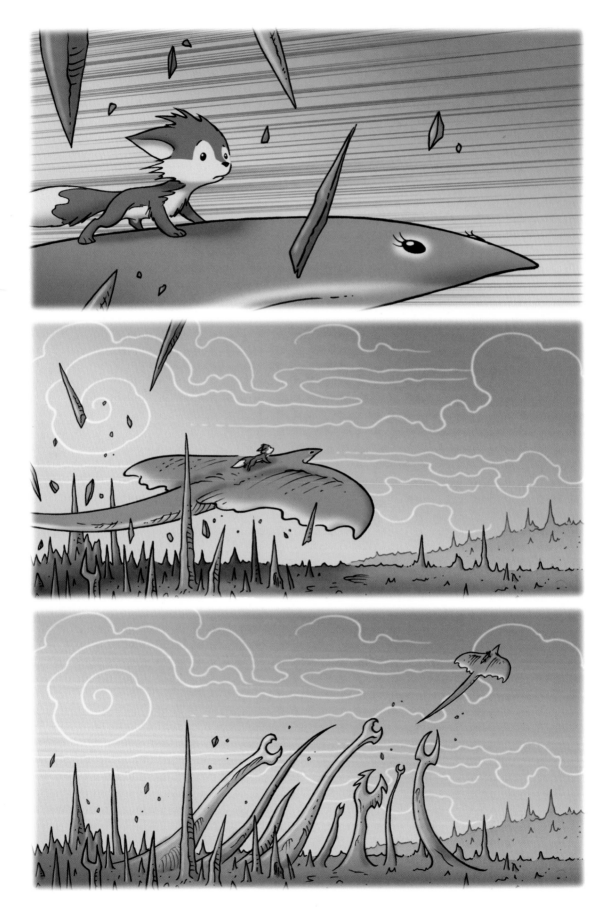

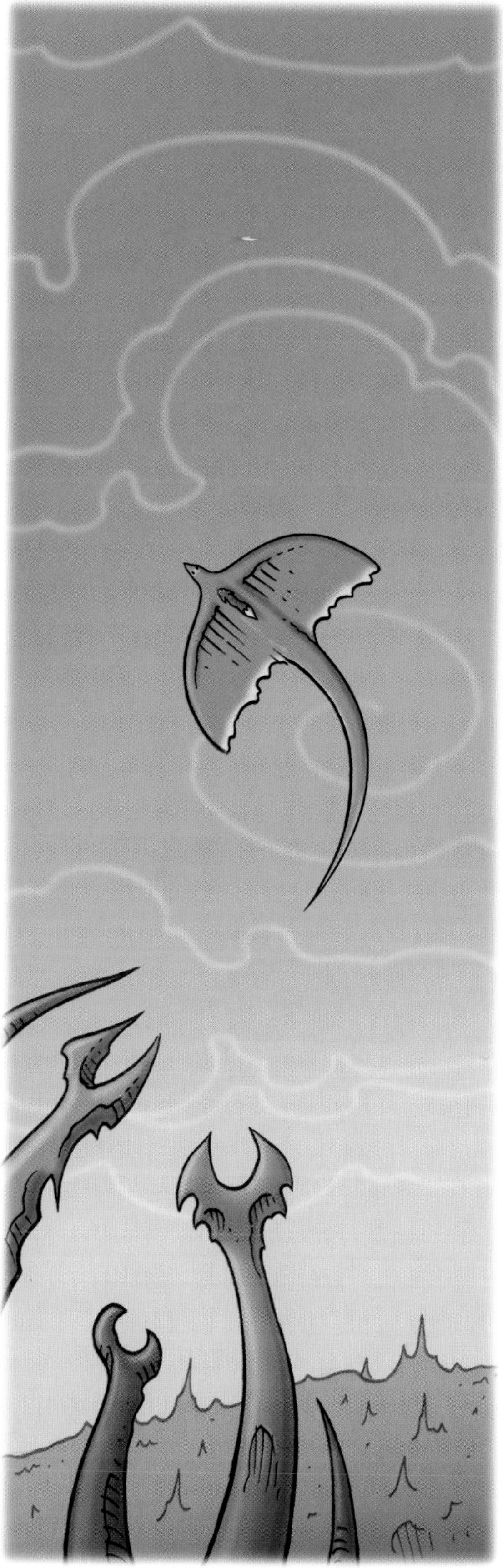
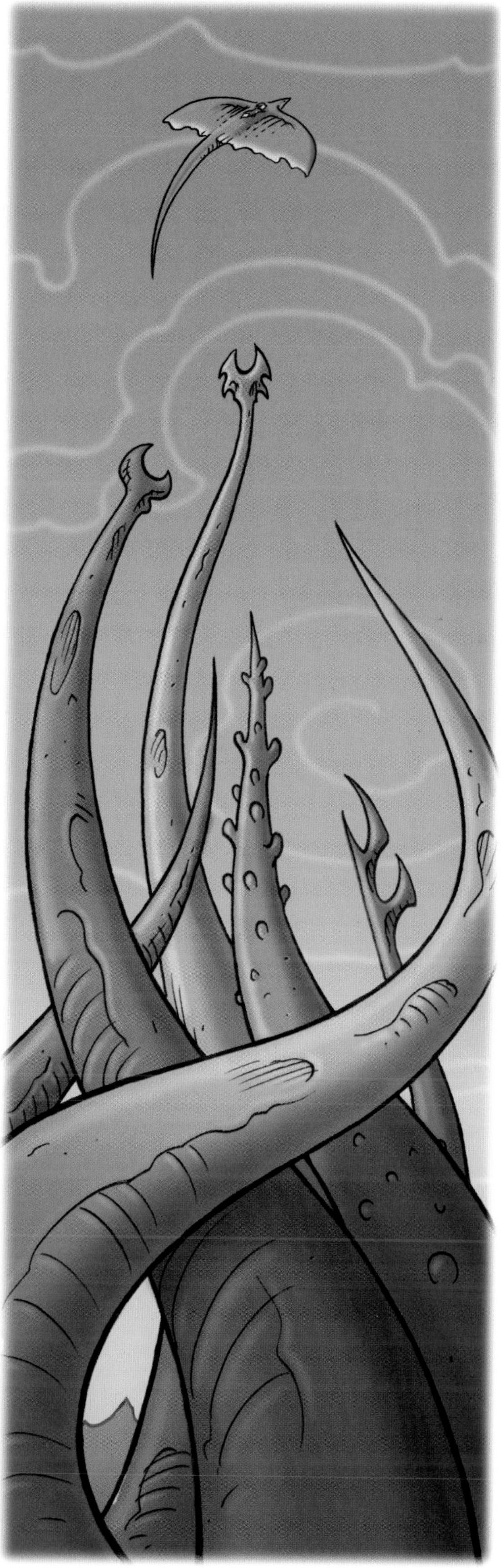

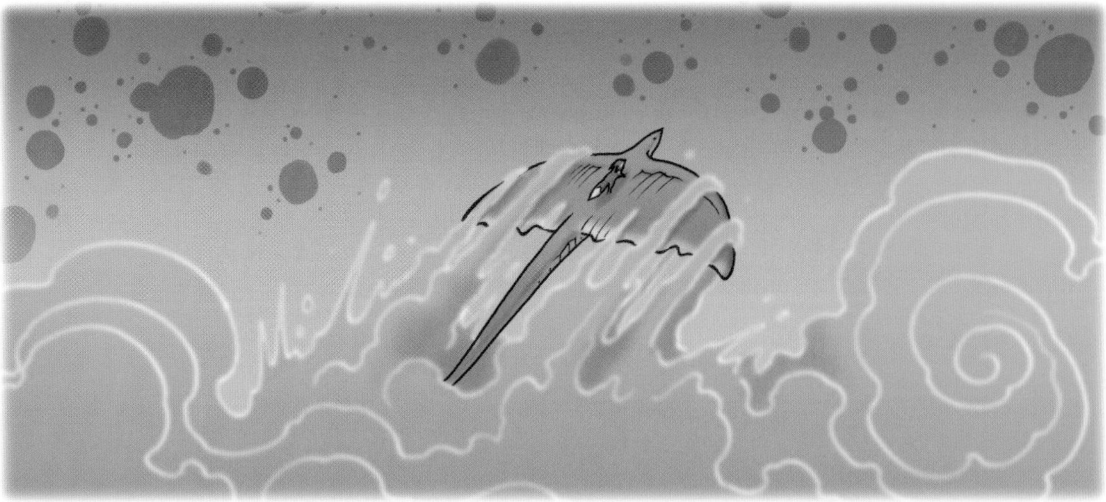

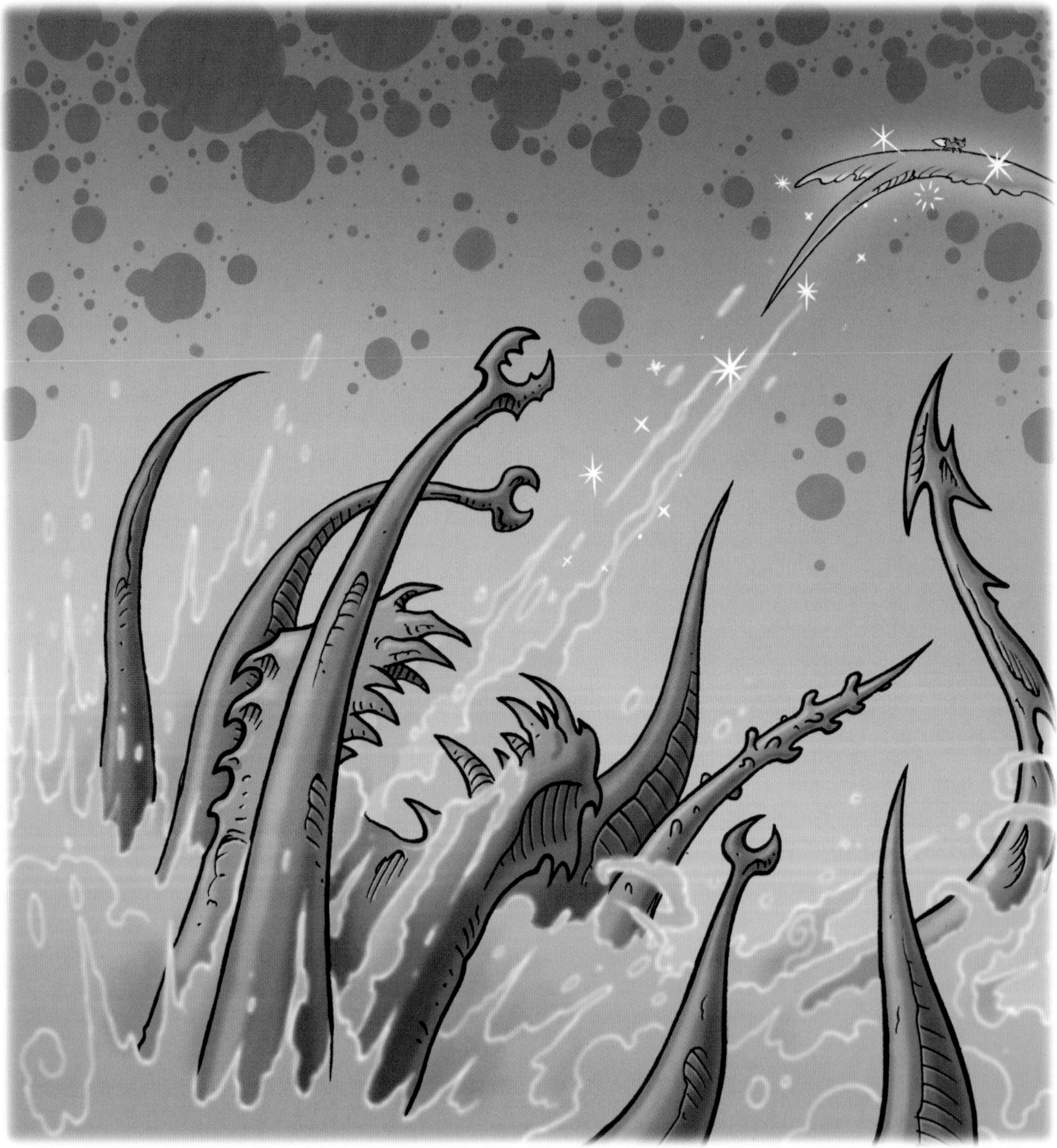

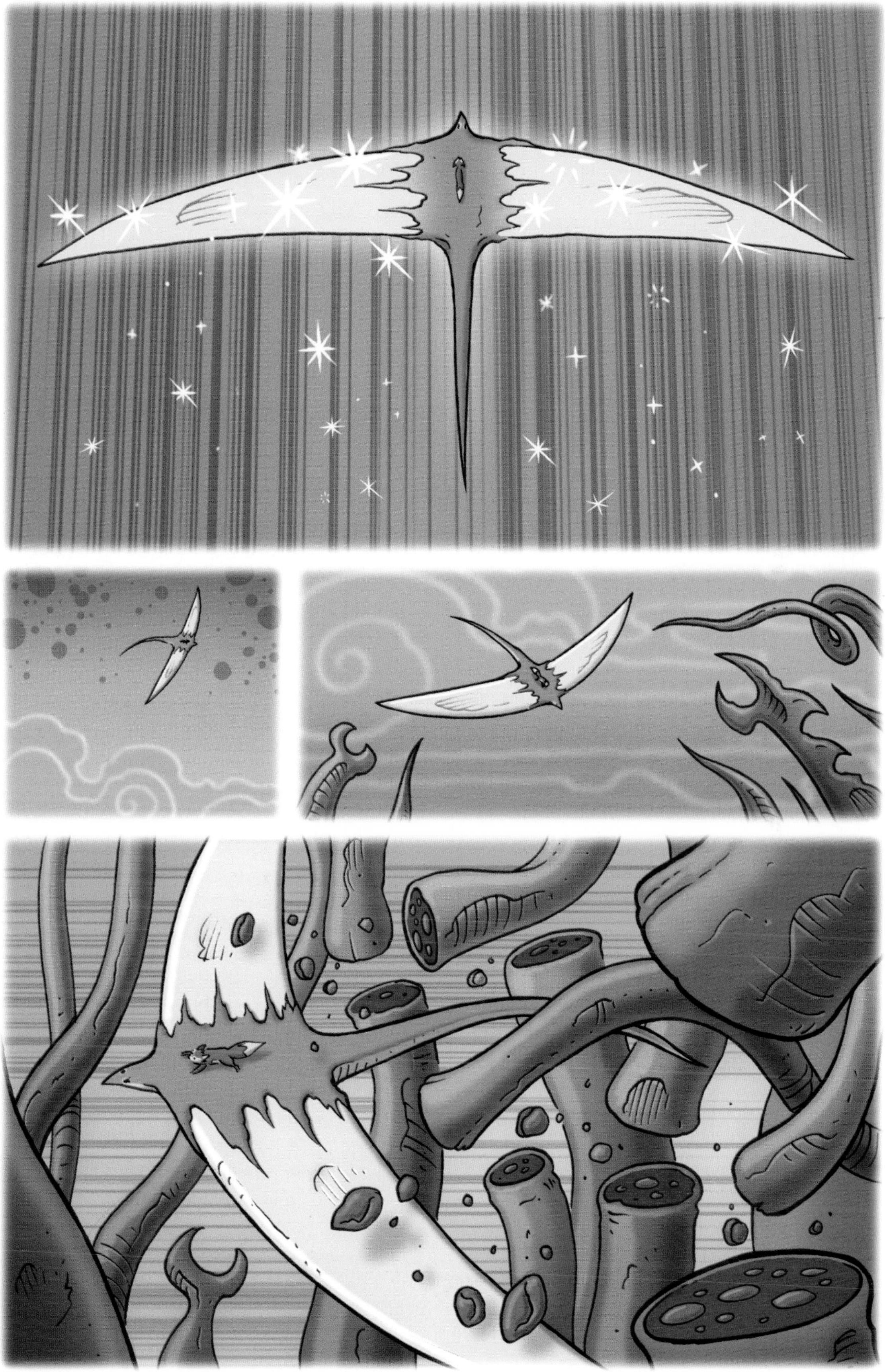

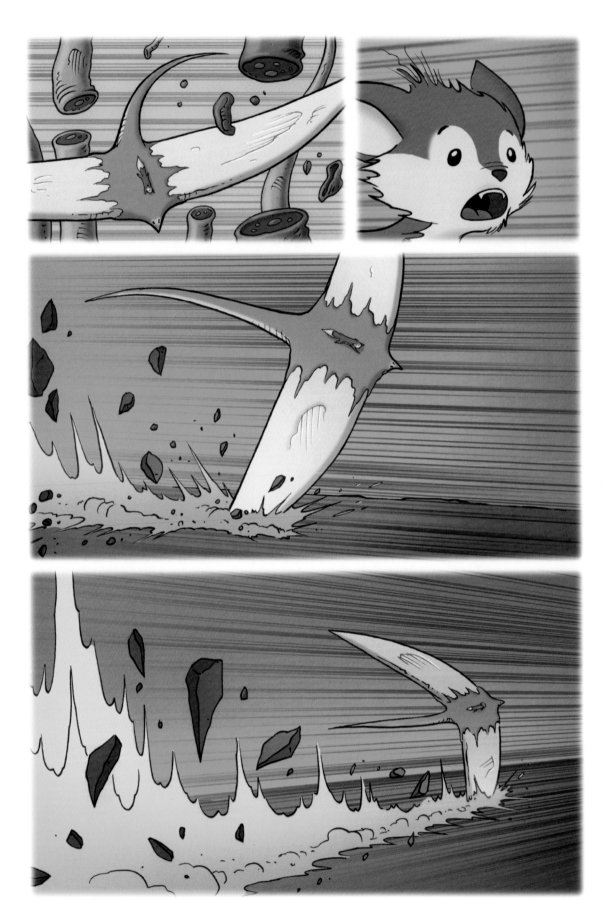

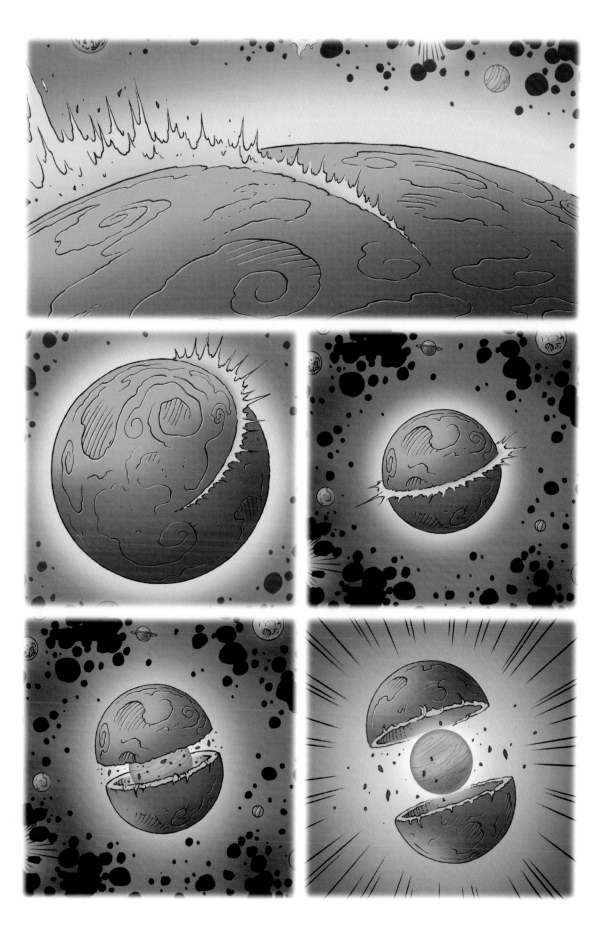

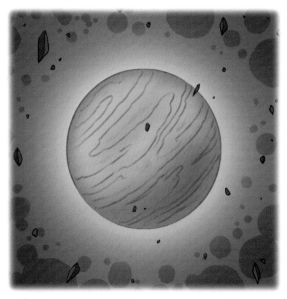

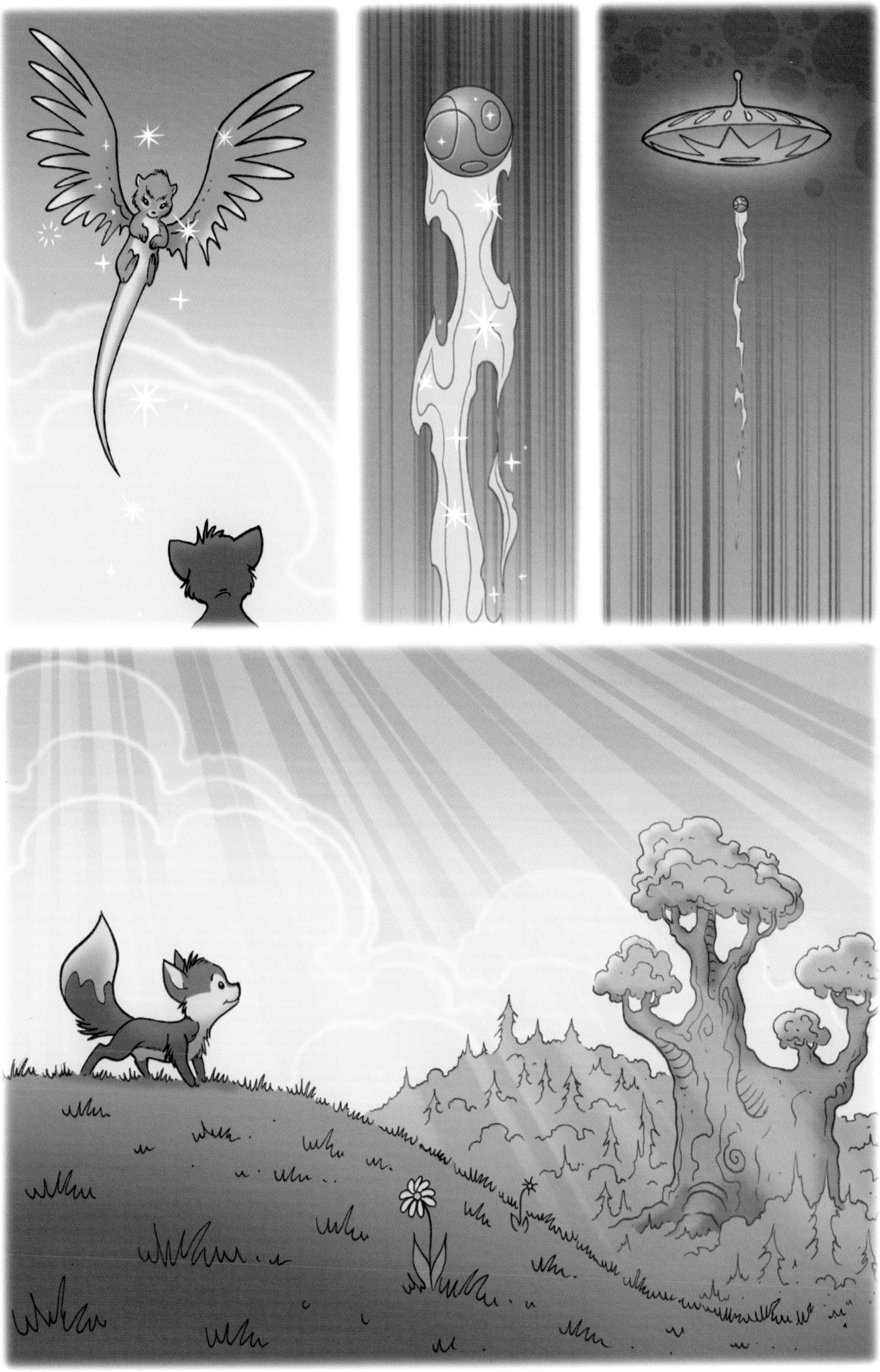

Solomon
Fix

by
Doug TenNapel

color by sean charmatz

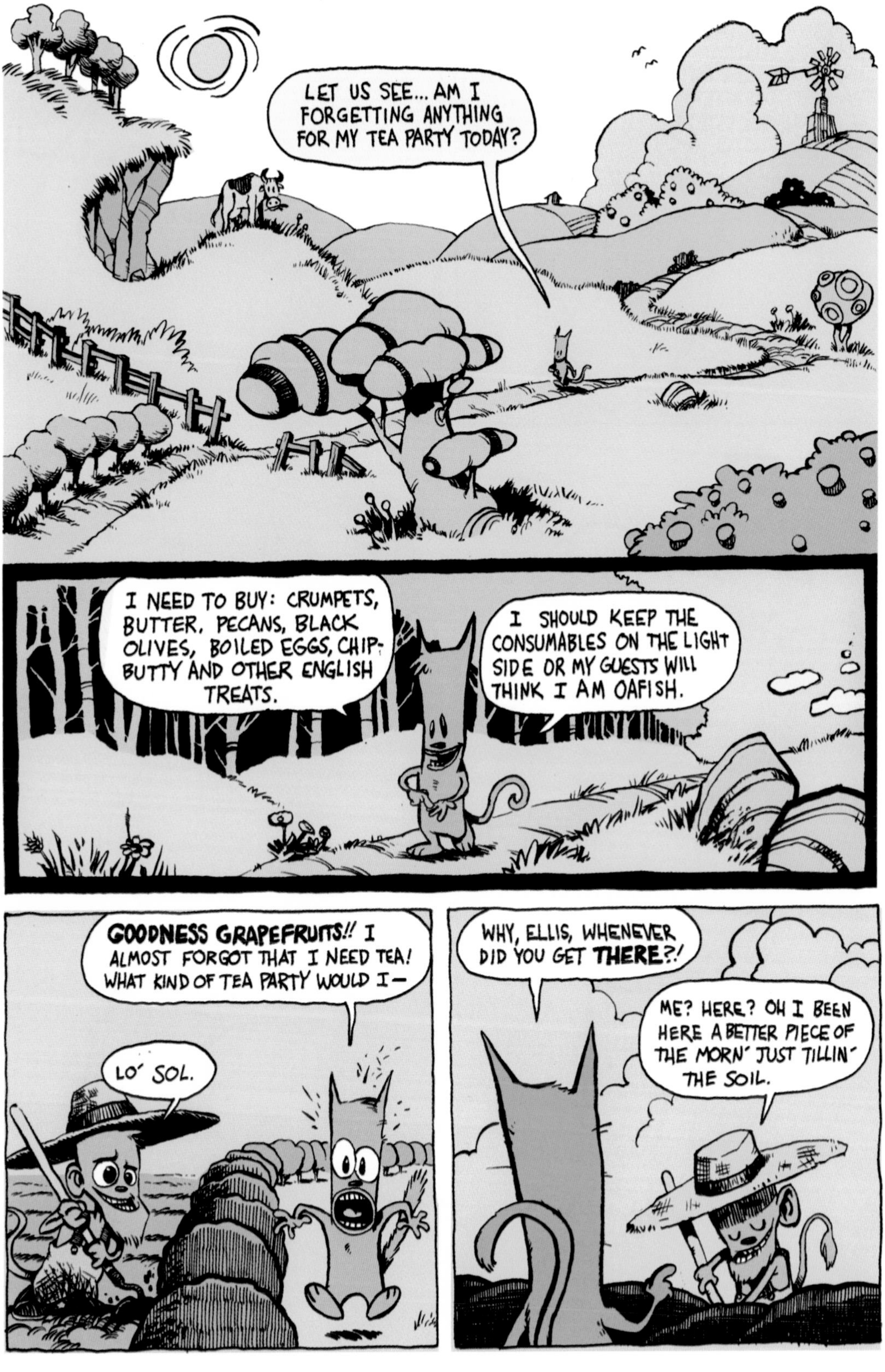
LET US SEE... AM I FORGETTING ANYTHING FOR MY TEA PARTY TODAY?
I NEED TO BUY: CRUMPETS, BUTTER, PECANS, BLACK OLIVES, BOILED EGGS, CHIP-BUTTY AND OTHER ENGLISH TREATS.
I SHOULD KEEP THE CONSUMABLES ON THE LIGHT SIDE OR MY GUESTS WILL THINK I AM OAFISH.
GOODNESS GRAPEFRUITS!! I ALMOST FORGOT THAT I NEED TEA! WHAT KIND OF TEA PARTY WOULD I—
LO' SOL.
WHY, ELLIS, WHENEVER DID YOU GET THERE?!
ME? HERE? OH I BEEN HERE A BETTER PIECE OF THE MORN' JUST TILLIN' THE SOIL.

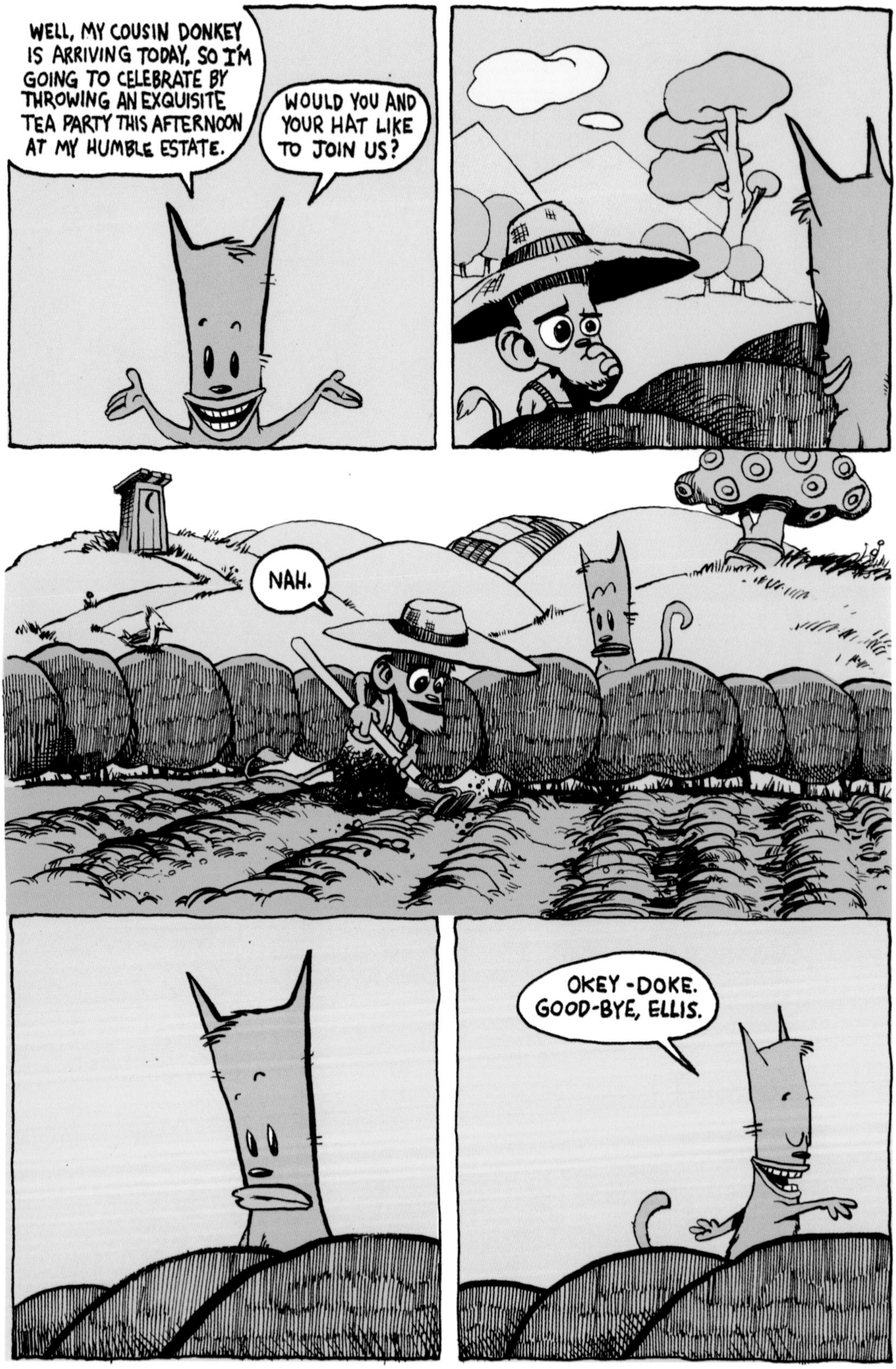
WELL, MY COUSIN DONKEY IS ARRIVING TODAY, SO I'M GOING TO CELEBRATE BY THROWING AN EXQUISITE TEA PARTY THIS AFTERNOON AT MY HUMBLE ESTATE.
WOULD YOU AND YOUR HAT LIKE TO JOIN US?
NAH.
OKEY-DOKE. GOOD-BYE, ELLIS.

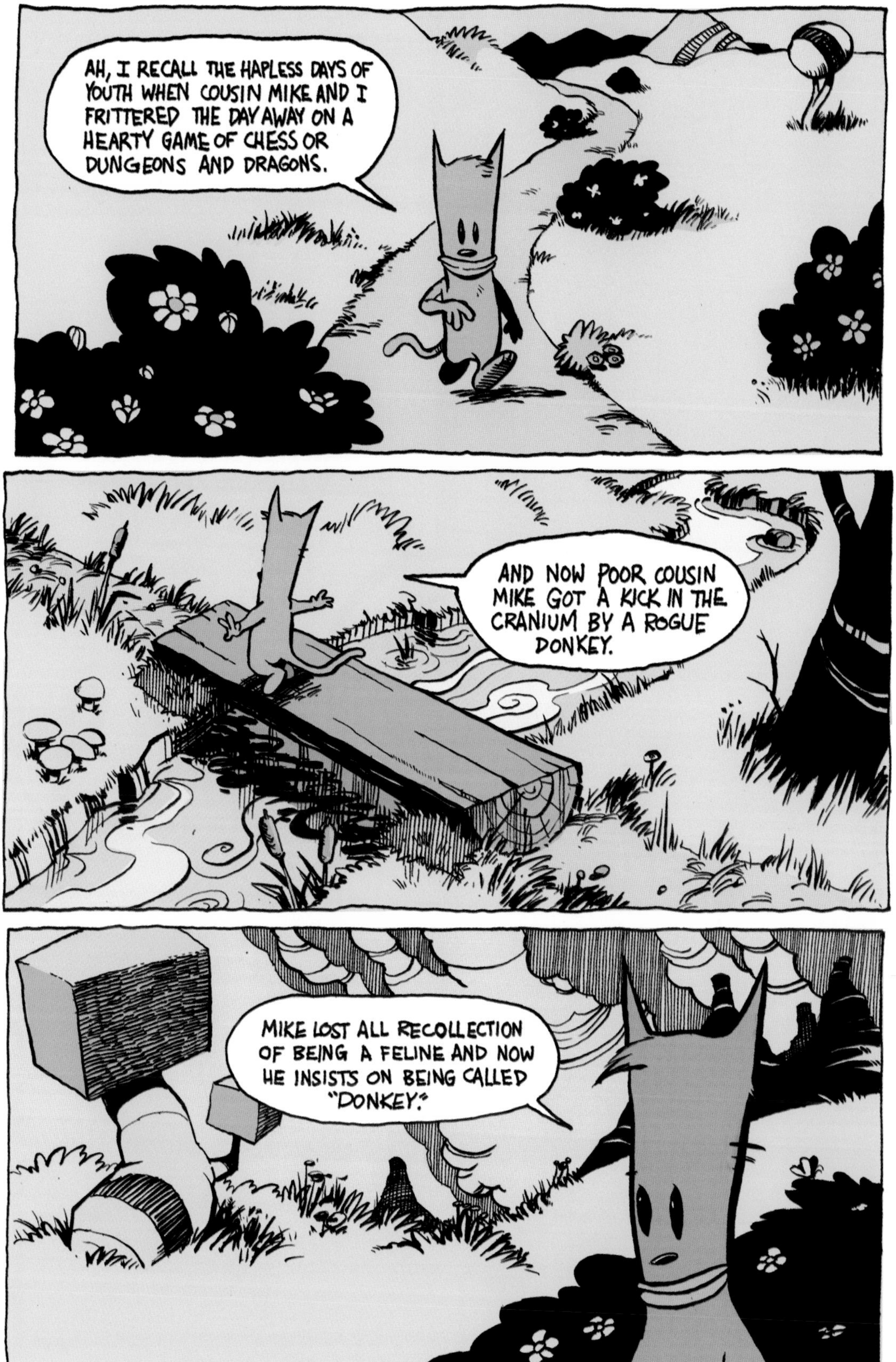
AH, I RECALL THE HAPLESS DAYS OF YOUTH WHEN COUSIN MIKE AND I FRITTERED THE DAY AWAY ON A HEARTY GAME OF CHESS OR DUNGEONS AND DRAGONS.
AND NOW POOR COUSIN MIKE GOT A KICK IN THE CRANIUM BY A ROGUE DONKEY.
MIKE LOST ALL RECOLLECTION OF BEING A FELINE AND NOW HE INSISTS ON BEING CALLED "DONKEY."

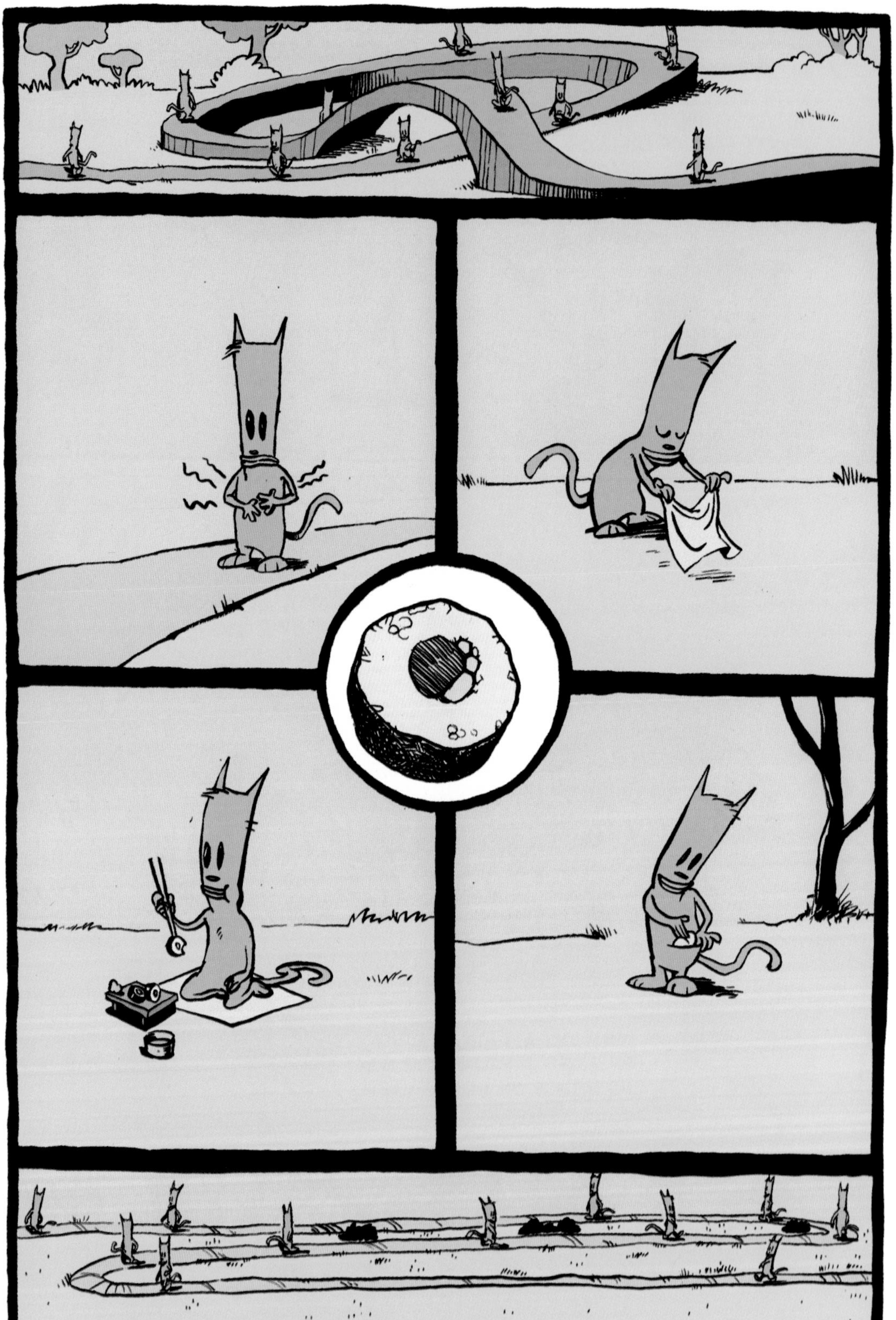

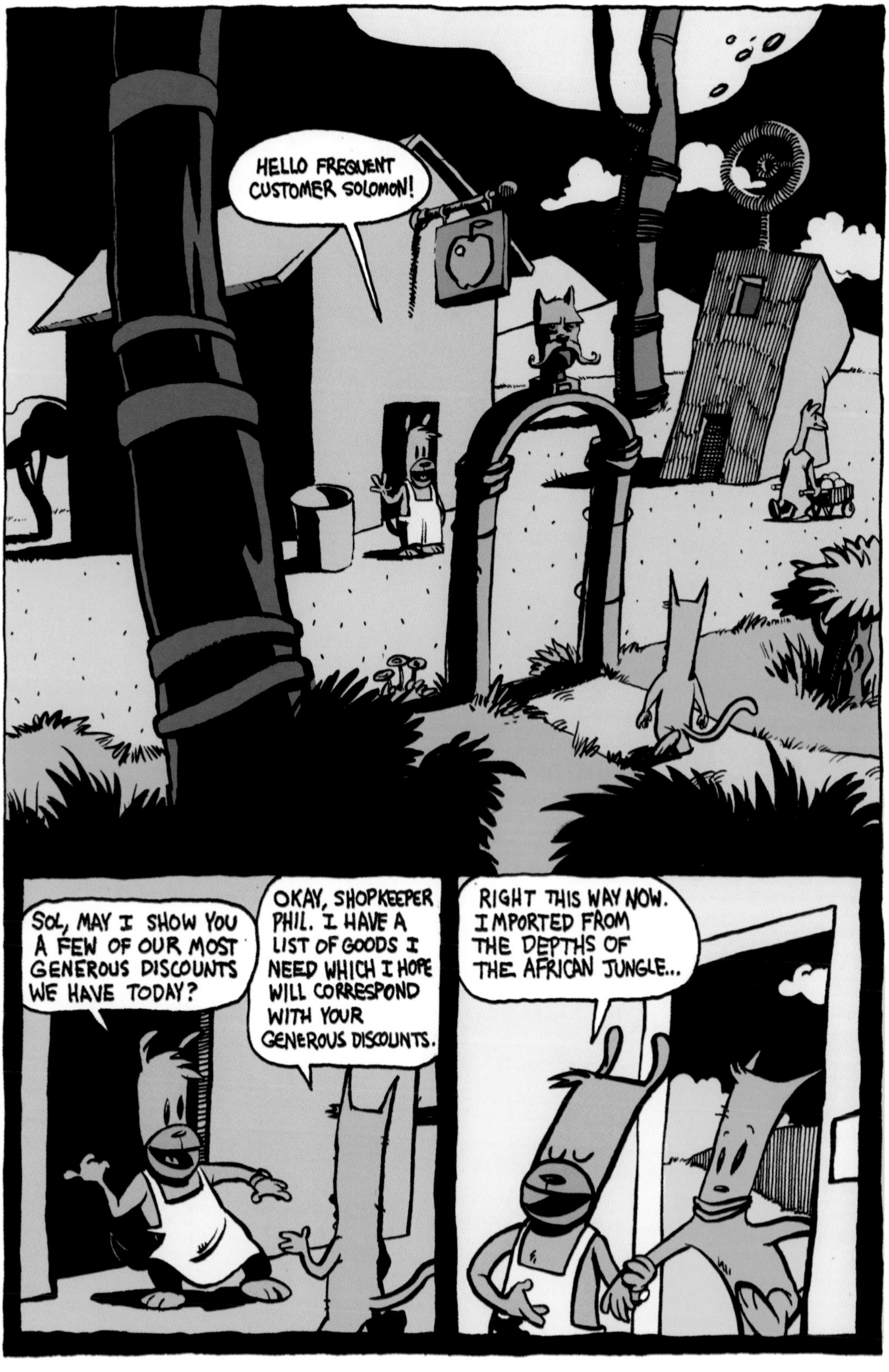
HELLO FREQUENT CUSTOMER SOLOMON!
SOL, MAY I SHOW YOU A FEW OF OUR MOST GENEROUS DISCOUNTS WE HAVE TODAY?
OKAY, SHOPKEEPER PHIL. I HAVE A LIST OF GOODS I NEED WHICH I HOPE WILL CORRESPOND WITH YOUR GENEROUS DISCOUNTS.
RIGHT THIS WAY NOW. IMPORTED FROM THE DEPTHS OF THE AFRICAN JUNGLE...

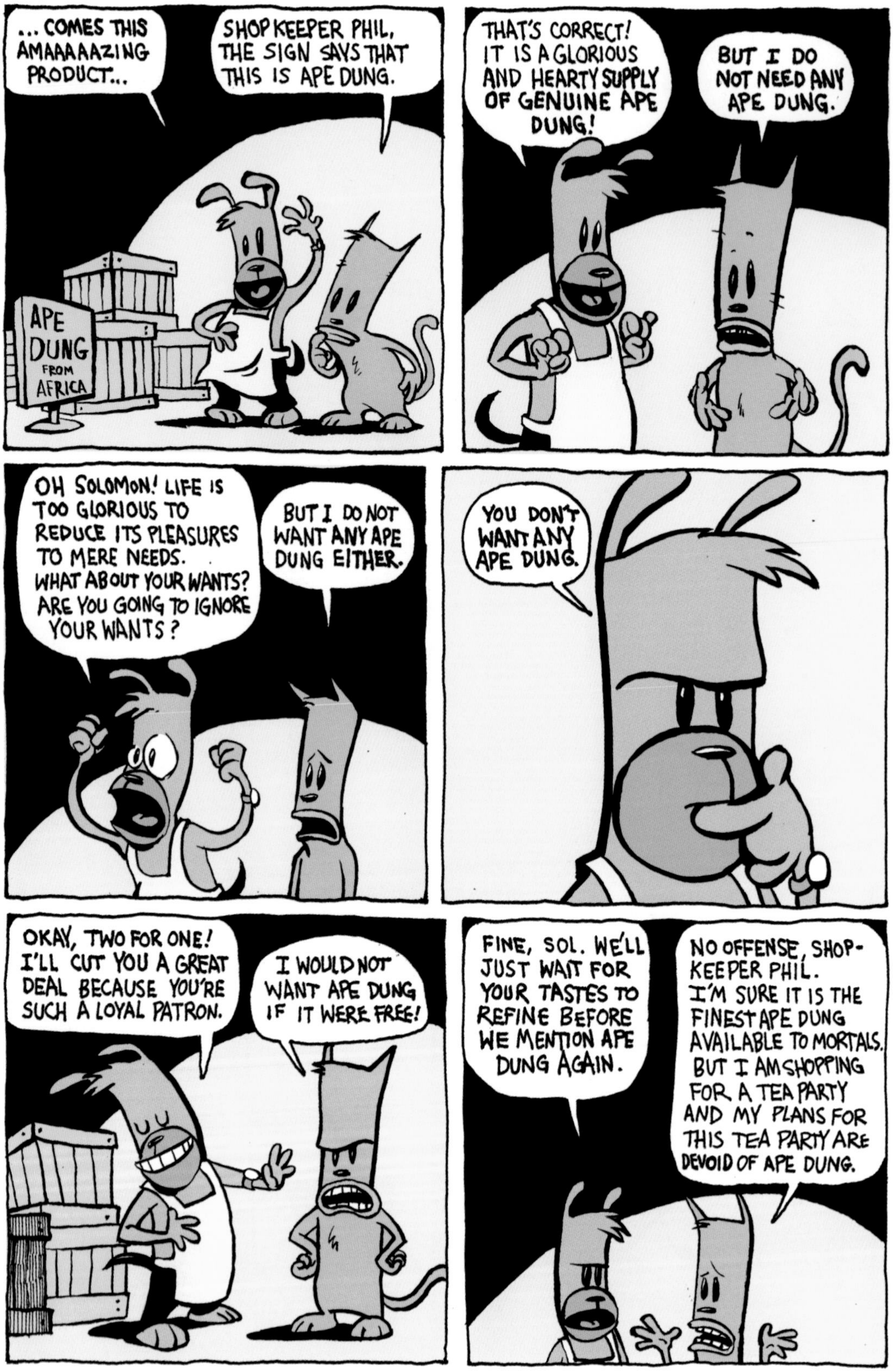

... COMES THIS AMAAAAAZING PRODUCT...
SHOP KEEPER PHIL, THE SIGN SAYS THAT THIS IS APE DUNG.
APE DUNG FROM AFRICA
THAT'S CORRECT! IT IS A GLORIOUS AND HEARTY SUPPLY OF GENUINE APE DUNG!
BUT I DO NOT NEED ANY APE DUNG.
OH SOLOMON! LIFE IS TOO GLORIOUS TO REDUCE ITS PLEASURES TO MERE NEEDS. WHAT ABOUT YOUR WANTS? ARE YOU GOING TO IGNORE YOUR WANTS?
BUT I DO NOT WANT ANY APE DUNG EITHER.
YOU DON'T WANT ANY APE DUNG.
OKAY, TWO FOR ONE! I'LL CUT YOU A GREAT DEAL BECAUSE YOU'RE SUCH A LOYAL PATRON.
I WOULD NOT WANT APE DUNG IF IT WERE FREE!
FINE, SOL. WE'LL JUST WAIT FOR YOUR TASTES TO REFINE BEFORE WE MENTION APE DUNG AGAIN.
NO OFFENSE, SHOP-KEEPER PHIL. I'M SURE IT IS THE FINEST APE DUNG AVAILABLE TO MORTALS. BUT I AM SHOPPING FOR A TEA PARTY AND MY PLANS FOR THIS TEA PARTY ARE DEVOID OF APE DUNG.

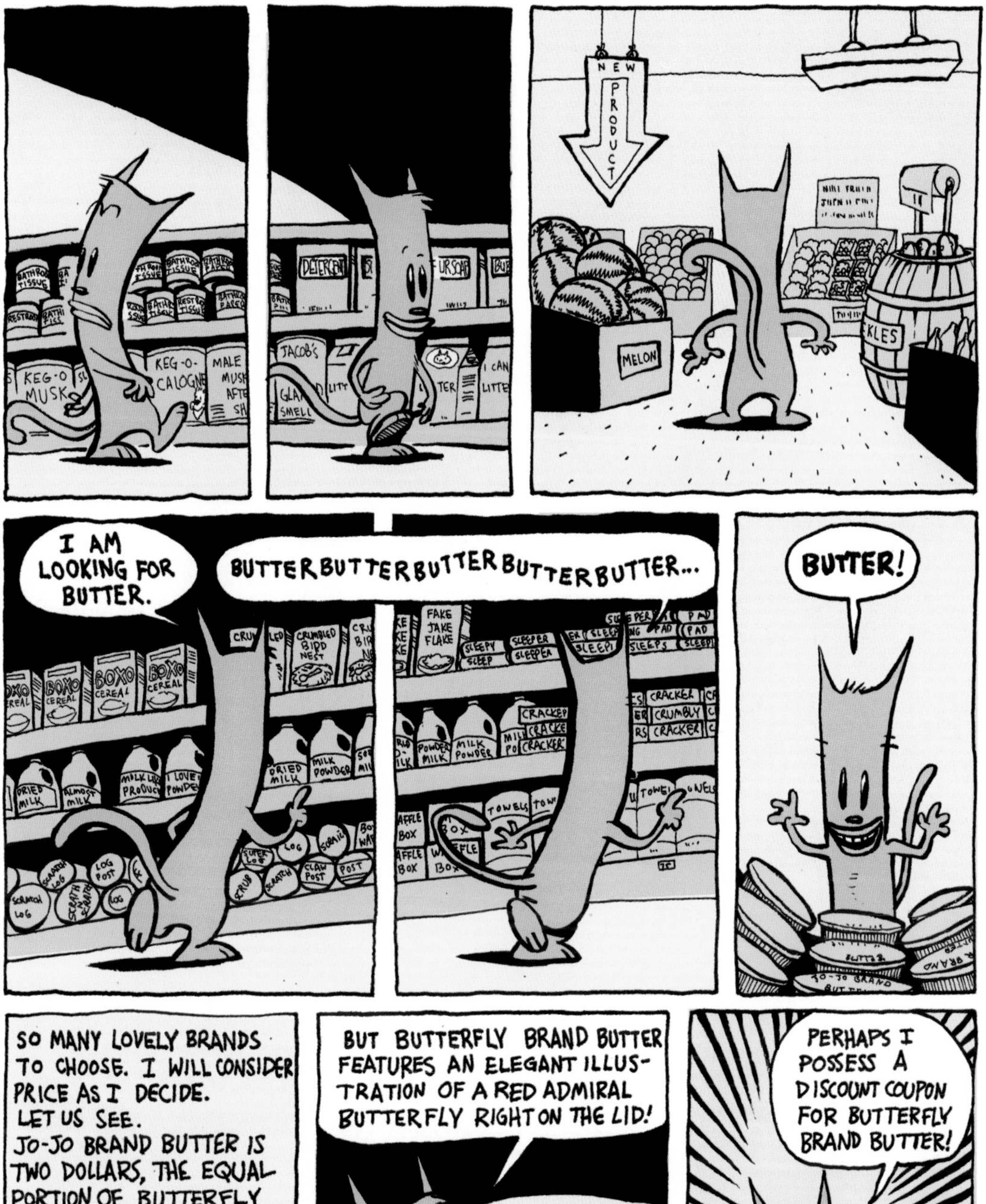
NEW PRODUCT
MELON
I AM LOOKING FOR BUTTER.
BUTTERBUTTERBUTTERBUTTERBUTTER...
BUTTER!
SO MANY LOVELY BRANDS TO CHOOSE. I WILL CONSIDER PRICE AS I DECIDE. LET US SEE. JO-JO BRAND BUTTER IS TWO DOLLARS, THE EQUAL PORTION OF BUTTERFLY BRAND BUTTER COSTS EIGHT DOLLARS.
BUT BUTTERFLY BRAND BUTTER FEATURES AN ELEGANT ILLUSTRATION OF A RED ADMIRAL BUTTERFLY RIGHT ON THE LID!
BUTTERFLY BRAND BUTTER
PERHAPS I POSSESS A DISCOUNT COUPON FOR BUTTERFLY BRAND BUTTER!
FLIP FLIP FLIP FLIP

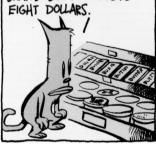

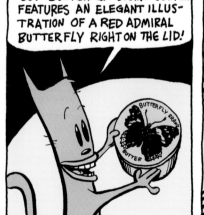

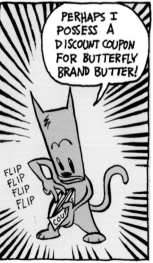

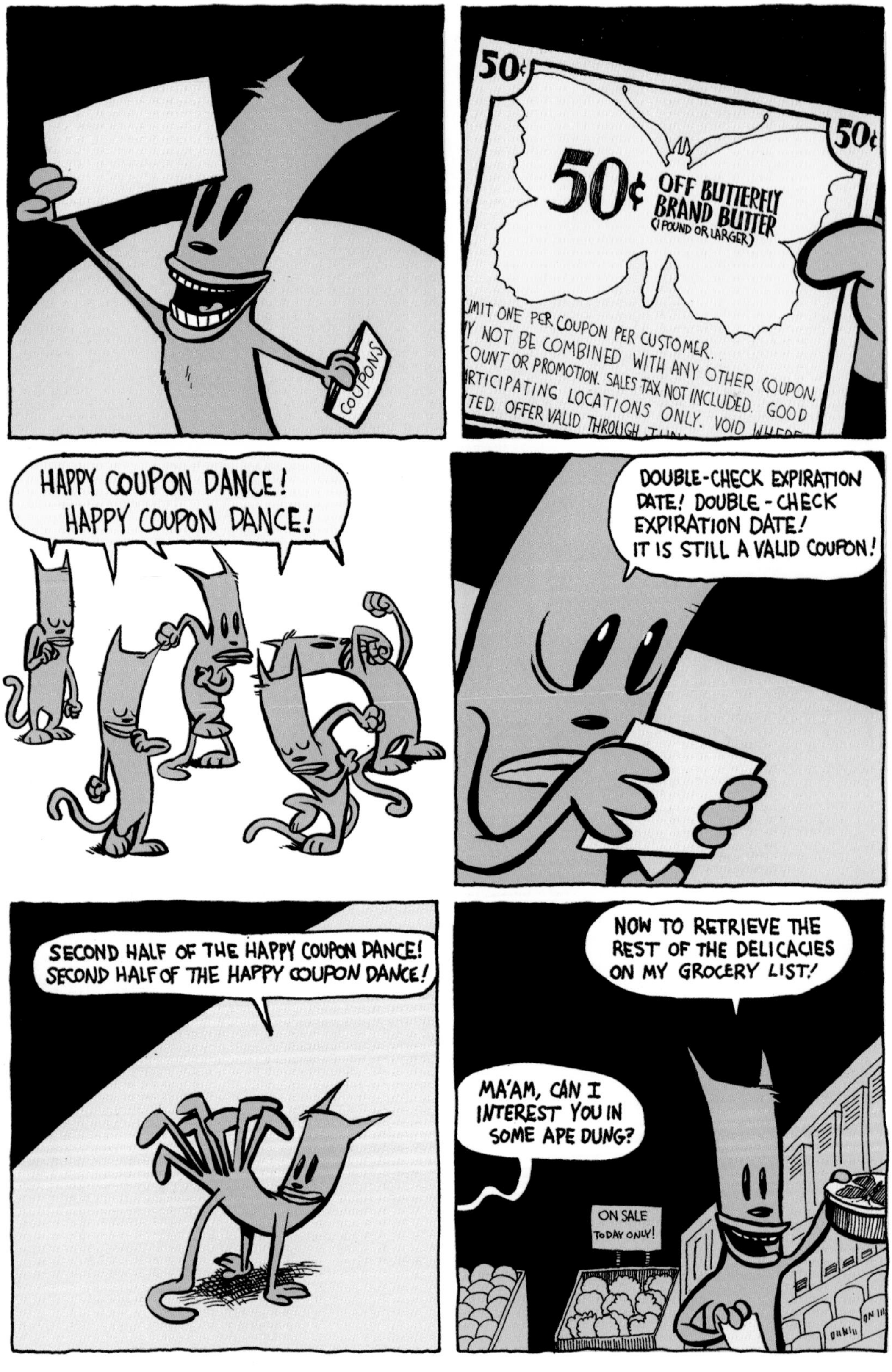
COUPONS
50¢
50¢
50¢ OFF BUTTERFLY BRAND BUTTER (1 POUND OR LARGER)
ONE PER COUPON PER CUSTOMER.
NOT BE COMBINED WITH ANY OTHER COUPON,
OR PROMOTION. SALES TAX NOT INCLUDED. GOOD
LOCATIONS ONLY. VOID
OFFER VALID THROUGH
HAPPY COUPON DANCE! HAPPY COUPON DANCE!
DOUBLE-CHECK EXPIRATION DATE! DOUBLE-CHECK EXPIRATION DATE! IT IS STILL A VALID COUPON!
SECOND HALF OF THE HAPPY COUPON DANCE! SECOND HALF OF THE HAPPY COUPON DANCE!
NOW TO RETRIEVE THE REST OF THE DELICACIES ON MY GROCERY LIST!
MA'AM, CAN I INTEREST YOU IN SOME APE DUNG?
ON SALE TODAY ONLY!

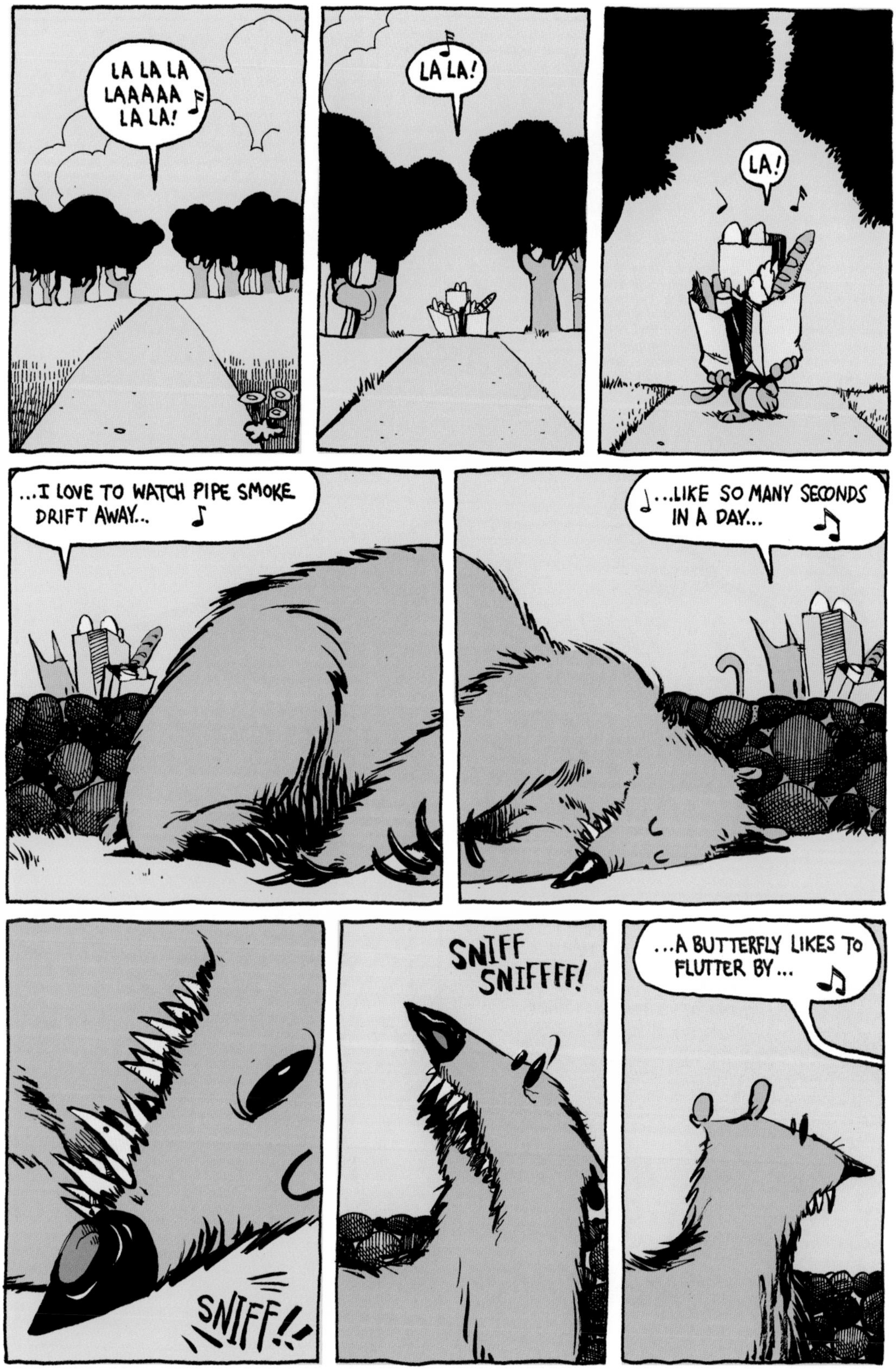
LA LA LA LAAAAA LA LA!
LA LA!
LA!
...I LOVE TO WATCH PIPE SMOKE DRIFT AWAY...
...LIKE SO MANY SECONDS IN A DAY...
SNIFF!!
SNIFF SNIFFFF!
...A BUTTERFLY LIKES TO FLUTTER BY...

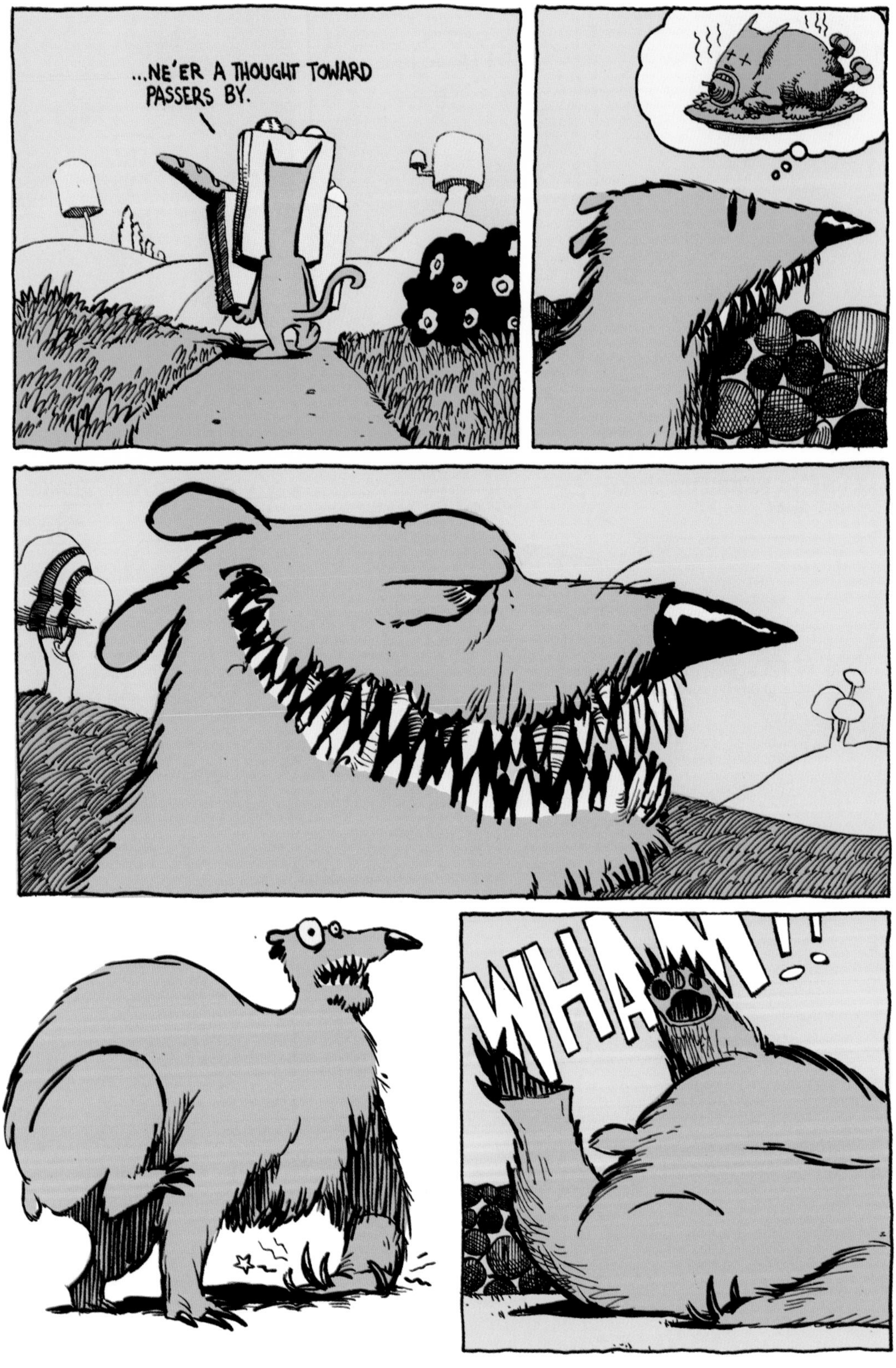
...NE'ER A THOUGHT TOWARD PASSERS BY.
WHAM!!

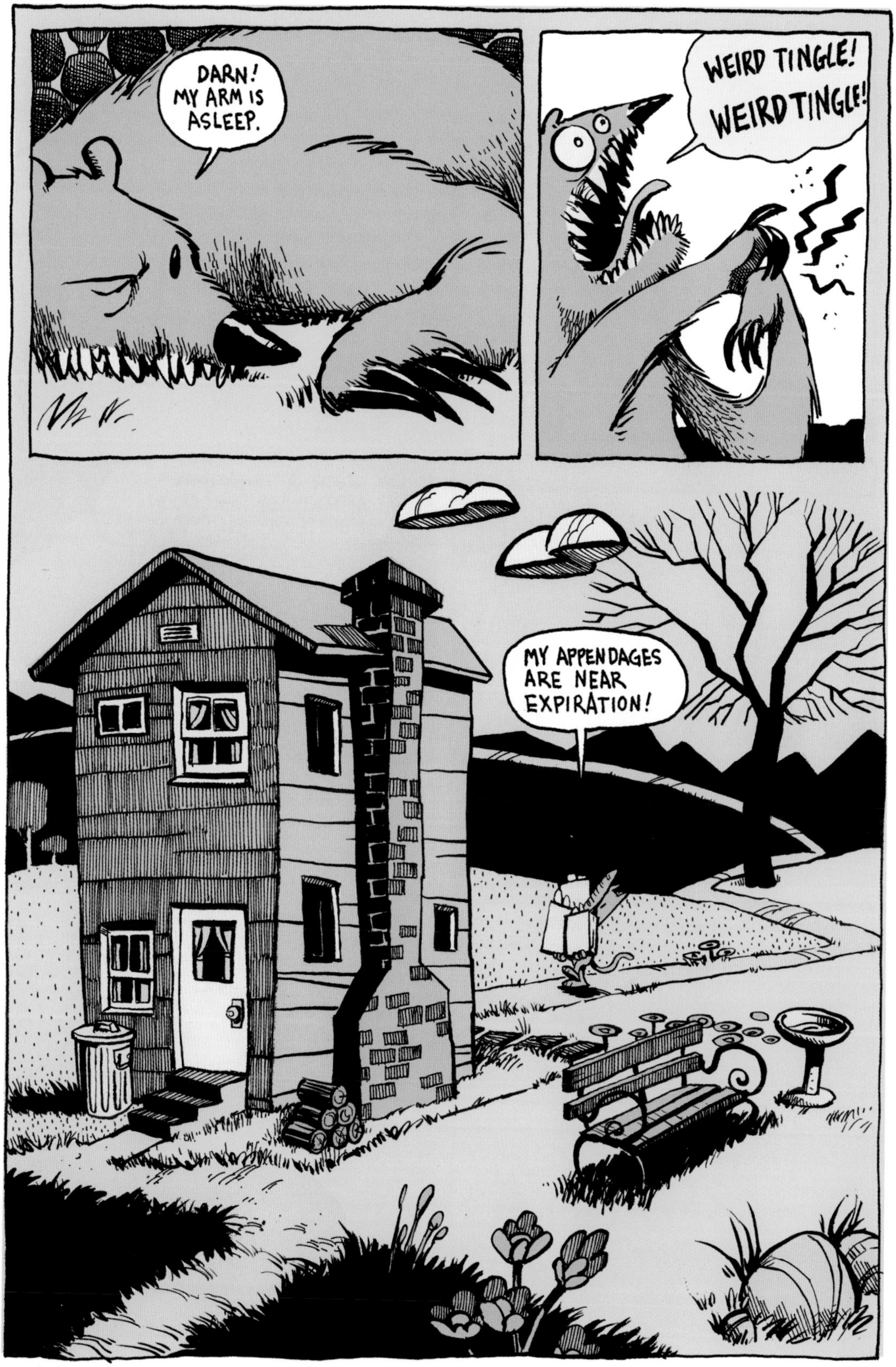
DARN! MY ARM IS ASLEEP.
WEIRD TINGLE! WEIRD TINGLE!
MY APPENDAGES ARE NEAR EXPIRATION!

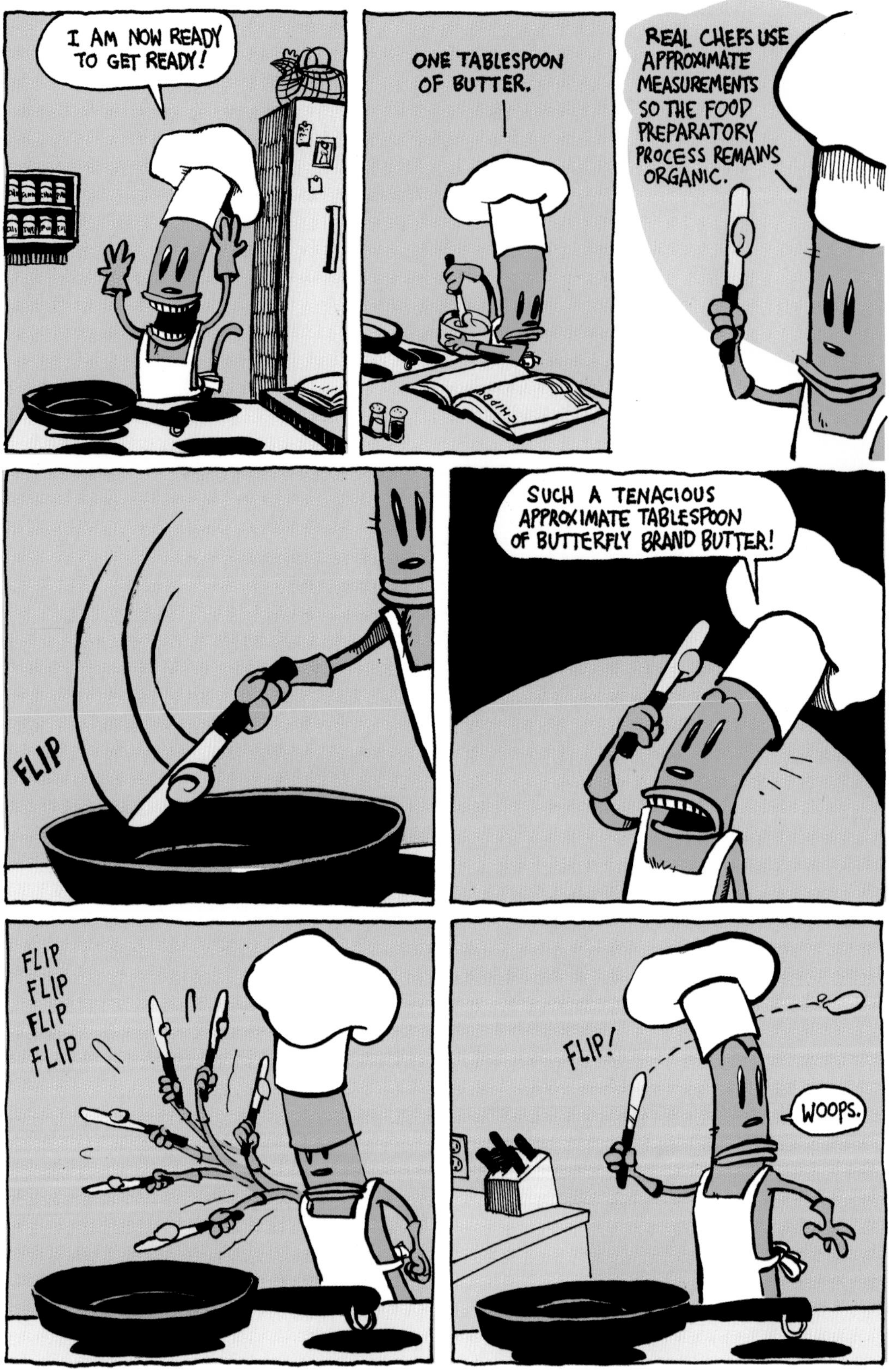
I AM NOW READY TO GET READY!
ONE TABLESPOON OF BUTTER.
REAL CHEFS USE APPROXIMATE MEASUREMENTS SO THE FOOD PREPARATORY PROCESS REMAINS ORGANIC.
FLIP
SUCH A TENACIOUS APPROXIMATE TABLESPOON OF BUTTERFLY BRAND BUTTER!
FLIP
FLIP
FLIP
FLIP
FLIP!
WOOPS.

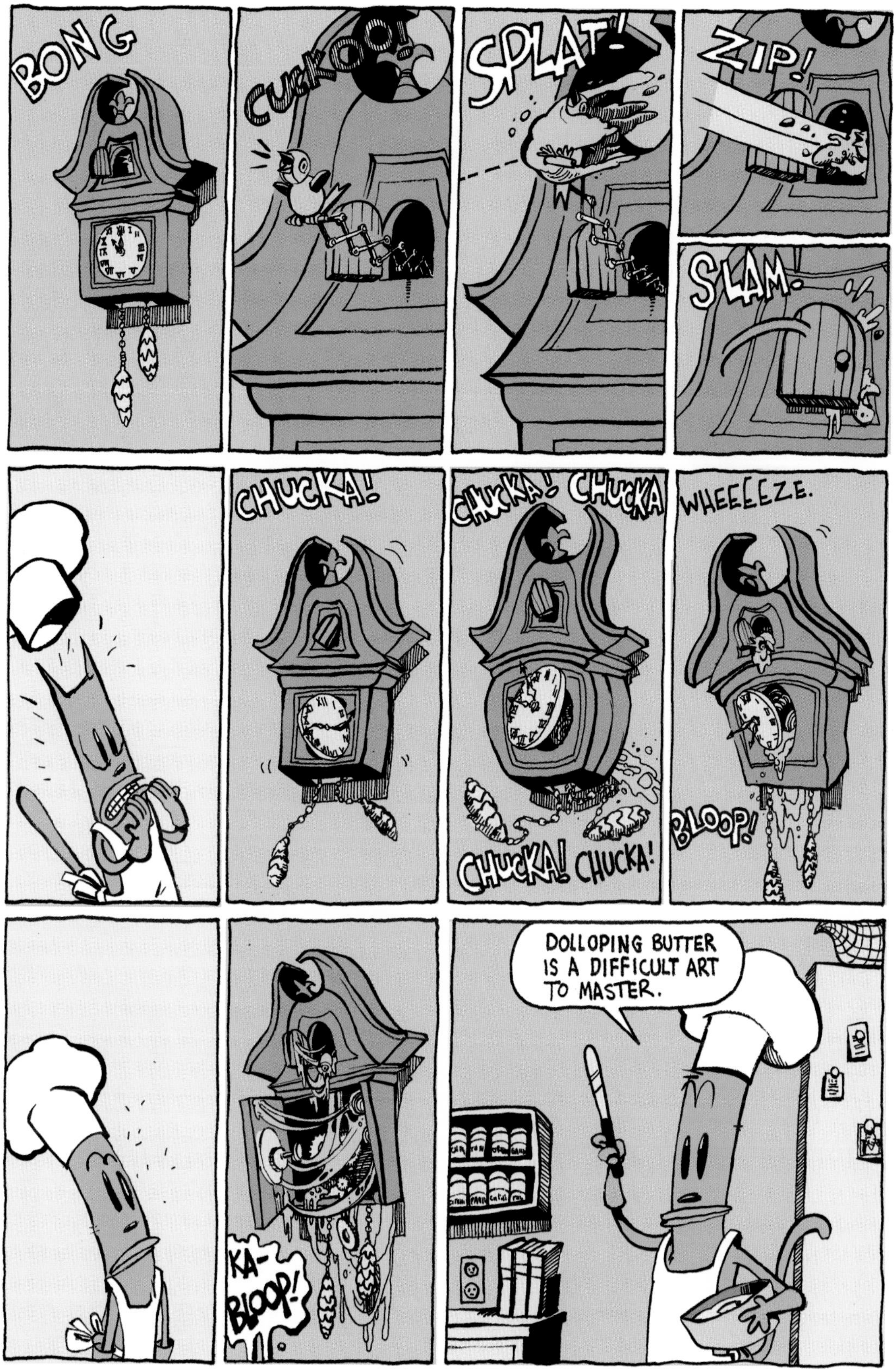
BONG
CUCKOO!
SPLAT!
ZIP!
SLAM.
CHUCKA!
CHUCKA! CHUCKA
CHUCKA! CHUCKA!
WHEEEEZE.
BLOOP!
KA-BLOOP!
DOLLOPING BUTTER IS A DIFFICULT ART TO MASTER.

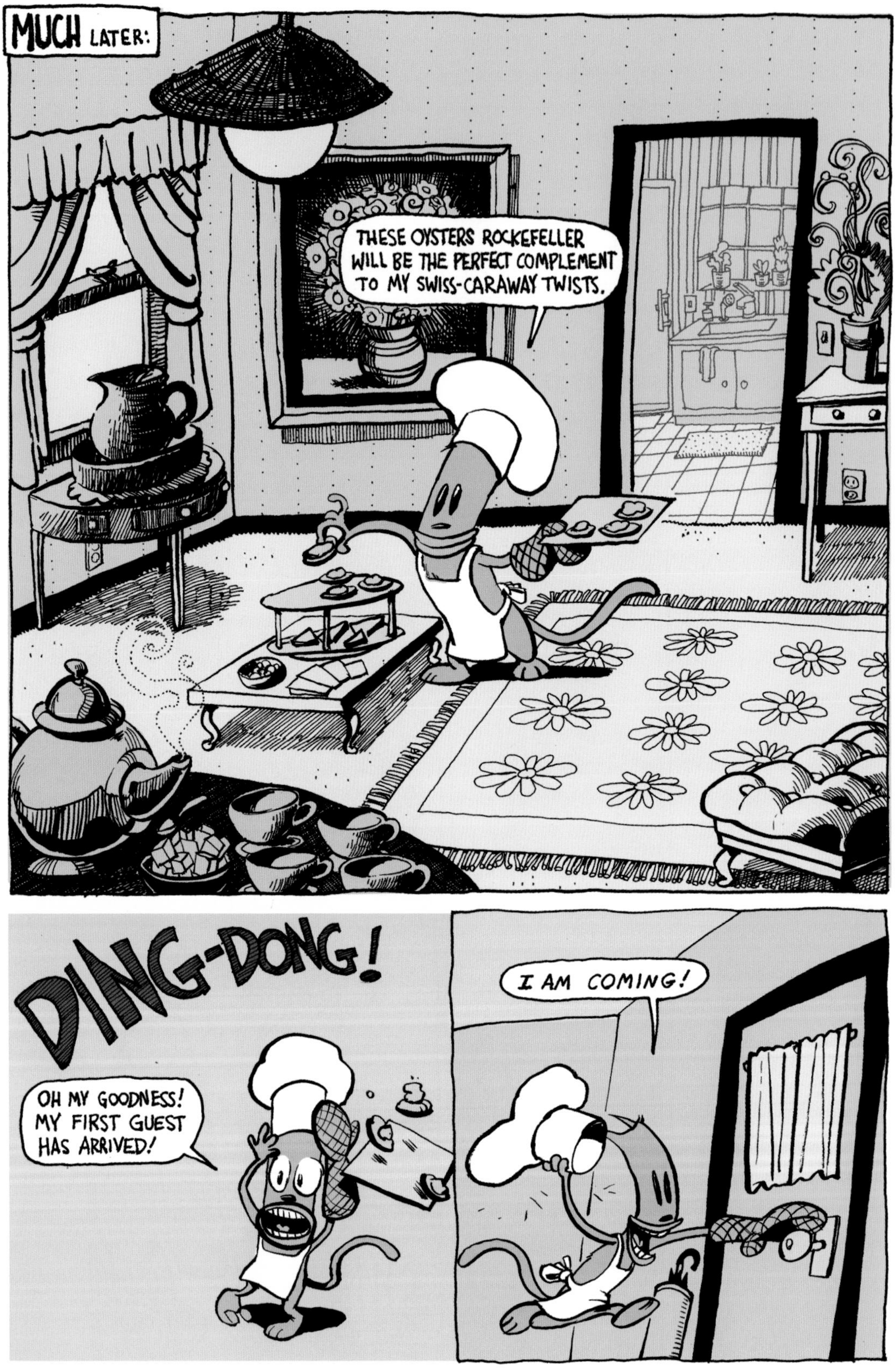
MUCH LATER:
THESE OYSTERS ROCKEFELLER WILL BE THE PERFECT COMPLEMENT TO MY SWISS-CARAWAY TWISTS.
DING-DONG!
OH MY GOODNESS! MY FIRST GUEST HAS ARRIVED!
I AM COMING!

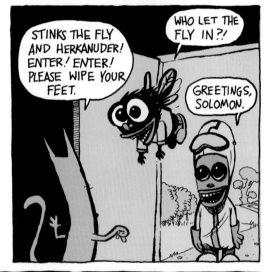

ALL OF MY ACQUAINTANCES APPEAR TO BE CONTENT WITH THE FESTIVITIES AND THE CONSUMABLES SEEM PRESENT IN VIRTUAL UBIQUITY.

DING-DONG!

THAT MUST BE COUSIN DONKEY!

THE WHOLE WORLD HAS TURNED INTO A COLOSSAL MOUNT OF HAIR AND FANG!

GRRRR.

GRAAAAR!!

URSUS HORRIBILIS! SHOO! SHOO BEAR! SHOO!

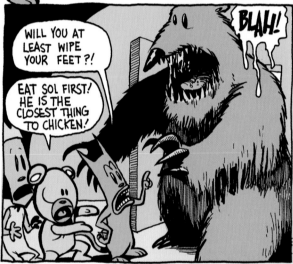

WILL YOU AT LEAST WIPE YOUR FEET?!

EAT SOL FIRST! HE IS THE CLOSEST THING TO CHICKEN!

BLAH!

MR. BEAR, PLEASE DO NOT CONSUME ME!

HERE, TRY A SPINACH PHYLLO TRIANGLE!

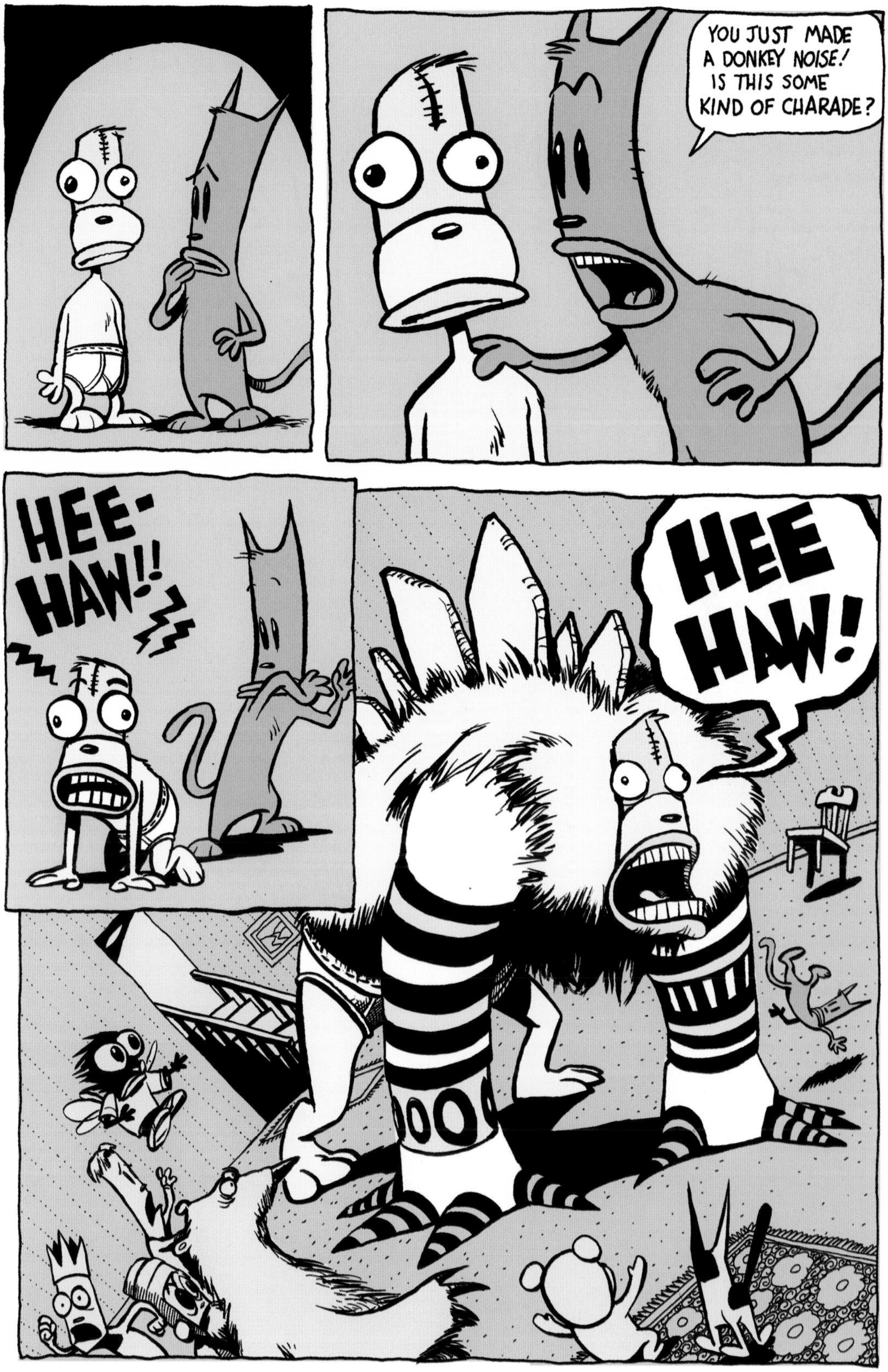
YOU JUST MADE A DONKEY NOISE! IS THIS SOME KIND OF CHARADE?
HEE-HAW!!
HEE HAW!

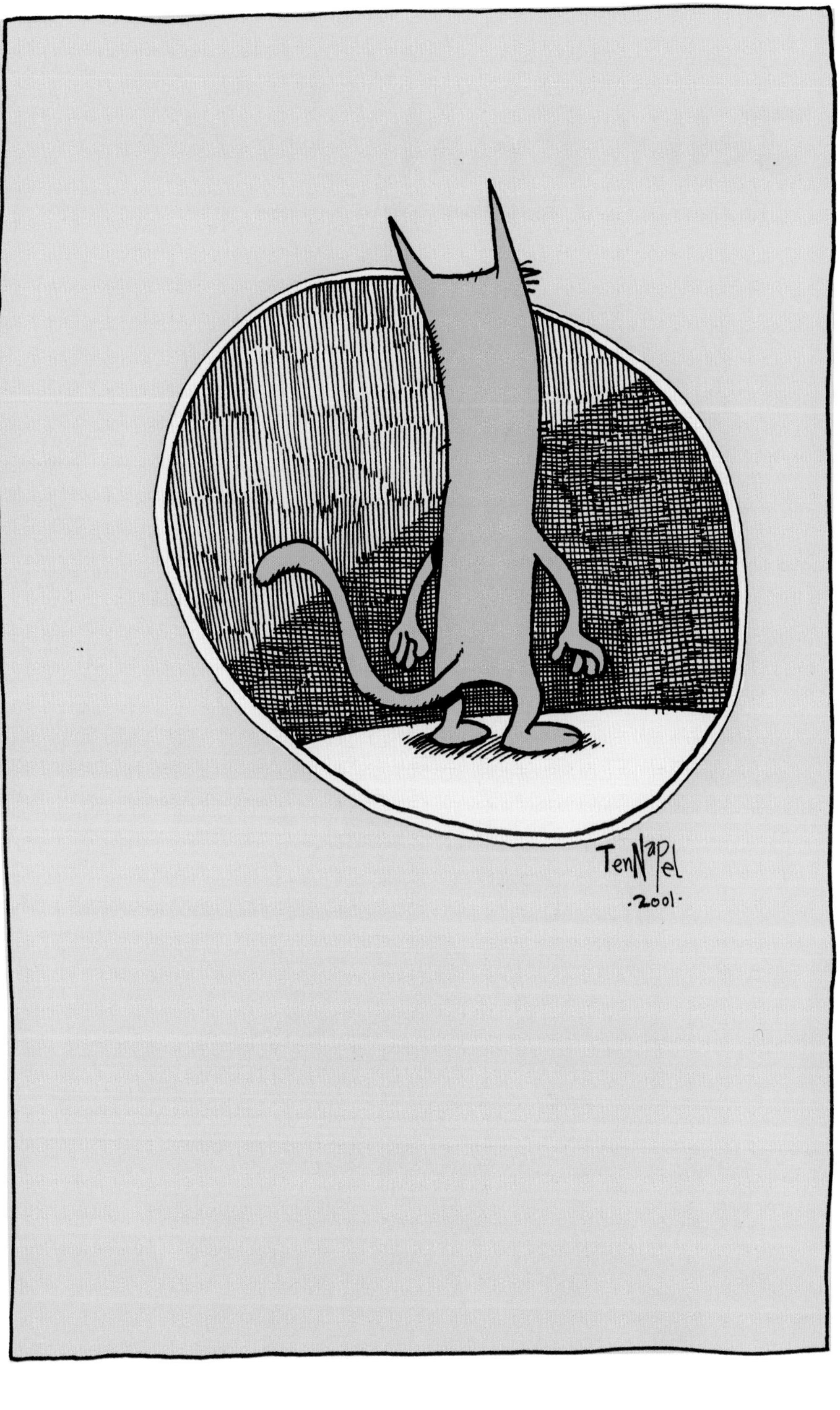
TenNapel
·2001·

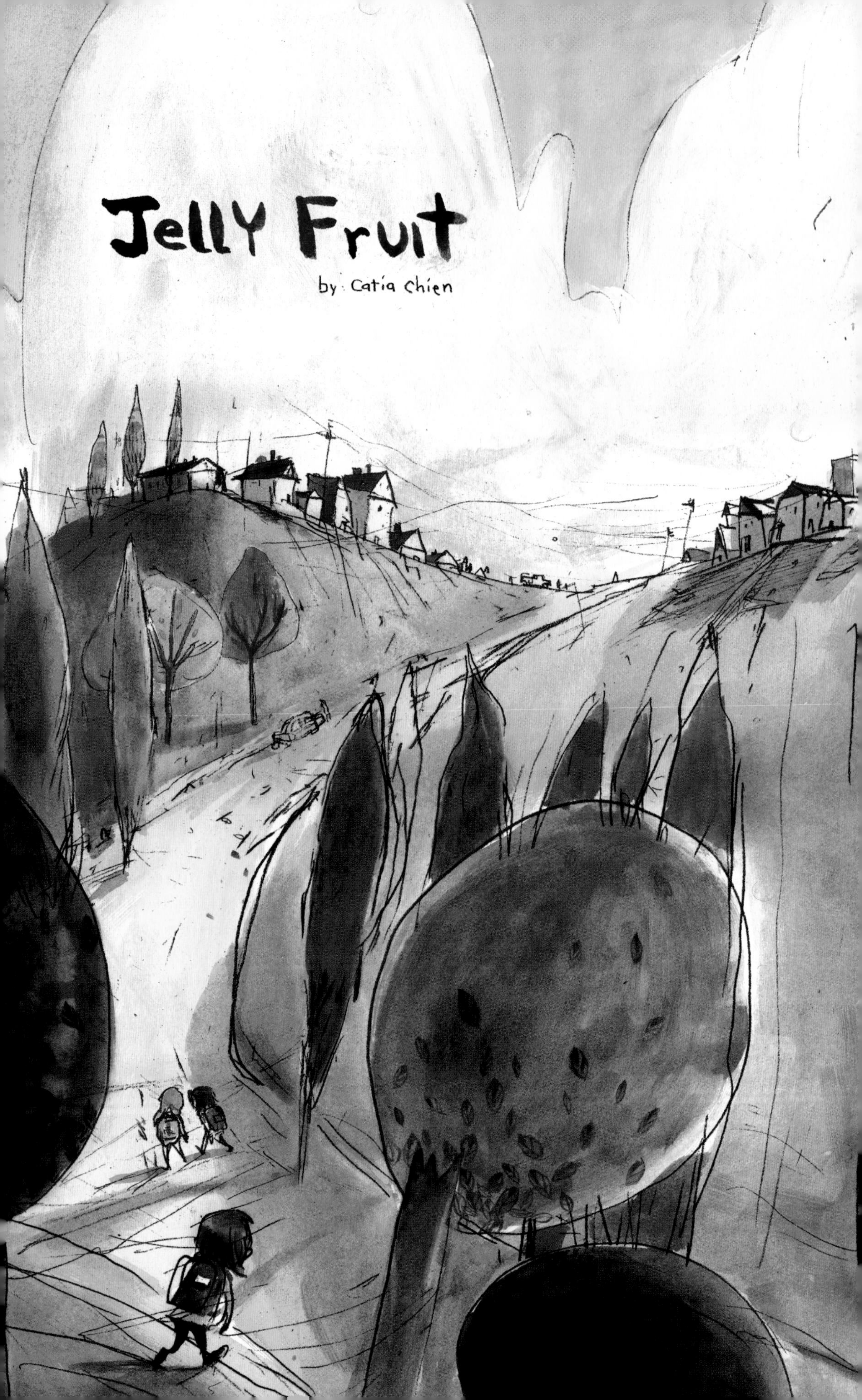
Jelly Fruit
by: Catia Chien

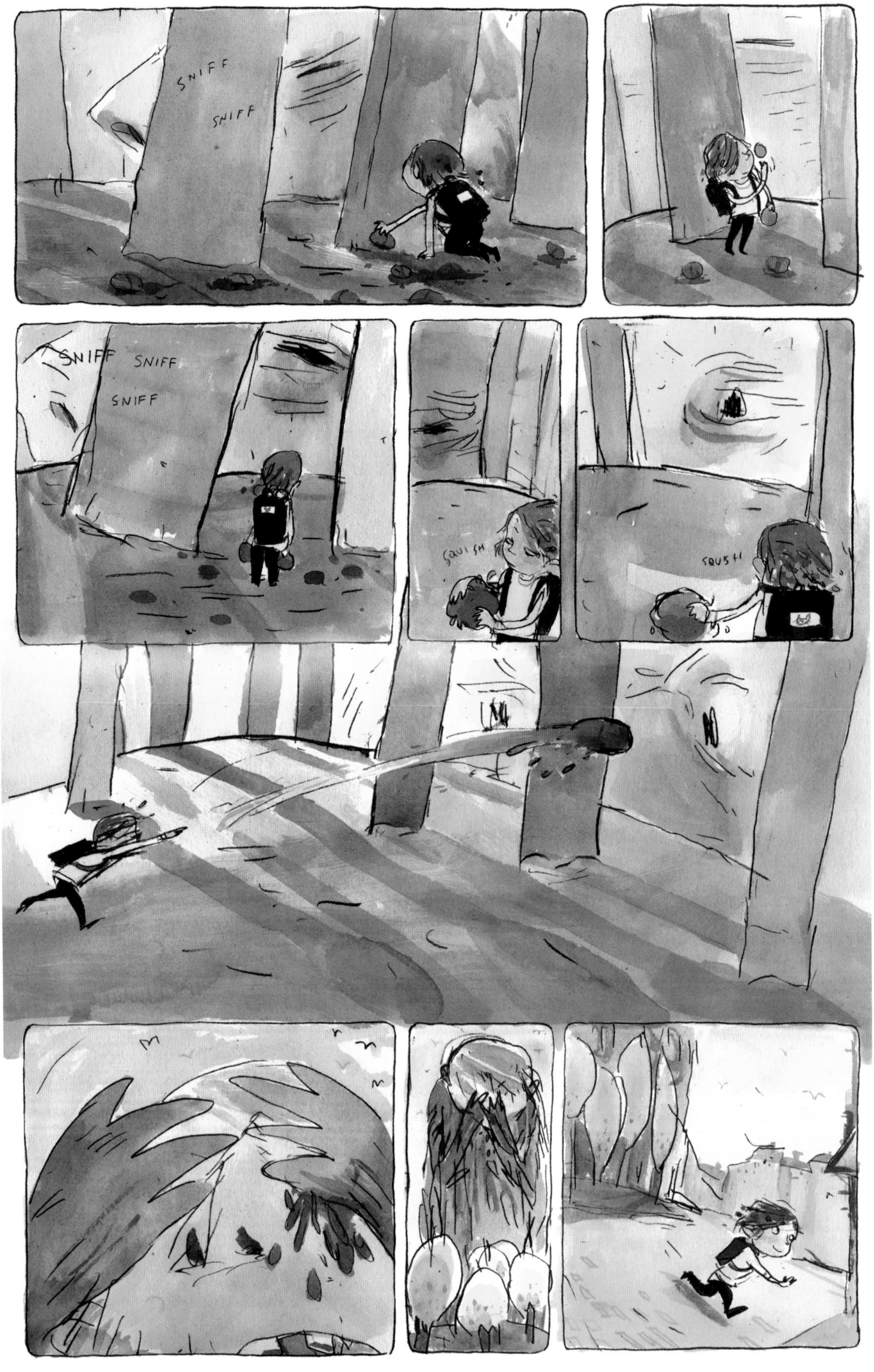
SNIFF
SNIFF
SNIFF SNIFF
SNIFF
SQUISH
SQUISH

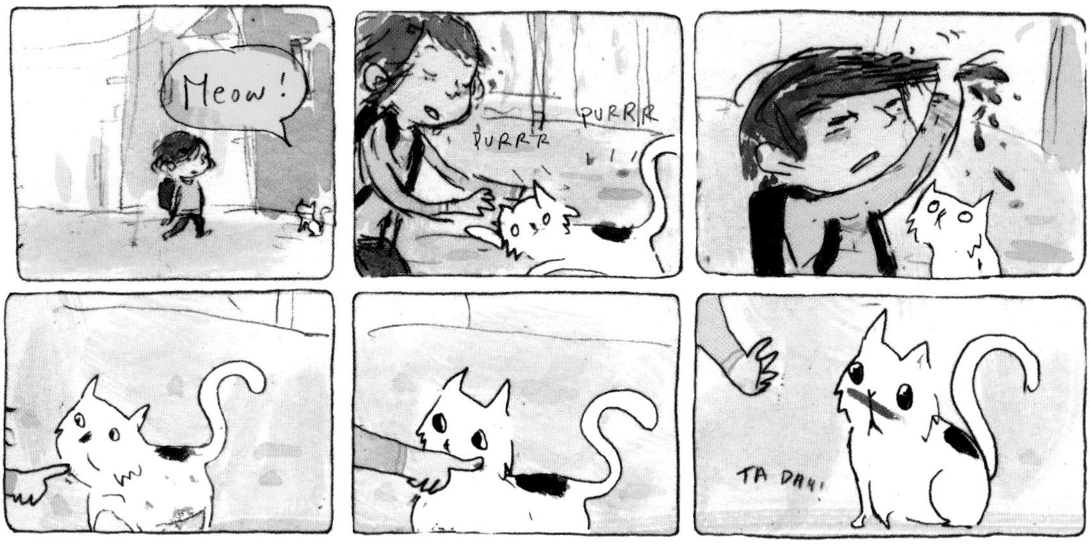
Meow!
PURRR
PURRR
TA DA!!

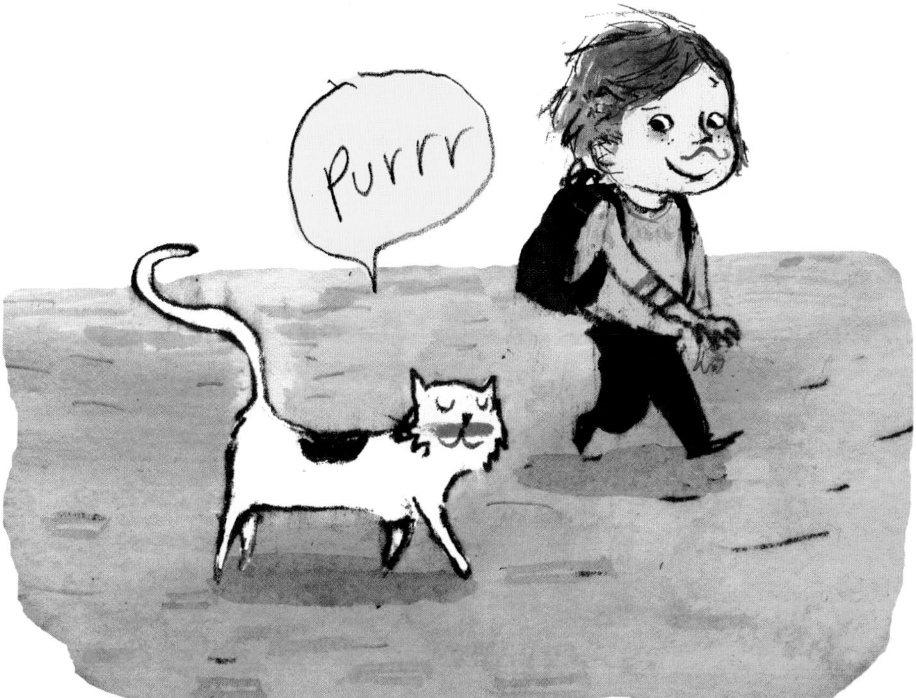
Purrr

The end

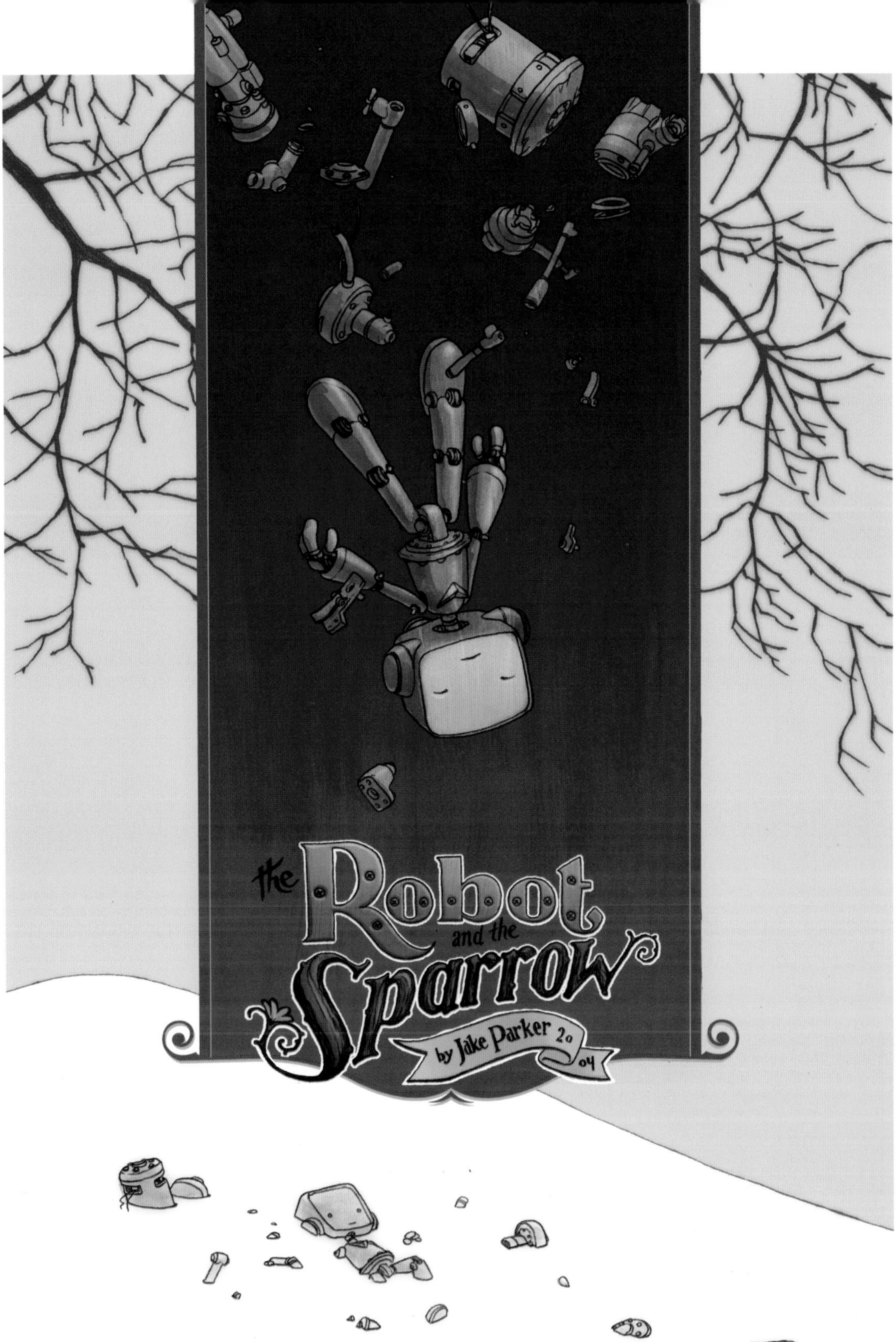
the Robot and the Sparrow
by Jake Parker 2004

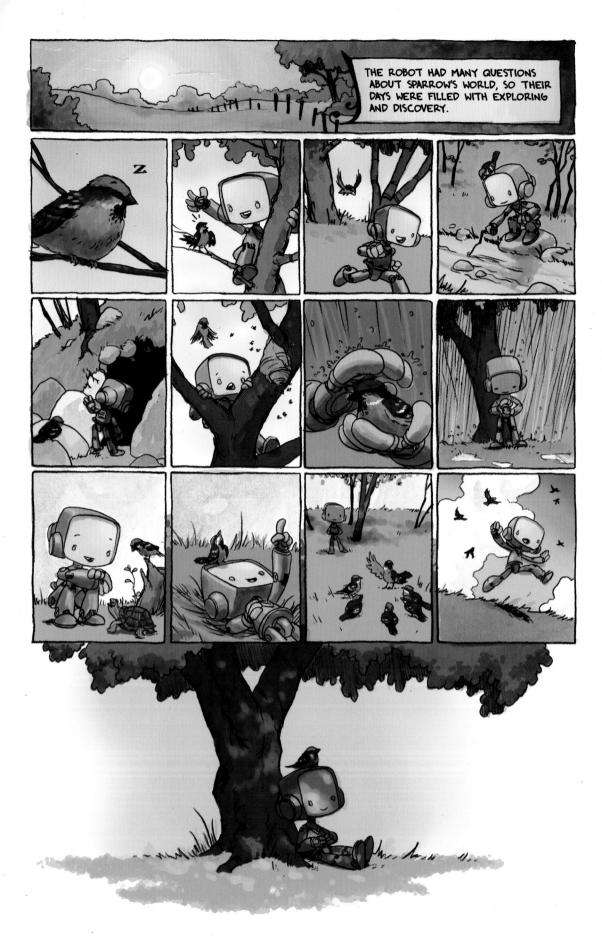

THE ROBOT HAD MANY QUESTIONS ABOUT SPARROW'S WORLD, SO THEIR DAYS WERE FILLED WITH EXPLORING AND DISCOVERY.

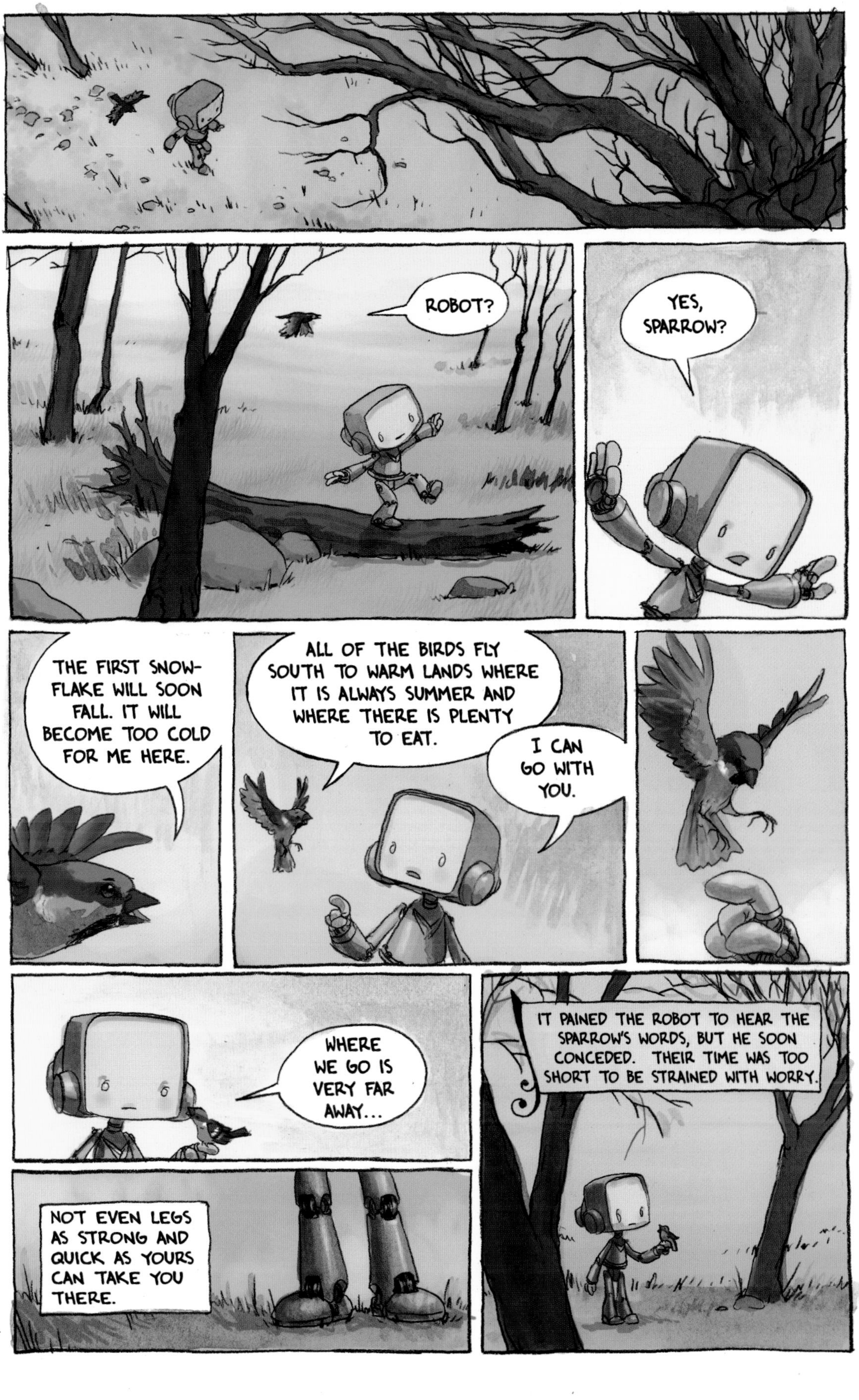
ROBOT?
YES, SPARROW?
THE FIRST SNOW-FLAKE WILL SOON FALL. IT WILL BECOME TOO COLD FOR ME HERE.
ALL OF THE BIRDS FLY SOUTH TO WARM LANDS WHERE IT IS ALWAYS SUMMER AND WHERE THERE IS PLENTY TO EAT.
I CAN GO WITH YOU.
WHERE WE GO IS VERY FAR AWAY...
NOT EVEN LEGS AS STRONG AND QUICK AS YOURS CAN TAKE YOU THERE.
IT PAINED THE ROBOT TO HEAR THE SPARROW'S WORDS, BUT HE SOON CONCEDED. THEIR TIME WAS TOO SHORT TO BE STRAINED WITH WORRY.

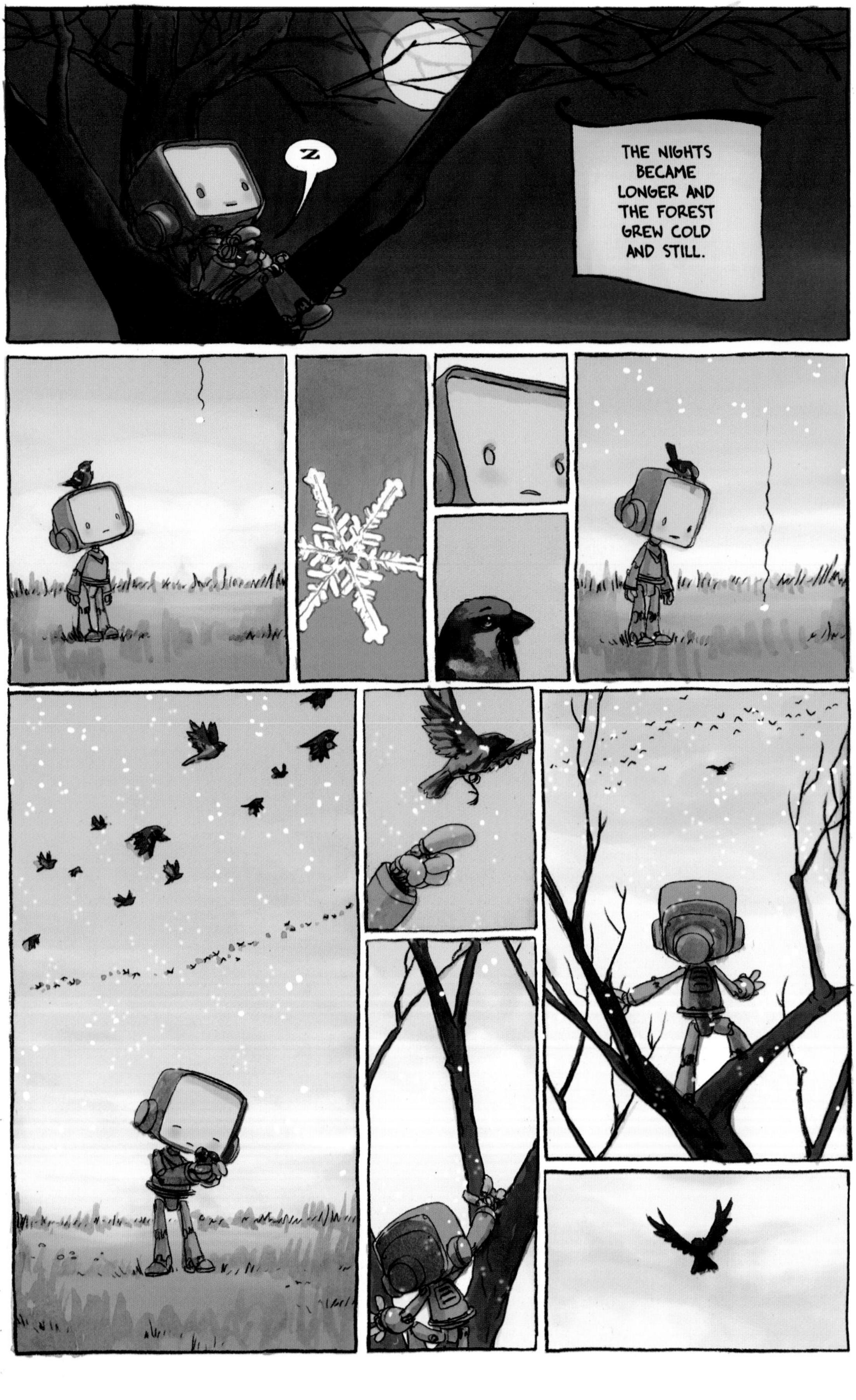
Z
THE NIGHTS BECAME LONGER AND THE FOREST GREW COLD AND STILL.

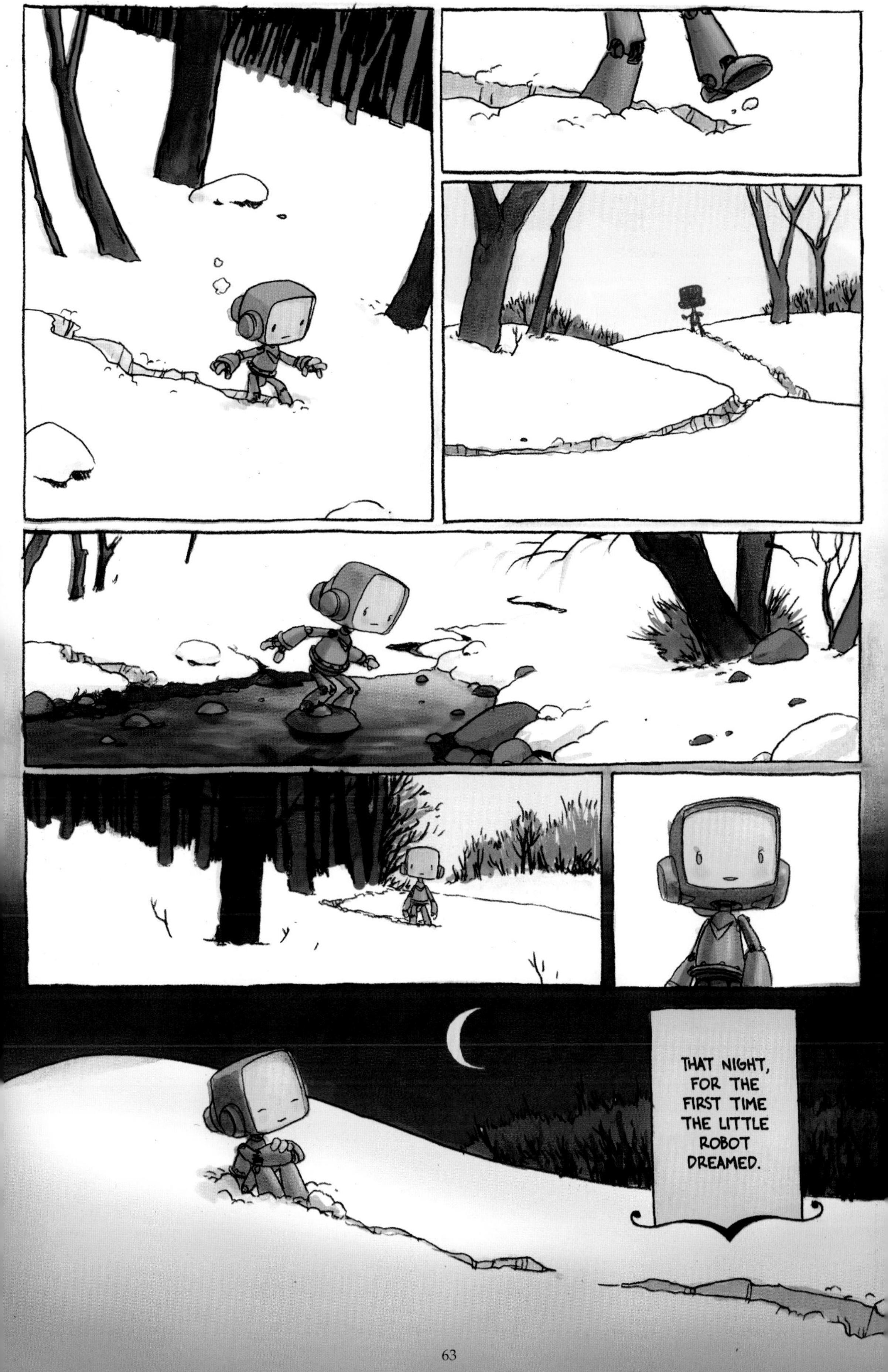
THAT NIGHT, FOR THE FIRST TIME THE LITTLE ROBOT DREAMED.

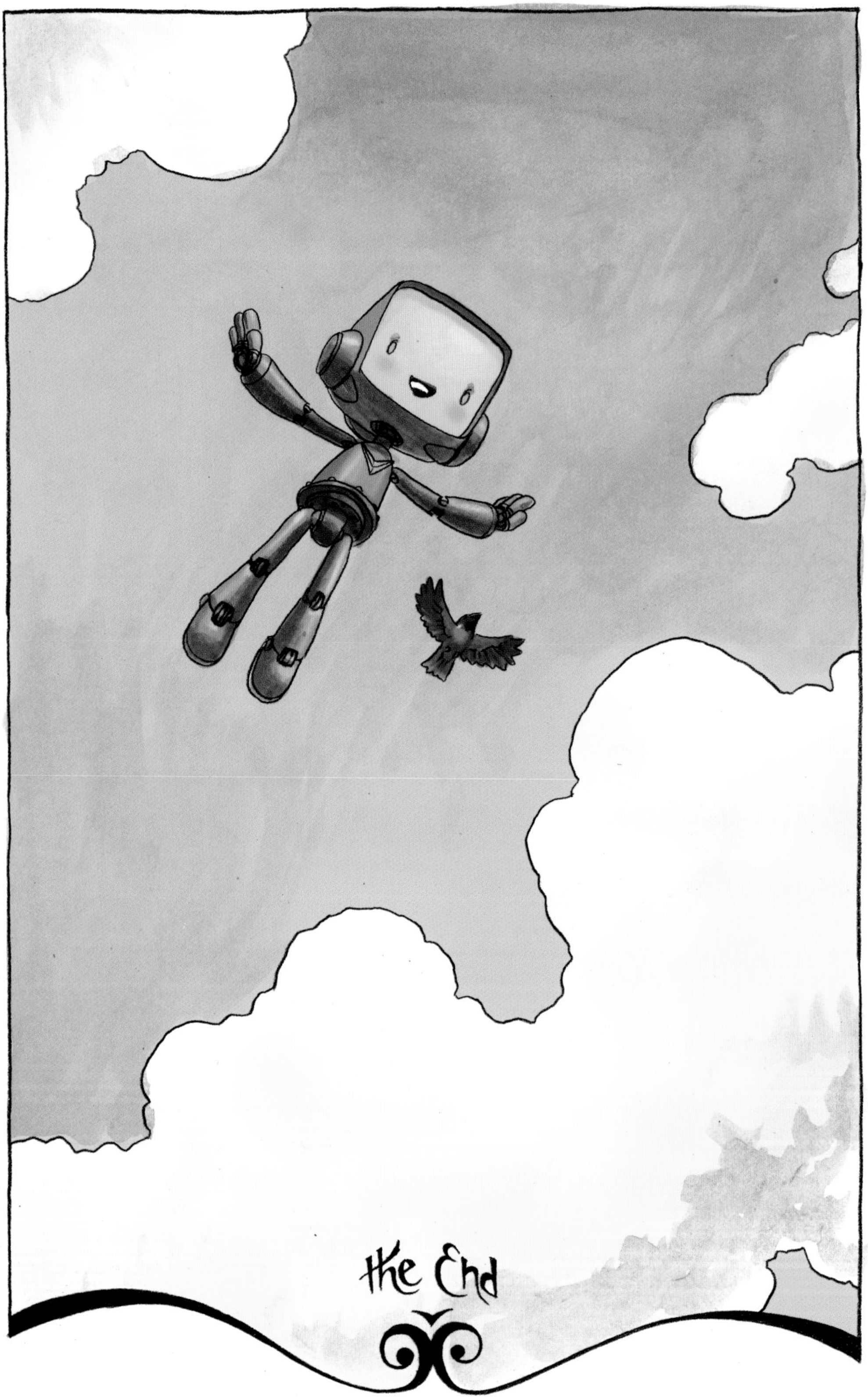
the End

DEAD SOUL'S · DAY OUT ·

A MALINKY ROBOT STORY

BY SONNY LIEW

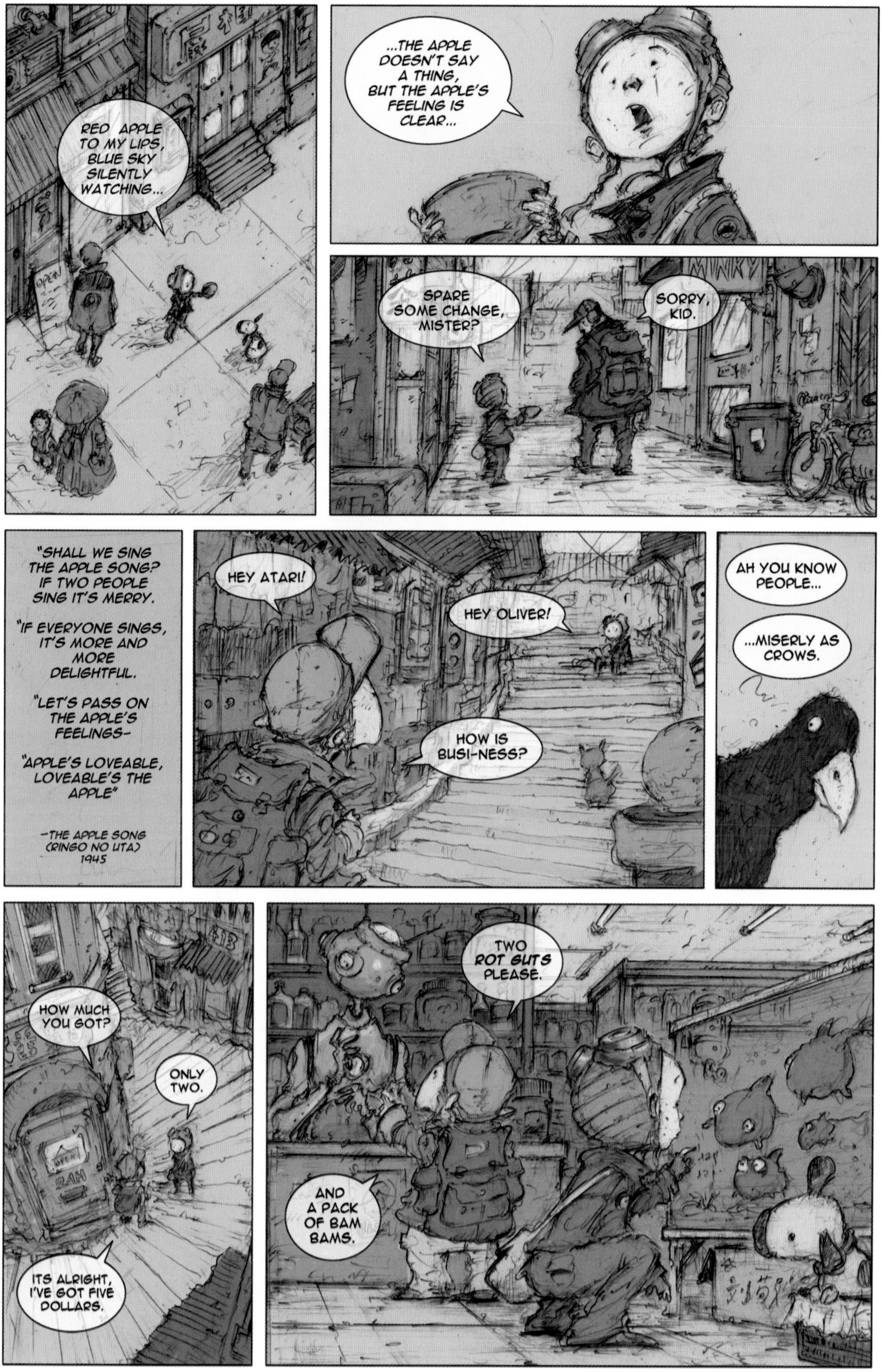
RED APPLE TO MY LIPS, BLUE SKY SILENTLY WATCHING...
OPEN
...THE APPLE DOESN'T SAY A THING, BUT THE APPLE'S FEELING IS CLEAR...
SPARE SOME CHANGE, MISTER?
SORRY, KID.
"SHALL WE SING THE APPLE SONG? IF TWO PEOPLE SING IT'S MERRY.
"IF EVERYONE SINGS, IT'S MORE AND MORE DELIGHTFUL.
"LET'S PASS ON THE APPLE'S FEELINGS-
"APPLE'S LOVEABLE, LOVEABLE'S THE APPLE"
-THE APPLE SONG (RINGO NO UTA) 1945
HEY ATARI!
HEY OLIVER!
HOW IS BUSI-NESS?
AH YOU KNOW PEOPLE...
...MISERLY AS CROWS.
HOW MUCH YOU GOT?
ONLY TWO.
ITS ALRIGHT, I'VE GOT FIVE DOLLARS.
TWO ROT GUTS PLEASE.
AND A PACK OF BAM BAMS.

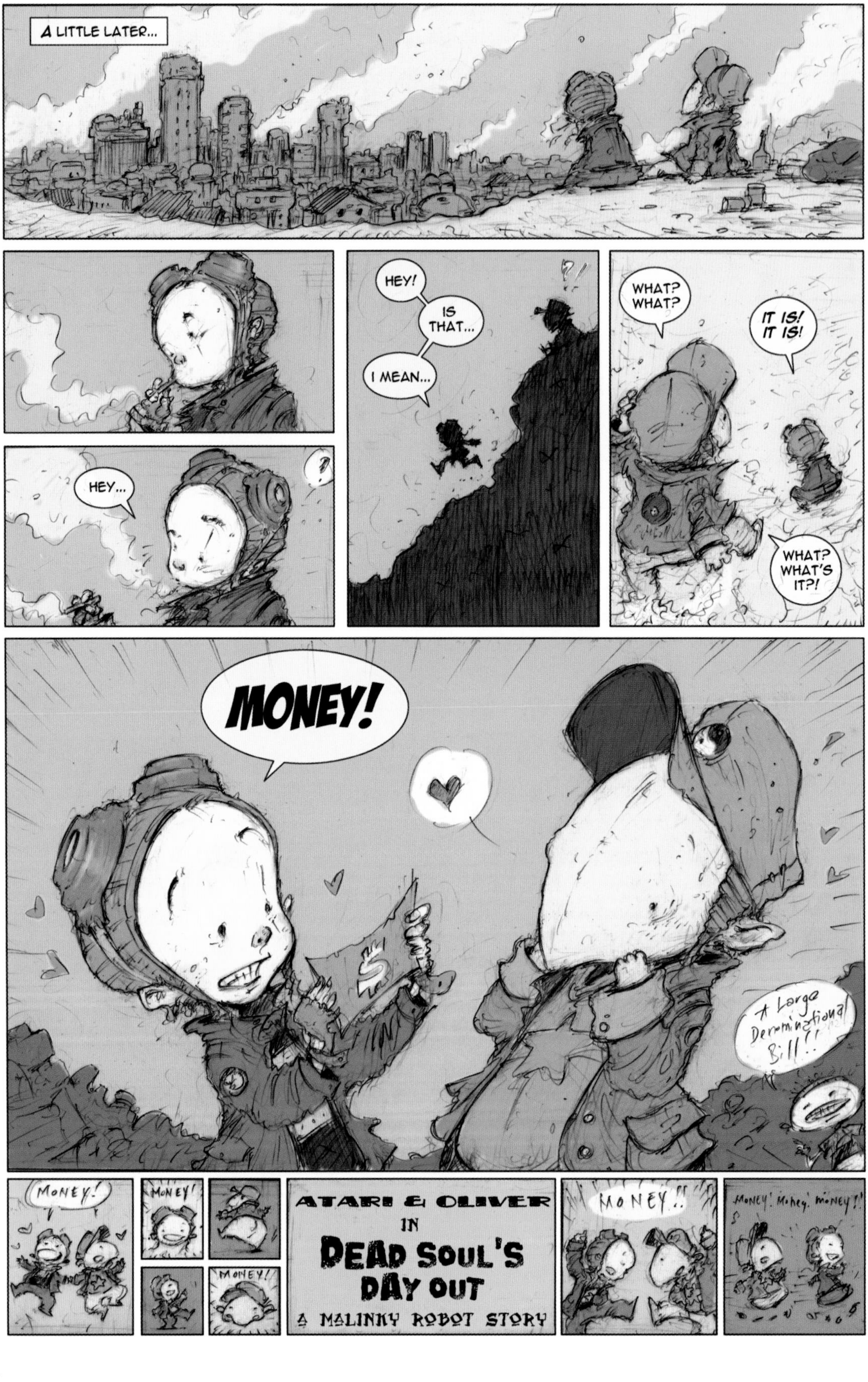
A LITTLE LATER...
HEY...
HEY!
IS THAT...
I MEAN...
?!
WHAT? WHAT?
IT IS! IT IS!
WHAT? WHAT'S IT?!
MONEY!
A Large Denominational Bill!!
MONEY!
MONEY!
MONEY!
ATARI & OLIVER
IN
DEAD SOUL'S DAY OUT
A MALINKY ROBOT STORY
MONEY!!
Money! Money! money!!

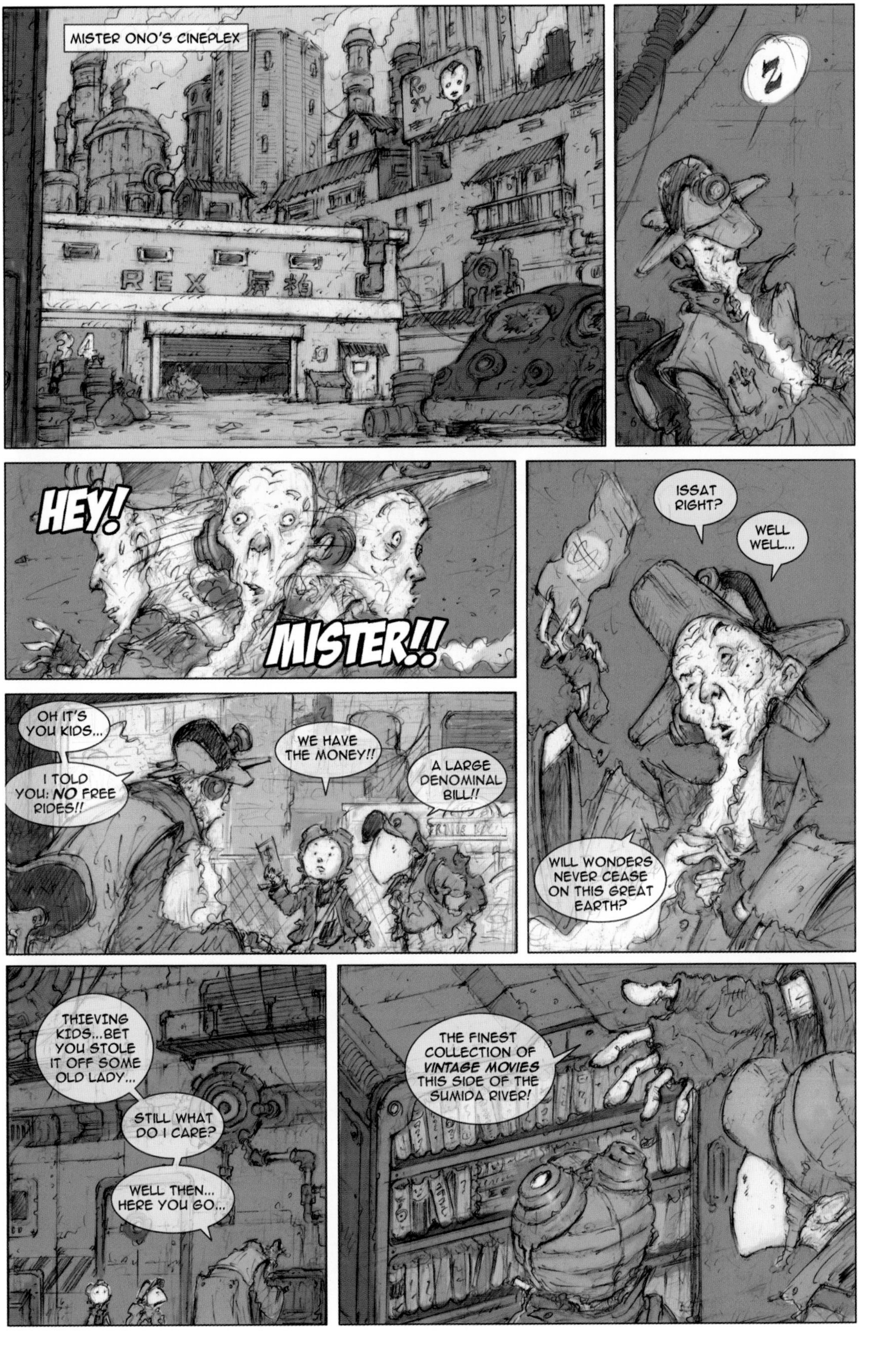
MISTER ONO'S CINEPLEX
REX
Z
HEY!
MISTER!!
OH IT'S YOU KIDS...
I TOLD YOU: NO FREE RIDES!!
WE HAVE THE MONEY!!
A LARGE DENOMINAL BILL!!
ISSAT RIGHT?
WELL WELL...
WILL WONDERS NEVER CEASE ON THIS GREAT EARTH?
THIEVING KIDS...BET YOU STOLE IT OFF SOME OLD LADY...
STILL WHAT DO I CARE?
WELL THEN... HERE YOU GO...
THE FINEST COLLECTION OF VINTAGE MOVIES THIS SIDE OF THE SUMIDA RIVER!

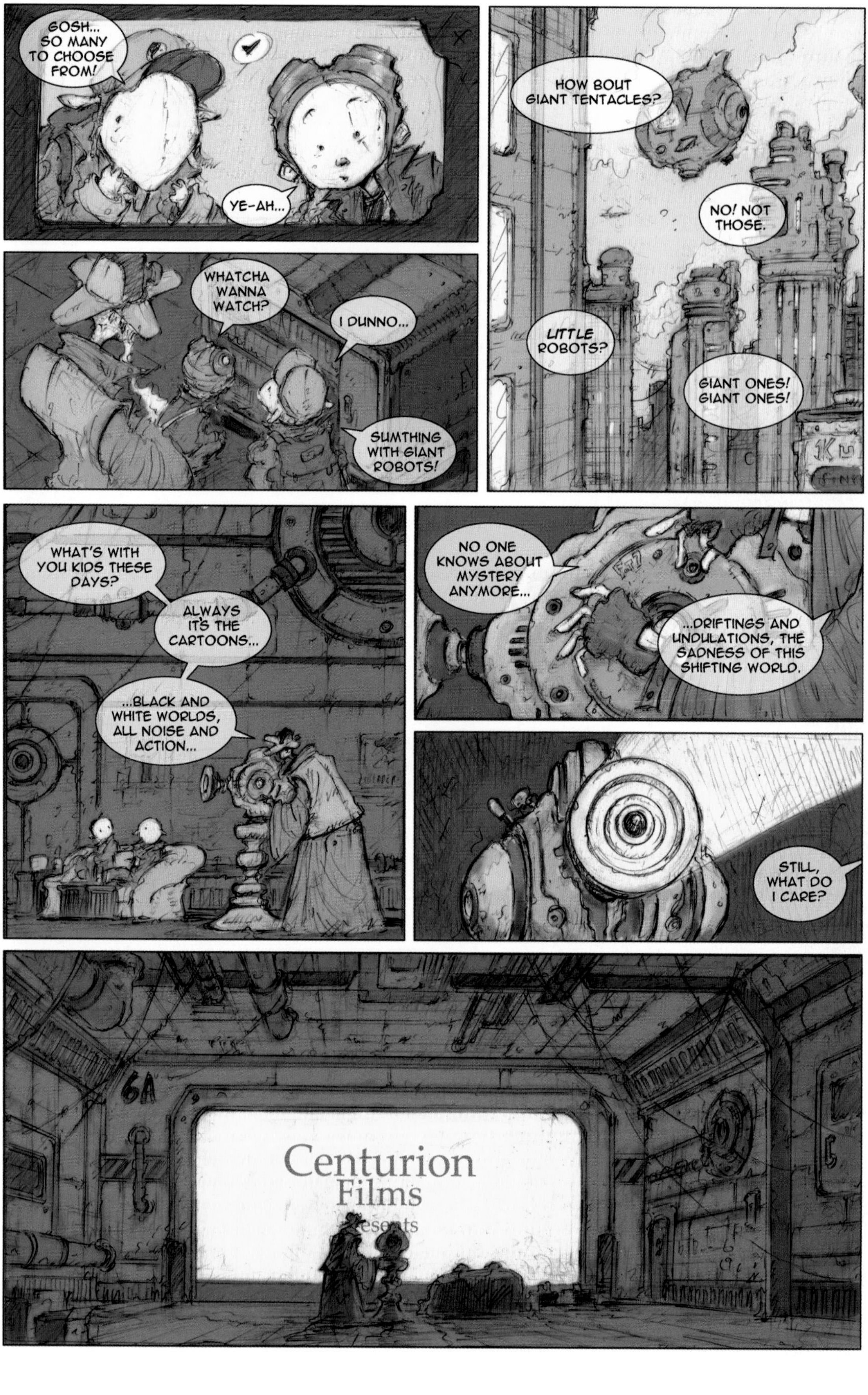
GOSH... SO MANY TO CHOOSE FROM!
YE-AH...
HOW BOUT GIANT TENTACLES?
NO! NOT THOSE.
LITTLE ROBOTS?
GIANT ONES! GIANT ONES!
WHATCHA WANNA WATCH?
I DUNNO...
SUMTHING WITH GIANT ROBOTS!
WHAT'S WITH YOU KIDS THESE DAYS?
ALWAYS IT'S THE CARTOONS...
...BLACK AND WHITE WORLDS, ALL NOISE AND ACTION...
NO ONE KNOWS ABOUT MYSTERY ANYMORE...
...DRIFTINGS AND UNDULATIONS, THE SADNESS OF THIS SHIFTING WORLD.
STILL, WHAT DO I CARE?
6A
Centurion
Films
Presents

"*DIE!* OPTIMETRIX PRIME!"

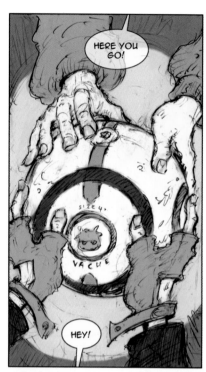

HERE YOU GO!

HEY!

CHECK IT OUT, OLIVER!

HA HA

THE *PSX-850!* THE LATEST ON THE MARKET!

IT'S BOO-TIFUL...

YOU WANNA PLAY A GAME, MISHA?

NAH...

HAFTA RUN, GOTTA HELP MY PARENTS PACK...

WHEN WILL YOU BE BACK?

FOR A VISIT?

DUNNO, A COUPLE OF MONTHS I GUESS...

I'LL SEND YOU GUYS A POSTCARD!

FOOM

SEEYA MISHA!

SEEYA ATARI!

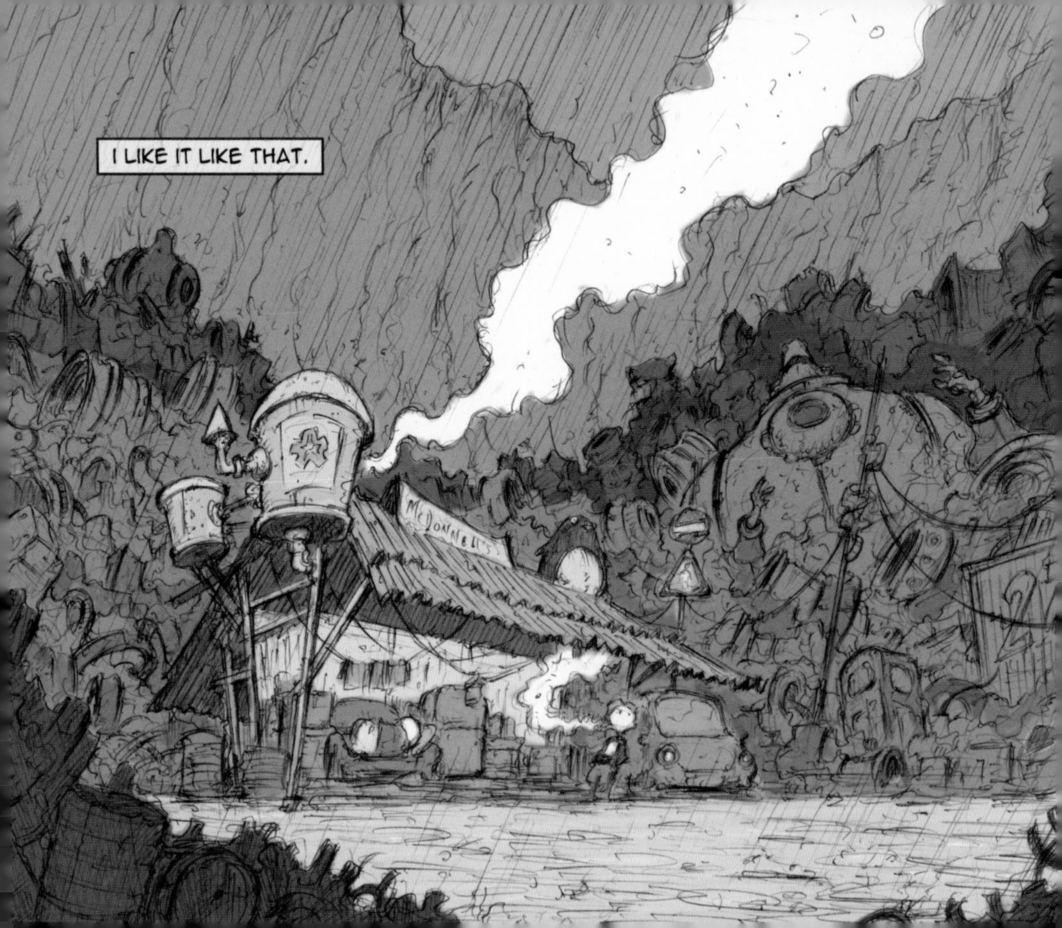
I LIKE IT LIKE THAT.

[redacted]

REWARD!

$5,000

ROCO ROJO'S MONSTER IS STILL AT LARGE

ATTENTION ALL SLAYERS

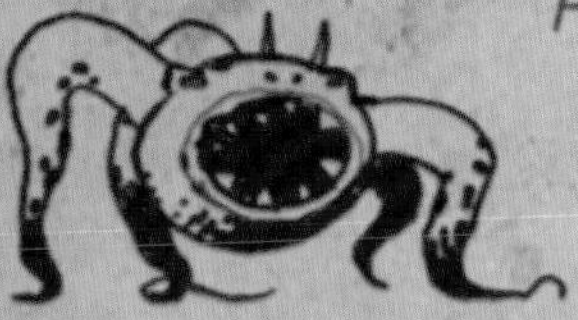

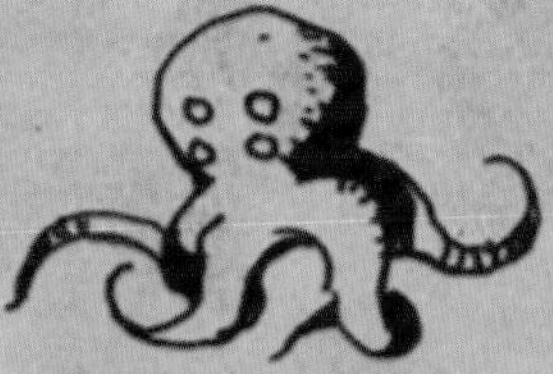

NOTE: MONSTER(S) MIGHT NOT LOOK LIKE DRAWINGS

[redacted]

THAT THING STINKS, MAN.

THEN TAKE IT OFF THE TABLE.

THE WAY YOU TACKLED THAT BEAST! MAN, I WAS AFRAID OF YOU!

HEY, EAT UP. YOU DON'T LOOK TOO GOOD.

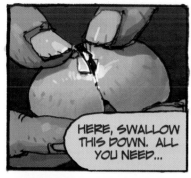

HERE, SWALLOW THIS DOWN. ALL YOU NEED...

...ARE A LITTLE NUTRIENTS!

THESE NOODLES... THEY TASTE OLD. AND THE SOUP LACKS FLAVOR. I SWEAR, ONE DAY I'LL HAVE MY OWN RESTAURANT AND-

YOU'LL QUIT THIS BUSINESS. I KNOW, I KNOW! WELL, A FEW MORE OF THESE BOUNTIES AND YOU JUST MIGHT SAVE ENOUGH MONEY FOR THAT DREAM OF YOURS.

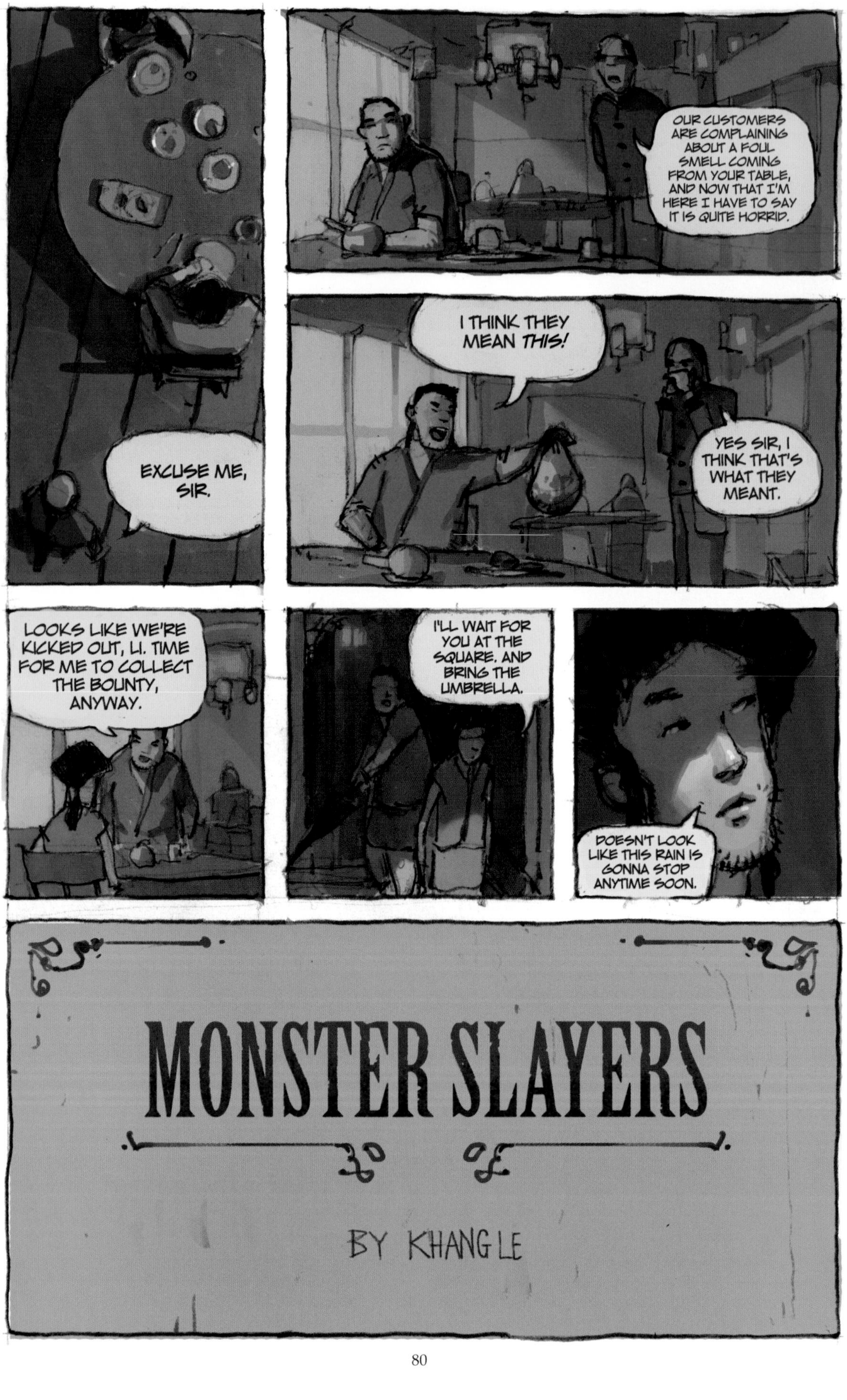
EXCUSE ME, SIR.
OUR CUSTOMERS ARE COMPLAINING ABOUT A FOUL SMELL COMING FROM YOUR TABLE, AND NOW THAT I'M HERE I HAVE TO SAY IT IS QUITE HORRID.
I THINK THEY MEAN *THIS!*
YES SIR, I THINK THAT'S WHAT THEY MEANT.
LOOKS LIKE WE'RE KICKED OUT, LI. TIME FOR ME TO COLLECT THE BOUNTY, ANYWAY.
I'LL WAIT FOR YOU AT THE SQUARE. AND BRING THE UMBRELLA.
DOESN'T LOOK LIKE THIS RAIN IS GONNA STOP ANYTIME SOON.
MONSTER SLAYERS
BY KHANG LE

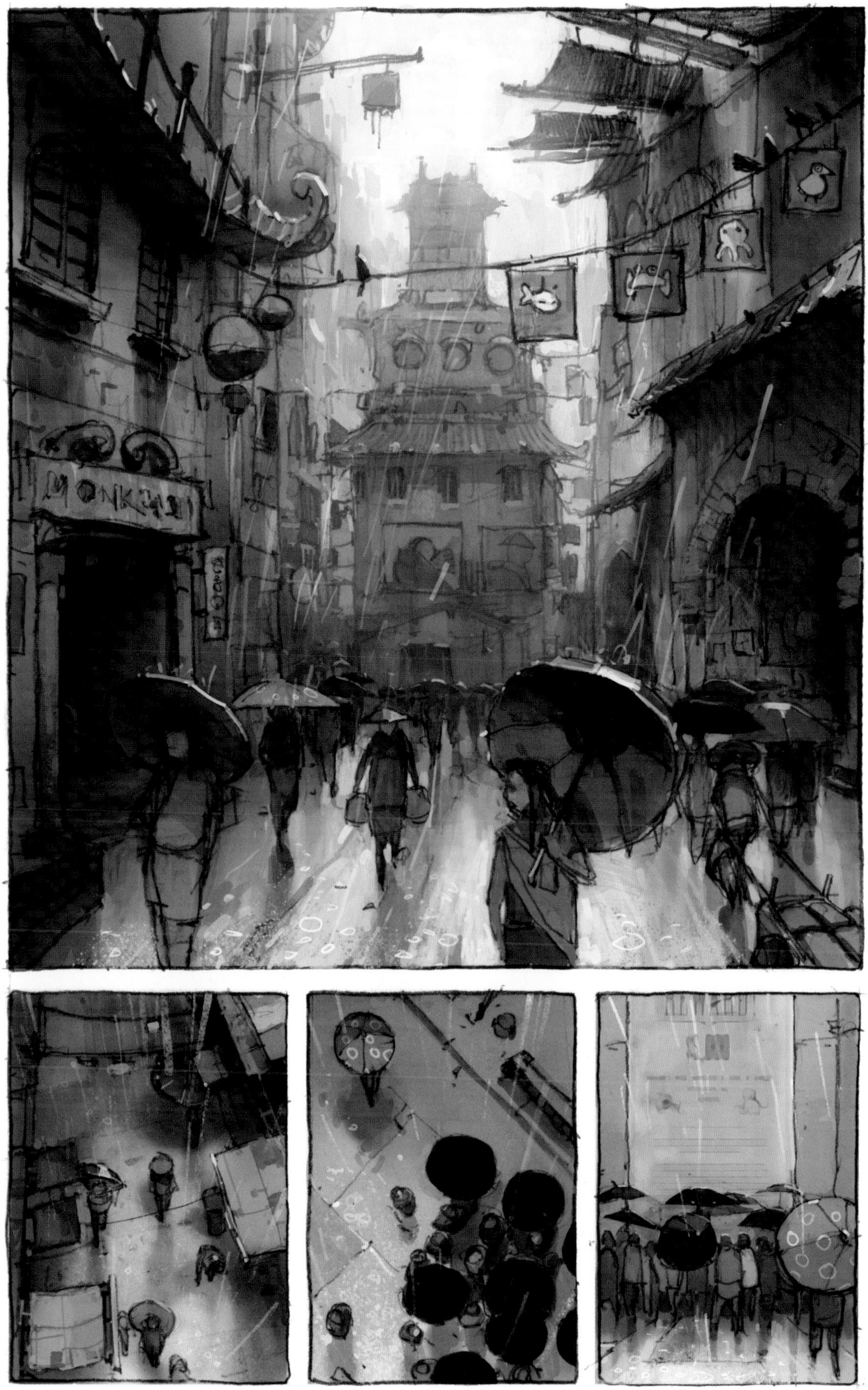

NO WAY AM I RISKING MY LIFE FOR THAT SMALL REWARD!

ROCO ROJO? WHAT A DUMP! A DESERT TOWN FULL OF SAVAGES!

5000? HAHAHA! BUNCH OF CHEAPSKATES.

THOSE BEASTS JUST SEEM TO POP UP EVERYWHERE THESE DAYS.

THOSE POOR SOULS, DYING OF THIRST IS A HORRIBLE WAY TO GO.

EXCUSE ME SIR, I CAN'T GET CLOSE ENOUGH TO SEE. IS THAT THE NEW BOUNTY?

YES, IT'S JUST A SMALL REWARD FOR A BEAST DWELLING IN THE WELL OF *ROCO ROJO*. IT'S A DESERT TOWN SO THEY'RE DESPERATE FOR HELP. THAT MONSTER—

IS NO MATCH FOR ME! I WILL **SLAUGHTER** THAT FORSAKEN BEAST WITH MY BARE HANDS—

WHO'S THIS GUY

FOR I AM *SIR AKIMA* !!!

WHAT A LOSER.

HEY HEY! WHERE ARE YOU GOING? DON'T YOU WANT TO HEAR MY STORY ABOUT SLAYING THE BEAST OF AGAMORA?

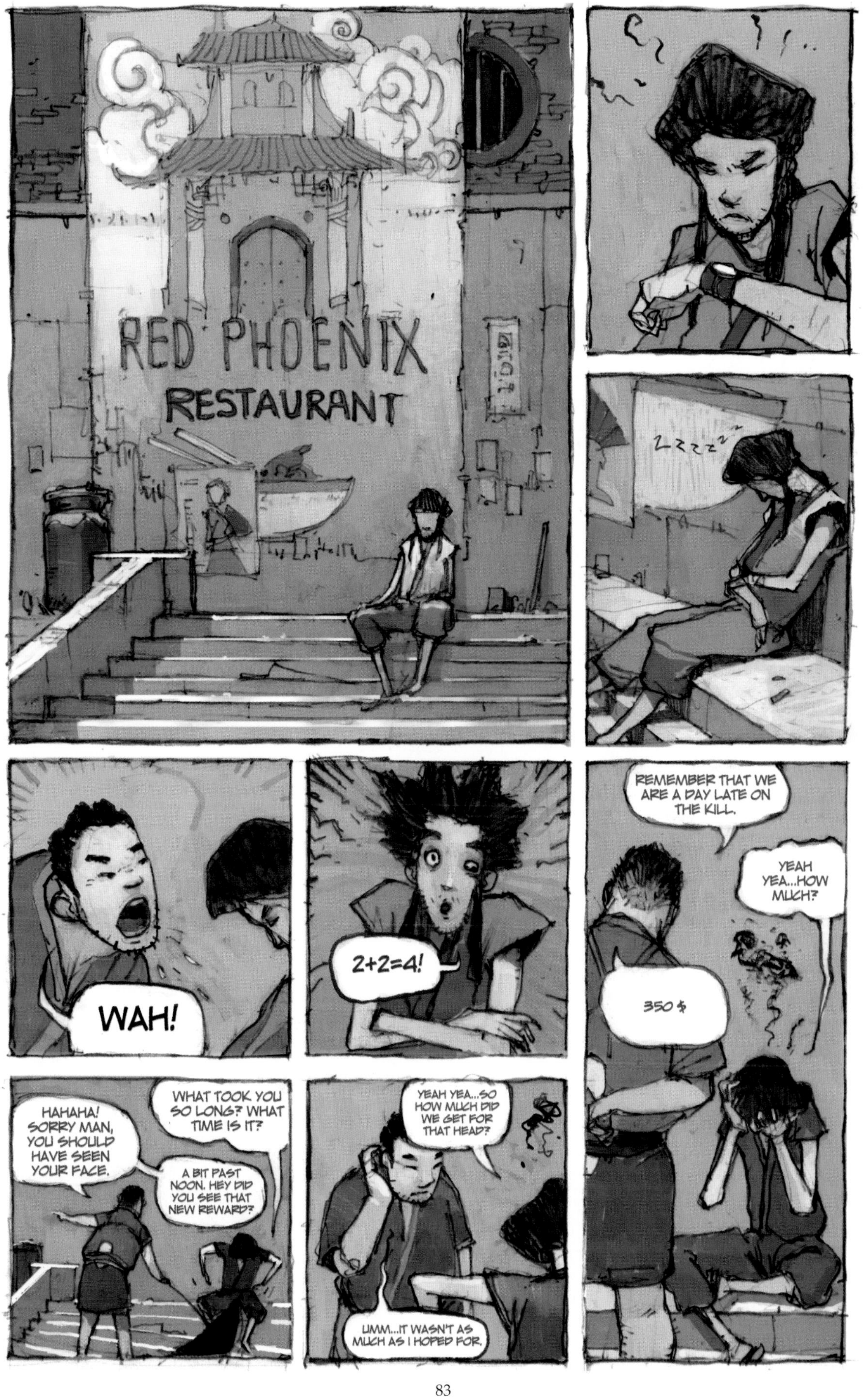
RED PHOENIX
RESTAURANT
Zzzzz
WAH!
2+2=4!
HAHAHA! SORRY MAN, YOU SHOULD HAVE SEEN YOUR FACE.
WHAT TOOK YOU SO LONG? WHAT TIME IS IT?
A BIT PAST NOON. HEY DID YOU SEE THAT NEW REWARD?
YEAH YEA...SO HOW MUCH DID WE GET FOR THAT HEAD?
UMM...IT WASN'T AS MUCH AS I HOPED FOR.
350 $
REMEMBER THAT WE ARE A DAY LATE ON THE KILL.
YEAH YEA...HOW MUCH?

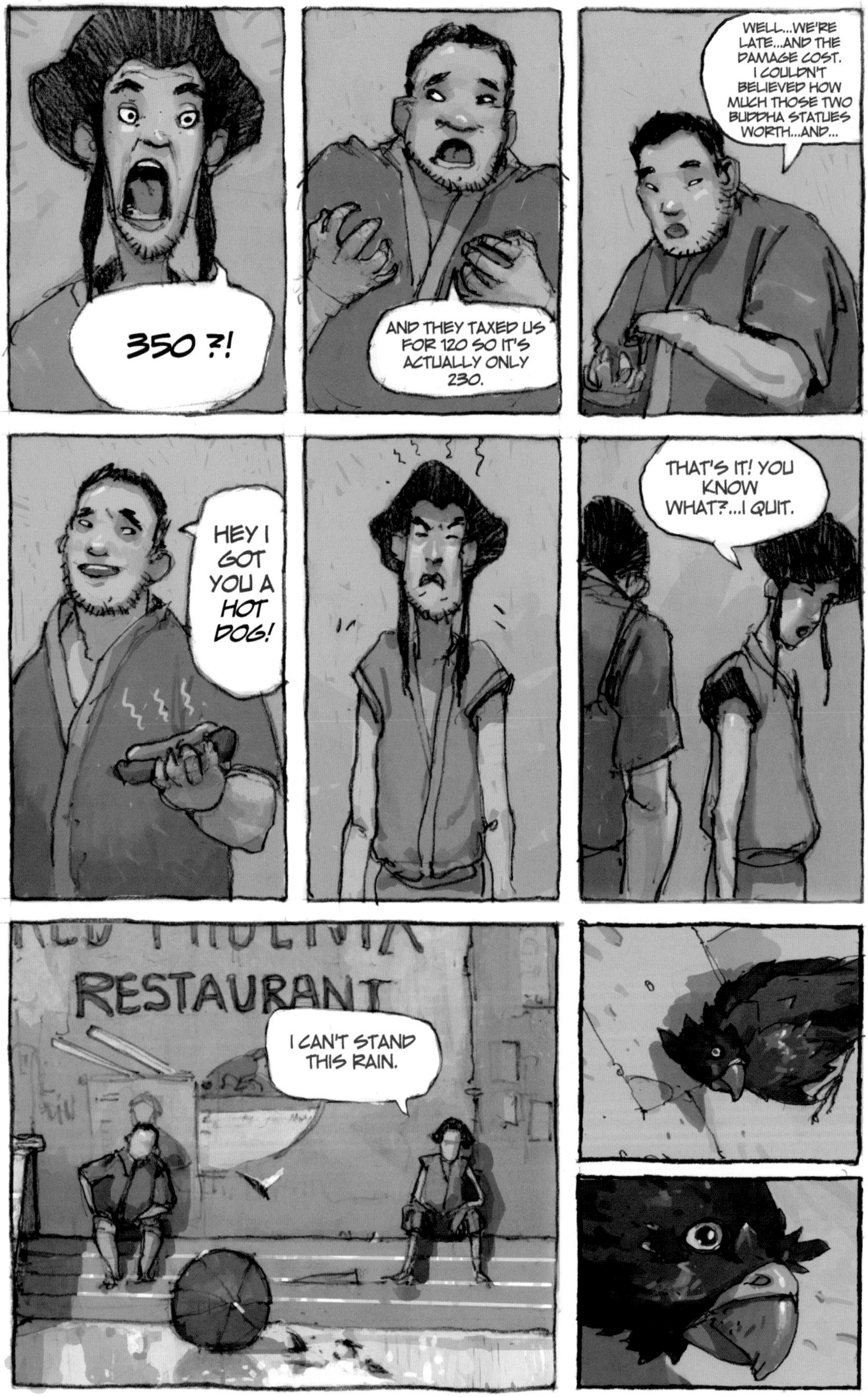
350 ?!
AND THEY TAXED US FOR 120 SO IT'S ACTUALLY ONLY 230.
WELL...WE'RE LATE...AND THE DAMAGE COST. I COULDN'T BELIEVED HOW MUCH THOSE TWO BUDDHA STATUES WORTH...AND...
HEY I GOT YOU A HOT DOG!
THAT'S IT! YOU KNOW WHAT?...I QUIT.
RESTAURANT
I CAN'T STAND THIS RAIN.

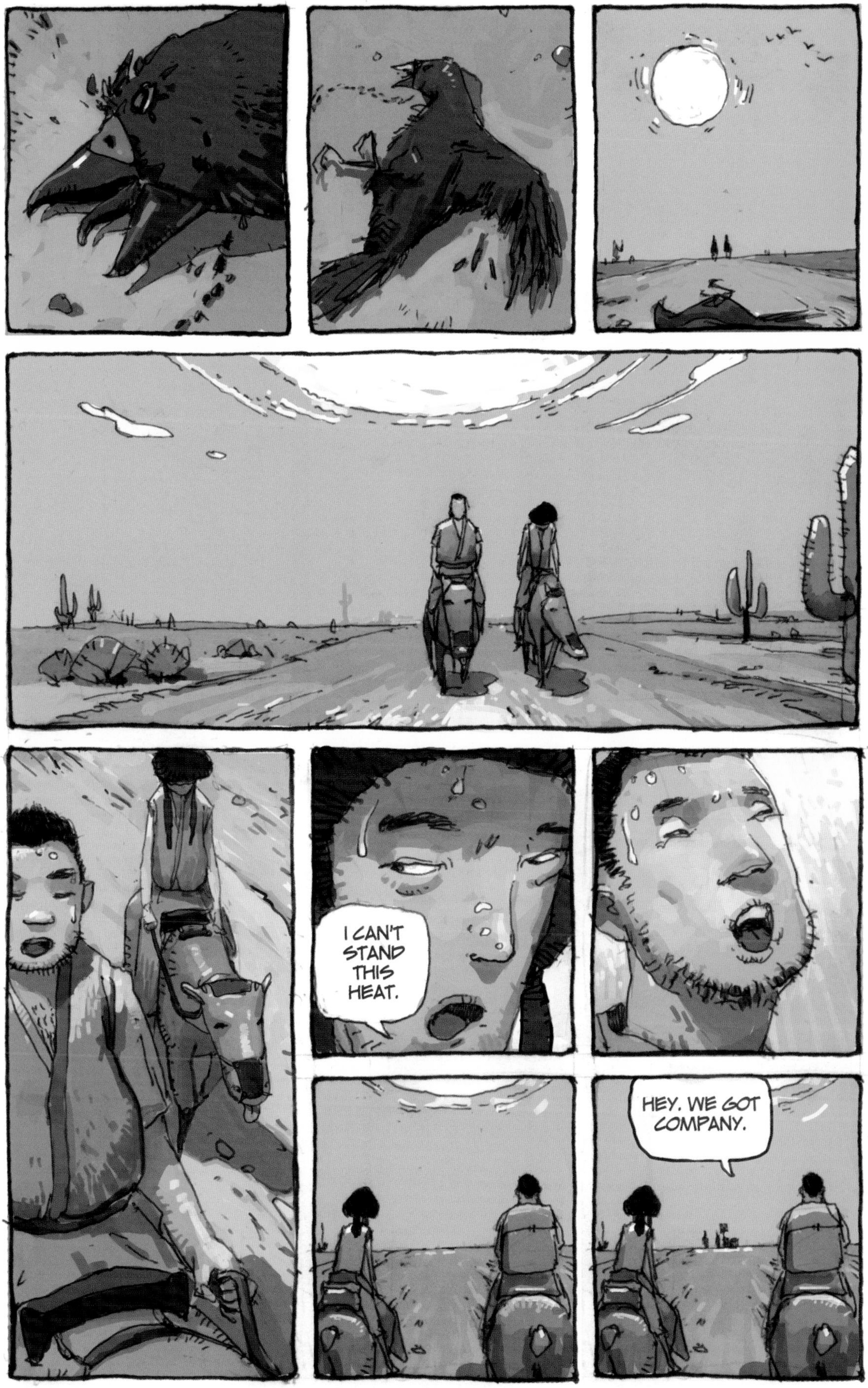
I CAN'T STAND THIS HEAT.
HEY. WE GOT COMPANY.

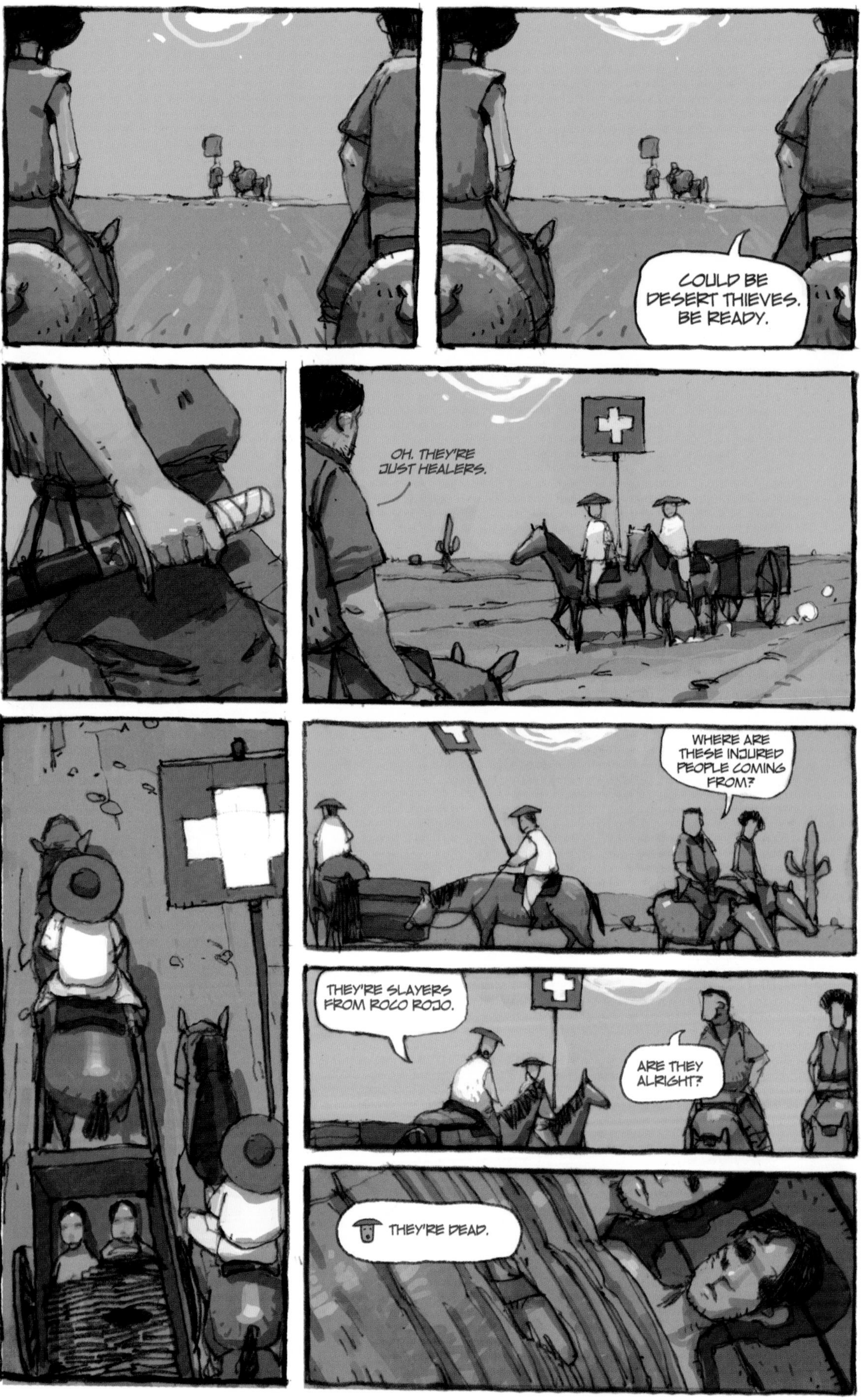
COULD BE DESERT THIEVES. BE READY.
OH. THEY'RE JUST HEALERS.
WHERE ARE THESE INJURED PEOPLE COMING FROM?
THEY'RE SLAYERS FROM ROCO ROJO.
ARE THEY ALRIGHT?
THEY'RE DEAD.

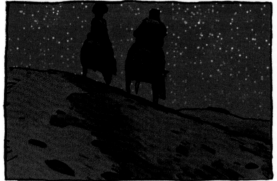

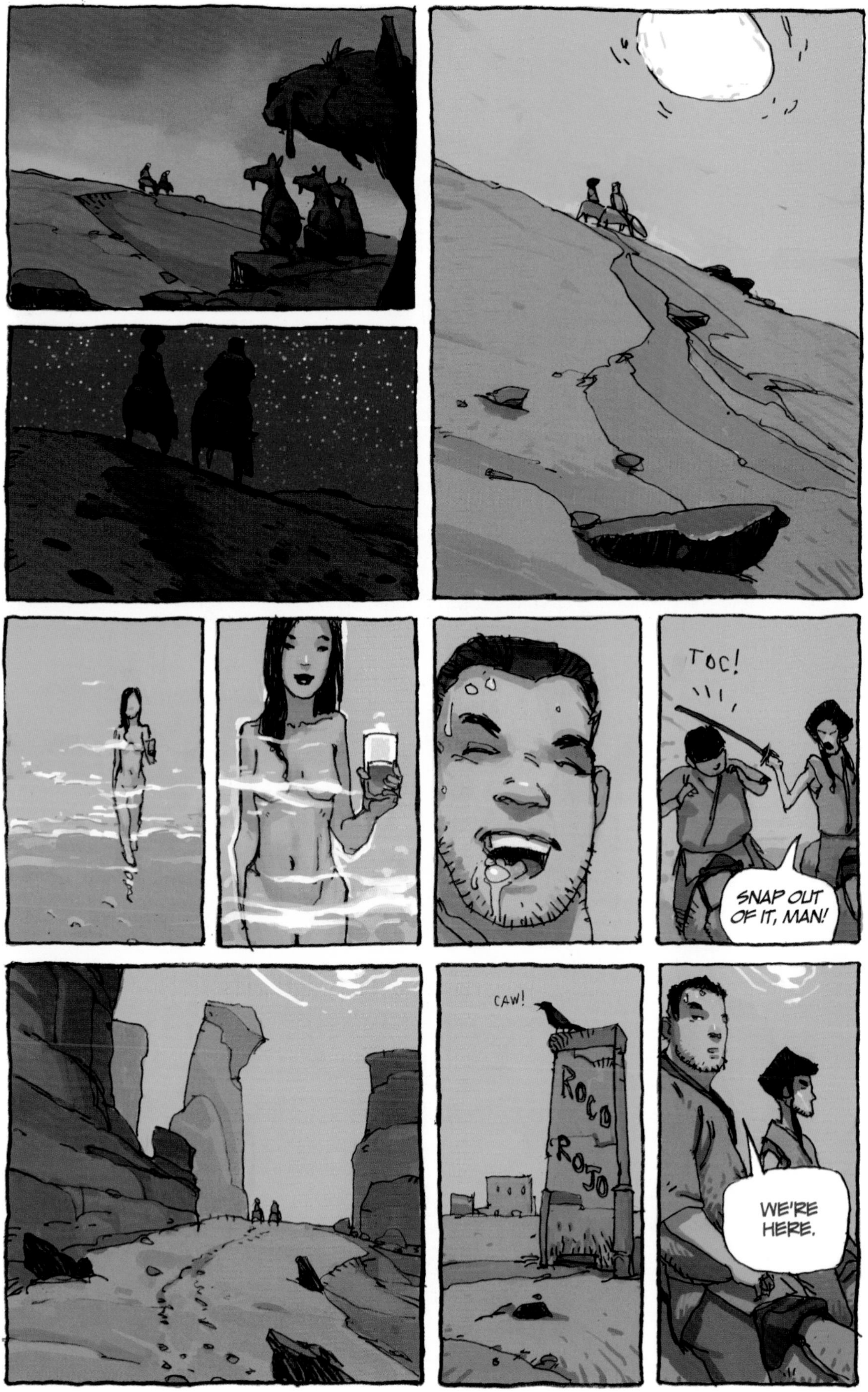
TOC!
SNAP OUT OF IT, MAN!
CAW!
ROCO ROJO
WE'RE HERE.

88

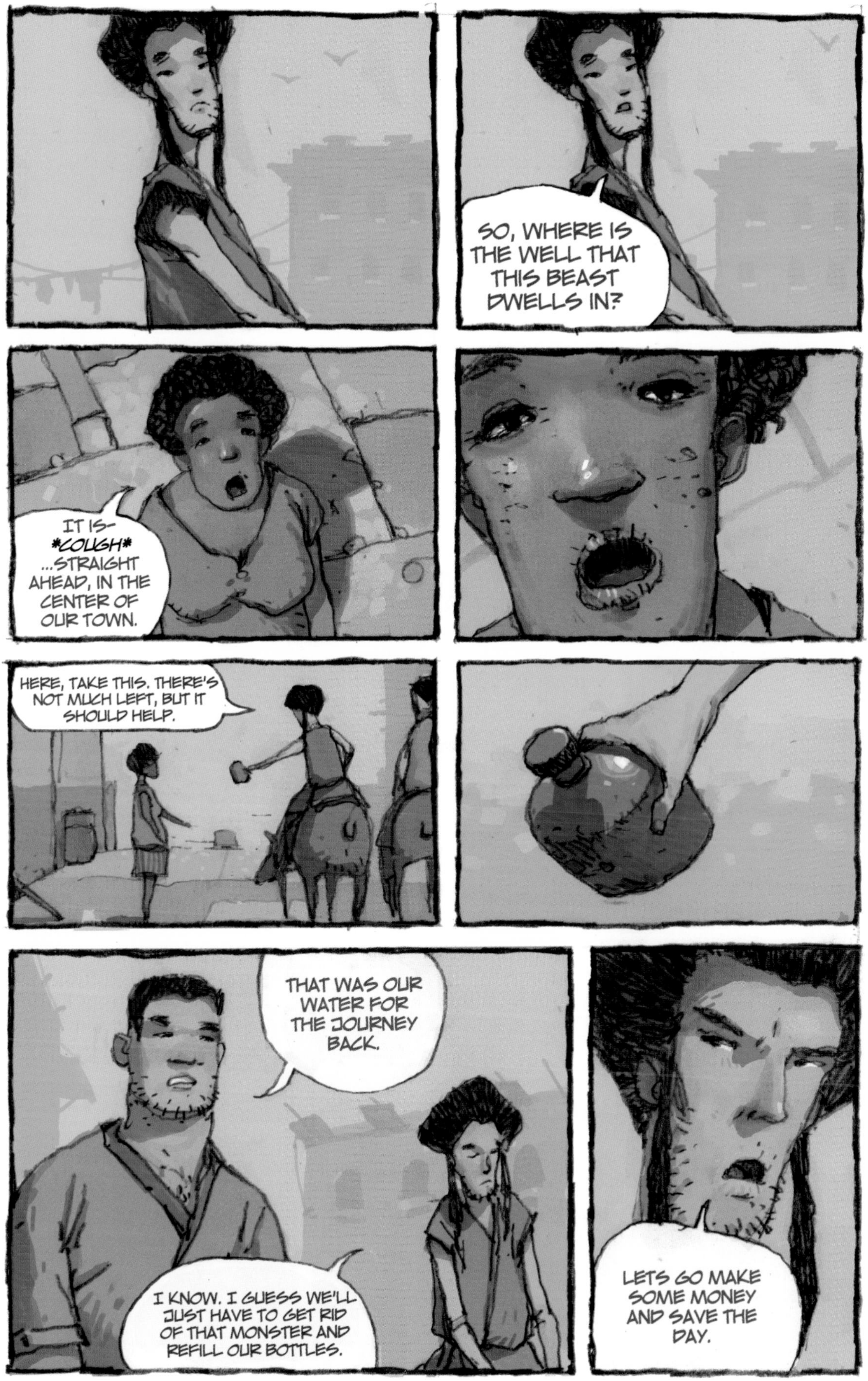
SO, WHERE IS THE WELL THAT THIS BEAST DWELLS IN?
IT IS- *COUGH* ...STRAIGHT AHEAD, IN THE CENTER OF OUR TOWN.
HERE, TAKE THIS. THERE'S NOT MUCH LEFT, BUT IT SHOULD HELP.
THAT WAS OUR WATER FOR THE JOURNEY BACK.
I KNOW. I GUESS WE'LL JUST HAVE TO GET RID OF THAT MONSTER AND REFILL OUR BOTTLES.
LETS GO MAKE SOME MONEY AND SAVE THE DAY.

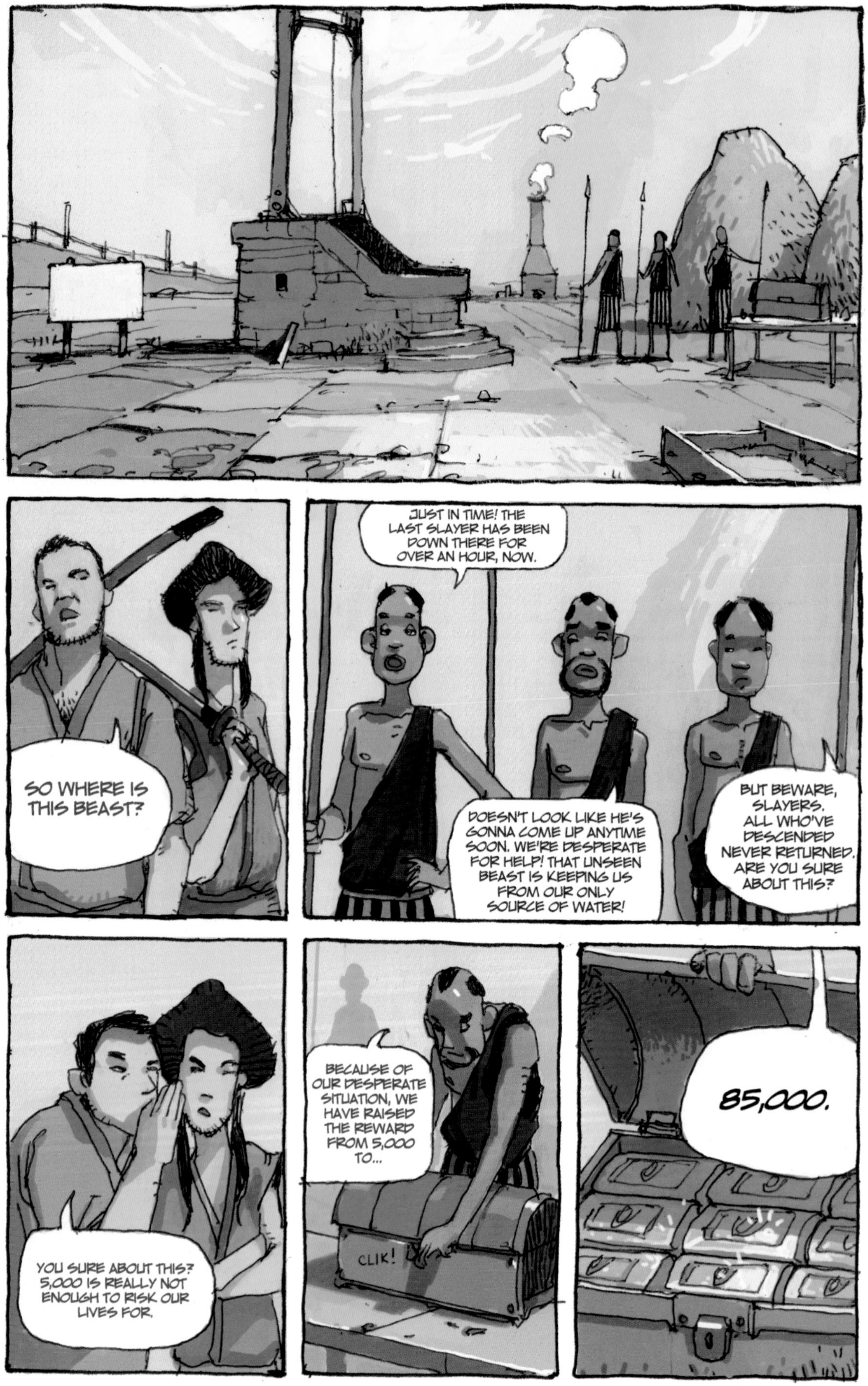
SO WHERE IS THIS BEAST?
JUST IN TIME! THE LAST SLAYER HAS BEEN DOWN THERE FOR OVER AN HOUR, NOW.
DOESN'T LOOK LIKE HE'S GONNA COME UP ANYTIME SOON. WE'RE DESPERATE FOR HELP! THAT UNSEEN BEAST IS KEEPING US FROM OUR ONLY SOURCE OF WATER!
BUT BEWARE, SLAYERS. ALL WHO'VE DESCENDED NEVER RETURNED. ARE YOU SURE ABOUT THIS?
YOU SURE ABOUT THIS? 5,000 IS REALLY NOT ENOUGH TO RISK OUR LIVES FOR.
BECAUSE OF OUR DESPERATE SITUATION, WE HAVE RAISED THE REWARD FROM 5,000 TO...
CLIK!
85,000.

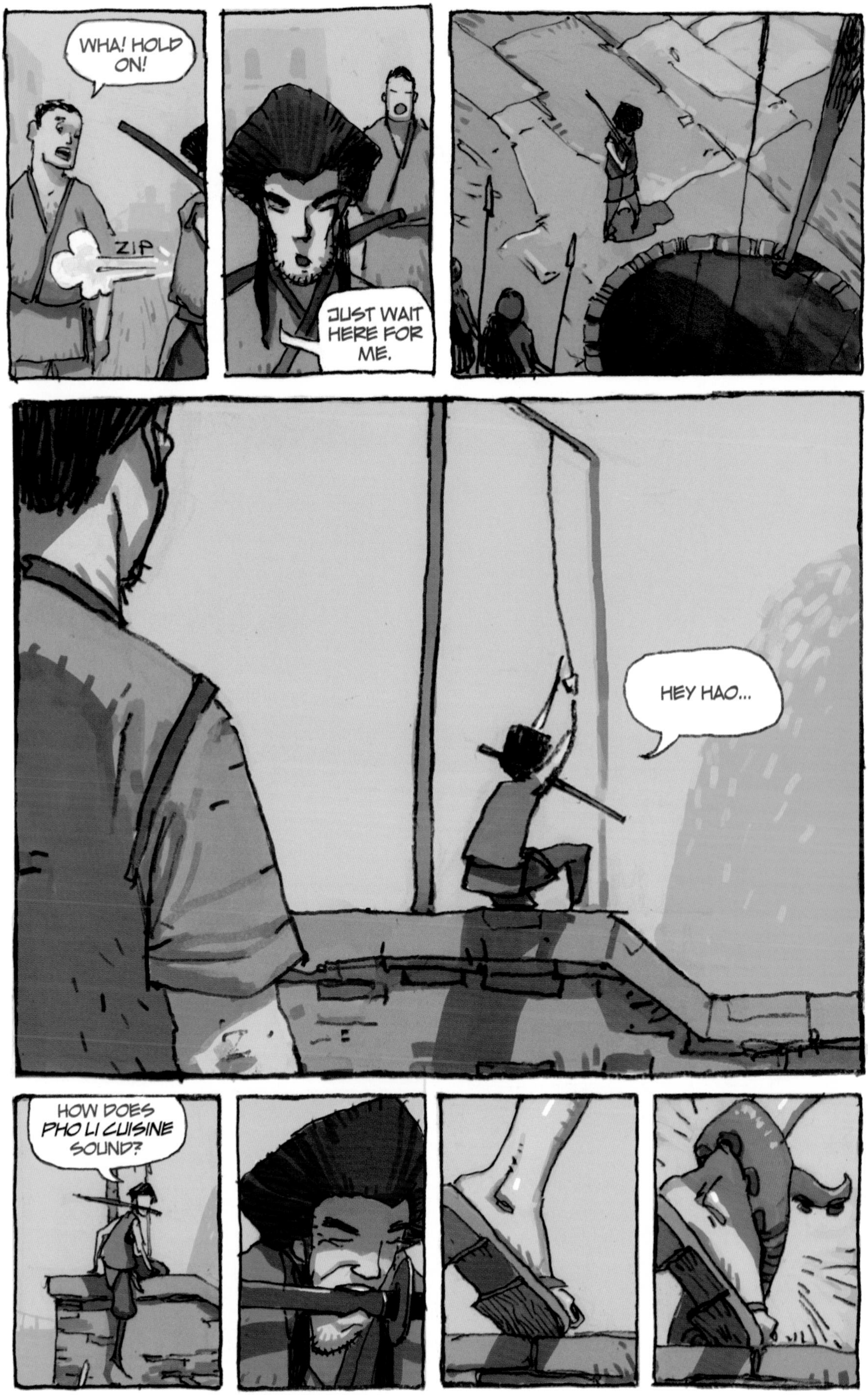
WHA! HOLD ON!
ZIP
JUST WAIT HERE FOR ME.
HEY HAO...
HOW DOES PHO LI CUISINE SOUND?

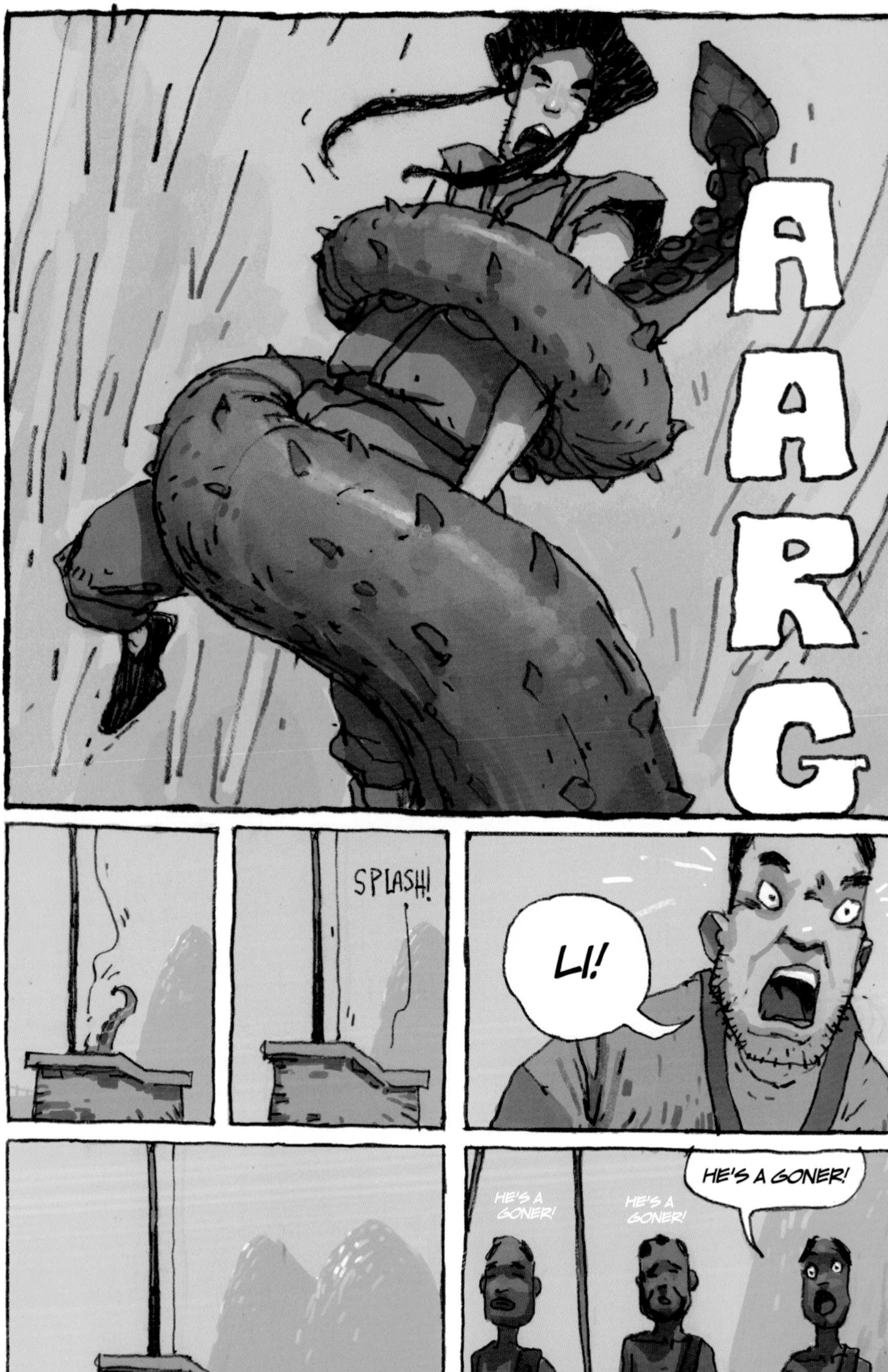

AARG
SPLASH!
LI!
HE'S A GONER!
HE'S A GONER!
HE'S A GONER!

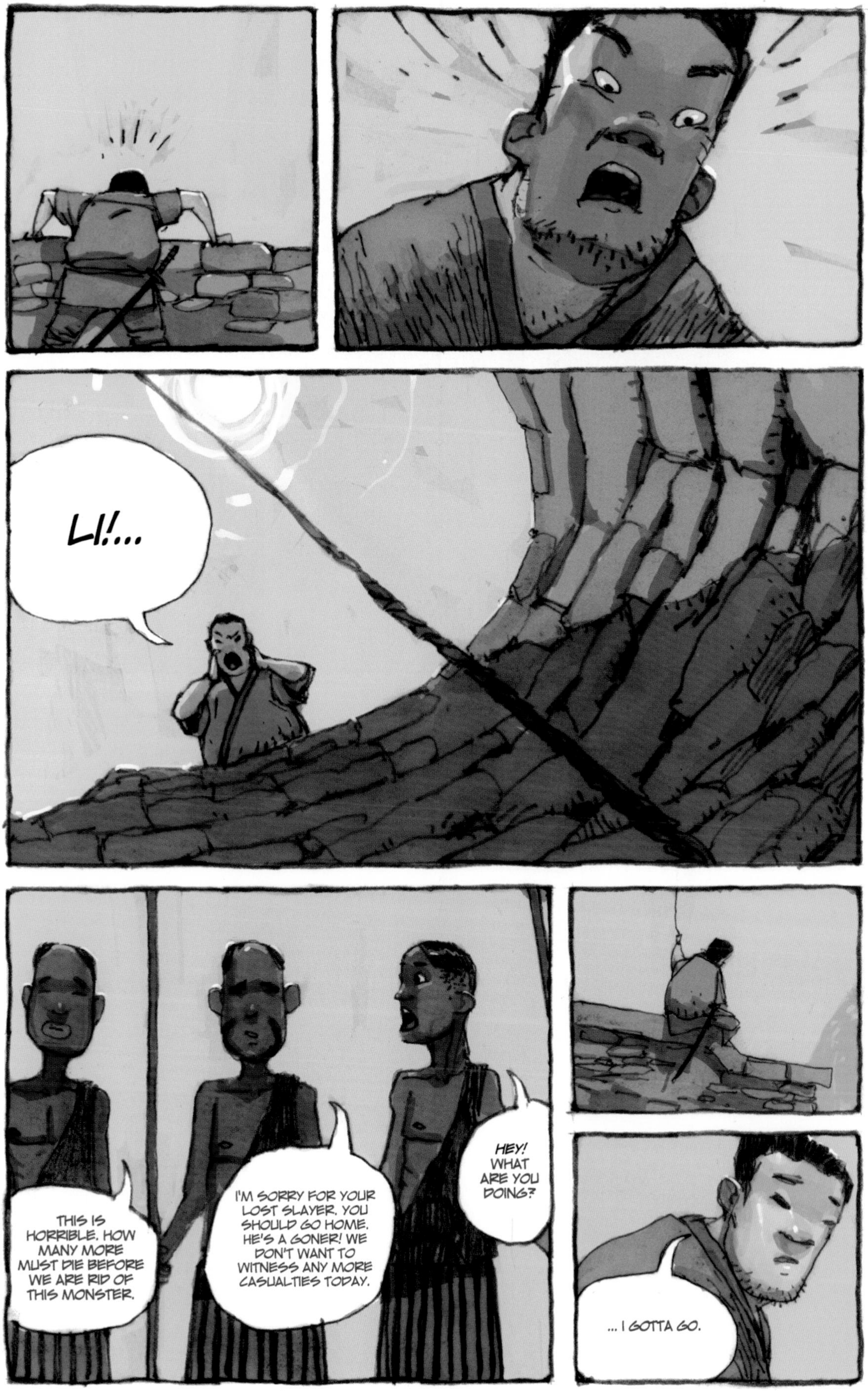
LI!...
THIS IS HORRIBLE. HOW MANY MORE MUST DIE BEFORE WE ARE RID OF THIS MONSTER.
I'M SORRY FOR YOUR LOST SLAYER. YOU SHOULD GO HOME. HE'S A GONER! WE DON'T WANT TO WITNESS ANY MORE CASUALTIES TODAY.
HEY! WHAT ARE YOU DOING?
... I GOTTA GO.

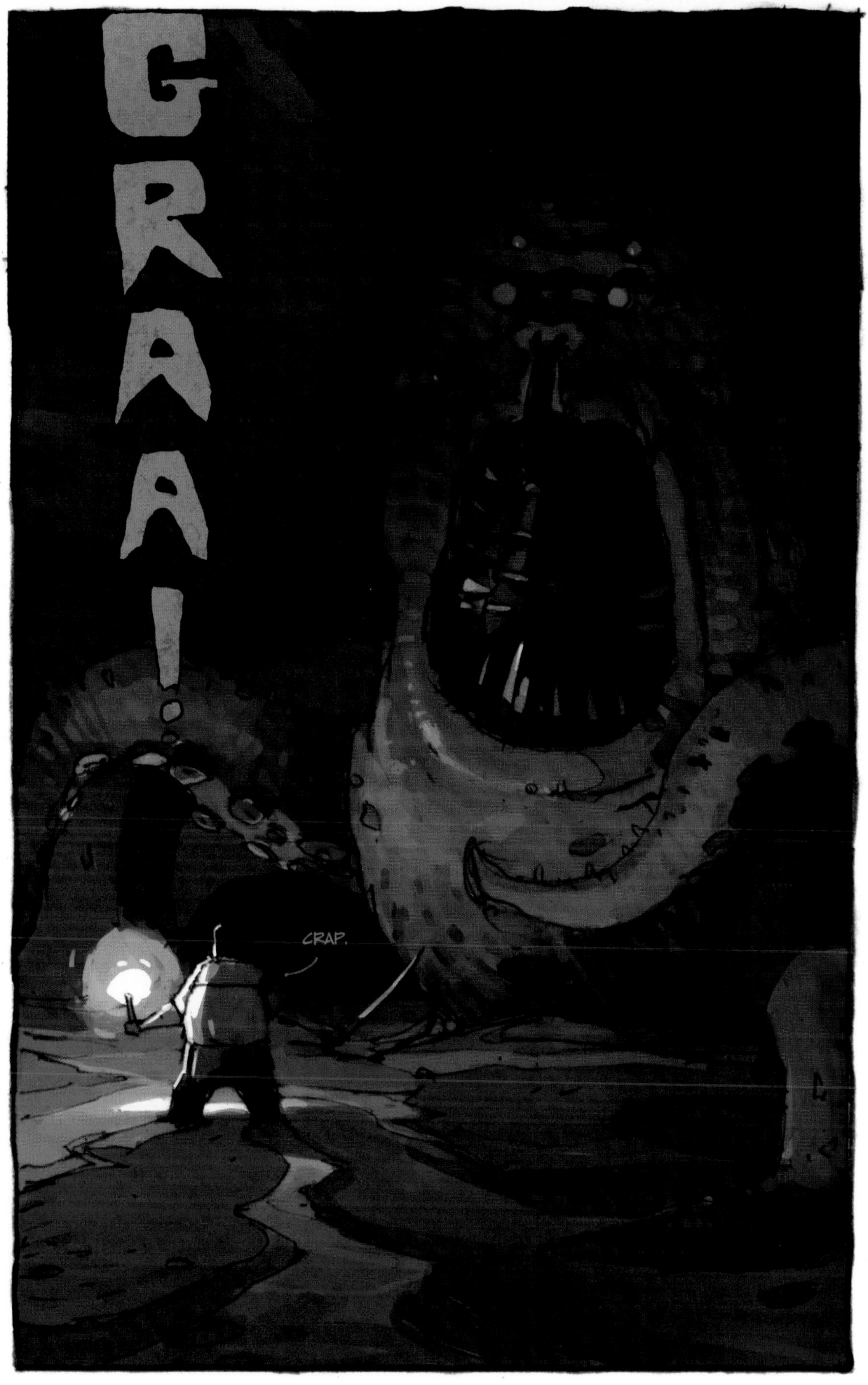
GRAA!
CRAP.

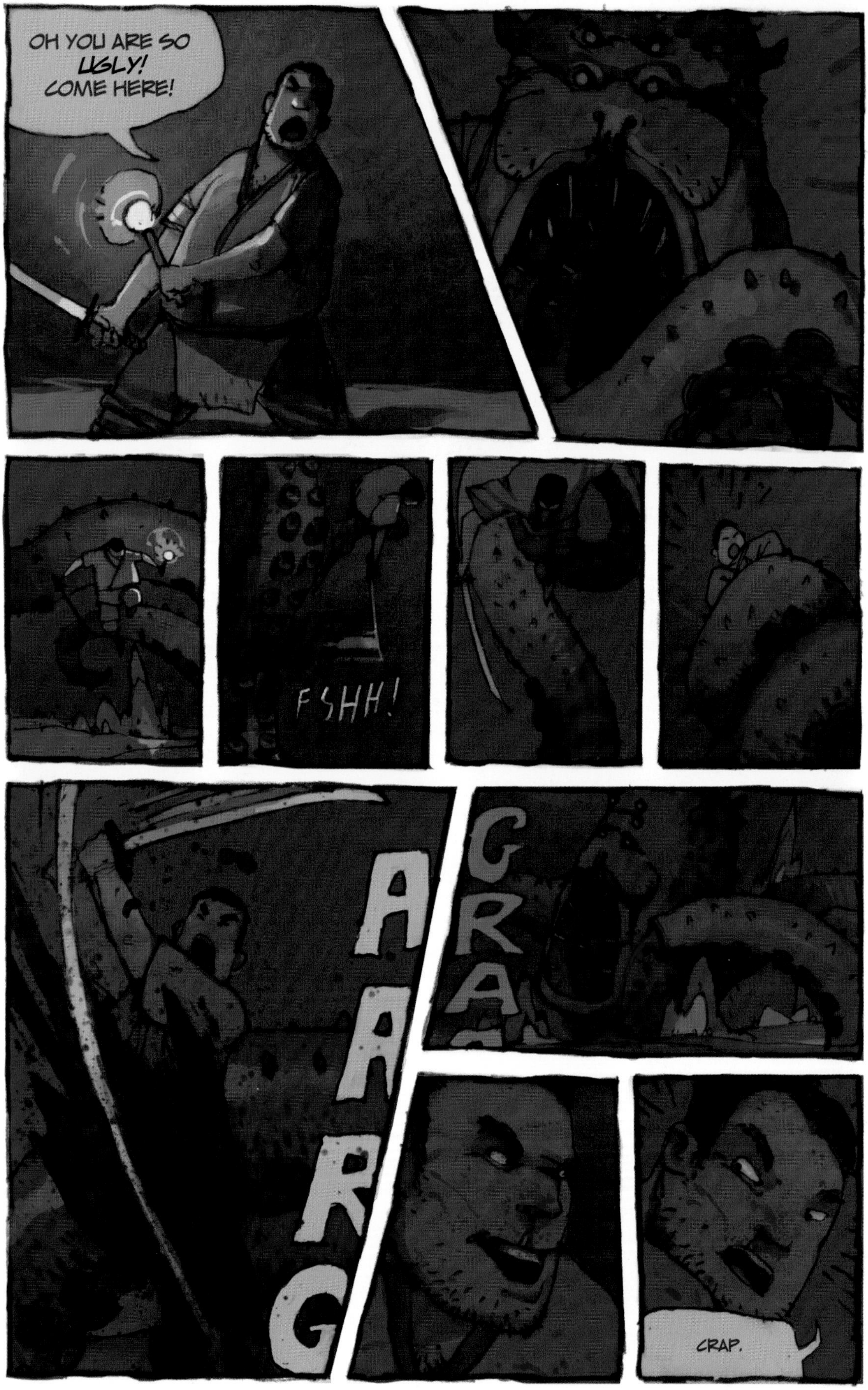
OH YOU ARE SO UGLY! COME HERE!
FSHH!
AARG
GRA
CRAP.

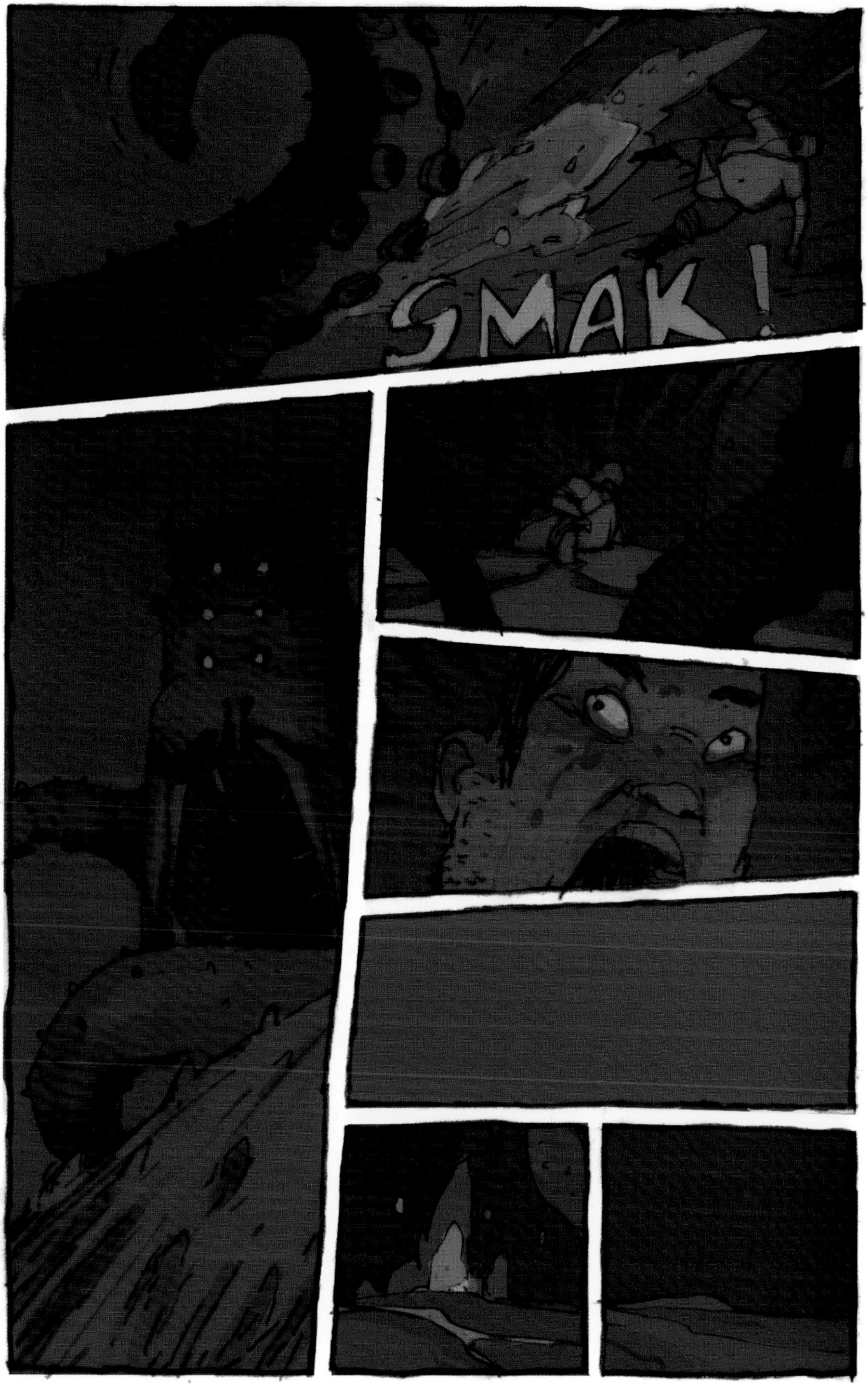
SMAK!

HAO!

WAKE UP HAO!

HAO!

WUH?...WHA?... WHERE ARE WE?

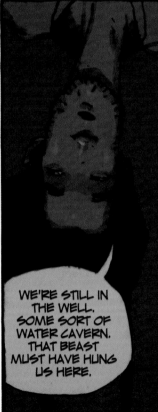

WE'RE STILL IN THE WELL. SOME SORT OF WATER CAVERN. THAT BEAST MUST HAVE HUNG US HERE.

AND IT'S POPPING OUT EGGS.

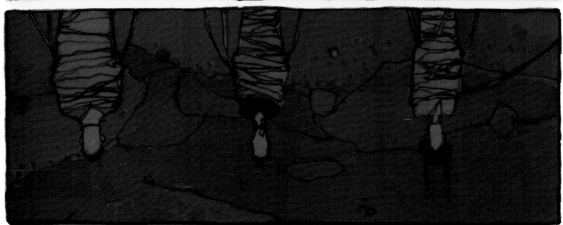

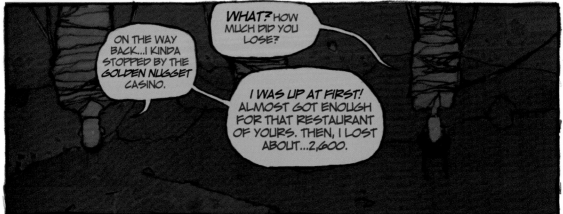

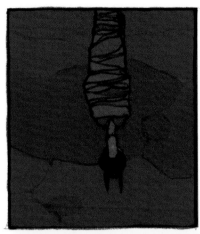

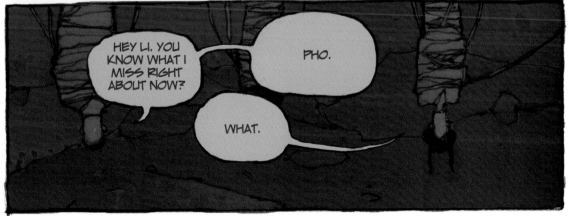

...ADDING SOME BEAN SPROUTS AND MINT LEAVES...

...SOME HOT SAUCE AND HOISIN SAUCE FOR EXTRA FLAVOR...

MMM...THAT HOT STEAMY BROTH WITH THIN TENDER SLICES OF RARE BEEF...

THEN A SQUEEZE OF LIME TO TOP IT OFF. DAMN LI...I'M SALIVATING...

HOW ABOUT YOU MAN...WHAT DO YOU MISS MOST FROM THIS WORLD?

...I DON'T KNOW.

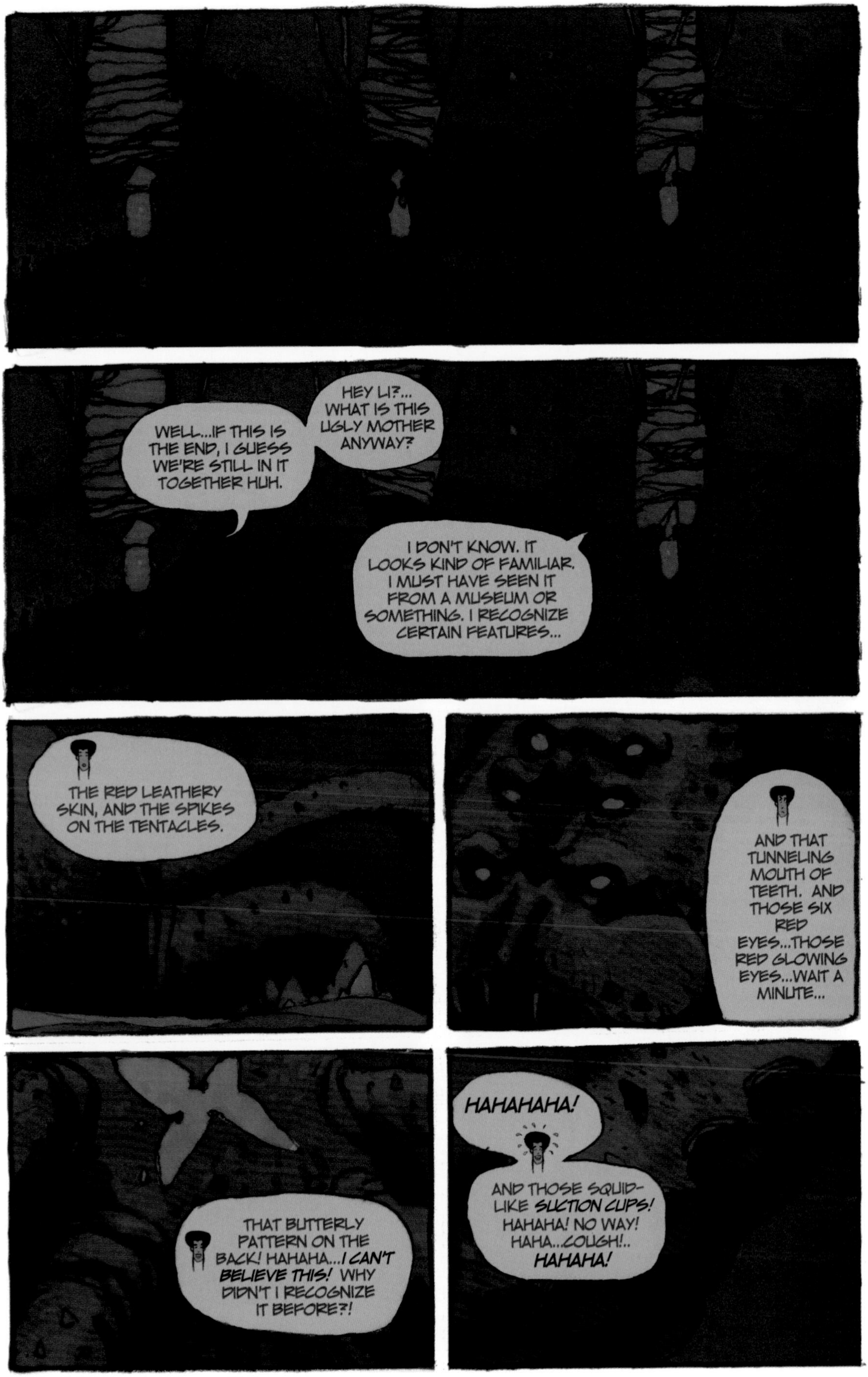
WELL...IF THIS IS THE END, I GUESS WE'RE STILL IN IT TOGETHER HUH.
HEY LI?... WHAT IS THIS UGLY MOTHER ANYWAY?
I DON'T KNOW. IT LOOKS KIND OF FAMILIAR. I MUST HAVE SEEN IT FROM A MUSEUM OR SOMETHING. I RECOGNIZE CERTAIN FEATURES...
THE RED LEATHERY SKIN, AND THE SPIKES ON THE TENTACLES.
AND THAT TUNNELING MOUTH OF TEETH. AND THOSE SIX RED EYES...THOSE RED GLOWING EYES...WAIT A MINUTE...
THAT BUTTERLY PATTERN ON THE BACK! HAHAHA...I CAN'T BELIEVE THIS! WHY DIDN'T I RECOGNIZE IT BEFORE?!
HAHAHAHA!
AND THOSE SQUID-LIKE SUCTION CUPS! HAHAHA! NO WAY! HAHA...COUGH!.. HAHAHA!

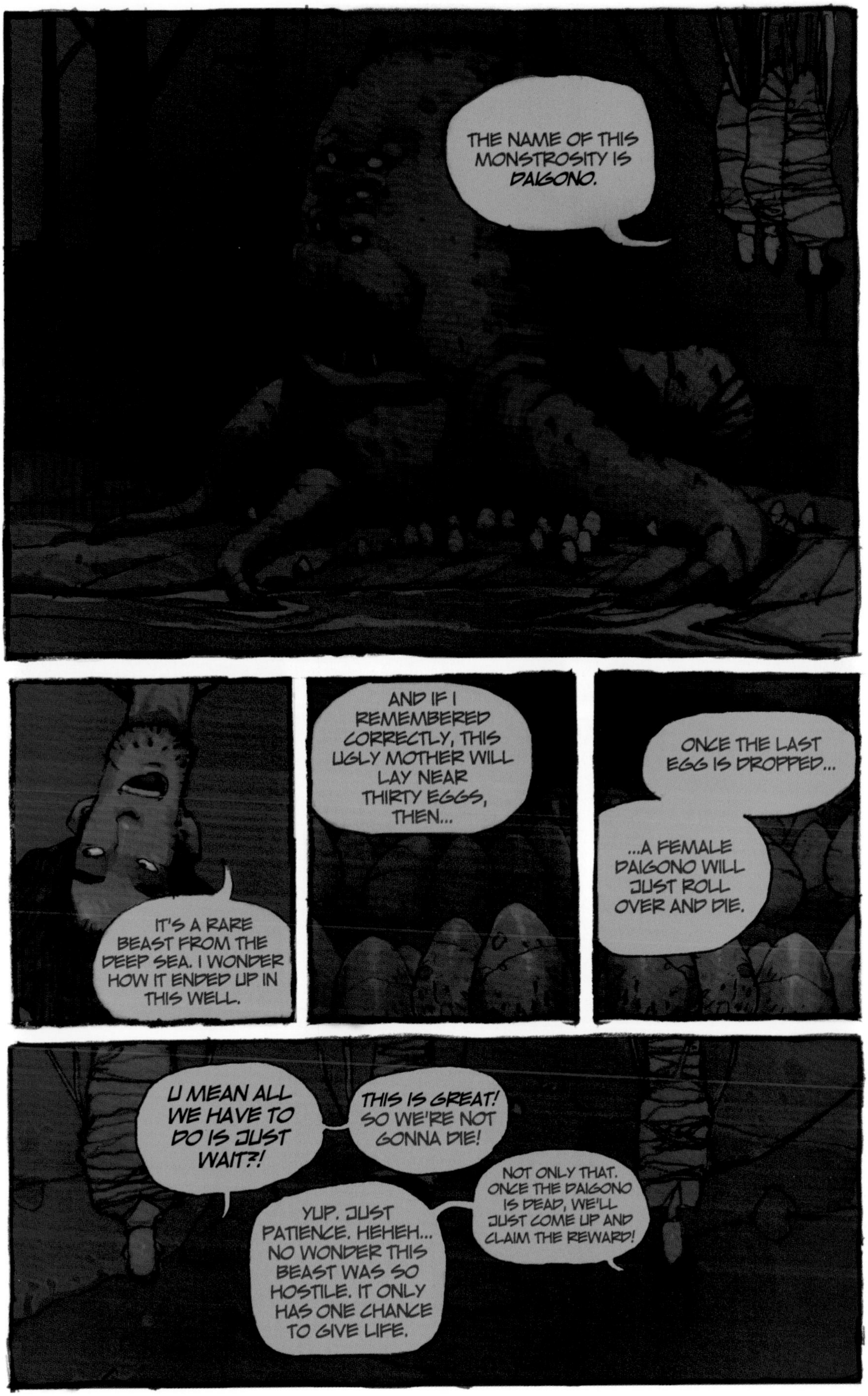
THE NAME OF THIS MONSTROSITY IS DAIGONO.
IT'S A RARE BEAST FROM THE DEEP SEA. I WONDER HOW IT ENDED UP IN THIS WELL.
AND IF I REMEMBERED CORRECTLY, THIS UGLY MOTHER WILL LAY NEAR THIRTY EGGS, THEN...
ONCE THE LAST EGG IS DROPPED...
...A FEMALE DAIGONO WILL JUST ROLL OVER AND DIE.
U MEAN ALL WE HAVE TO DO IS JUST WAIT?!
THIS IS GREAT! SO WE'RE NOT GONNA DIE!
YUP. JUST PATIENCE. HEHEH... NO WONDER THIS BEAST WAS SO HOSTILE. IT ONLY HAS ONE CHANCE TO GIVE LIFE.
NOT ONLY THAT. ONCE THE DAIGONO IS DEAD, WE'LL JUST COME UP AND CLAIM THE REWARD!

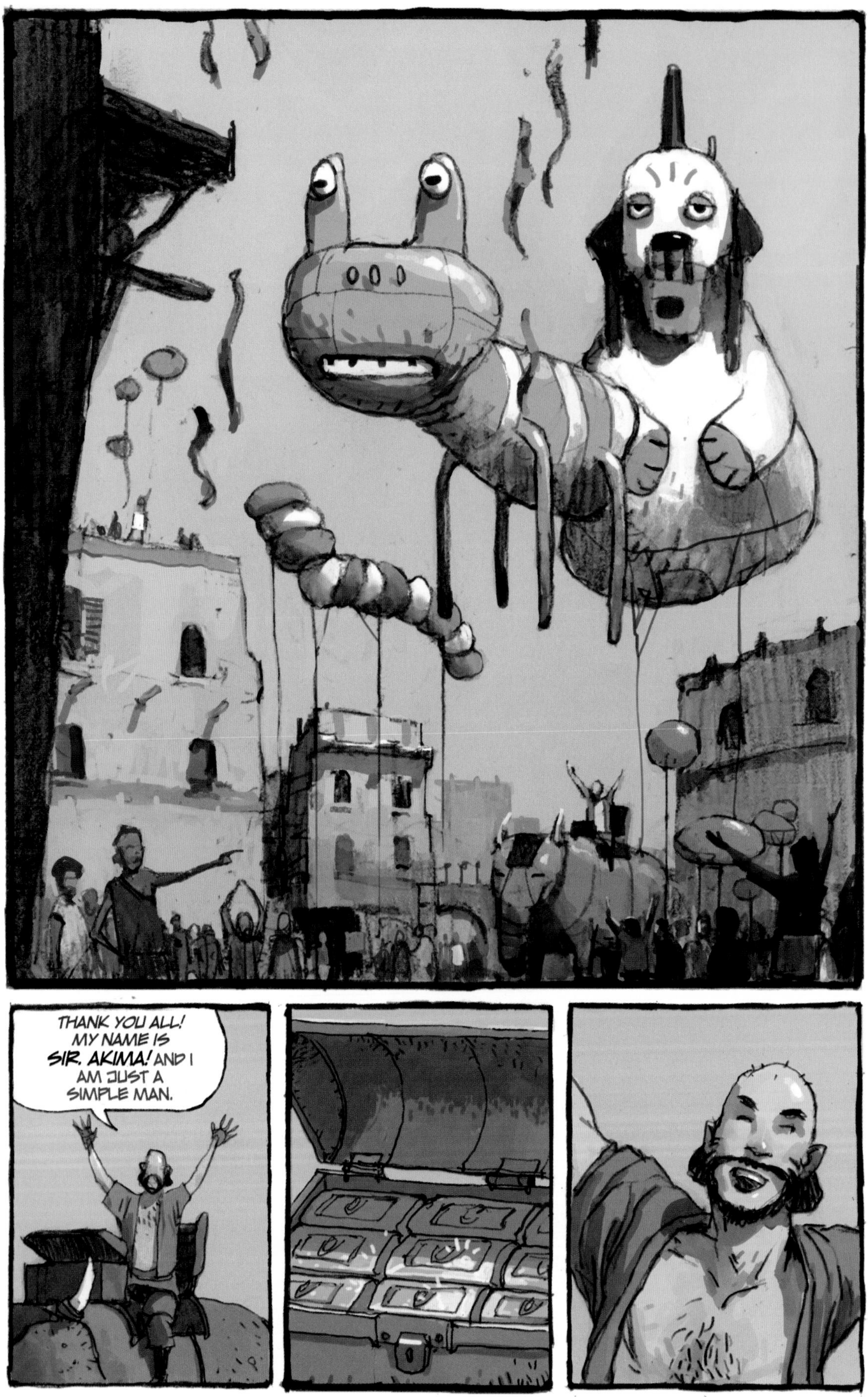
THANK YOU ALL! MY NAME IS SIR. AKIMA! AND I AM JUST A SIMPLE MAN.

111

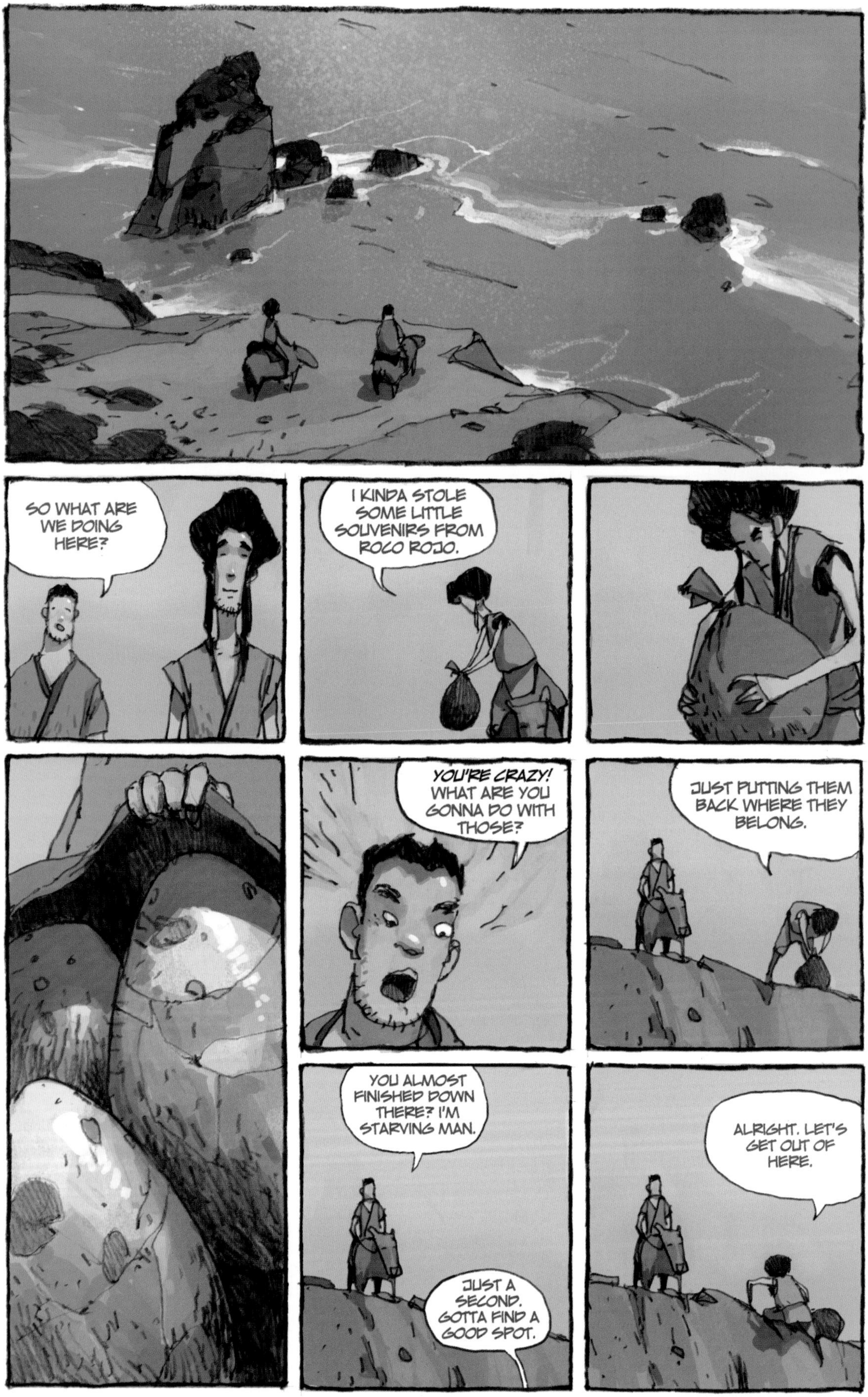
SO WHAT ARE WE DOING HERE?
I KINDA STOLE SOME LITTLE SOUVENIRS FROM ROCO ROJO.
YOU'RE CRAZY! WHAT ARE YOU GONNA DO WITH THOSE?
JUST PUTTING THEM BACK WHERE THEY BELONG.
YOU ALMOST FINISHED DOWN THERE? I'M STARVING MAN.
JUST A SECOND. GOTTA FIND A GOOD SPOT.
ALRIGHT. LET'S GET OUT OF HERE.

YEAH...I FELT KIND OF BAD FOR THAT UGLY MOTHER TOO.

YEAH...SAME HERE. THAT'S WHY I DECIDED TO SAVED THE TWO EGGS.

TWO? I THOUGHT I SAW THREE EGGS IN THE SACK. WHAT HAPPENED TO THE THIRD ONE?

DINNER!

AHAHAHA! YOU BAD?! I NEVER HAD MONSTER'S EGG BEFORE, WONDER WHAT IT'LL TASTE LIKE.

I'M TELLING YOU LI! I WAS UP LIKE 13,000! IT WAS ALMOST ENOUGH FOR YOUR RESTAURANT AND...

I GUESS WE'LL FIND OUT. AHEM...SOOO...YOU LOST 2,600 AT THE GOLDEN NUGGET?..

YEAH...YEA... WHATEVER MAN. THAT'S THE LAST TIME I LET YOU GO COLLECT THE BOUNTY.

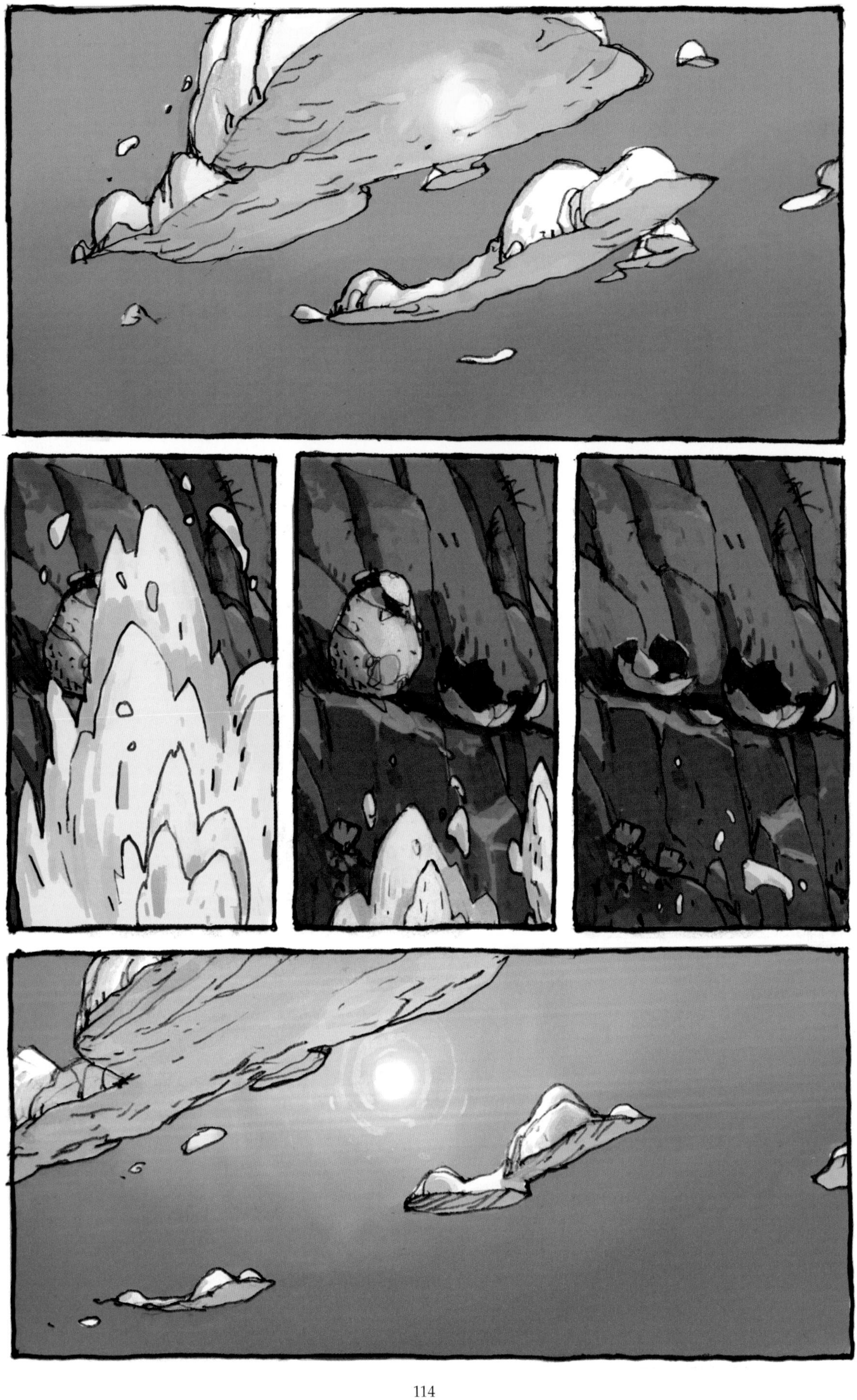

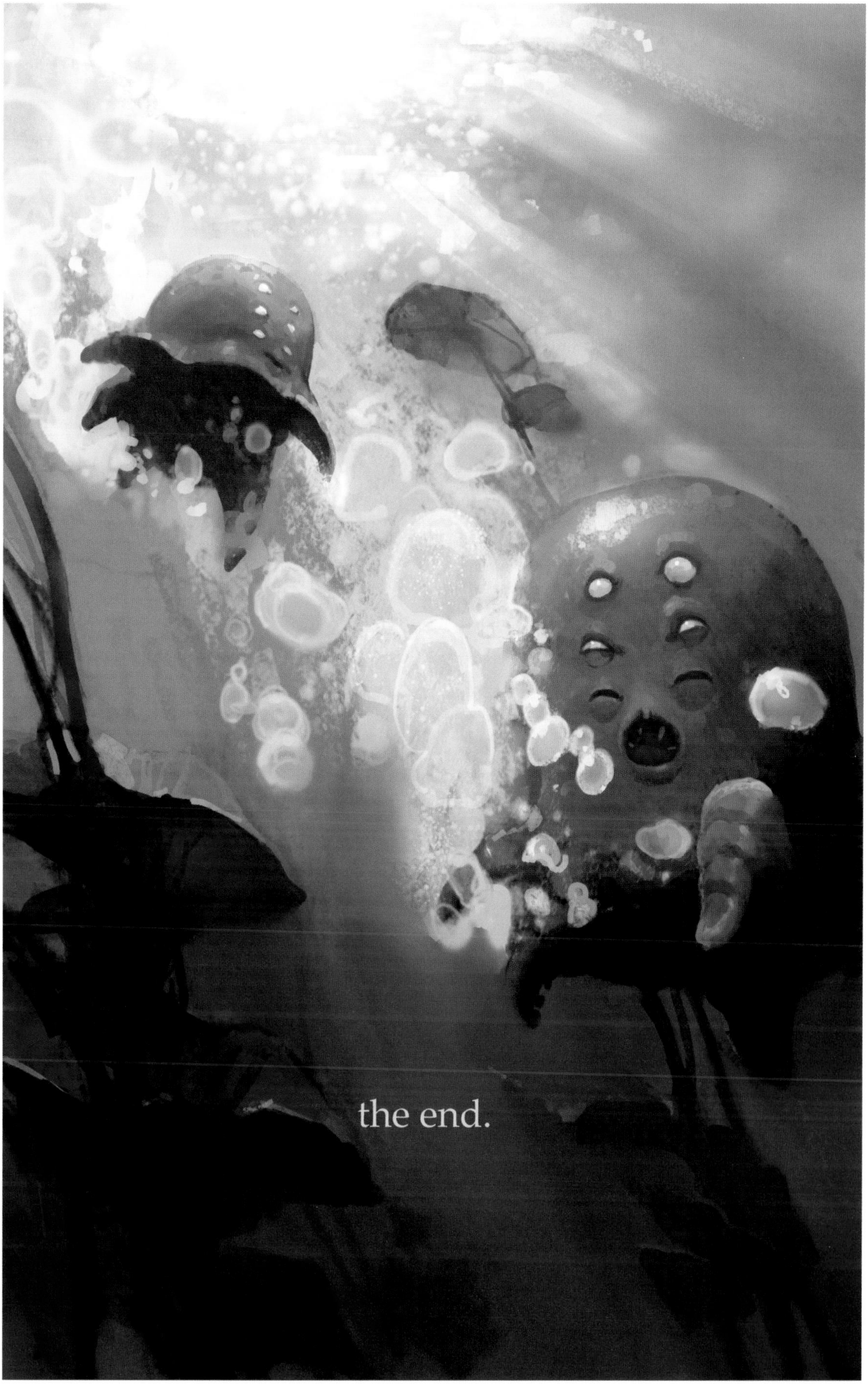
the end.

The Golden Temple

continued from "Taj Mahal,"
Flight: Volume One

Written & Illustrated
by Neil Babra

I used to live here when I was a kid.

I had a precocious command of the languages, according to my father.

Sometime after we left, I forgot.

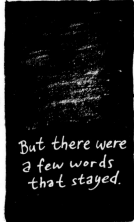
But there were a few words that stayed.

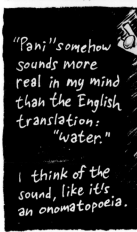
"Pani" somehow sounds more real in my mind than the English translation: "water."

I think of the sound, like it's an onomatopoeia.

And I remember splashing around in a monsoon...

...Just one second before it ended.

It's hard to explain how a casual word could feel like, a secret...

117

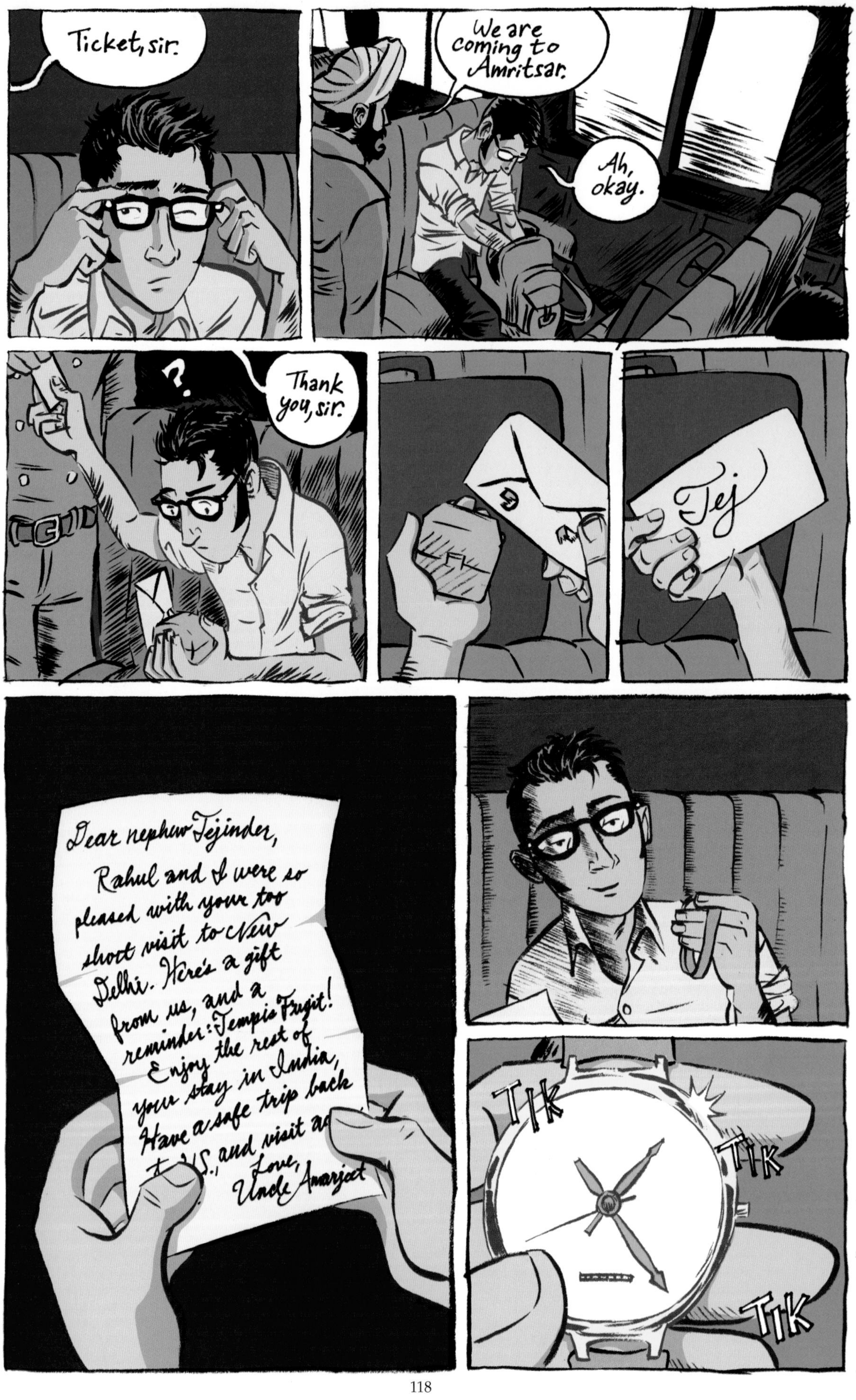
Ticket, sir.
We are coming to Amritsar.
Ah, okay.
?
Thank you, sir.
Tej
Dear nephew Tejinder,
Rahul and I were so
pleased with your too
short visit to New
Delhi. Here's a gift
from us, and a
reminder: Tempis Fugit!
Enjoy the rest of
your stay in India,
Have a safe trip back
to U.S., and visit a
Love,
Uncle Amarjeet
TIK
TIK
TIK

Hey this looks pretty.

We can see the monument if you like.

Is this familiar to you?

I know it's really weird, but I don't remember much at all.

DEDICATED
MASSACRE OF
DS OF INNO-
INDUS, SIKHS,
LIMS AT THE
OF TROOPS
DED BY THE
BRITISH ARMY.
YER

No... That must have been, sixteen years ago?

Things here must seem strange, having grown up abroad.

A little, but it's interesting. Have you read any Edward Said? Sometimes an exile has the best perspective.

An exile?

In a manner of speaking.

But you're an American!

WHERE THE
BULLET HOLES
ARE STILL VISI
IN THE PARK WA

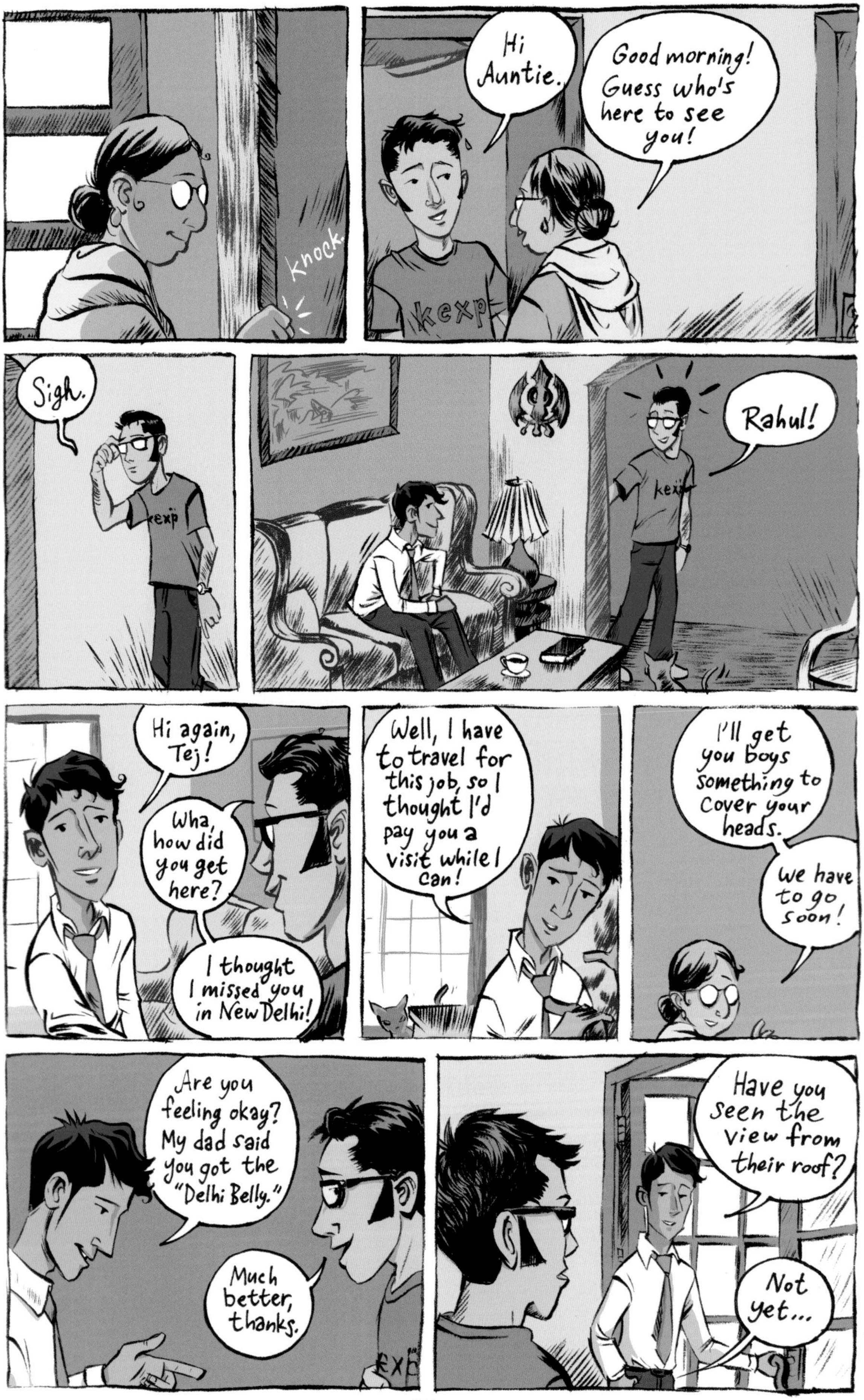
knock.
Hi Auntie.
Good morning! Guess who's here to see you!
Sigh.
Rahul!
kexp
Hi again, Tej!
Wha, how did you get here?
I thought I missed you in New Delhi!
Well, I have to travel for this job, so I thought I'd pay you a visit while I can!
I'll get you boys something to cover your heads.
We have to go soon!
Are you feeling okay? My dad said you got the "Delhi Belly."
Much better, thanks.
Have you seen the view from their roof?
Not yet...

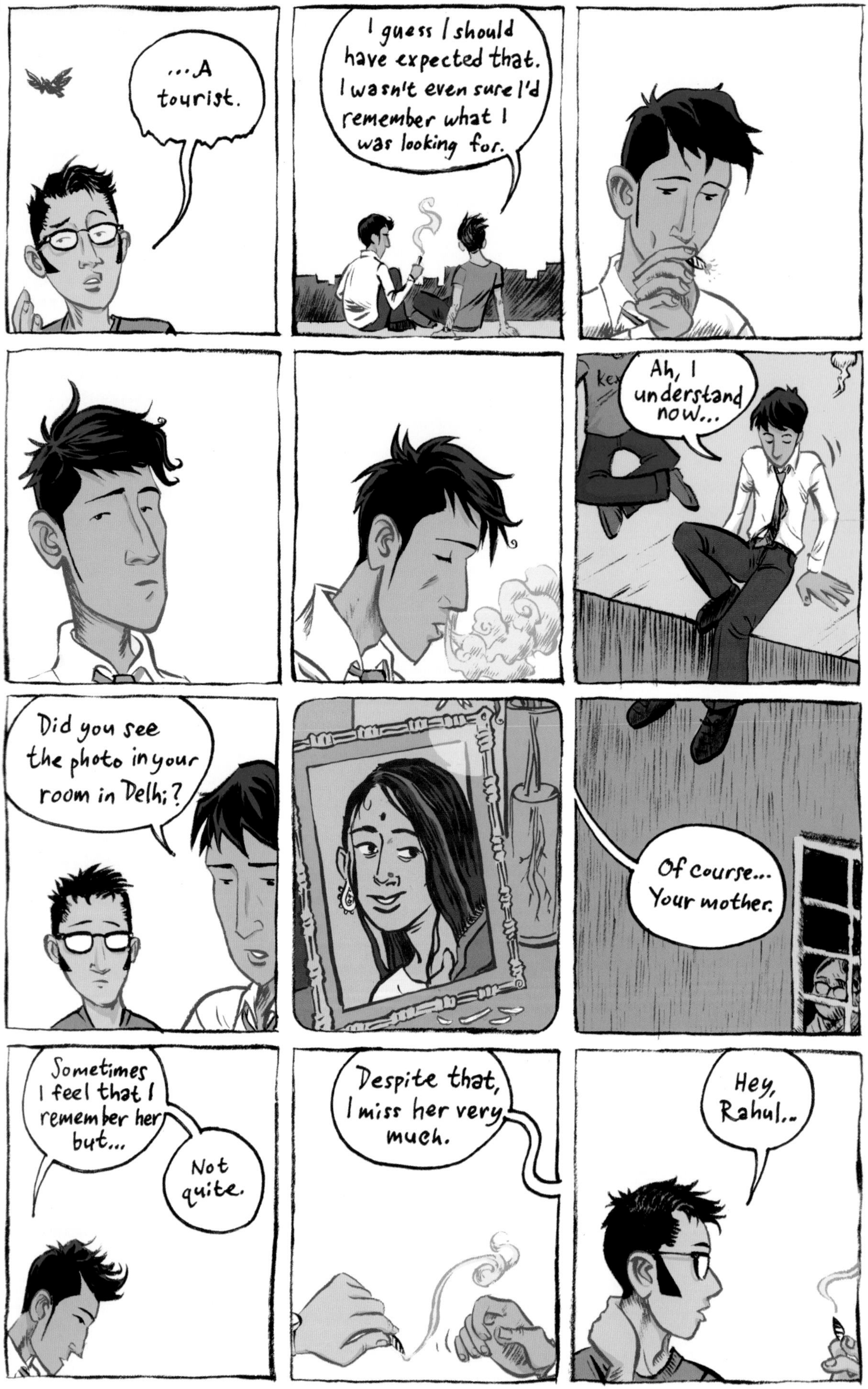

...A tourist.
I guess I should have expected that. I wasn't even sure I'd remember what I was looking for.
Ah, I understand now...
Did you see the photo in your room in Delhi?
Of course... Your mother.
Sometimes I feel that I remember her but...
Not quite.
Despite that, I miss her very much.
Hey, Rahul..

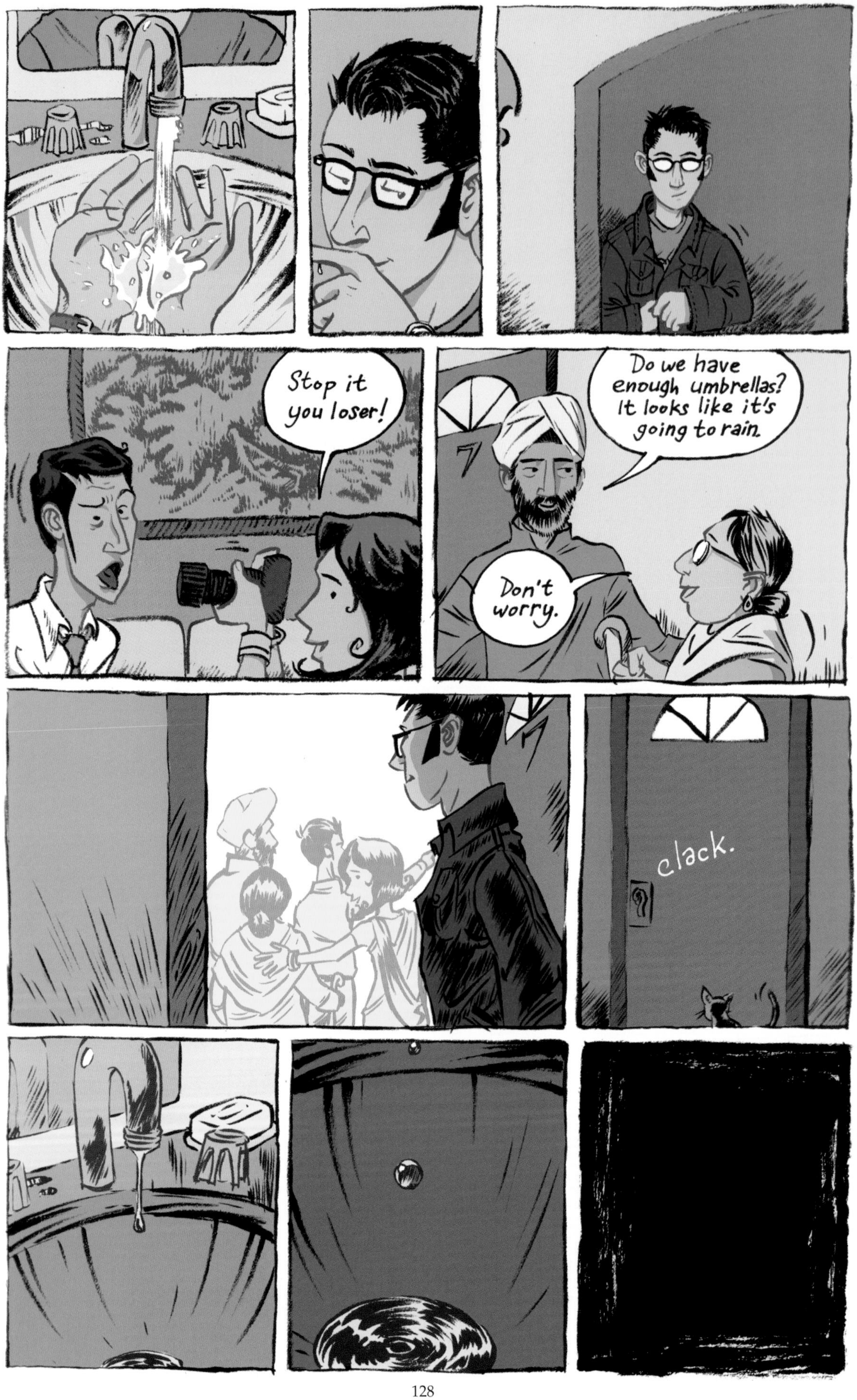
Stop it you loser!
Do we have enough umbrellas? It looks like it's going to rain.
Don't worry.
clack.

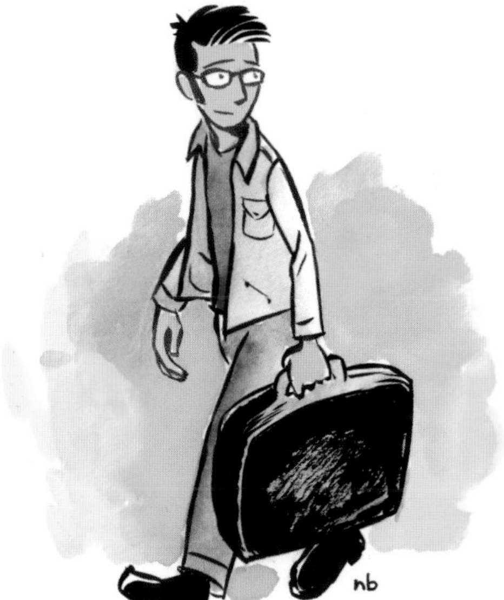
nb

"DANCE OF the SUGAR PLUMS"

OR, LAST MONTH ON EARTH

BY DON HERTZFELDT

POPULAR SHRILL MUSIC PIPED
IN FROM NEARBY RESTAURANT

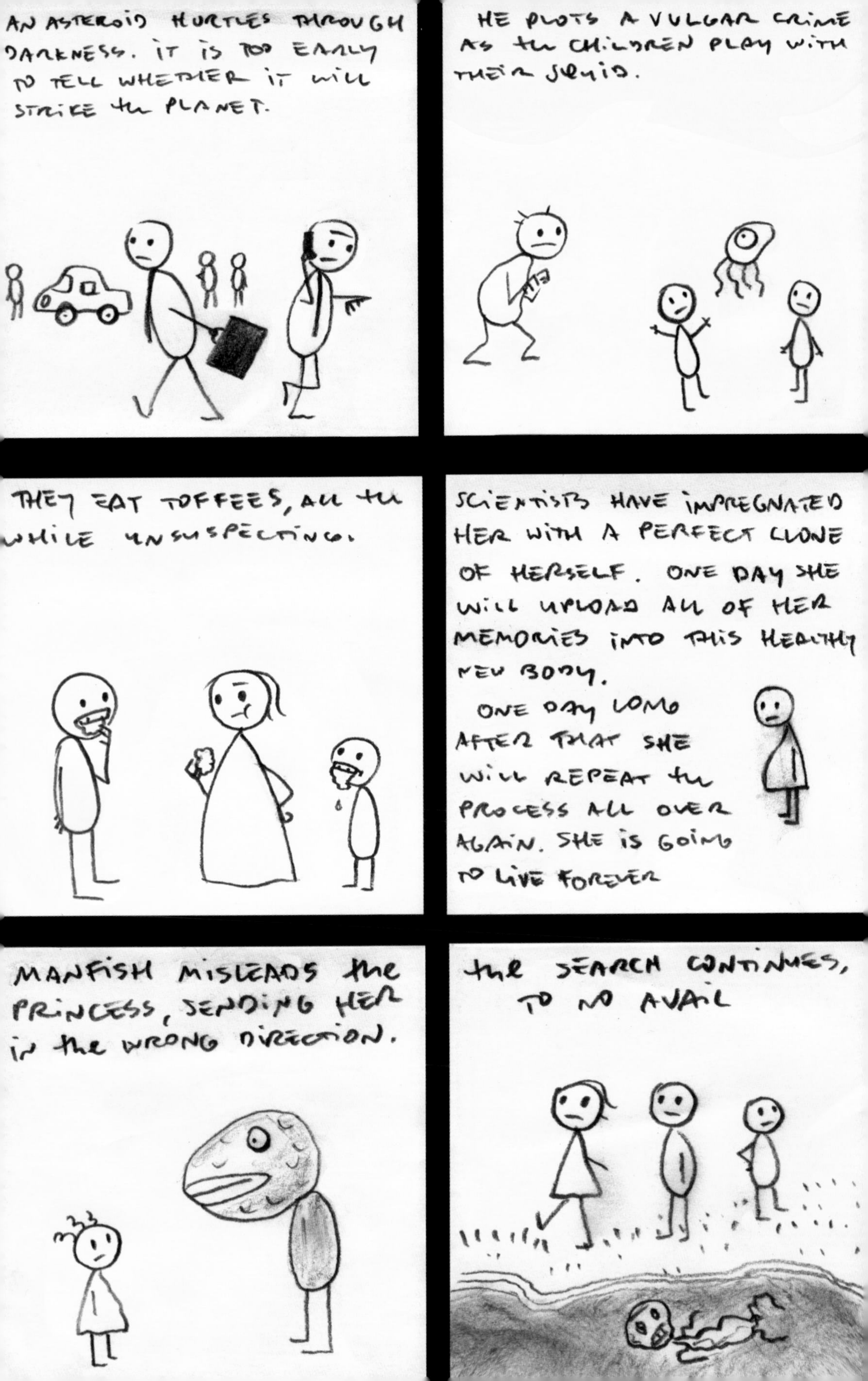
AN ASTEROID HURTLES THROUGH DARKNESS. IT IS TOO EARLY TO TELL WHETHER IT WILL STRIKE the PLANET.
HE PLOTS A VULGAR CRIME AS the CHILDREN PLAY WITH THEIR SQUID.
THEY EAT TOFFEES, ALL the WHILE UNSUSPECTING.
SCIENTISTS HAVE IMPREGNATED HER WITH A PERFECT CLONE OF HERSELF. ONE DAY SHE WILL UPLOAD ALL OF HER MEMORIES INTO THIS HEALTHY NEW BODY.
ONE DAY LONG AFTER THAT SHE WILL REPEAT the PROCESS ALL OVER AGAIN. SHE IS GOING TO LIVE FOREVER
MANFISH MISLEADS the PRINCESS, SENDING HER in the WRONG DIRECTION.
the SEARCH CONTINUES, TO NO AVAIL

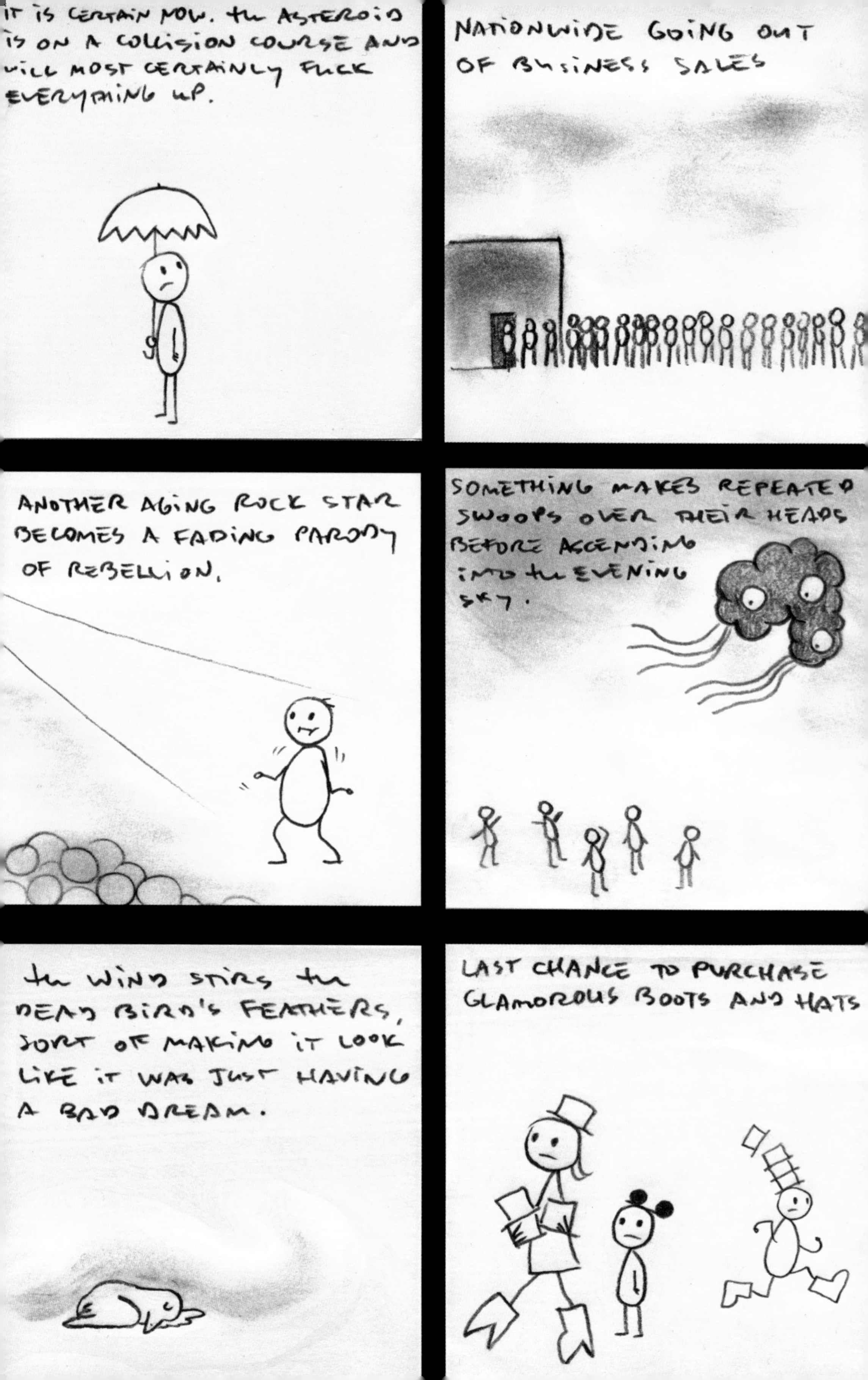
IT IS CERTAIN NOW. THE ASTEROID IS ON A COLLISION COURSE AND WILL MOST CERTAINLY FUCK EVERYTHING UP.
NATIONWIDE GOING OUT OF BUSINESS SALES
ANOTHER AGING ROCK STAR BECOMES A FADING PARODY OF REBELLION.
SOMETHING MAKES REPEATED SWOOPS OVER THEIR HEADS BEFORE ASCENDING INTO THE EVENING SKY.
THE WIND STIRS THE DEAD BIRD'S FEATHERS, SORT OF MAKING IT LOOK LIKE IT WAS JUST HAVING A BAD DREAM.
LAST CHANCE TO PURCHASE GLAMOROUS BOOTS AND HATS

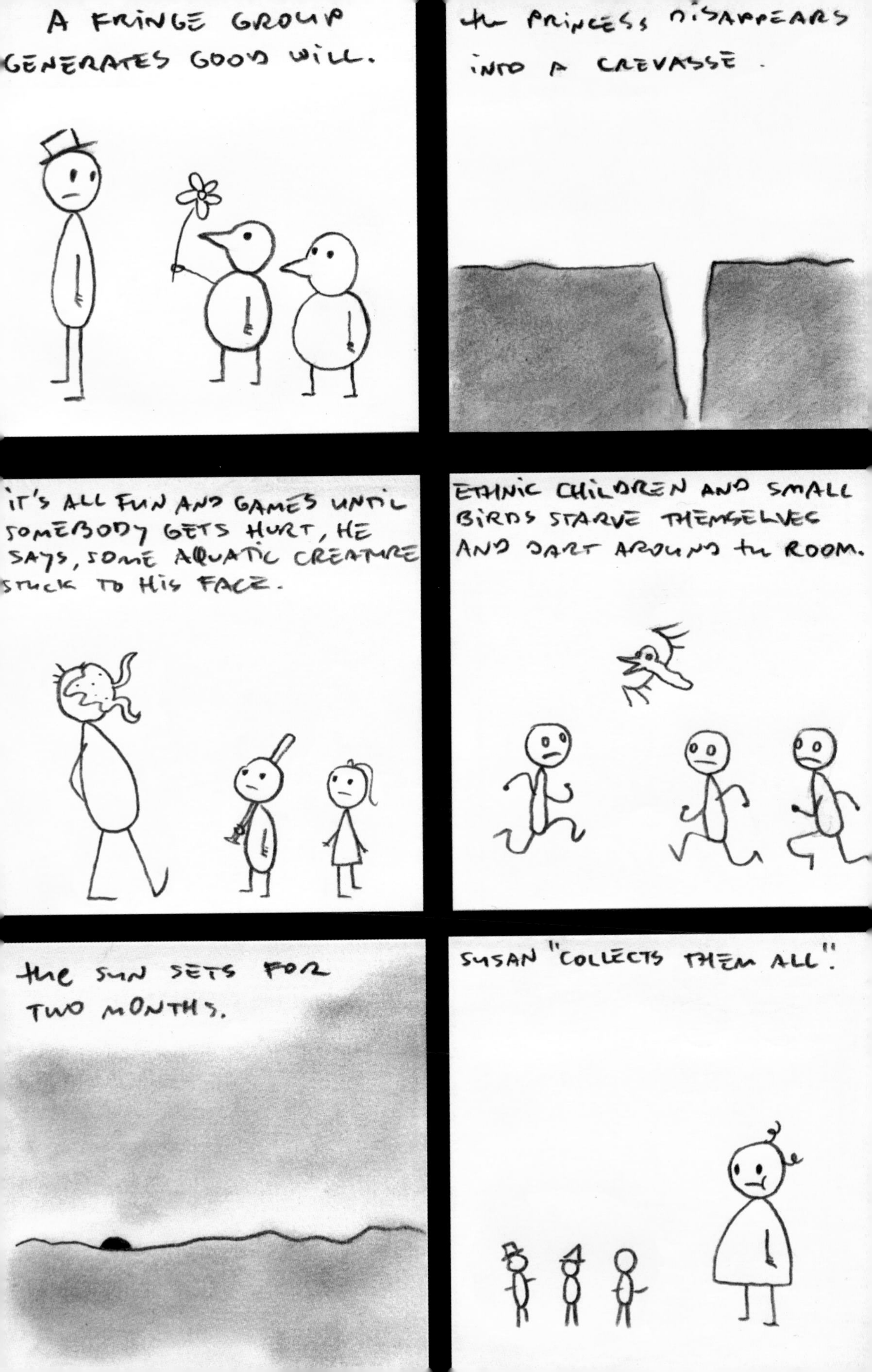
A FRINGE GROUP GENERATES GOOD WILL.
the PRINCESS DISAPPEARS INTO A CREVASSE.
IT'S ALL FUN AND GAMES UNTIL SOMEBODY GETS HURT, HE SAYS, SOME AQUATIC CREATURE STUCK TO HIS FACE.
ETHNIC CHILDREN AND SMALL BIRDS STARVE THEMSELVES AND DART AROUND the ROOM.
the SUN SETS FOR TWO MONTHS.
SUSAN "COLLECTS THEM ALL".

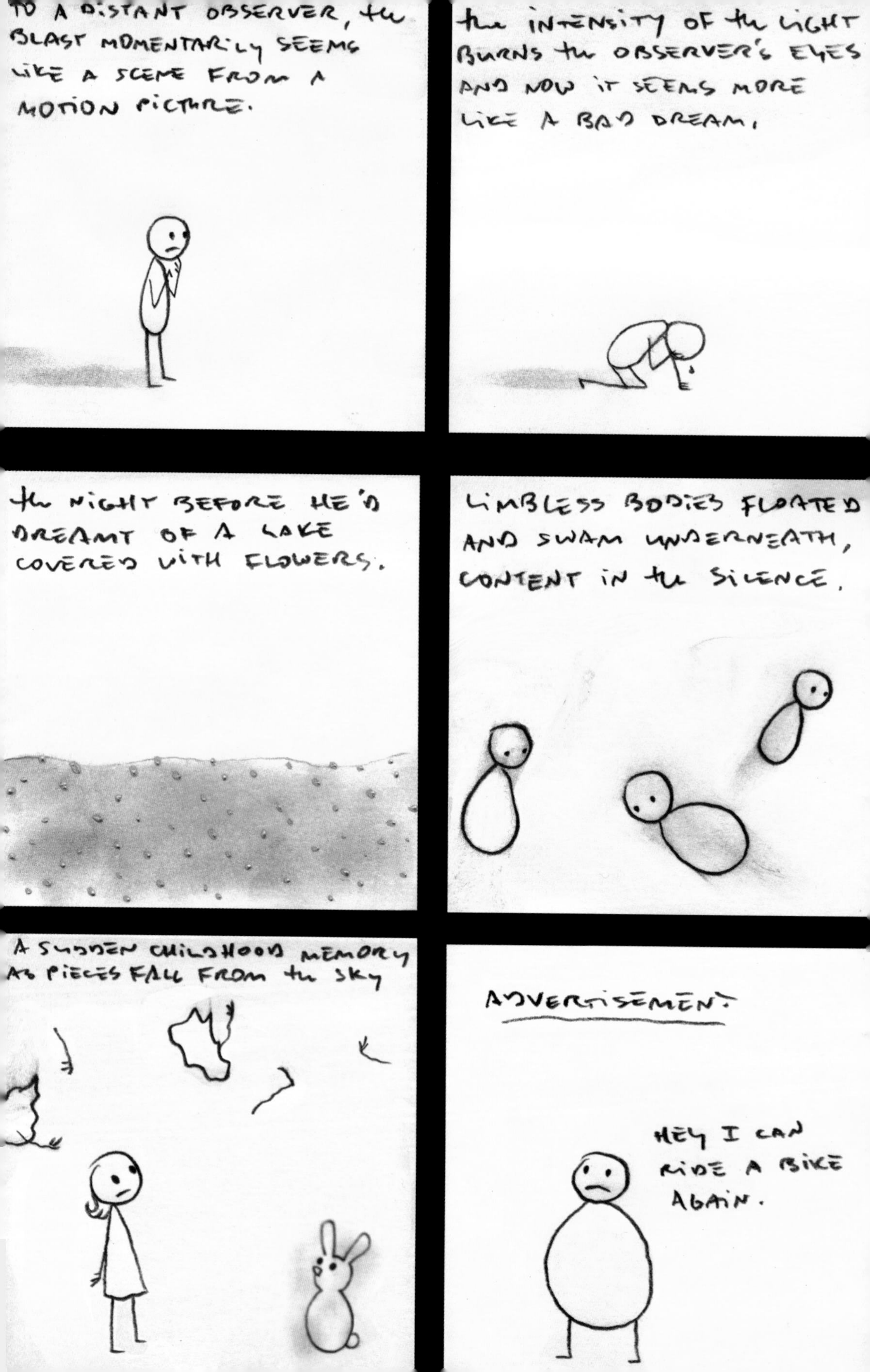
TO A DISTANT OBSERVER, the BLAST MOMENTARILY SEEMS LIKE A SCENE FROM A MOTION PICTURE.
the INTENSITY OF the LIGHT BURNS the OBSERVER'S EYES AND NOW IT SEEMS MORE LIKE A BAD DREAM.
the NIGHT BEFORE HE'D DREAMT OF A LAKE COVERED WITH FLOWERS.
LIMBLESS BODIES FLOATED AND SWAM UNDERNEATH, CONTENT IN the SILENCE.
A SUDDEN CHILDHOOD MEMORY AS PIECES FALL FROM the SKY
ADVERTISEMENT:
HEY I CAN RIDE A BIKE AGAIN.

HIDING IN HOMES AND
SAYING GOOD BYE

CARTOON MARATHON
ON TELEVISION

A PLASTIC BAG RATTLES ON
tu END OF A BROKEN POLE.

MASS CRUSTACEAN SUICIDES

DID SHE FORGET TO
WATER tu CACTUS?

SOMEBODY LOST A BUTTON.

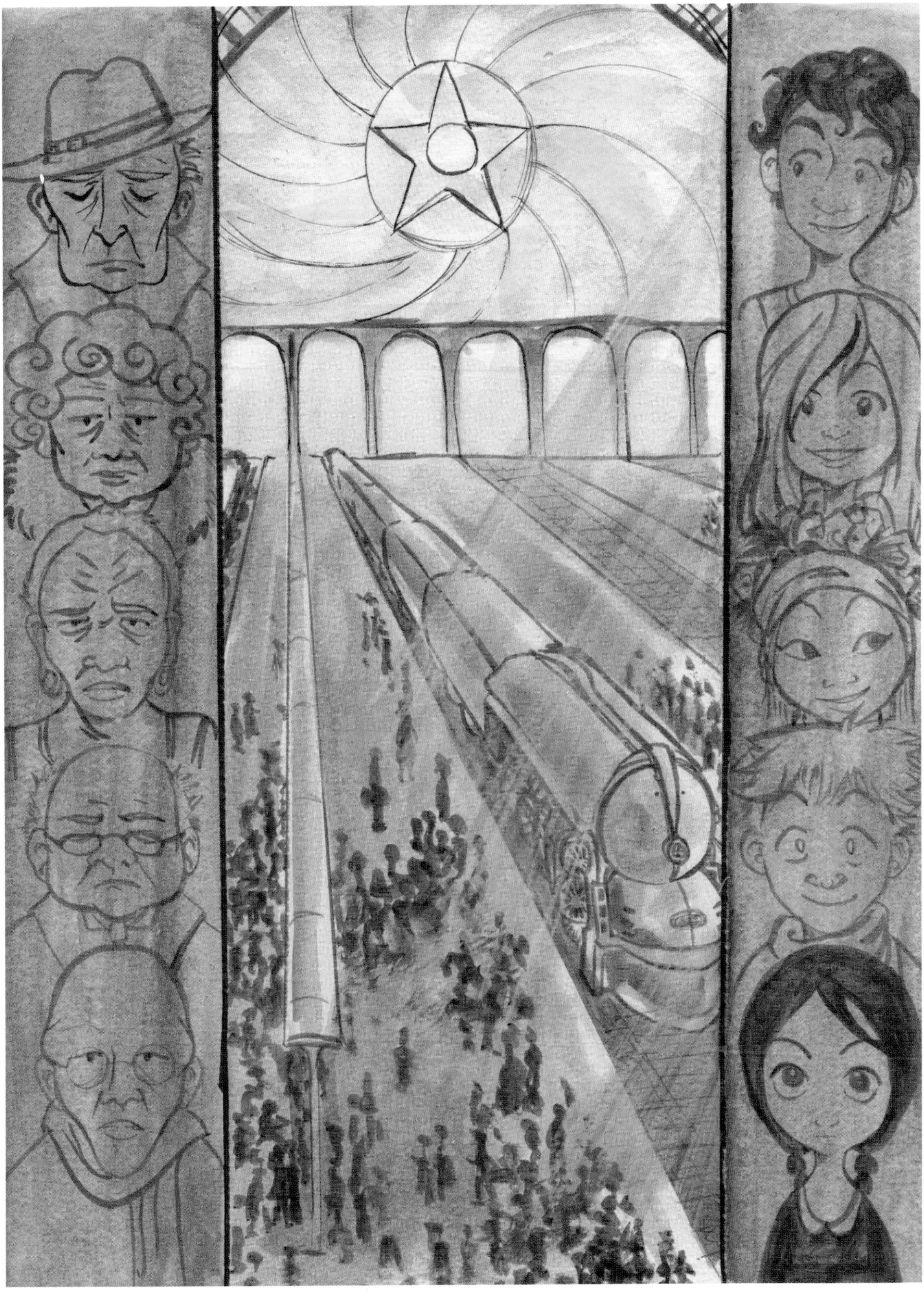

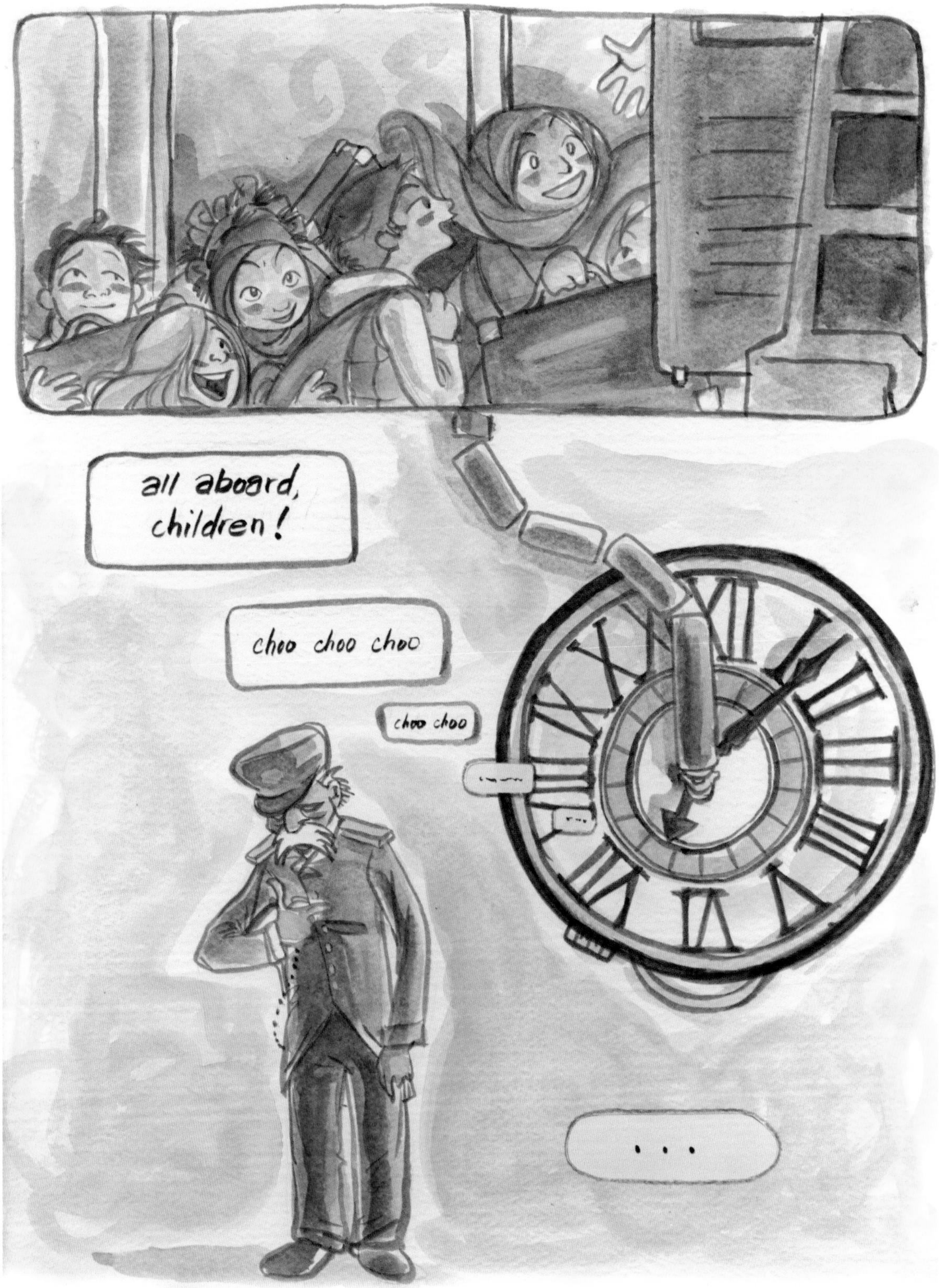
all aboard,
children!
choo choo choo
choo choo
. . .

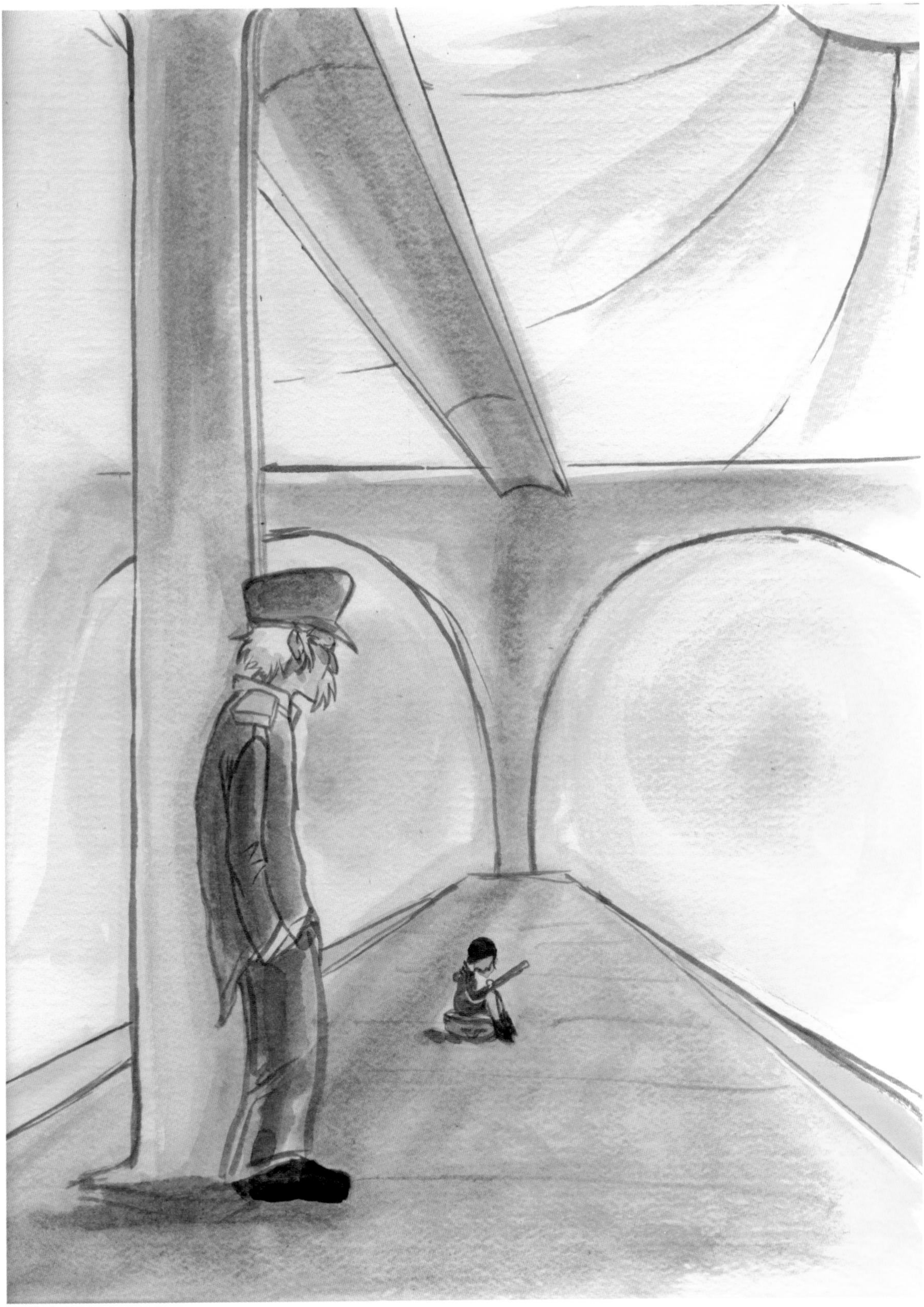

On my way here I sat across from a fortune teller. She enjoyed my drawing very much and asked for a portrait of herself in exchange for a reading. I obliged innocently, not realizing the consequences of learning one's fate on a destiny train. She said only this to me:

In the next stage of your life, you will make a <u>mistake</u>.

A mistake so grave it could alter your experience of the world.

While her reading left me perplexed, I would not have considered staying if I hadn't noticed the two gentlemen waiting with me on the transfer station.

One man stood tall and pert, not a sign of misfortune upon his attractive form. His manner was clumsy, but he blushed and hummed to himself with a sincerity only reserved for the happiest children...

The two couldn't have been very far in age but their souls told a story generations apart.

The other wore an expression of weariness, bundles of rugged scarves barely concealing the years of injustice and cynicism imprinted on his face. He moved very little, but when he did, he maneuvered with a grace only possible through long-term exertion.

It was seeing them that triggered my decision to stay.

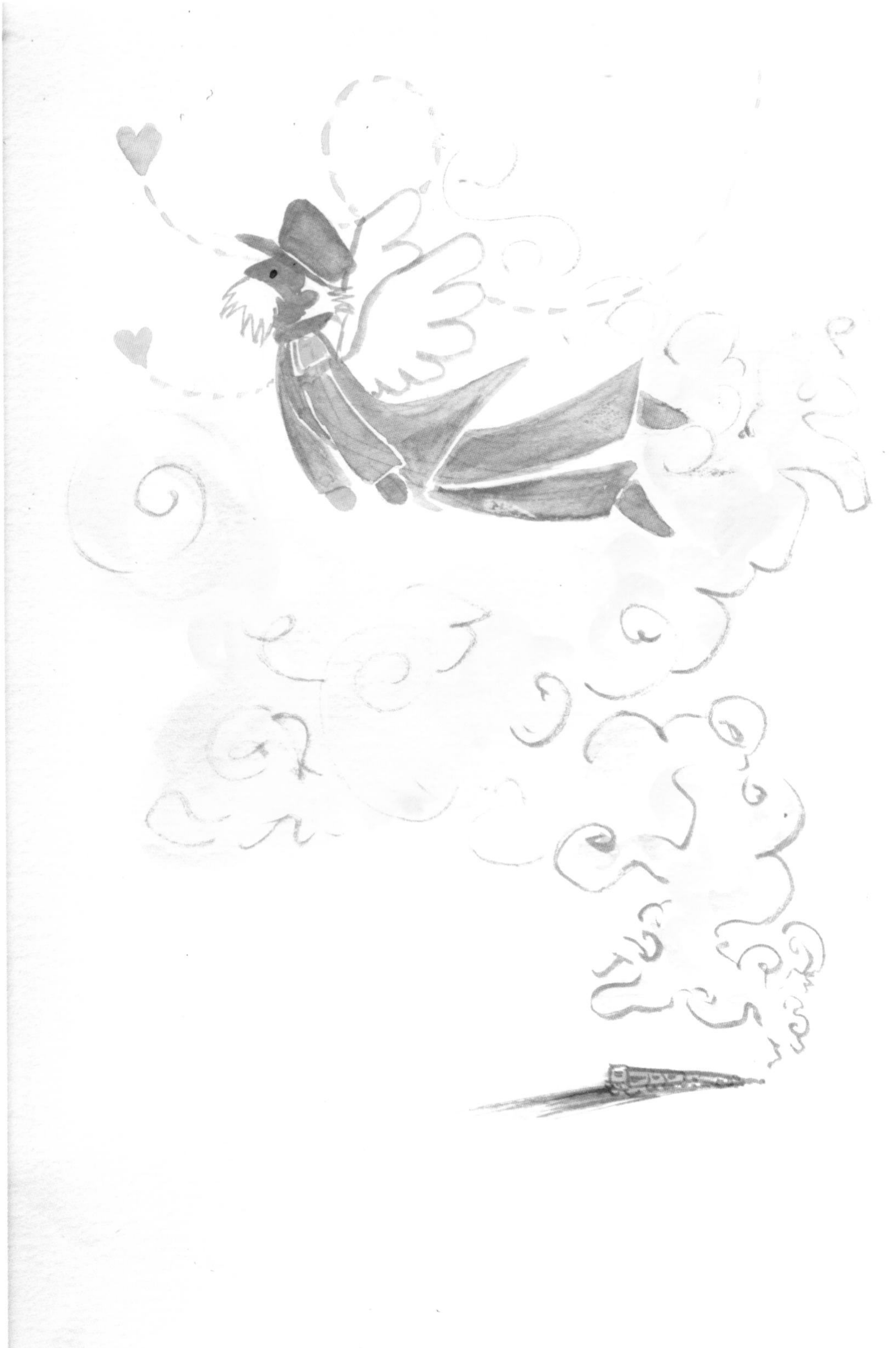

The Orange Grove

by Kazu Kibuishi

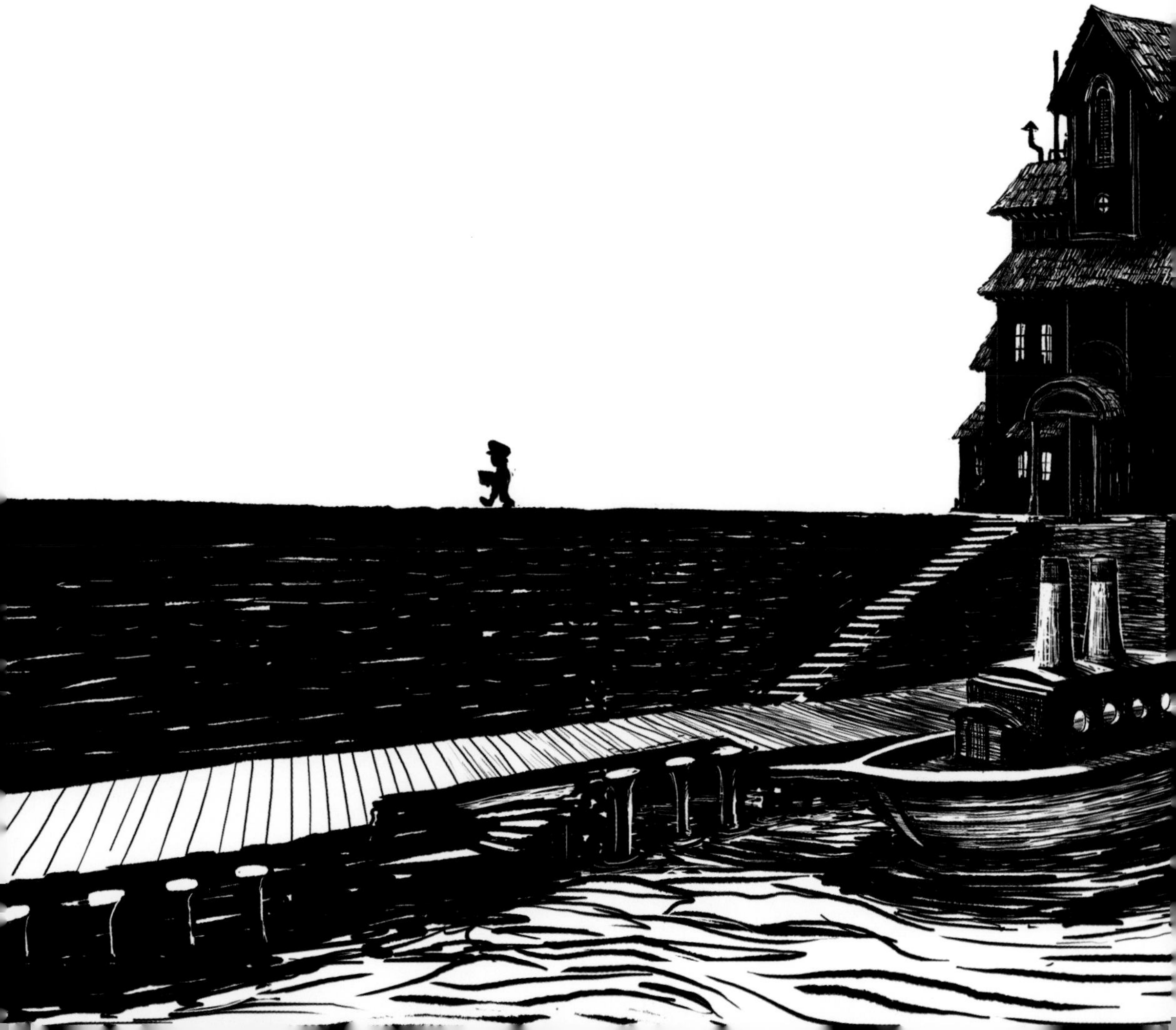

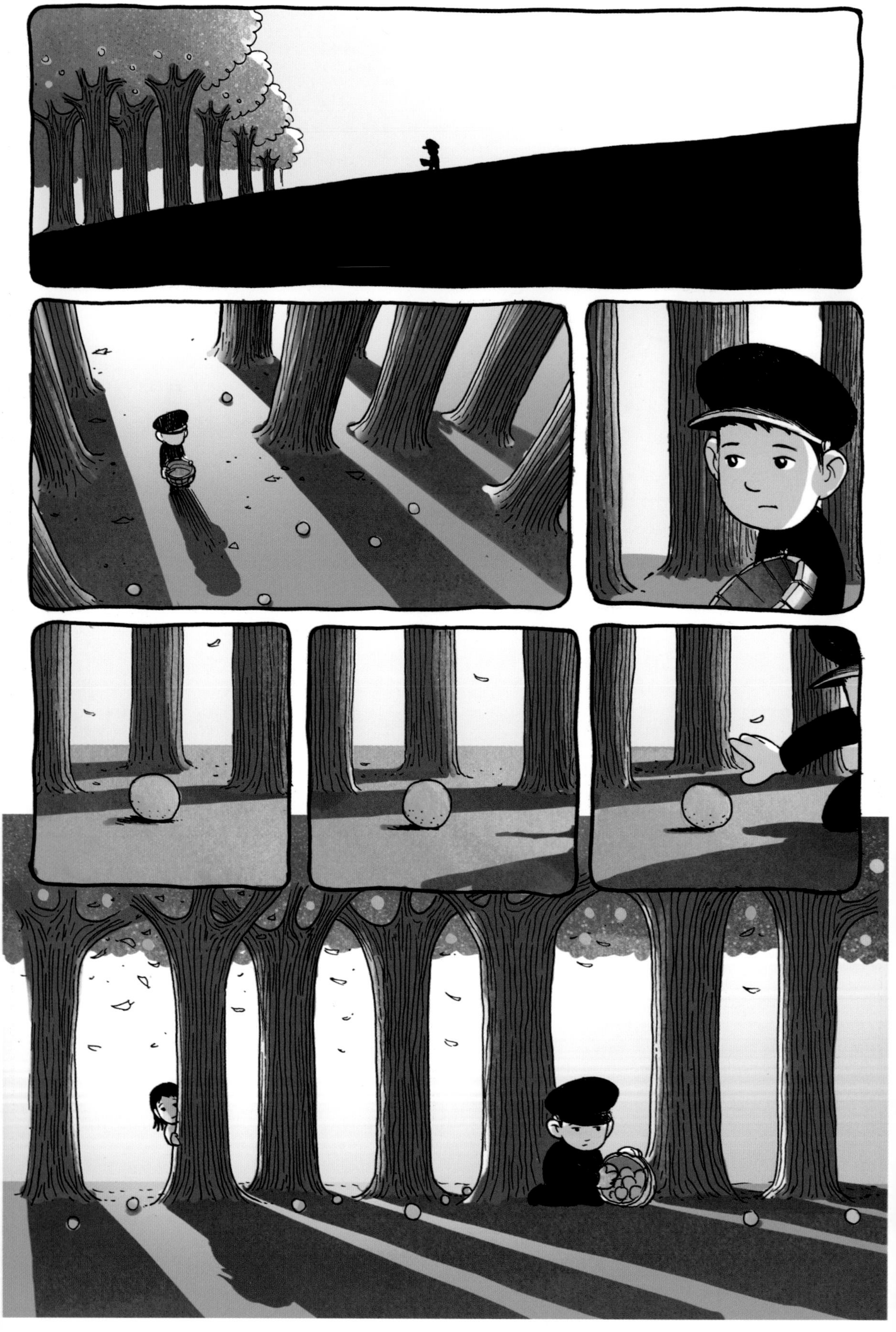

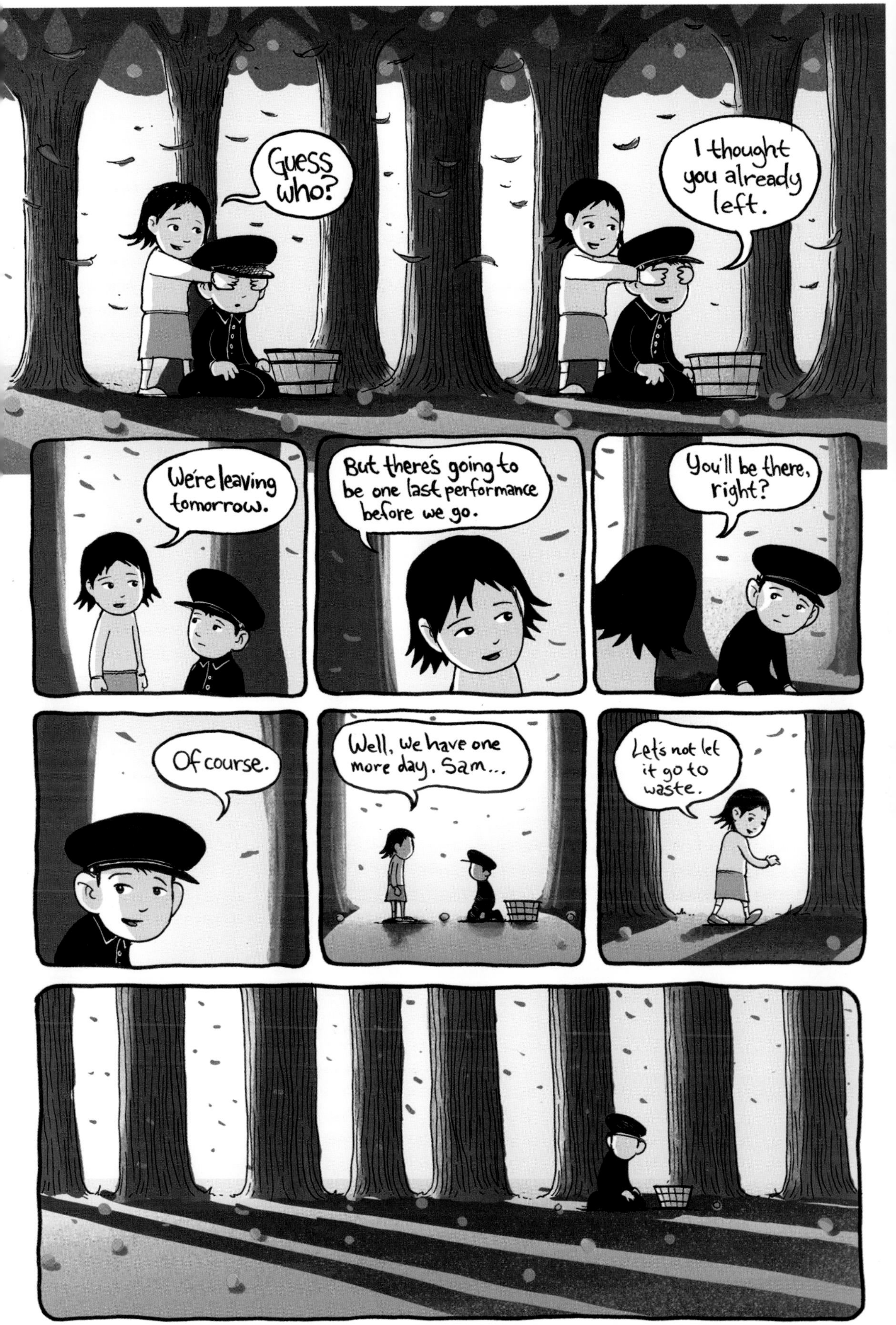
Guess who?
I thought you already left.
We're leaving tomorrow.
But there's going to be one last performance before we go.
You'll be there, right?
Of course.
Well, we have one more day, Sam...
Let's not let it go to waste.

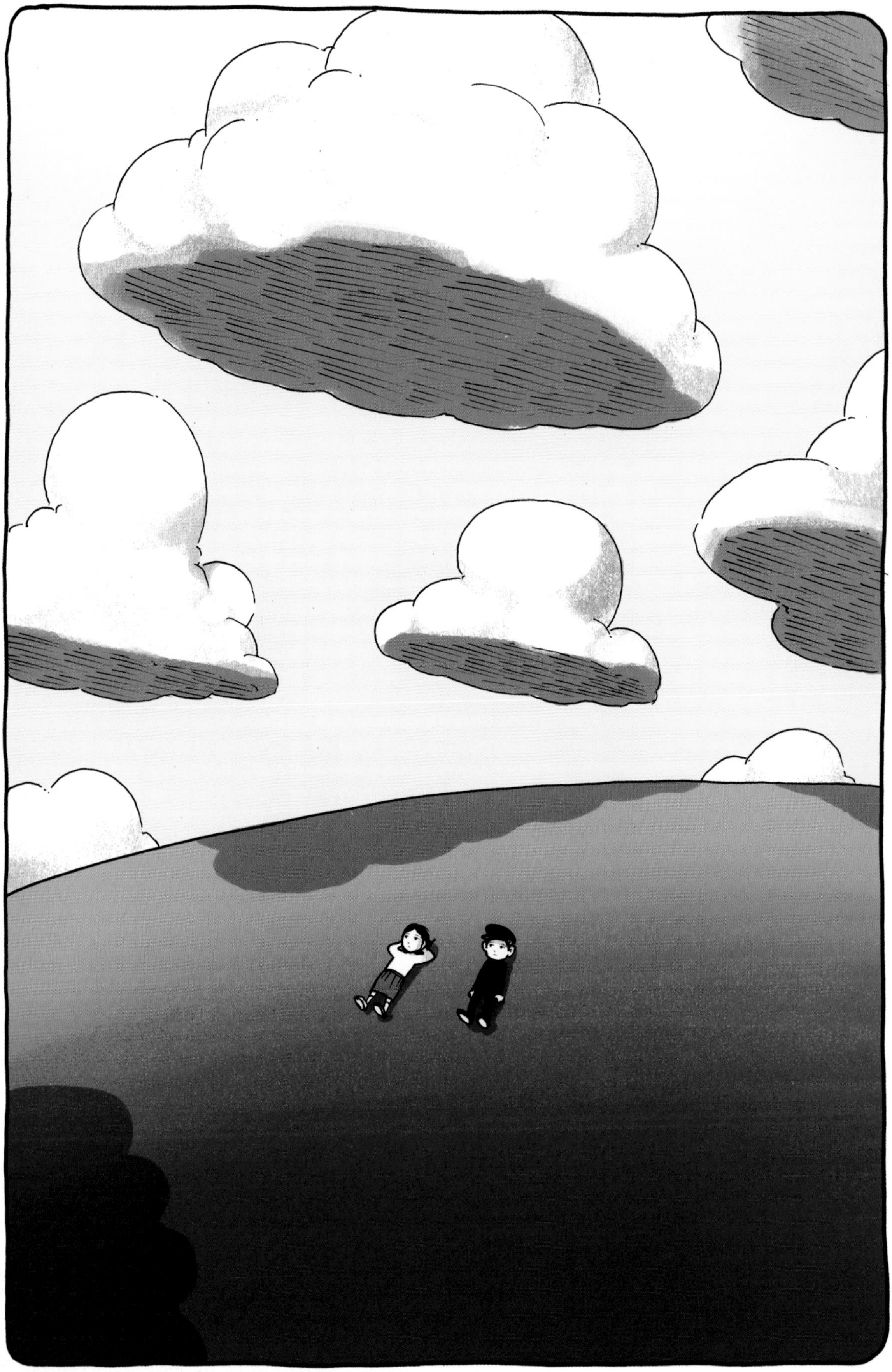

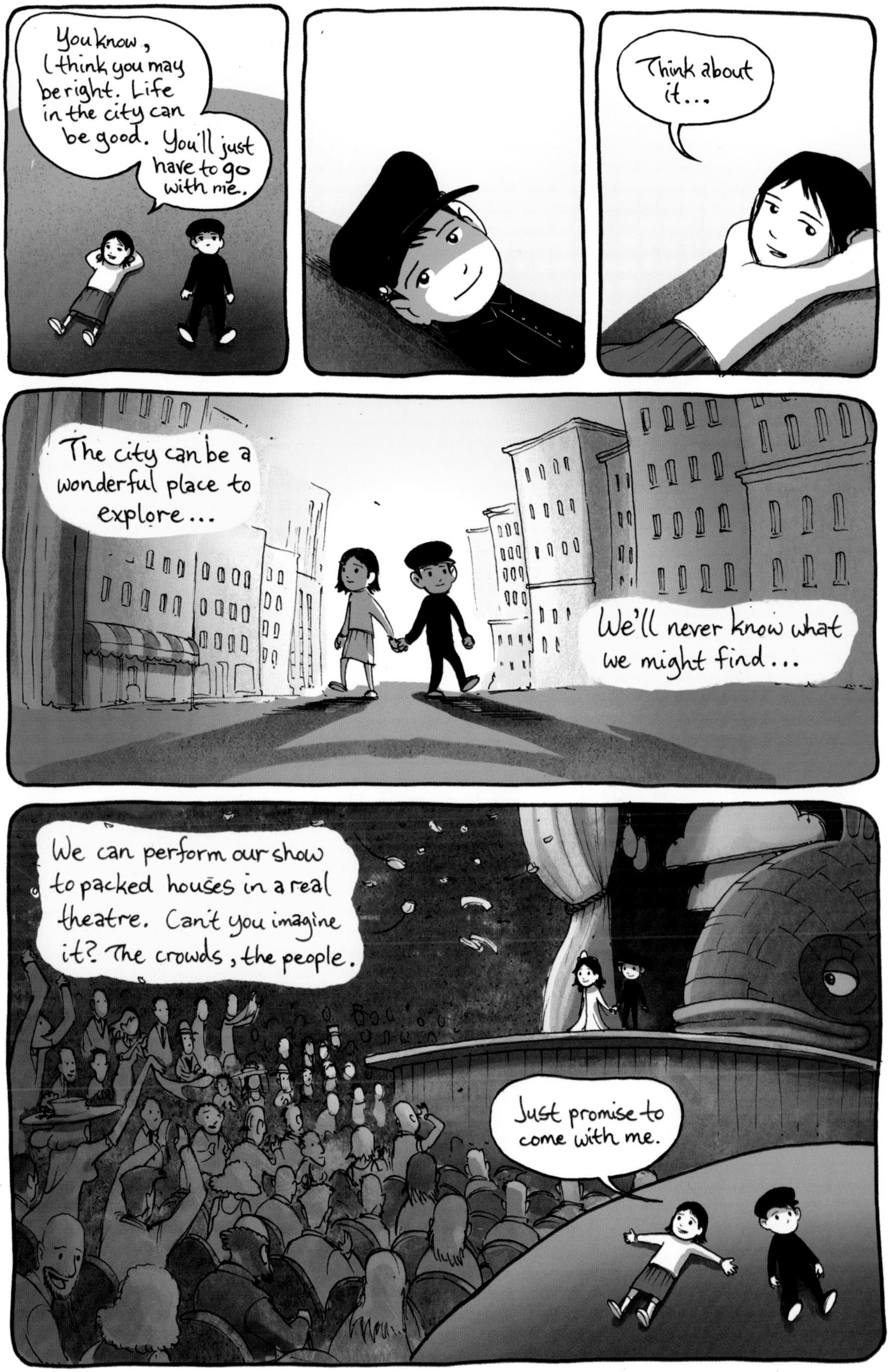
You know, I think you may be right. Life in the city can be good. You'll just have to go with me.
Think about it...
The city can be a wonderful place to explore...
We'll never know what we might find...
We can perform our show to packed houses in a real theatre. Can't you imagine it? The crowds, the people.
Just promise to come with me.

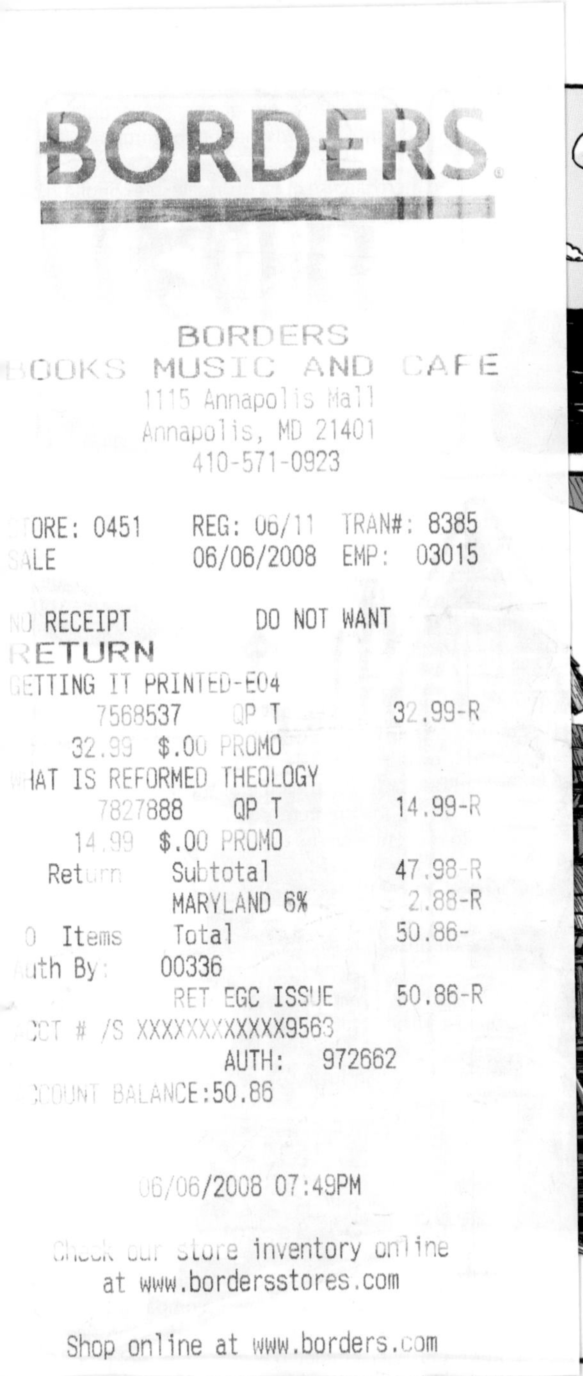

BORDERS

BORDERS
BOOKS MUSIC AND CAFE
1115 Annapolis Mall
Annapolis, MD 21401
410-571-0923

TORE: 0451 REG: 06/11 TRAN#: 8385
SALE 06/06/2008 EMP: 03015

NO RECEIPT DO NOT WANT
RETURN
GETTING IT PRINTED-E04
7568537 QP T 32.99-R
32.99 $.00 PROMO
WHAT IS REFORMED THEOLOGY
7827888 QP T 14.99-R
14.99 $.00 PROMO
Return Subtotal 47.98-R
MARYLAND 6% 2.88-R
0 Items Total 50.86-
Auth By: 00336
RET EGC ISSUE 50.86-R
ACCT # /S XXXXXXXXXXXX9563
AUTH: 972662
ACCOUNT BALANCE:50.86

06/06/2008 07:49PM

Check our store inventory online
at www.bordersstores.com

Shop online at www.borders.com

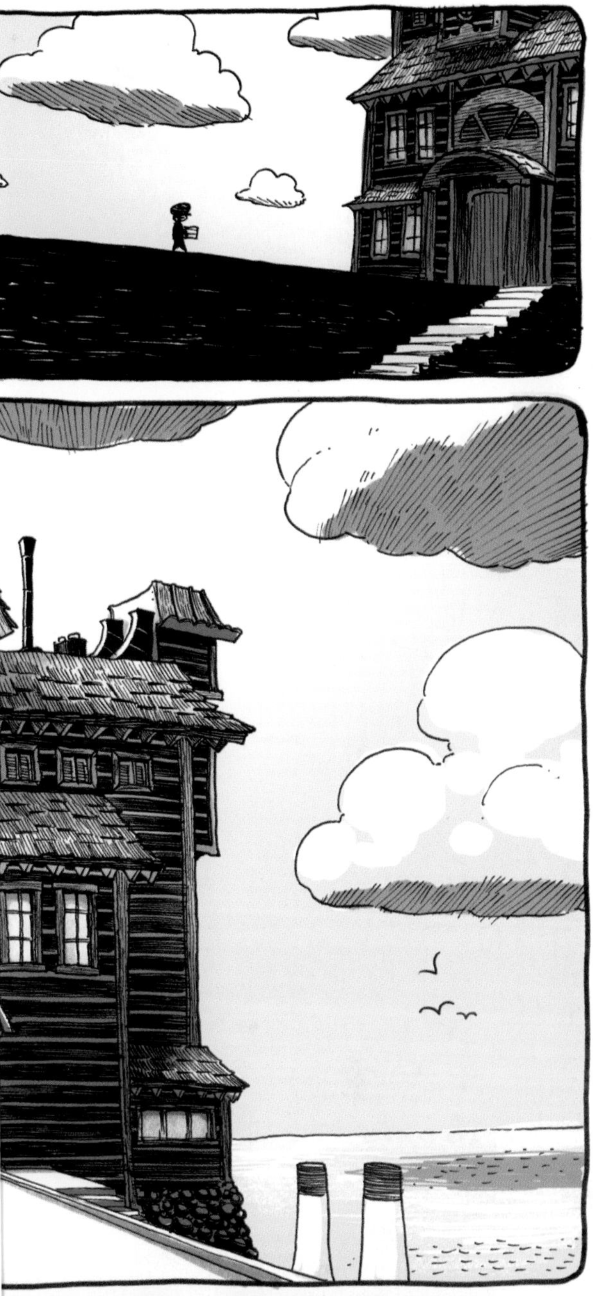

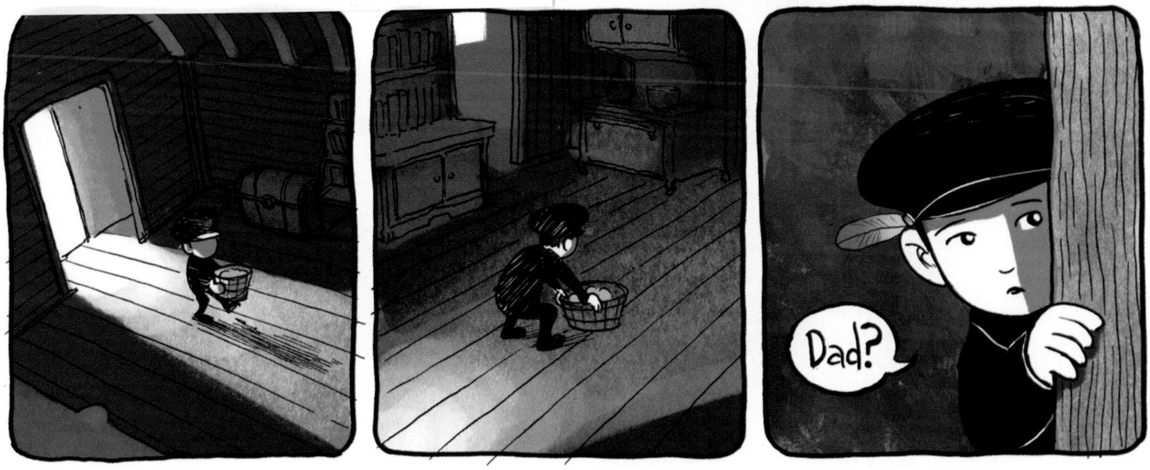
Dad?

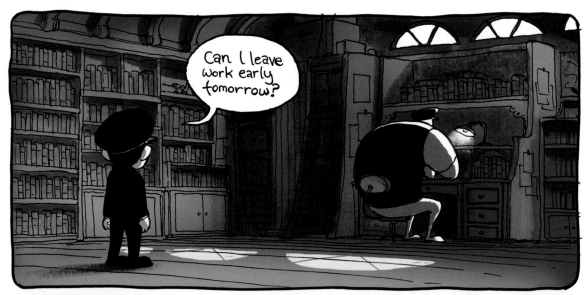

158

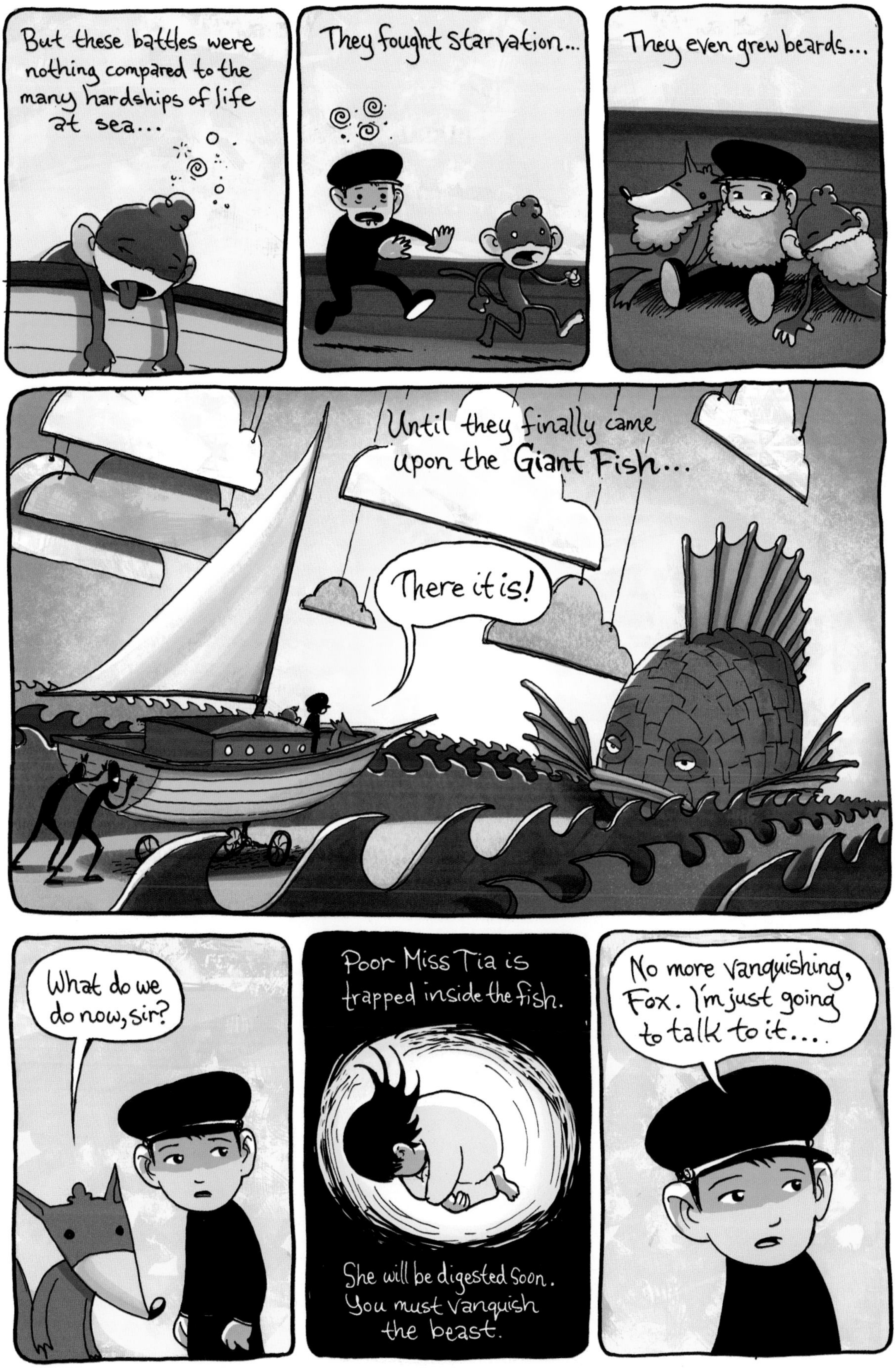
But these battles were nothing compared to the many hardships of life at sea...
They fought starvation...
They even grew beards...
Until they finally came upon the Giant Fish...
There it is!
What do we do now, sir?
Poor Miss Tia is trapped inside the fish.
She will be digested soon. You must vanquish the beast.
No more vanquishing, Fox. I'm just going to talk to it...

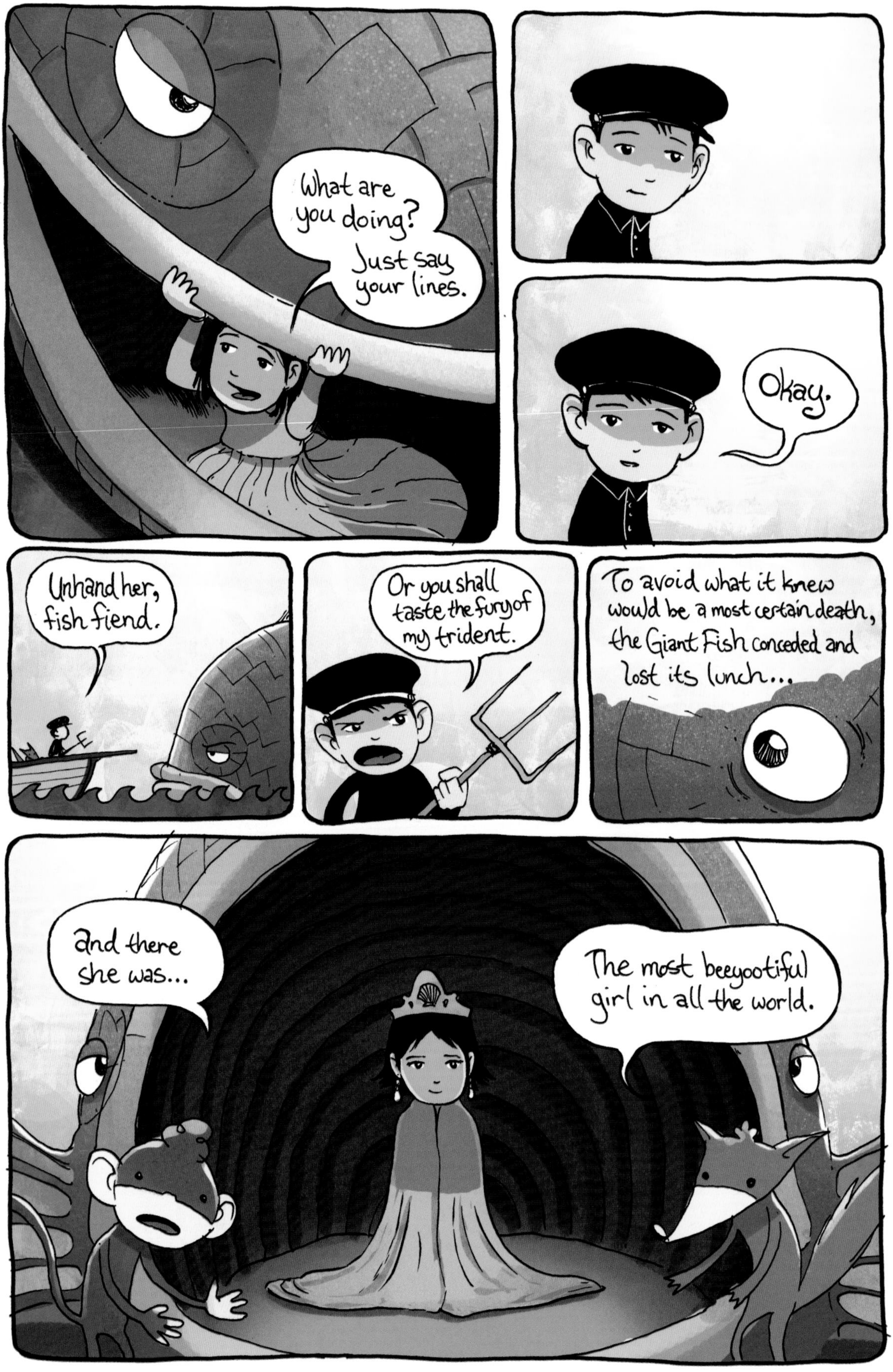
What are you doing?
Just say your lines.
Okay.
Unhand her, fish fiend.
Or you shall taste the fury of my trident.
To avoid what it knew would be a most certain death, the Giant Fish conceded and lost its lunch...
And there she was...
The most beeyootiful girl in all the world.

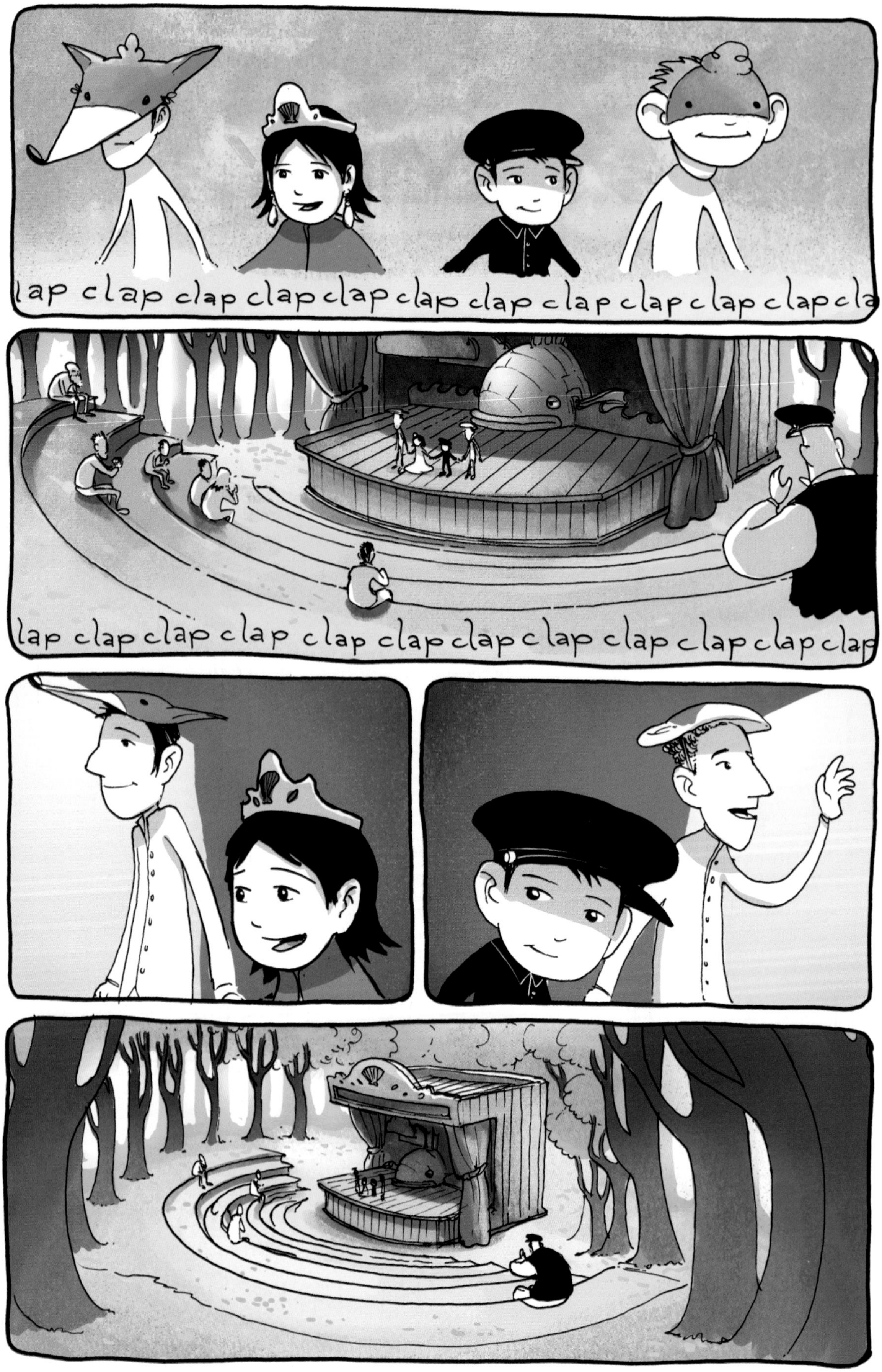
lap clap clap clap clap clap clap clap clap clap clap cla
lap clap clap clap clap clap clap clap clap clap clap clap

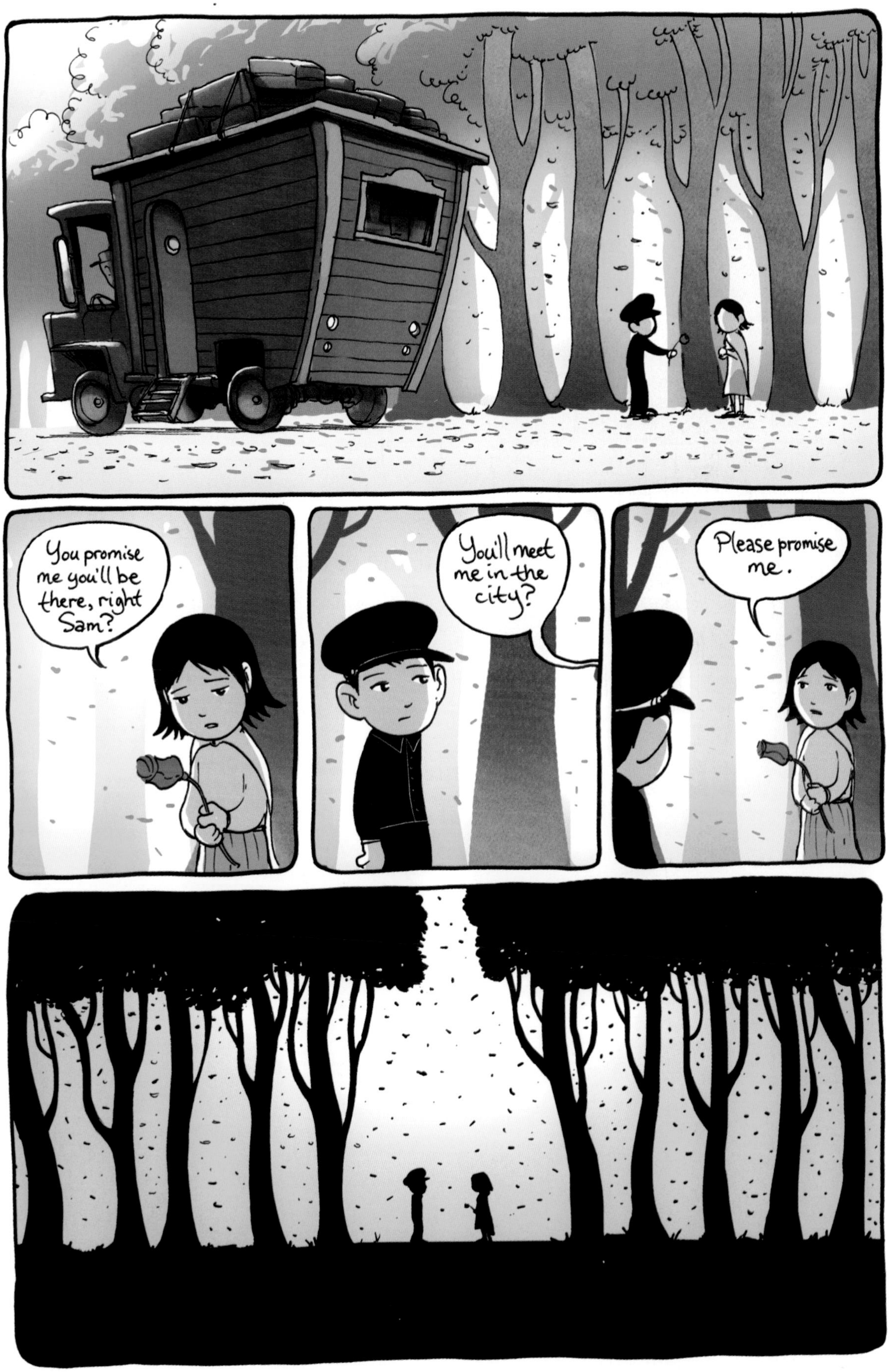
You promise me you'll be there, right Sam?
You'll meet me in the city?
Please promise me.

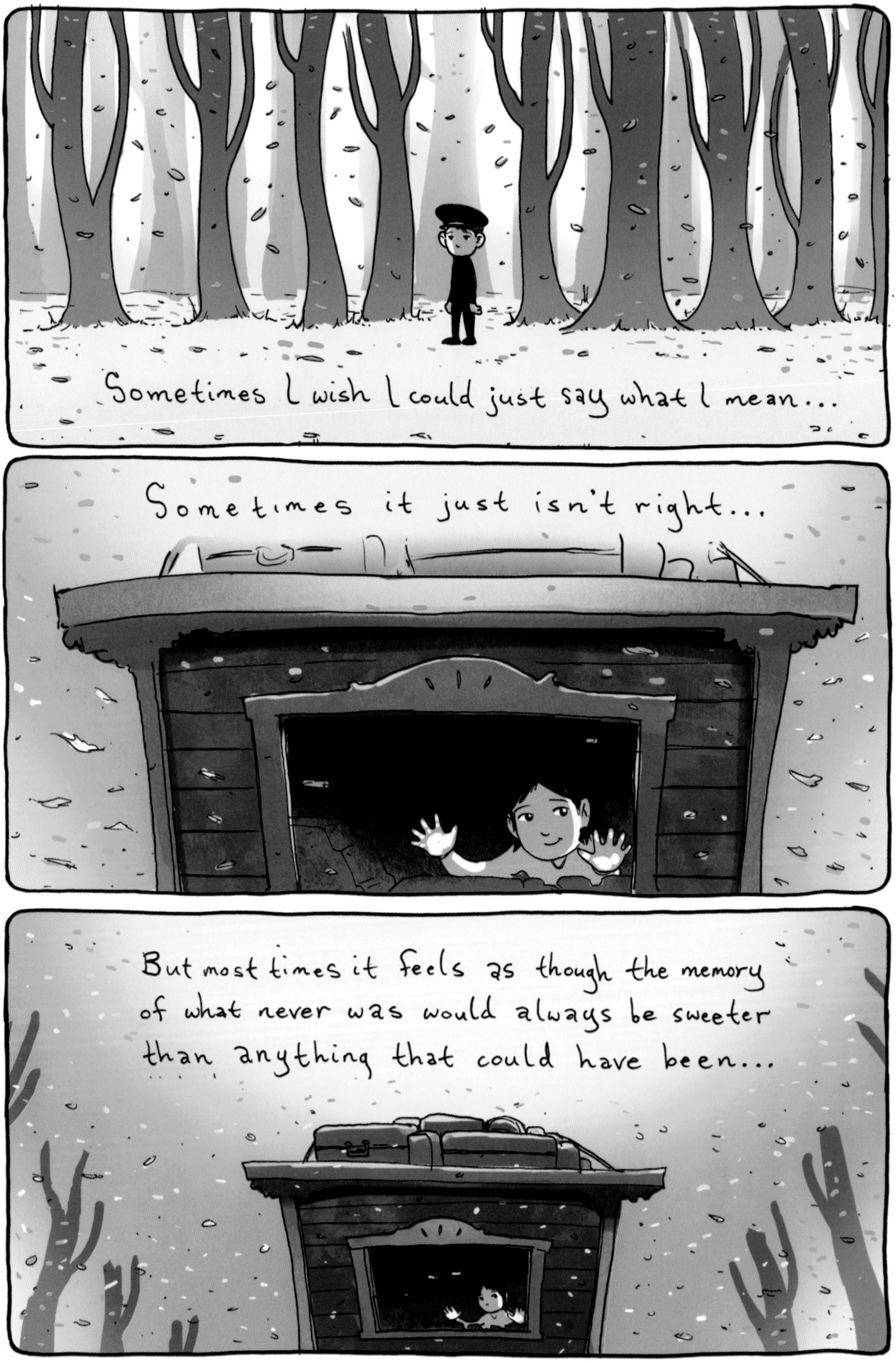
Sometimes I wish I could just say what I mean...
Sometimes it just isn't right...
But most times it feels as though the memory of what never was would always be sweeter than anything that could have been...

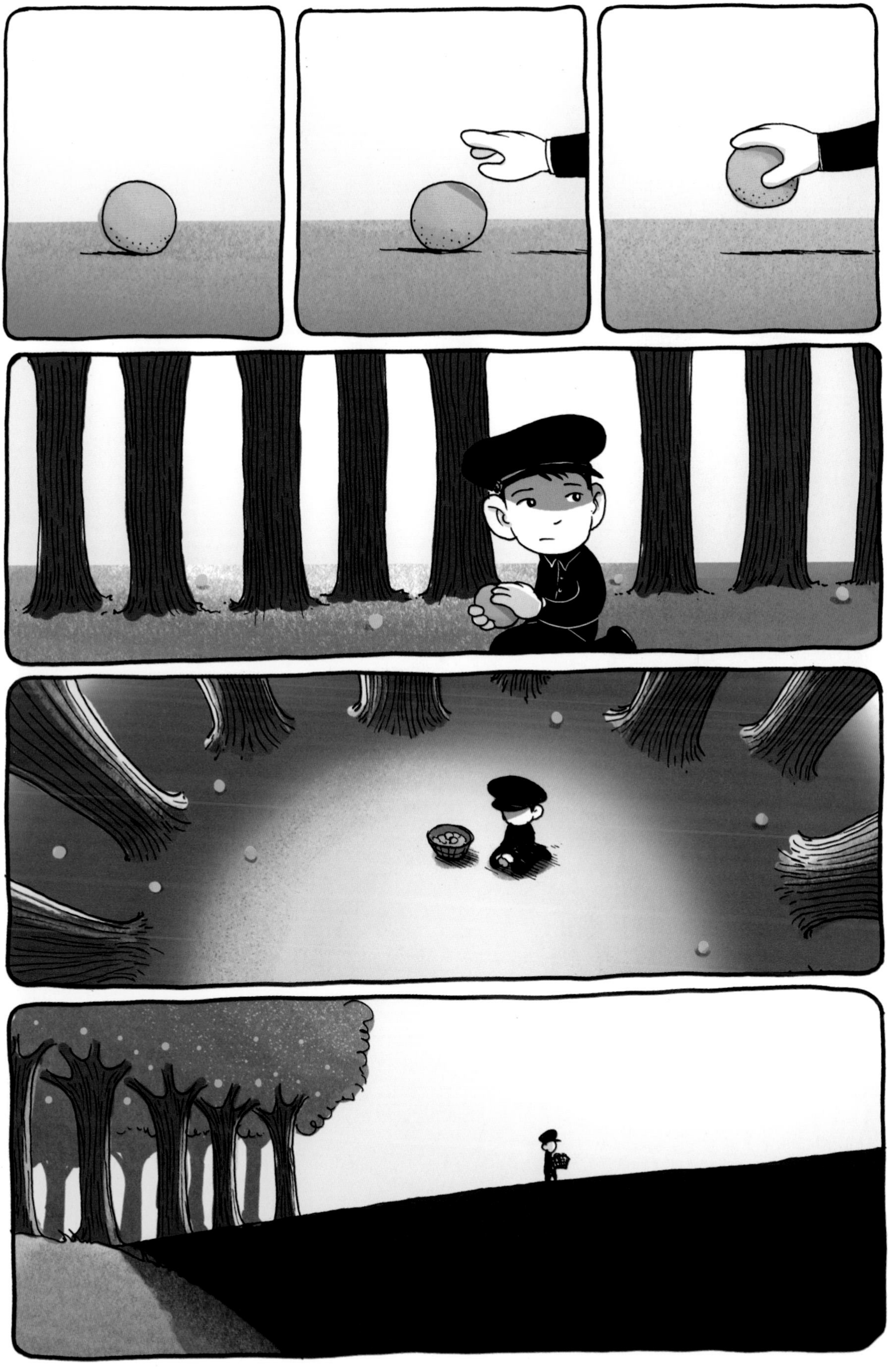

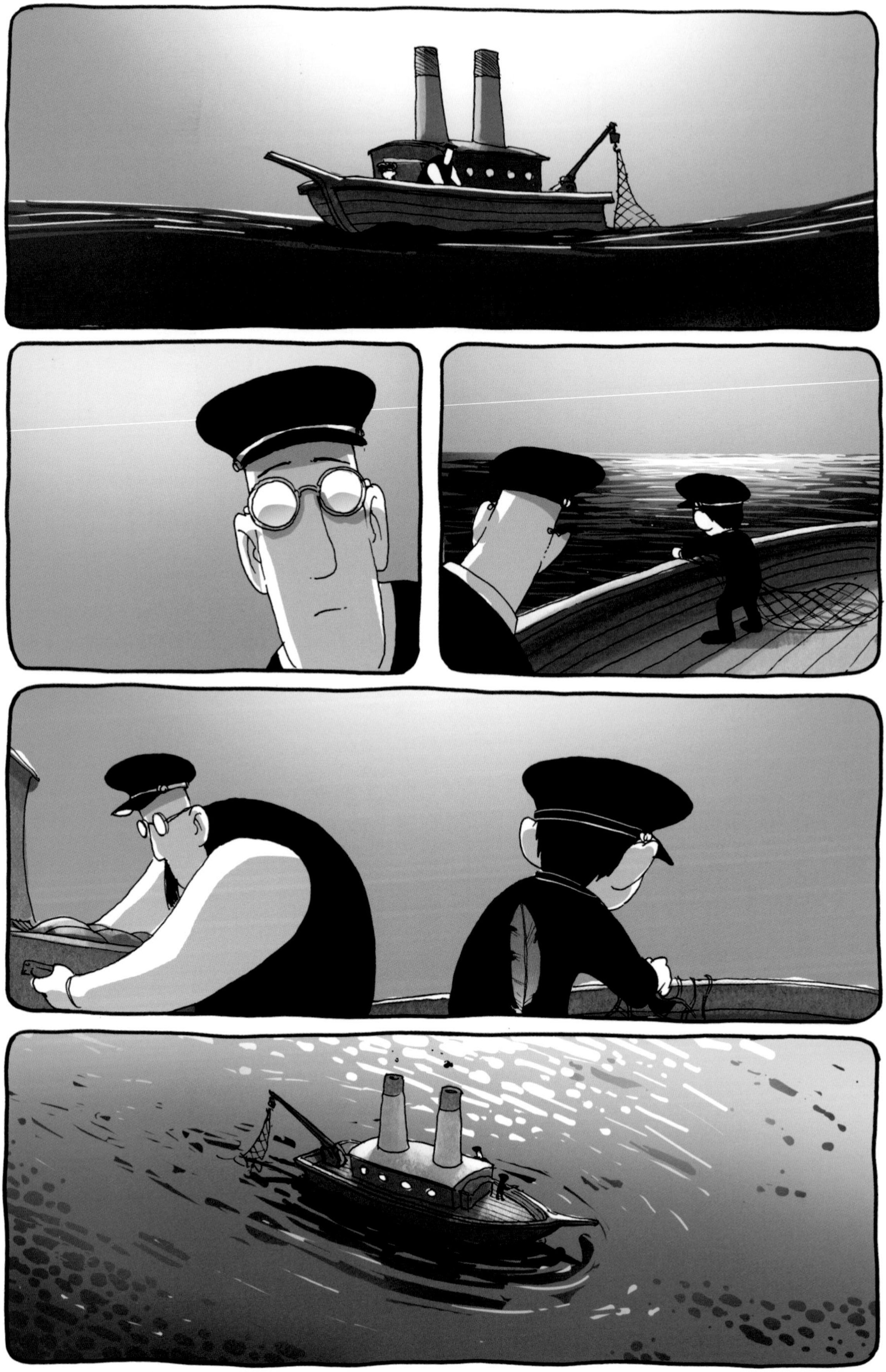

WeatherVain

by Hope Larson

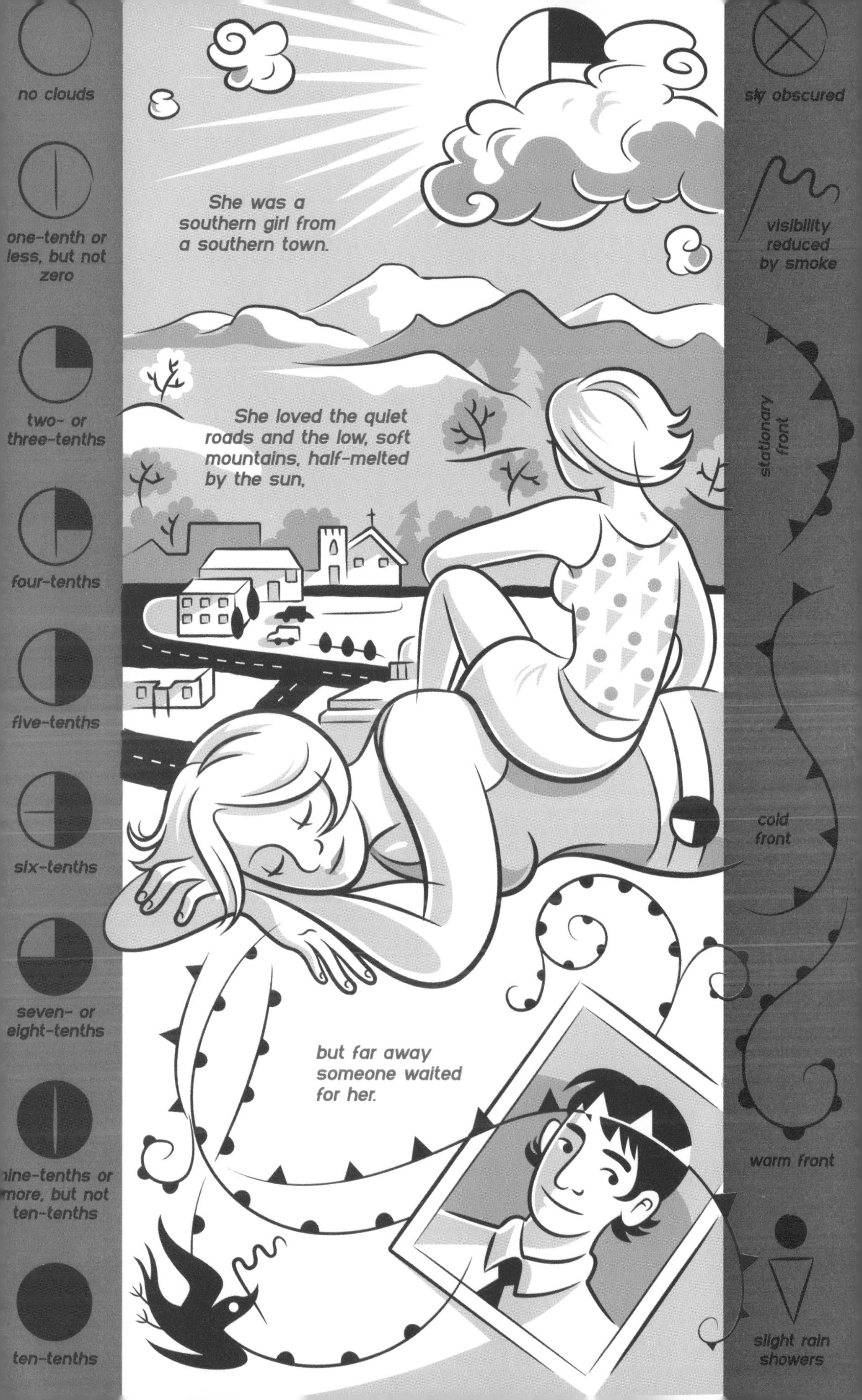

no clouds
one-tenth or less, but not zero
two- or three-tenths
four-tenths
five-tenths
six-tenths
seven- or eight-tenths
ine-tenths or more, but not ten-tenths
ten-tenths
She was a southern girl from a southern town.
She loved the quiet roads and the low, soft mountains, half-melted by the sun,
but far away someone waited for her.
sky obscured
visibility reduced by smoke
stationary front
cold front
warm front
slight rain showers

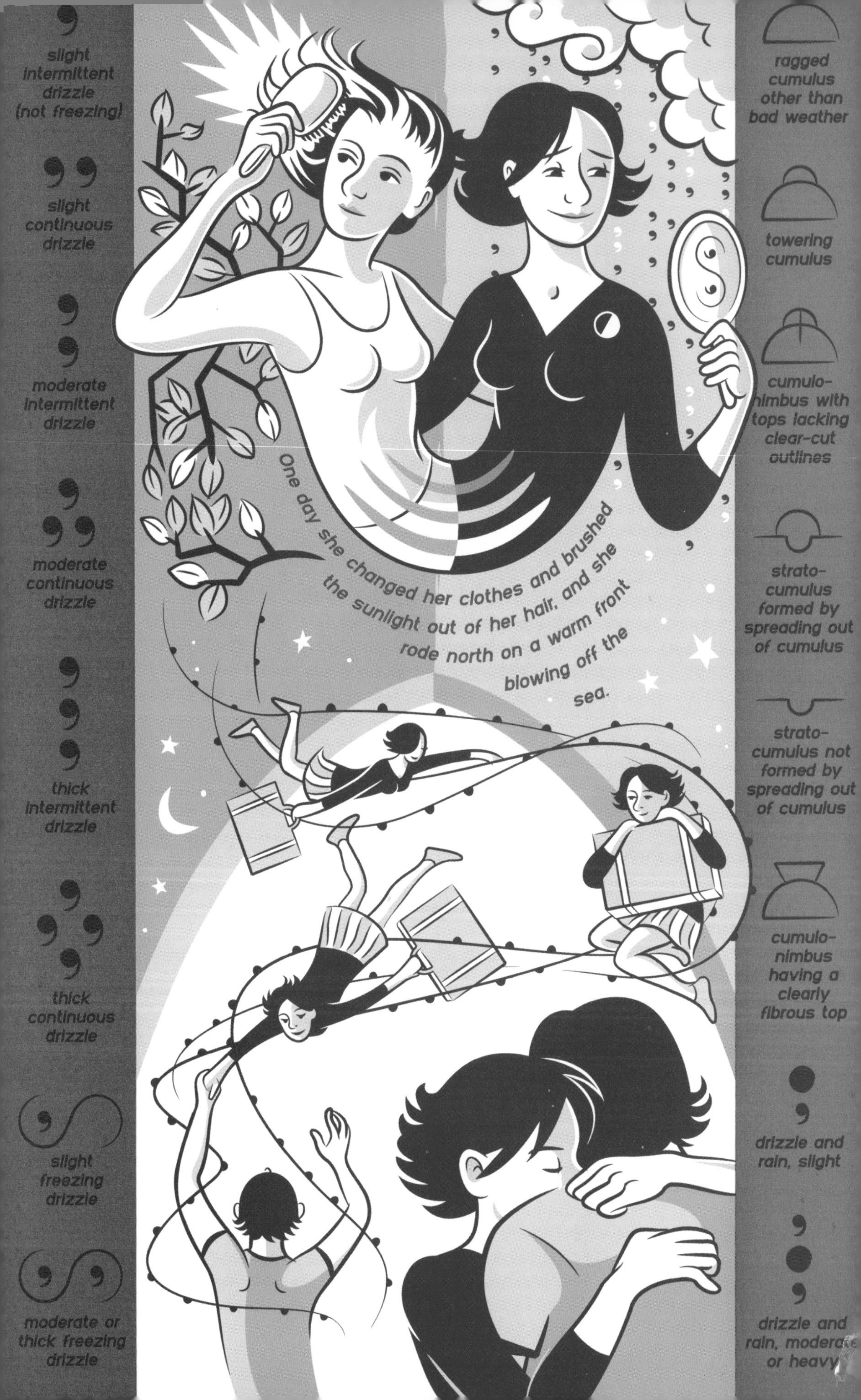
slight intermittent drizzle (not freezing)
slight continuous drizzle
moderate intermittent drizzle
moderate continuous drizzle
thick intermittent drizzle
thick continuous drizzle
slight freezing drizzle
moderate or thick freezing drizzle
One day she changed her clothes and brushed the sunlight out of her hair, and she rode north on a warm front blowing off the sea.
ragged cumulus other than bad weather
towering cumulus
cumulonimbus with tops lacking clear-cut outlines
stratocumulus formed by spreading out of cumulus
stratocumulus not formed by spreading out of cumulus
cumulonimbus having a clearly fibrous top
drizzle and rain, slight
drizzle and rain, moderate or heavy

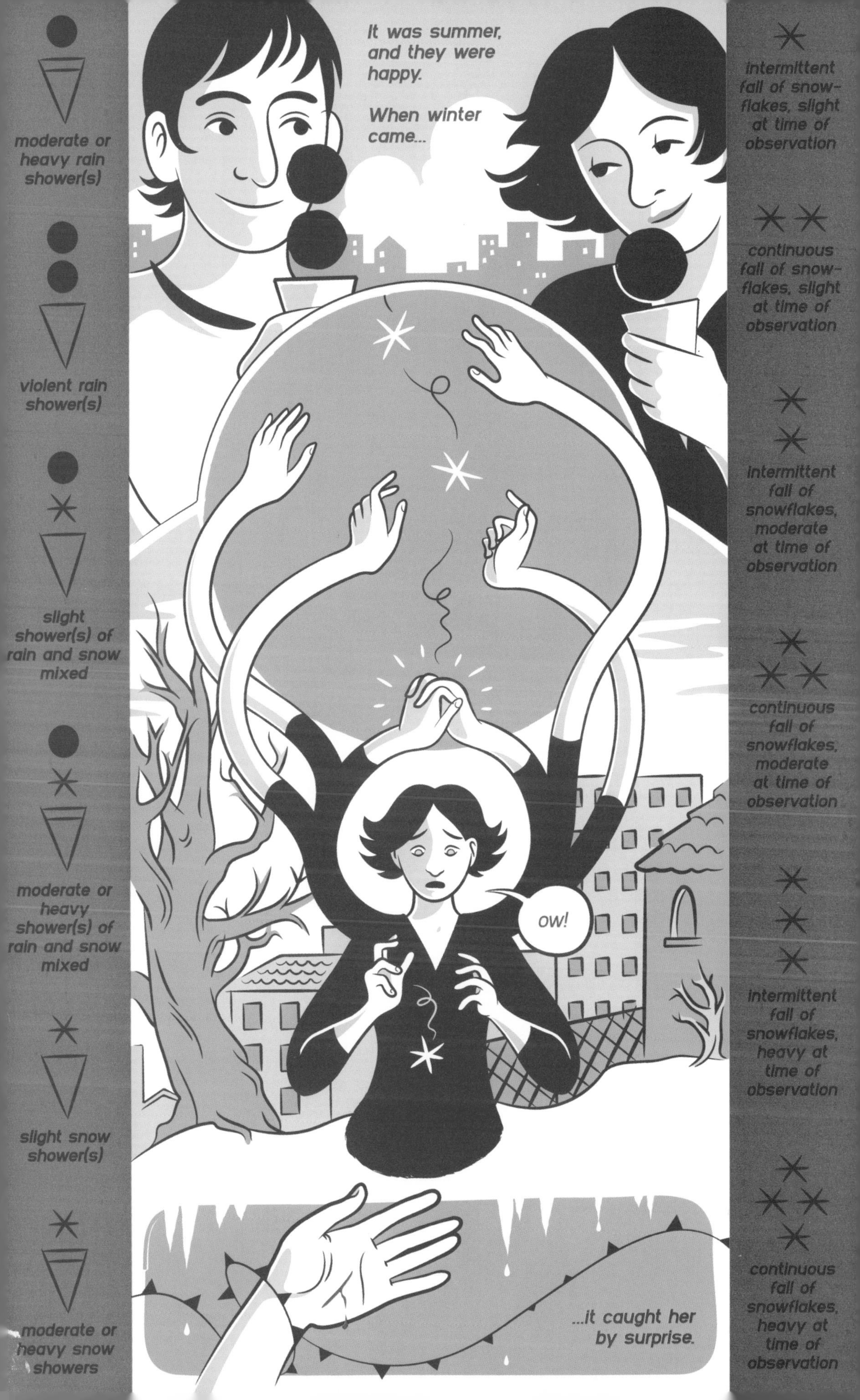
It was summer, and they were happy.
When winter came...
OW!
...it caught her by surprise.
moderate or heavy rain shower(s)
violent rain shower(s)
slight shower(s) of rain and snow mixed
moderate or heavy shower(s) of rain and snow mixed
slight snow shower(s)
moderate or heavy snow showers
intermittent fall of snow-flakes, slight at time of observation
continuous fall of snow-flakes, slight at time of observation
intermittent fall of snowflakes, moderate at time of observation
continuous fall of snowflakes, moderate at time of observation
intermittent fall of snowflakes, heavy at time of observation
continuous fall of snowflakes, heavy at time of observation

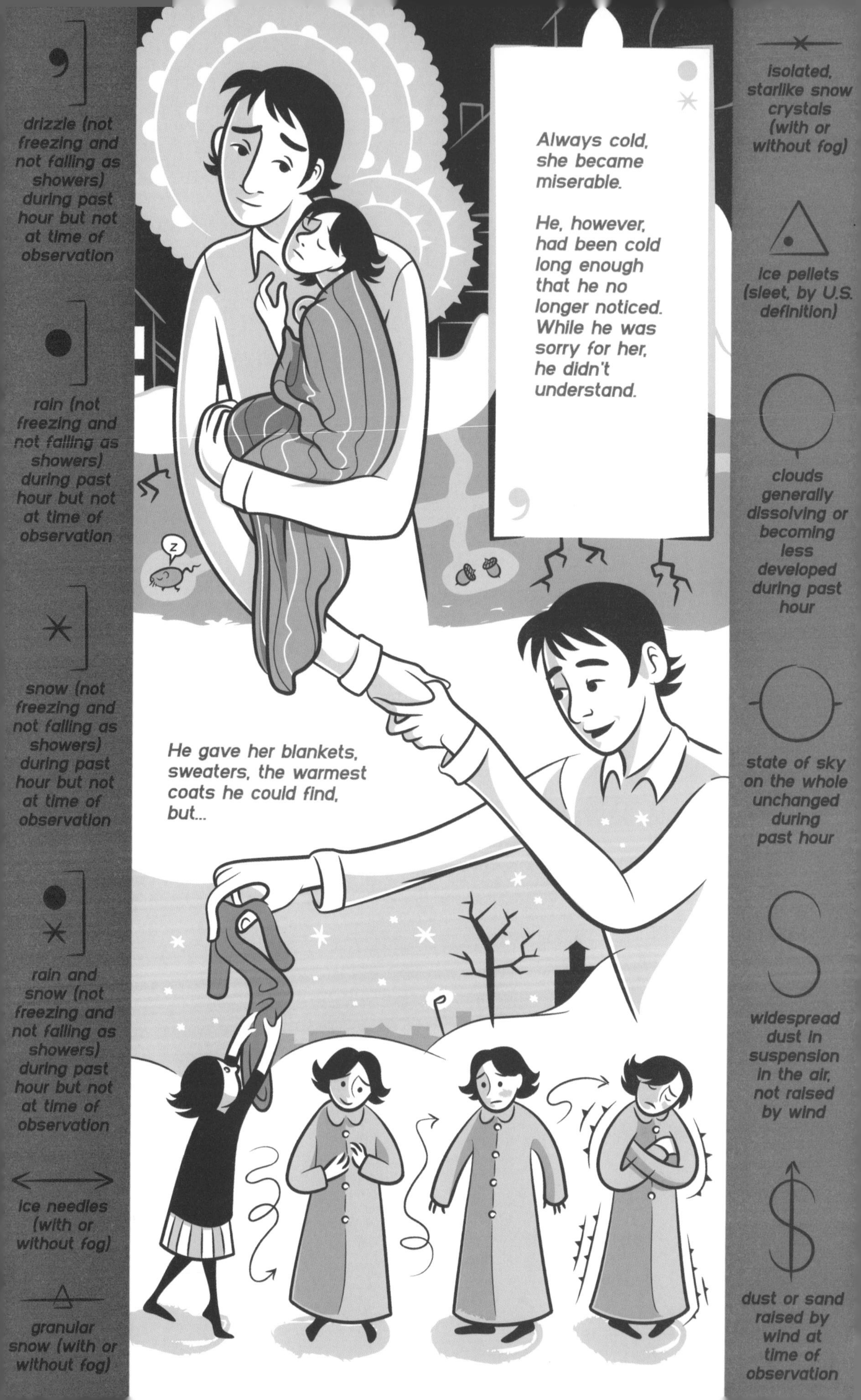
drizzle (not freezing and not falling as showers) during past hour but not at time of observation
rain (not freezing and not falling as showers) during past hour but not at time of observation
snow (not freezing and not falling as showers) during past hour but not at time of observation
rain and snow (not freezing and not falling as showers) during past hour but not at time of observation
ice needles (with or without fog)
granular snow (with or without fog)
Always cold, she became miserable.
He, however, had been cold long enough that he no longer noticed. While he was sorry for her, he didn't understand.
He gave her blankets, sweaters, the warmest coats he could find, but...
isolated, starlike snow crystals (with or without fog)
ice pellets (sleet, by U.S. definition)
clouds generally dissolving or becoming less developed during past hour
state of sky on the whole unchanged during past hour
widespread dust in suspension in the air, not raised by wind
dust or sand raised by wind at time of observation

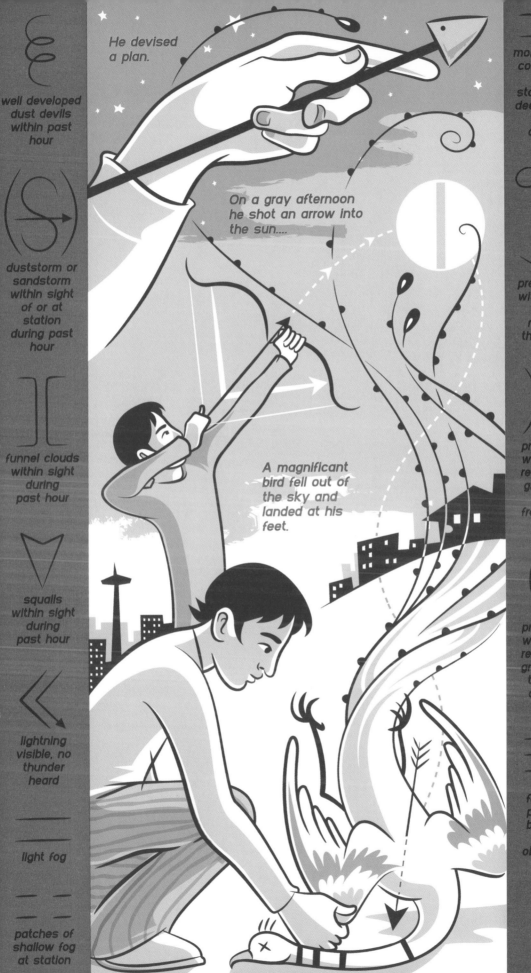

He devised a plan.

On a gray afternoon he shot an arrow into the sun....

A magnificant bird fell out of the sky and landed at his feet.

well developed dust devils within past hour

duststorm or sandstorm within sight of or at station during past hour

funnel clouds within sight during past hour

squalls within sight during past hour

lightning visible, no thunder heard

light fog

patches of shallow fog at station

more or less continuous fog at station, not deeper than 6 feet on land

haze

precipitation within sight, but not reaching the ground

precipitation within sight, reaching the ground, but distant from station

precipitation within sight, reaching the ground, near to but not at station

fog during past hour, but not at time of observation

showers

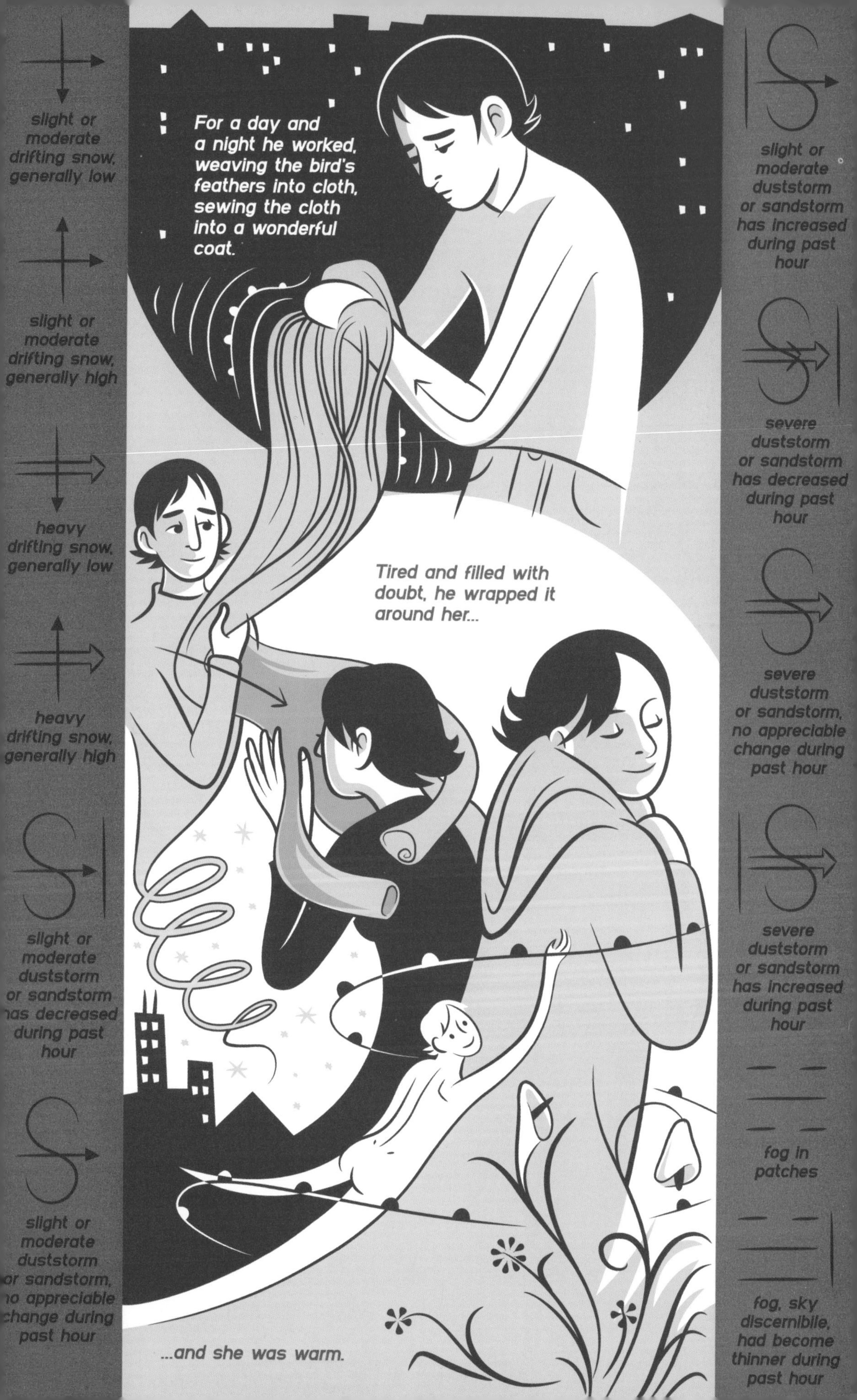
slight or moderate drifting snow, generally low
slight or moderate drifting snow, generally high
heavy drifting snow, generally low
heavy drifting snow, generally high
slight or moderate duststorm or sandstorm has decreased during past hour
slight or moderate duststorm or sandstorm, no appreciable change during past hour
For a day and a night he worked, weaving the bird's feathers into cloth, sewing the cloth into a wonderful coat.
Tired and filled with doubt, he wrapped it around her...
...and she was warm.
slight or moderate duststorm or sandstorm has increased during past hour
severe duststorm or sandstorm has decreased during past hour
severe duststorm or sandstorm, no appreciable change during past hour
severe duststorm or sandstorm has increased during past hour
fog in patches
fog, sky discernibile, had become thinner during past hour

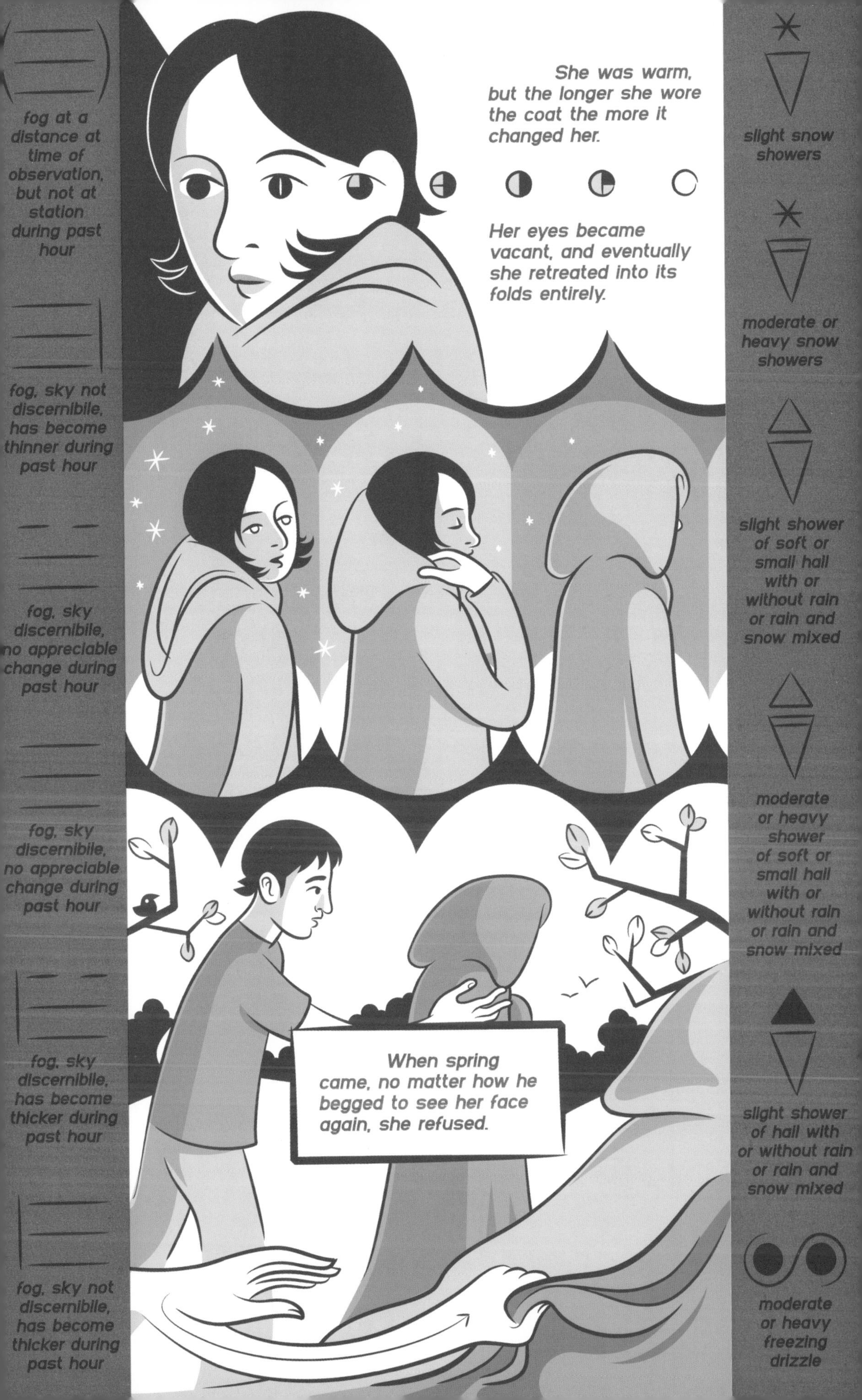
fog at a distance at time of observation, but not at station during past hour
fog, sky not discernibile, has become thinner during past hour
fog, sky discernibile, no appreciable change during past hour
fog, sky discernibile, no appreciable change during past hour
fog, sky discernibile, has become thicker during past hour
fog, sky not discernibile, has become thicker during past hour
She was warm, but the longer she wore the coat the more it changed her.
Her eyes became vacant, and eventually she retreated into its folds entirely.
When spring came, no matter how he begged to see her face again, she refused.
slight snow showers
moderate or heavy snow showers
slight shower of soft or small hail with or without rain or rain and snow mixed
moderate or heavy shower of soft or small hail with or without rain or rain and snow mixed
slight shower of hail with or without rain or rain and snow mixed
moderate or heavy freezing drizzle

thunderstorm, with or without precipitation

slight or moderate thunderstorm with hail at time of observation

heavy thunderstorm with hail at time of observation

slight rain at time of observation; thunderstorm during past hour but not at time of observation

moderate or heavy rain at time of observation; thunderstorm during past hour but not at time of observation

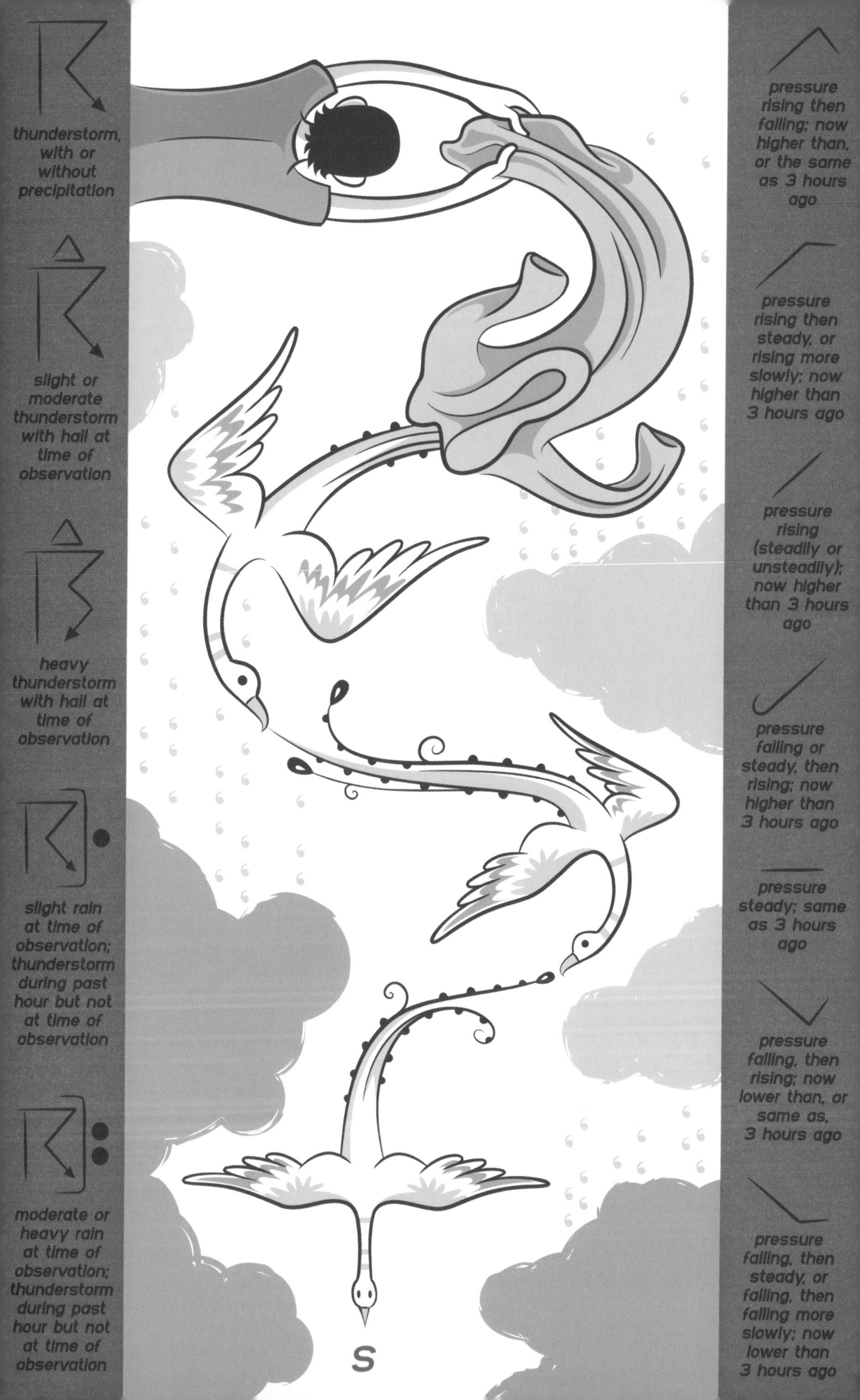

S

pressure rising then falling; now higher than, or the same as 3 hours ago

pressure rising then steady, or rising more slowly; now higher than 3 hours ago

pressure rising (steadily or unsteadily); now higher than 3 hours ago

pressure falling or steady, then rising; now higher than 3 hours ago

pressure steady; same as 3 hours ago

pressure falling, then rising; now lower than, or same as, 3 hours ago

pressure falling, then steady, or falling, then falling more slowly; now lower than 3 hours ago

the end.

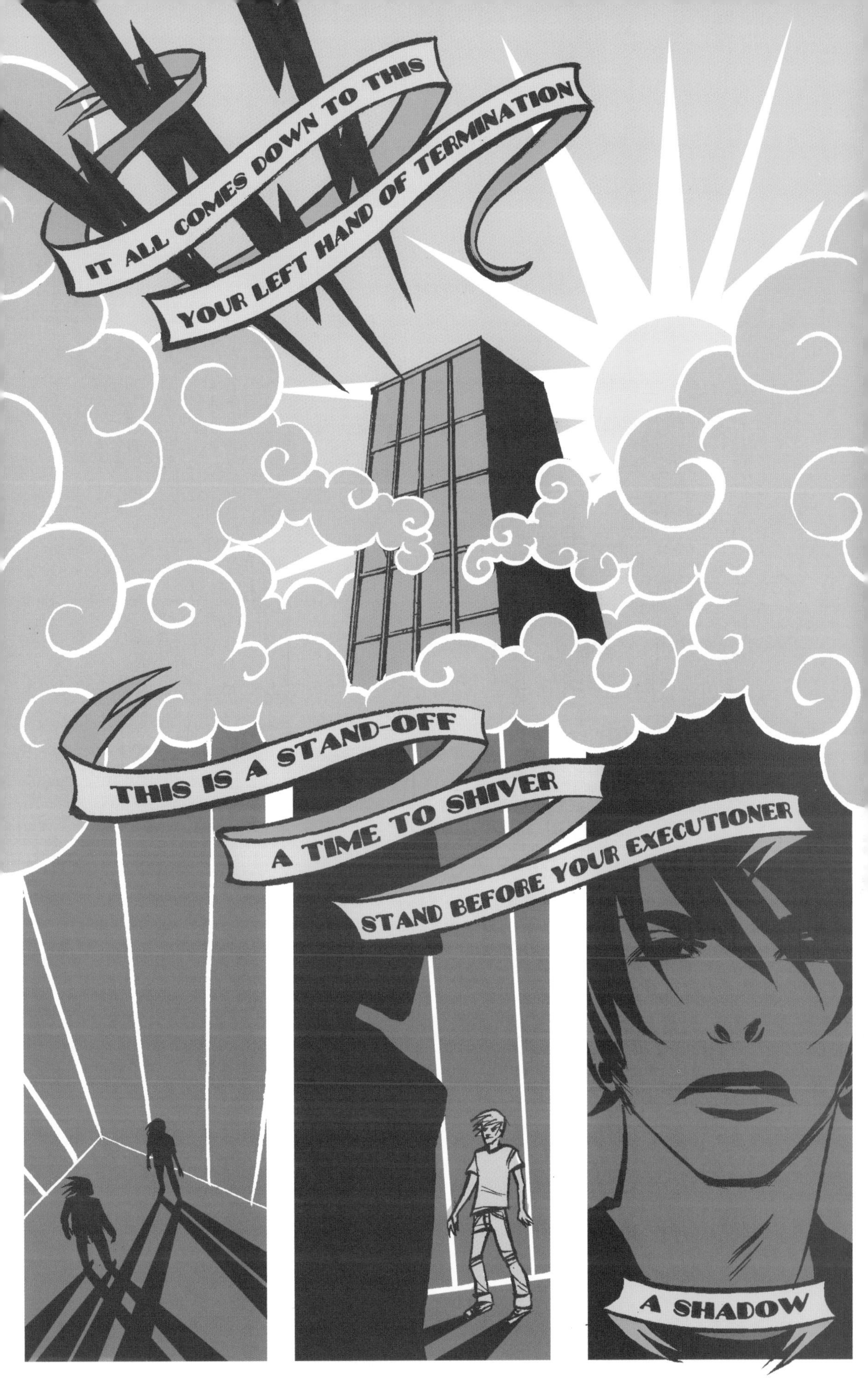
IT ALL COMES DOWN TO THIS
YOUR LEFT HAND OF TERMINATION
THIS IS A STAND-OFF
A TIME TO SHIVER
STAND BEFORE YOUR EXECUTIONER
A SHADOW

TIPS AND TOES, AIRBORNE TOUCHING GROUND
TAKE A DEEP BREATH
AND FLOOD WITH YOU

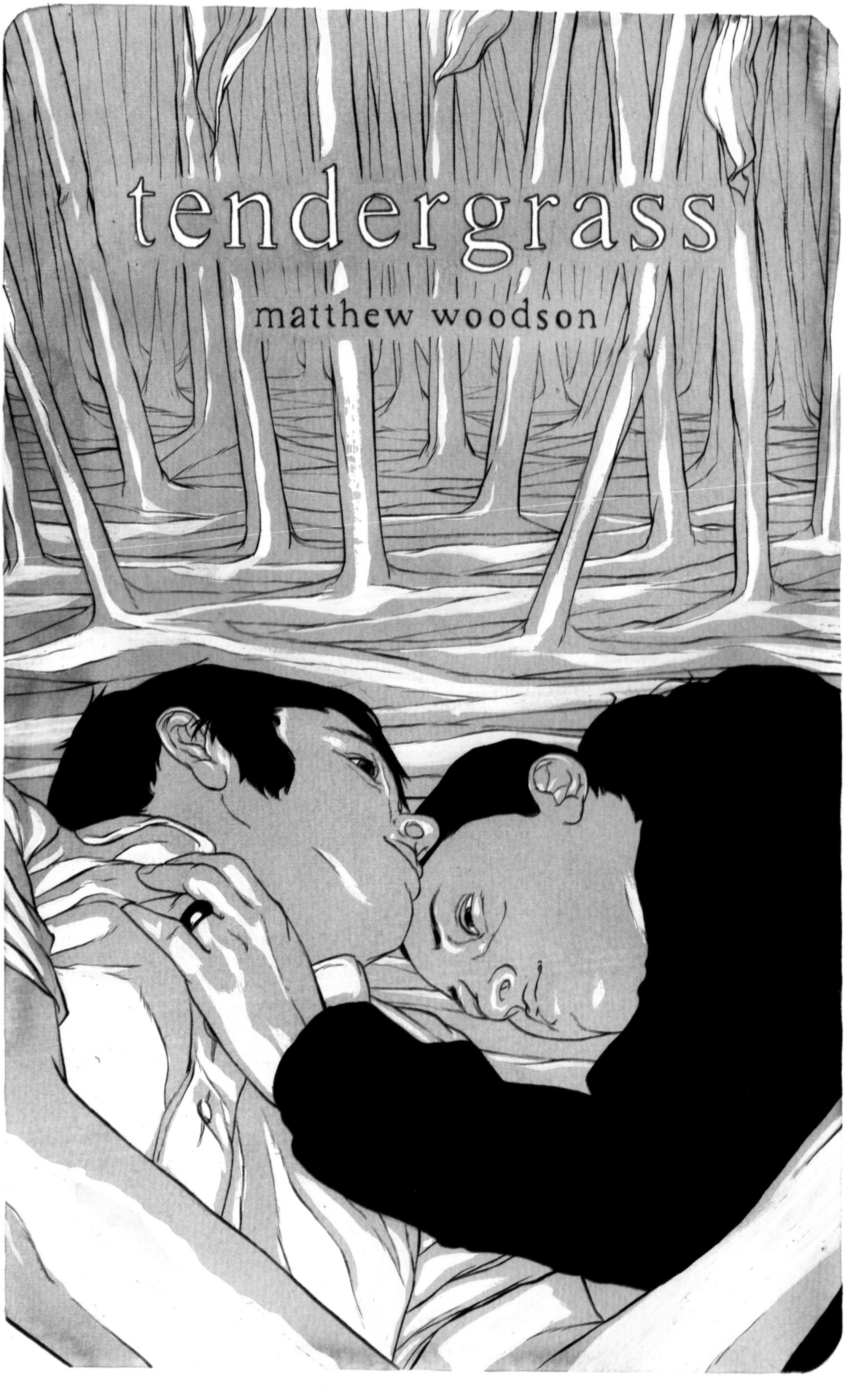
tendergrass
matthew woodson

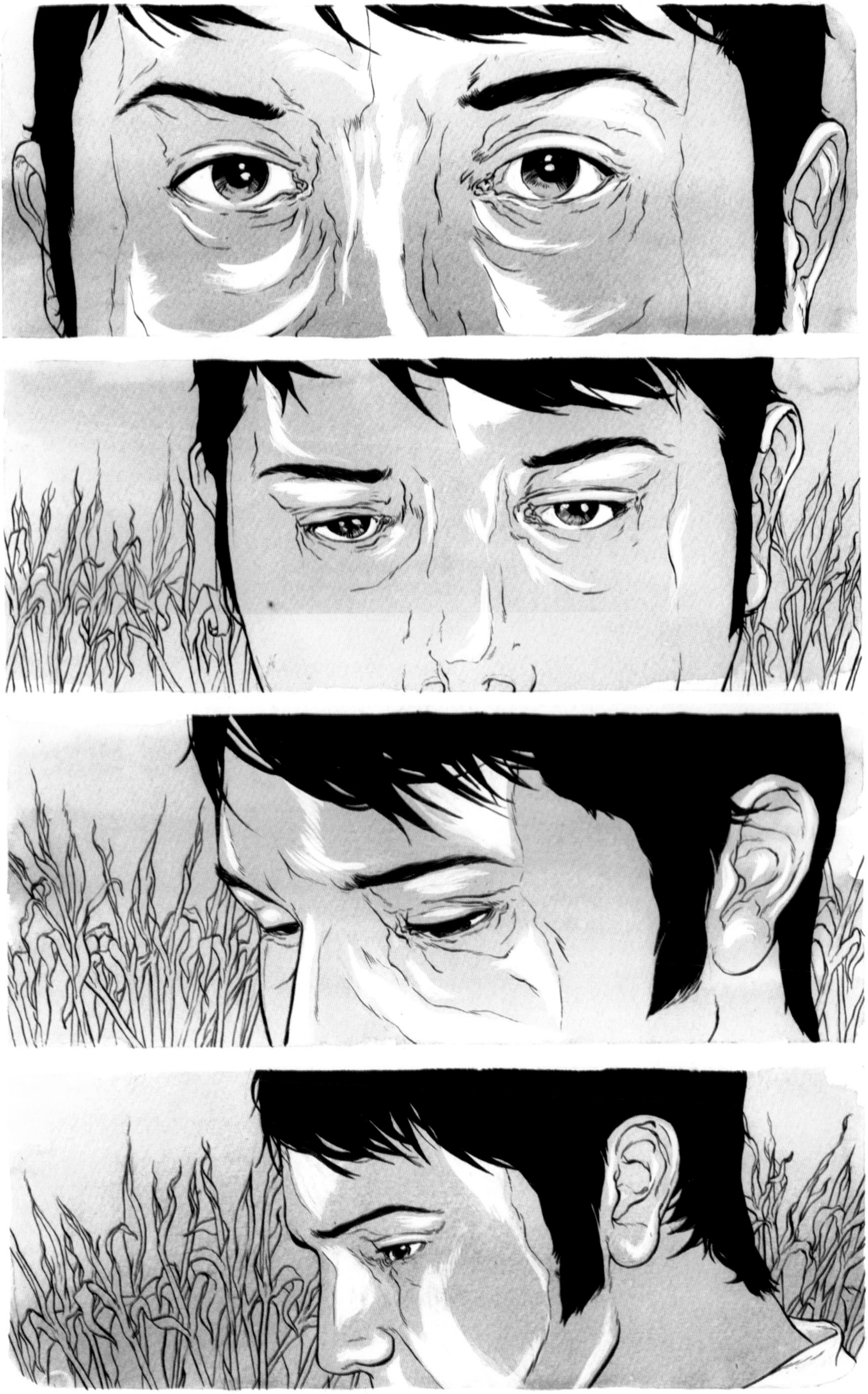

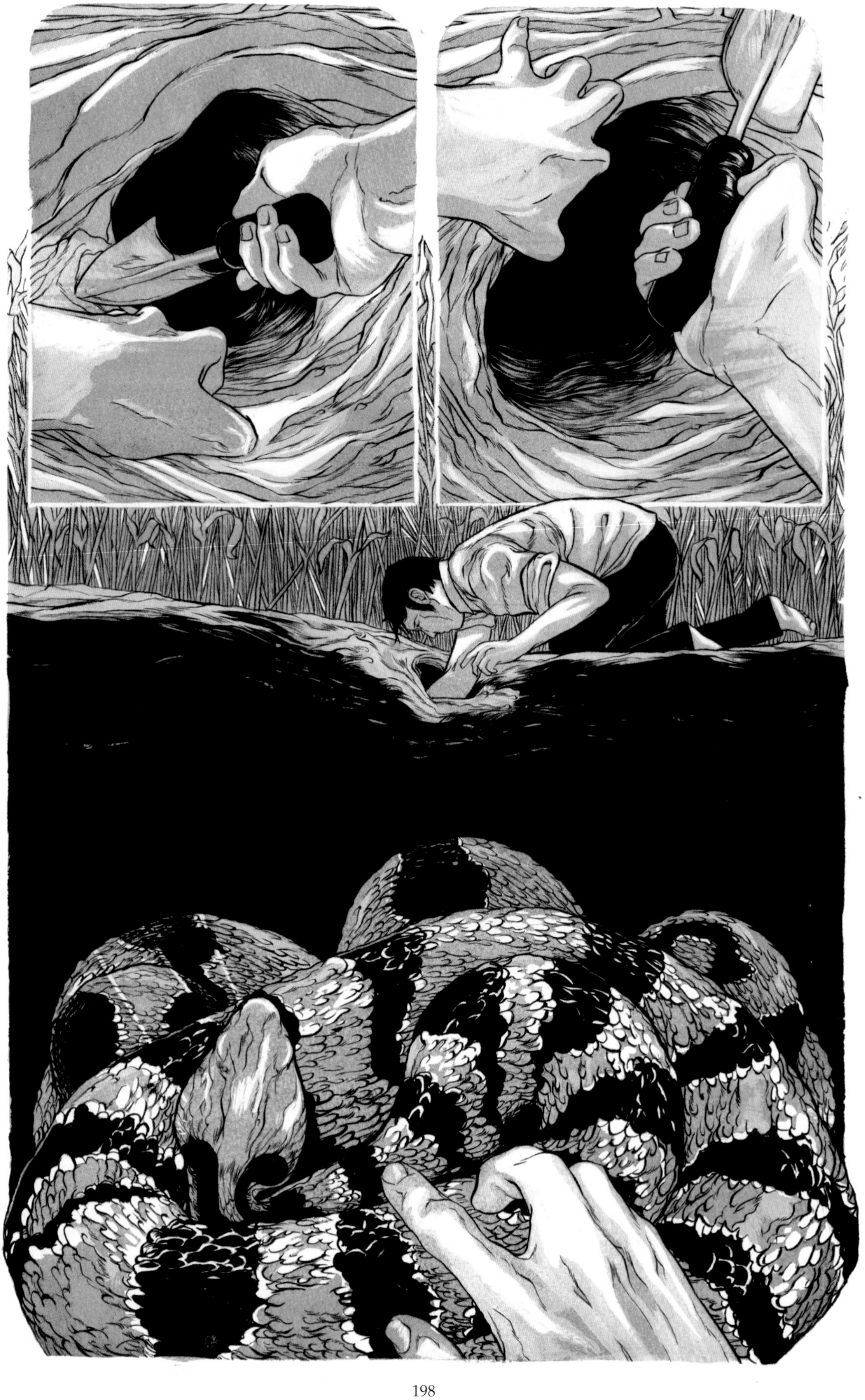

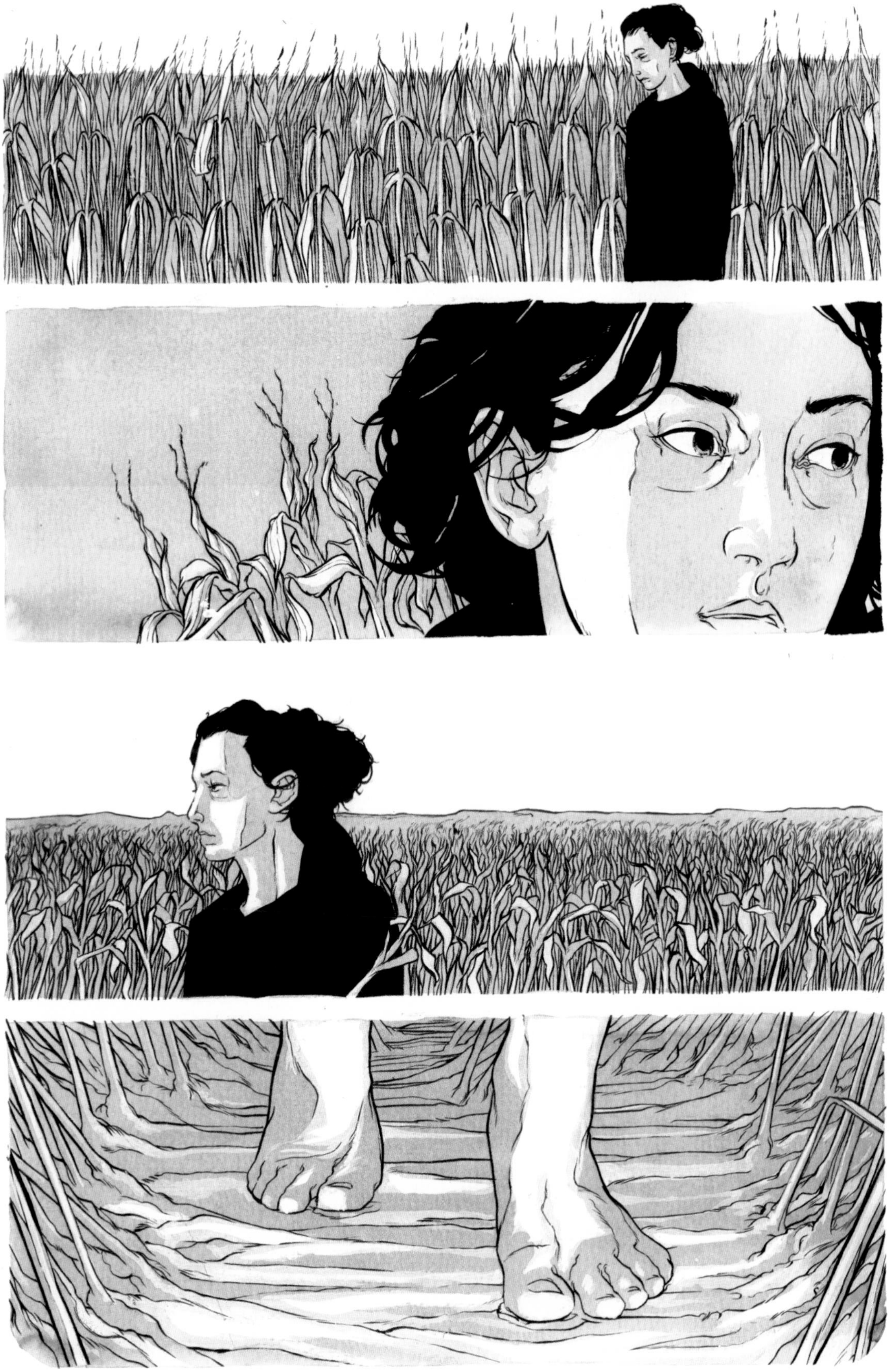

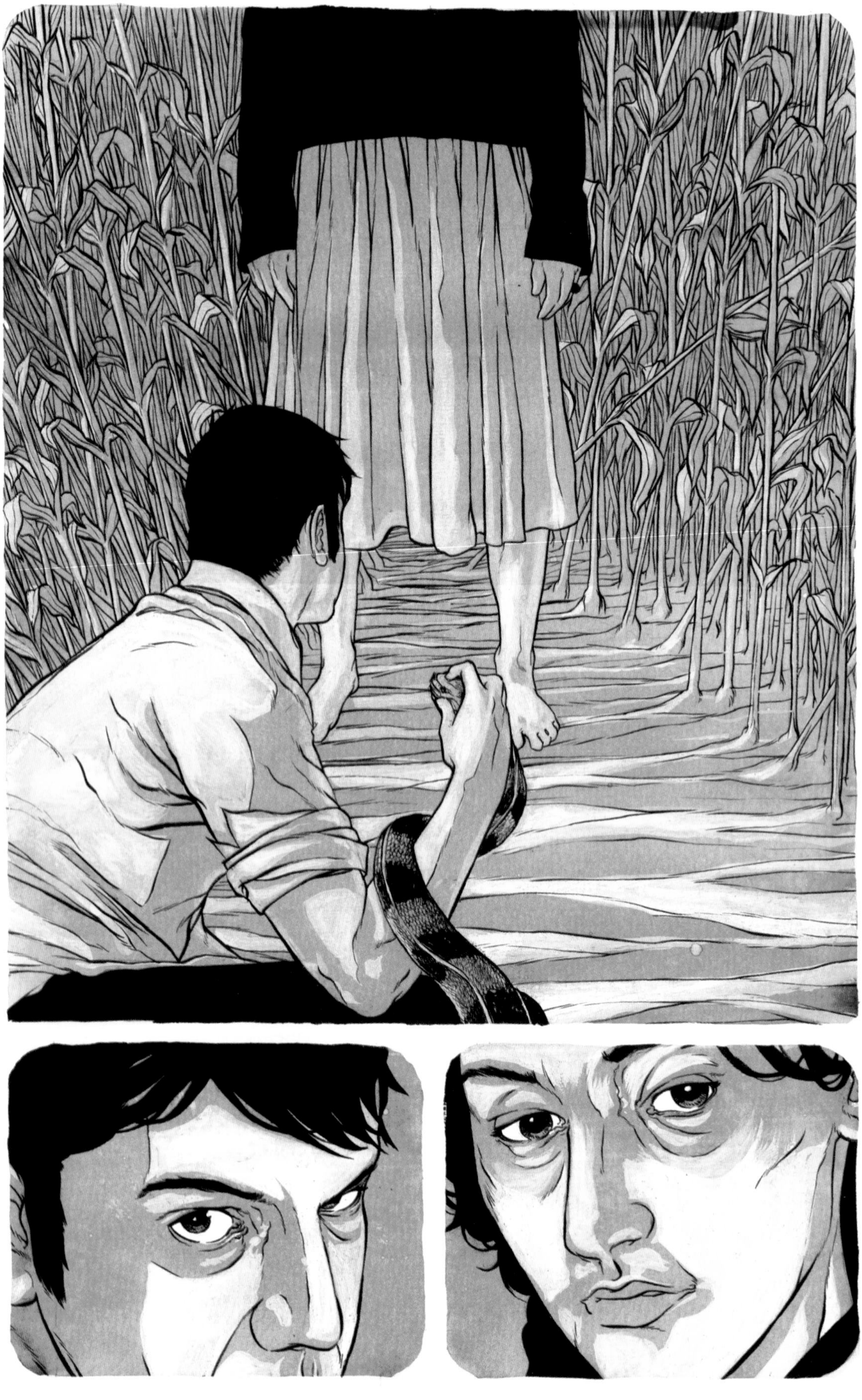

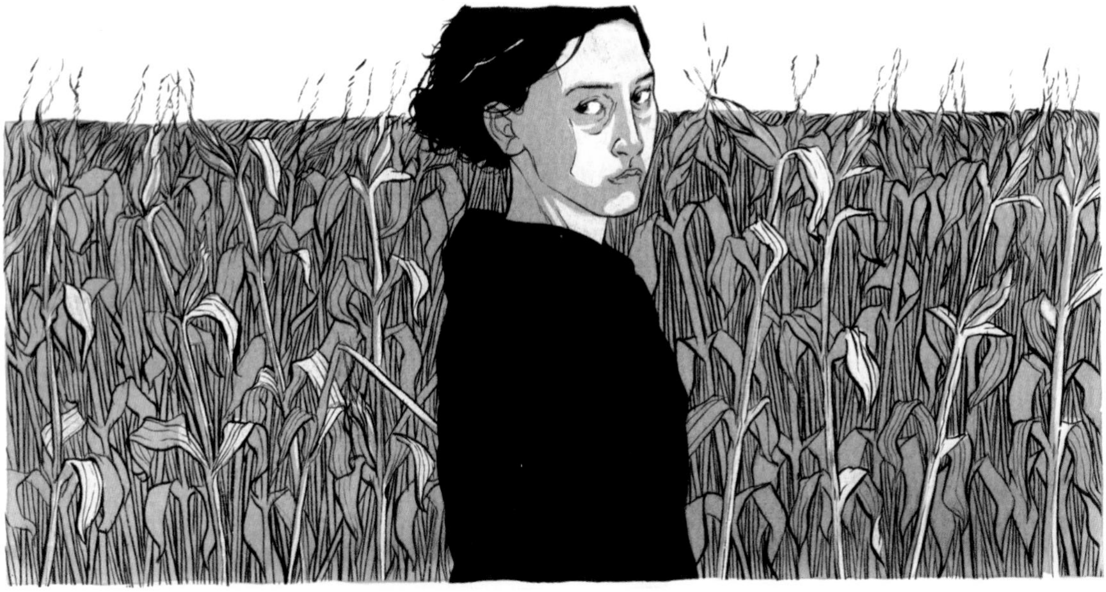

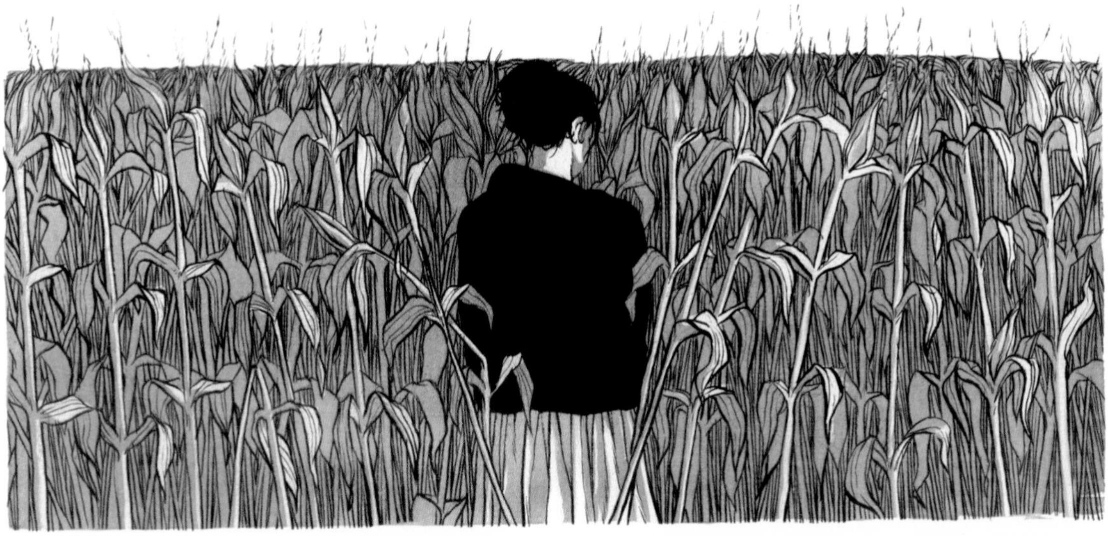

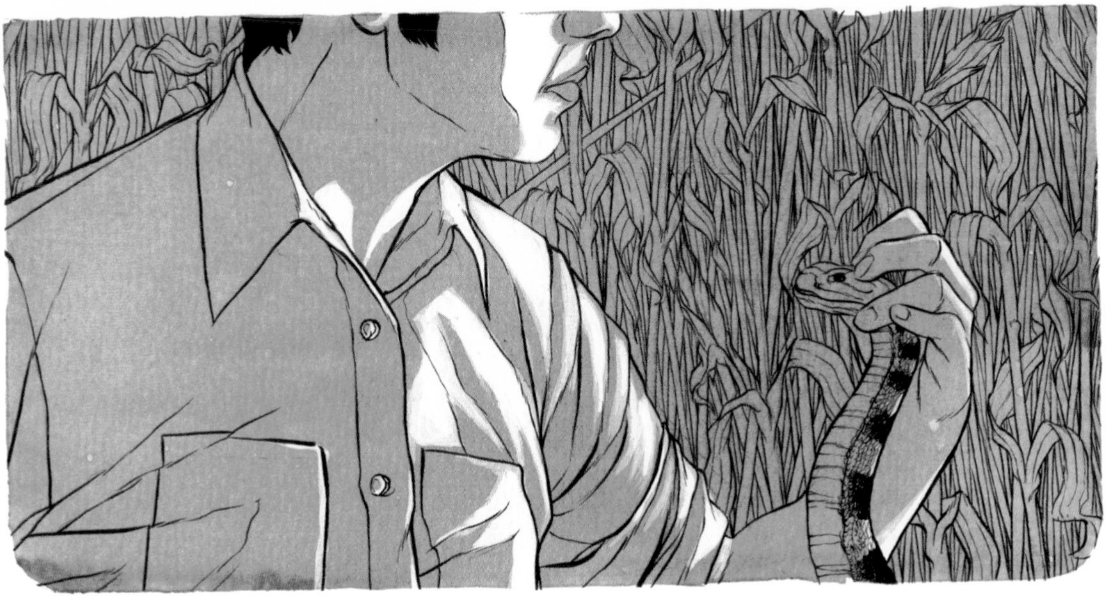

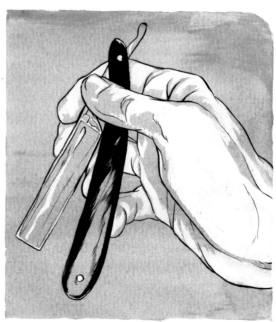
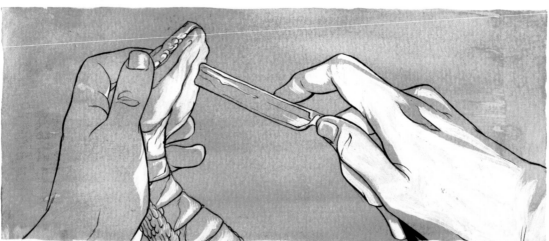

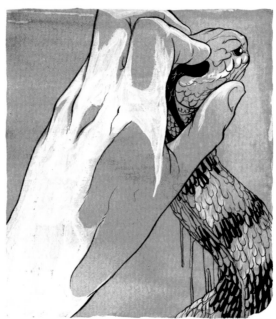

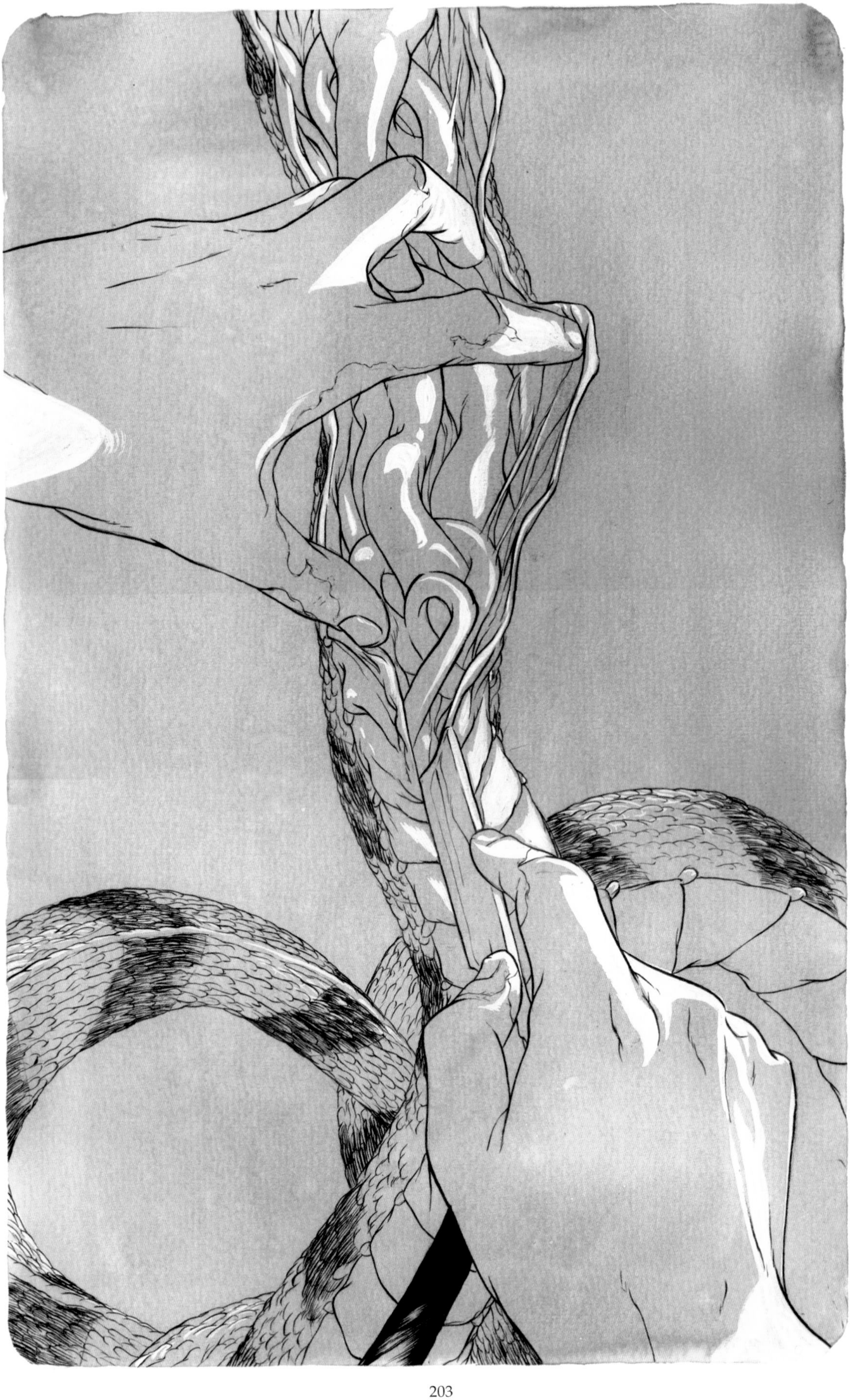

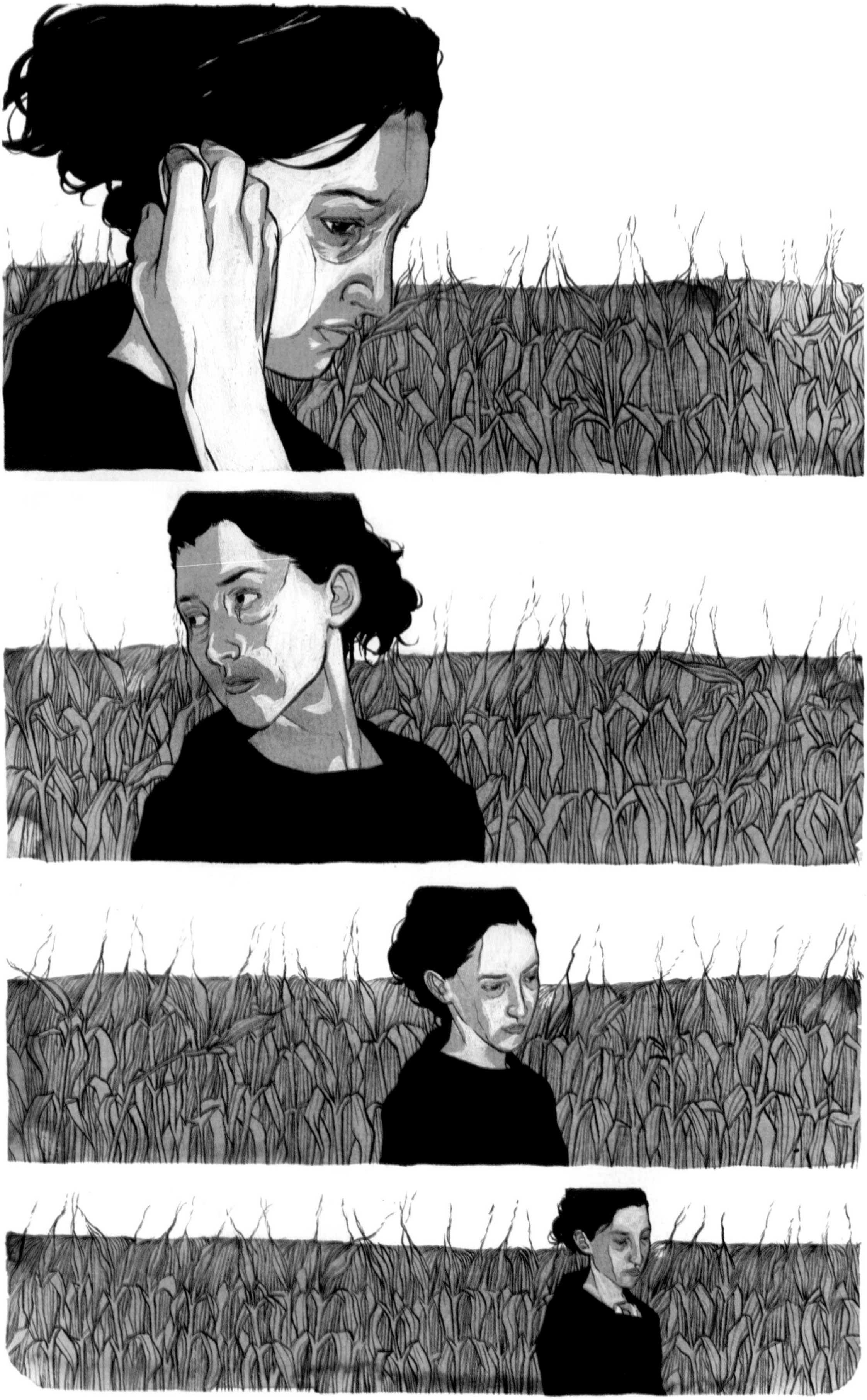

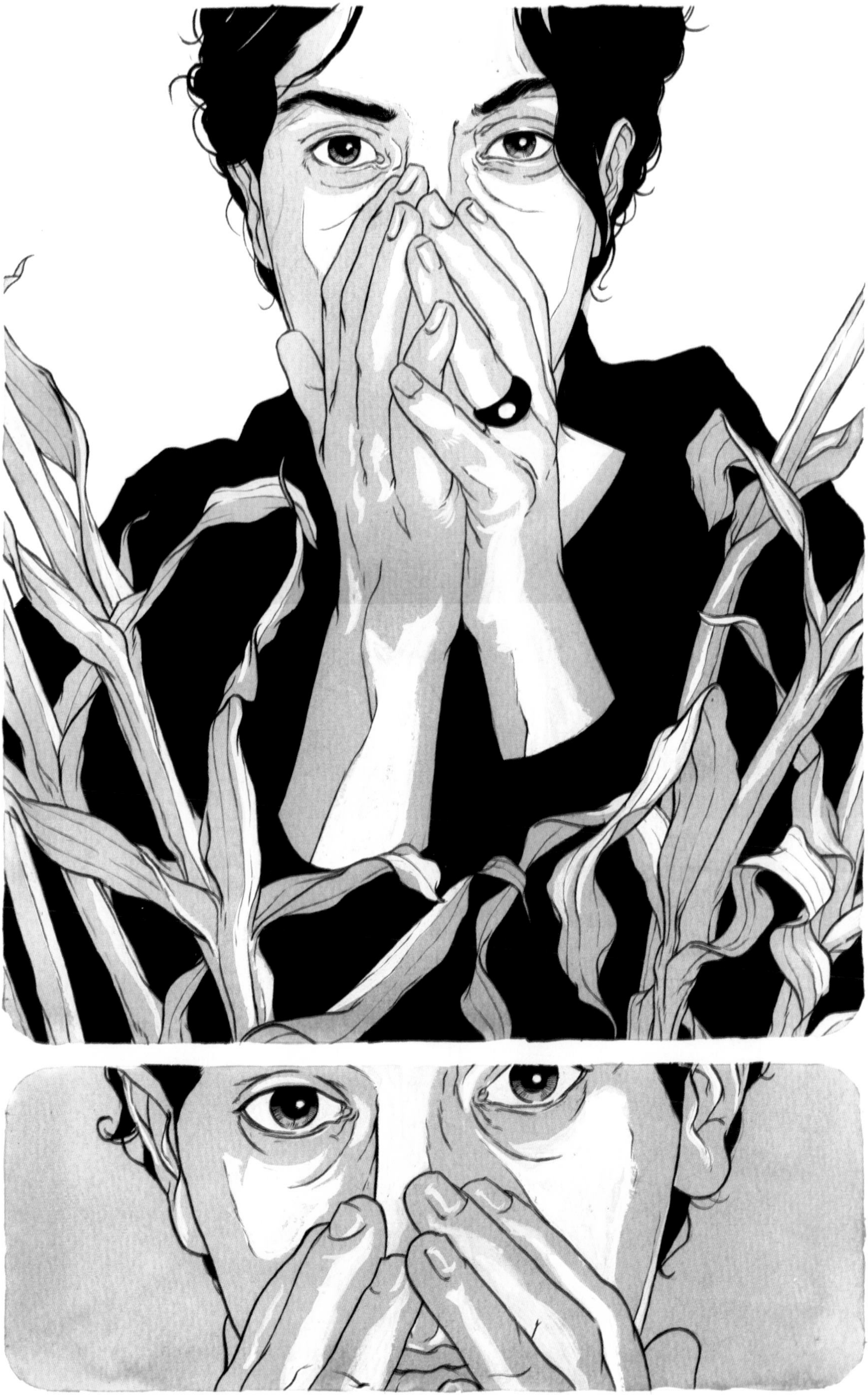

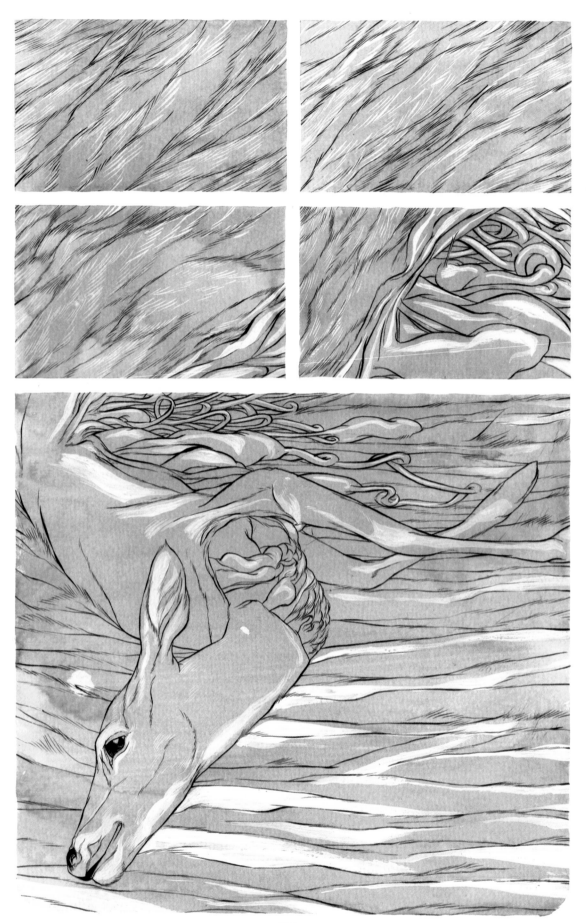

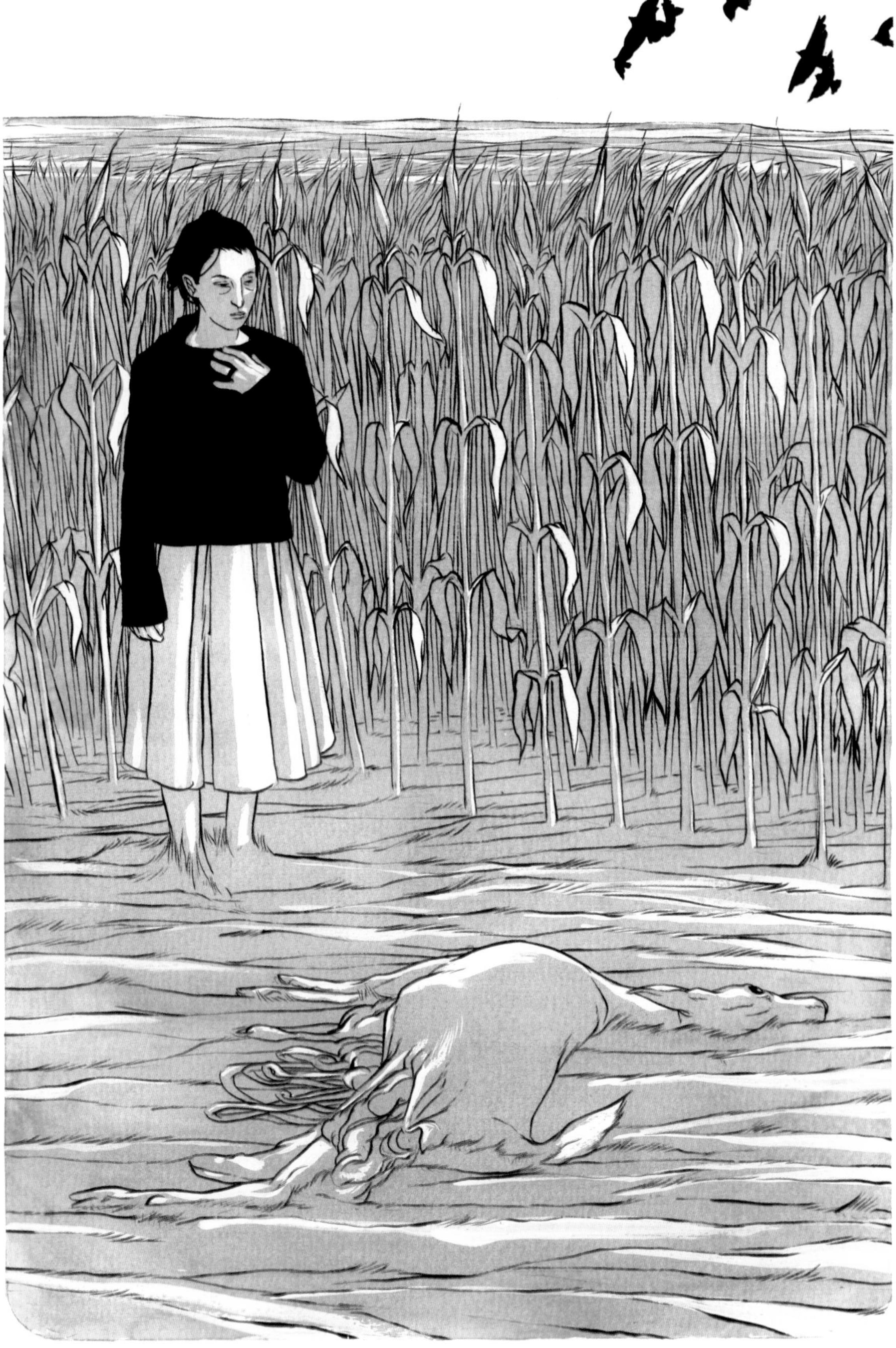

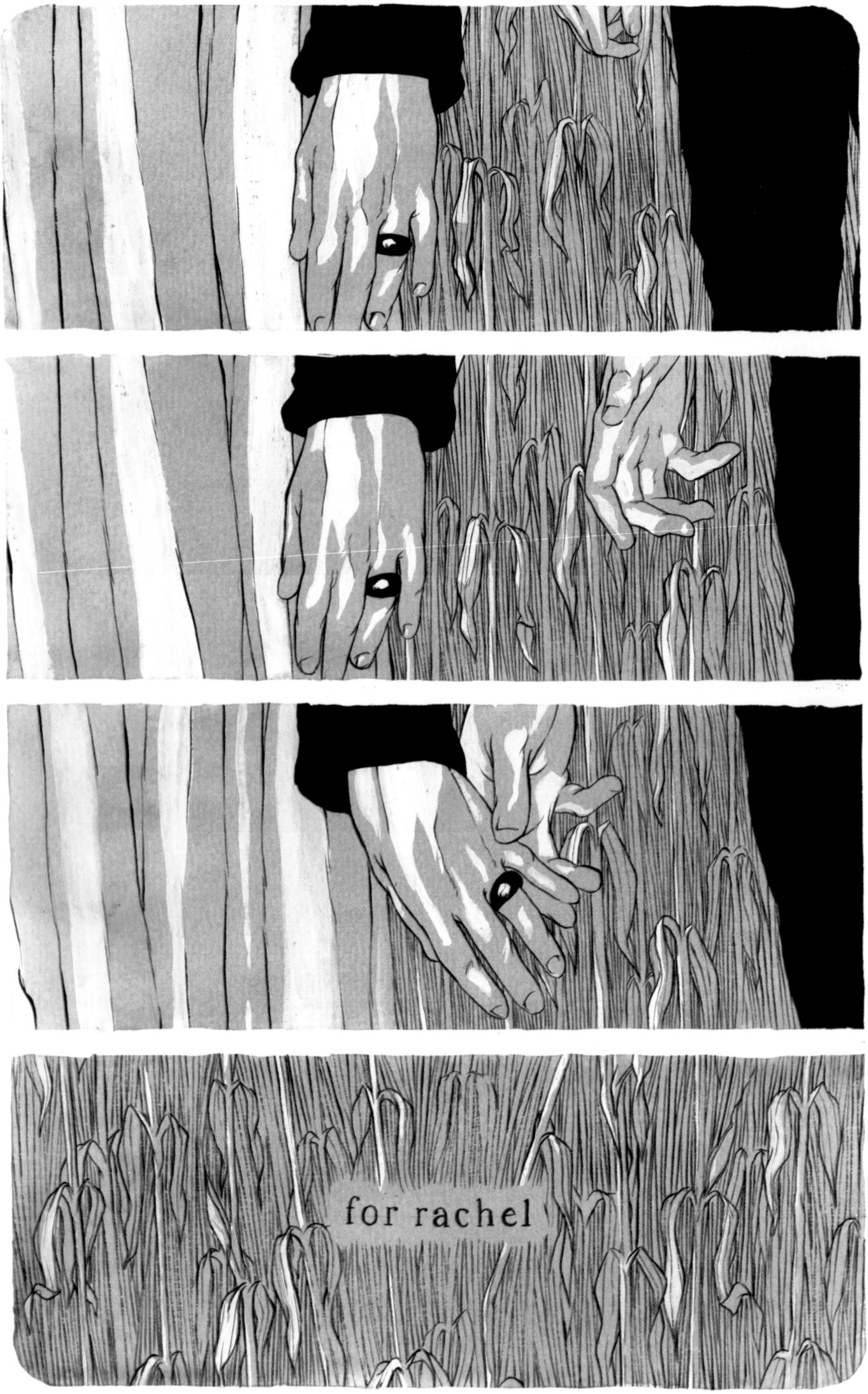
for rachel

last**things**last

by kean soo

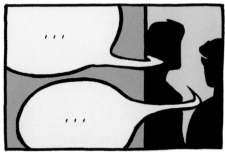

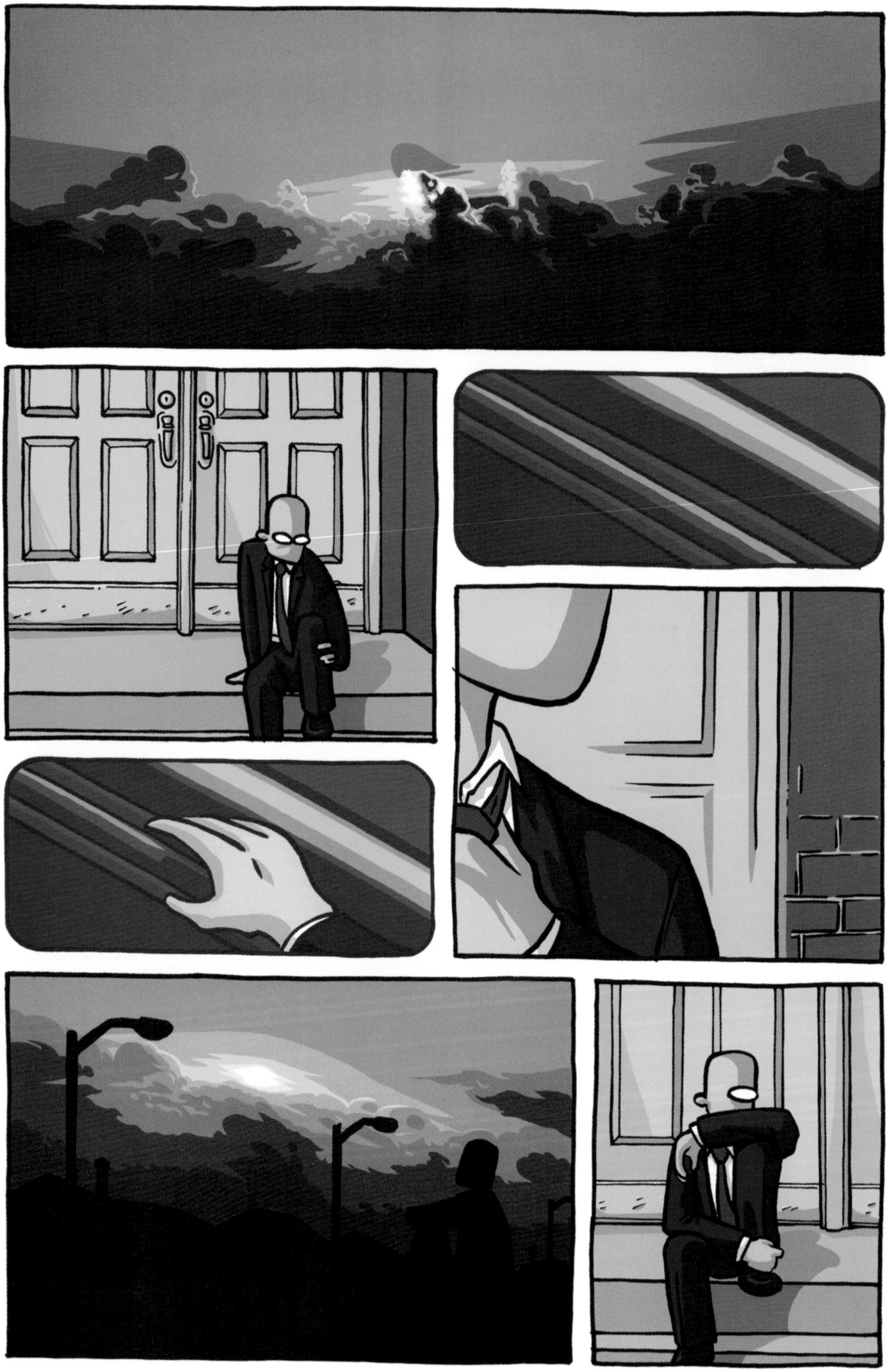

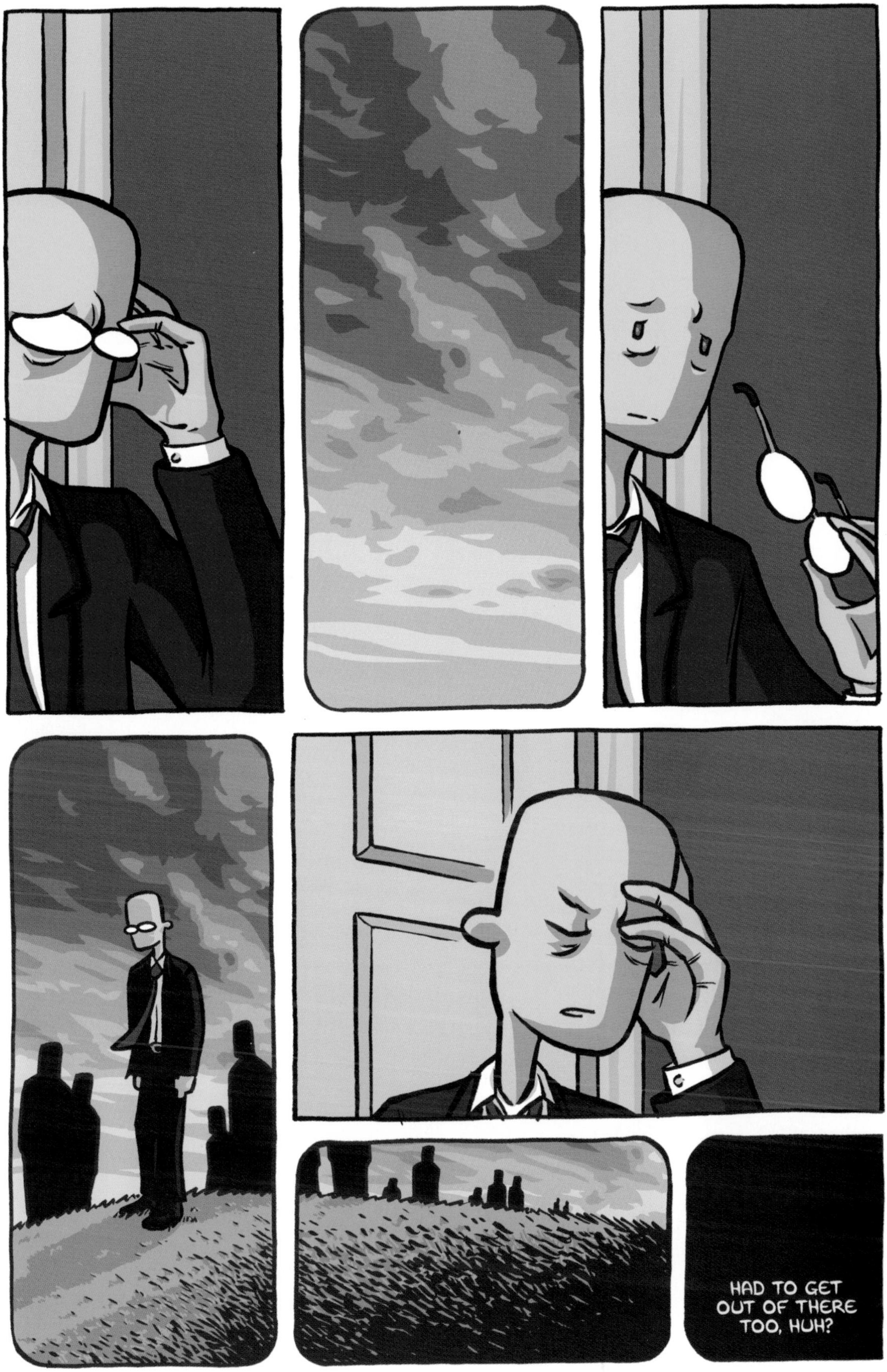
HAD TO GET
OUT OF THERE
TOO, HUH?

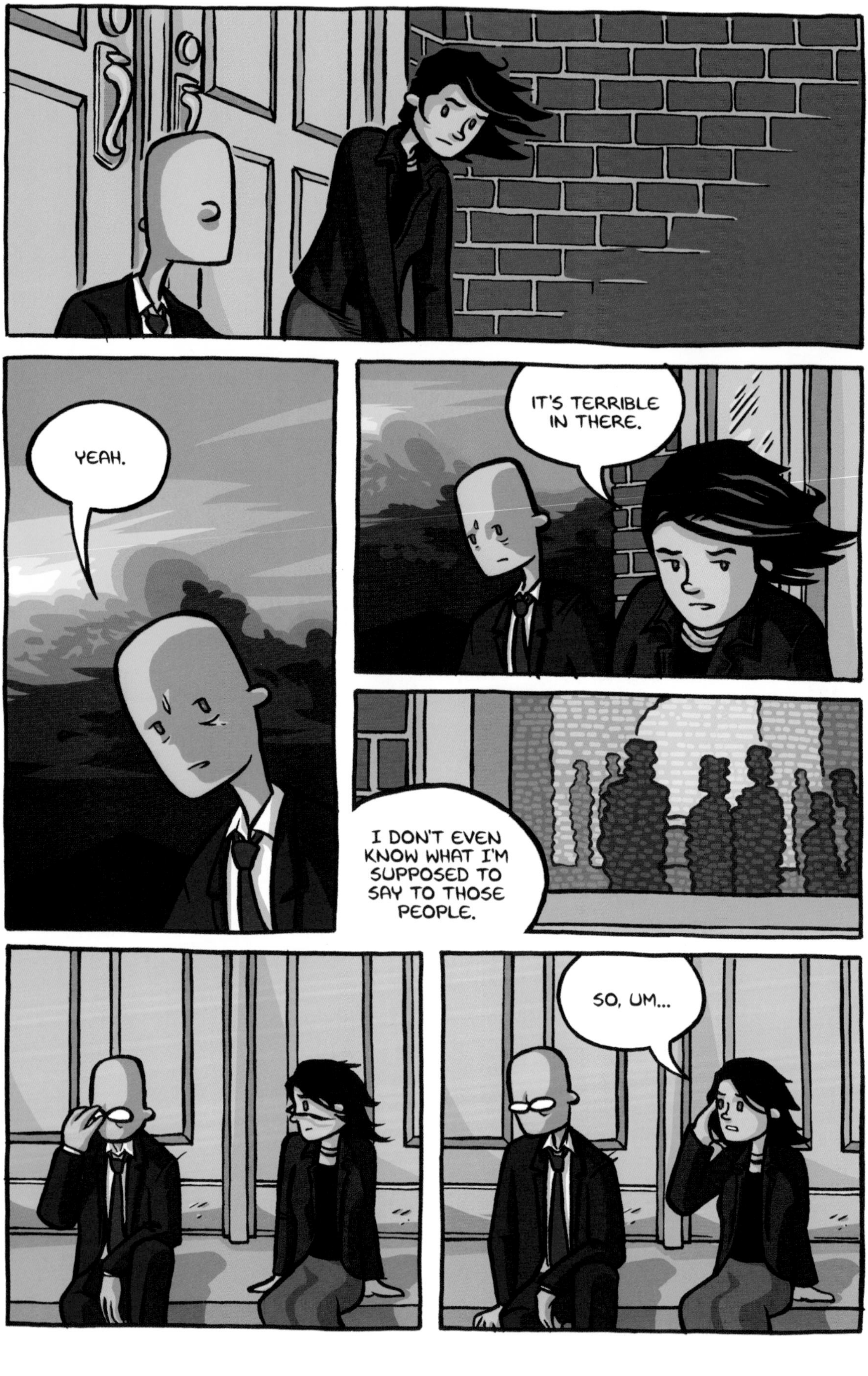
YEAH.
IT'S TERRIBLE IN THERE.
I DON'T EVEN KNOW WHAT I'M SUPPOSED TO SAY TO THOSE PEOPLE.
SO, UM...

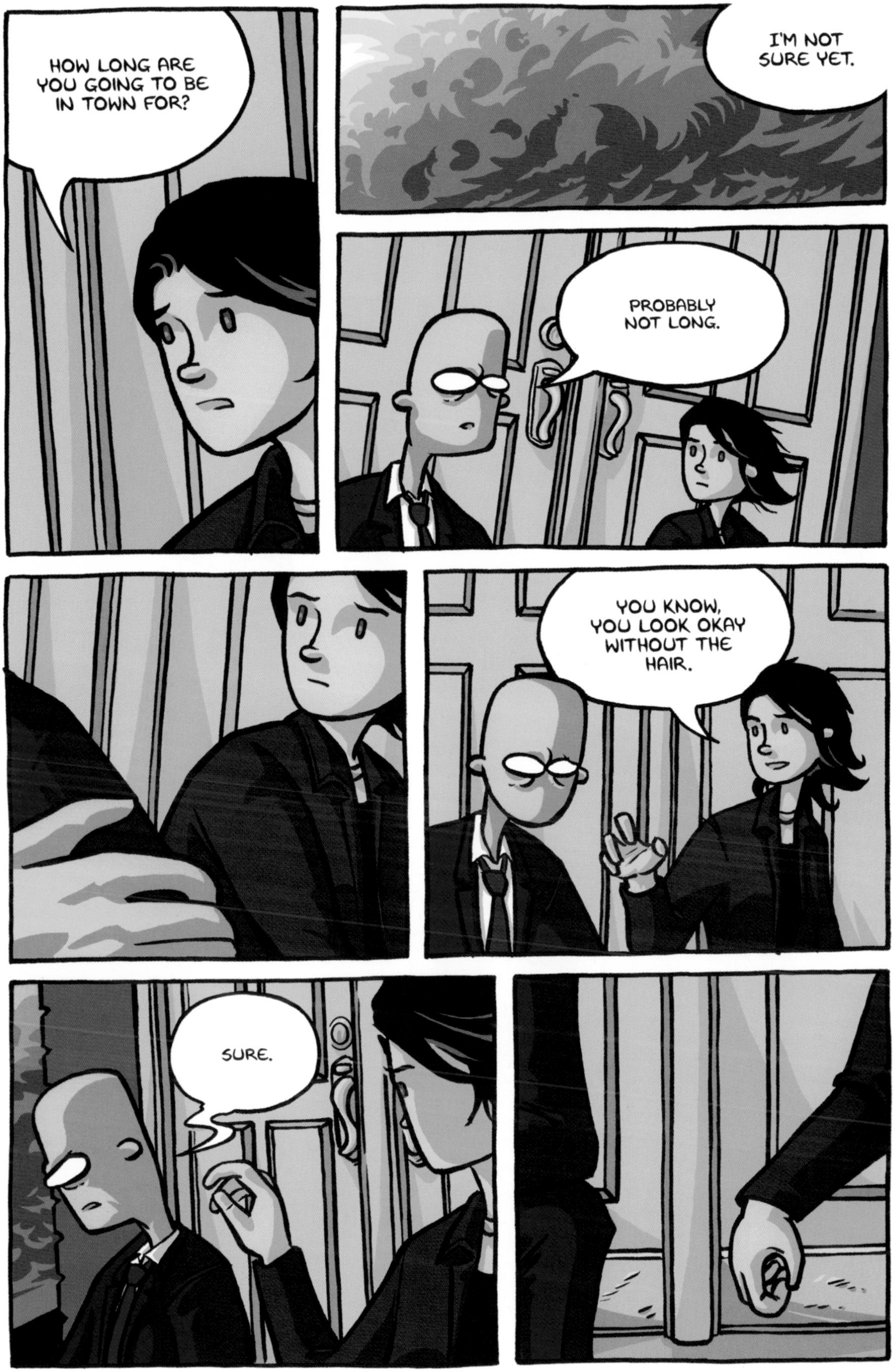

HOW LONG ARE YOU GOING TO BE IN TOWN FOR?
I'M NOT SURE YET.
PROBABLY NOT LONG.
YOU KNOW, YOU LOOK OKAY WITHOUT THE HAIR.
SURE.

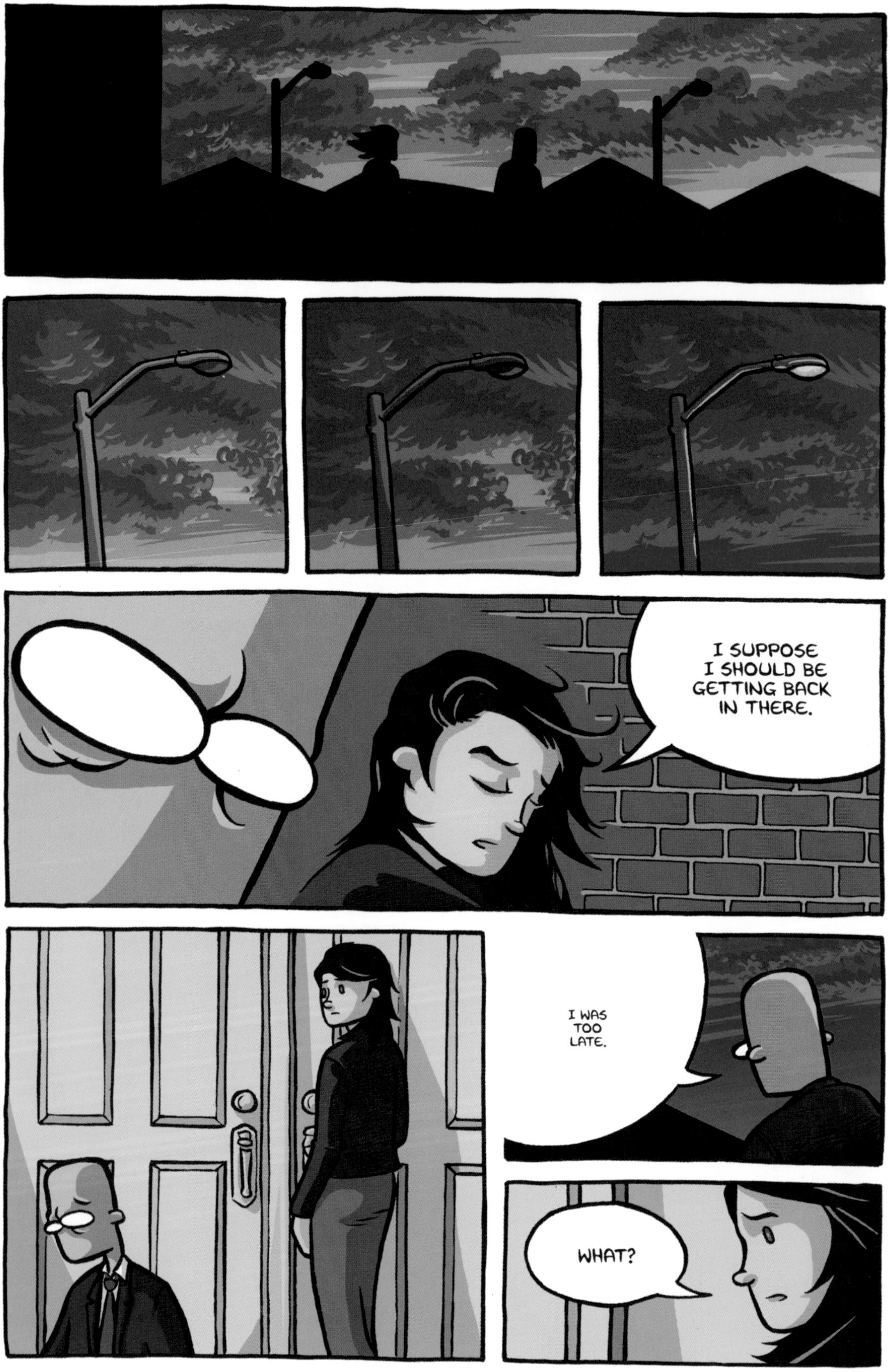
I SUPPOSE I SHOULD BE GETTING BACK IN THERE.
I WAS TOO LATE.
WHAT?

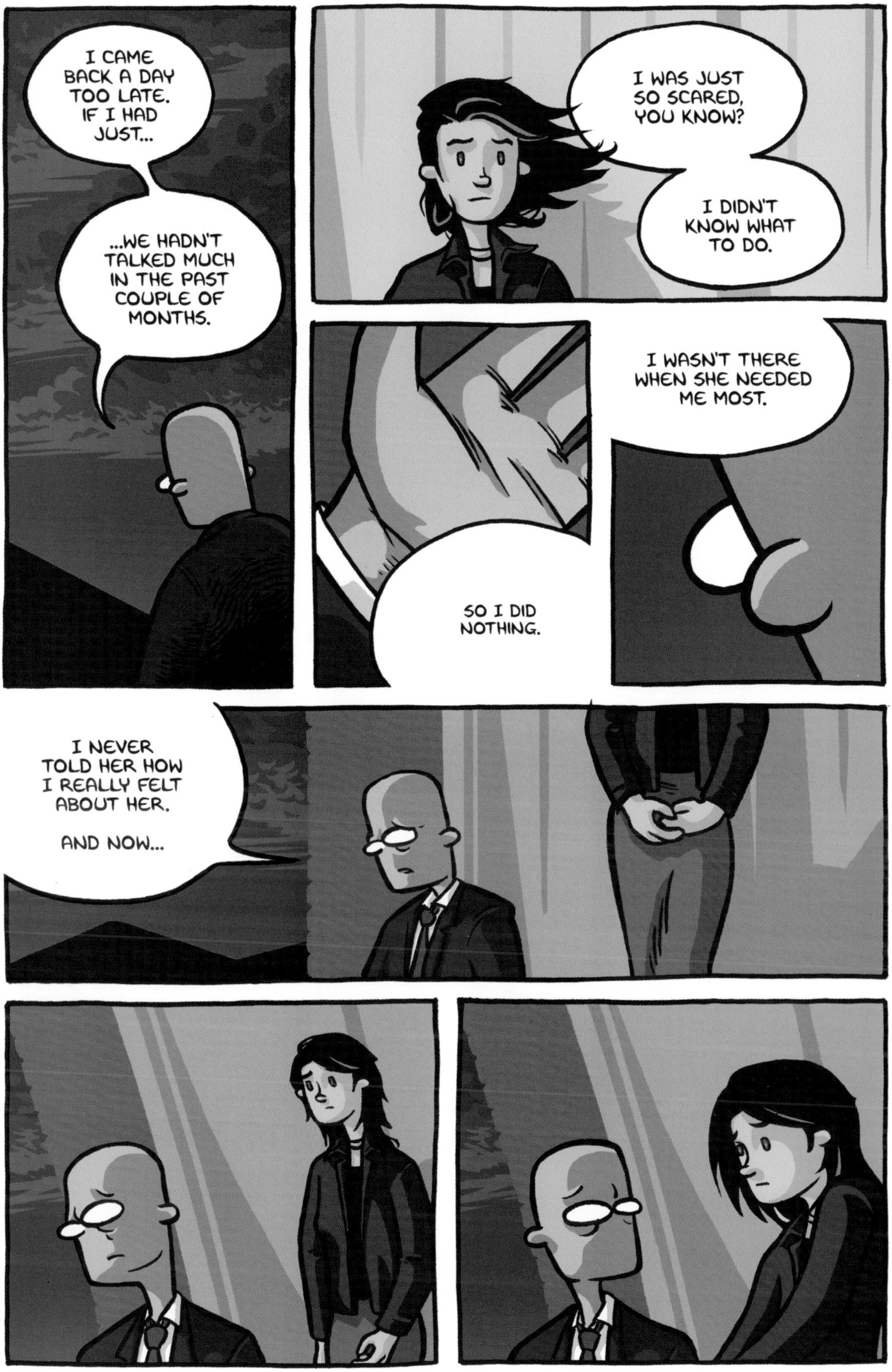
I CAME BACK A DAY TOO LATE. IF I HAD JUST...
...WE HADN'T TALKED MUCH IN THE PAST COUPLE OF MONTHS.
I WAS JUST SO SCARED, YOU KNOW?
I DIDN'T KNOW WHAT TO DO.
I WASN'T THERE WHEN SHE NEEDED ME MOST.
SO I DID NOTHING.
I NEVER TOLD HER HOW I REALLY FELT ABOUT HER.
AND NOW...

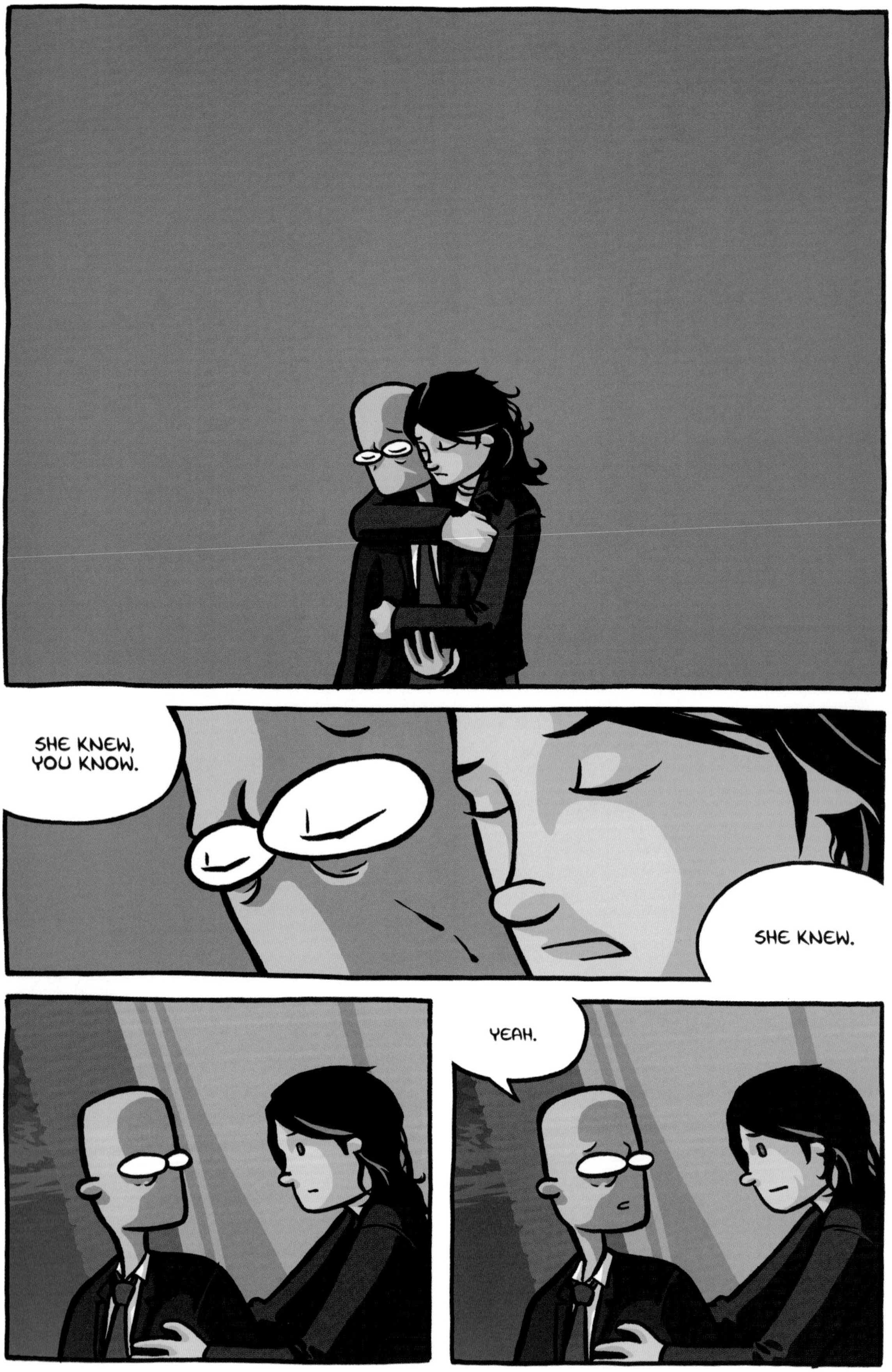
SHE KNEW,
YOU KNOW.
SHE KNEW.
YEAH.

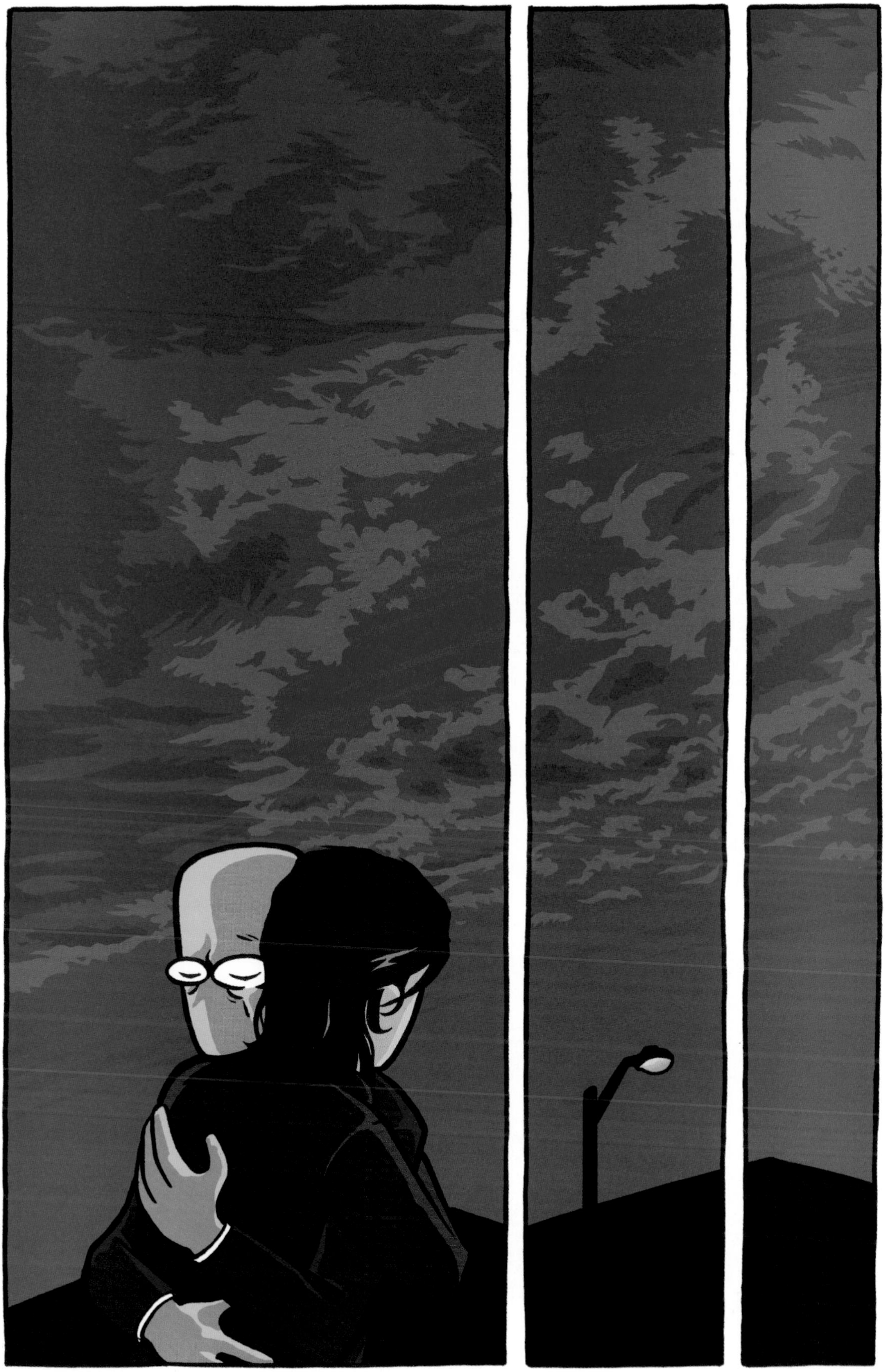

CELLMATES

by Phil Craven

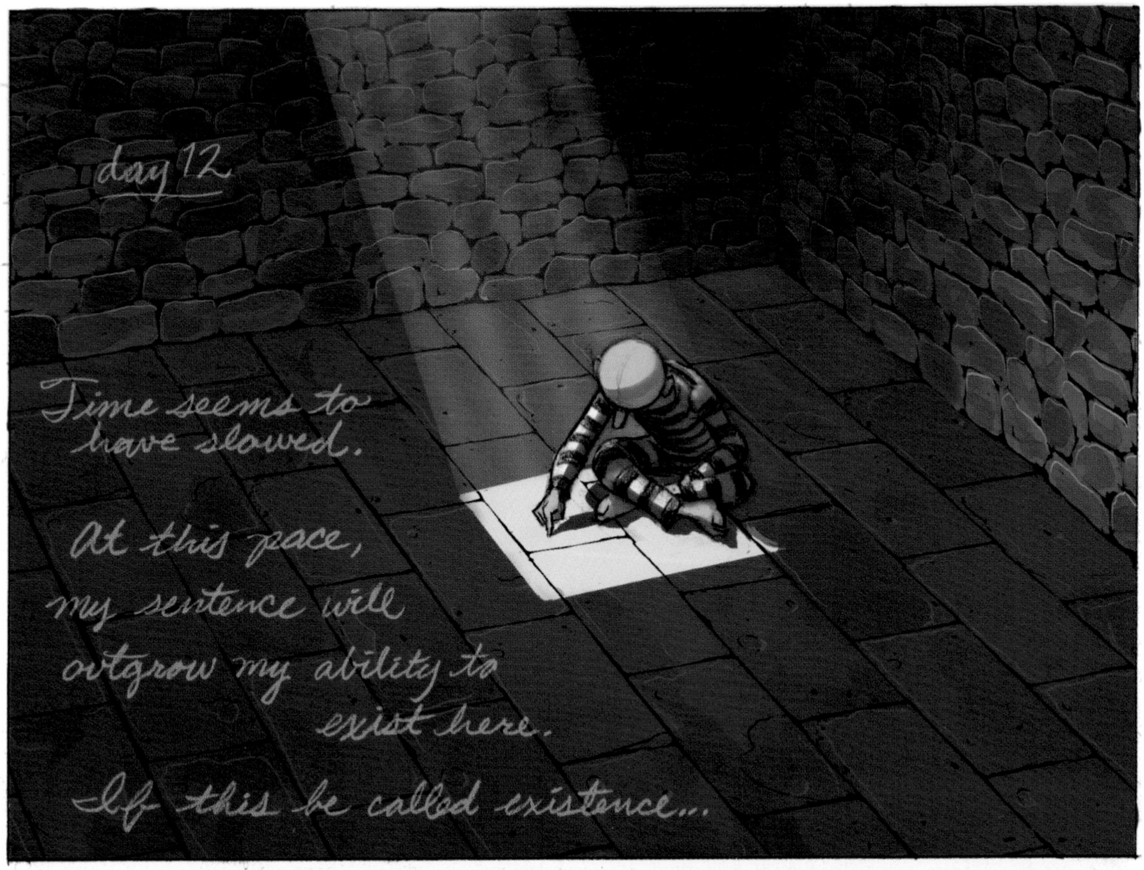
day 12
Time seems to have slowed.
At this pace, my sentence will outgrow my ability to exist here.
If this be called existence...

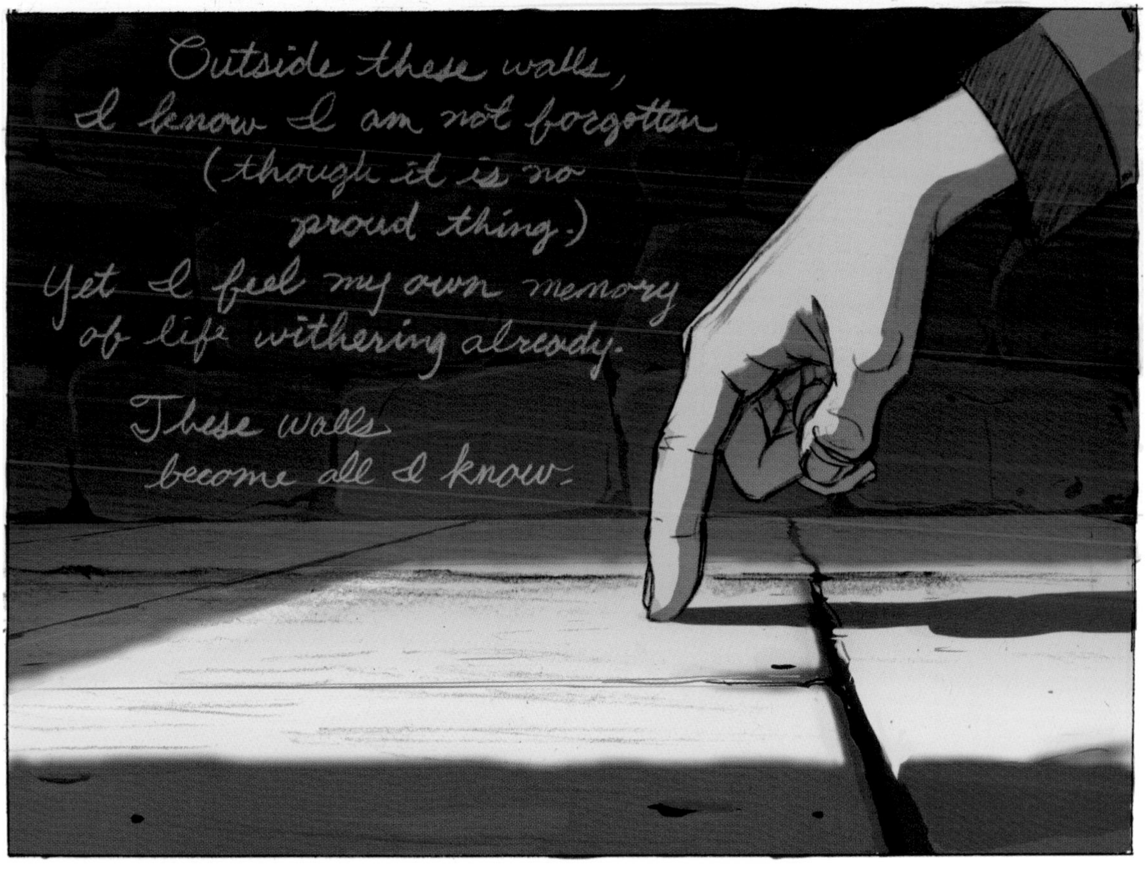
Outside these walls, I know I am not forgotten (though it is no proud thing.)
Yet I feel my own memory of life withering already.
These walls become all I know.

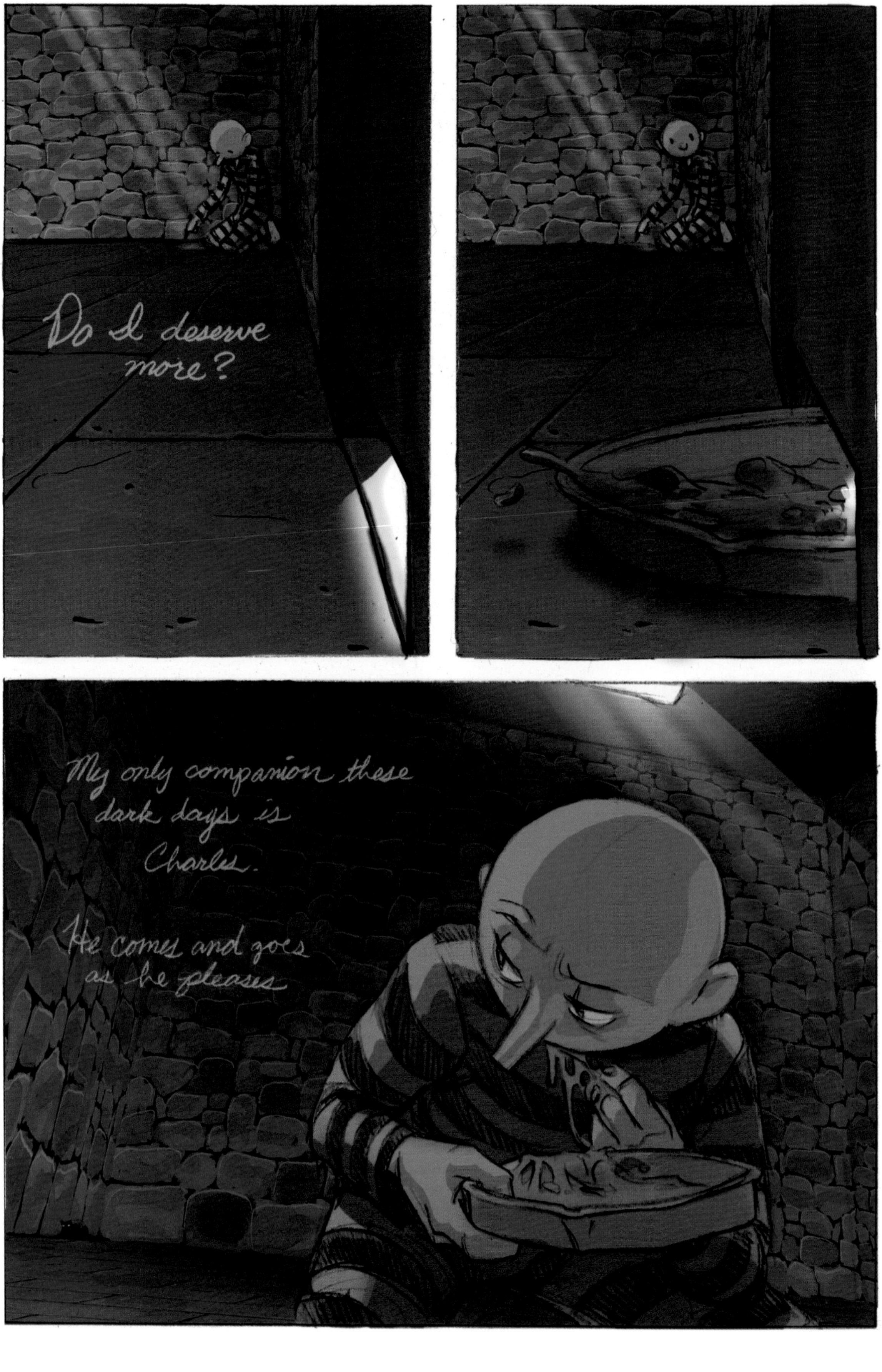
Do I deserve more?
My only companion these dark days is Charles.
He comes and goes as he pleases

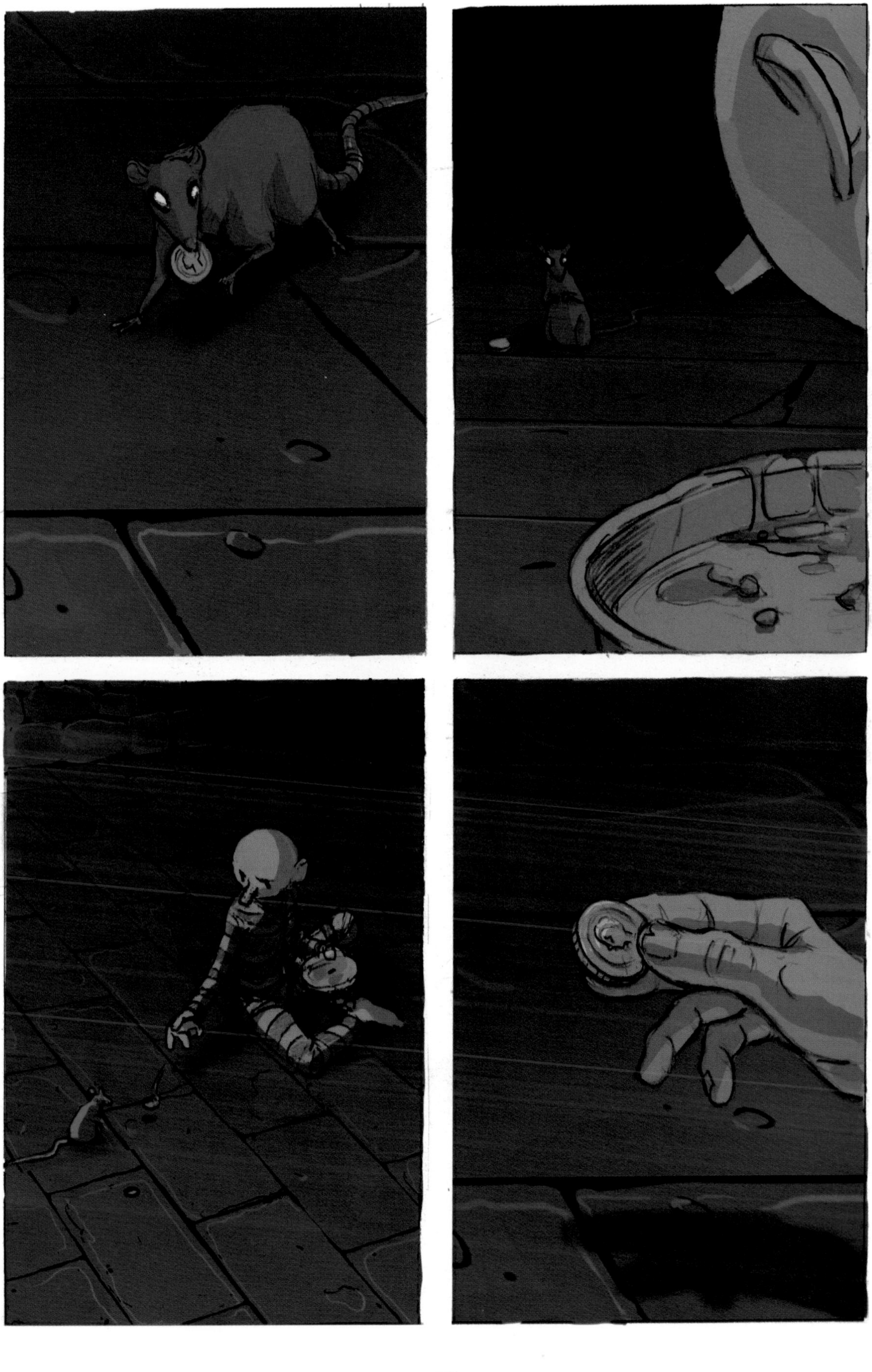

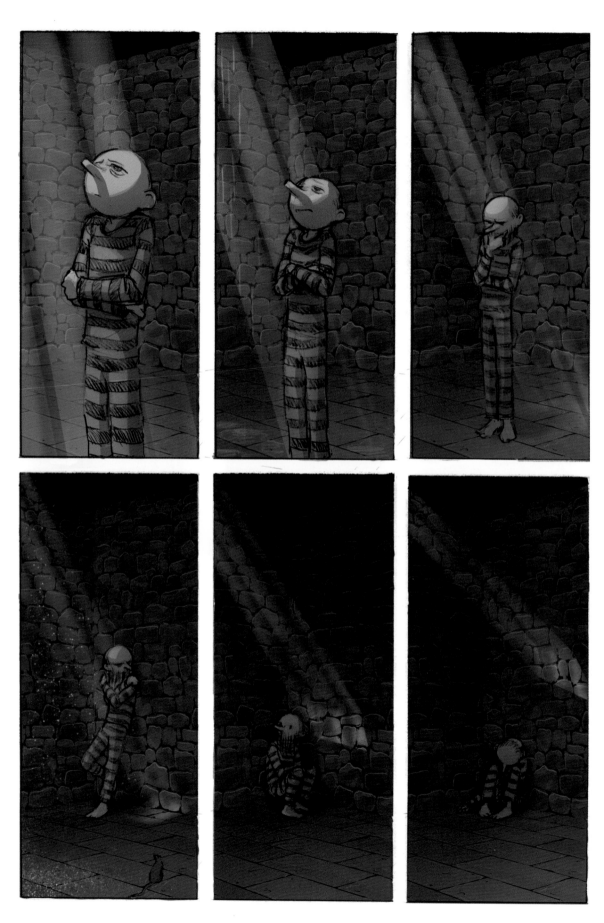

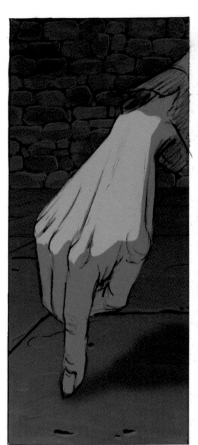

a leaf!
a twig...
bits of the
world

a world I remain in,
but not with

except for Charles

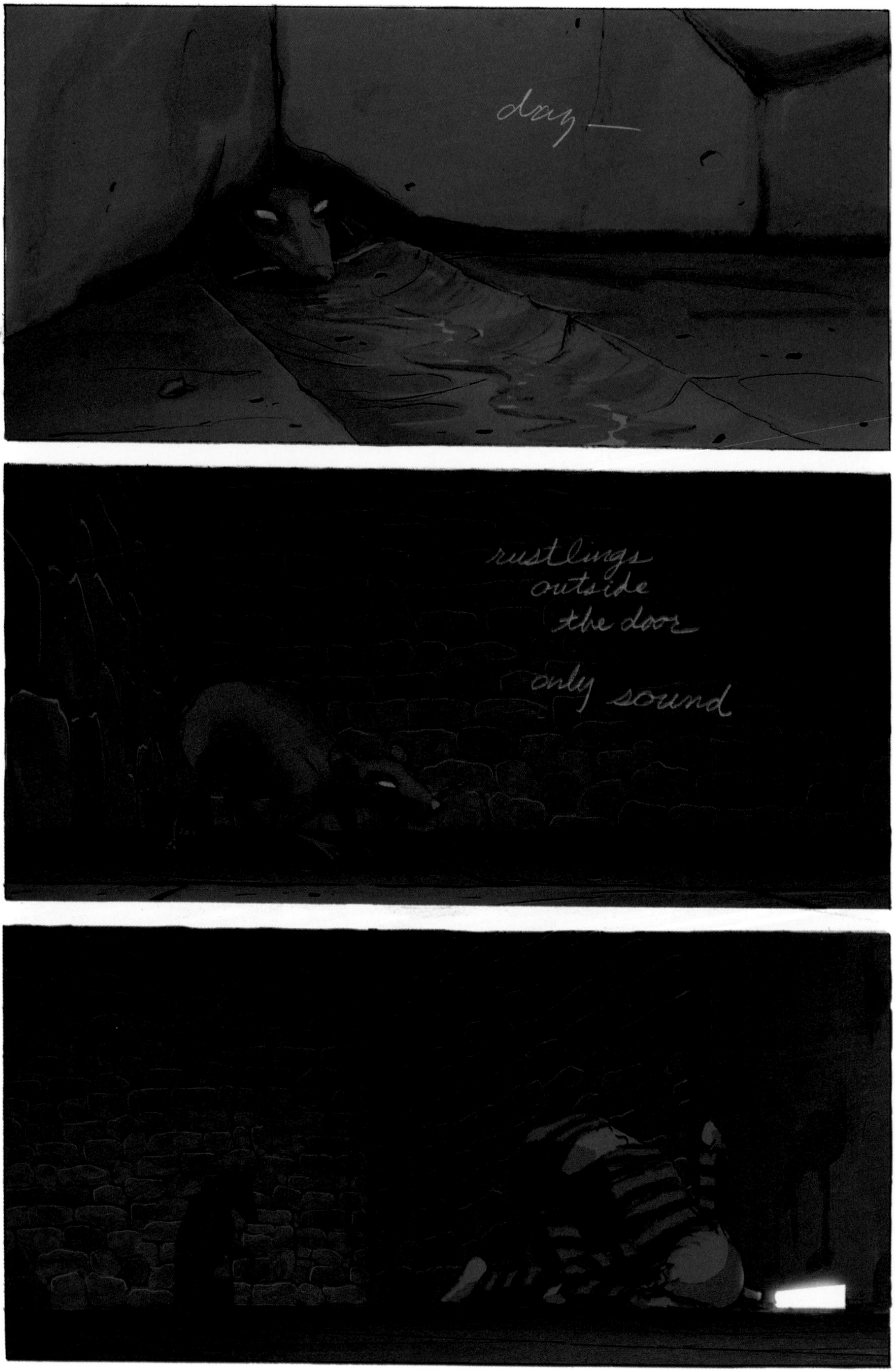
day—
rustlings outside the door—
only sound

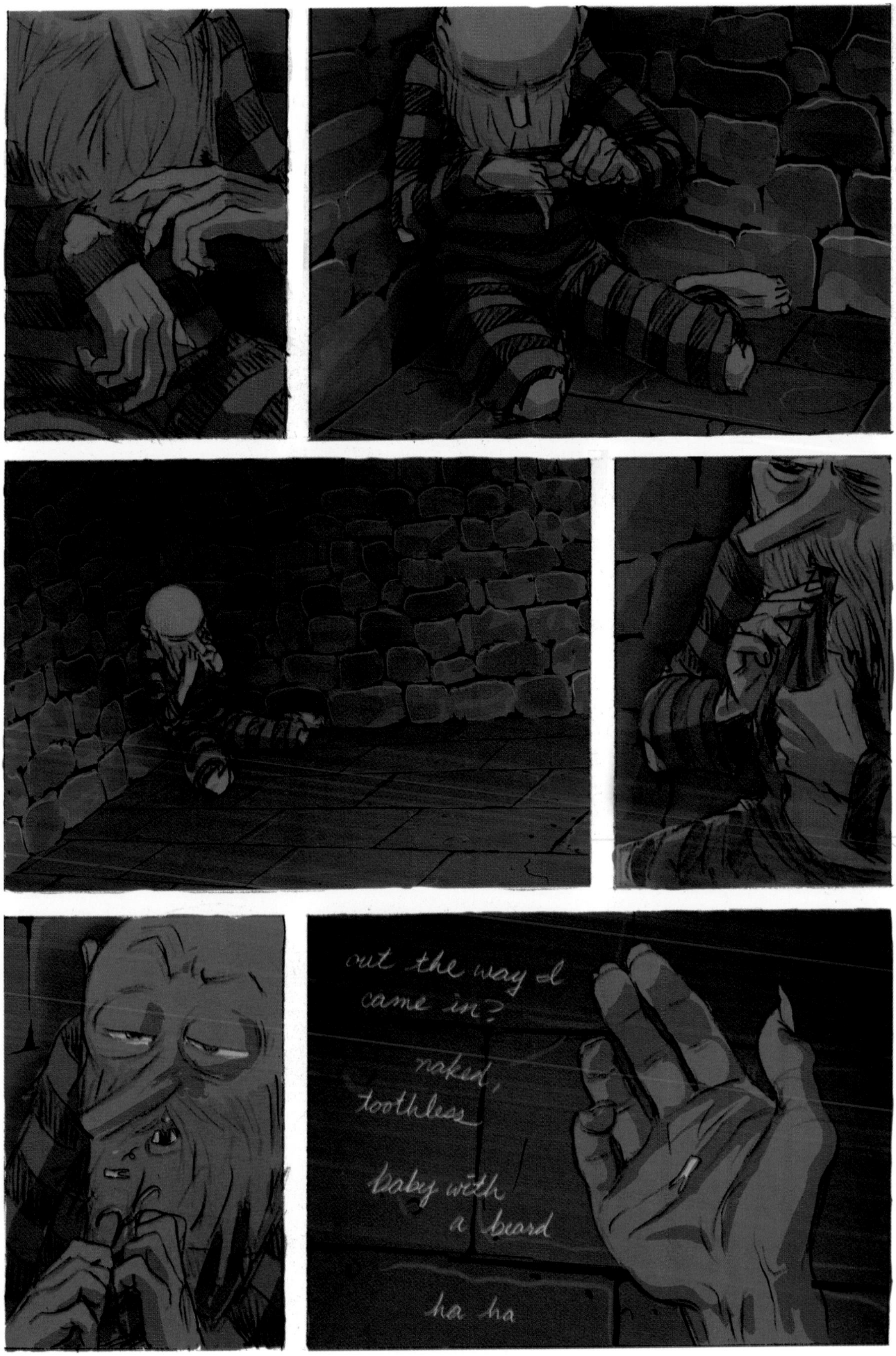
out the way I
came in?
naked,
toothless
baby with
a beard
ha ha

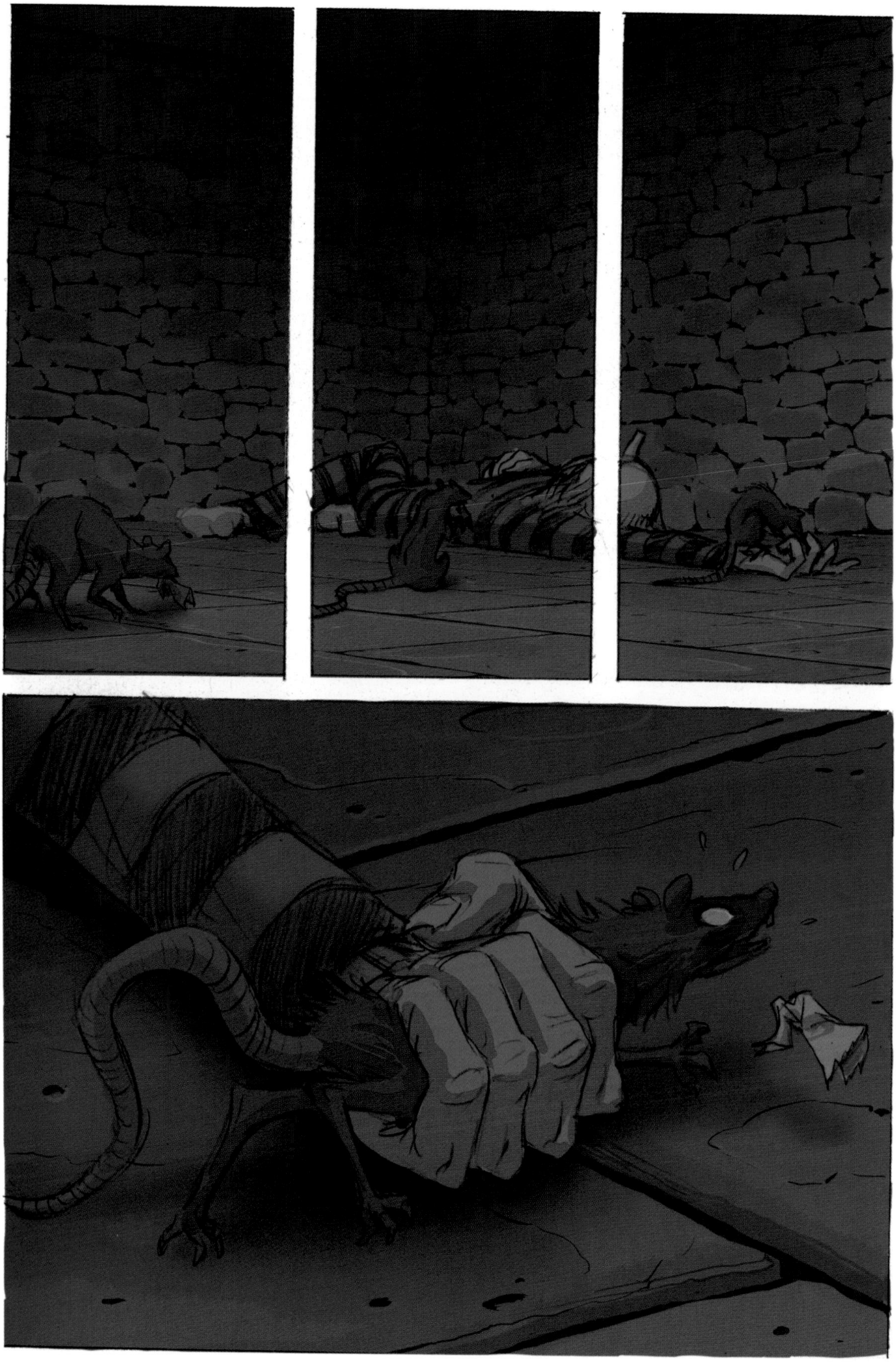

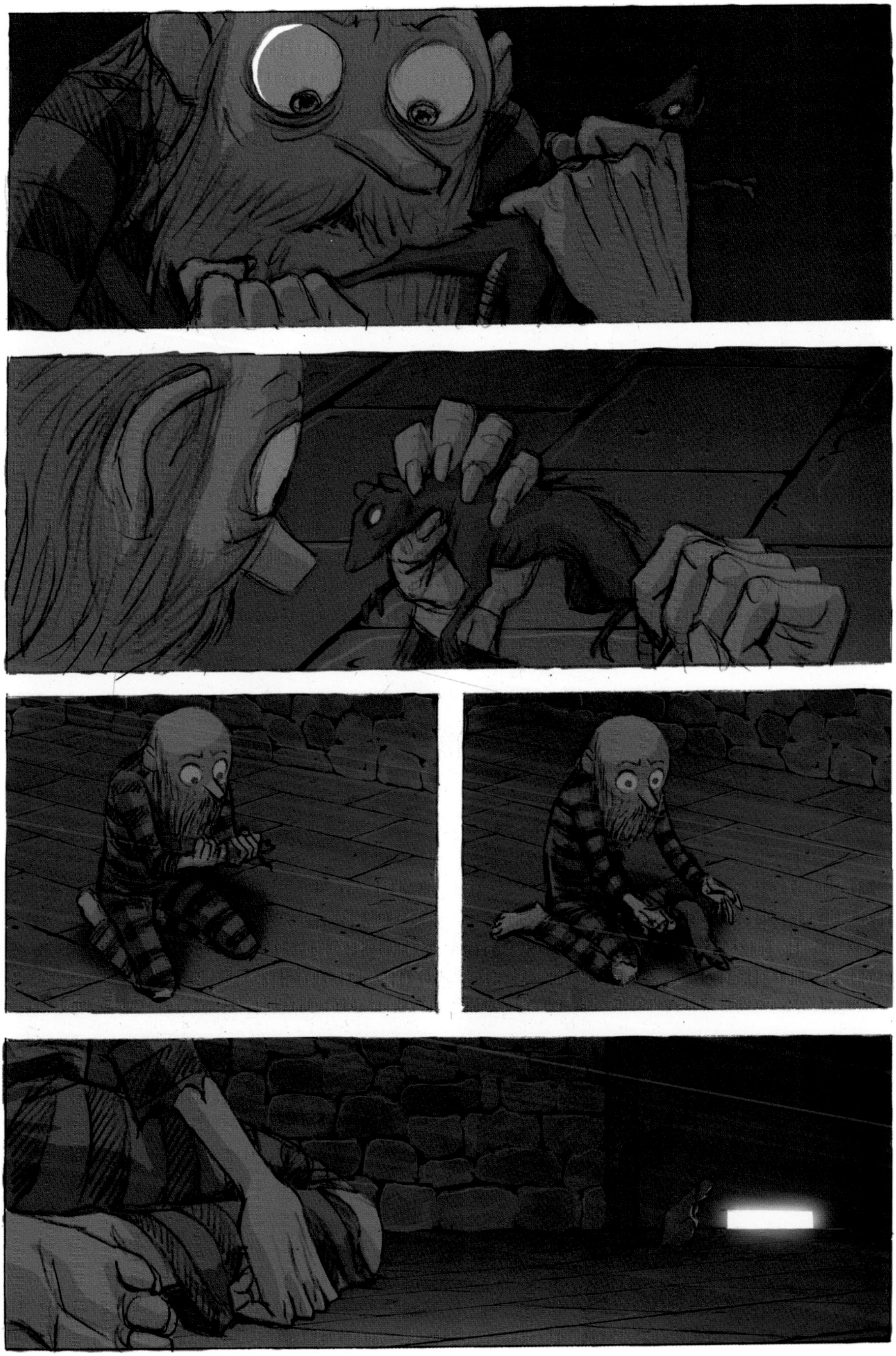

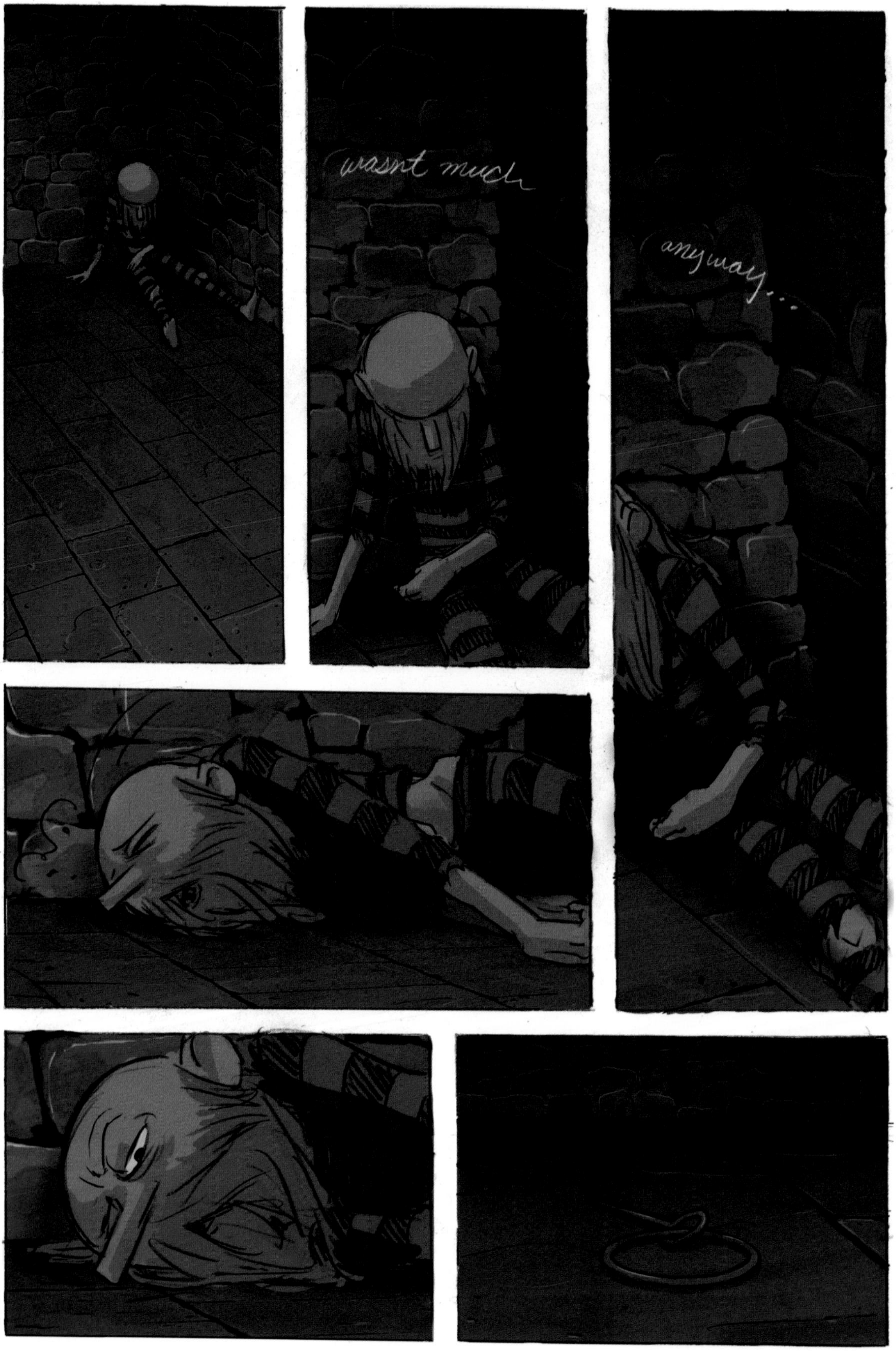
wasnt much
anyway...

The End

THE RIDE

STORY AND ART RODOLPHE GUENODEN
COLORS KAZU KIBUISHI

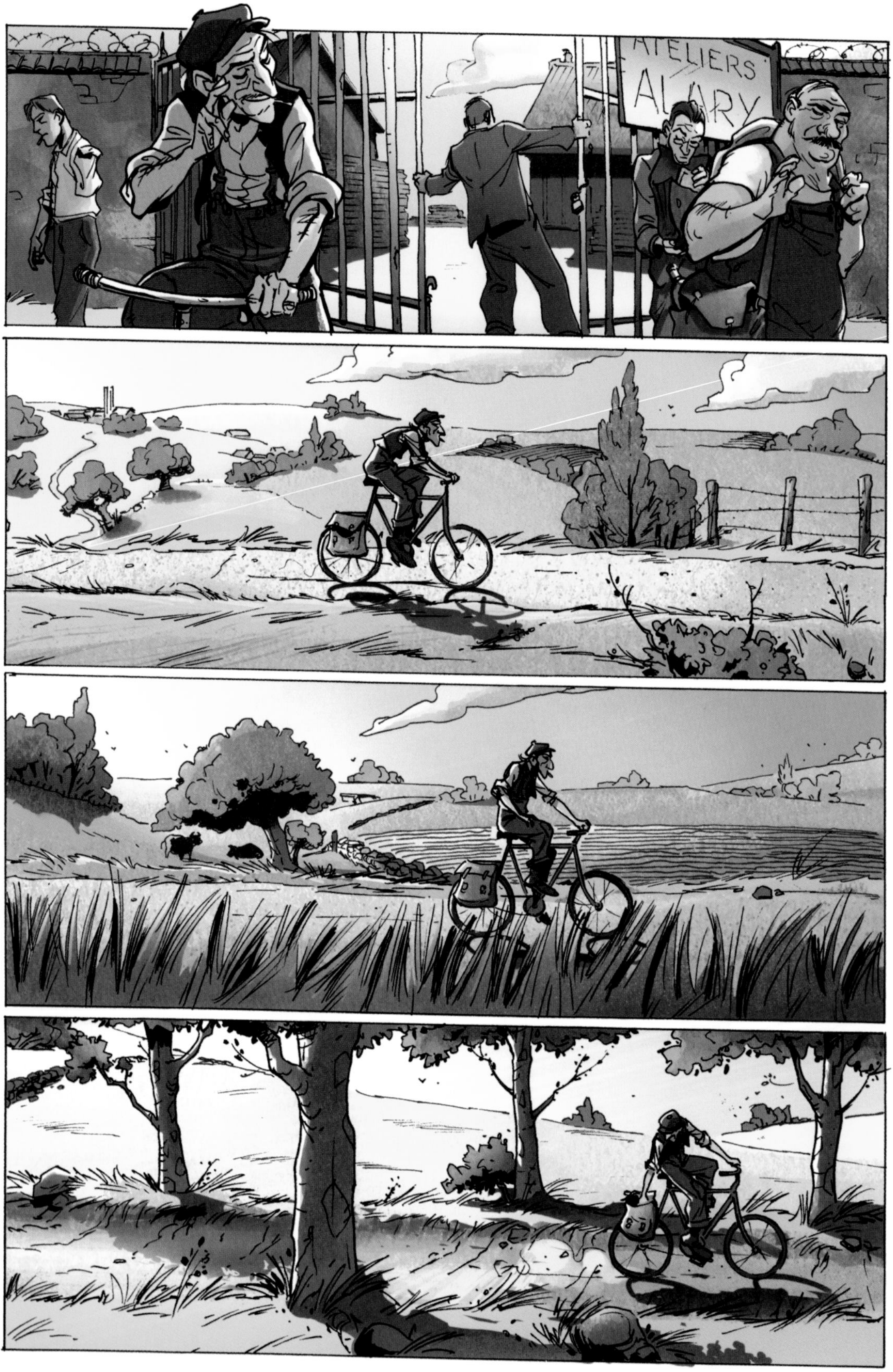
ATELIERS

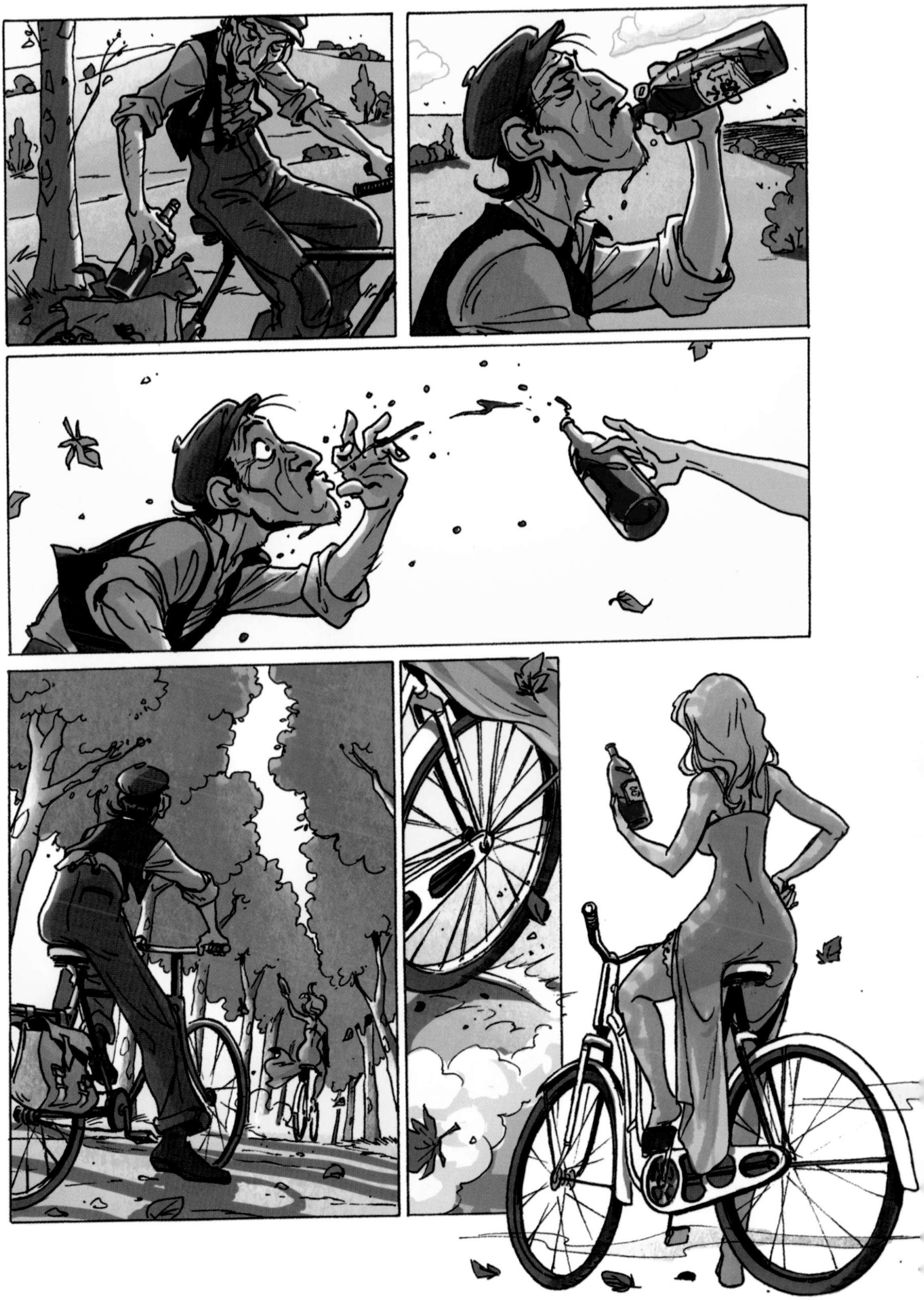

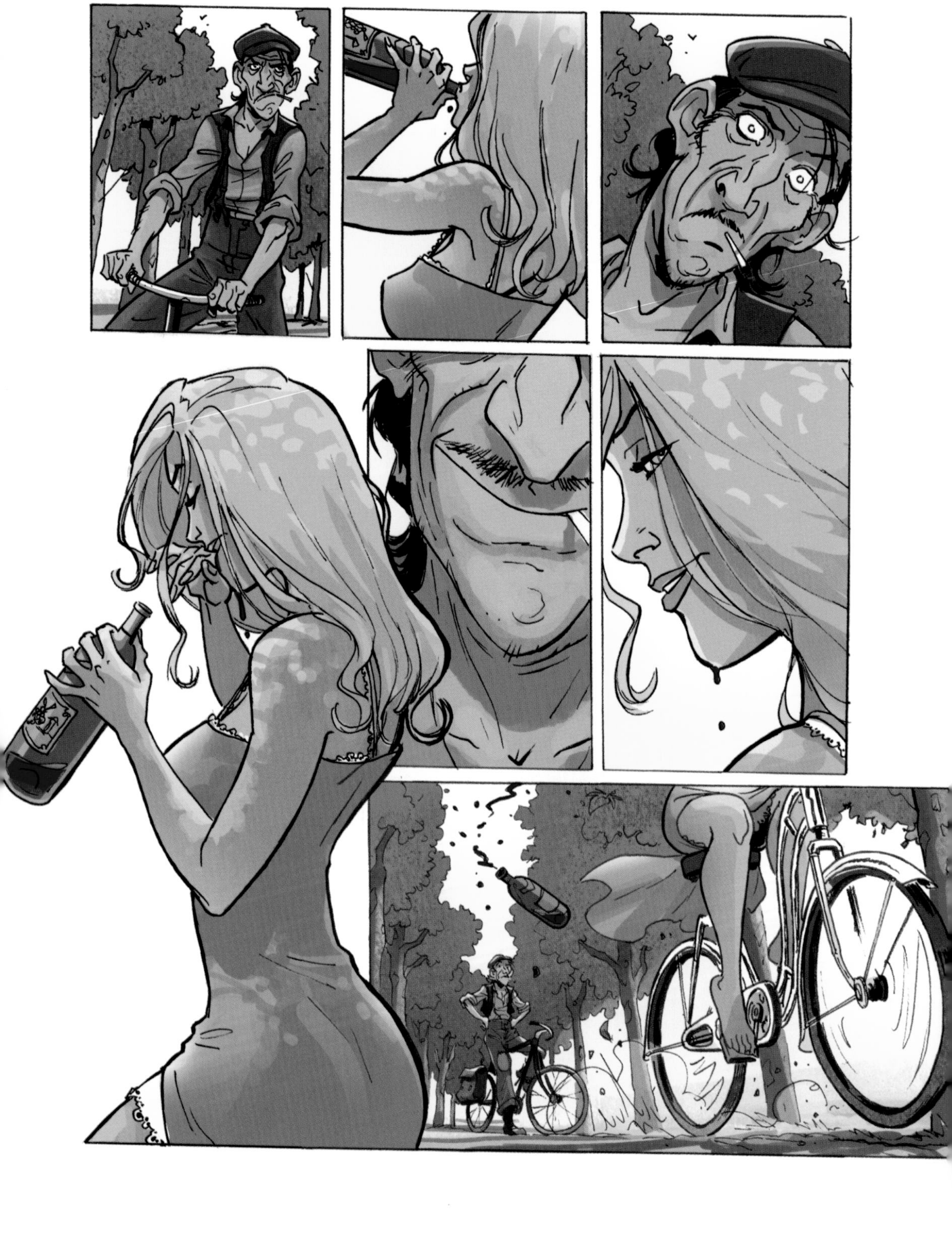

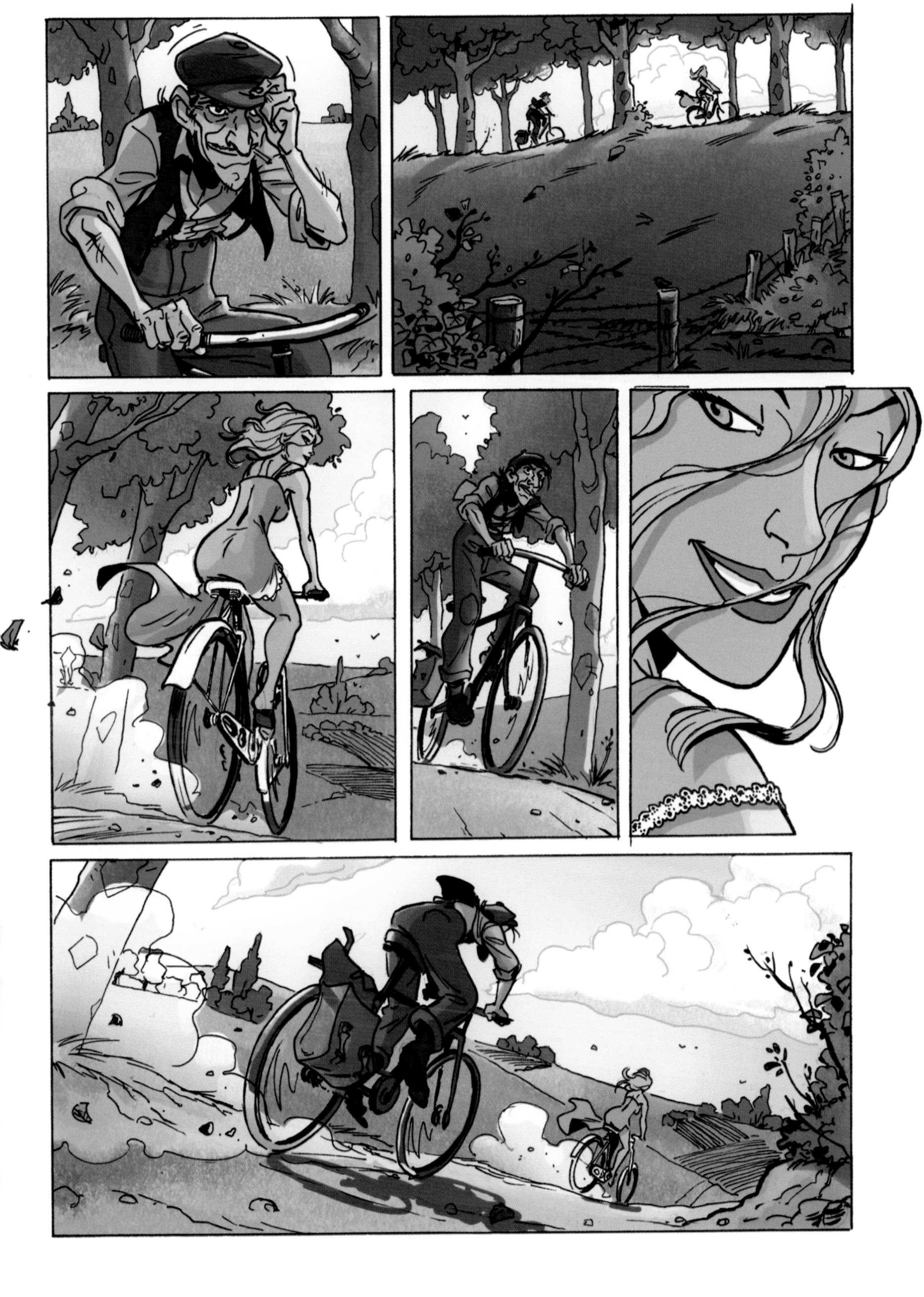

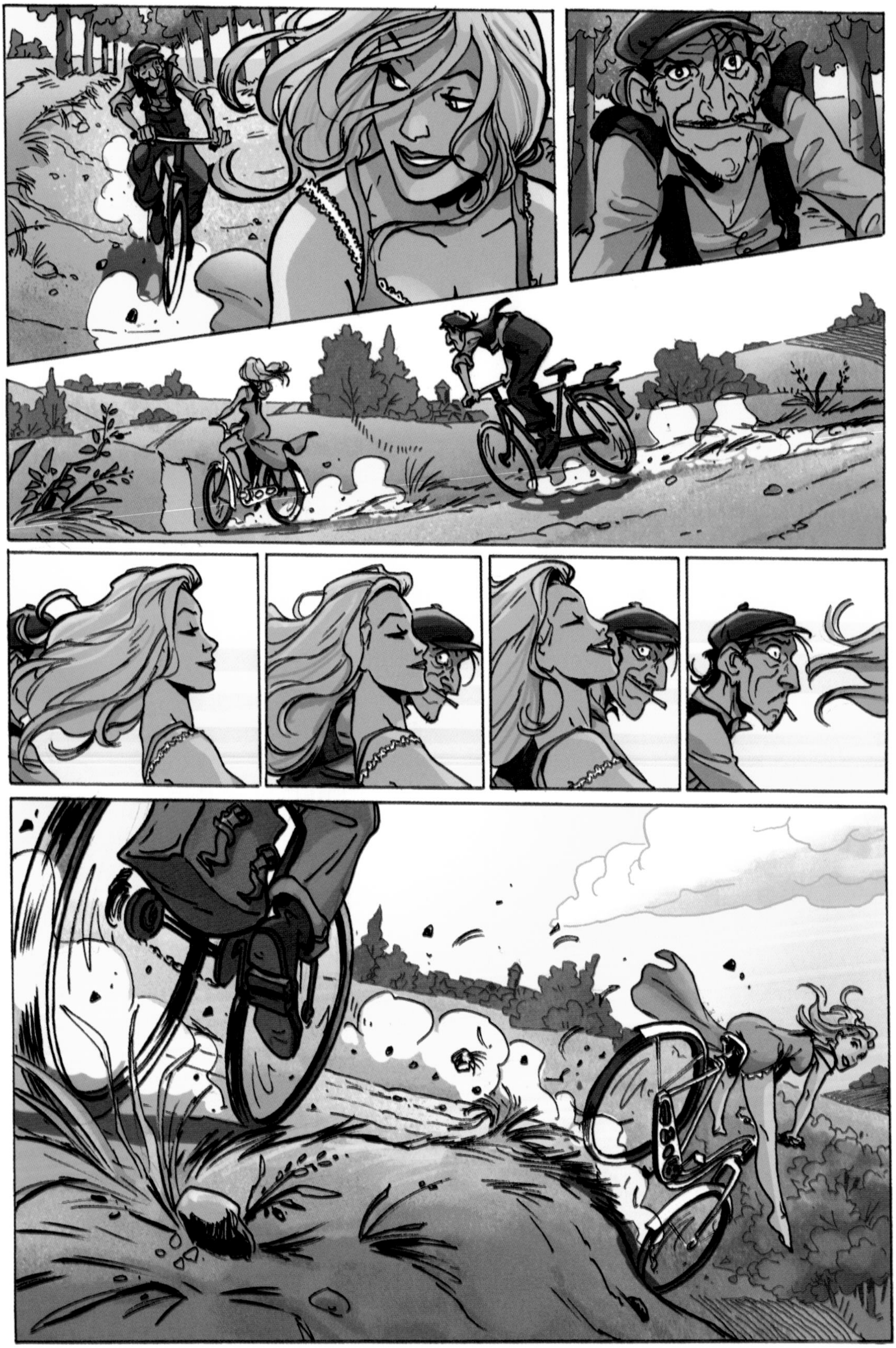

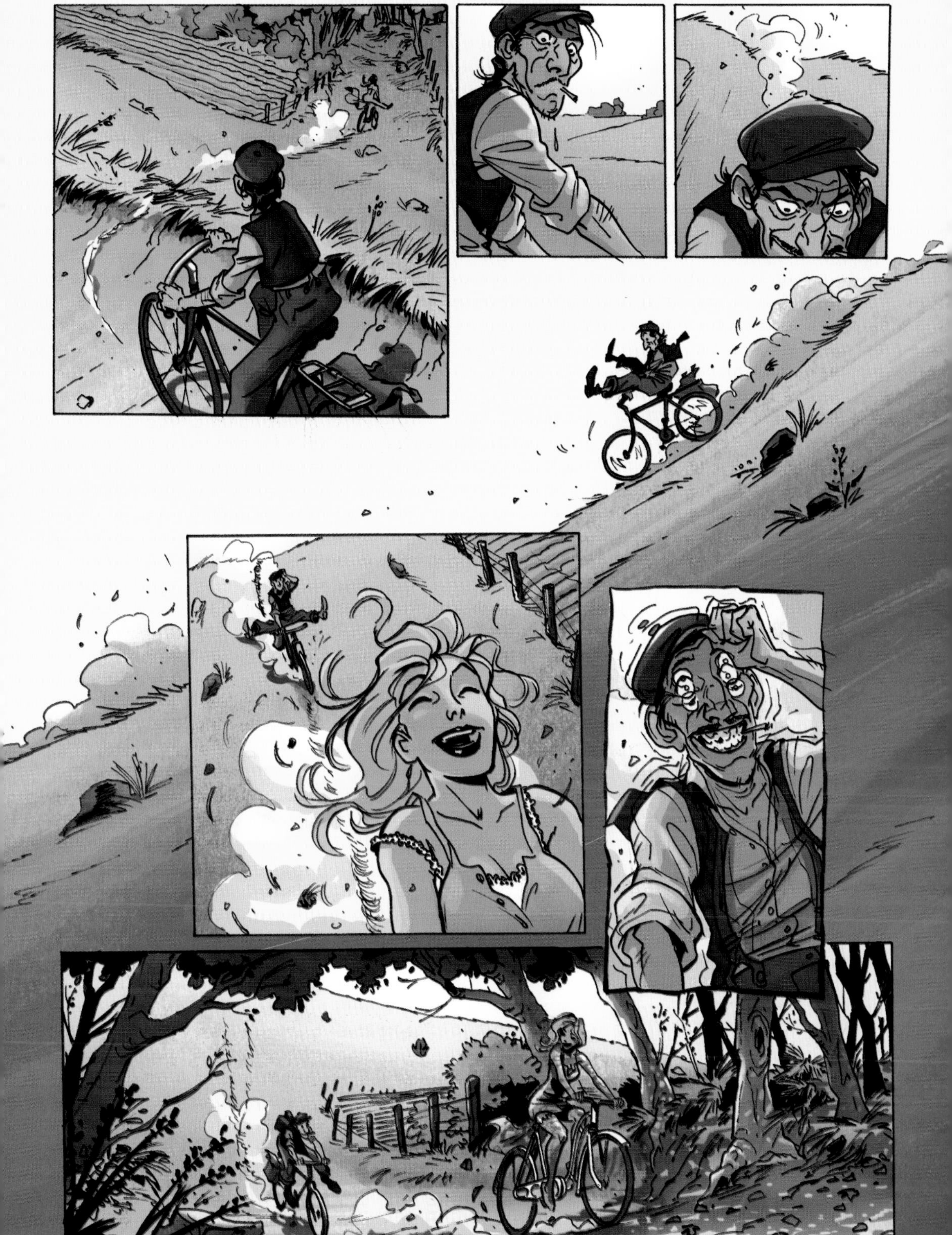

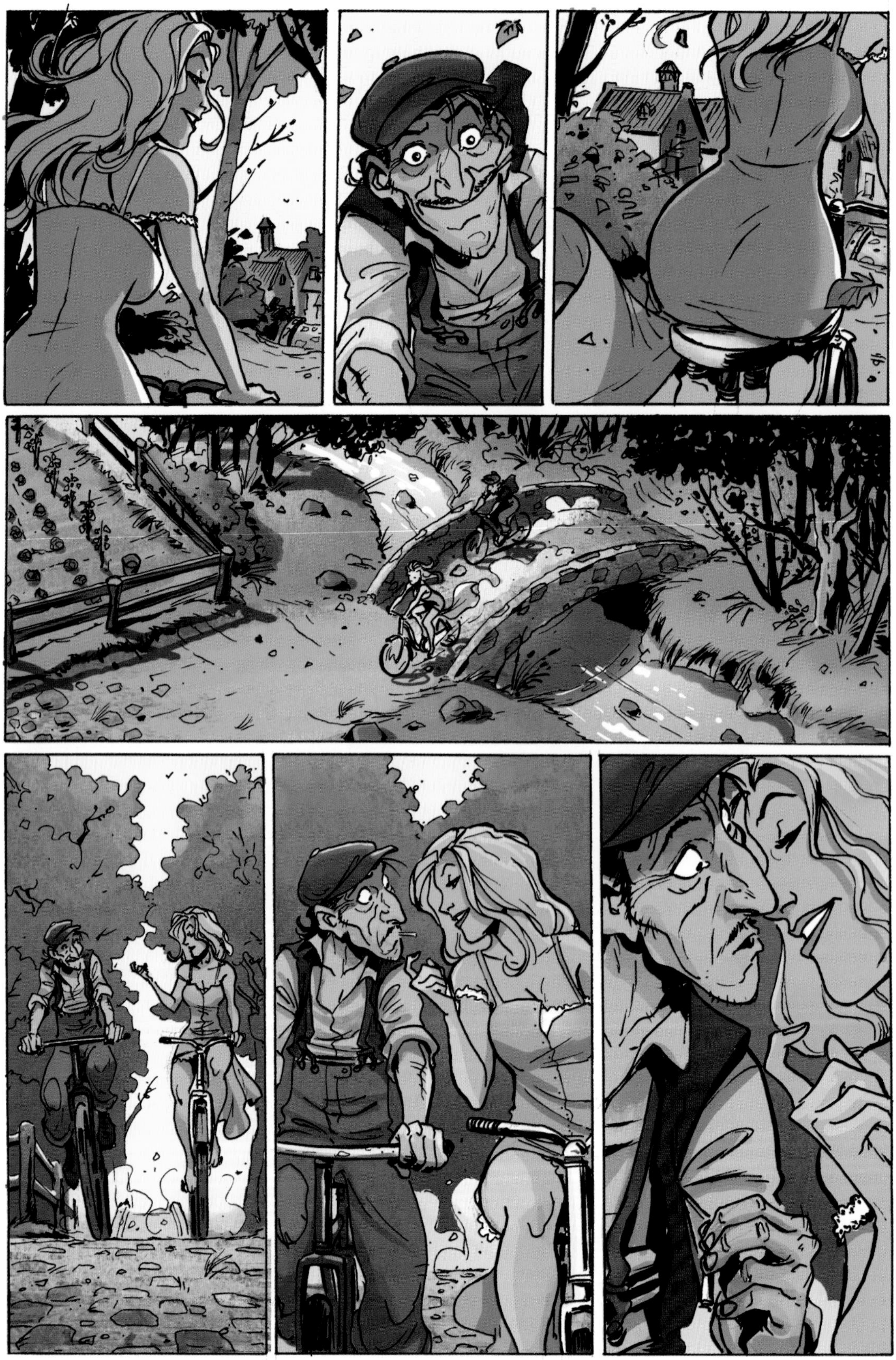

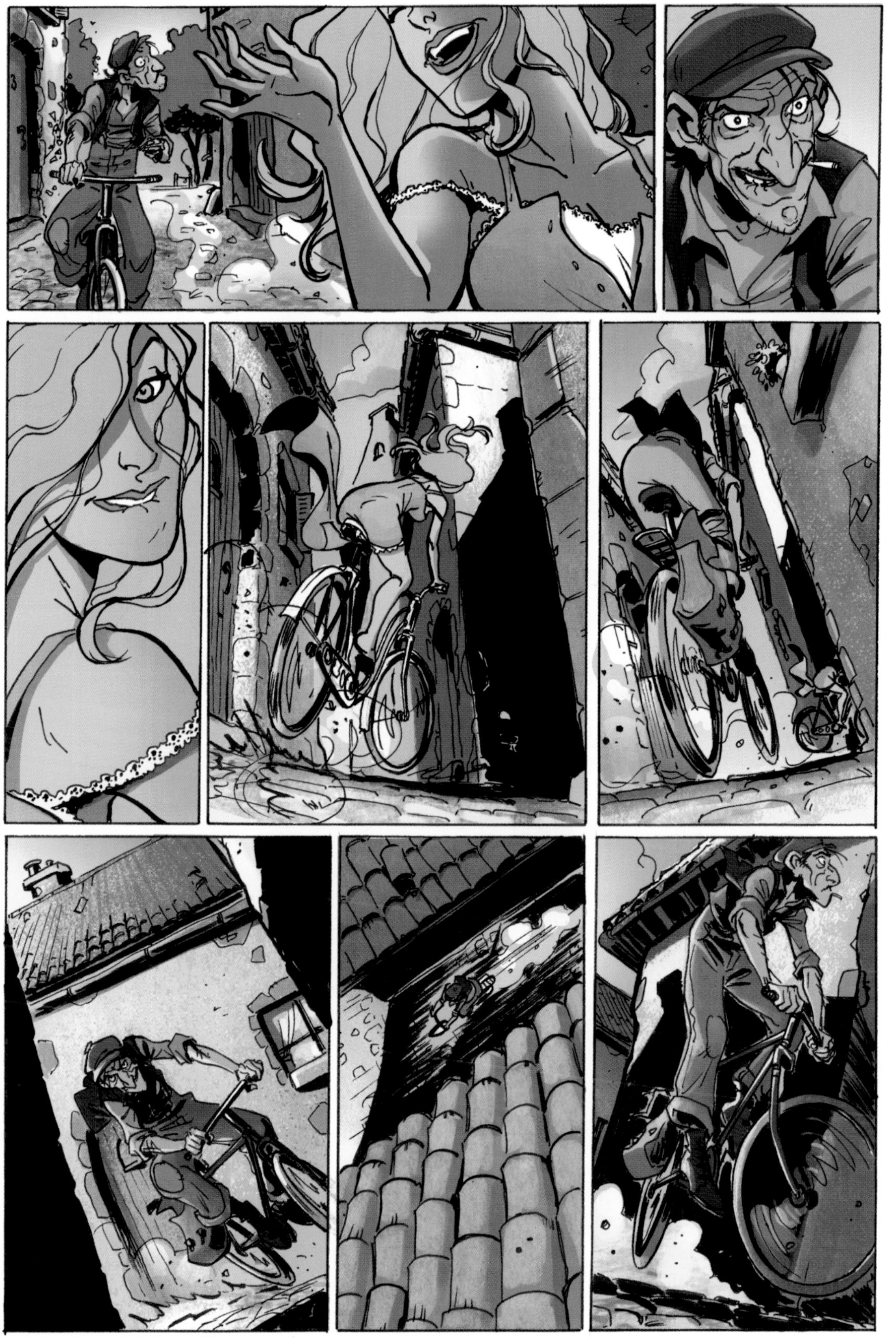

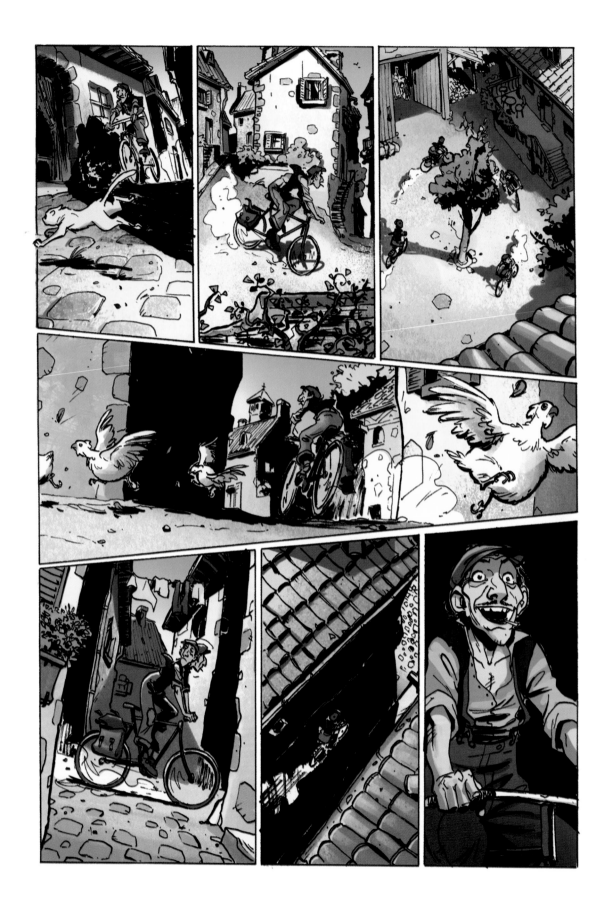

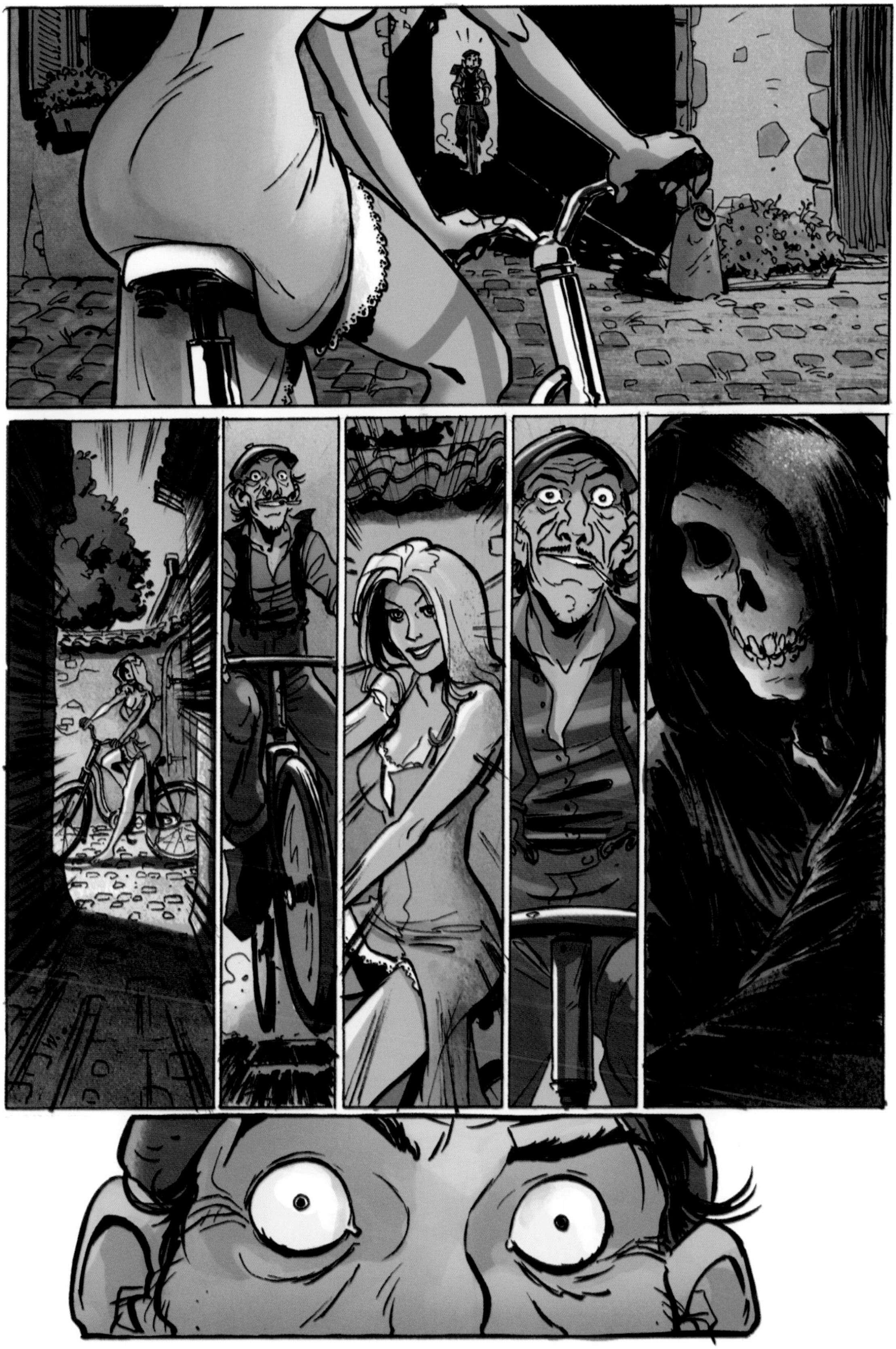

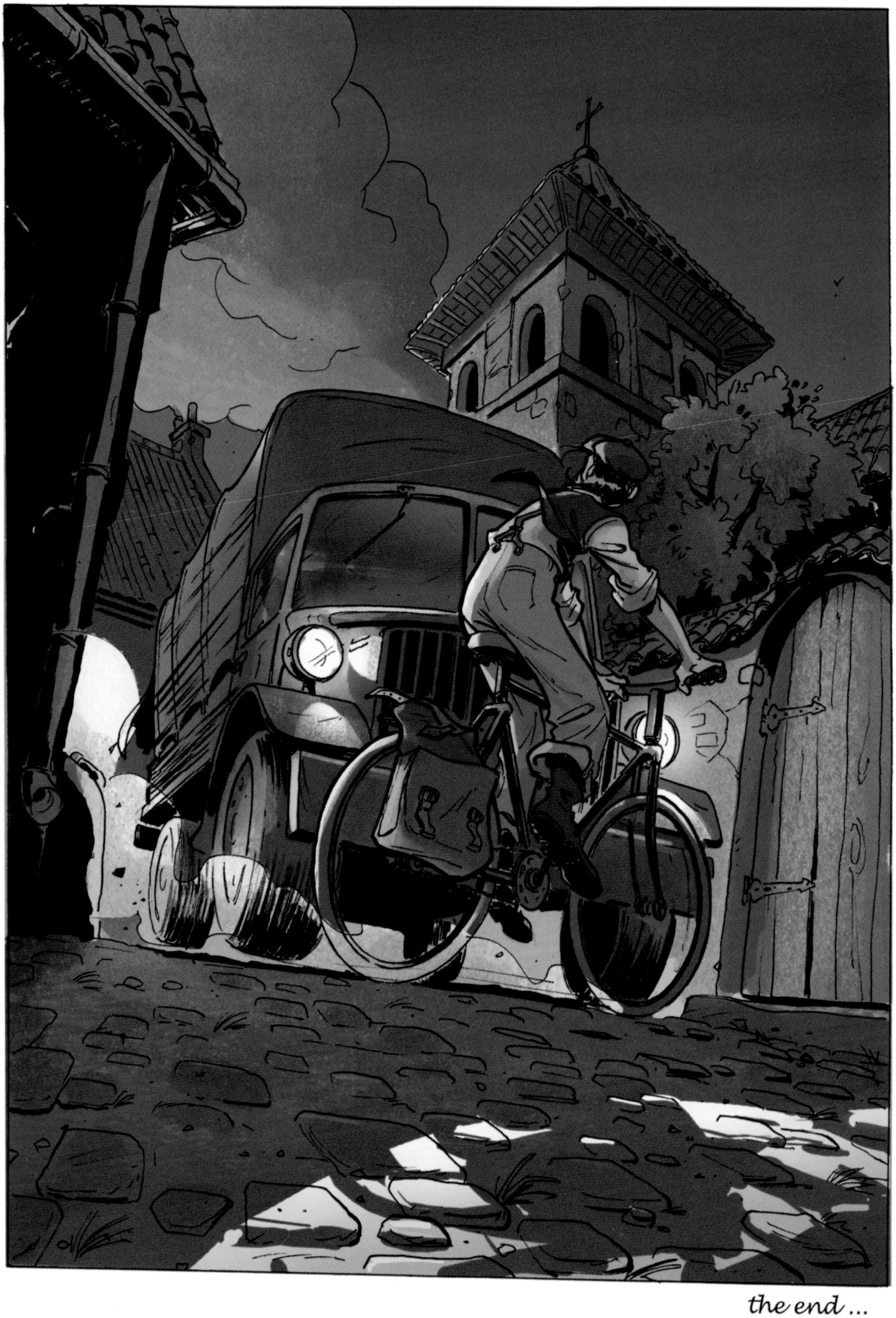

the end ...

★ LAiKA ★

BY DOUG HOLGATE

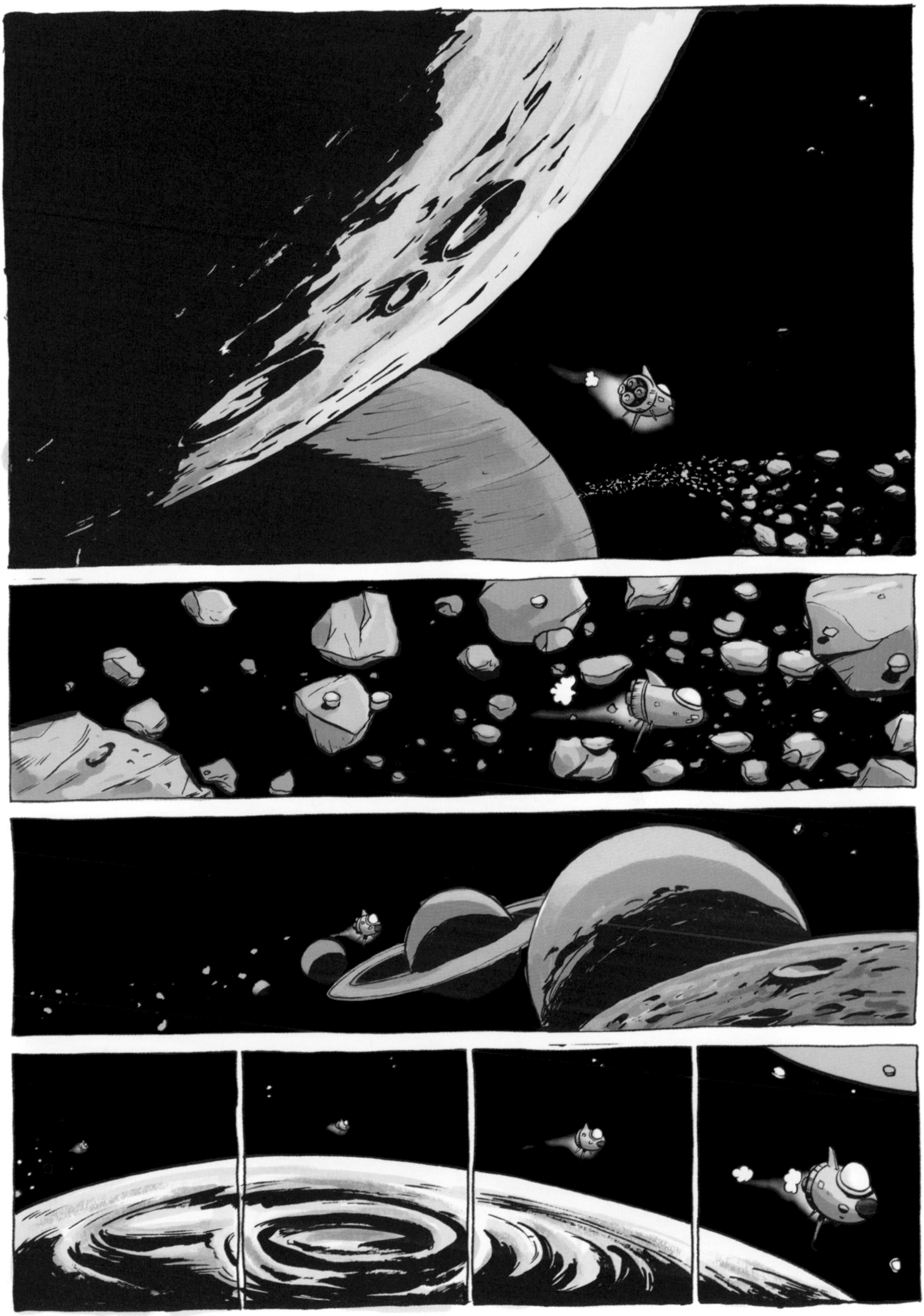

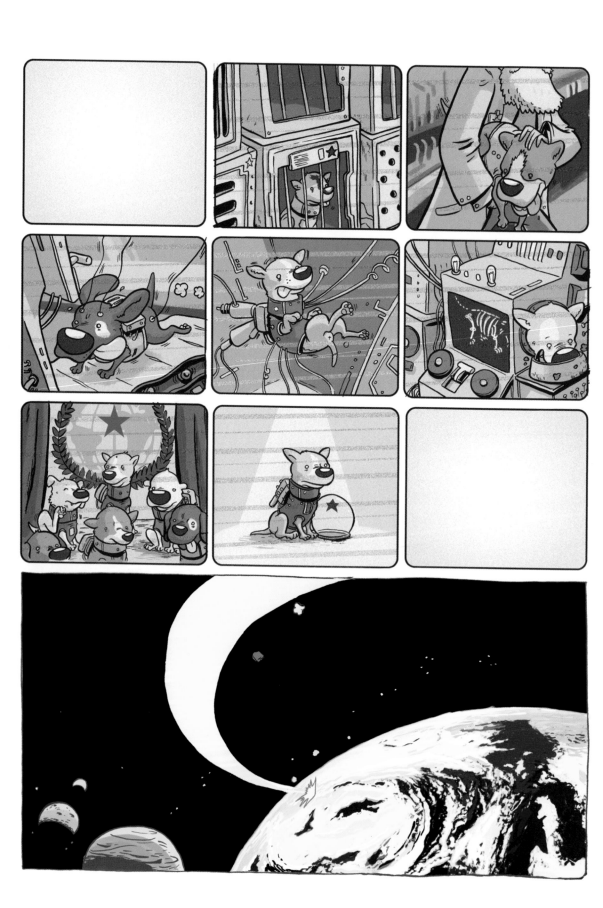

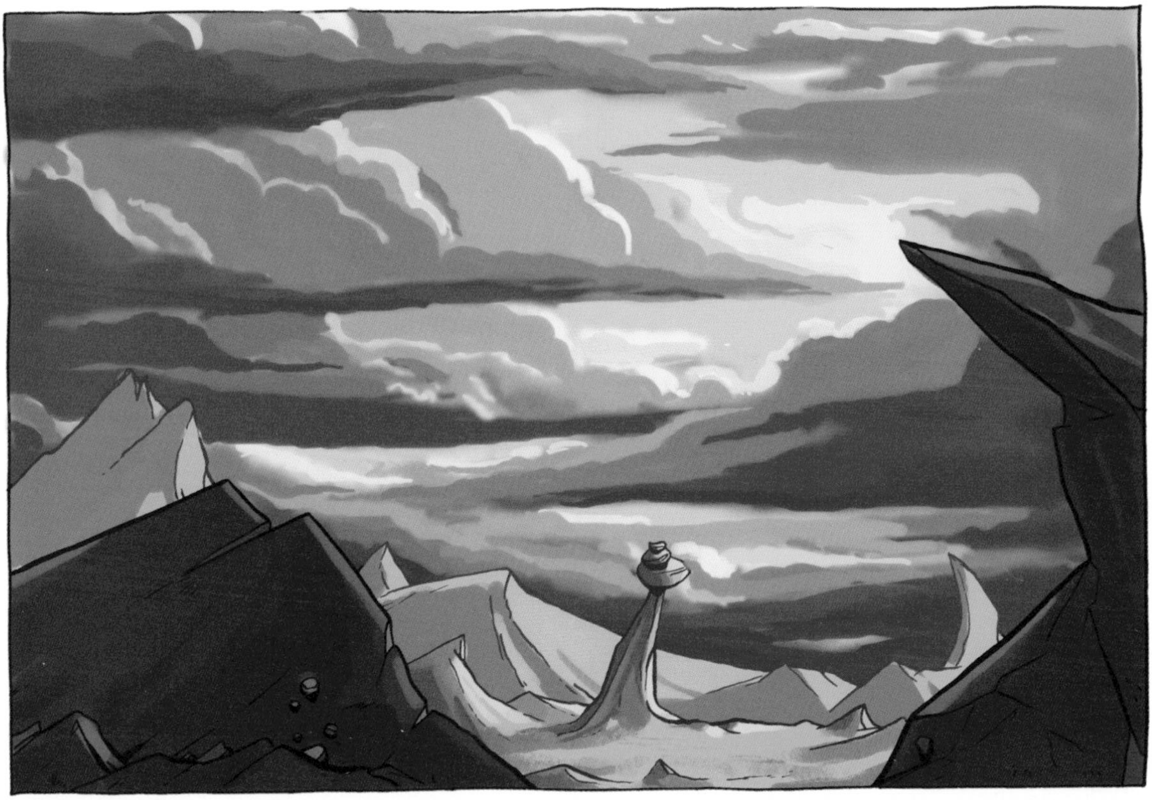

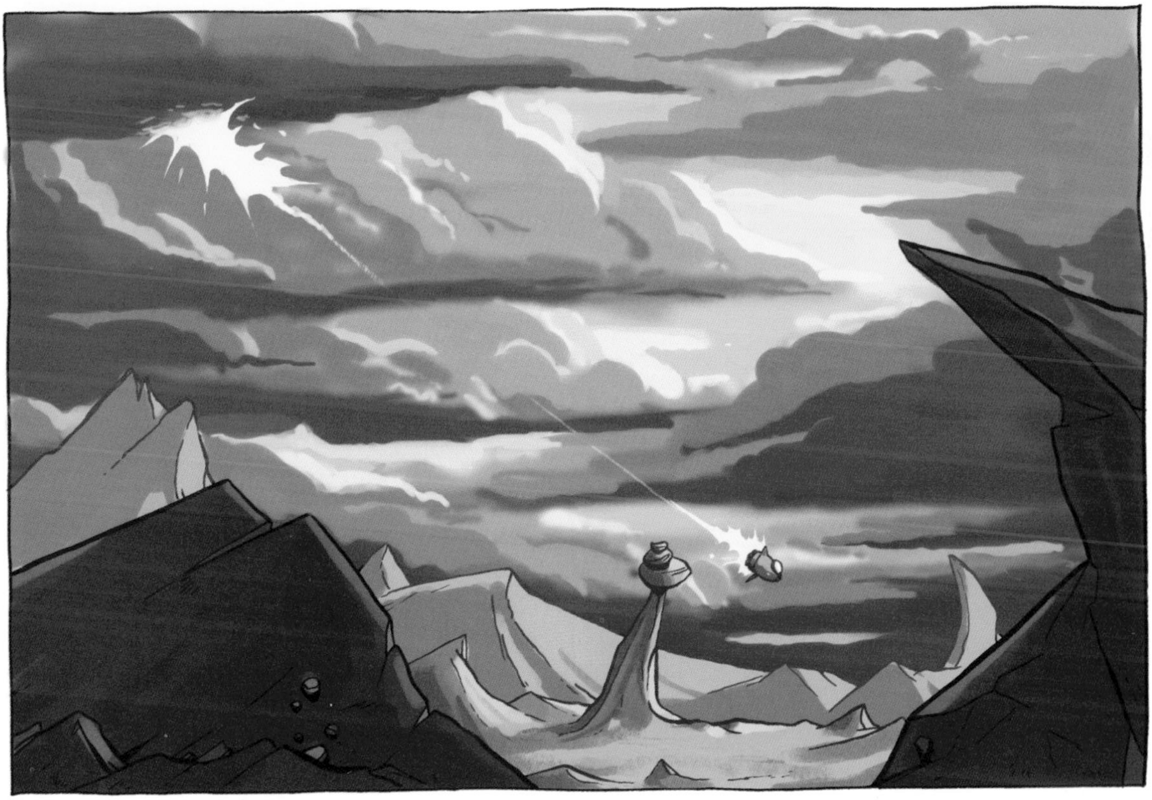

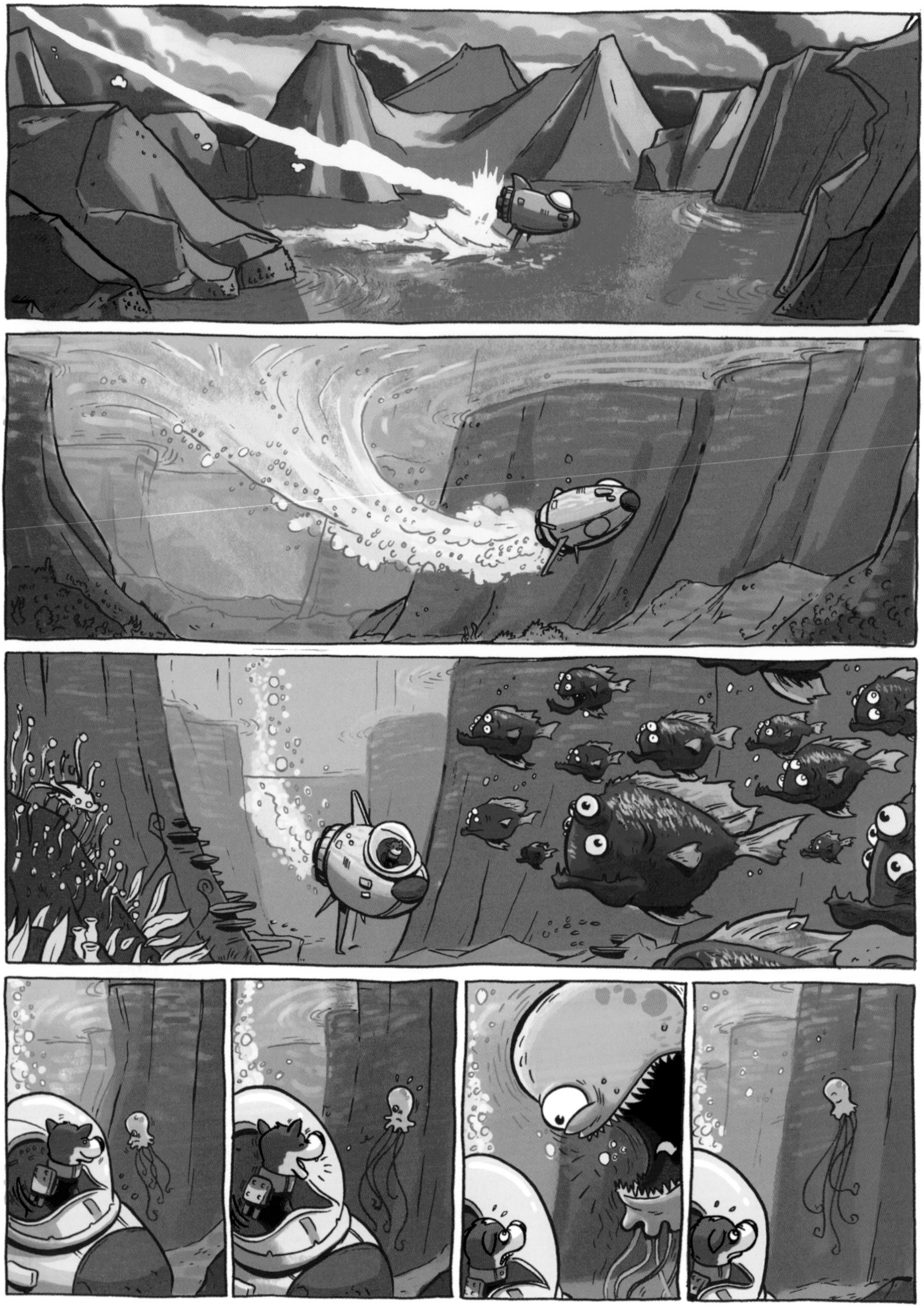

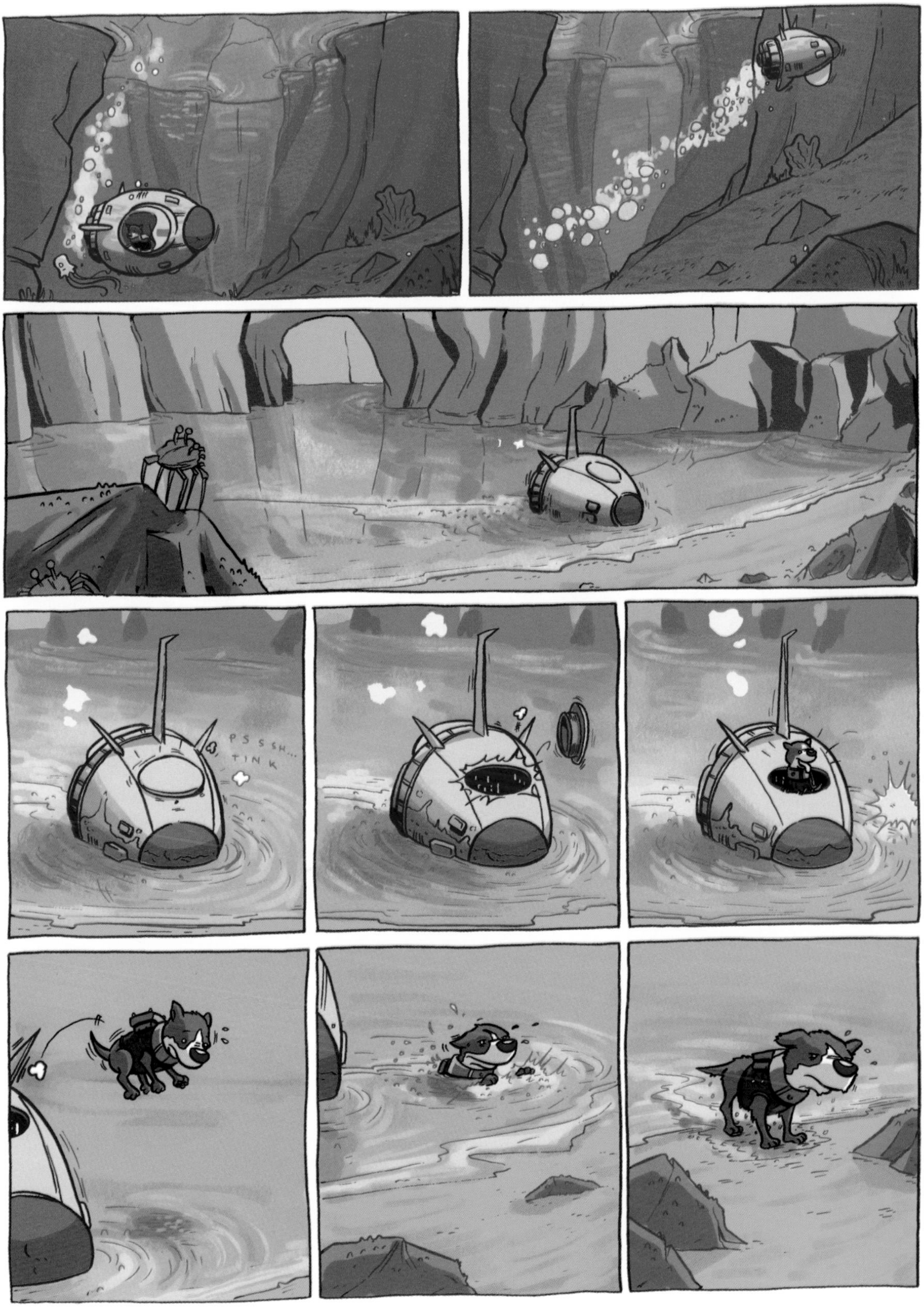
PSSSH...
TINK

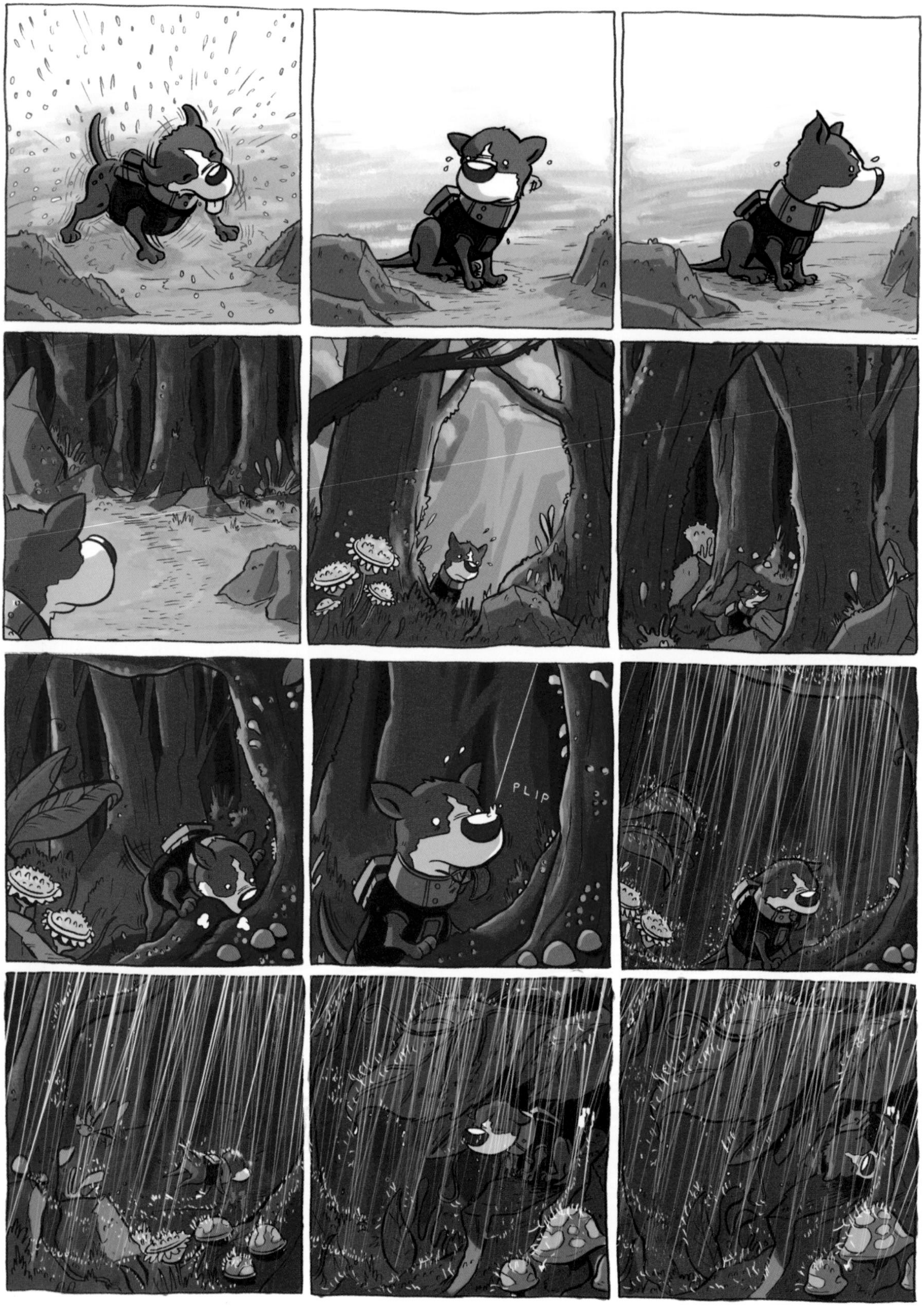
PLIP

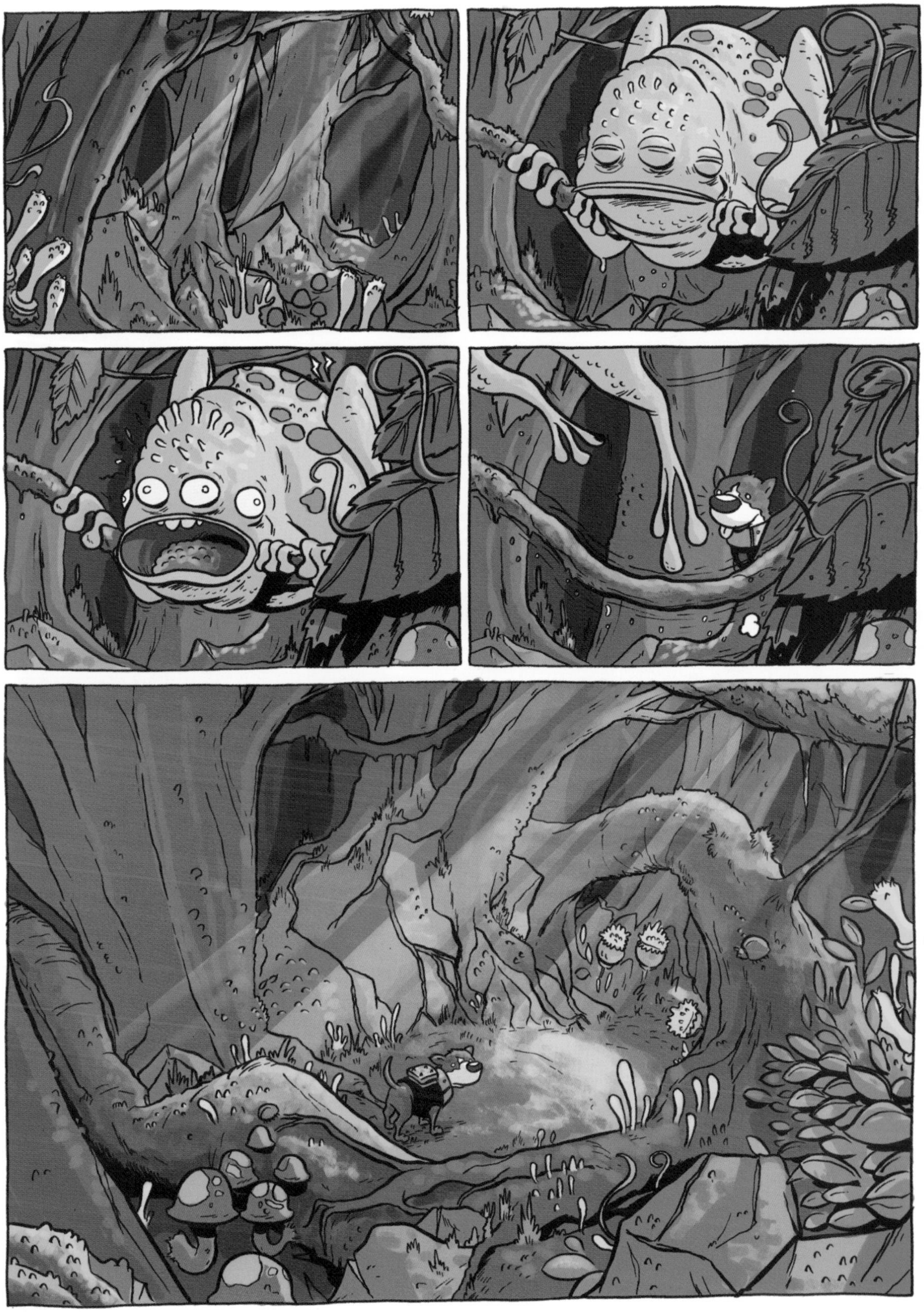

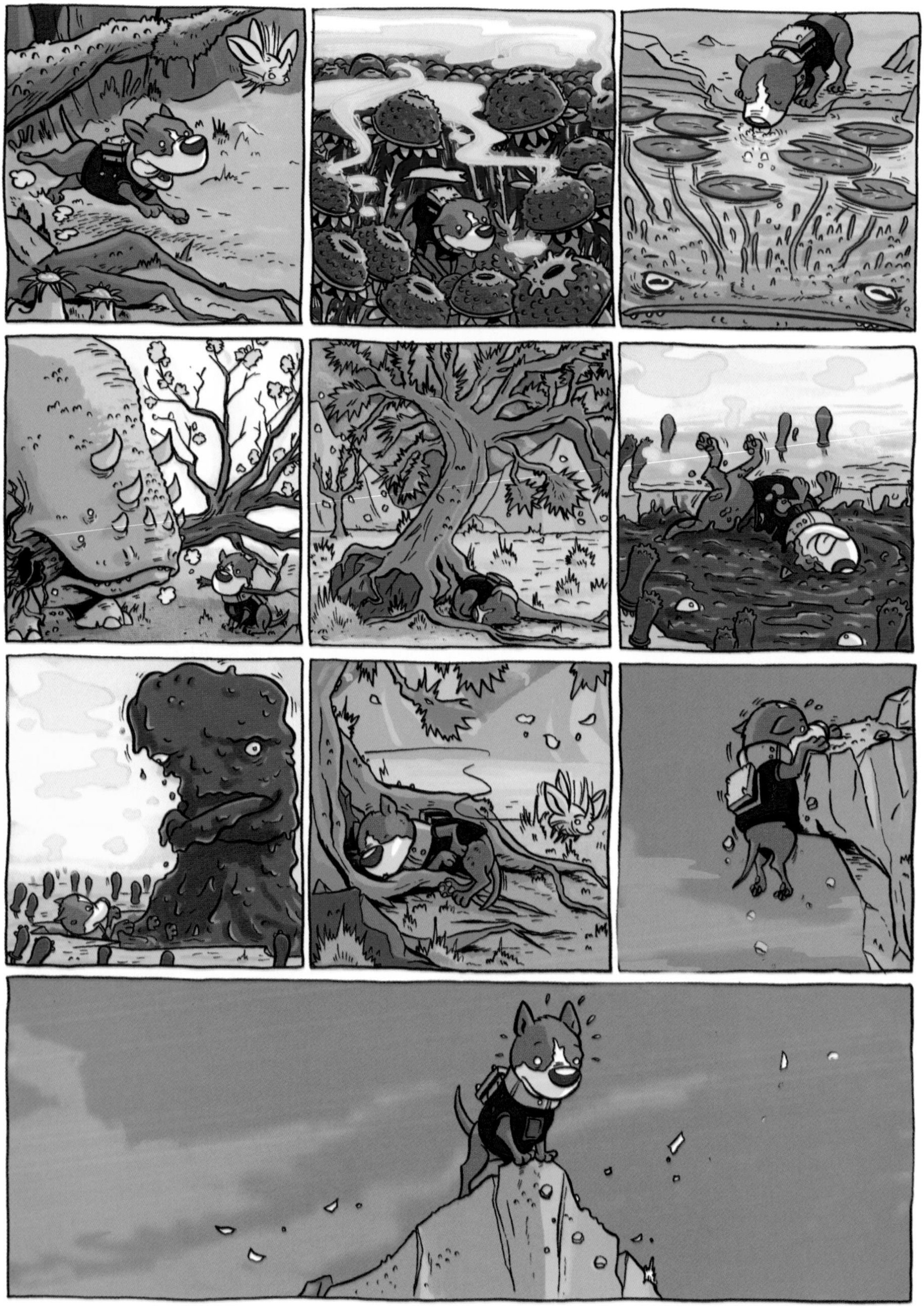

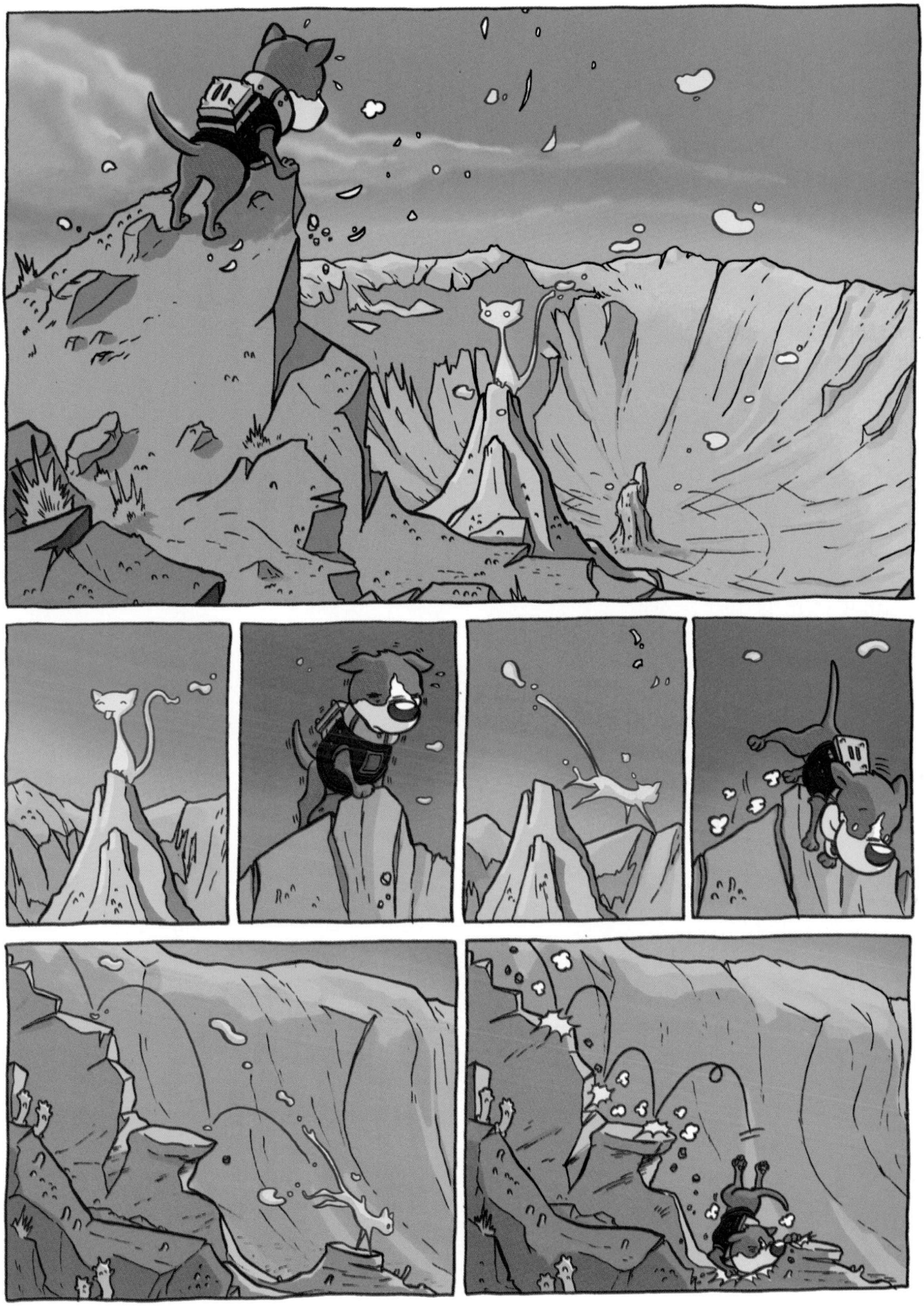

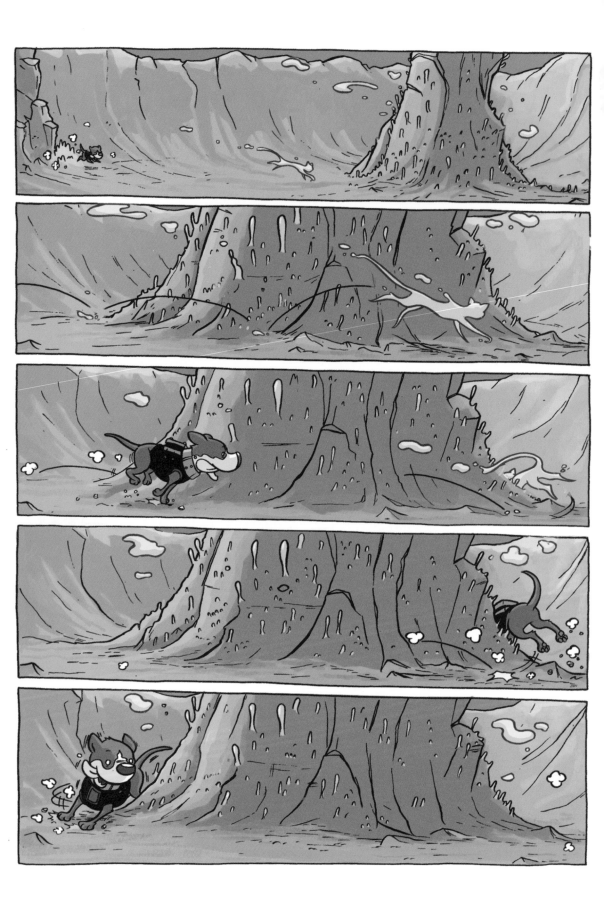

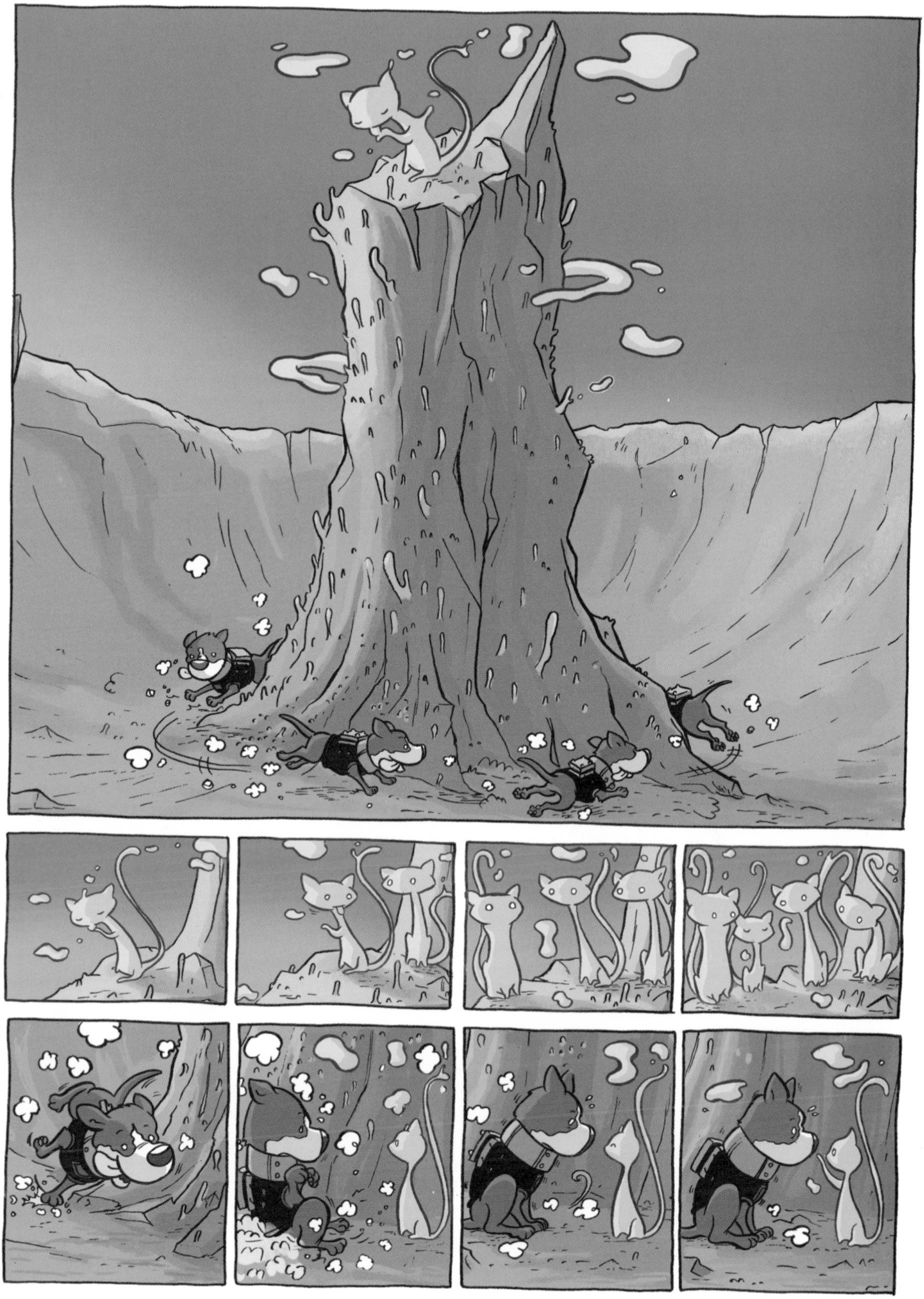

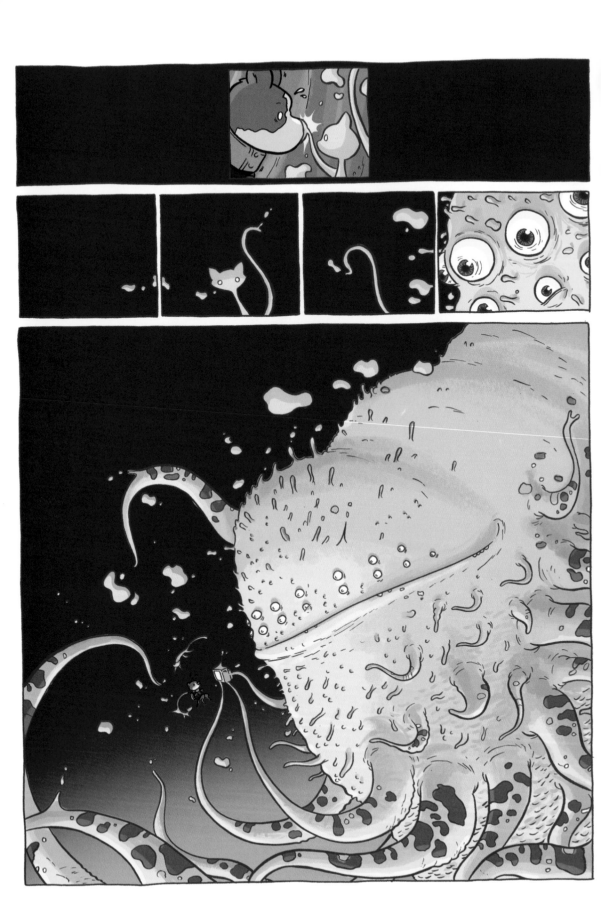

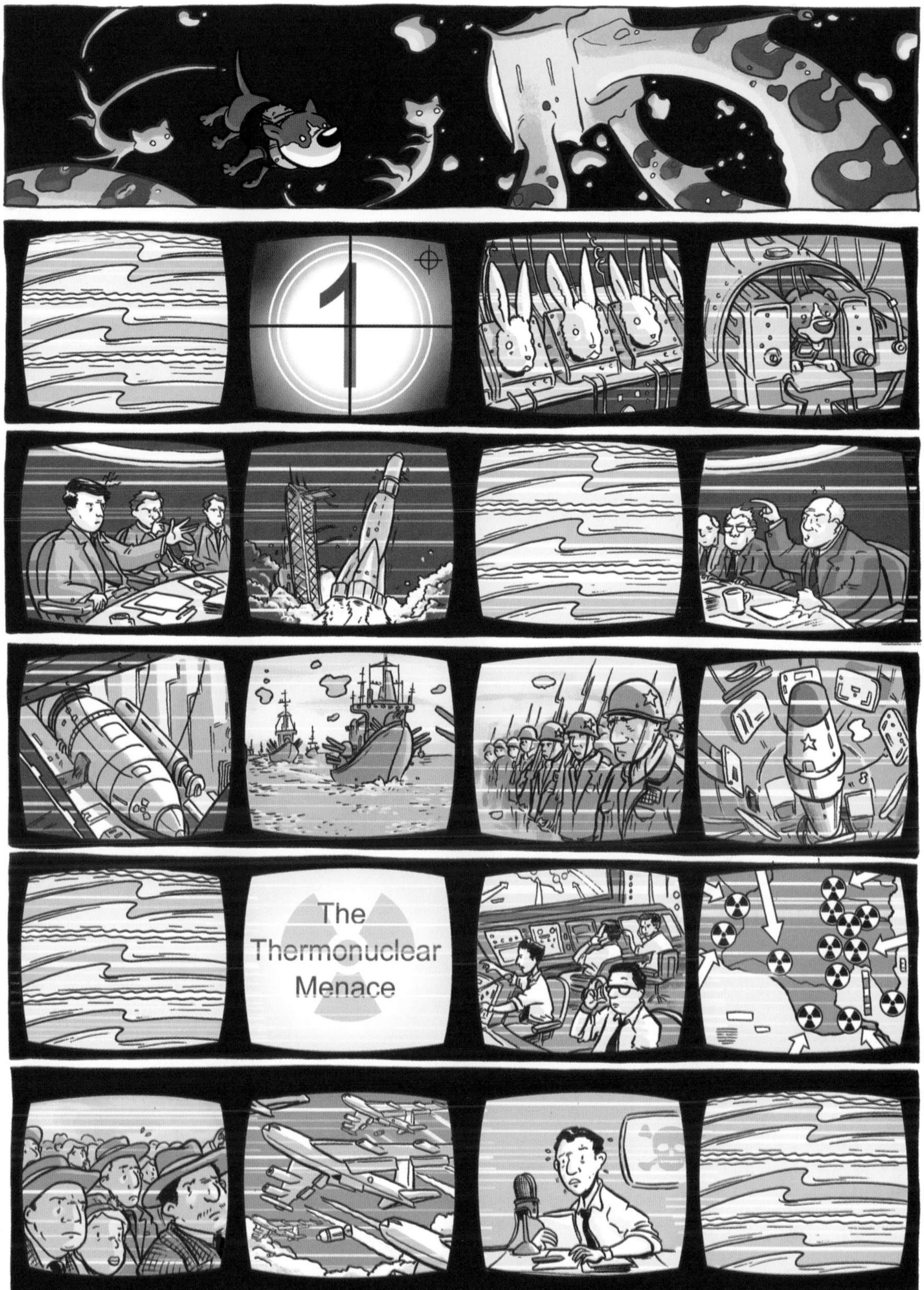
1
The
Thermonuclear
Menace

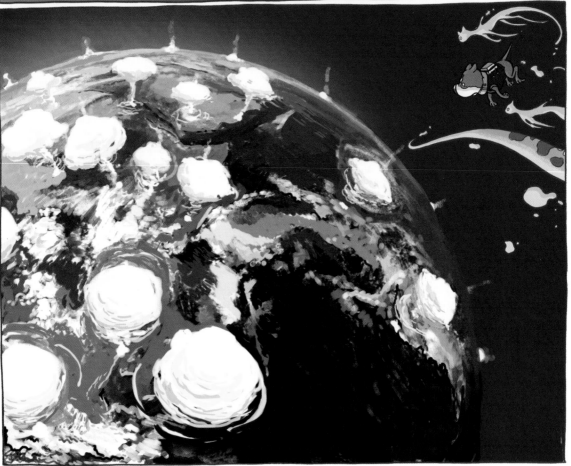

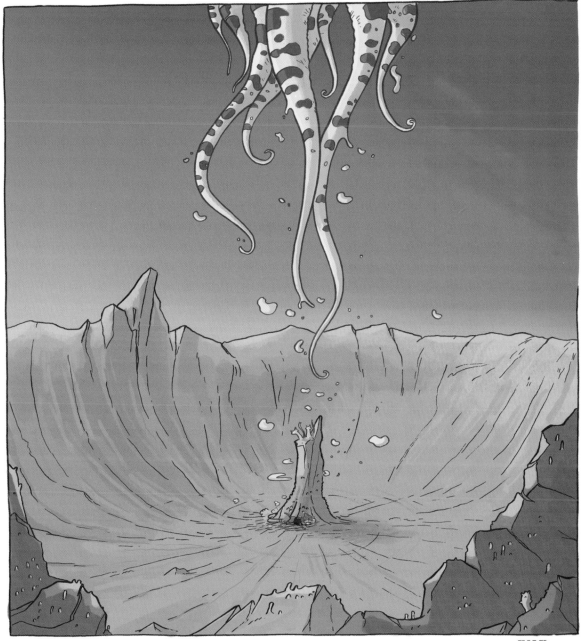

★ END ★

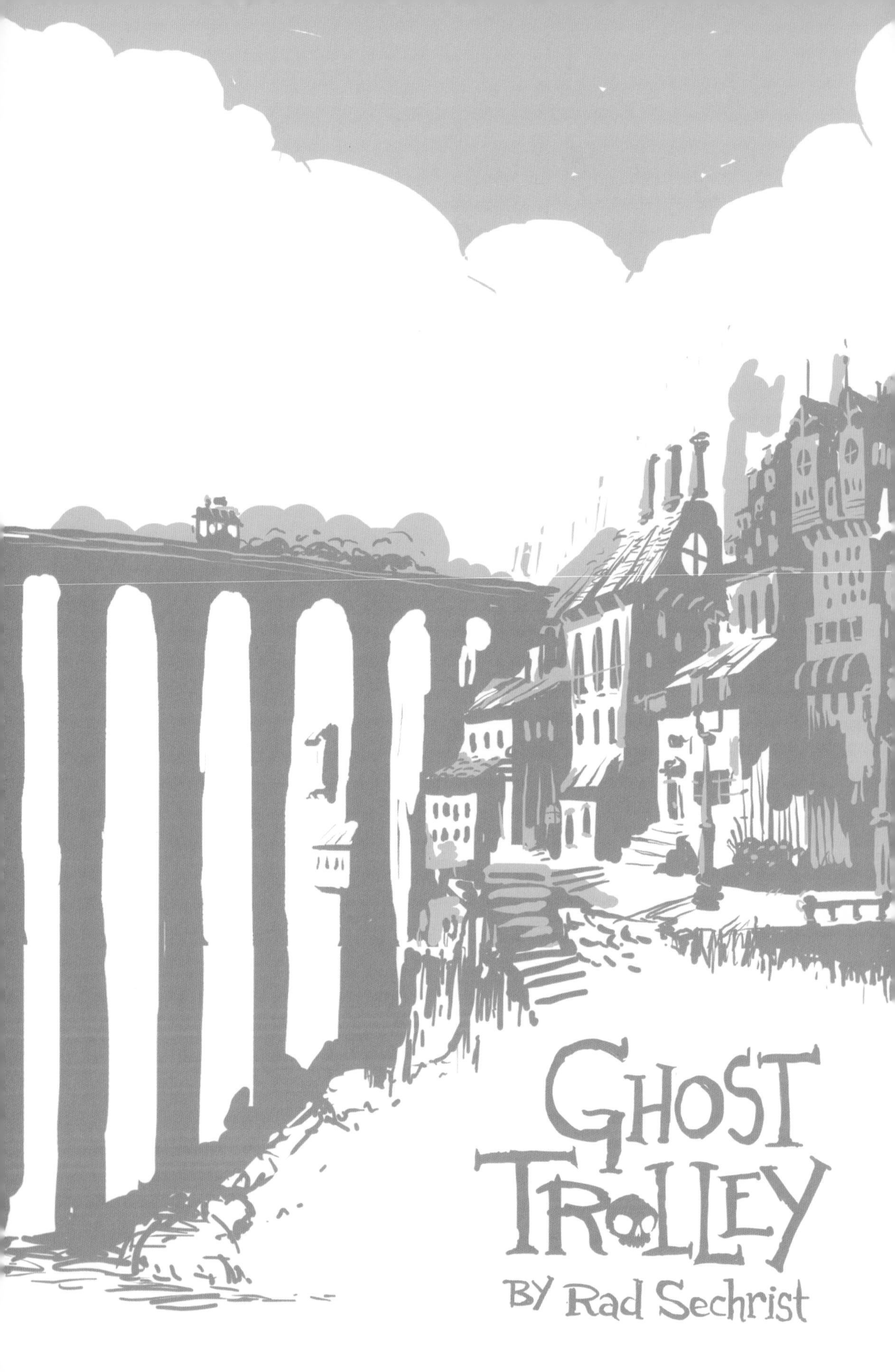
GHOST
TROLLEY
BY Rad Sechrist

SCRCH!

LAST STOP!

ROOTPORT

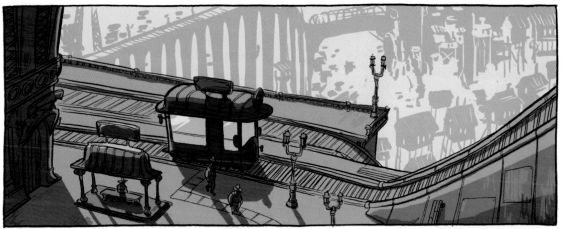

SLAM!

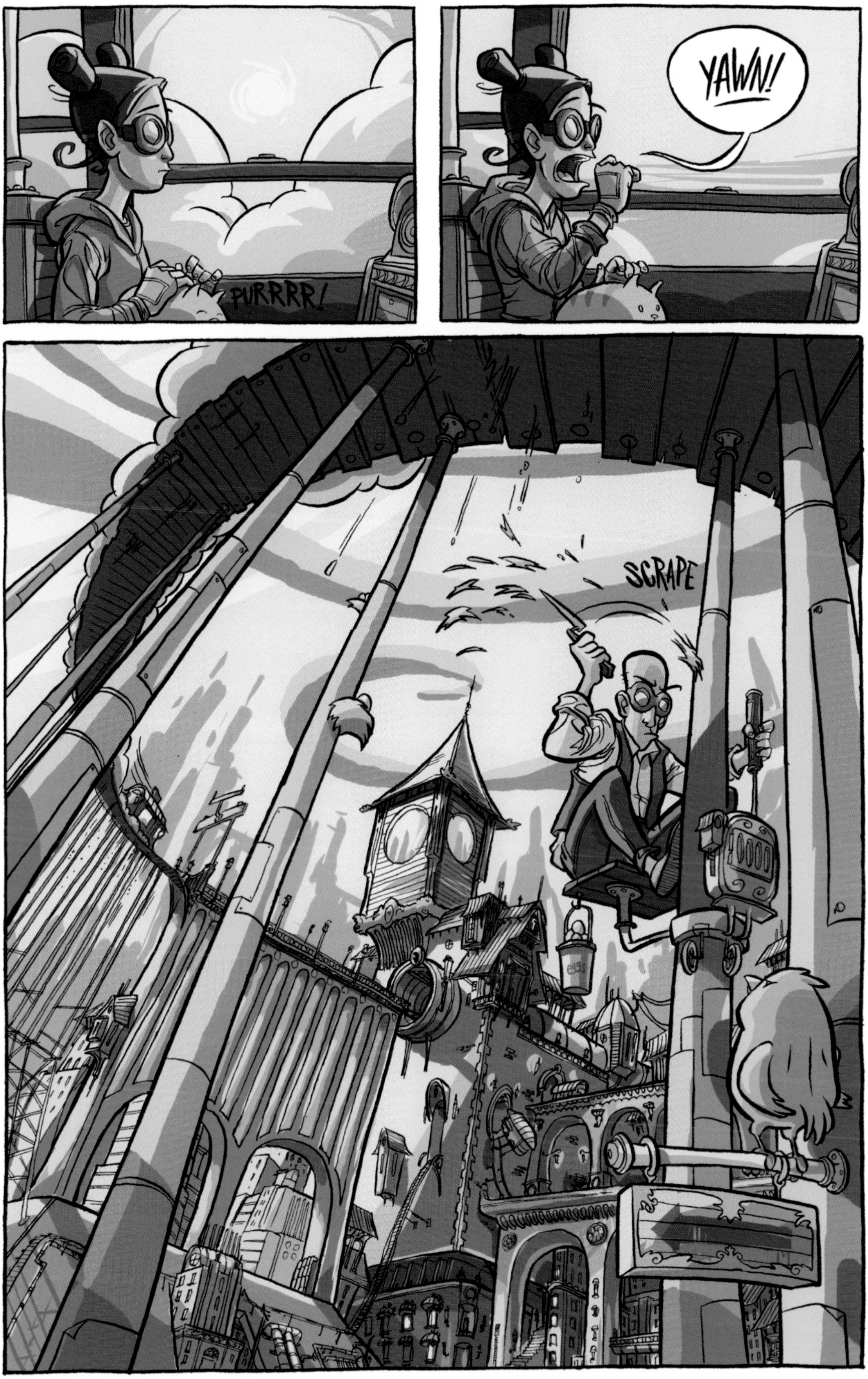
PURRRR!
YAWN!
SCRAPE
EGGS

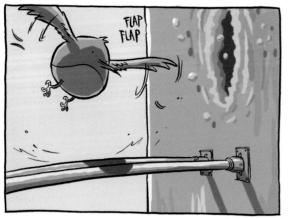

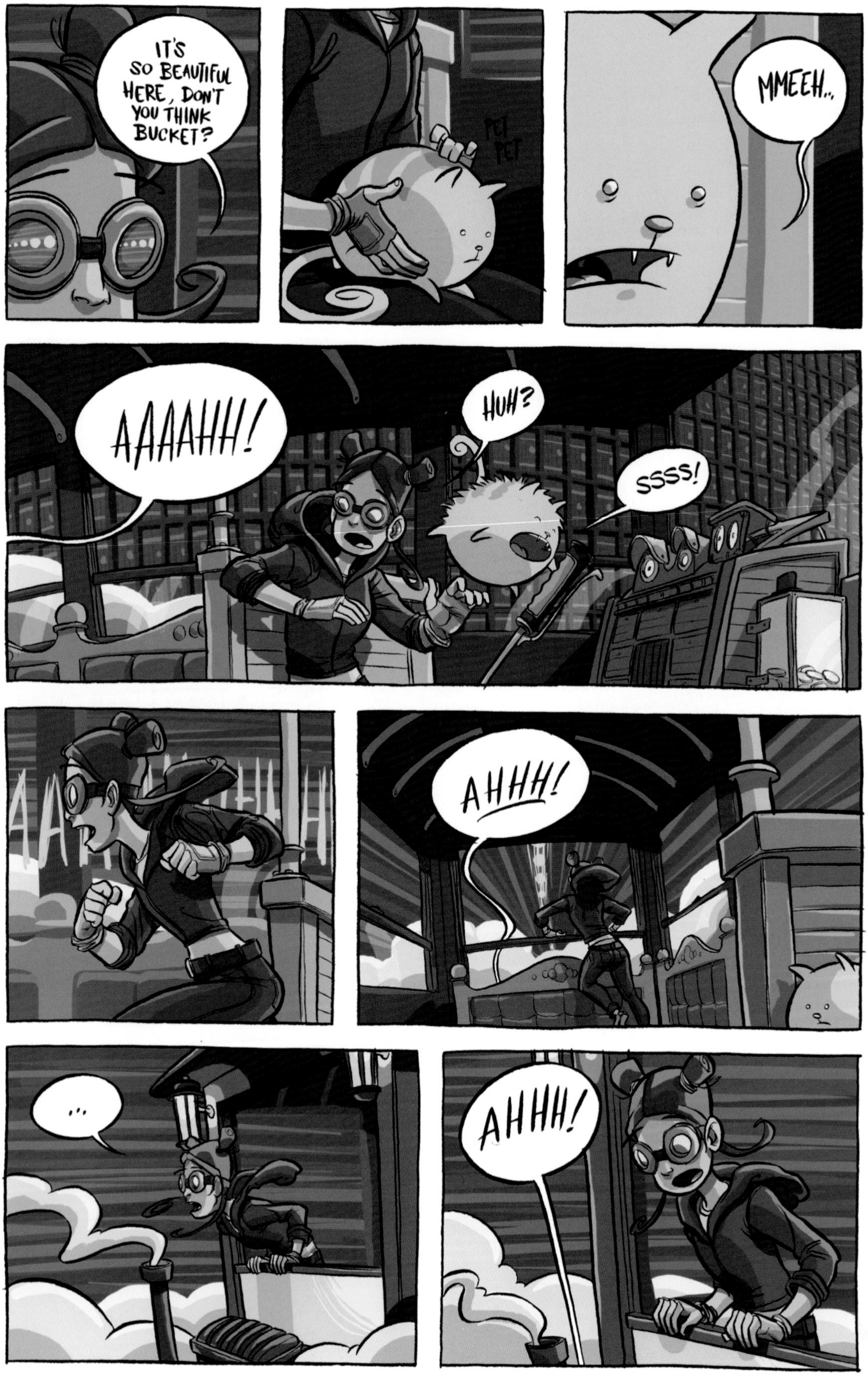
IT'S SO BEAUTIFUL HERE, DON'T YOU THINK BUCKET?
PET PET
MMEEH...
AAAAHH!
HUH?
SSSS!
AHHH!
...
AHHH!

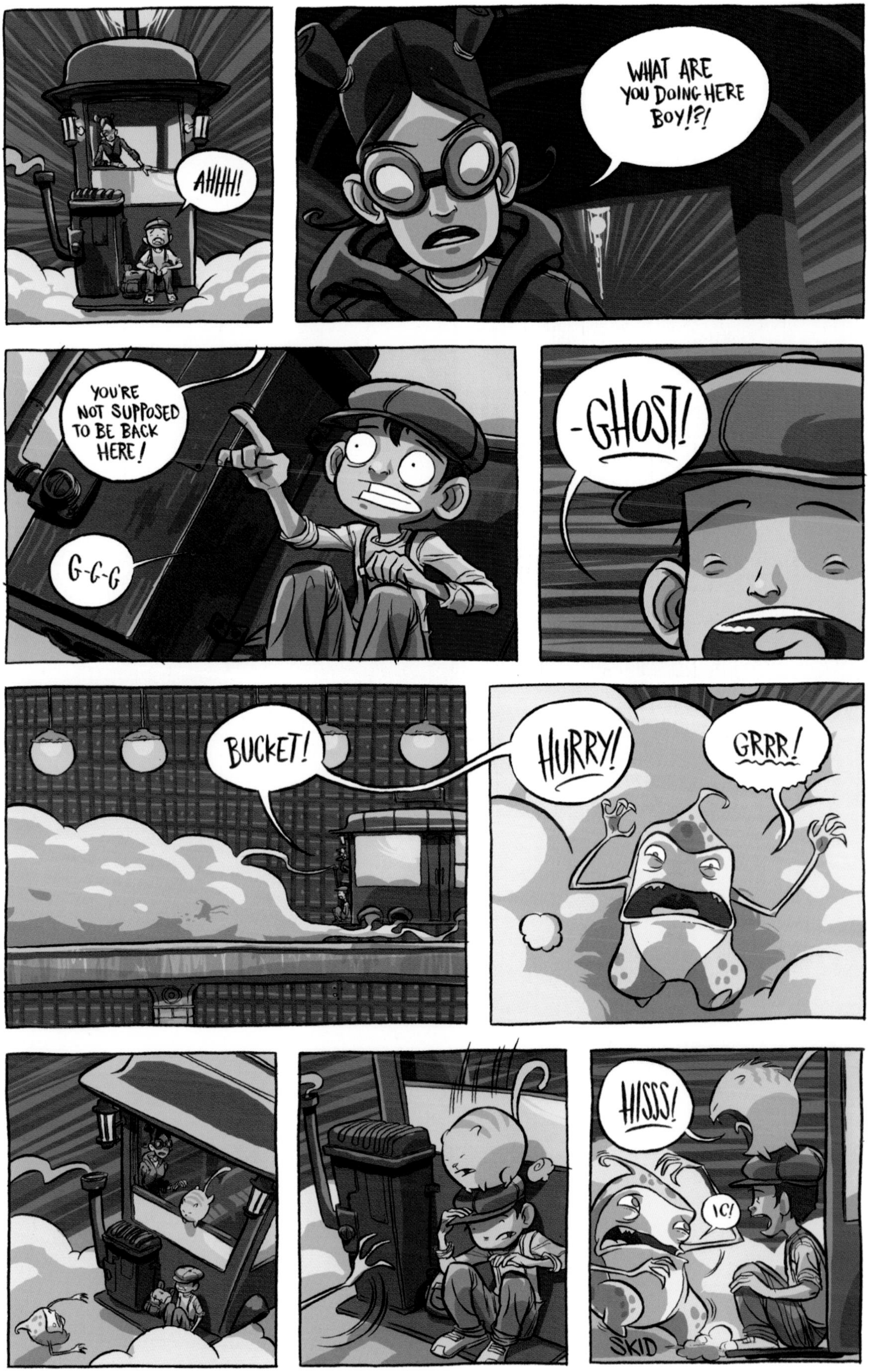
AHHH!
WHAT ARE YOU DOING HERE BOY!?!
YOU'RE NOT SUPPOSED TO BE BACK HERE!
G-G-G
-GHOST!
BUCKET!
HURRY!
GRRR!
HISSS!
IC!
SKID

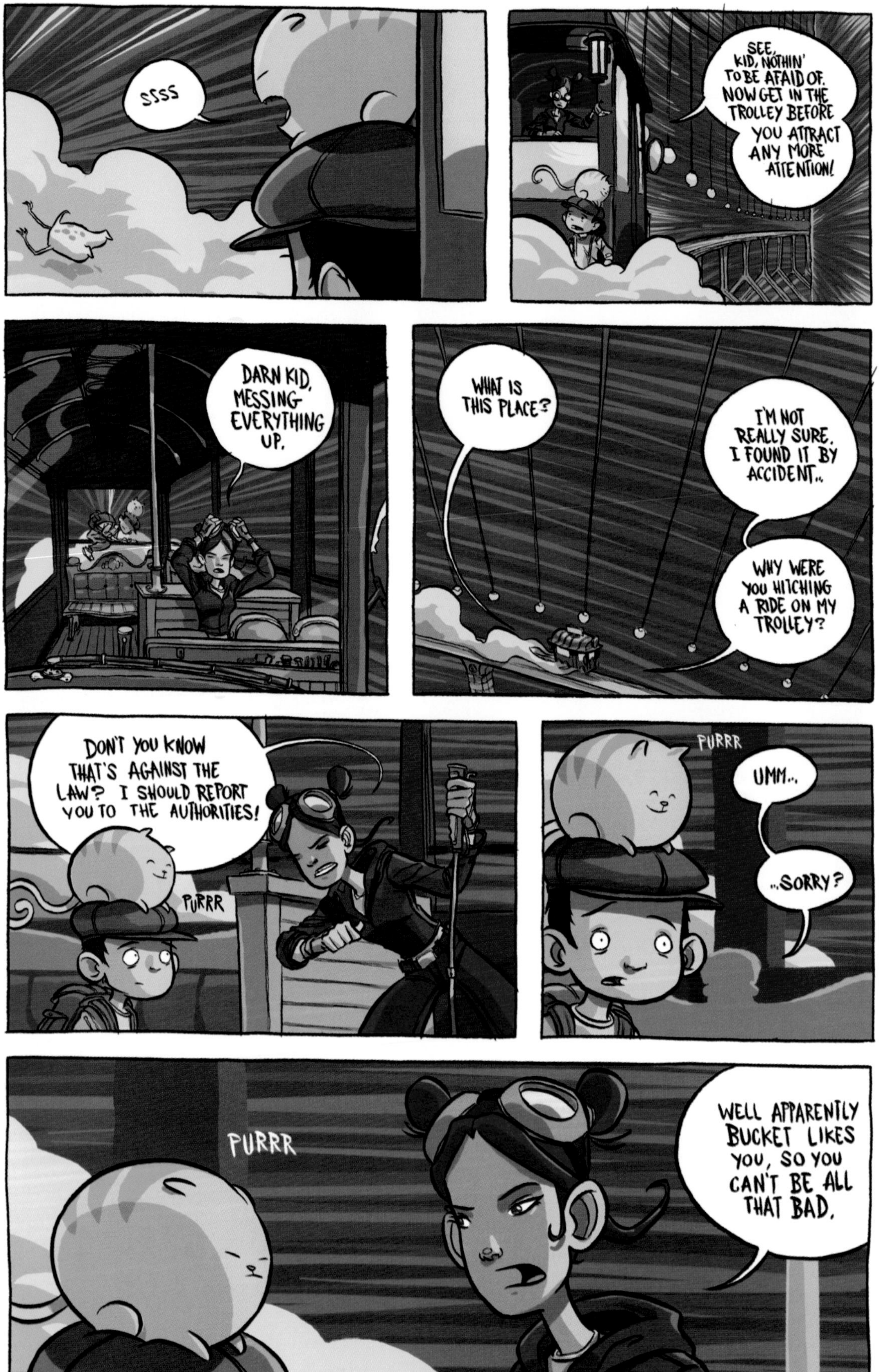
SSSS
SEE, KID, NOTHIN' TO BE AFAID OF. NOW GET IN THE TROLLEY BEFORE YOU ATTRACT ANY MORE ATTENTION!
DARN KID, MESSING EVERYTHING UP.
WHAT IS THIS PLACE?
I'M NOT REALLY SURE. I FOUND IT BY ACCIDENT..
WHY WERE YOU HITCHING A RIDE ON MY TROLLEY?
DON'T YOU KNOW THAT'S AGAINST THE LAW? I SHOULD REPORT YOU TO THE AUTHORITIES!
PURRR
PURRR
UMM..
..SORRY?
PURRR
WELL APPARENTLY BUCKET LIKES YOU, SO YOU CAN'T BE ALL THAT BAD.

YEP.

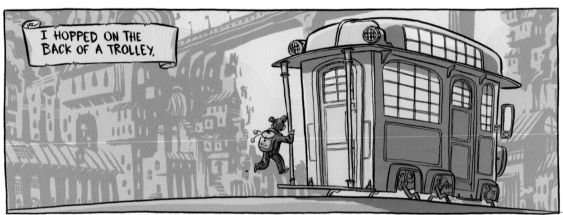

I HOPPED ON THE BACK OF A TROLLEY.

IT WAS SO BEAUTIFUL...

... I'D NEVER RIDDEN ON A TROLLEY BEFORE.

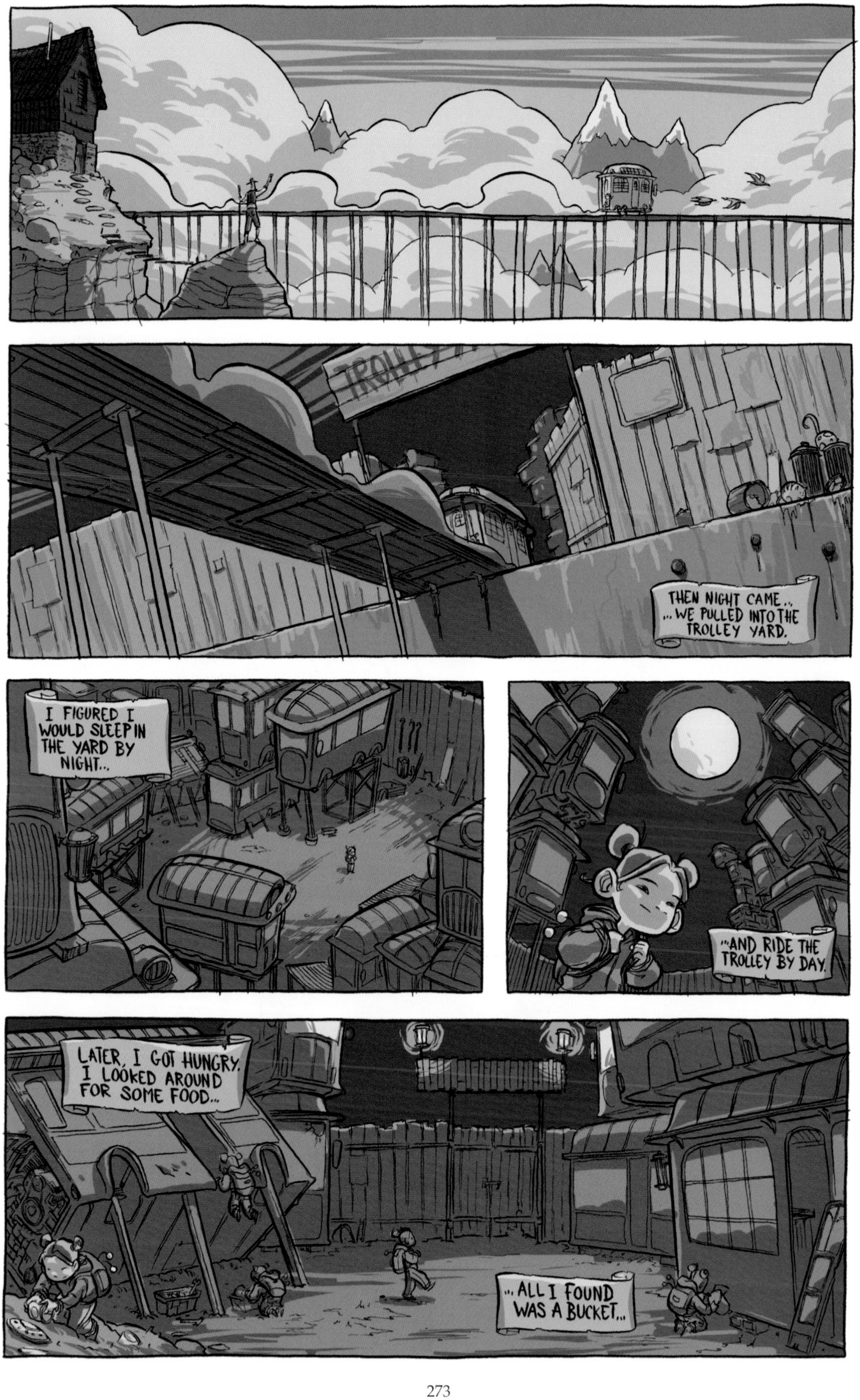
THEN NIGHT CAME...
...WE PULLED INTO THE TROLLEY YARD.
I FIGURED I WOULD SLEEP IN THE YARD BY NIGHT...
...AND RIDE THE TROLLEY BY DAY.
LATER, I GOT HUNGRY. I LOOKED AROUND FOR SOME FOOD...
...ALL I FOUND WAS A BUCKET...

276

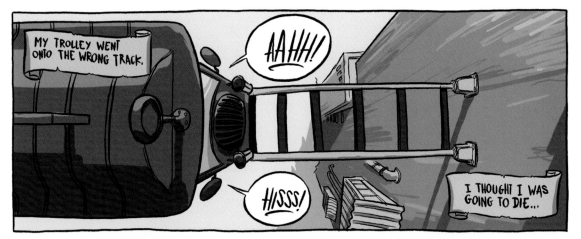

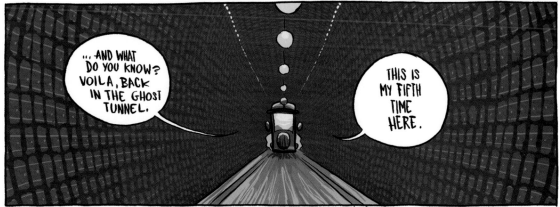

279

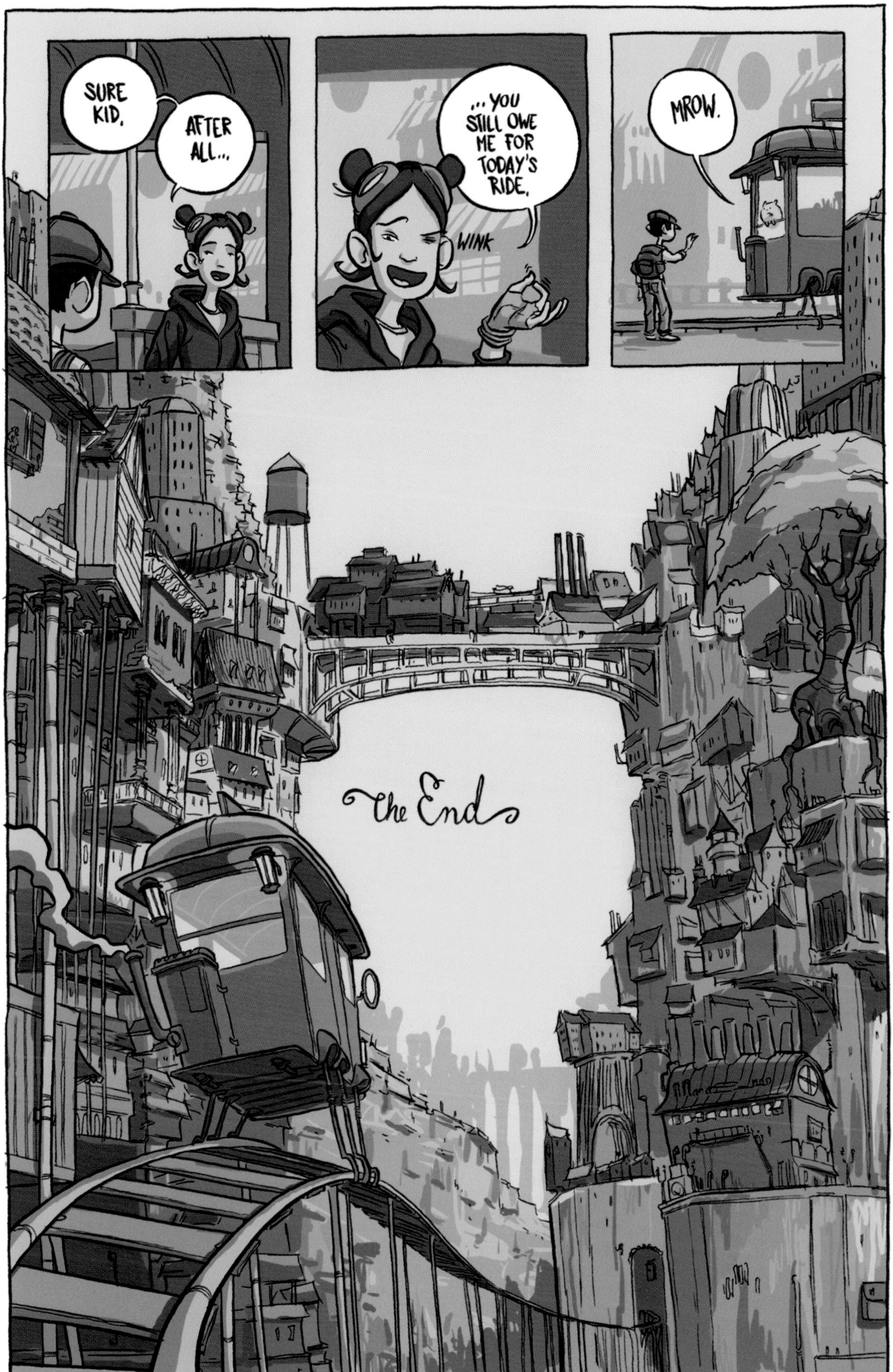
SURE KID.
AFTER ALL...
...YOU STILL OWE ME FOR TODAY'S RIDE.
WINK
MROW.
the End

Wilford's Stroll

by
Justin Ridge

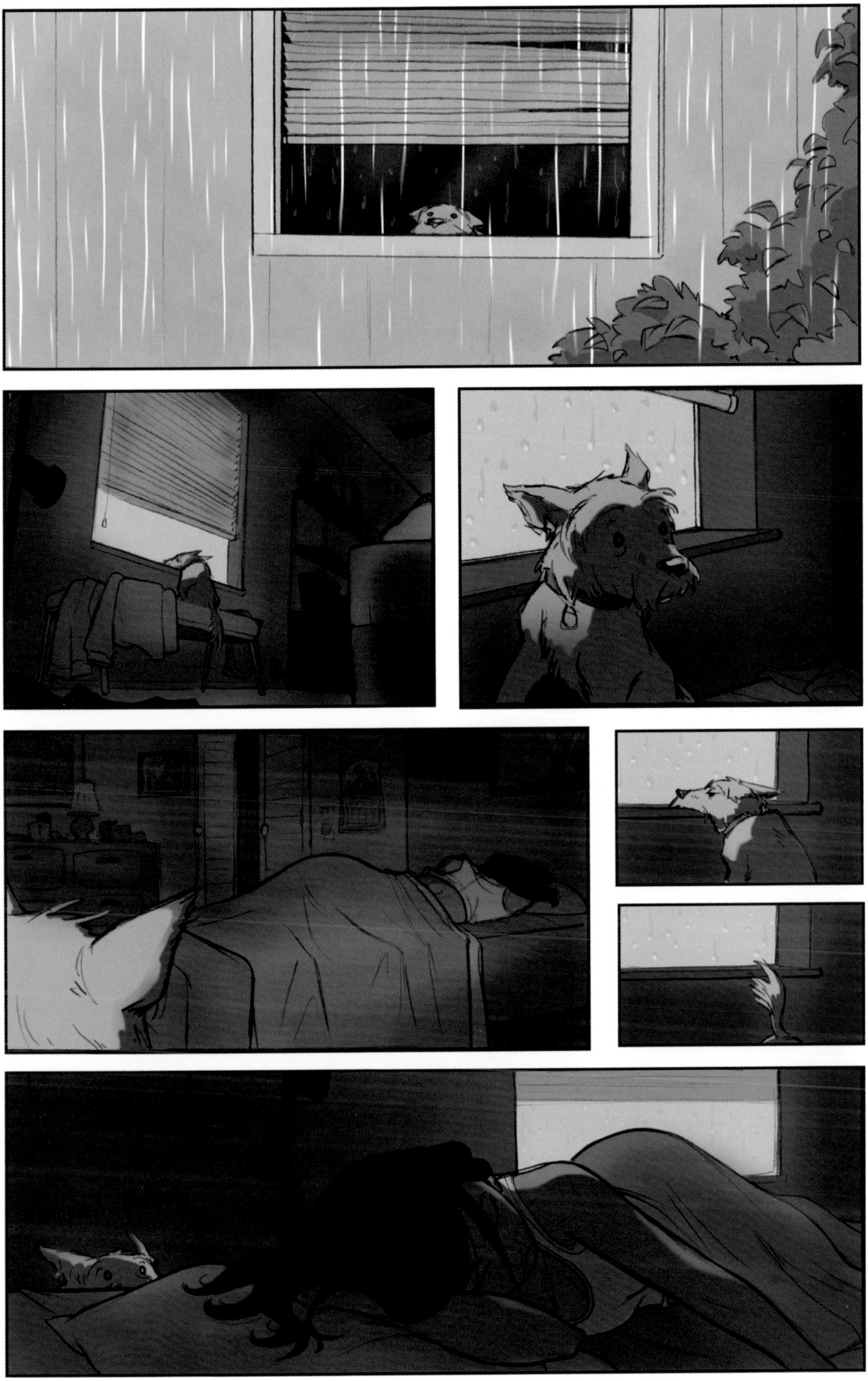

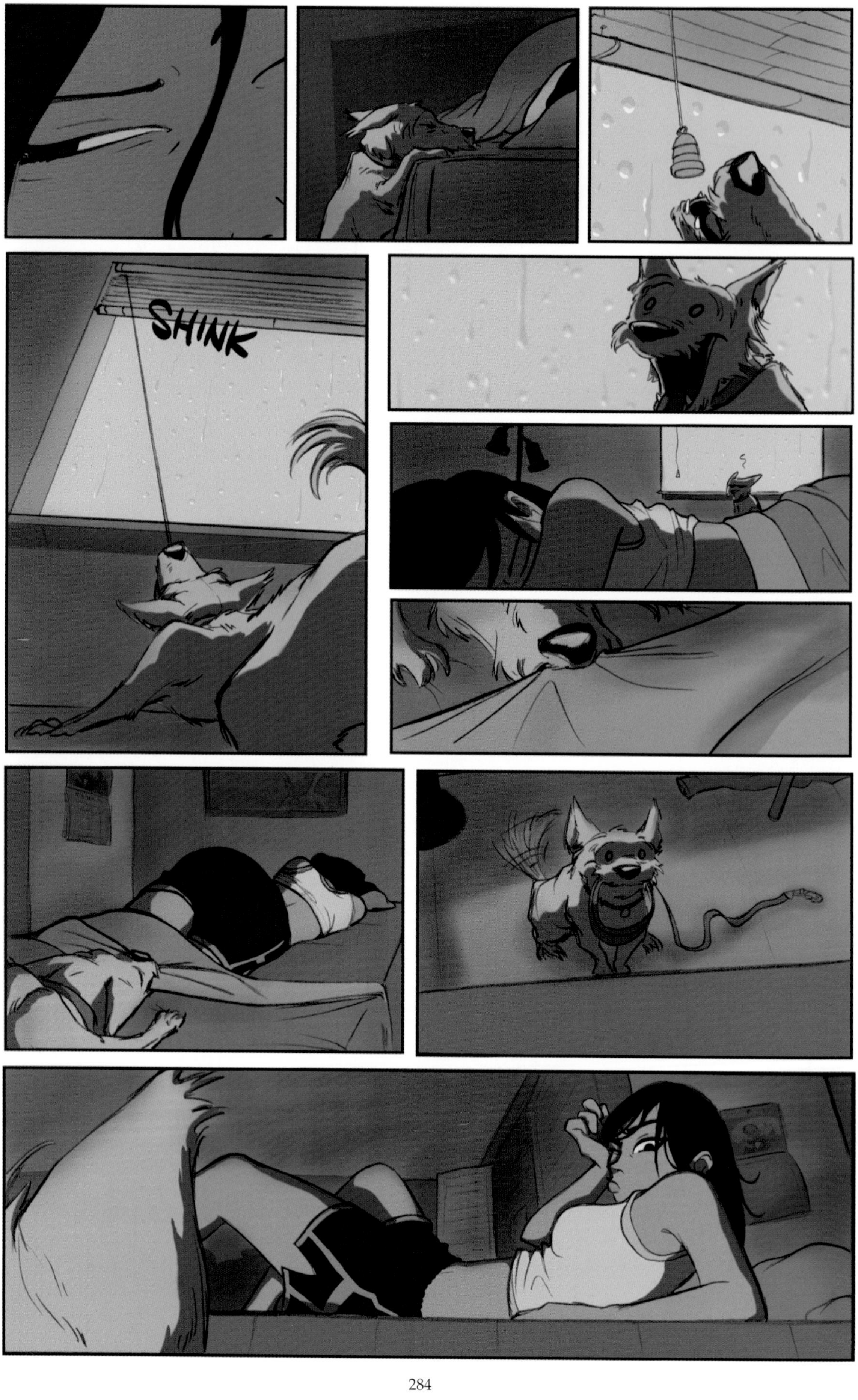
SHINK

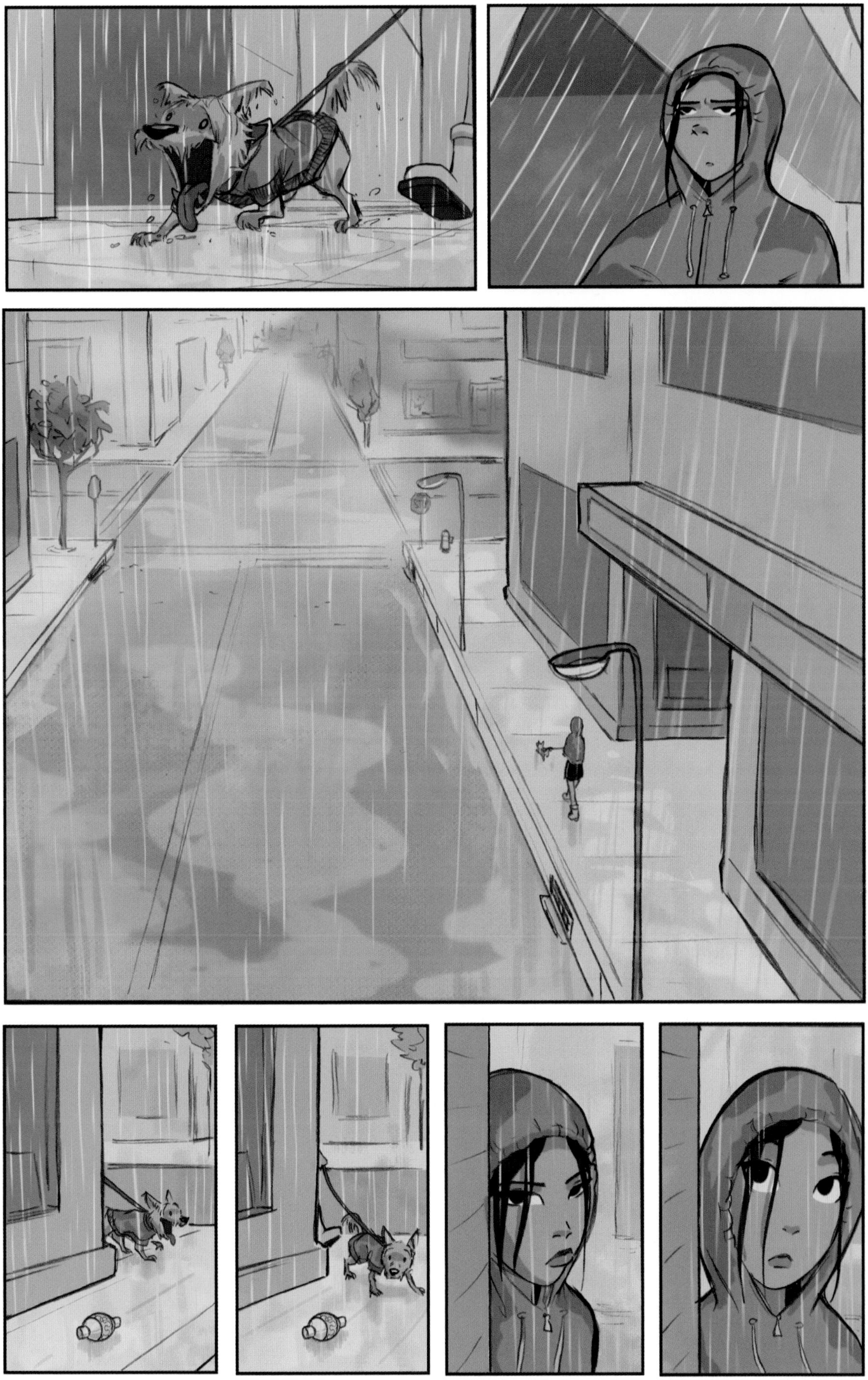

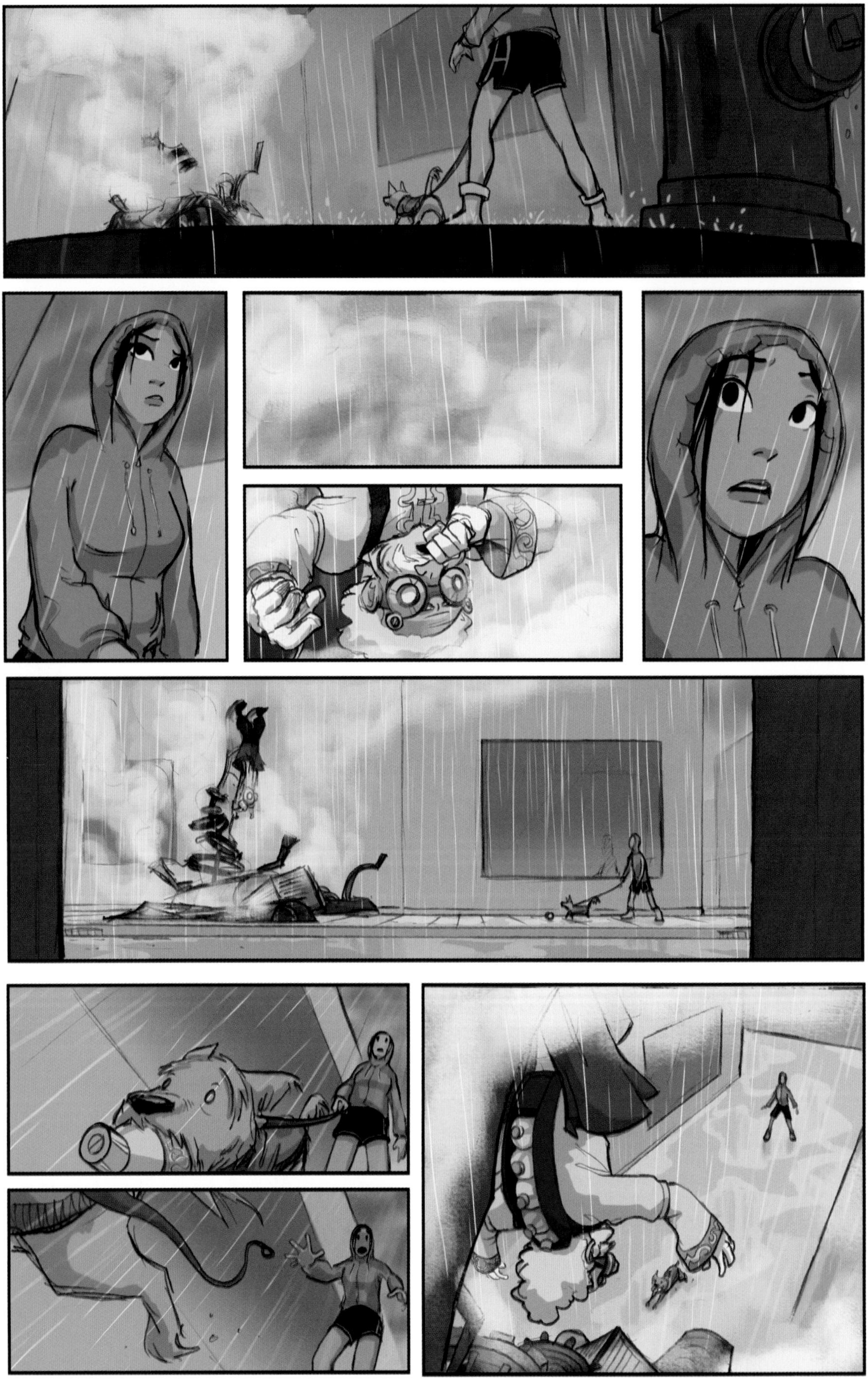

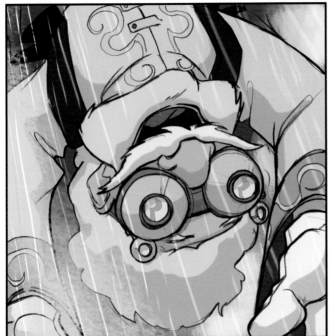

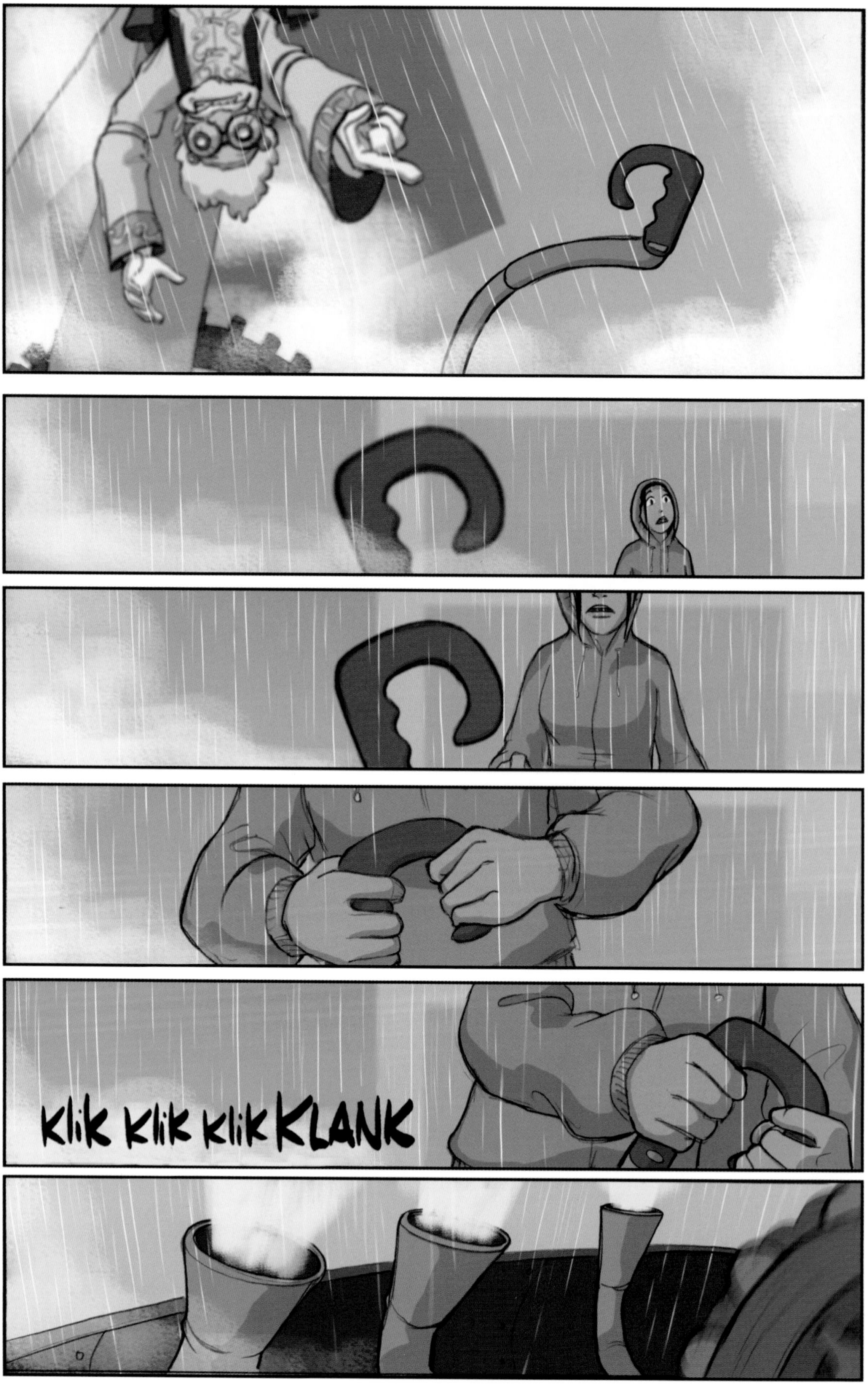
KLIK KLIK KLIK KLANK

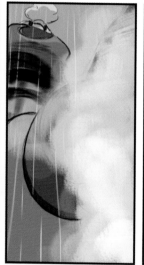

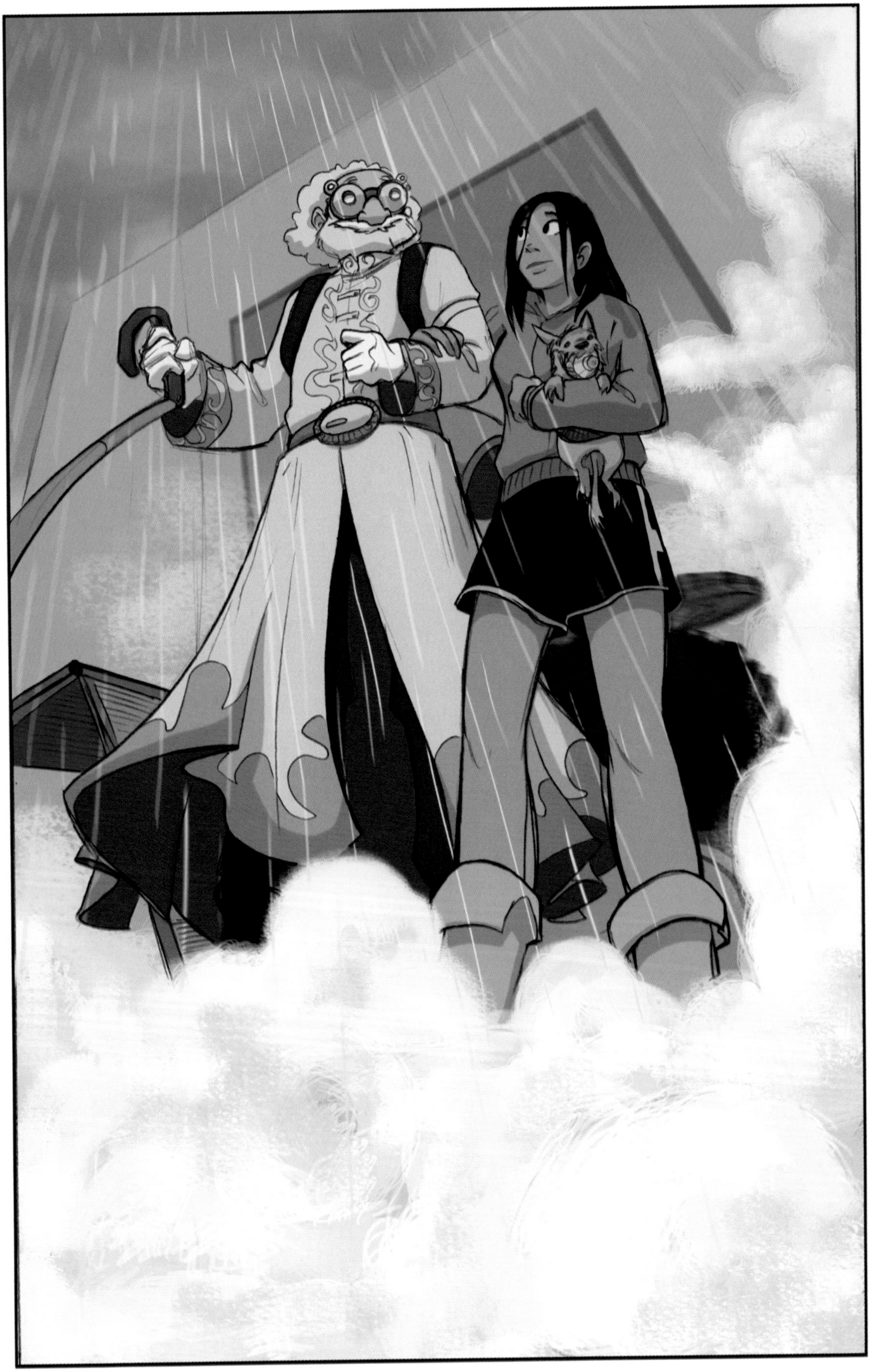

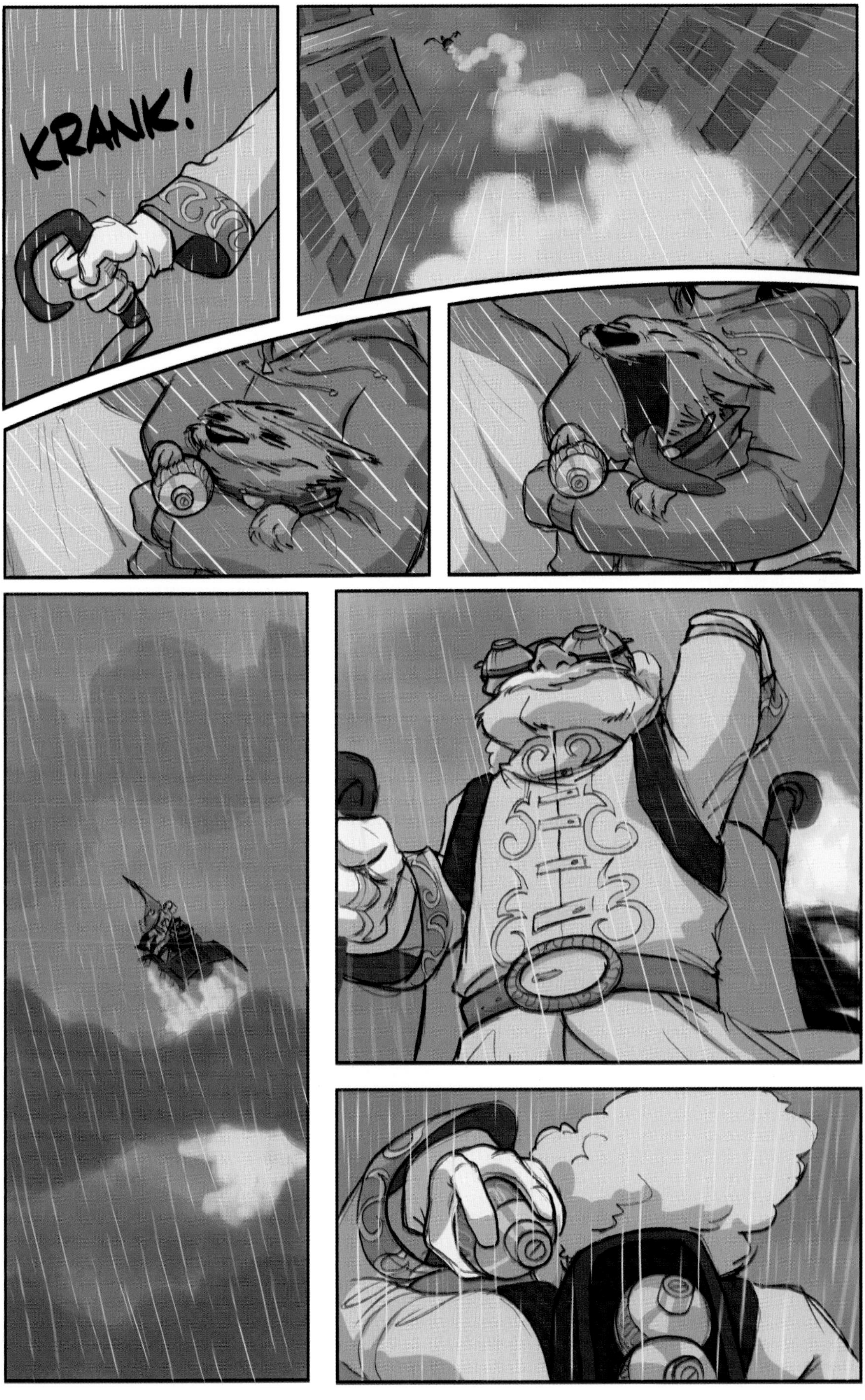
KRANK!

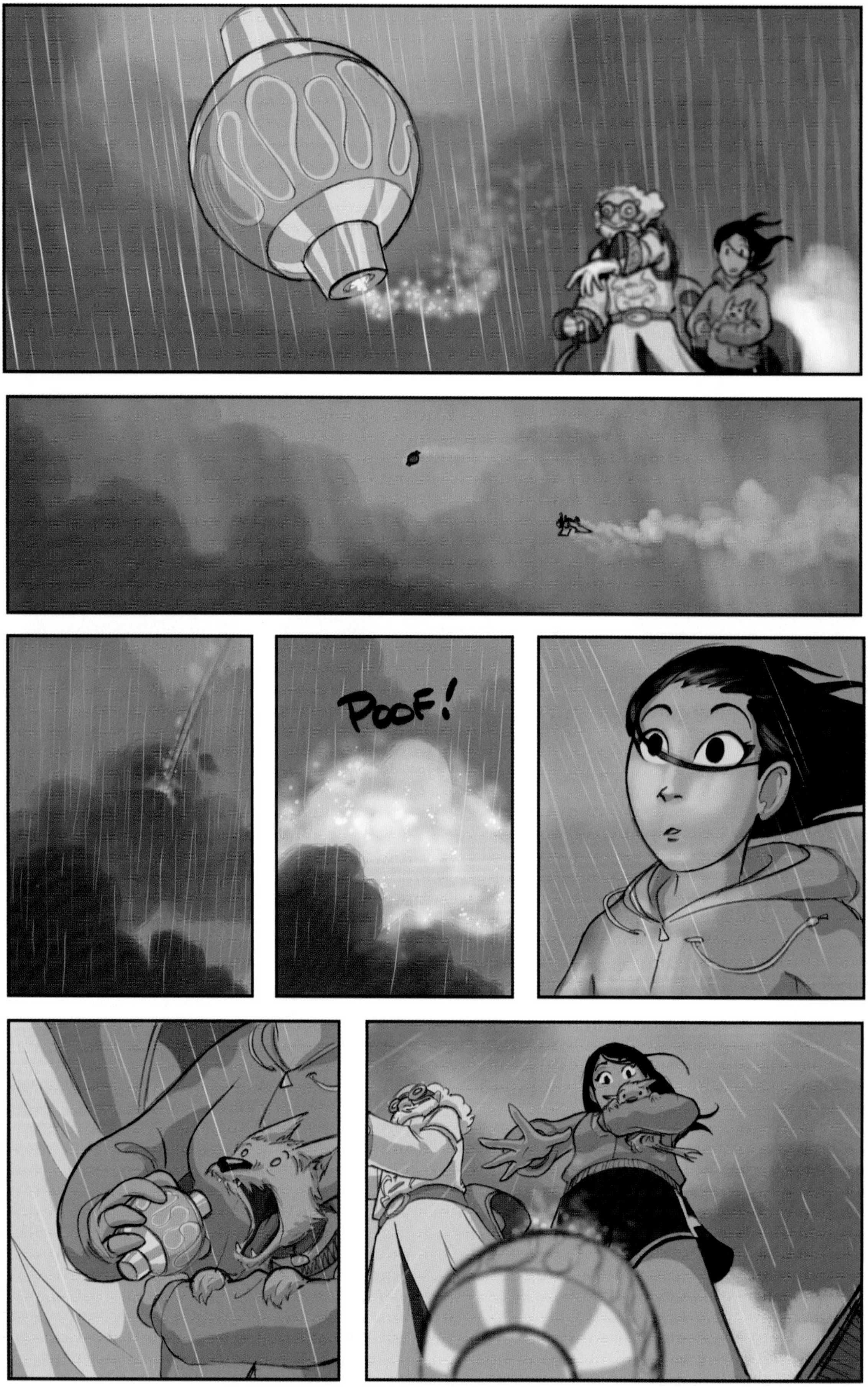
POOF!

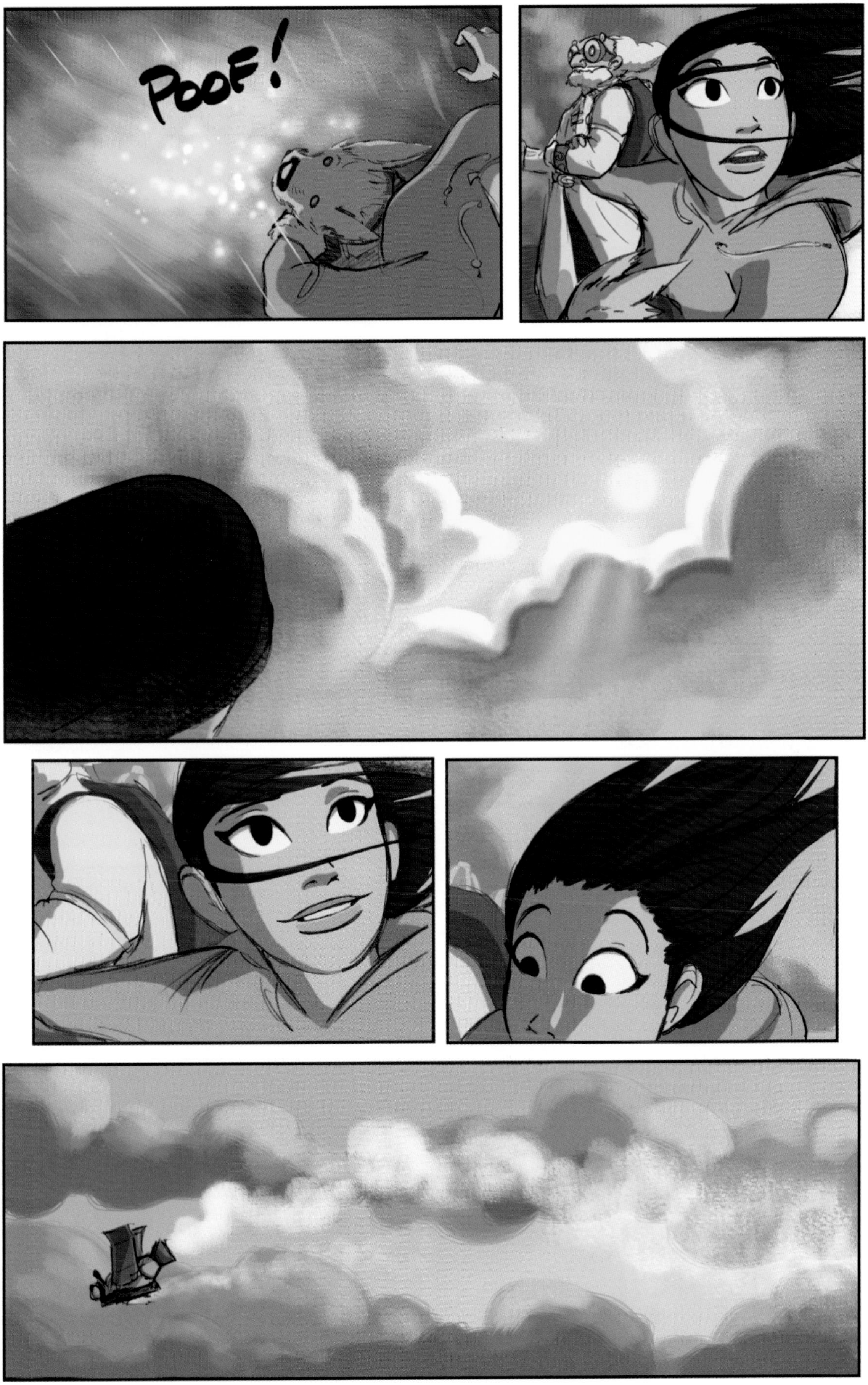
POOF!

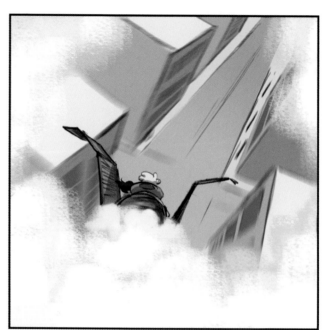

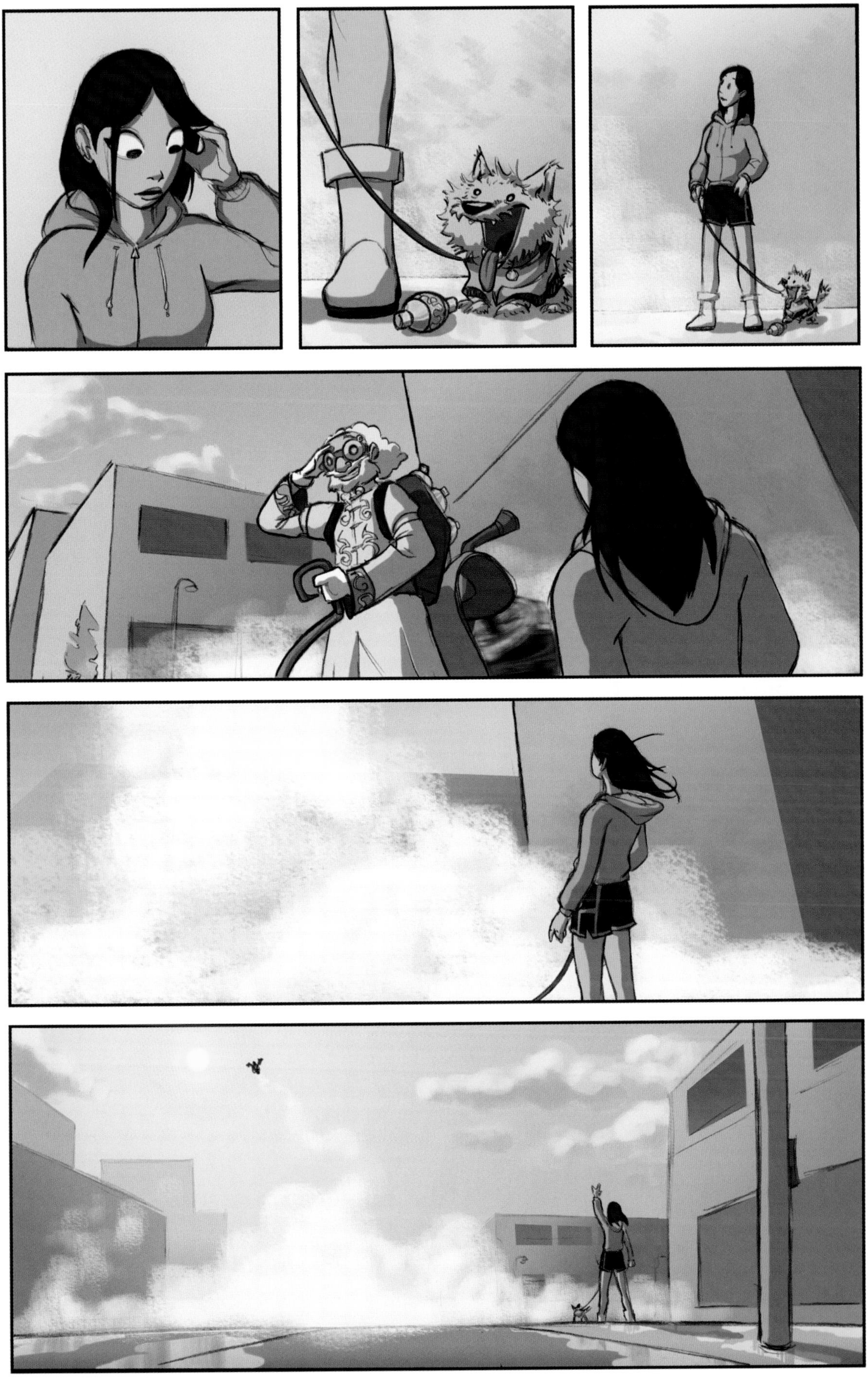

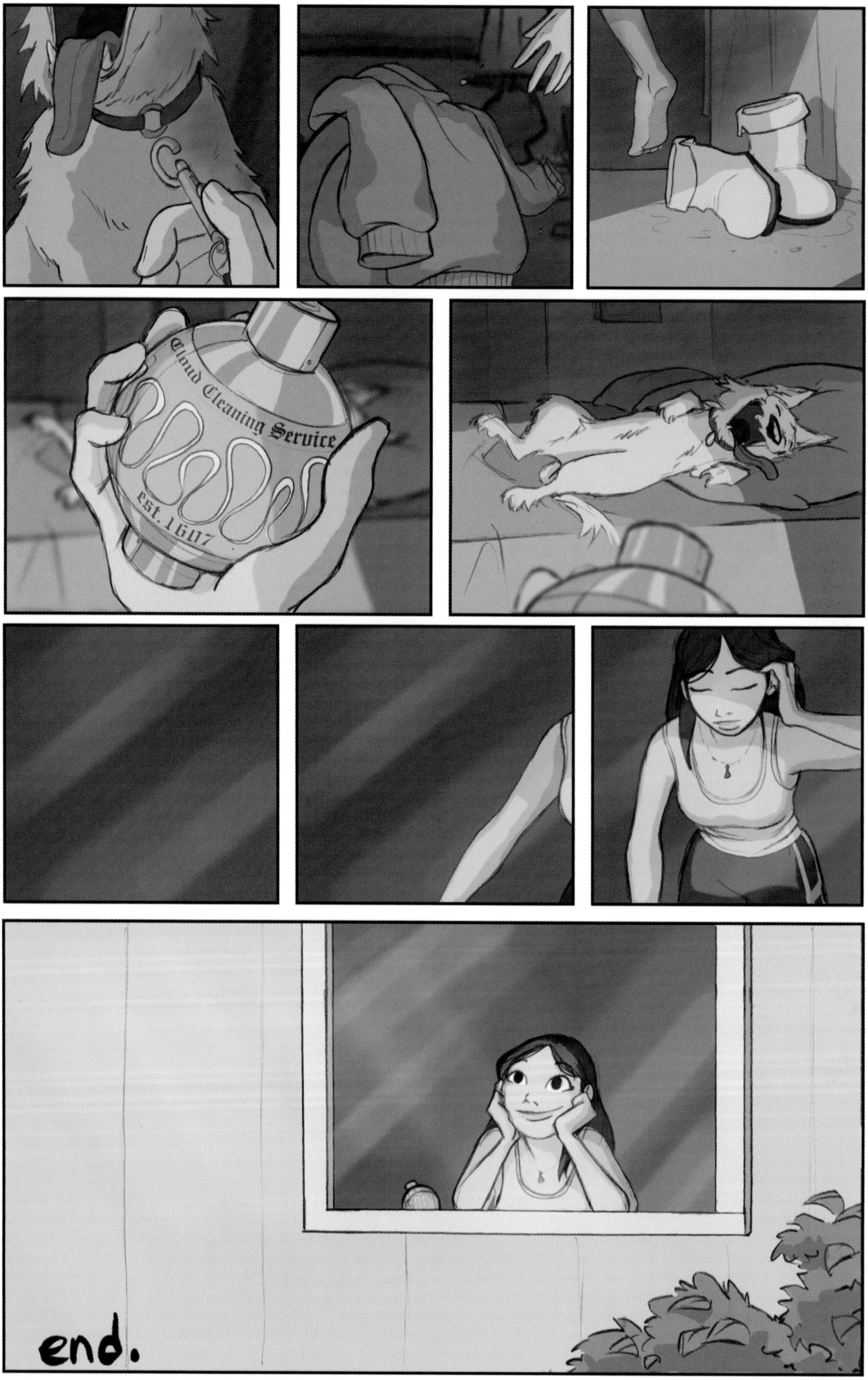
Cloud Cleaning Service
est. 1607
end.

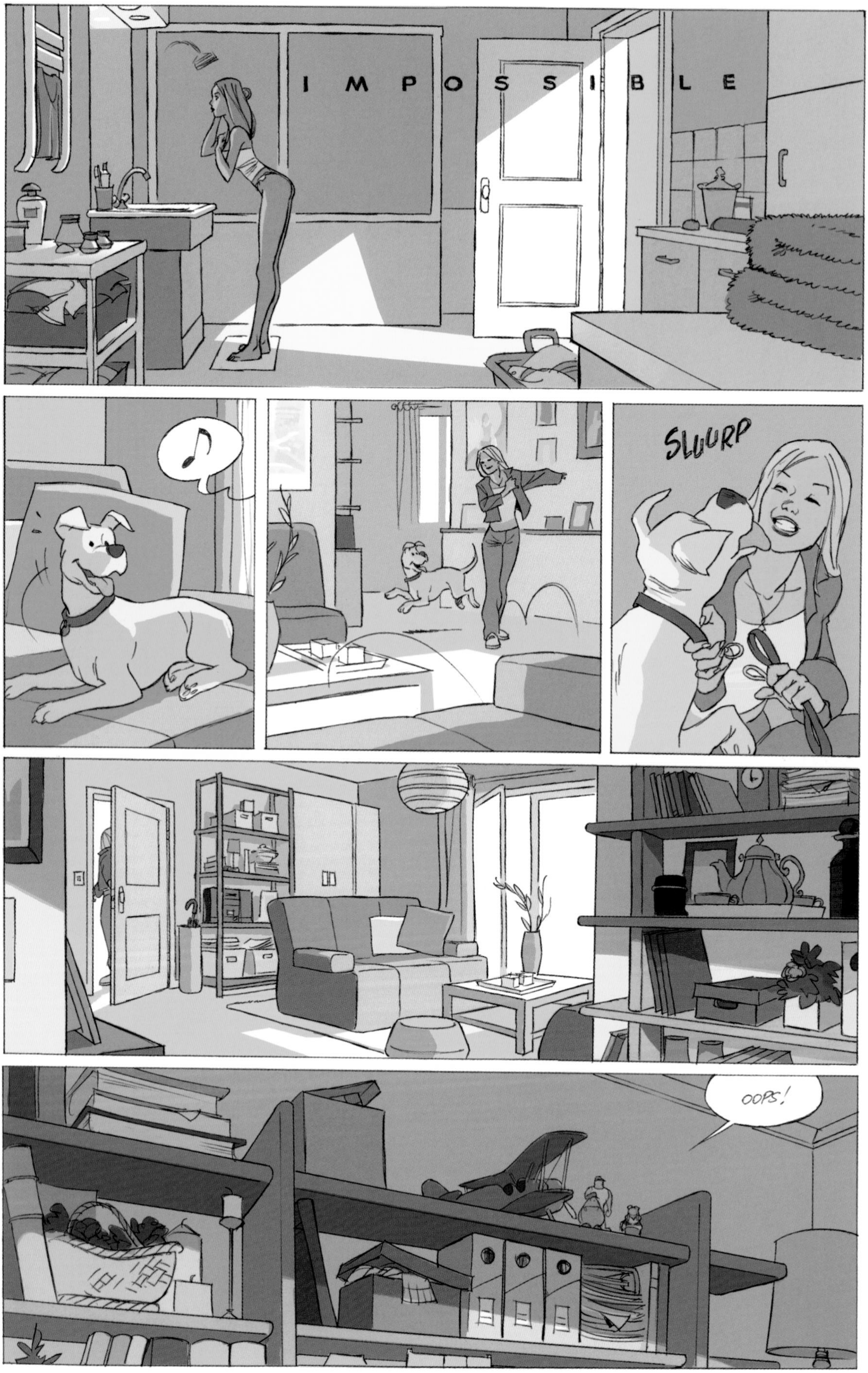

IMPOSSIBLE
SLUURP
OOPS!

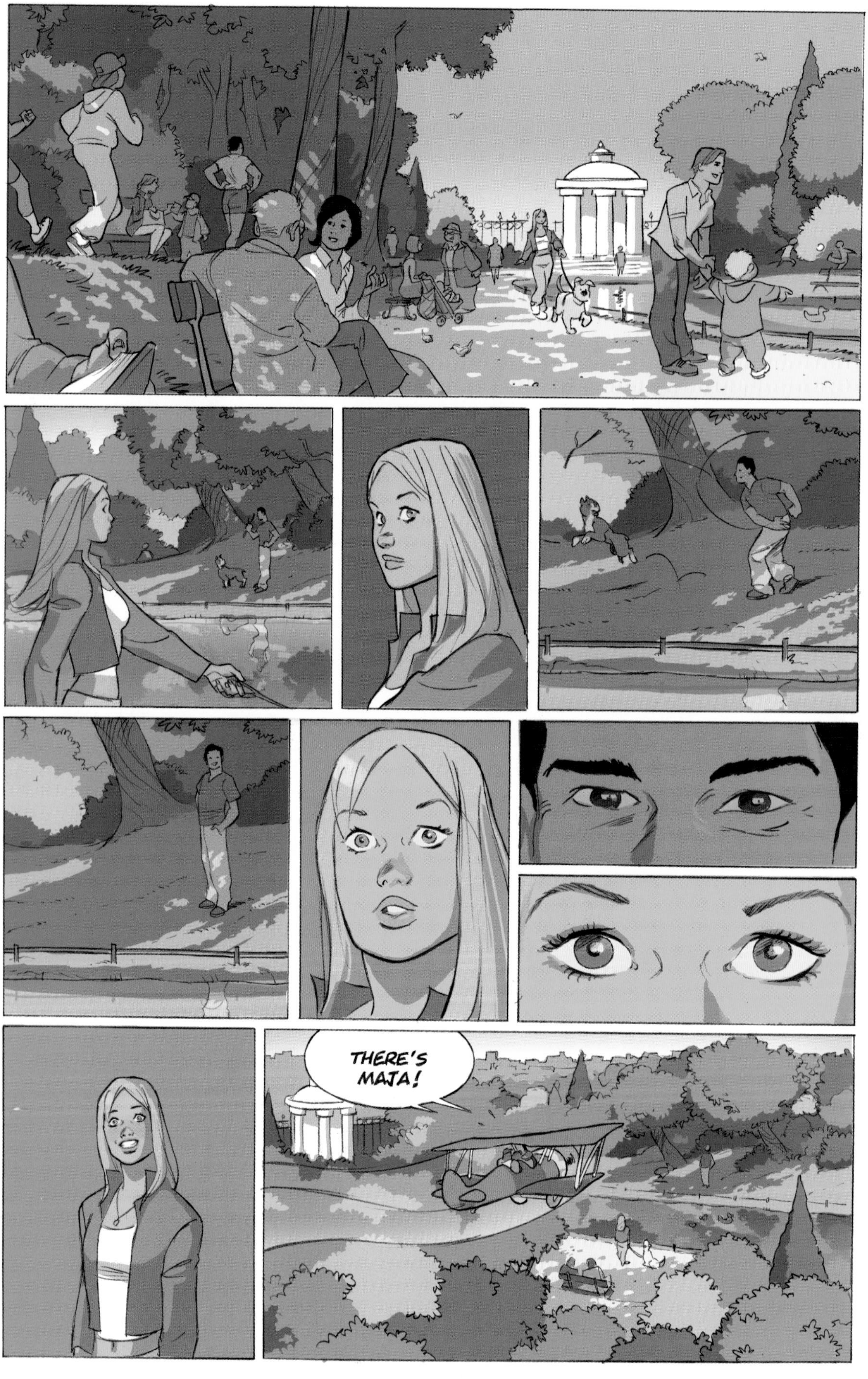
THERE'S MAJA!

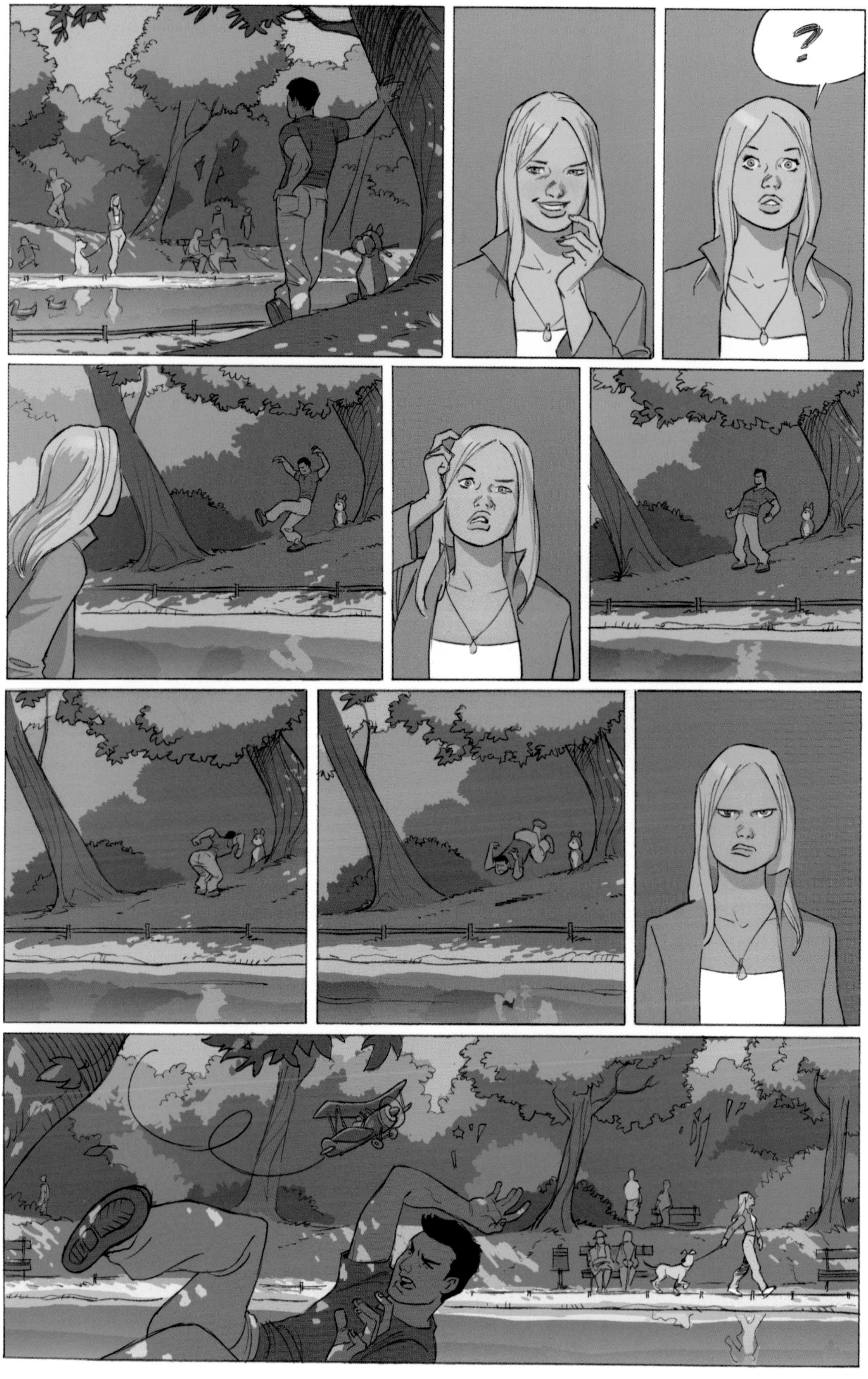
?

IMPOSSIBLE

ILLUSTRATIONS BY **HERVAL**   STORY BY **ARIS**

Dust on the Shelves

Story and Art
Bannister

Colors
Corentin Jaffré

Thanks to
Dean Trippe
for the english adaptation.

AFTER MY MOVE TO THE BIG CITY, I VERY QUICKLY DISCOVERED THE COMICS STORE.

COMICS · B.D · NOVE

HELLO.

HI.

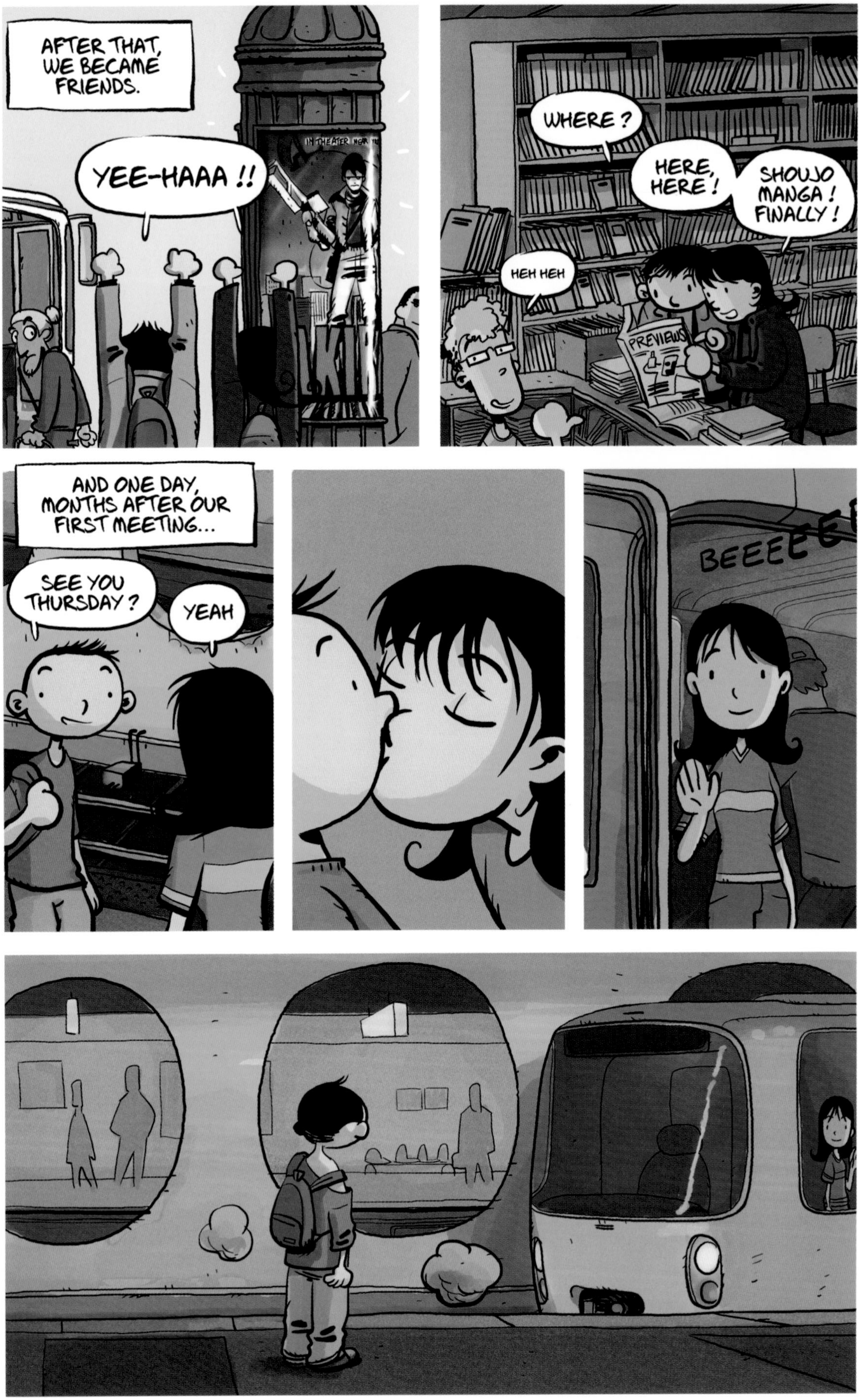
AFTER THAT, WE BECAME FRIENDS.
YEE-HAAA !!
WHERE ?
HERE, HERE !
SHOUJO MANGA ! FINALLY !
HEH HEH
PREVIEWS
AND ONE DAY, MONTHS AFTER OUR FIRST MEETING...
SEE YOU THURSDAY ?
YEAH
BEEEEE

WE DON'T GET OVER TO THE BOOKSHOP MUCH NOW, BECAUSE WE LIVE TOO FAR.

BUT EVERYTIME I OPEN THE DOOR —THAT DOESN'T CLOSE WELL— EVERYTHING COMES RIGHT BACK.

THE OLD FRIENDS ARE STILL THERE. THE DUST ON THE SHELVES TOO.

NOTHING'S CHANGED.

AT LEAST, I'M HOPING THESE LITTLE THINGS WON'T.

SOME CHANGES ARE INEVITABLE THOUGH...

IT WAS FIFTEEN YEARS AGO, THE FIRST TIME I STEPPED INTO THIS BOOKSHOP. IT WILL ALWAYS BE THE PLACE MY LIFE CHANGED FOREVER.

COMICS-BD

THE END?

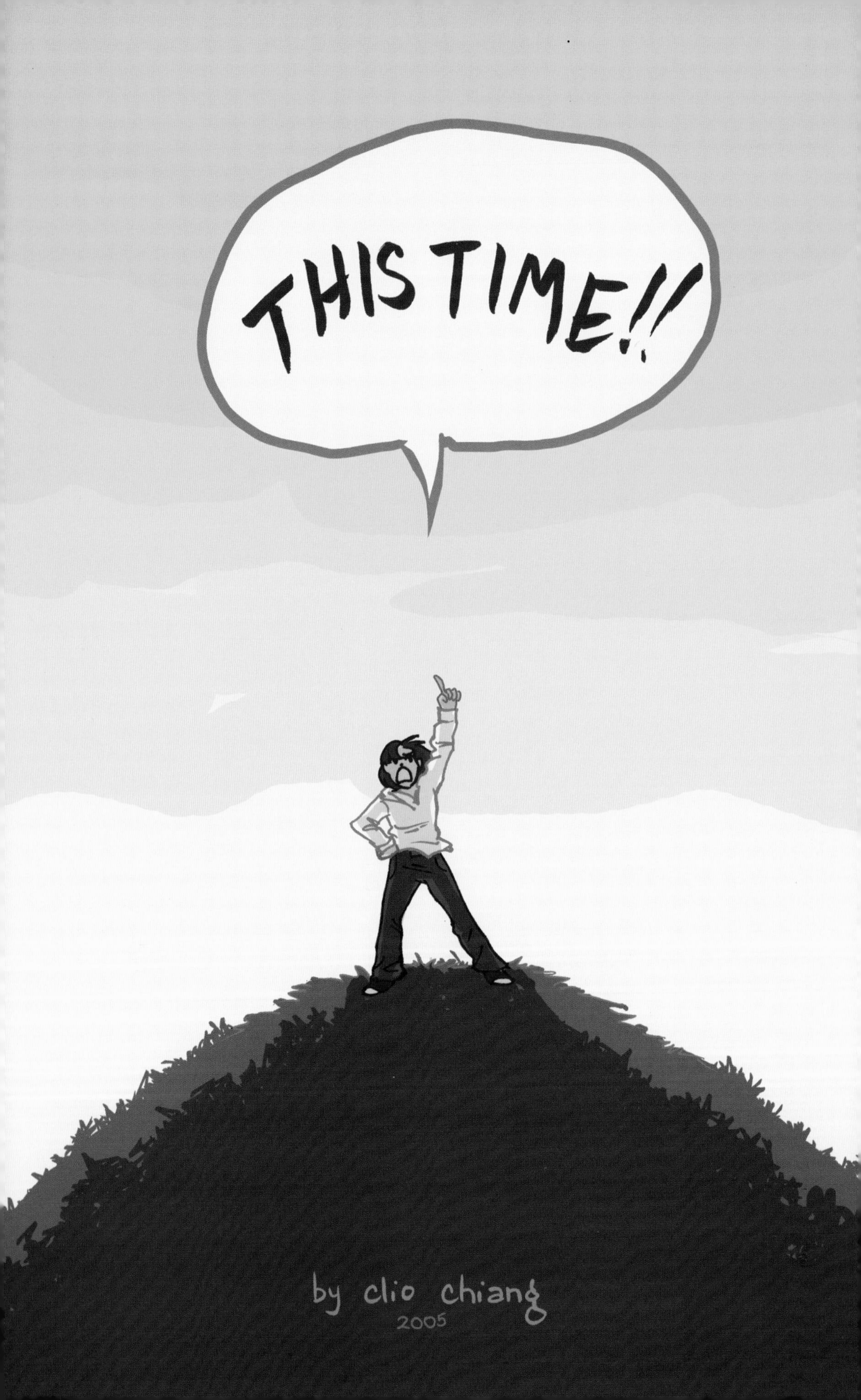
THIS TIME!!
by clio chiang
2005

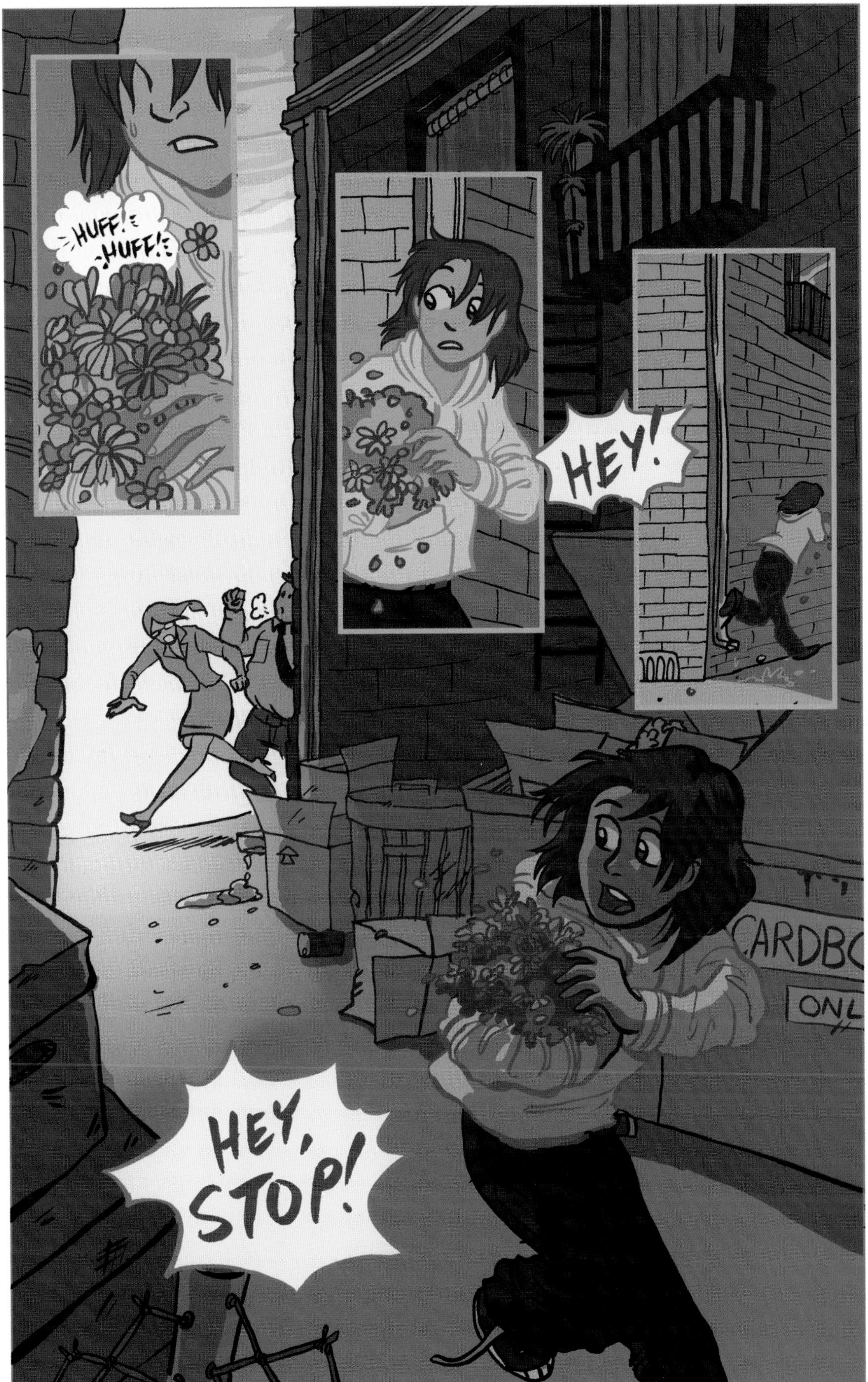
HUFF! HUFF!
HEY!
CARDBO
ONL
HEY, STOP!

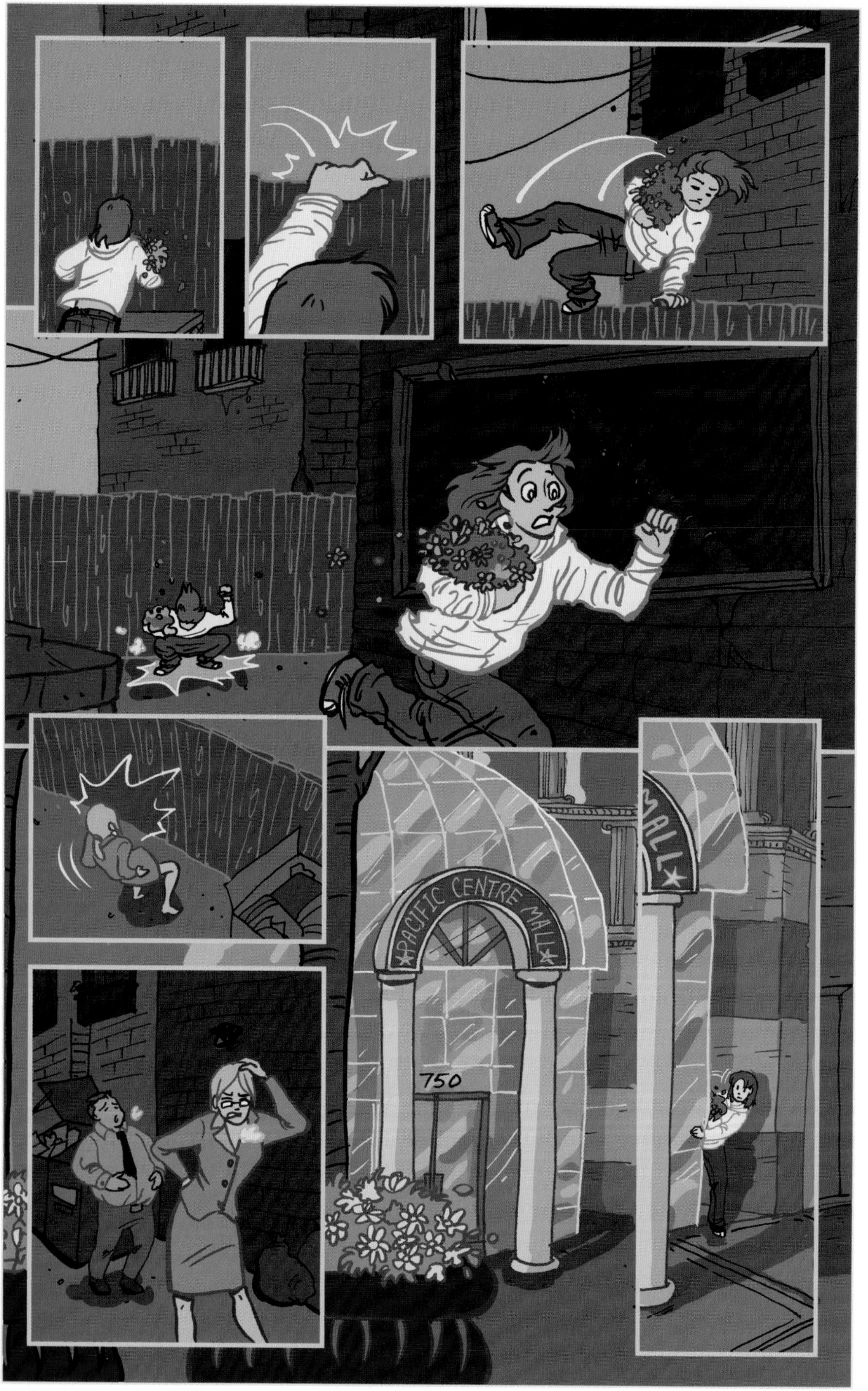
PACIFIC CENTRE MALL
750
MALL

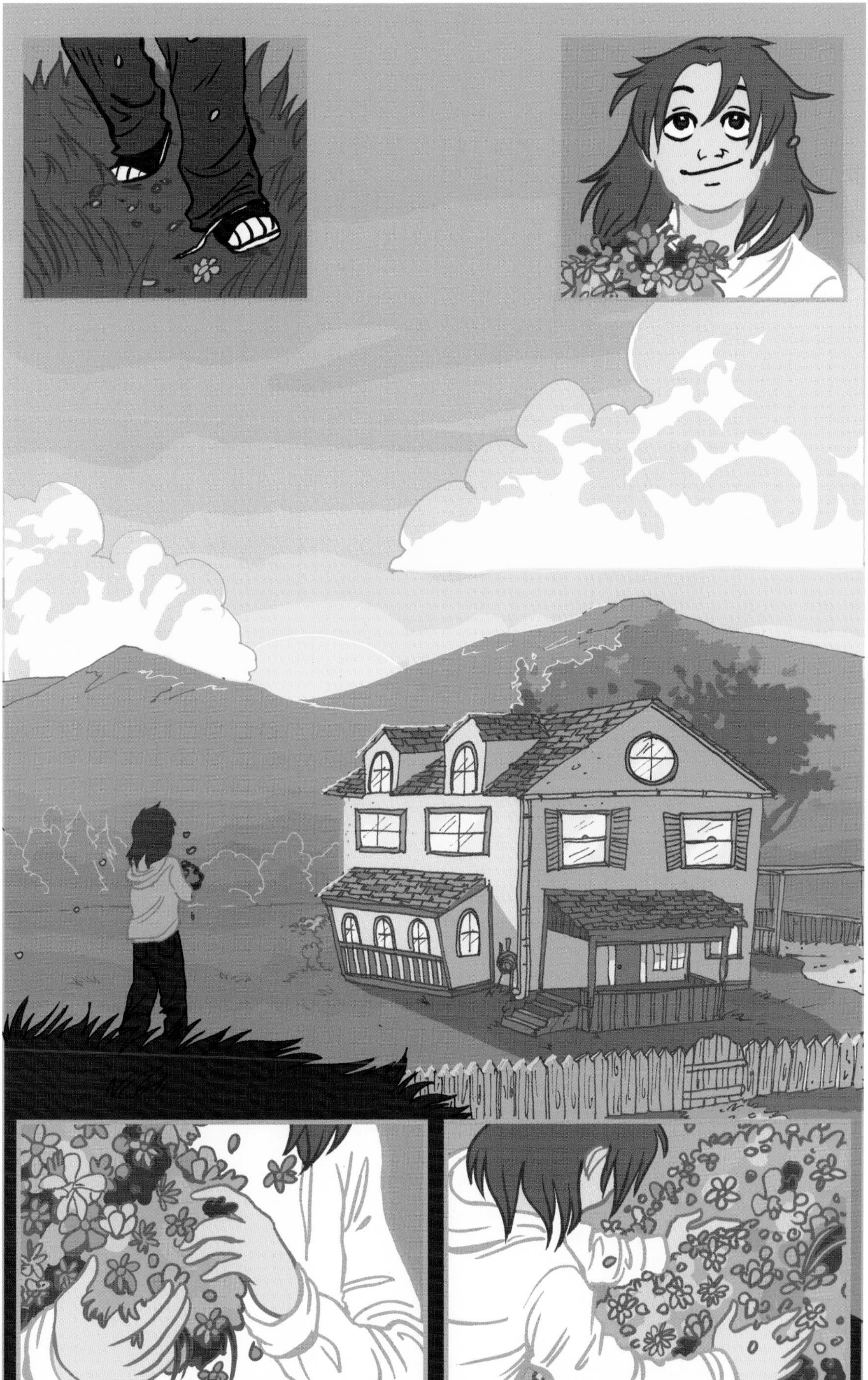

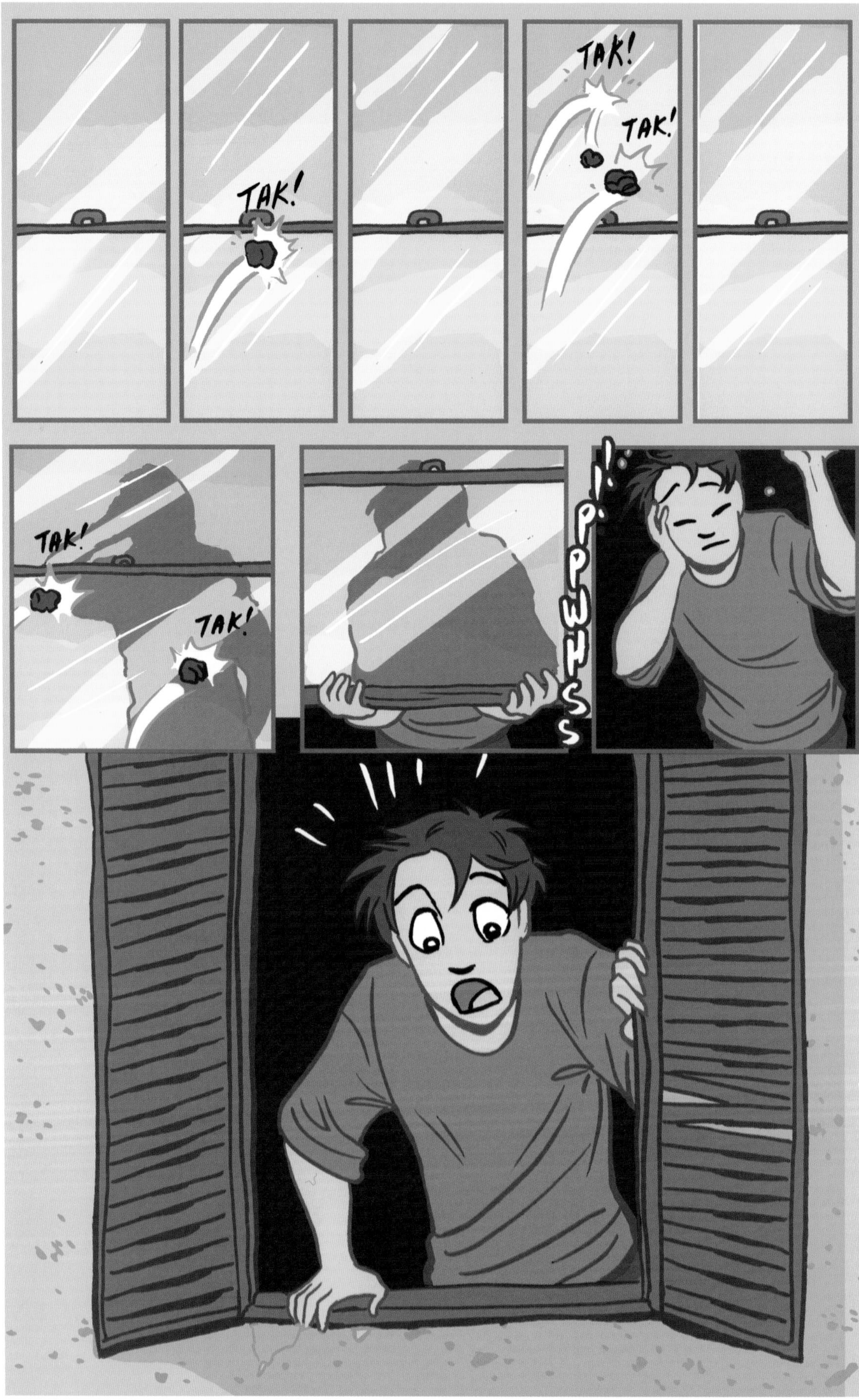
TAK!
TAK!
TAK!
TAK!
TAK!
!!
PPWHSS

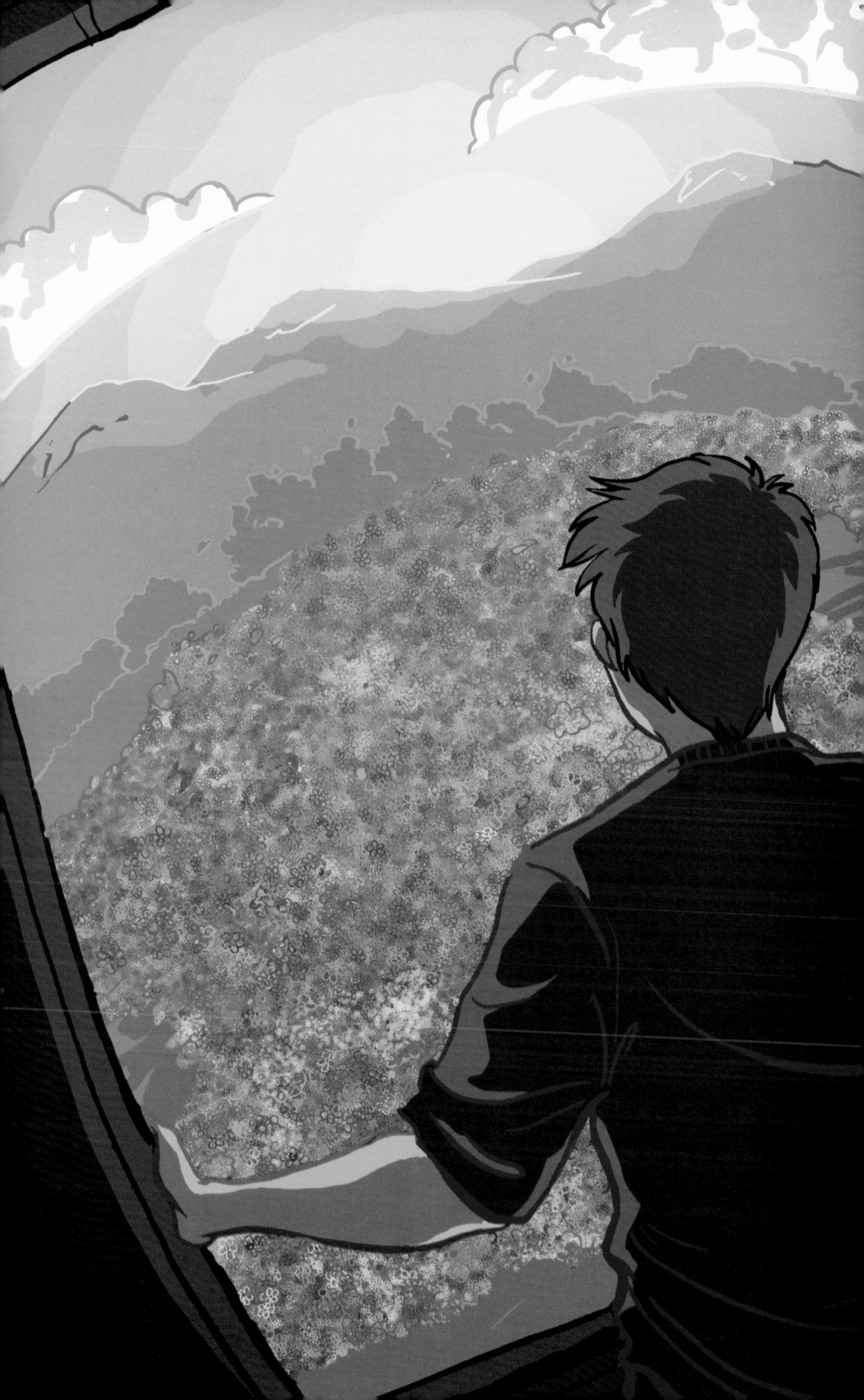

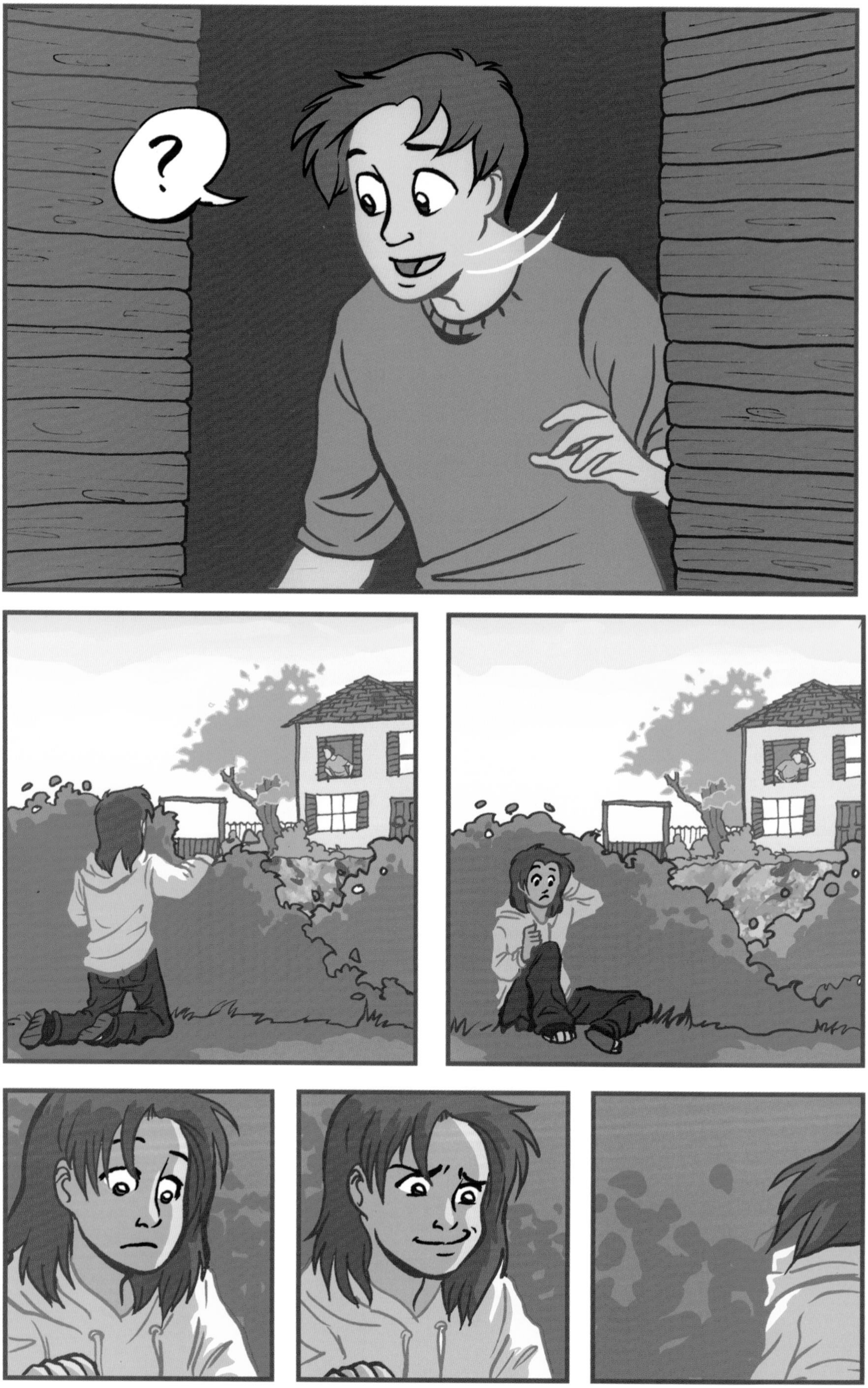
?

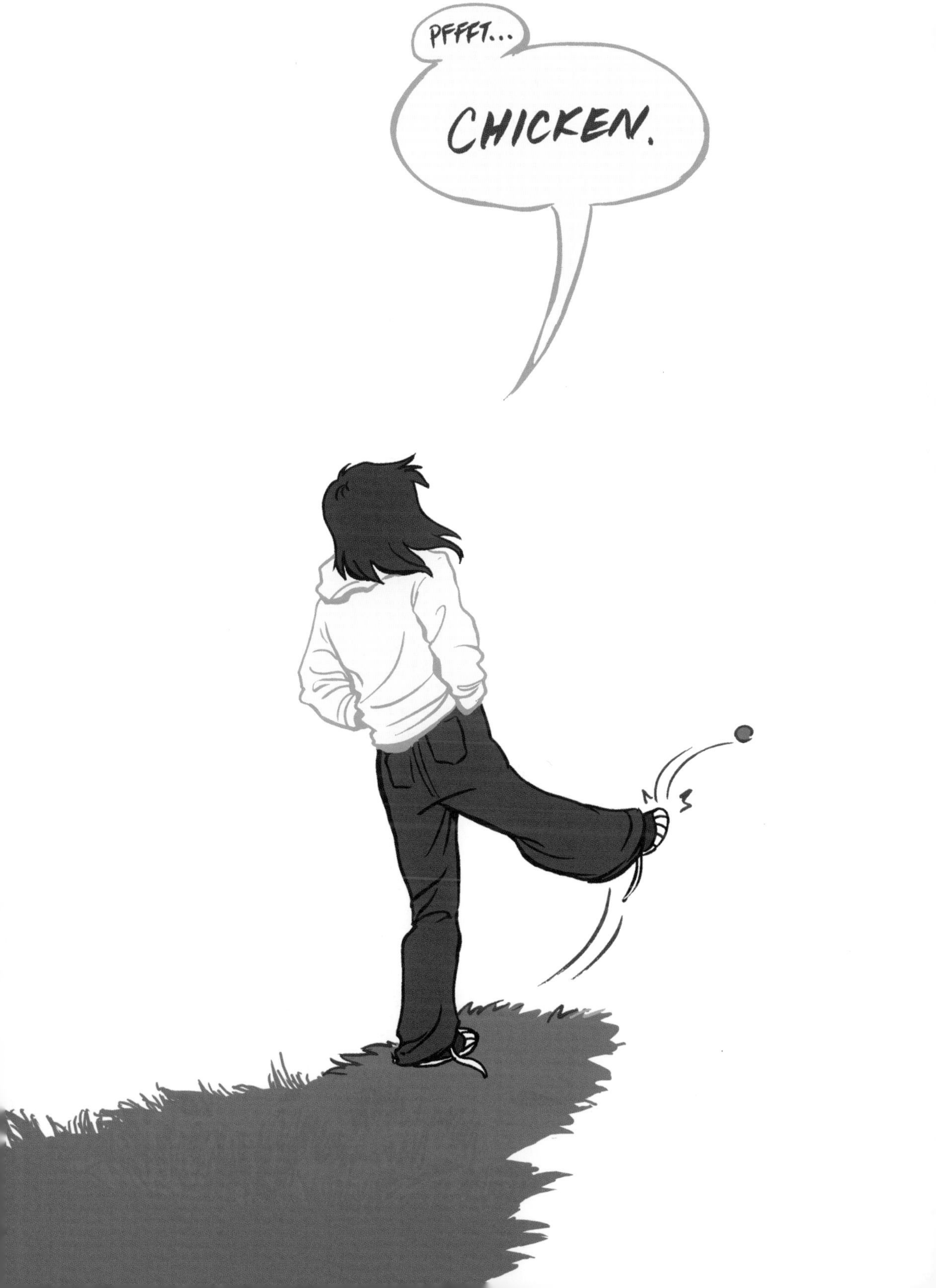
PFFFT...
CHICKEN.

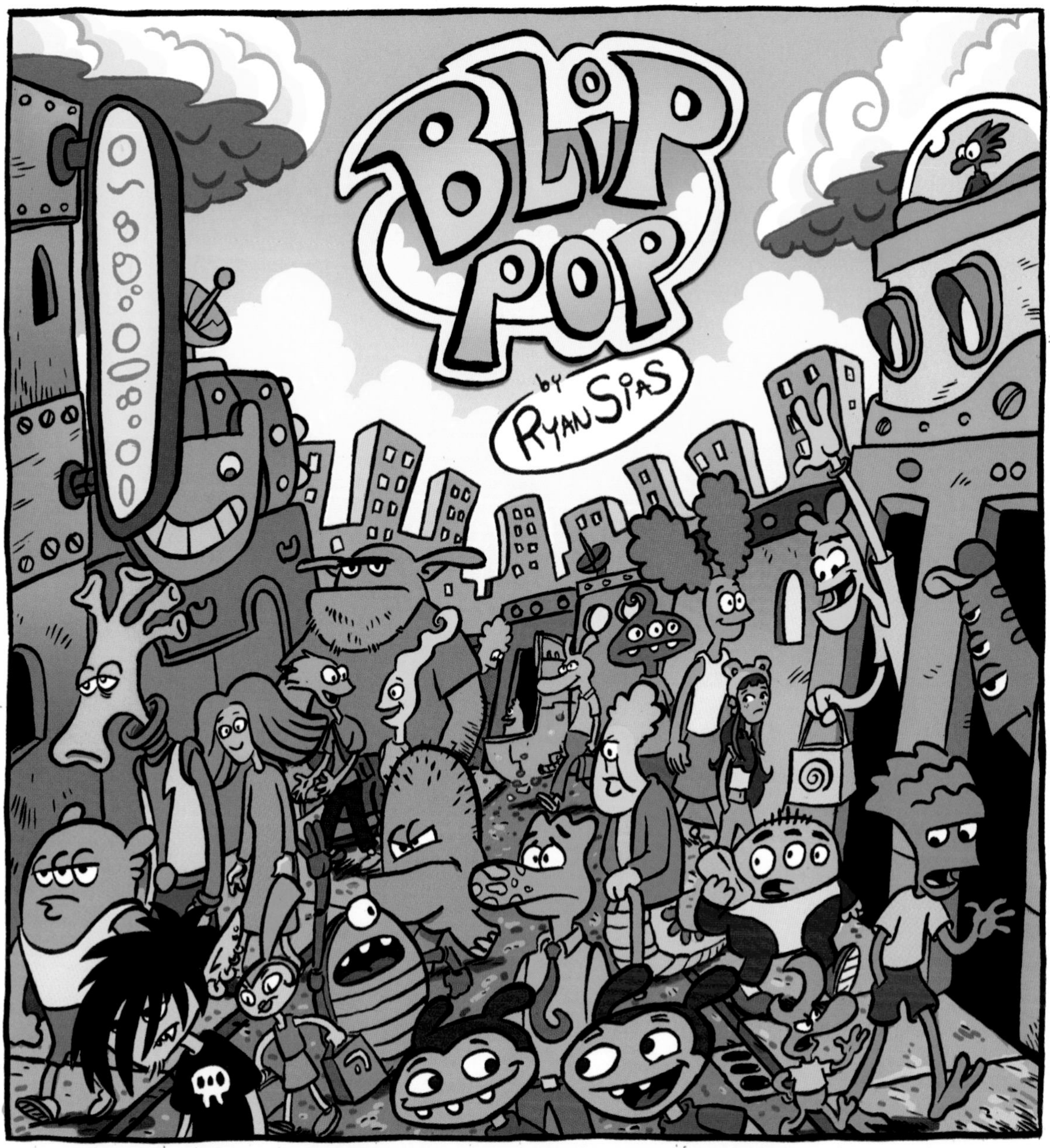
BLIP POP
by RYAN SIAS

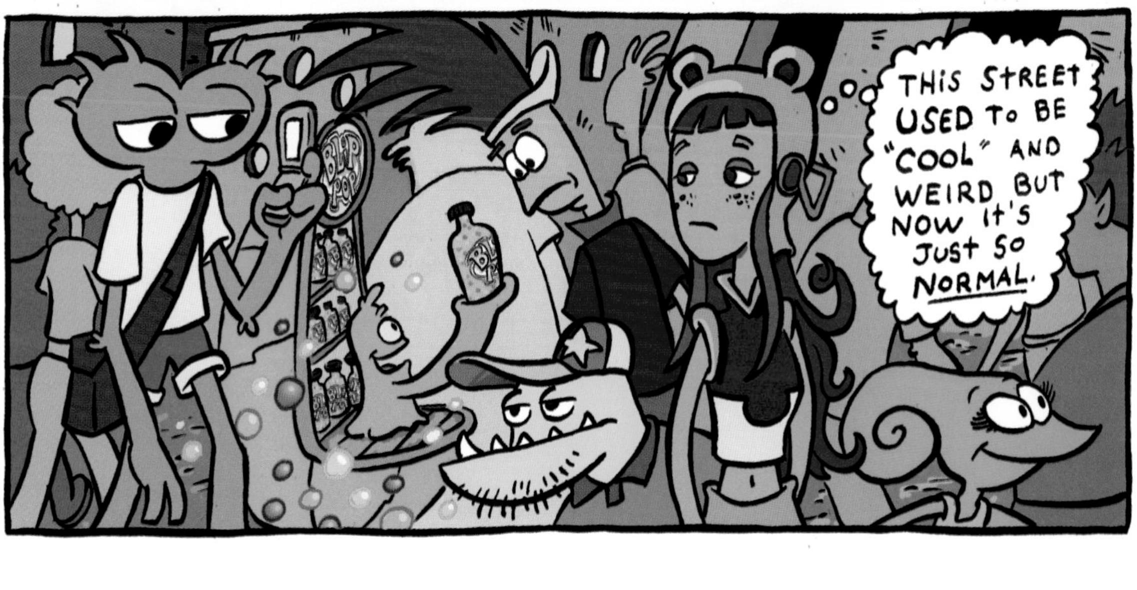
THIS STREET USED TO BE "COOL" AND WEIRD BUT NOW IT'S JUST SO NORMAL.

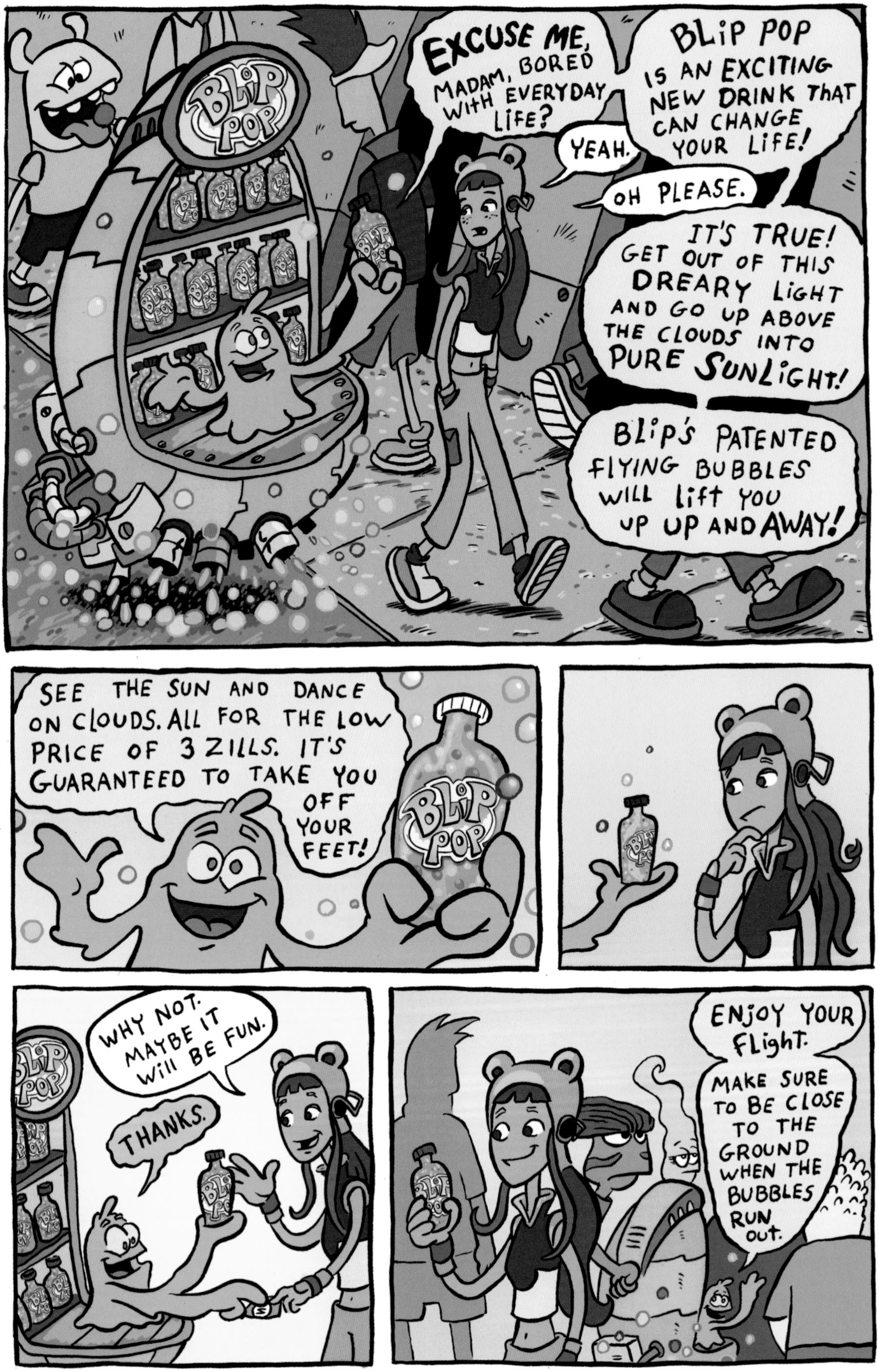
BLIP POP
EXCUSE ME, MADAM, BORED WITH EVERYDAY LIFE?
YEAH.
BLIP POP IS AN EXCITING NEW DRINK THAT CAN CHANGE YOUR LIFE!
OH PLEASE.
IT'S TRUE! GET OUT OF THIS DREARY LIGHT AND GO UP ABOVE THE CLOUDS INTO PURE SUNLIGHT!
BLIP'S PATENTED FLYING BUBBLES WILL LIFT YOU UP UP AND AWAY!
SEE THE SUN AND DANCE ON CLOUDS. ALL FOR THE LOW PRICE OF 3 ZILLS. IT'S GUARANTEED TO TAKE YOU OFF YOUR FEET!
BLIP POP
WHY NOT. MAYBE IT WILL BE FUN.
THANKS.
ENJOY YOUR FLIGHT.
MAKE SURE TO BE CLOSE TO THE GROUND WHEN THE BUBBLES RUN OUT.

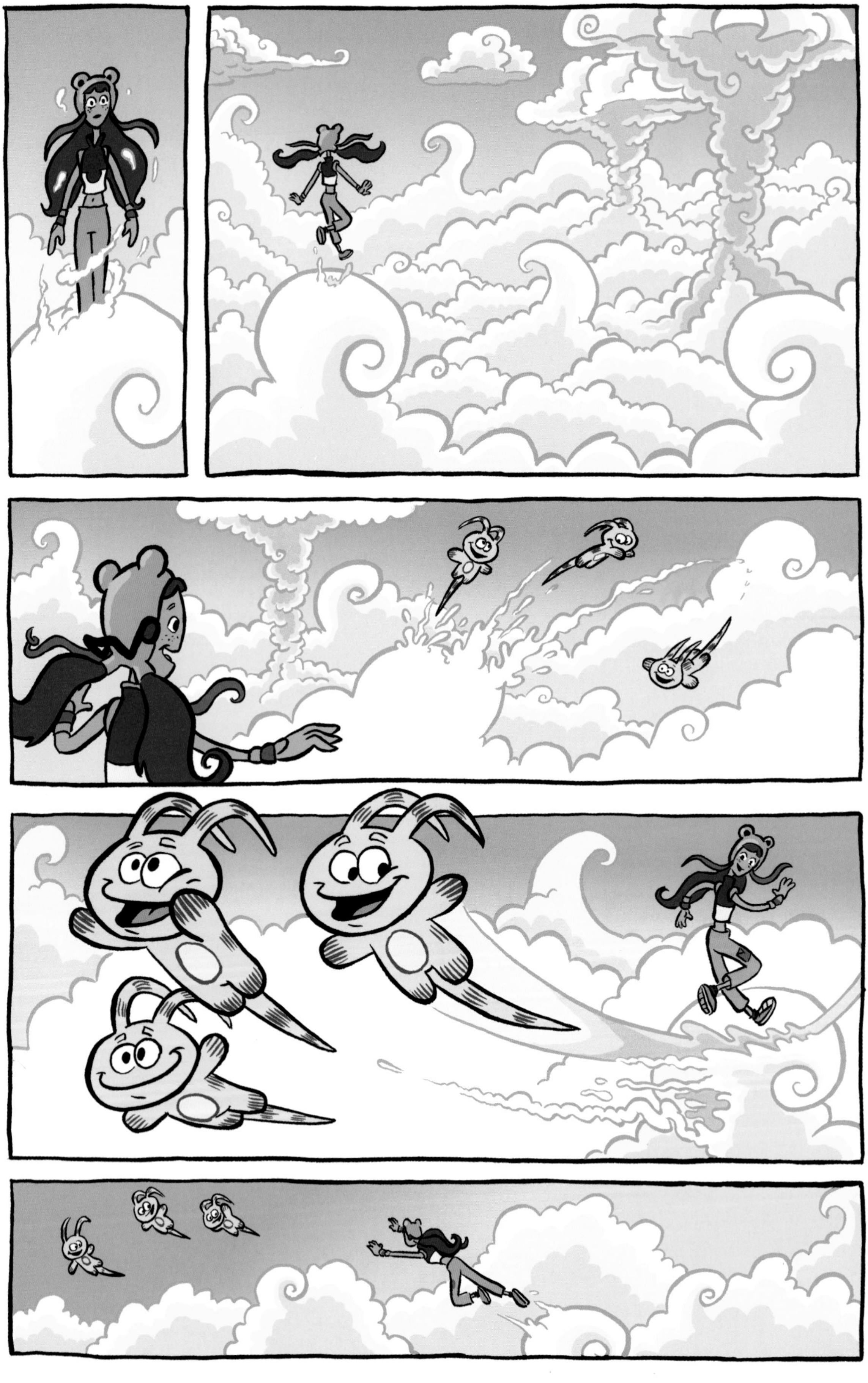

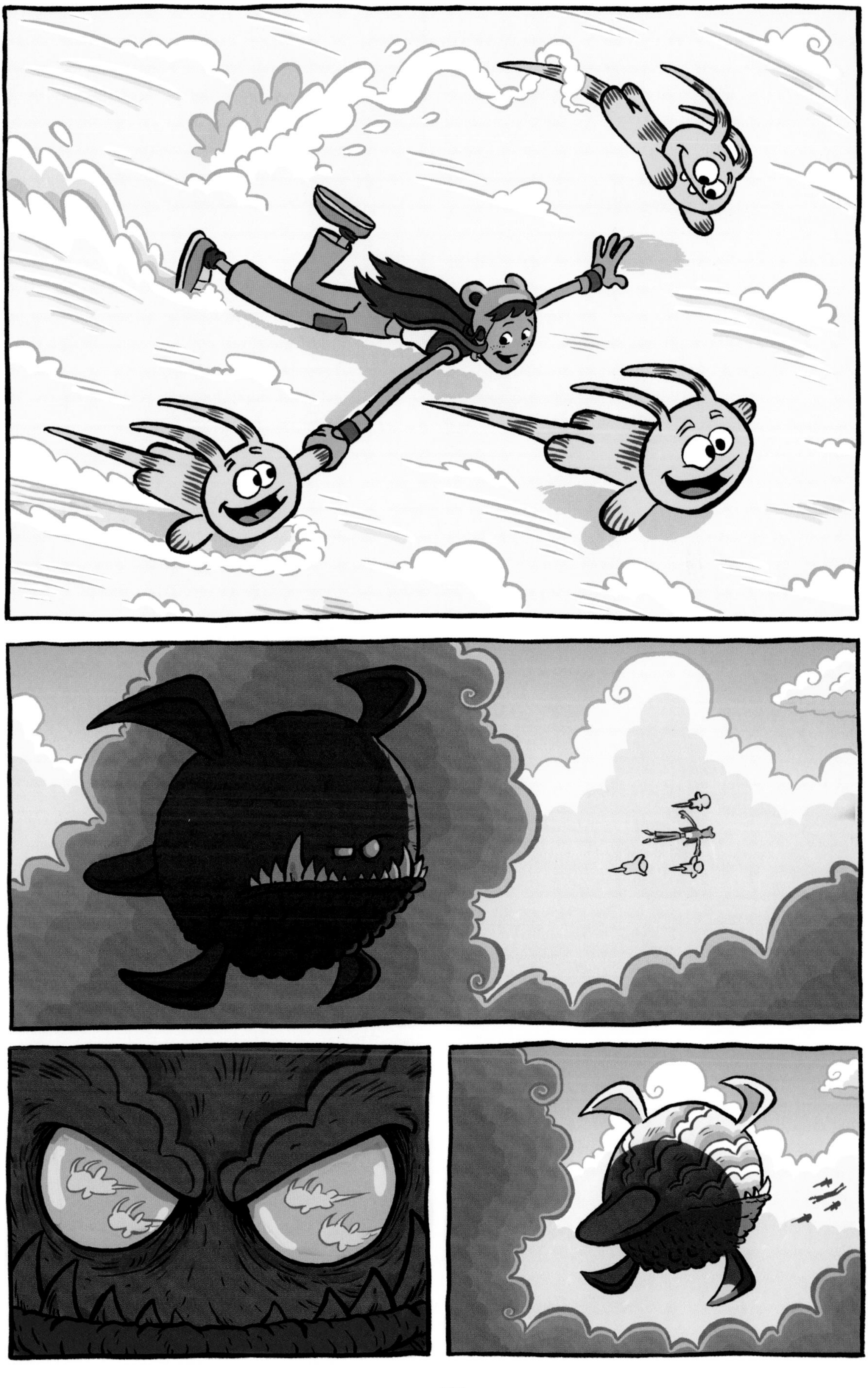

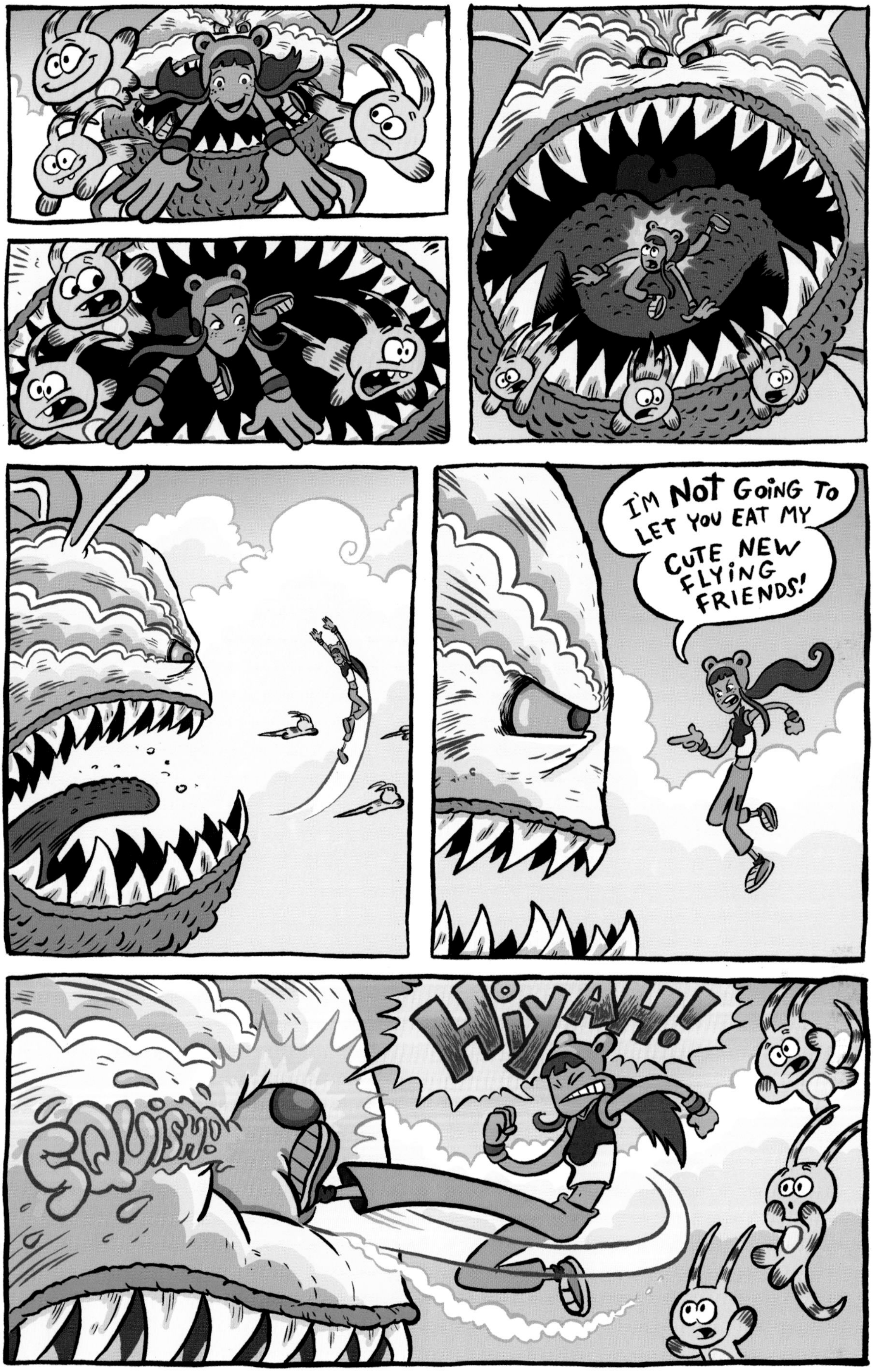
I'M NOT GOING TO LET YOU EAT MY CUTE NEW FLYING FRIENDS!
HiYAH!
SQUISH!

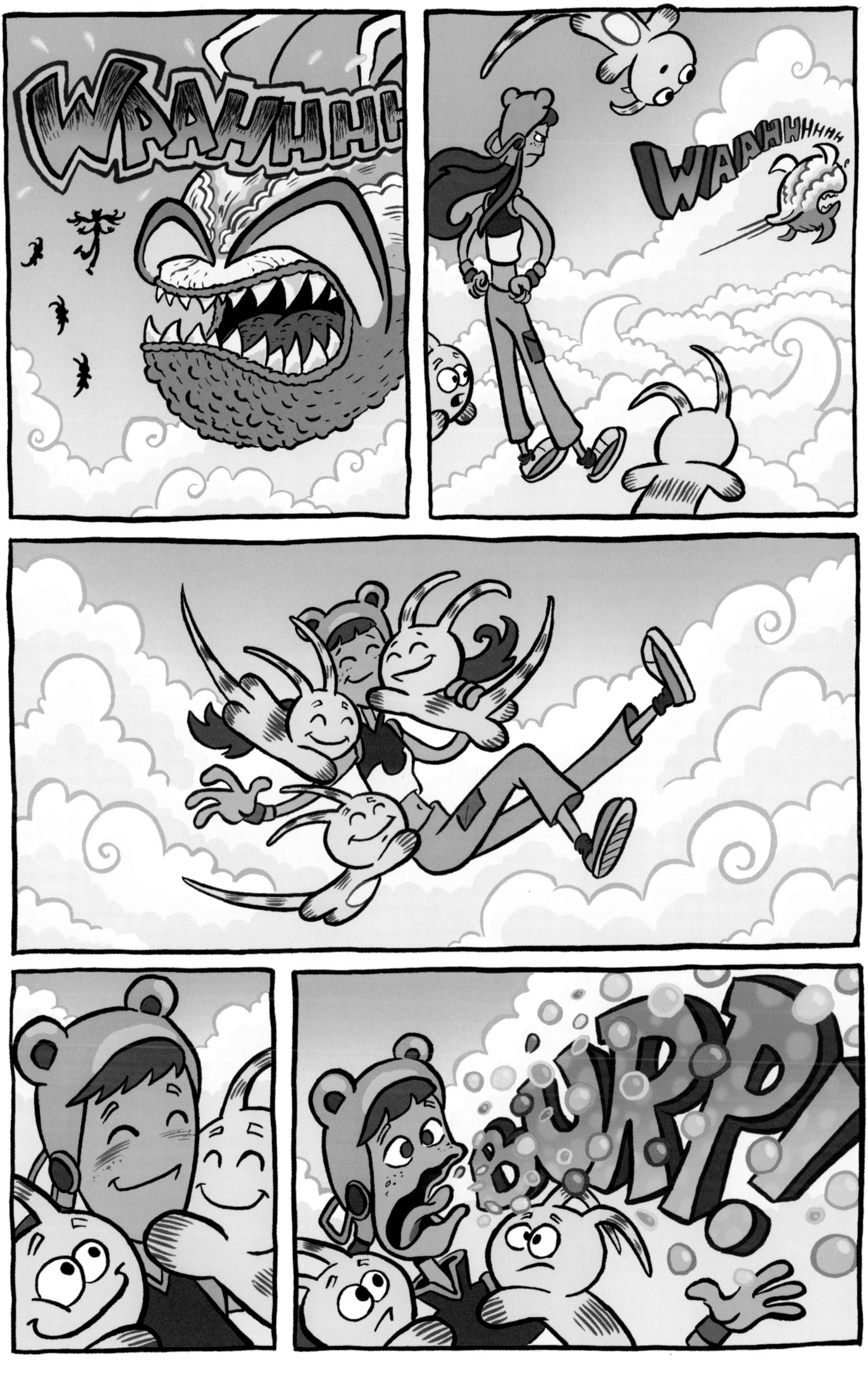
WAAHHHH
WAAHHHHHHH
BURP!

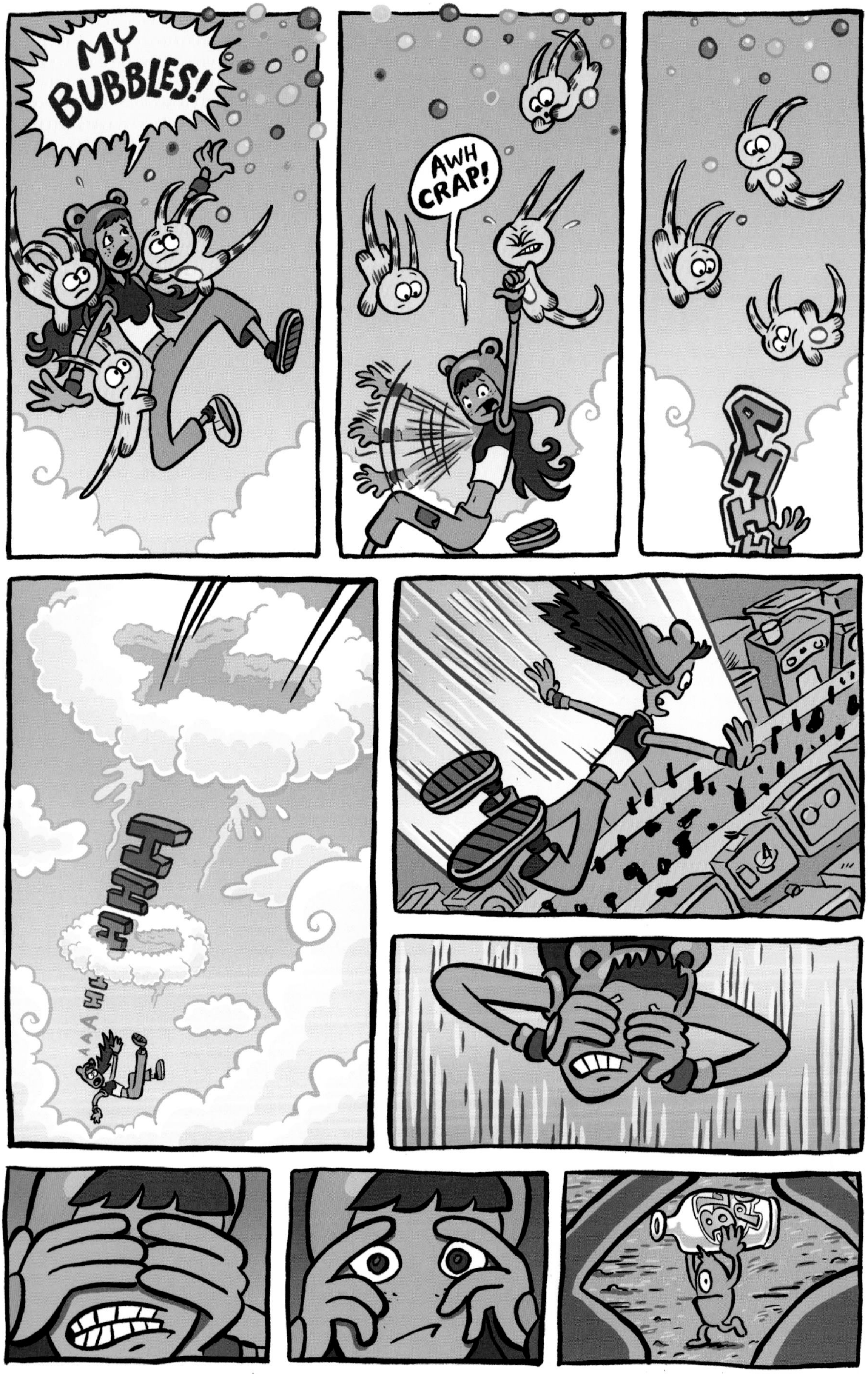
MY BUBBLES!
AWH CRAP!

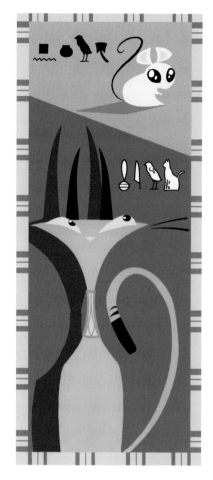

▲ MOUSETRAP ▲

STORY AND ART
JOHANE MATTE

COLOR
GHISLAIN BARBE

SPECIAL THANKS TO
ERIC BAPTIZAT

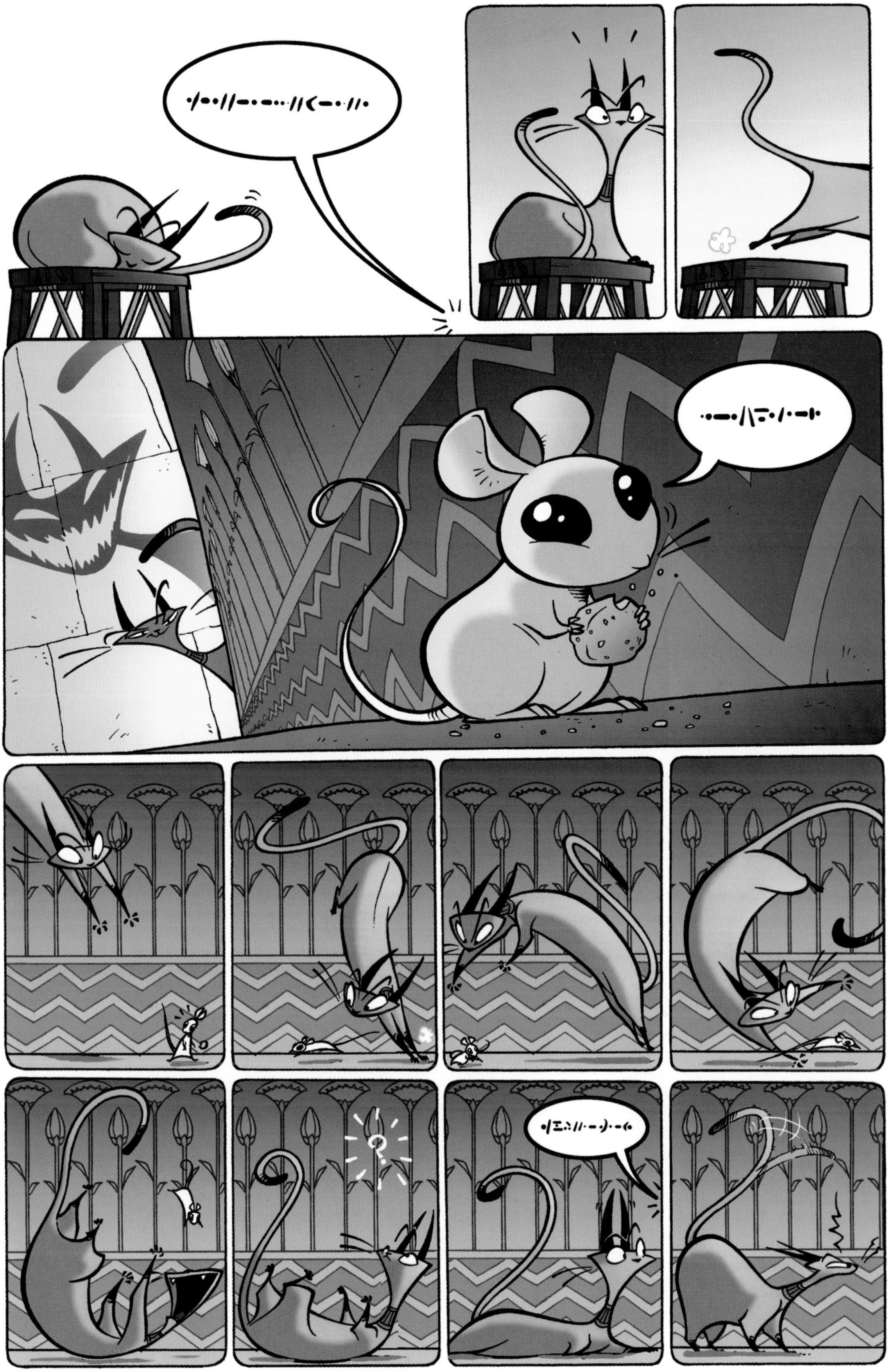

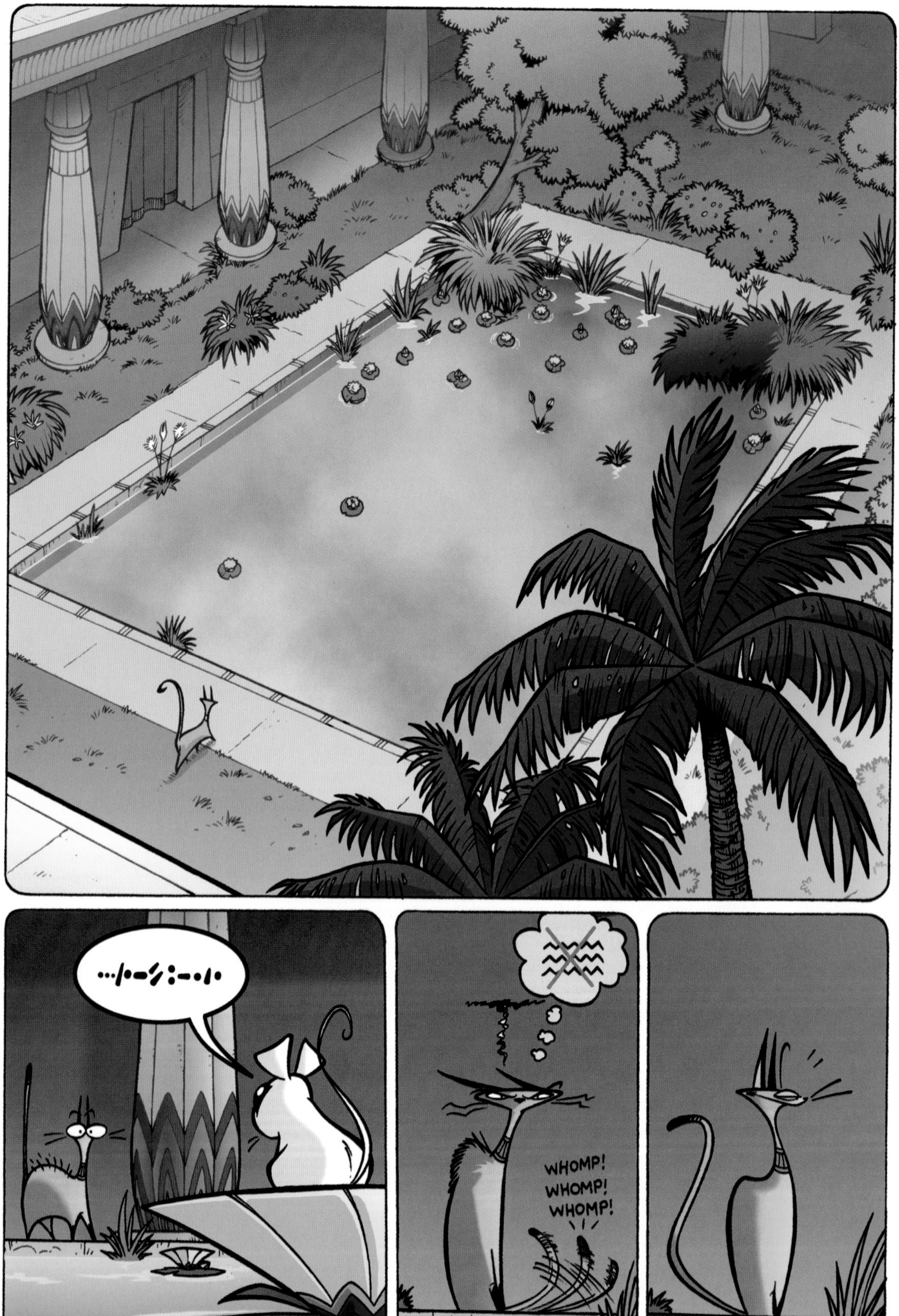
WHOMP!
WHOMP!
WHOMP!

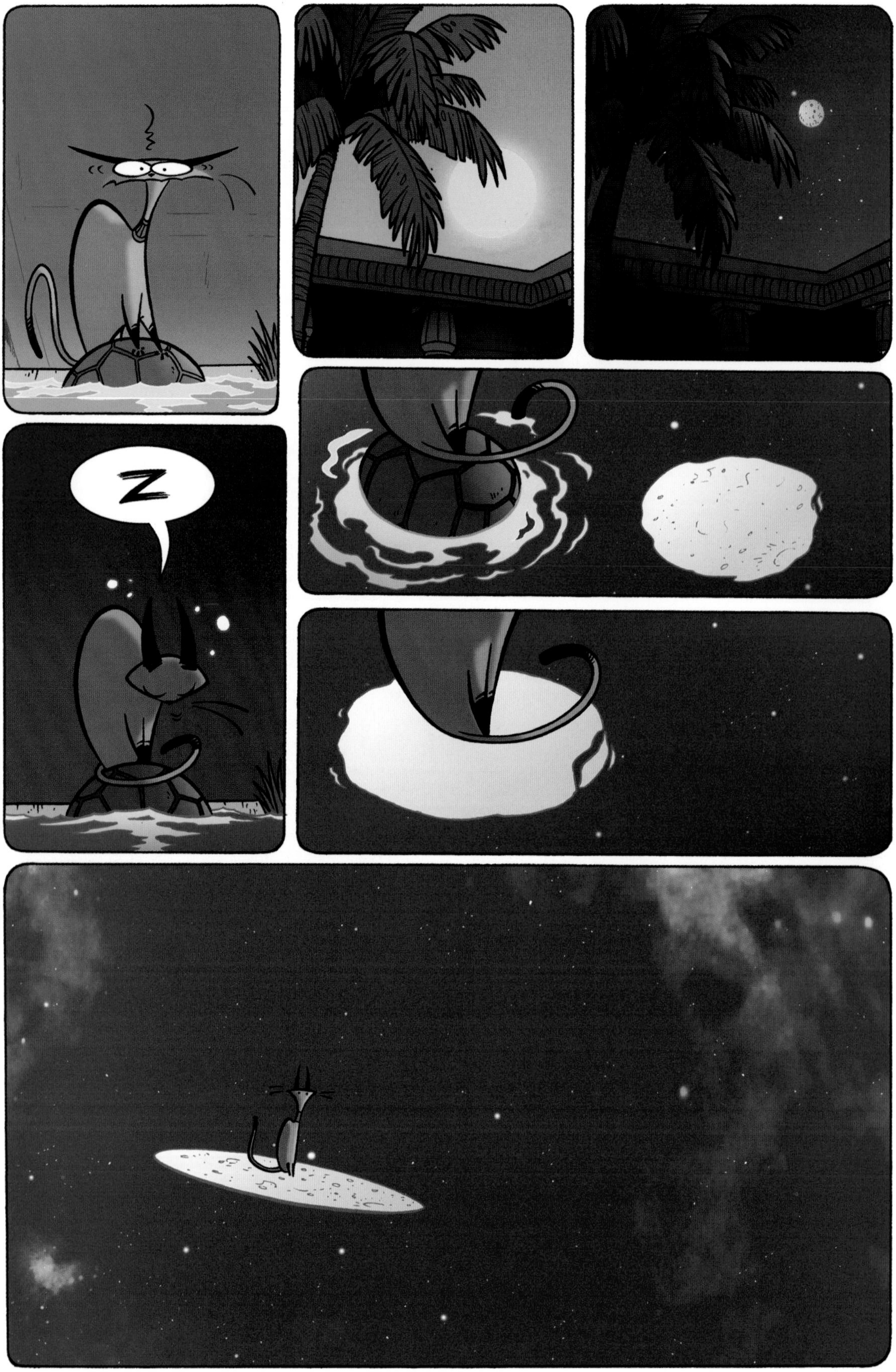
Z

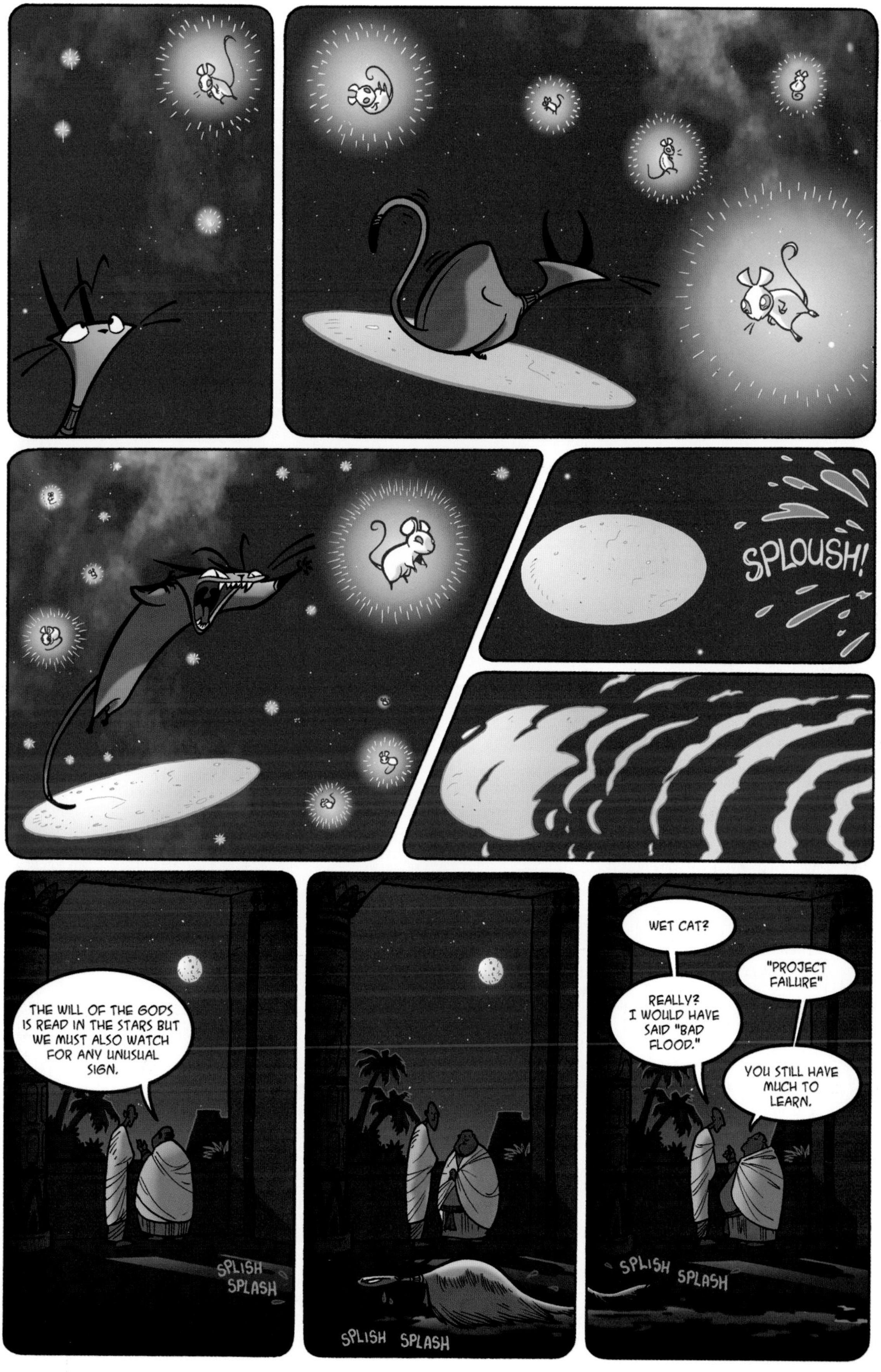
SPLOUSH!
THE WILL OF THE GODS IS READ IN THE STARS BUT WE MUST ALSO WATCH FOR ANY UNUSUAL SIGN.
SPLISH SPLASH
SPLISH SPLASH
WET CAT?
"PROJECT FAILURE"
REALLY? I WOULD HAVE SAID "BAD FLOOD."
YOU STILL HAVE MUCH TO LEARN.
SPLISH SPLASH

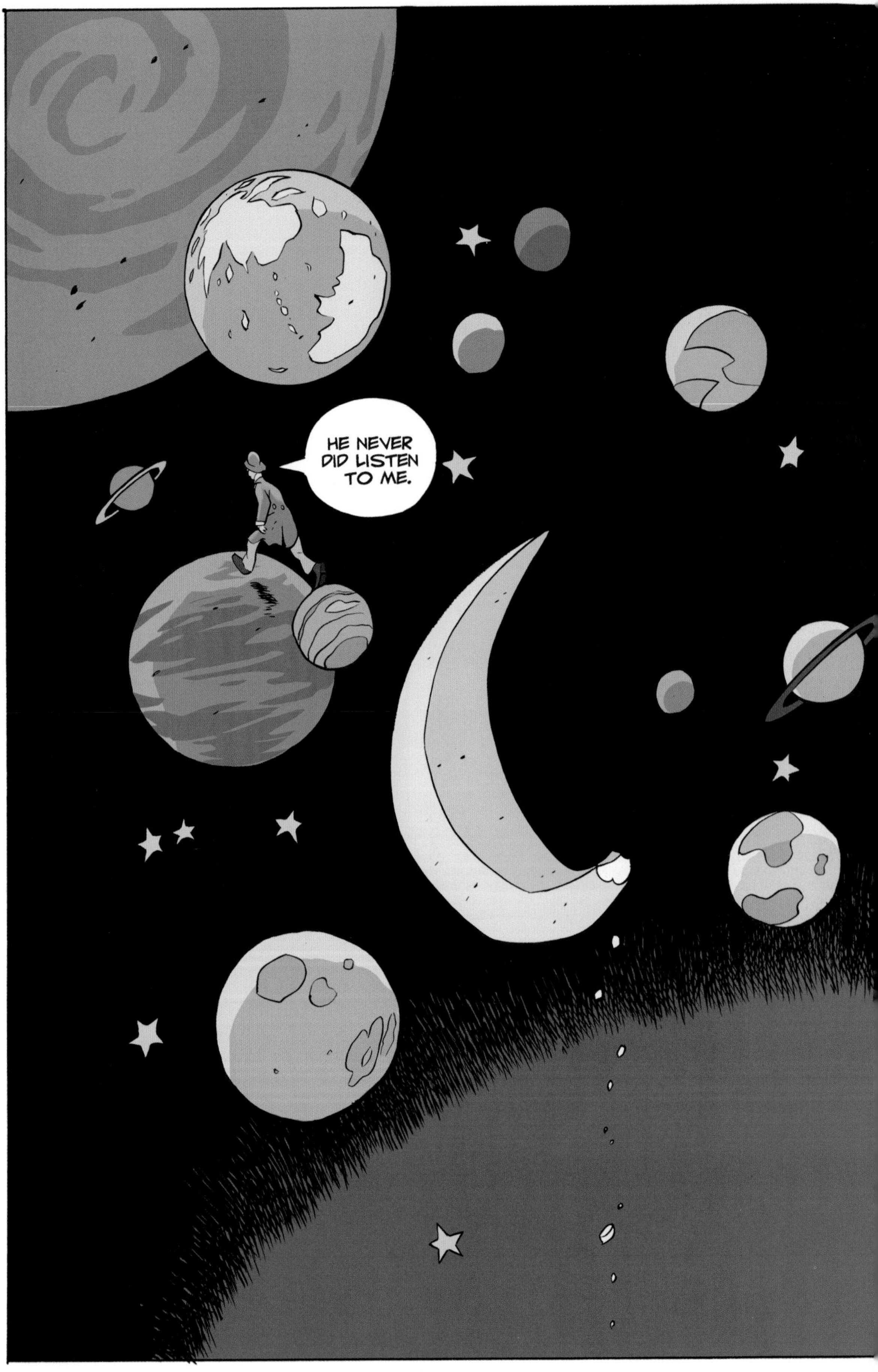
HE NEVER DID LISTEN TO ME.

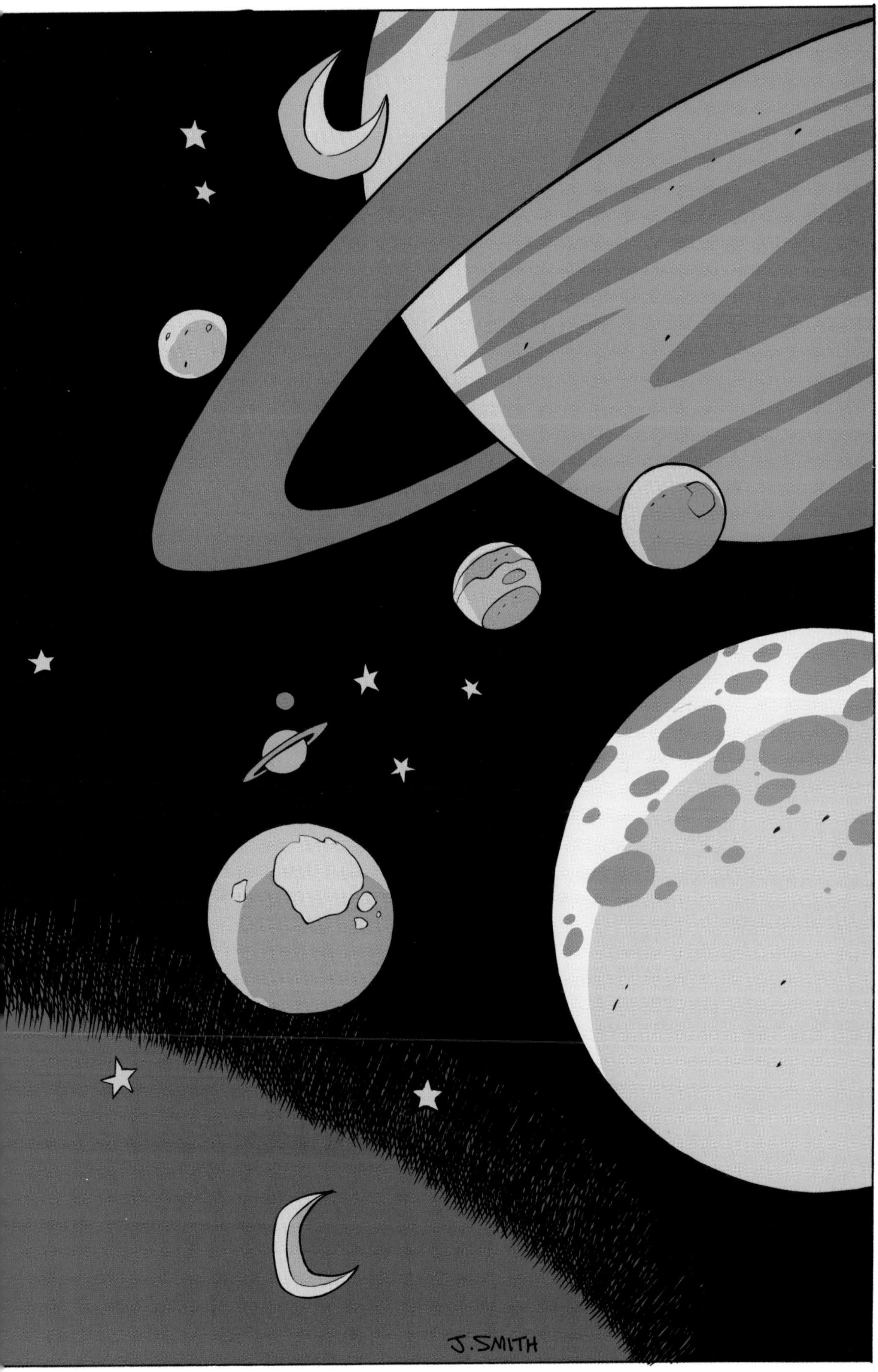
J.SMITH

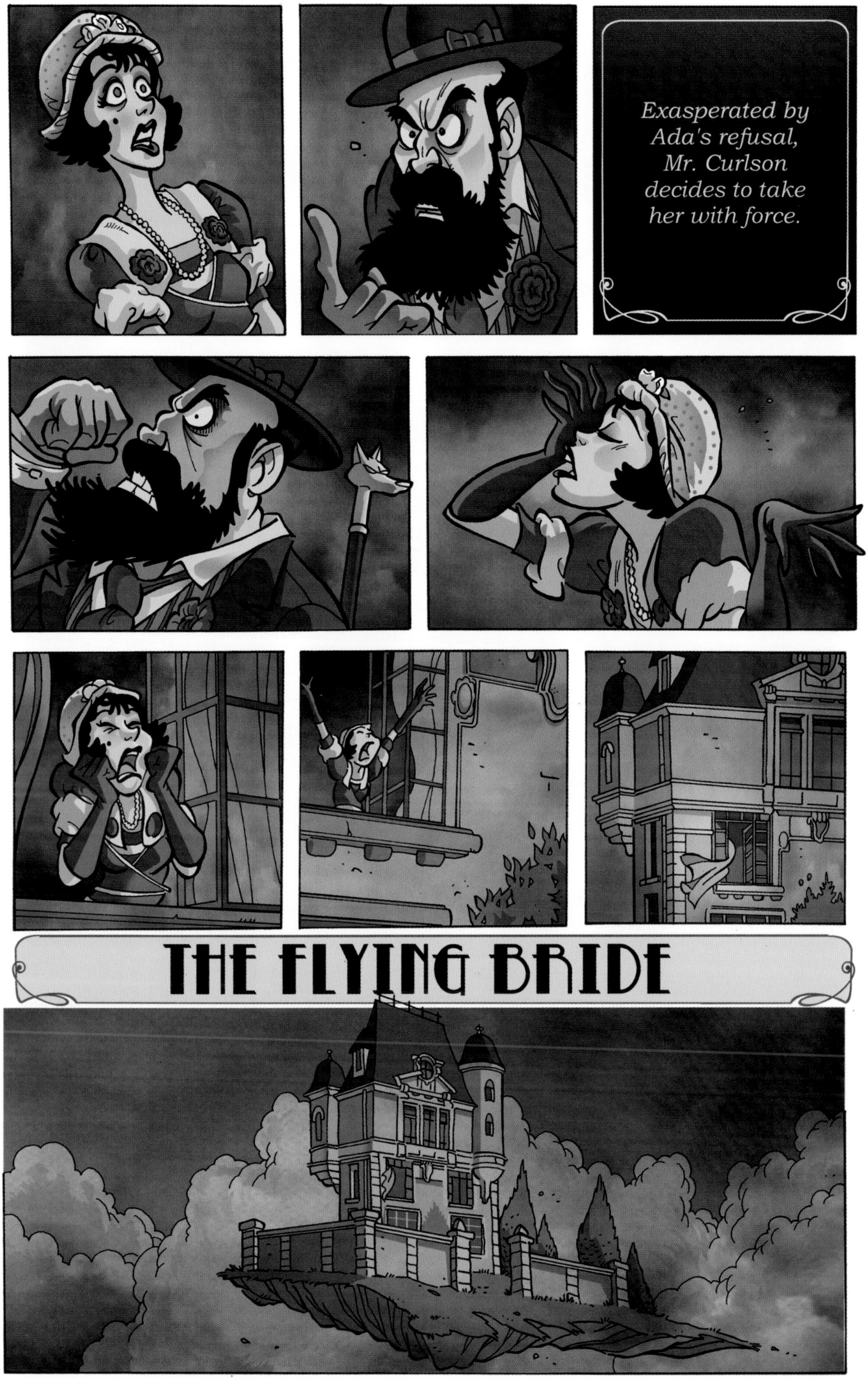
Exasperated by Ada's refusal, Mr. Curlson decides to take her with force.
THE FLYING BRIDE

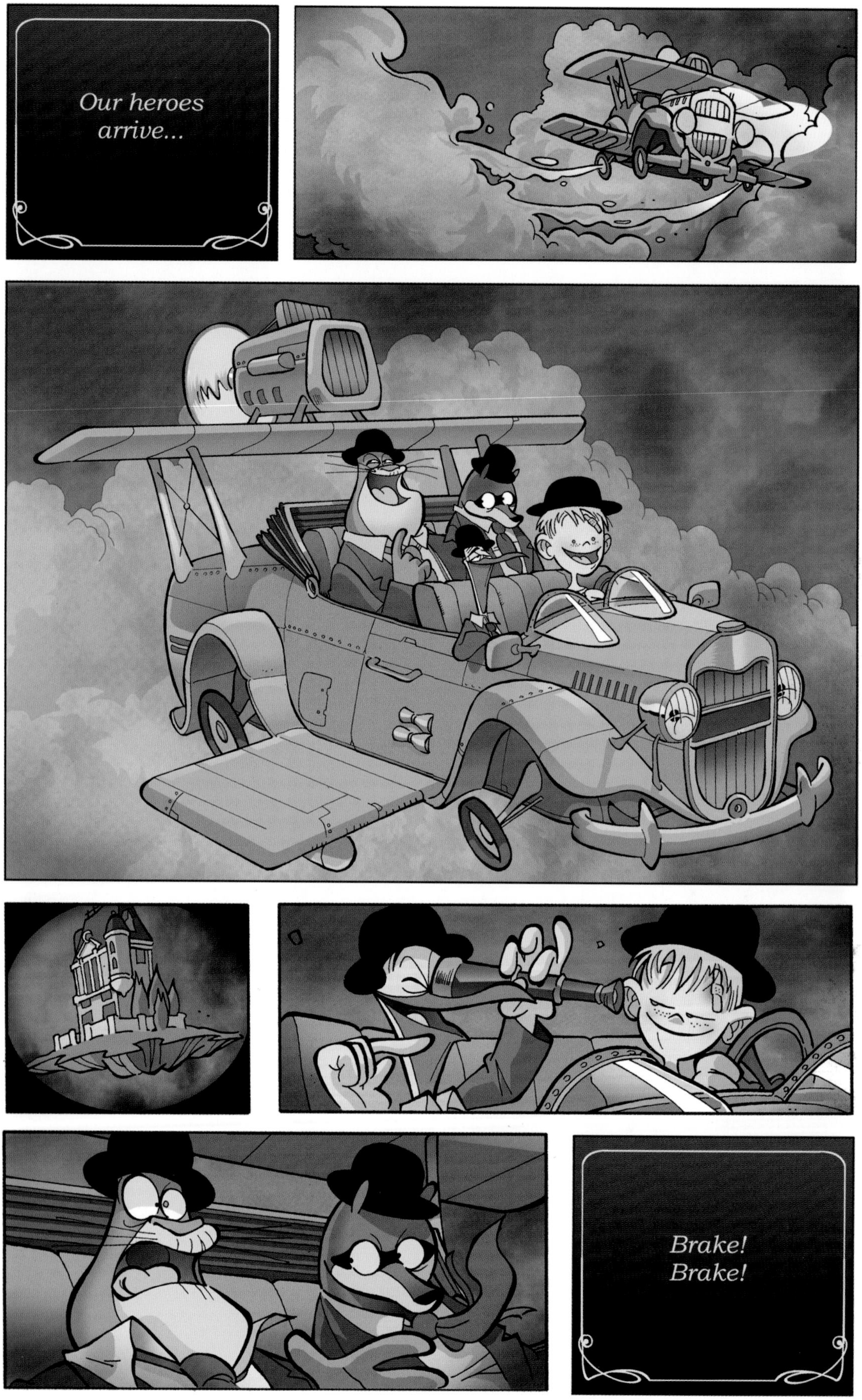
Our heroes arrive...
Brake! Brake!

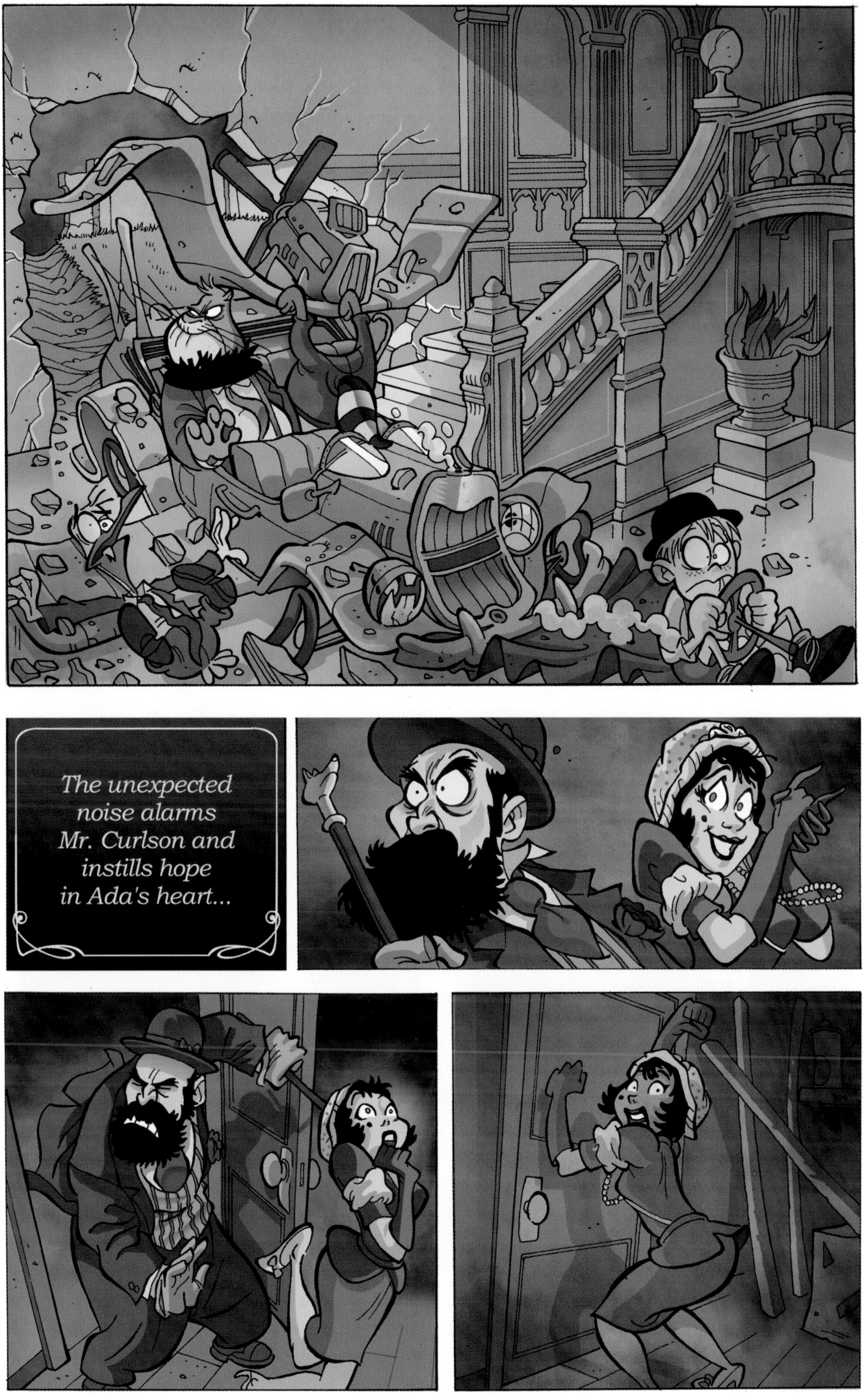
The unexpected noise alarms Mr. Curlson and instills hope in Ada's heart...

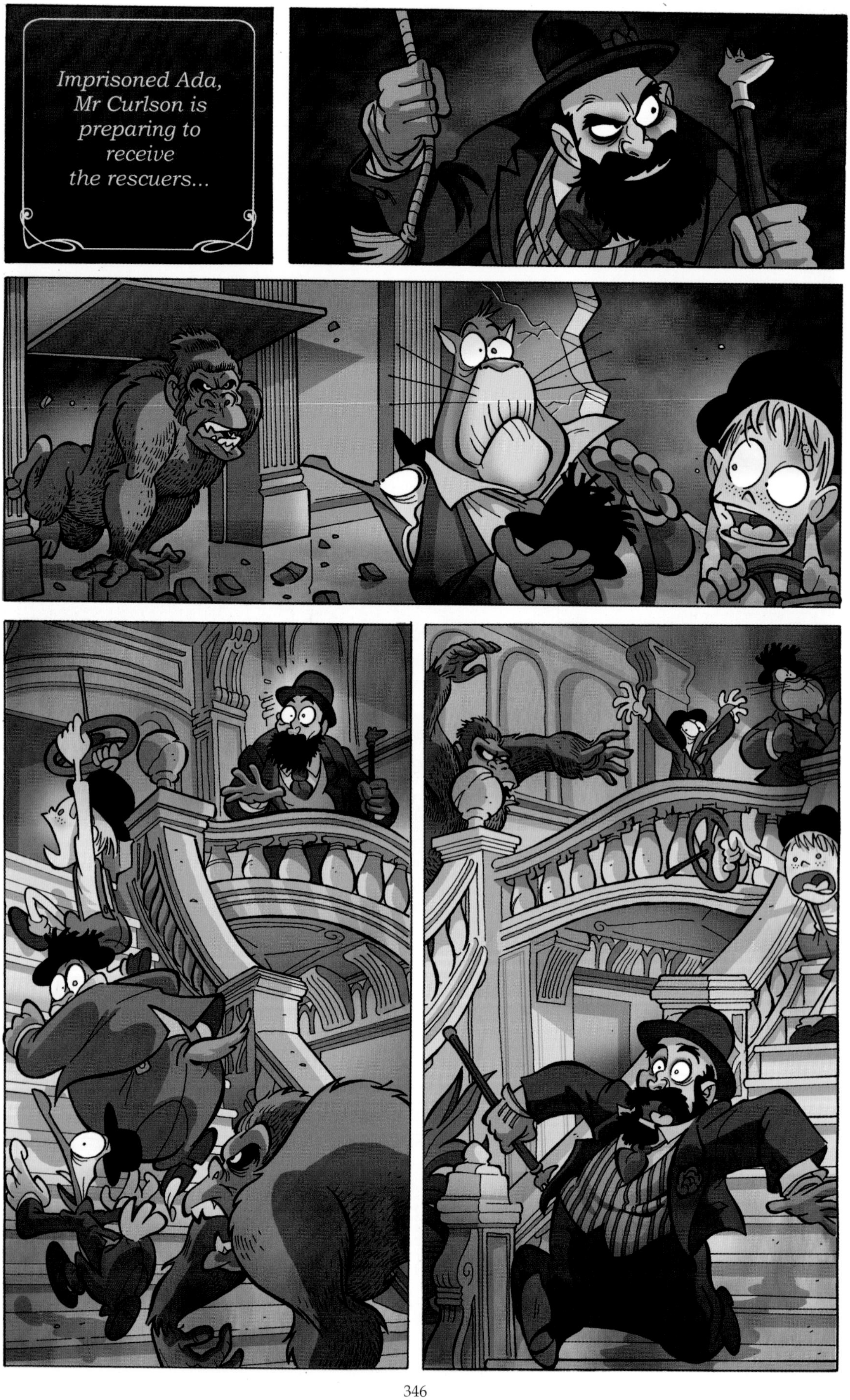
Imprisoned Ada, Mr Curlson is preparing to receive the rescuers...

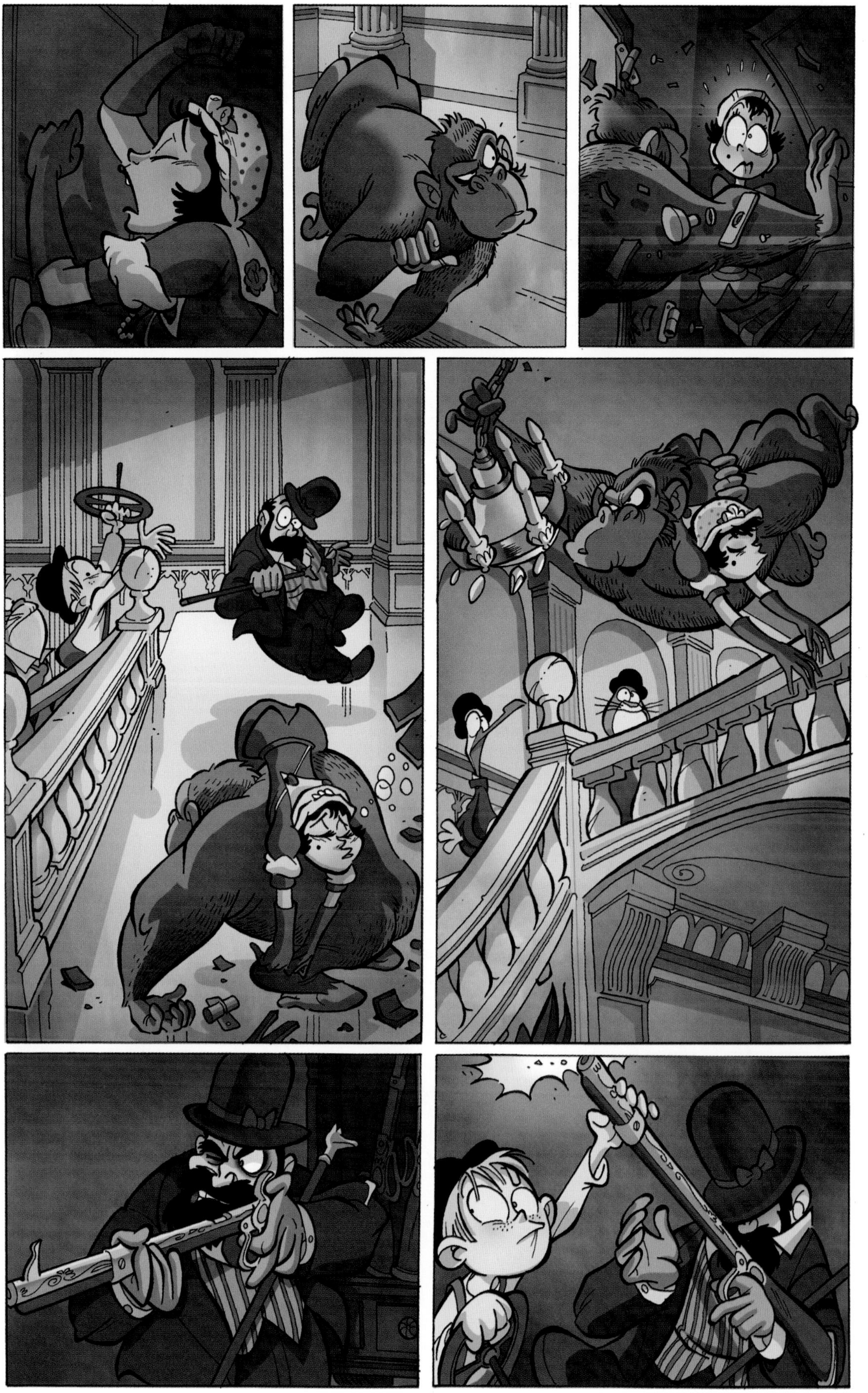

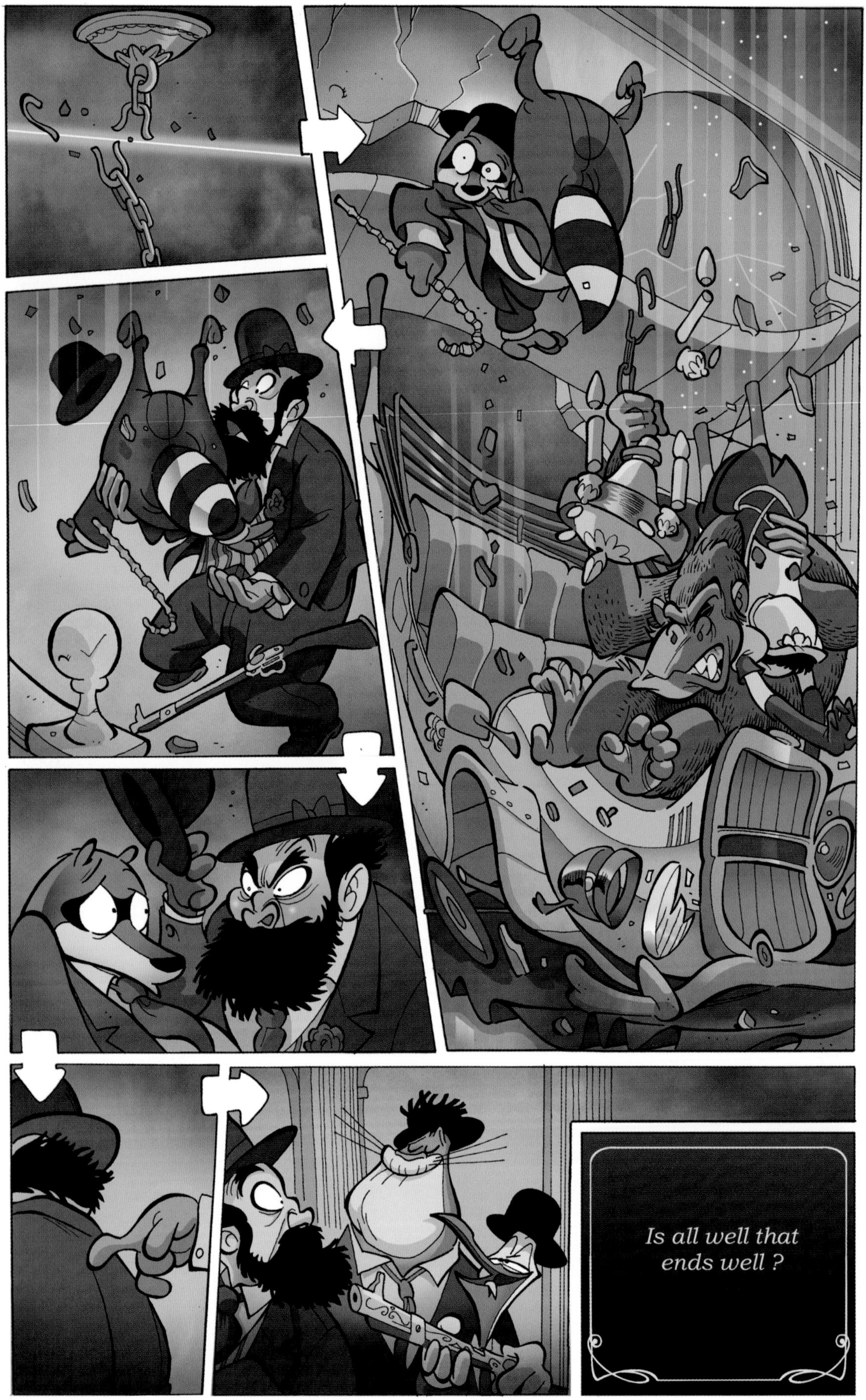
Is all well that ends well ?

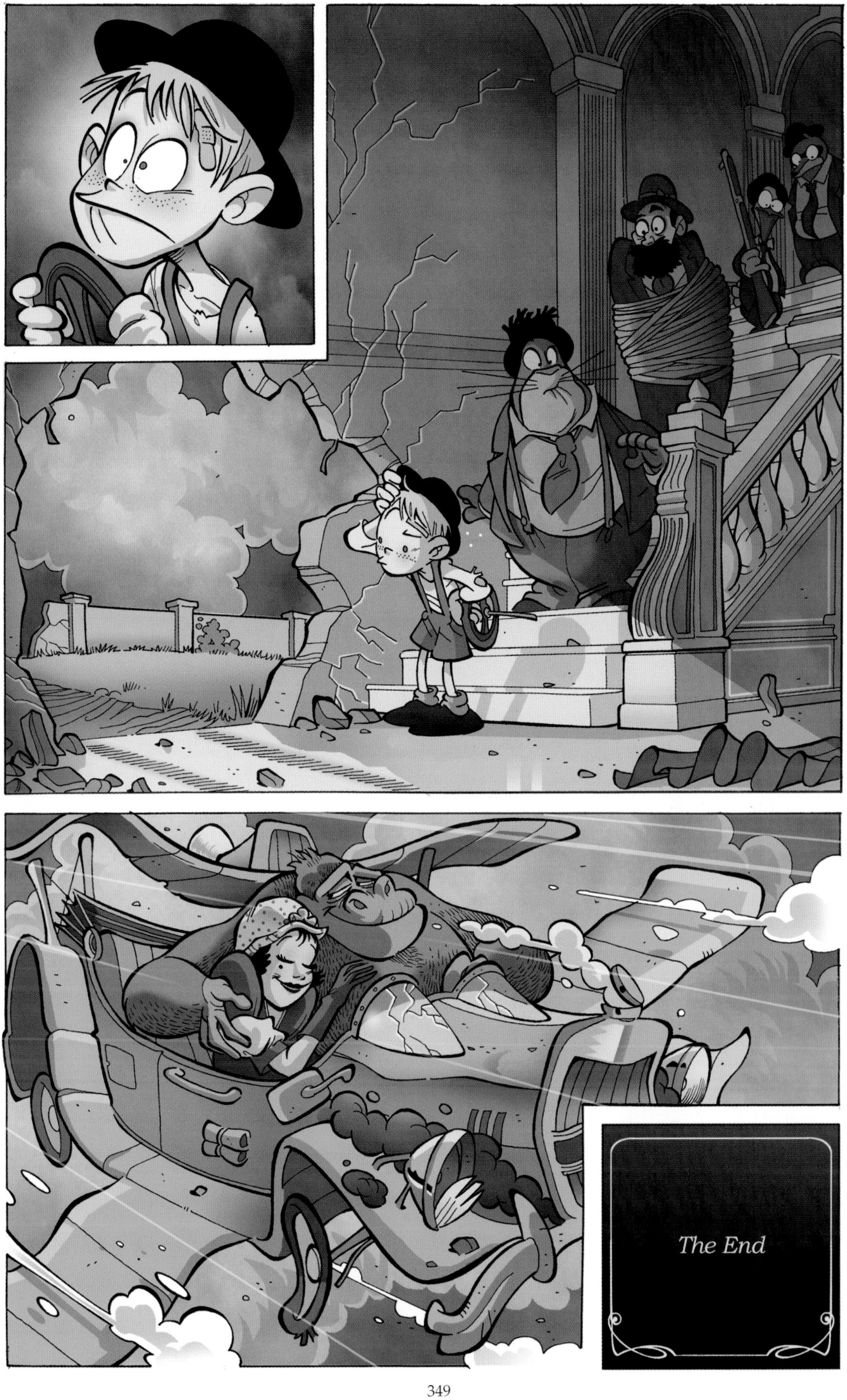
The End

THE PLANK

BY BEN HATKE

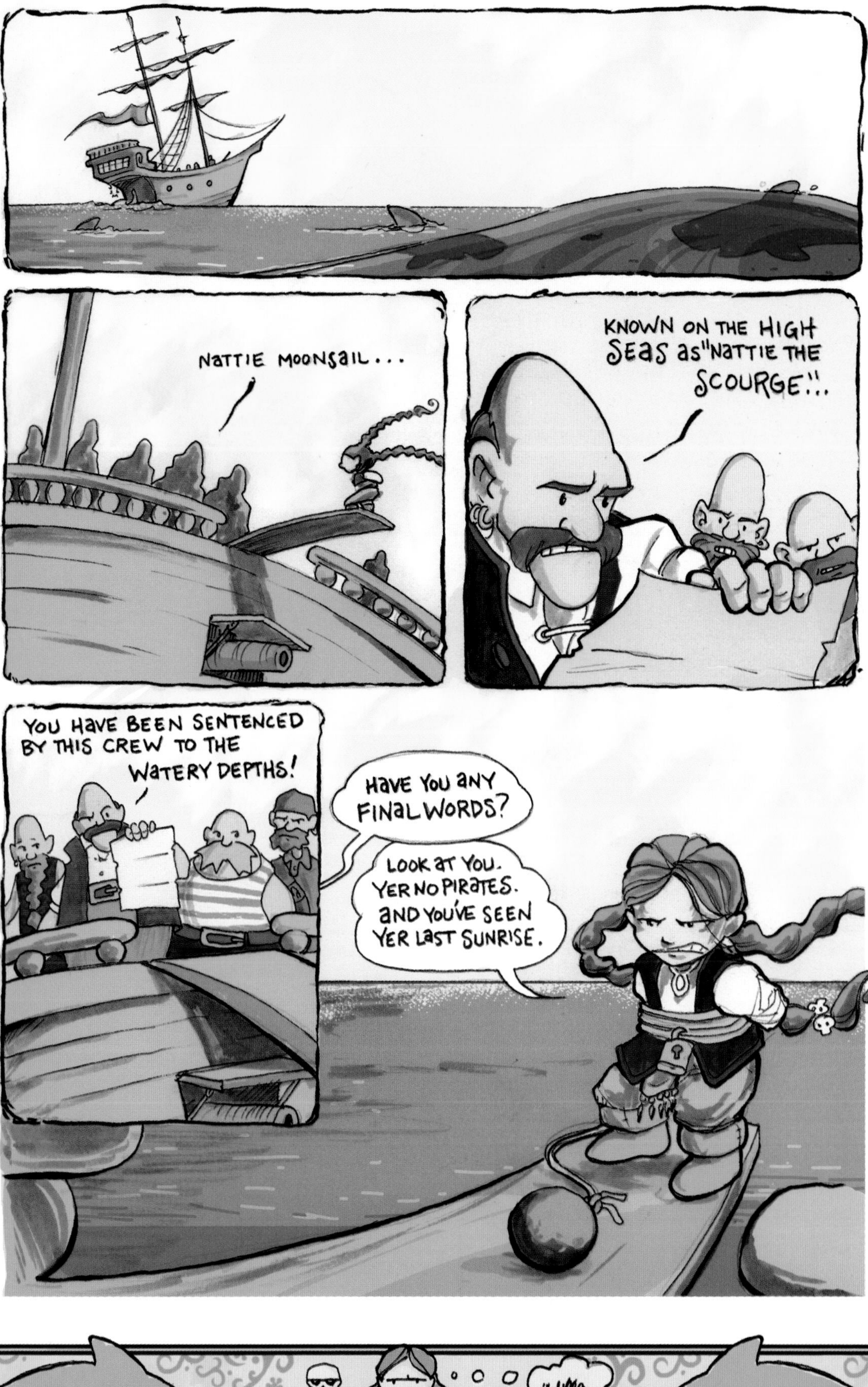
NATTIE MOONSAIL...
KNOWN ON THE HIGH SEAS AS "NATTIE THE SCOURGE"!..
YOU HAVE BEEN SENTENCED BY THIS CREW TO THE WATERY DEPTHS!
HAVE YOU ANY FINAL WORDS?
LOOK AT YOU. YER NO PIRATES. AND YOU'VE SEEN YER LAST SUNRISE.

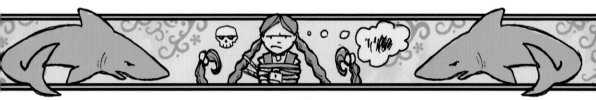

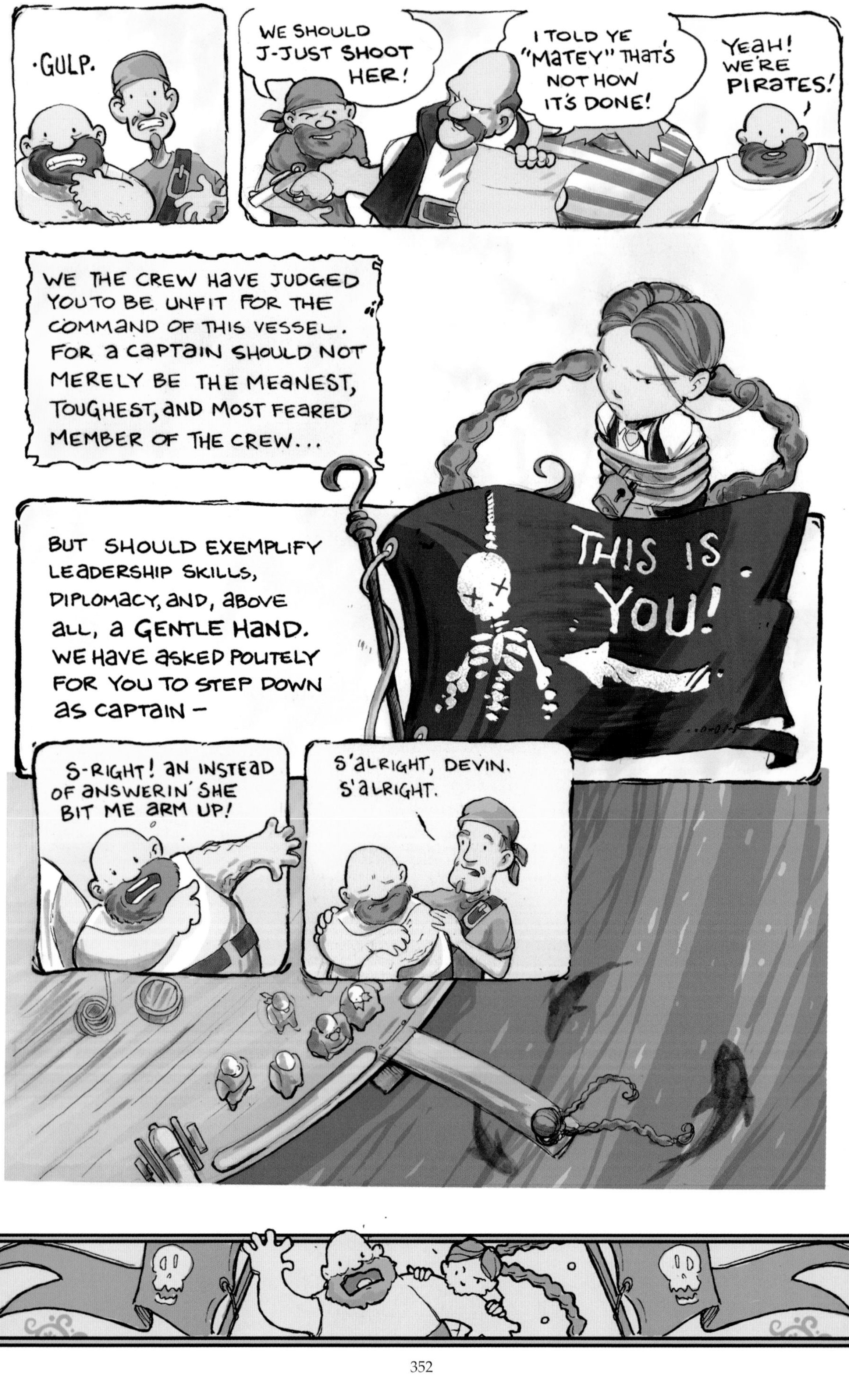
·GULP·
WE SHOULD J-JUST SHOOT HER!
I TOLD YE "MATEY" THAT'S NOT HOW IT'S DONE!
YEAH! WE'RE PIRATES!
WE THE CREW HAVE JUDGED YOU TO BE UNFIT FOR THE COMMAND OF THIS VESSEL. FOR A CAPTAIN SHOULD NOT MERELY BE THE MEANEST, TOUGHEST, AND MOST FEARED MEMBER OF THE CREW...
BUT SHOULD EXEMPLIFY LEADERSHIP SKILLS, DIPLOMACY, AND, ABOVE ALL, A GENTLE HAND. WE HAVE ASKED POLITELY FOR YOU TO STEP DOWN AS CAPTAIN -
THIS IS YOU!
S-RIGHT! AN INSTEAD OF ANSWERIN' SHE BIT ME ARM UP!
S'ALRIGHT, DEVIN. S'ALRIGHT.

ICARUS

Story and Art
Johane Matte

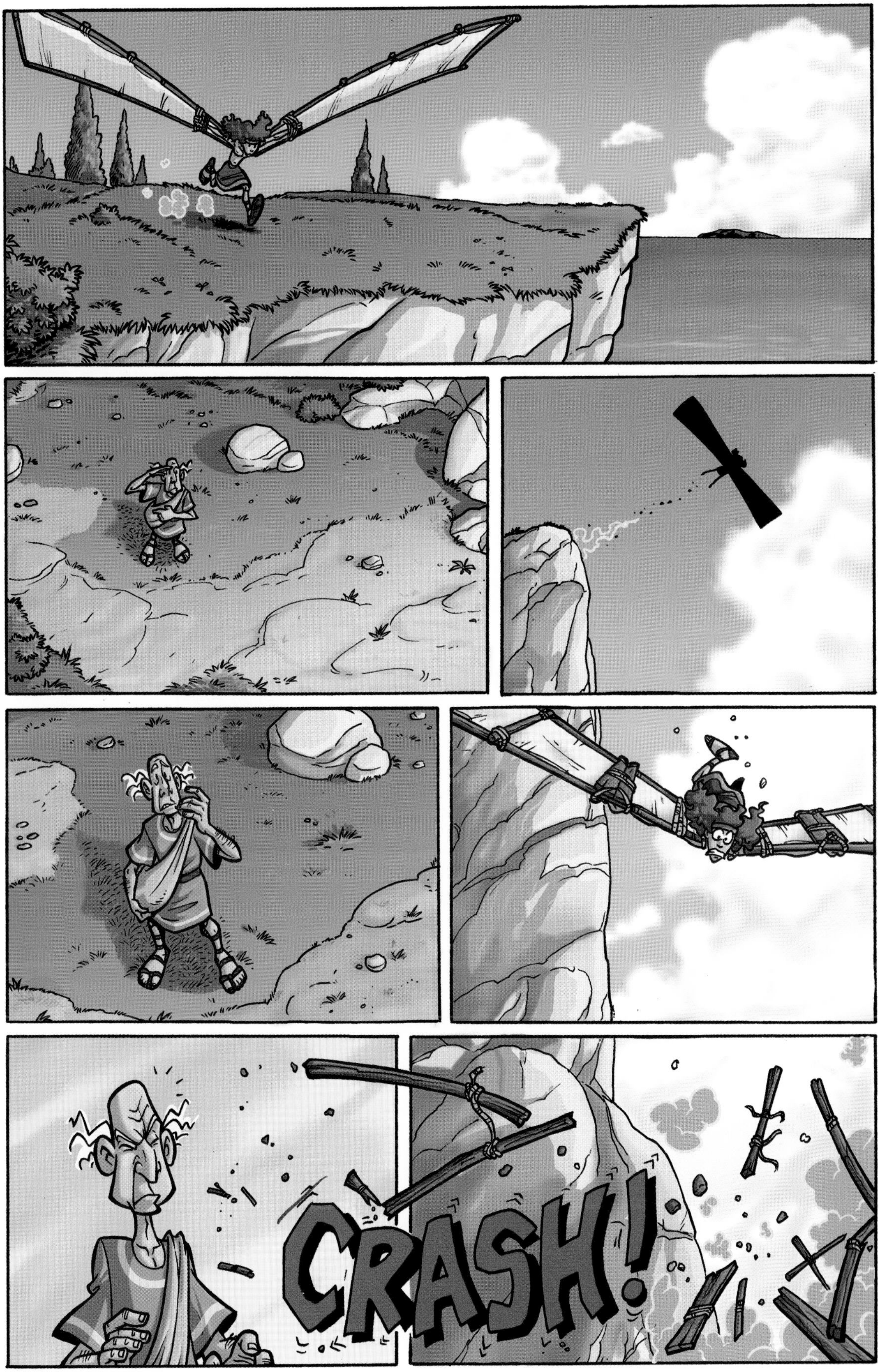
CRASH!

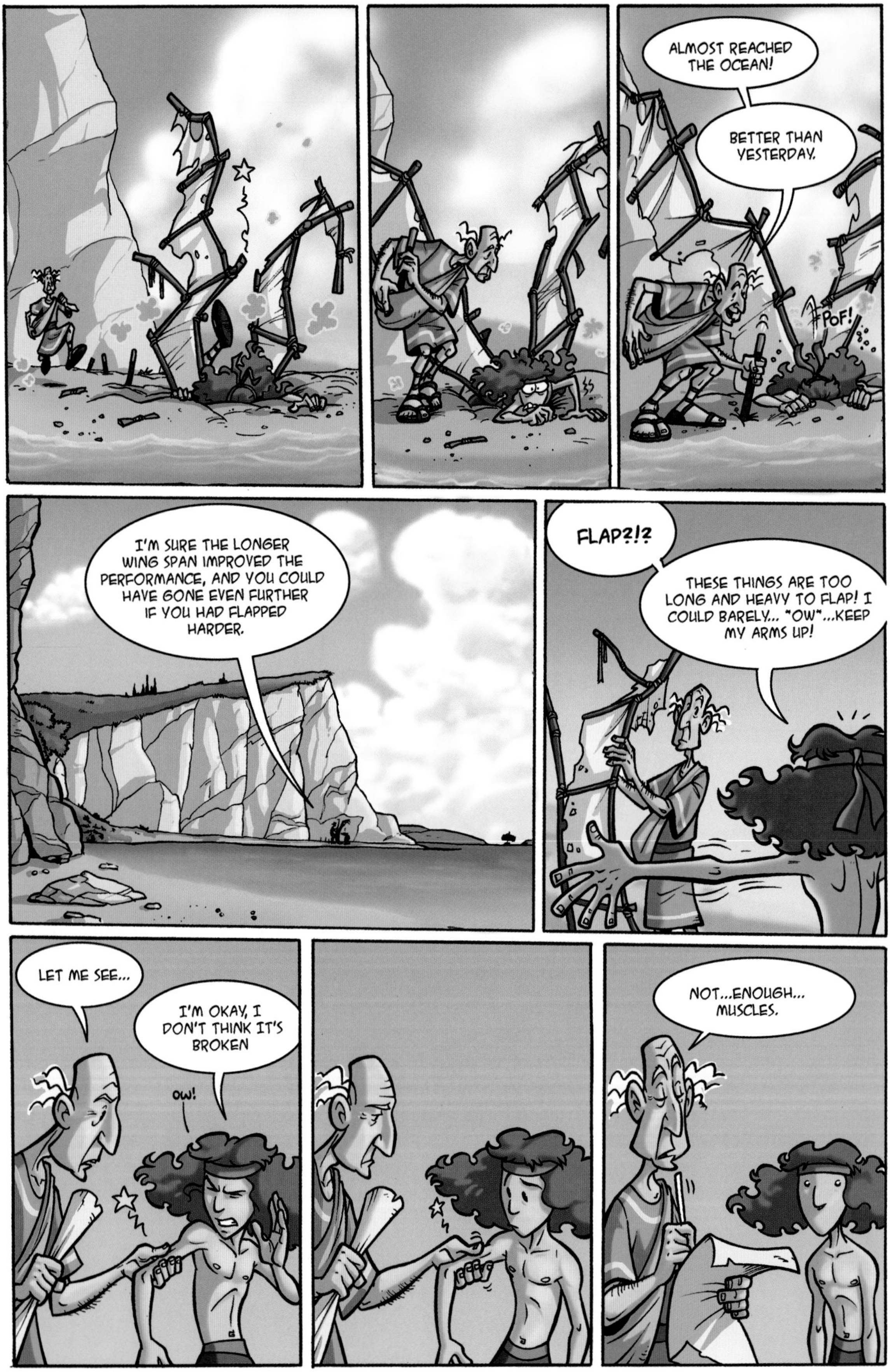
ALMOST REACHED THE OCEAN!
BETTER THAN YESTERDAY.
POF!
I'M SURE THE LONGER WING SPAN IMPROVED THE PERFORMANCE, AND YOU COULD HAVE GONE EVEN FURTHER IF YOU HAD FLAPPED HARDER.
FLAP?!?
THESE THINGS ARE TOO LONG AND HEAVY TO FLAP! I COULD BARELY... "OW"...KEEP MY ARMS UP!
LET ME SEE...
I'M OKAY, I DON'T THINK IT'S BROKEN
OW!
NOT...ENOUGH... MUSCLES.

364

BEFORE MY FATHER DIED, HE ALWAYS TAUGHT ME THAT I COULD LIVE WITHOUT USING THE MAGIC THAT WAS GIVEN TO ME BY THE GODS.

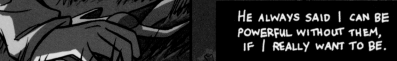

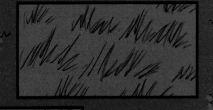

HE ALWAYS SAID I CAN BE POWERFUL WITHOUT THEM, IF I REALLY WANT TO BE.

NOW THAT HE'S GONE, I LIVE WITH RAED, THE LEADER OF THE MILITIA KNOWN AS "KEEPERS." HE SAYS USING MY MAGIC IS ESSENTIAL.

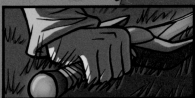

HE TELLS ME MY POWERS ARE A PART OF WHO I AM, AND USING THEM IS THE ONLY WAY I WILL EVER BE SUCCESSFUL.

BUT I STILL LIKE TO THINK THAT I CAN BE POWERFUL WITHOUT THEM...

A TEST FOR CENRI

BY AMY KIM GANTER

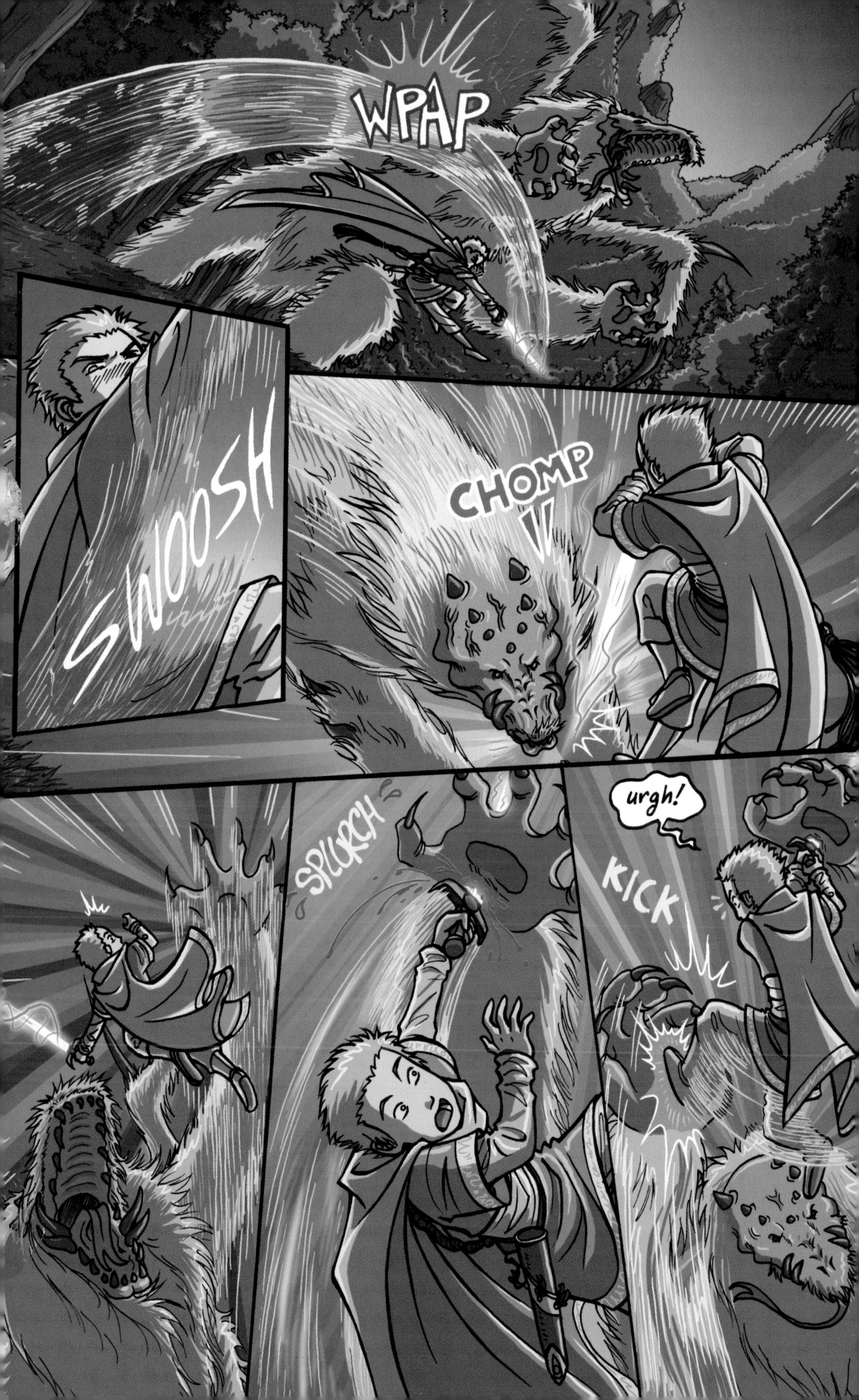
WPAP
SWOOSH
CHOMP
SPLURCH
urgh!
KICK

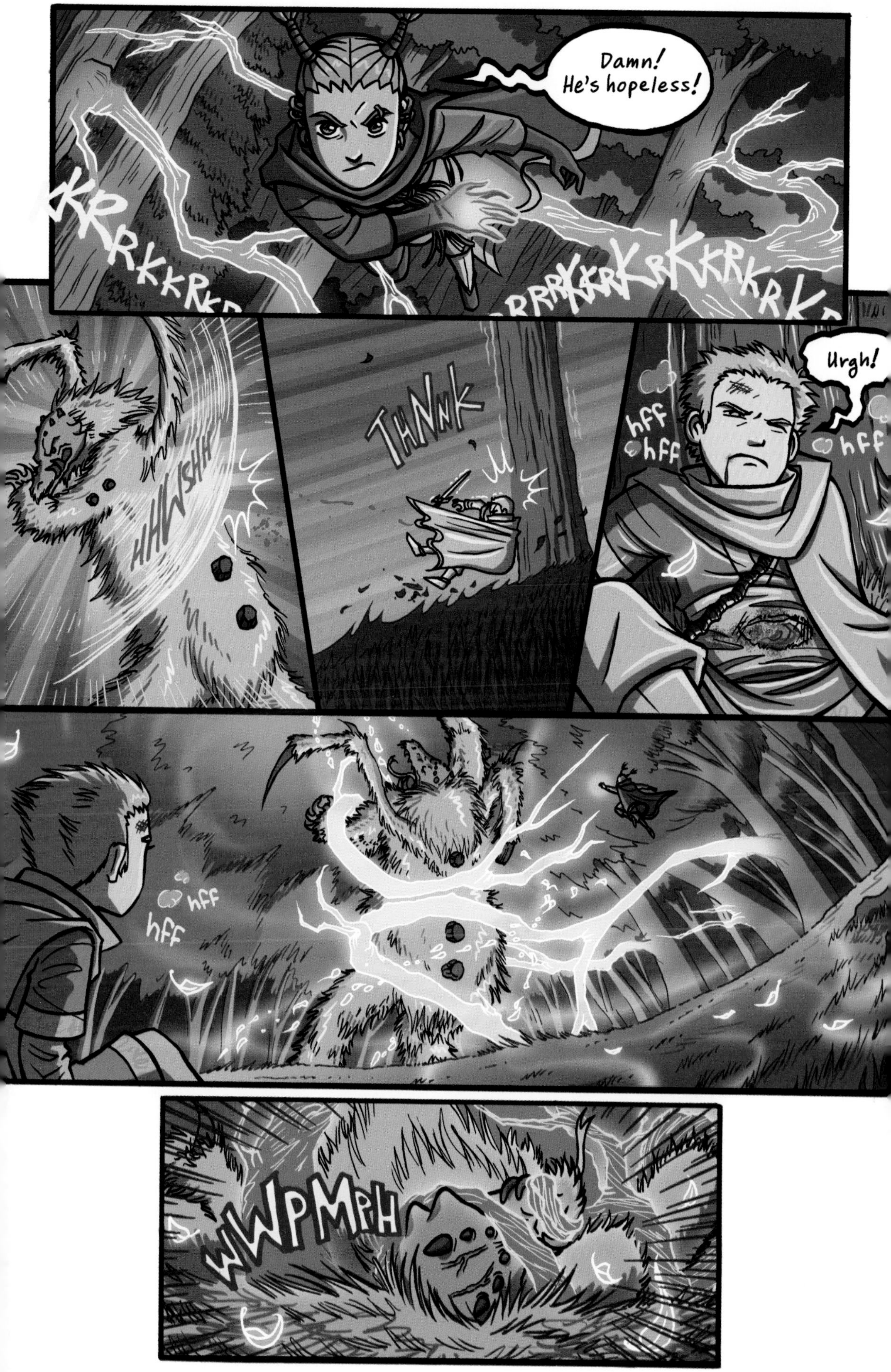
Damn!
He's hopeless!
THNNK
HHWSHH
Urgh!
hff
hff
hff
hff
hff
WWPMPH

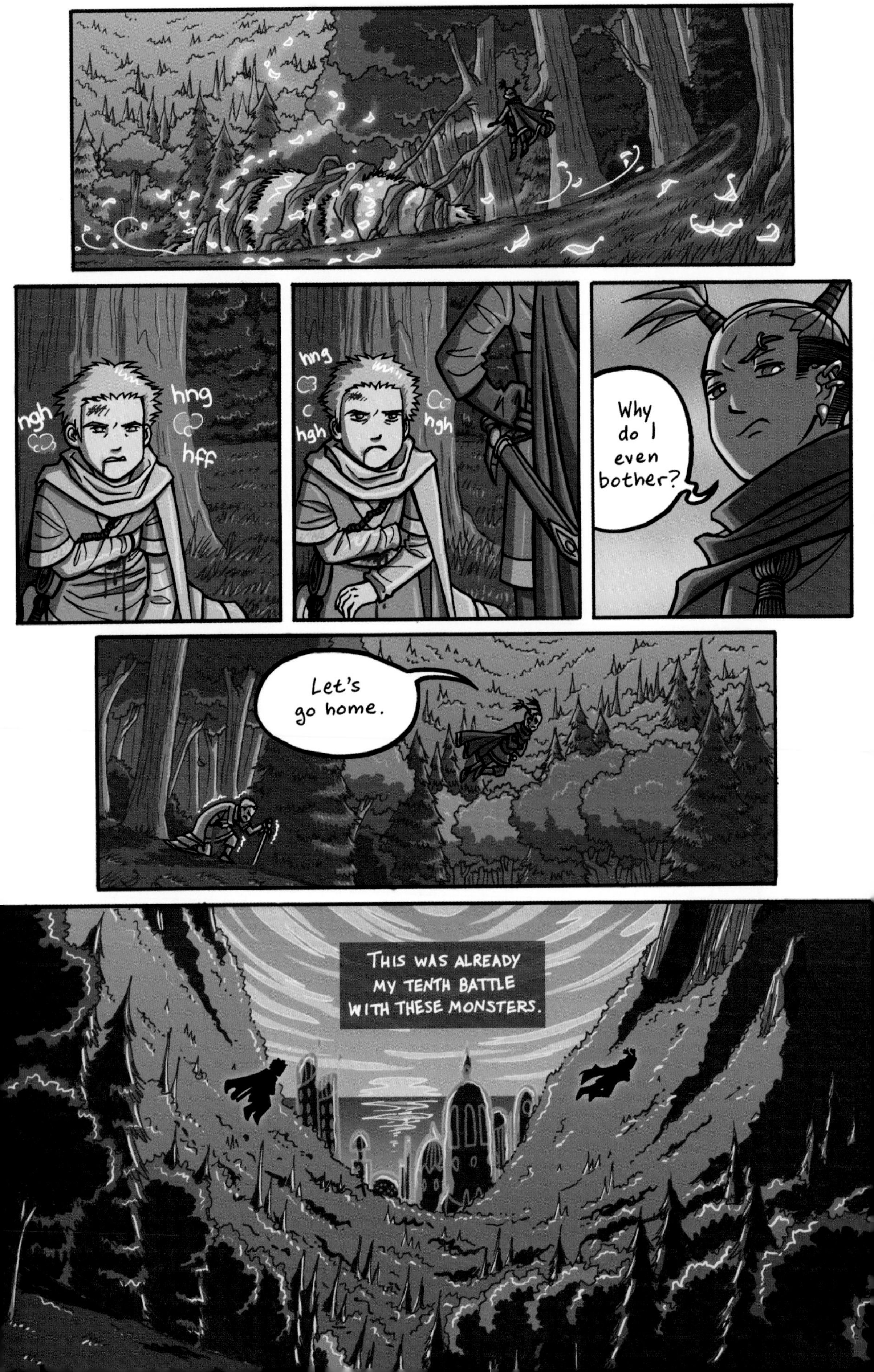
ngh
hng
hff
hng
hgh
ngh
Why do I even bother?
Let's go home.
THIS WAS ALREADY MY TENTH BATTLE WITH THESE MONSTERS.

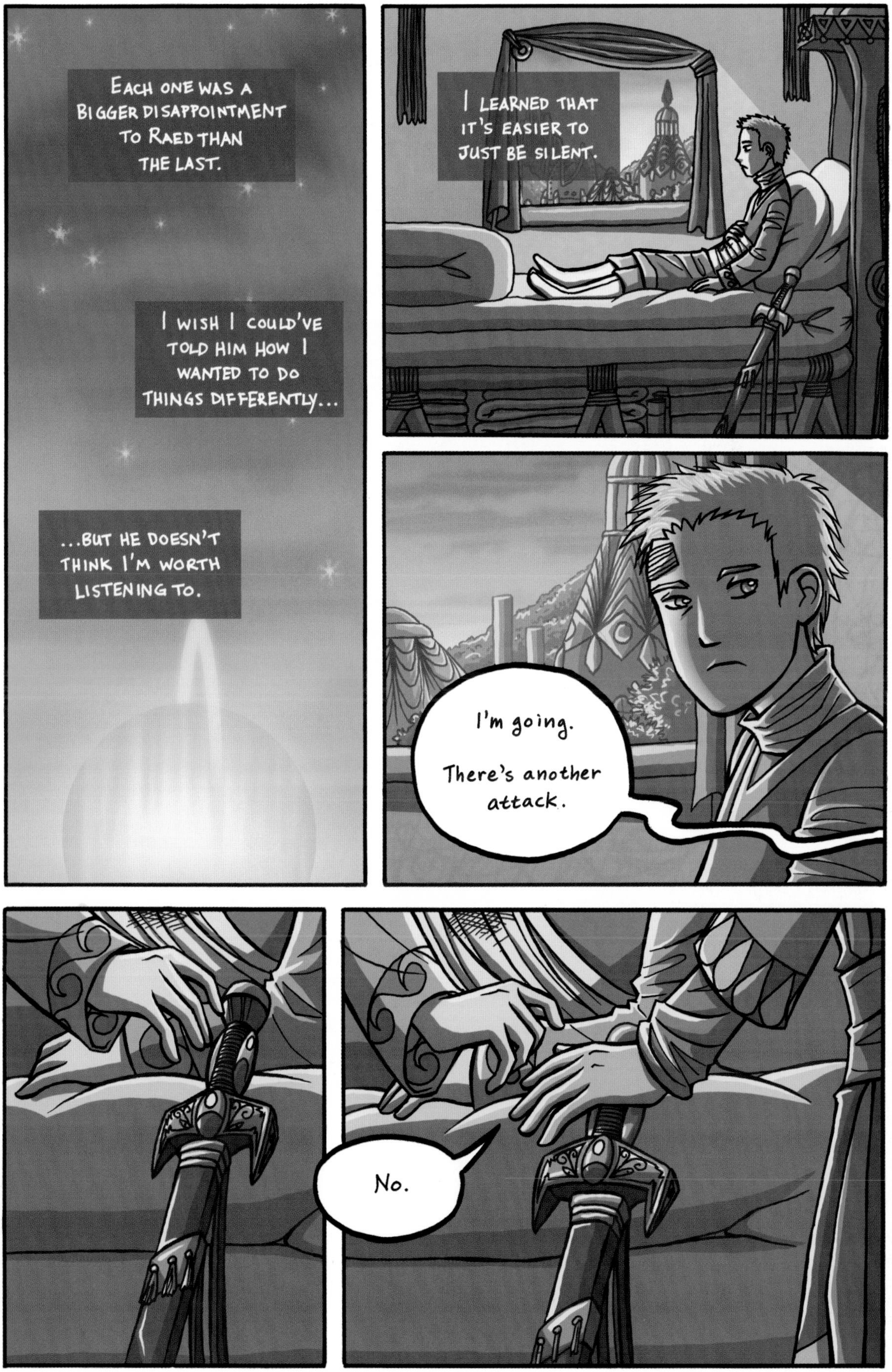
EACH ONE WAS A BIGGER DISAPPOINTMENT TO RAED THAN THE LAST.
I WISH I COULD'VE TOLD HIM HOW I WANTED TO DO THINGS DIFFERENTLY...
...BUT HE DOESN'T THINK I'M WORTH LISTENING TO.
I LEARNED THAT IT'S EASIER TO JUST BE SILENT.
I'm going.
There's another attack.
No.

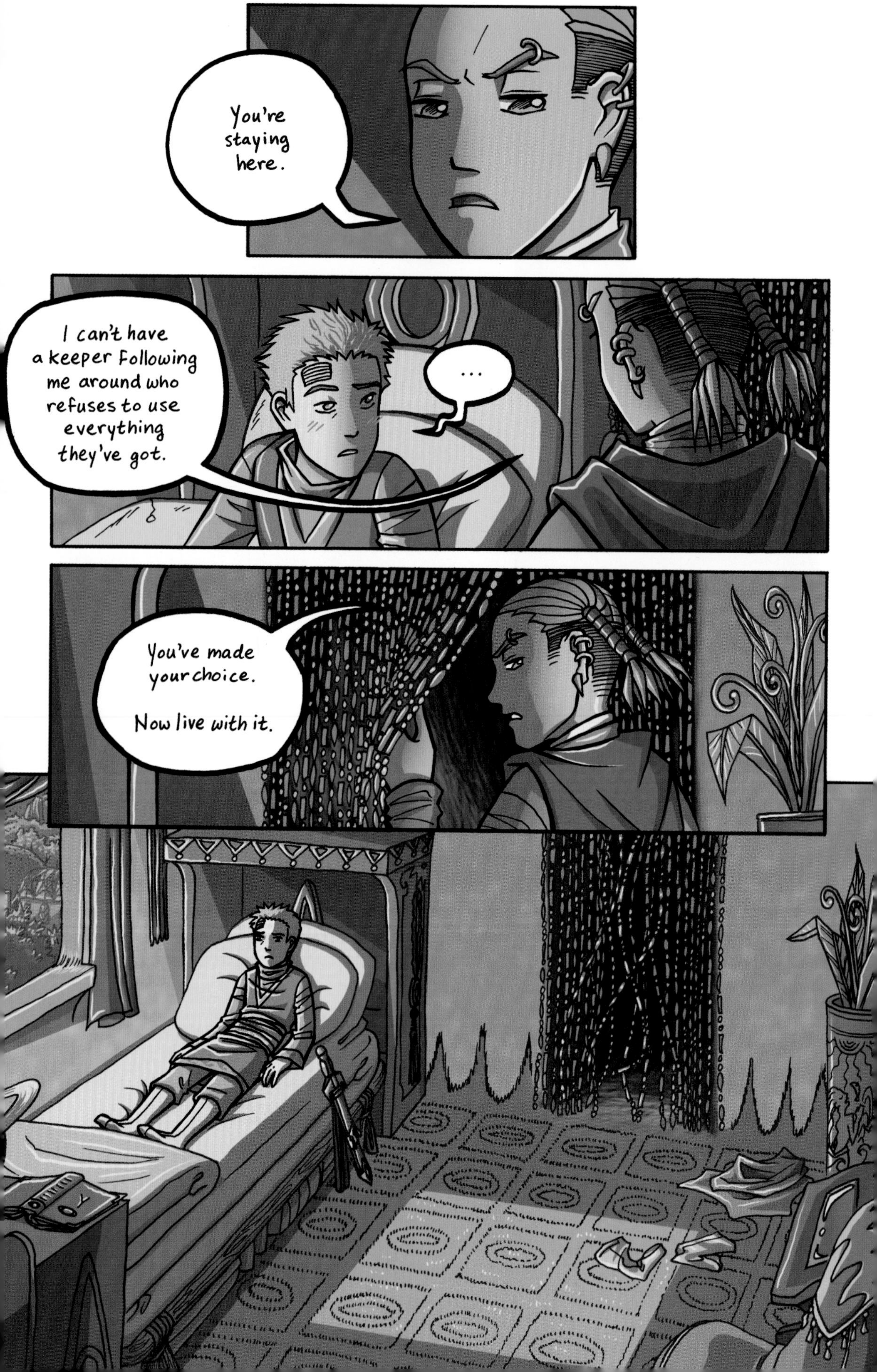
You're staying here.
I can't have a keeper following me around who refuses to use everything they've got.
...
You've made your choice.
Now live with it.

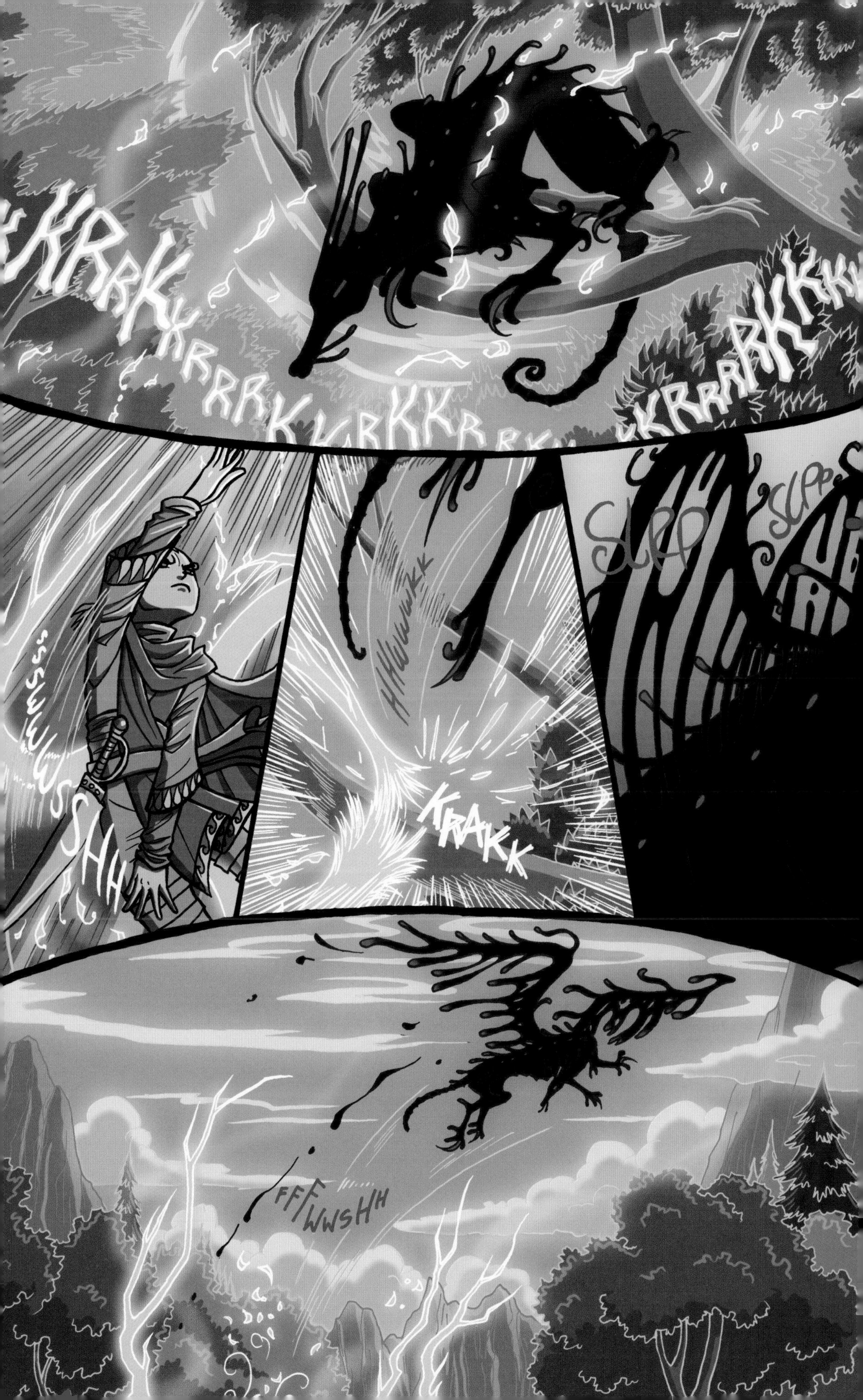
KRAKK
SLRP
FFFWWSHH

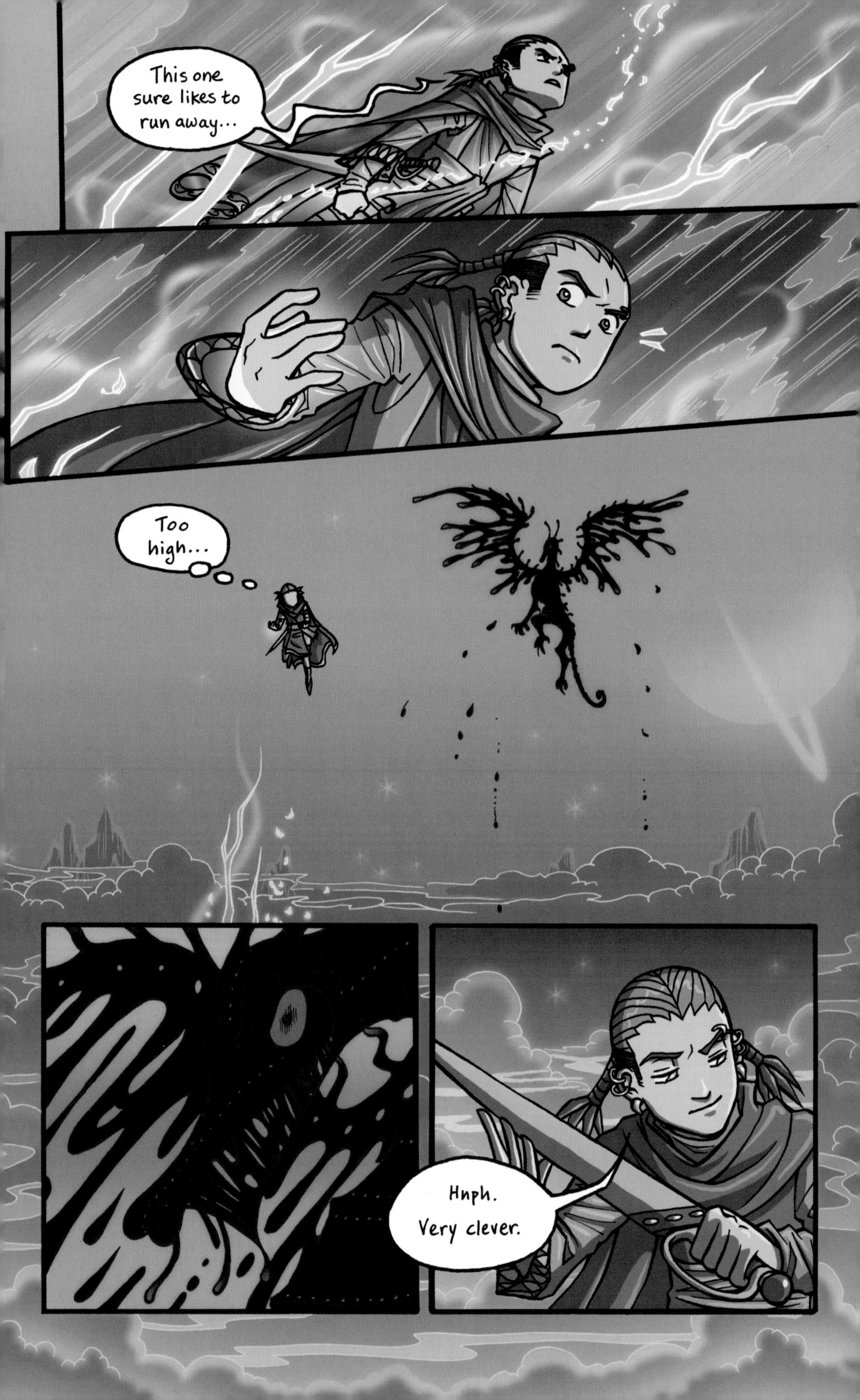
This one sure likes to run away...
Too high...
Hnph.
Very clever.

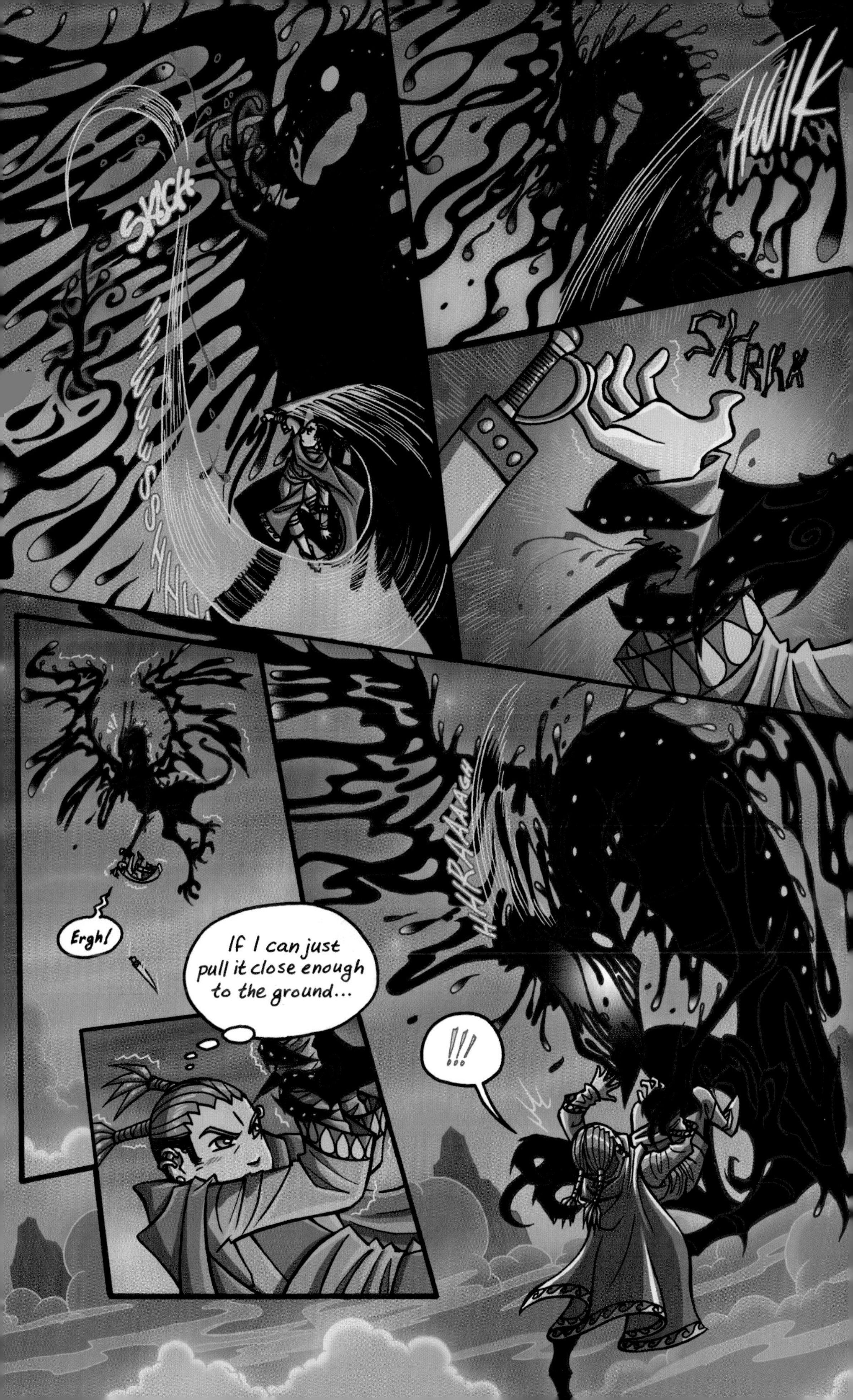
SKICH
HHWWUSSSHH
HWUK
SKRKK
Ergh!
If I can just pull it close enough to the ground...
HHRAAAAGH
!!!

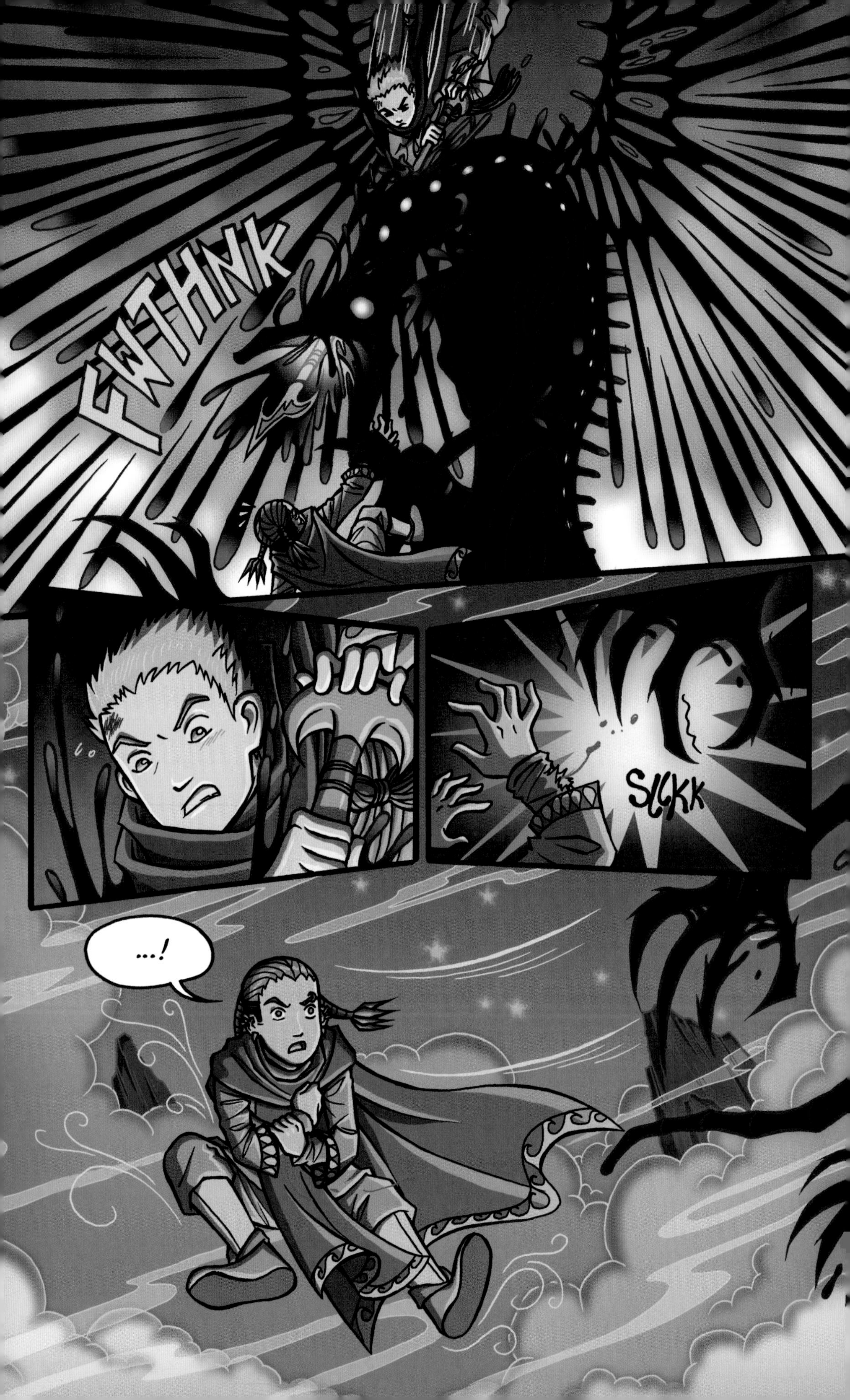
FWTHNK
SLCKK
...!

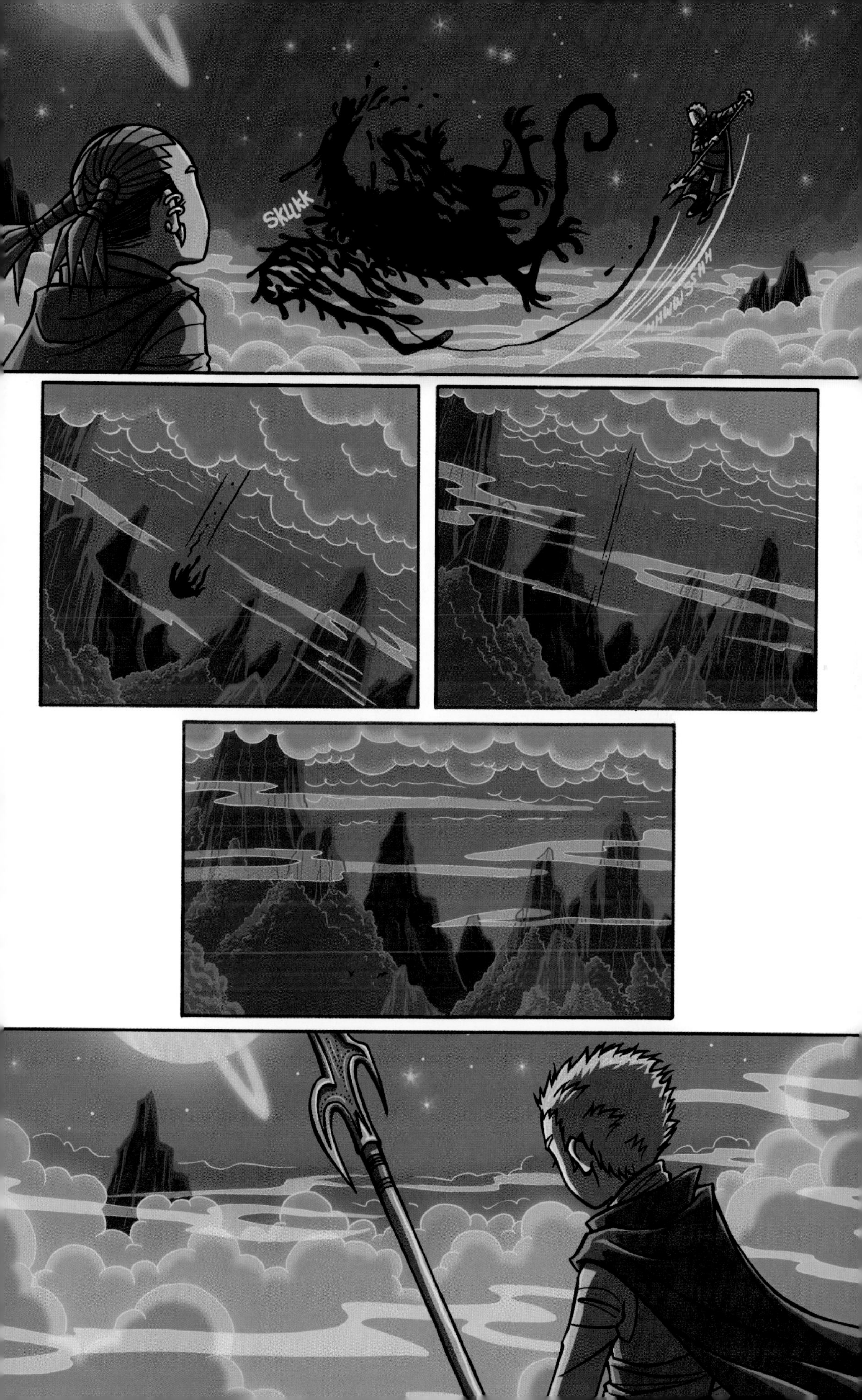
SKUKK
MHWWSSHH

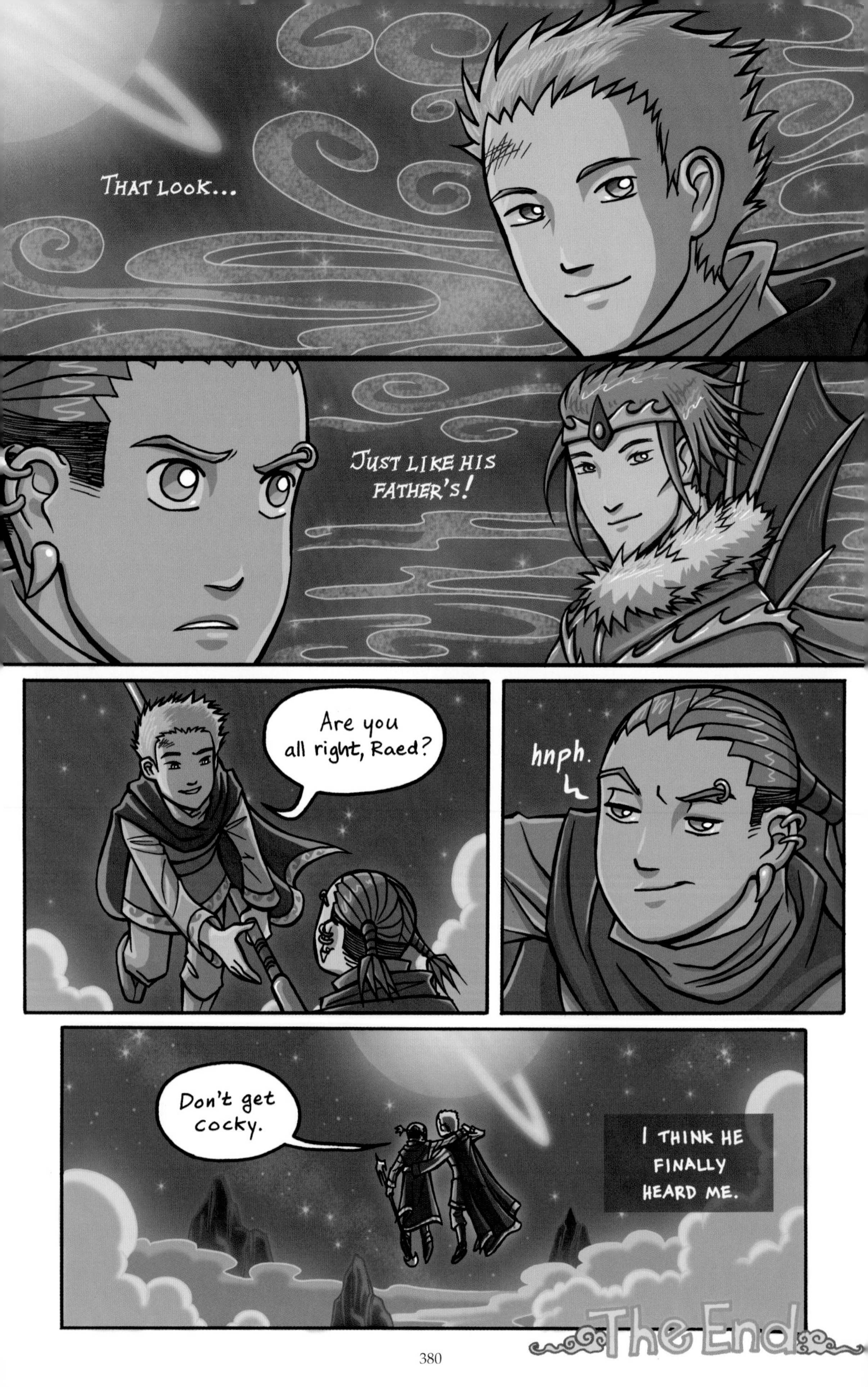
THAT LOOK...
JUST LIKE HIS FATHER'S!
Are you all right, Raed?
hnph.
Don't get cocky.
I THINK HE FINALLY HEARD ME.
The End

La Sonadora

by Joana Carneiro ★ Colors by Paulo Visgueiro

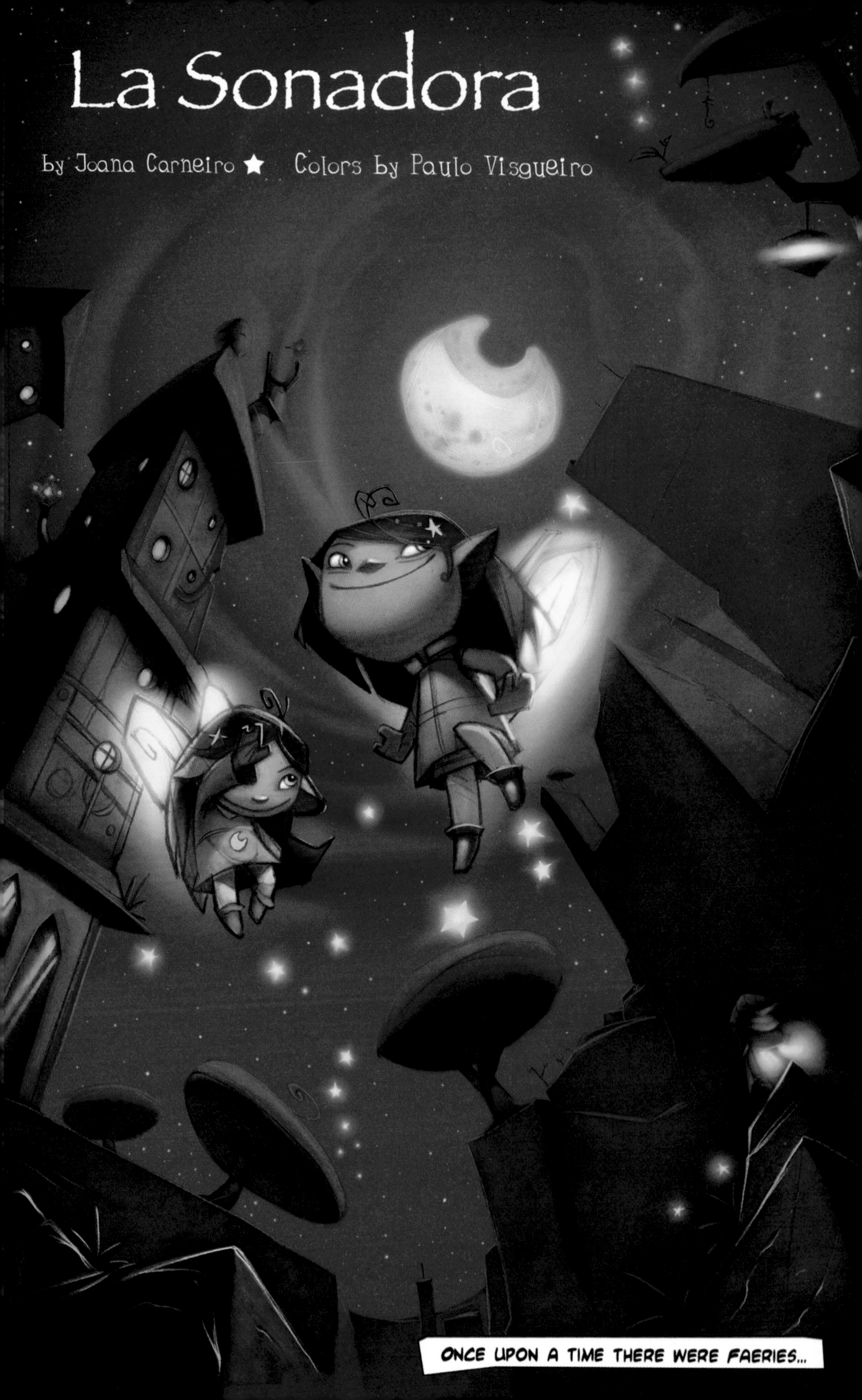
ONCE UPON A TIME THERE WERE FAERIES...

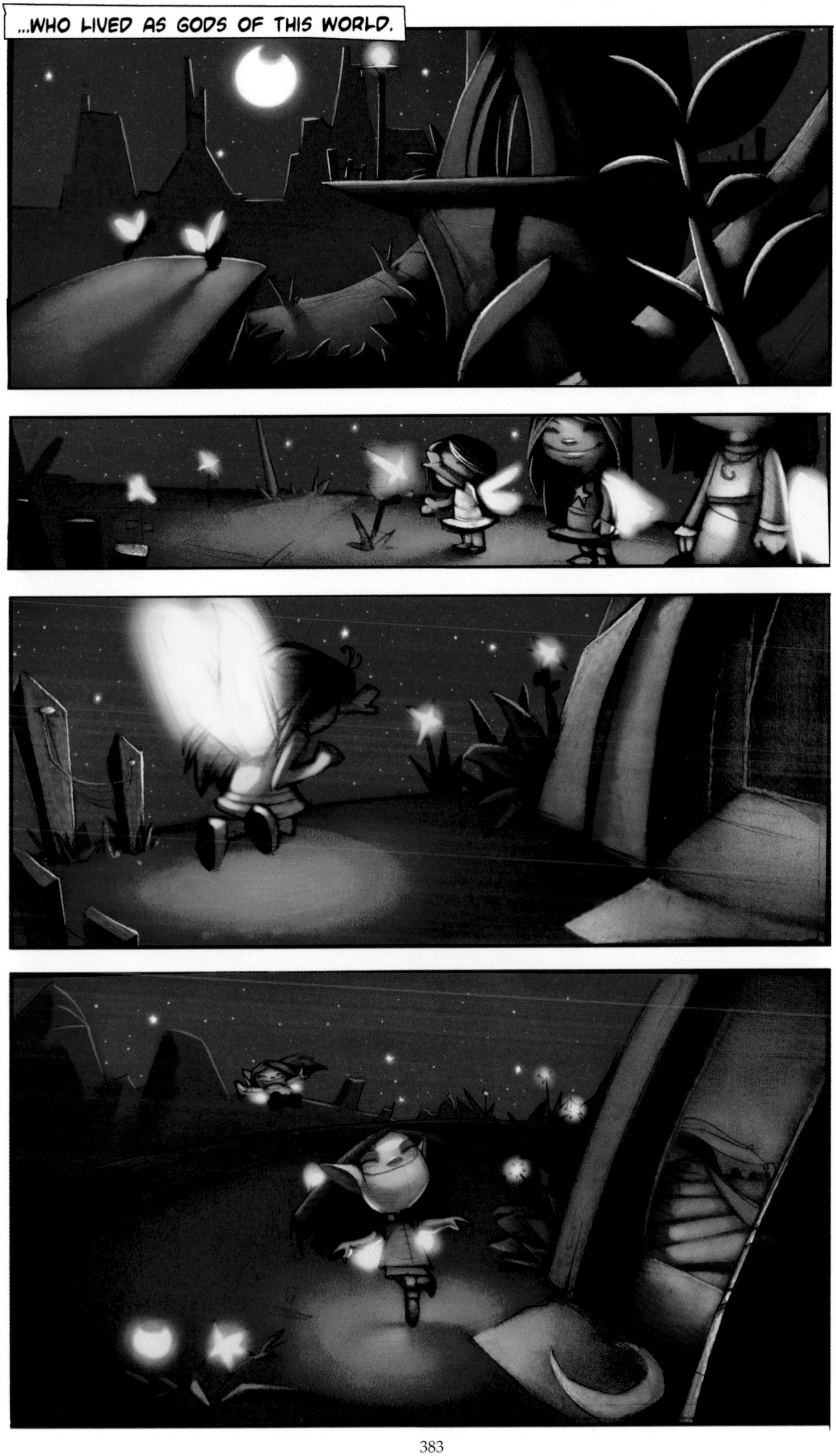
...WHO LIVED AS GODS OF THIS WORLD.

THEY LIVED CAREFREE LIVES...

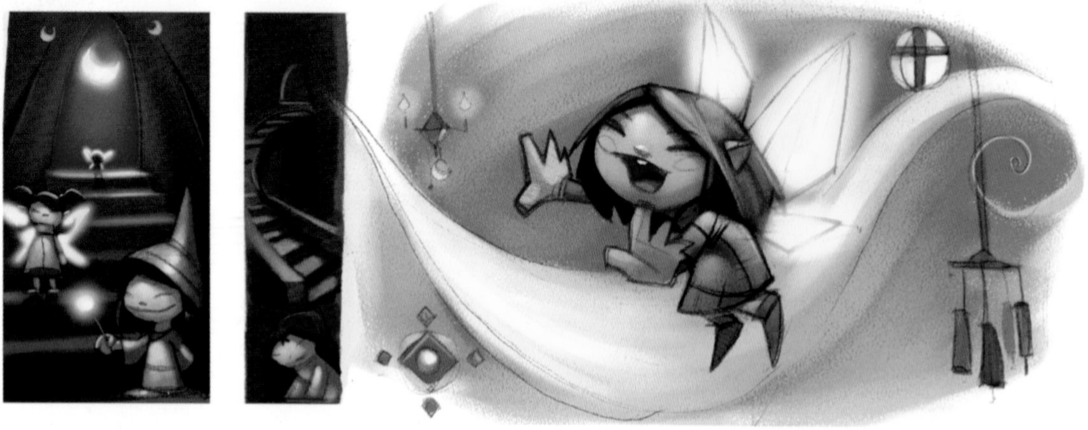

NEITHER BEING BAD ENOUGH TO BE PUNISHED, NOR GOOD ENOUGH TO BE SAVED.

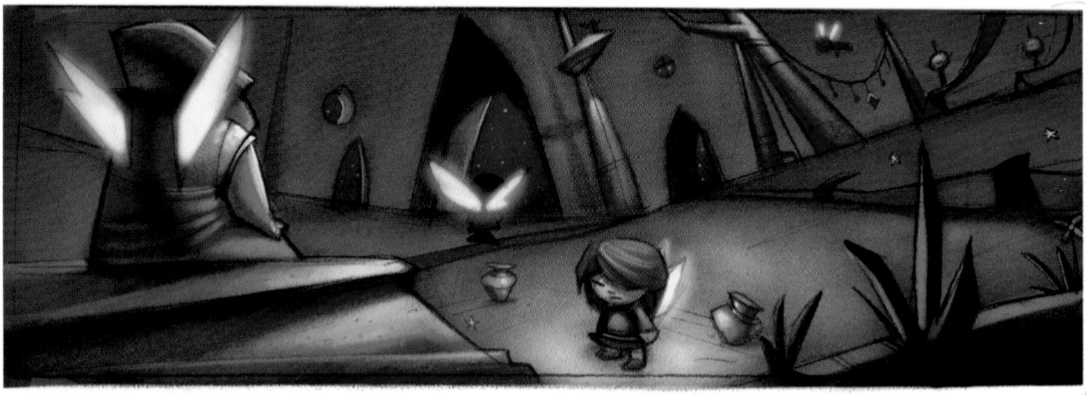

THE FAERIES WERE RULED BY THEIR FAERIE GODMOTHER. SHE WAS THE QUEEN OF ALL LIGHT AND ENCHANTMENTS, AND WAS RESPECTED THROUGHOUT HER KINGDOM BY ALL LIVING CREATURES.

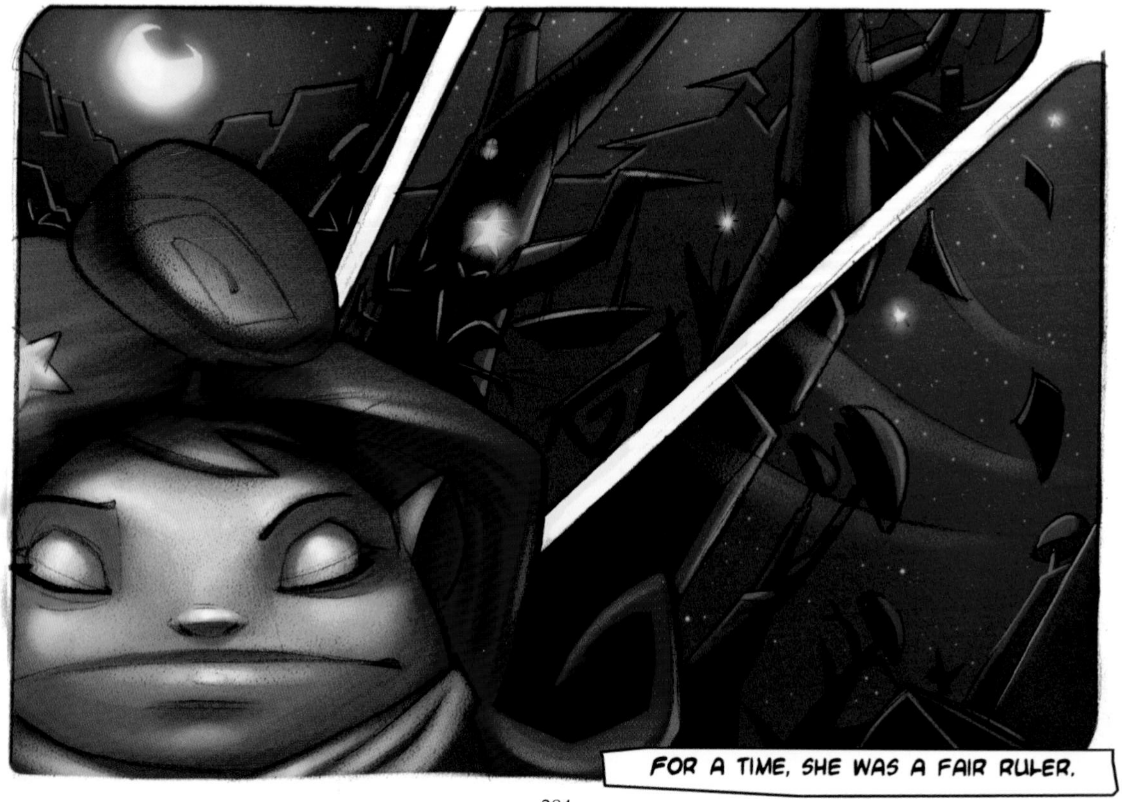
FOR A TIME, SHE WAS A FAIR RULER.

BUT AS TIME PASSED ON, THE FAERIE QUEEN BECAME CORRUPTED BY THE POWER BESTOWED UPON HER BY THE STARS.

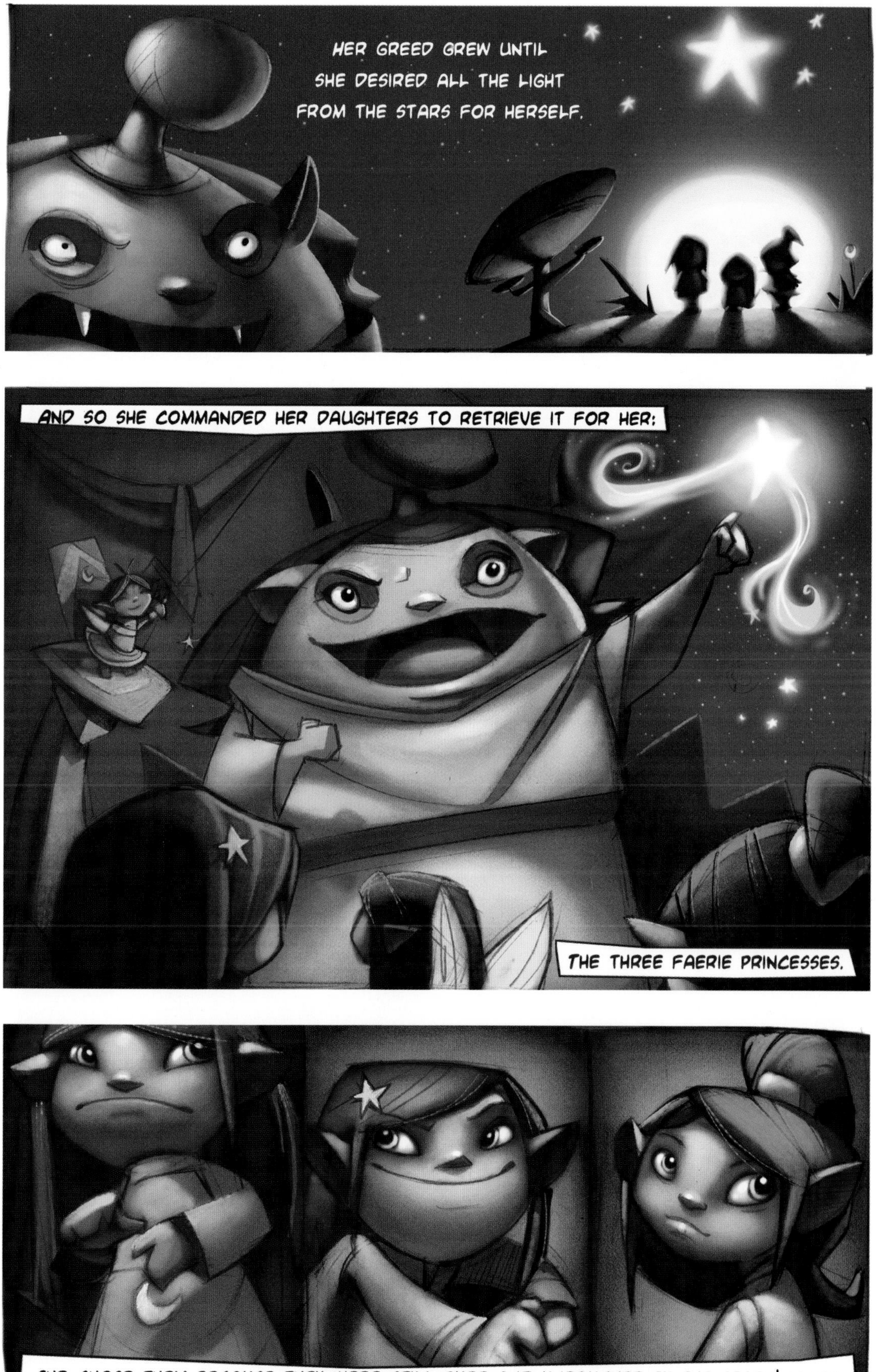
HER GREED GREW UNTIL SHE DESIRED ALL THE LIGHT FROM THE STARS FOR HERSELF.
AND SO SHE COMMANDED HER DAUGHTERS TO RETRIEVE IT FOR HER:
THE THREE FAERIE PRINCESSES.
SHE CHOSE THEM BECAUSE THEY WERE STILL PURE AND UNTOUCHED BY THE STARS' POWER.

TO HELP THEM ON THEIR QUEST, THE QUEEN GAVE THE PRINCESSES A MAGIC LANTERN
TO COLLECT THE LIGHT OF THE STARS.

OOOOOOH!

"THE LIGHT OF THE STARS, MOM?"
ASKED THE FIRST PRINCESS.

"AM I ALLOWED TO DO SO?"

SHE WAS VERY SCARED.

SO SHE FLEW TOWARD THE VERY FIRST STAR,

AND TOOK ONLY HALF OF ITS LIGHT.

BUT IT WAS NOT ENOUGH.

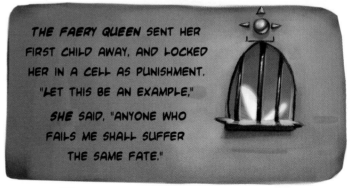

THE FAERY QUEEN SENT HER
FIRST CHILD AWAY, AND LOCKED
HER IN A CELL AS PUNISHMENT.
"LET THIS BE AN EXAMPLE,"
SHE SAID, "ANYONE WHO
FAILS ME SHALL SUFFER
THE SAME FATE."

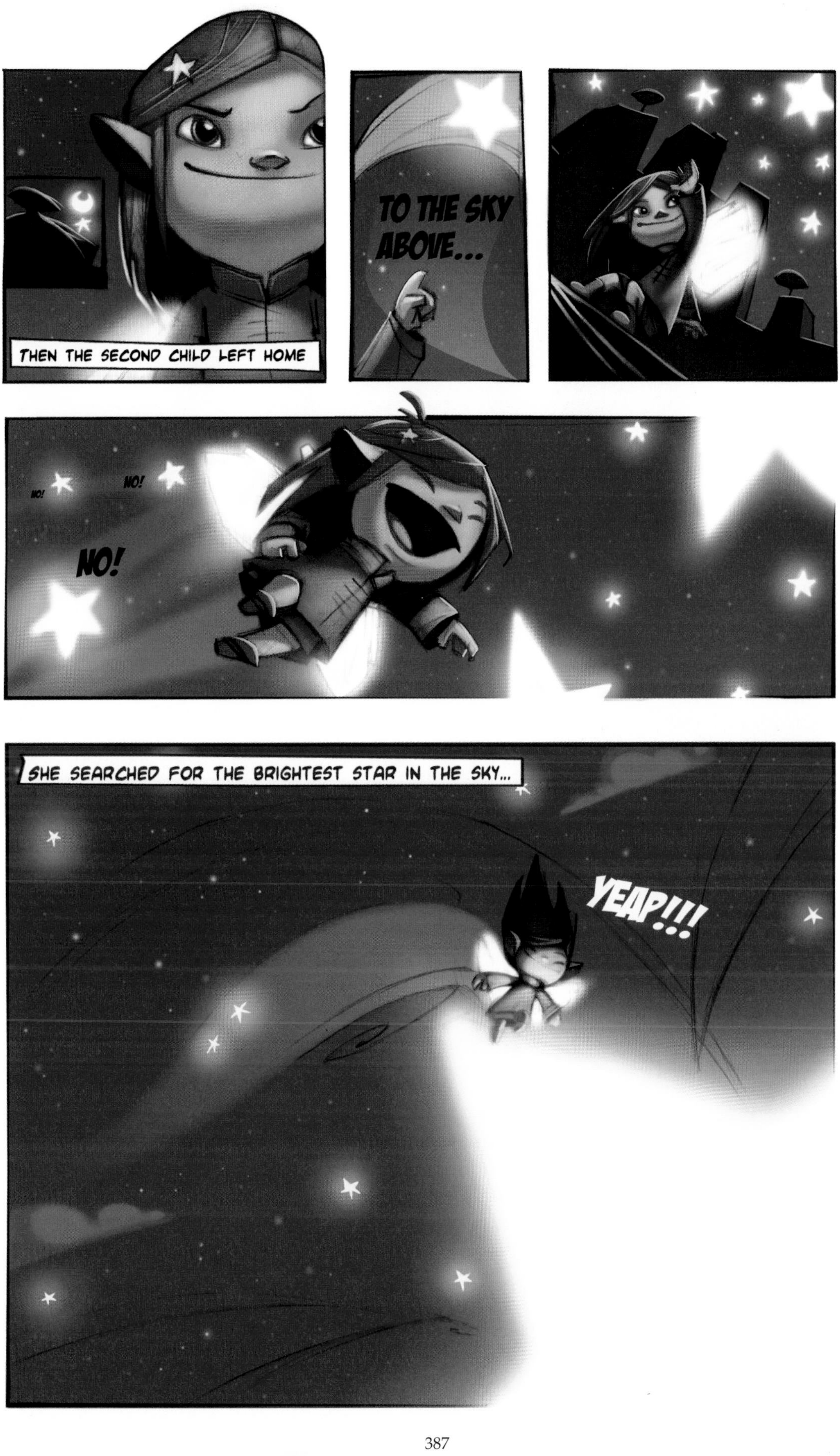
THEN THE SECOND CHILD LEFT HOME
TO THE SKY ABOVE...
NO!
NO!
NO!
SHE SEARCHED FOR THE BRIGHTEST STAR IN THE SKY...
YEAP!!!

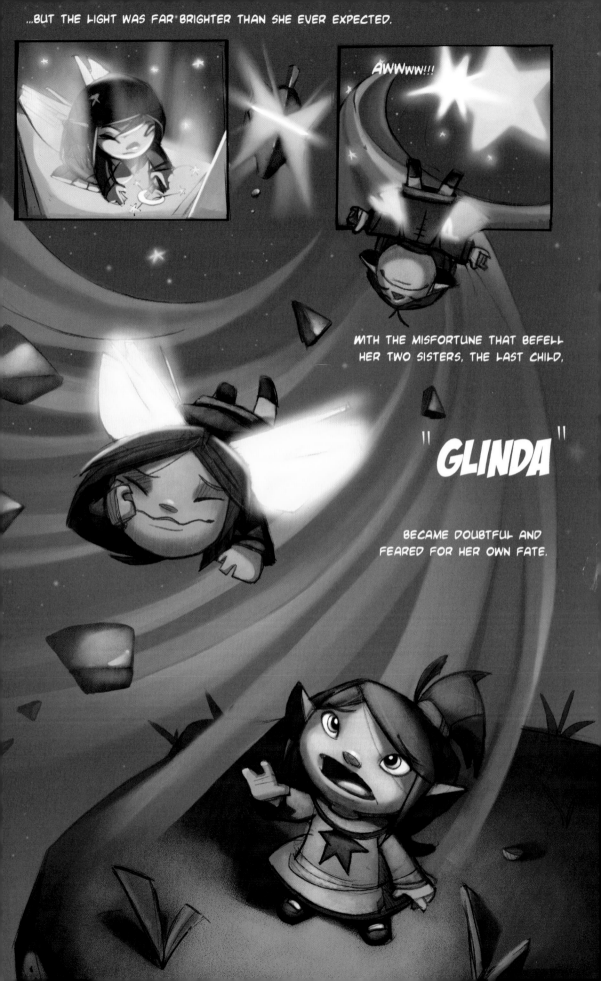

GLINDA WAS THE YOUNGEST AND THE LAST OF THE THREE PRINCESSES LEFT TO PURSUE THE LIGHT OF THE STARS. UNLIKE HER OTHER SISTERS, GLINDA WAS BORN WITHOUT WINGS, BUT SHE WAS GIFTED WITH THE ABILITY TO DREAM DURING THE DAYTIME.

WHEN SHE WAS A CHILD, GLINDA WOULD OFTEN DREAM OF FLYING UP TO THE STARS. HER MOTHER ONCE TOLD GLINDA THAT HER WINGS COULD ONLY RISE FROM HER SHOULDERS WHEN THE TIME WAS RIGHT, AND THAT SHE WOULD HAVE TO OVERCOME GREAT ADVERSITY TO DO SO. ONLY THEN WOULD SHE BECOME A TRUE FAERIE SPIRIT.

TIME PASSED, BUT GLINDA WAS NEVER BLESSED WITH WINGS. UNABLE TO FLY, SHE HAD NO OTHER CHOICE BUT TO ASK FOR SPIRITUAL GUIDANCE.

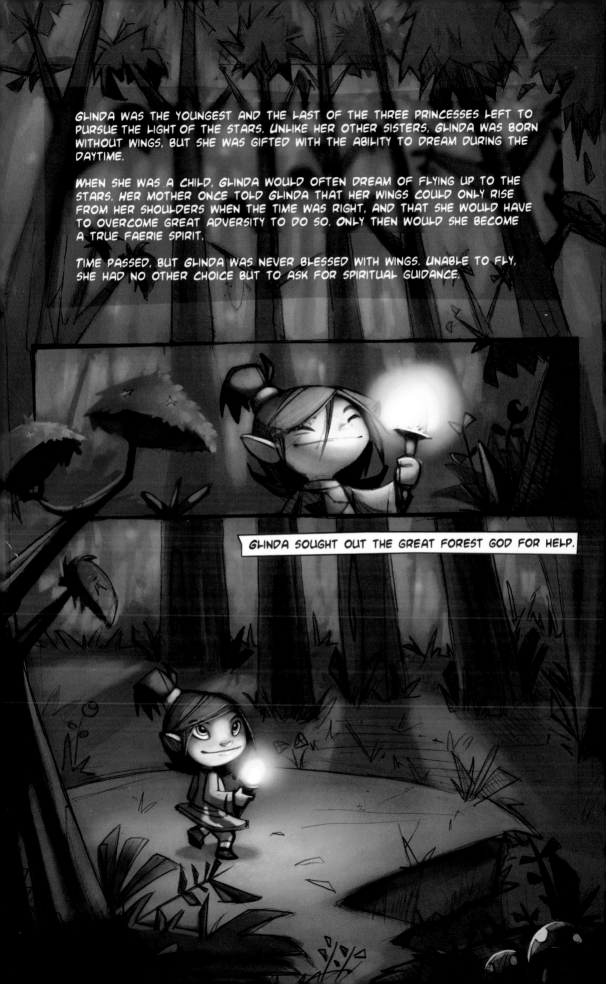

GLINDA SOUGHT OUT THE GREAT FOREST GOD FOR HELP.

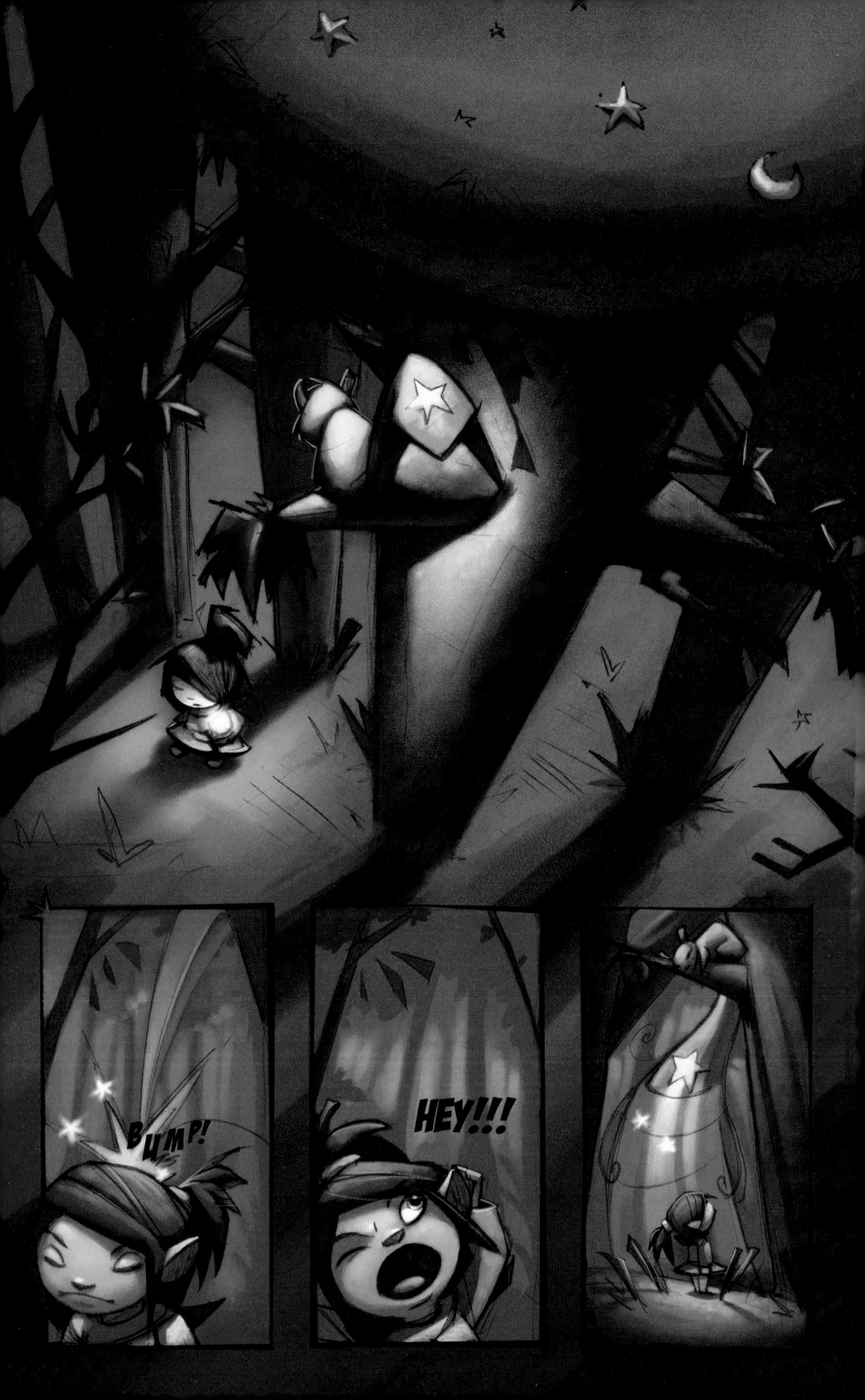
BUMP!
HEY!!!

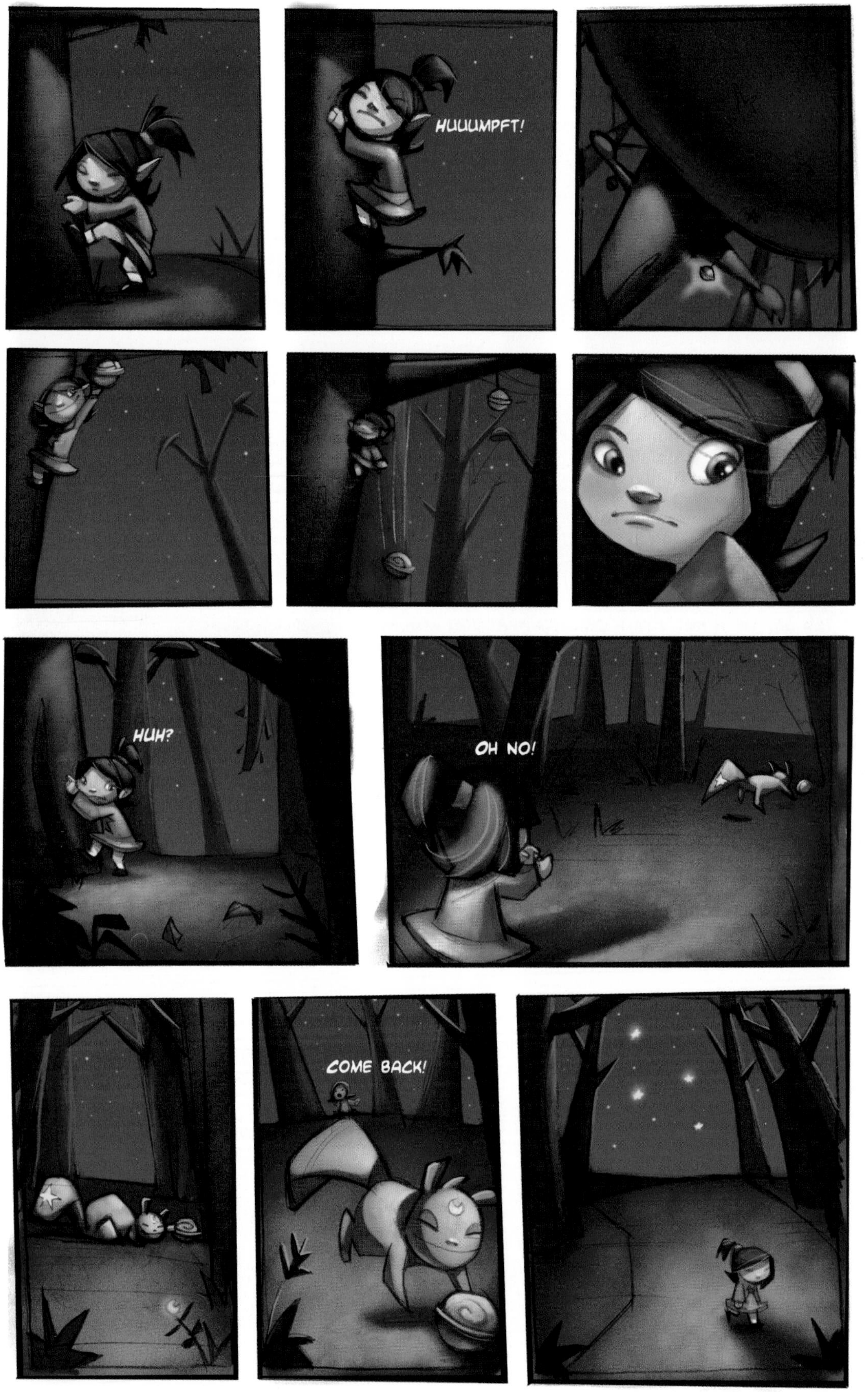
HUUUMPFT!
HUH?
OH NO!
COME BACK!

BUT LUCK NEVER TRULY LEAVES THOSE WHO HAVE HOPE.

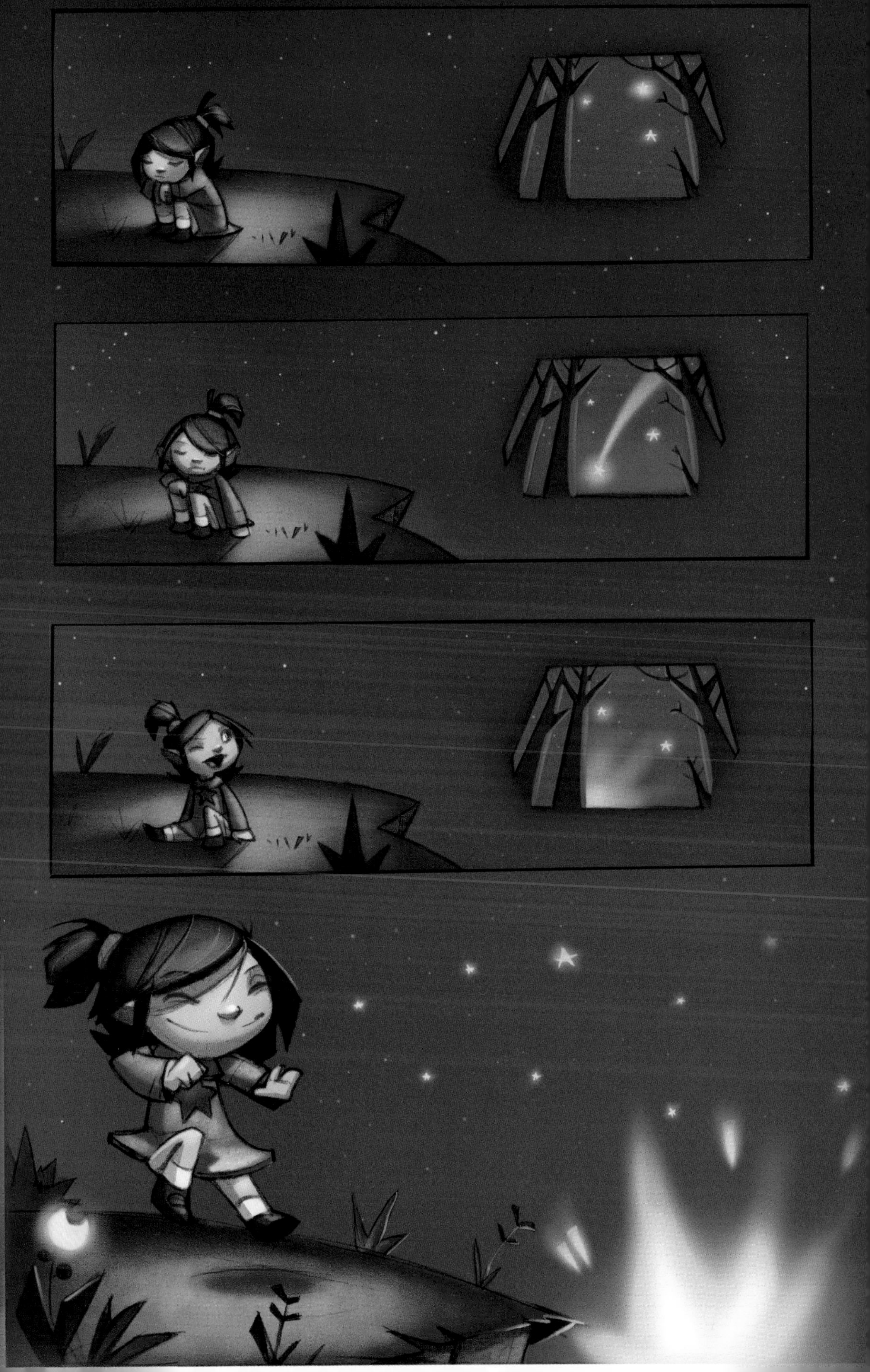

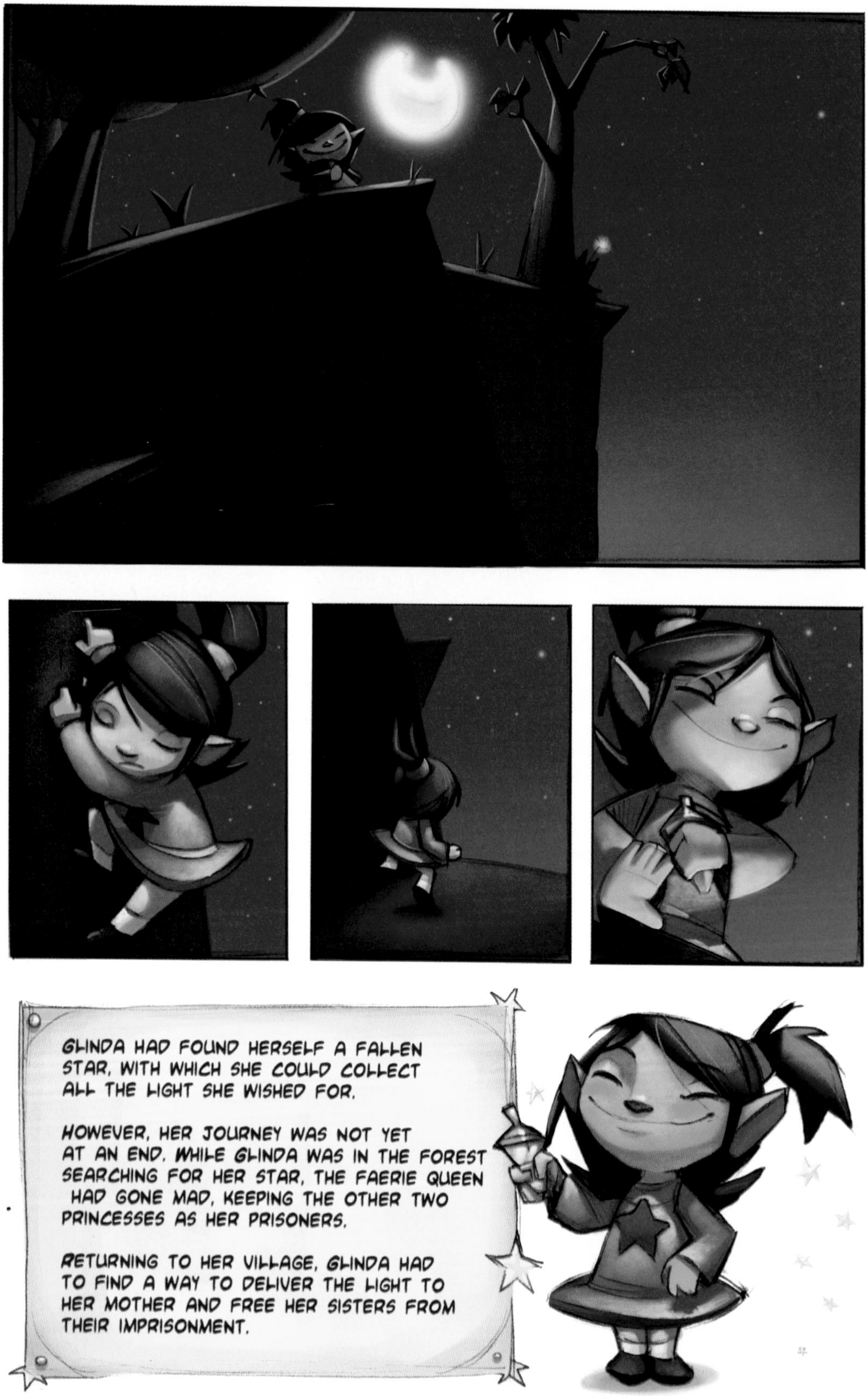
GLINDA HAD FOUND HERSELF A FALLEN STAR, WITH WHICH SHE COULD COLLECT ALL THE LIGHT SHE WISHED FOR.
HOWEVER, HER JOURNEY WAS NOT YET AT AN END. WHILE GLINDA WAS IN THE FOREST SEARCHING FOR HER STAR, THE FAERIE QUEEN HAD GONE MAD, KEEPING THE OTHER TWO PRINCESSES AS HER PRISONERS.
RETURNING TO HER VILLAGE, GLINDA HAD TO FIND A WAY TO DELIVER THE LIGHT TO HER MOTHER AND FREE HER SISTERS FROM THEIR IMPRISONMENT.

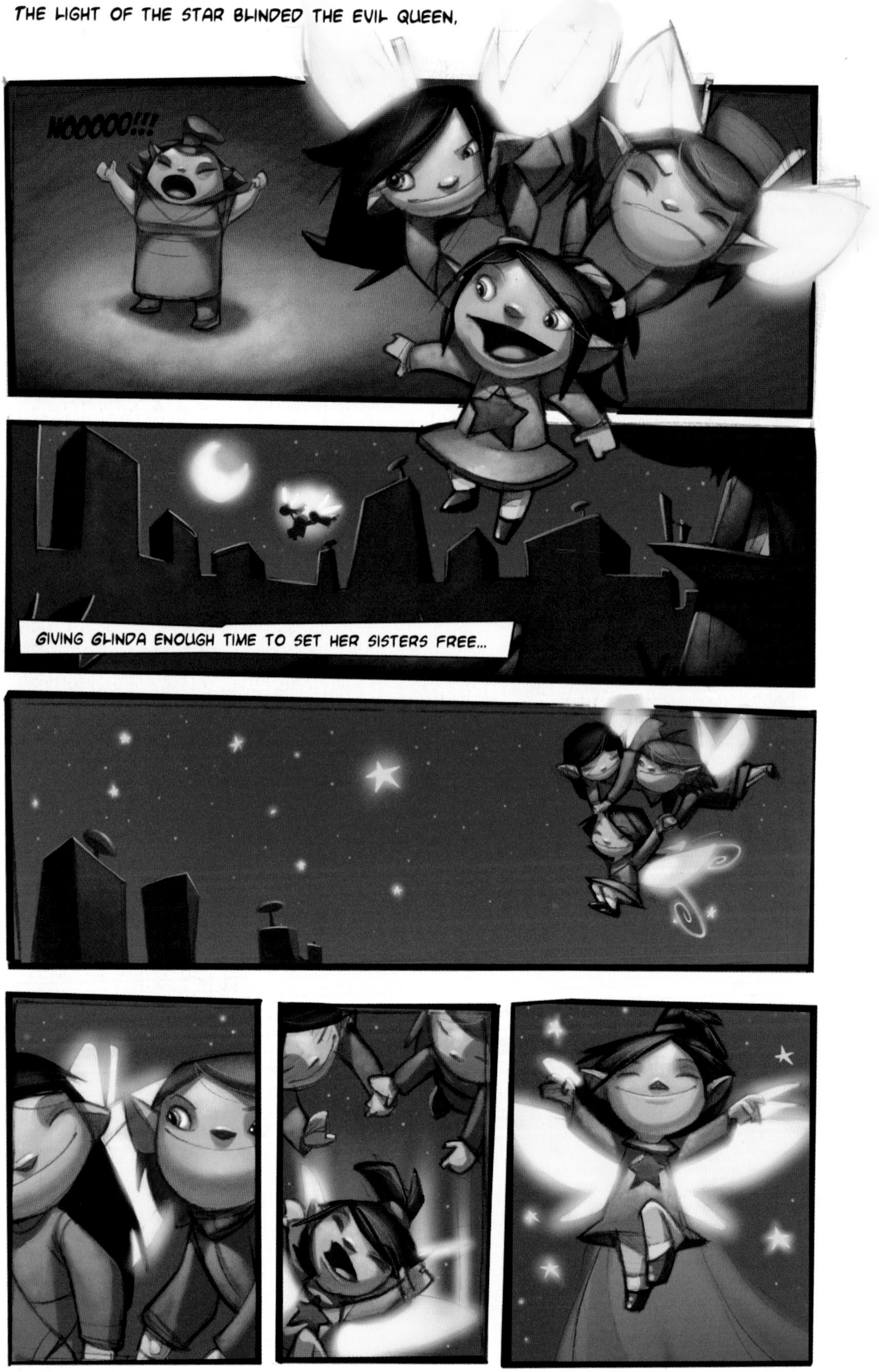
THE LIGHT OF THE STAR BLINDED THE EVIL QUEEN,
NOOOOO!!!
GIVING GLINDA ENOUGH TIME TO SET HER SISTERS FREE...

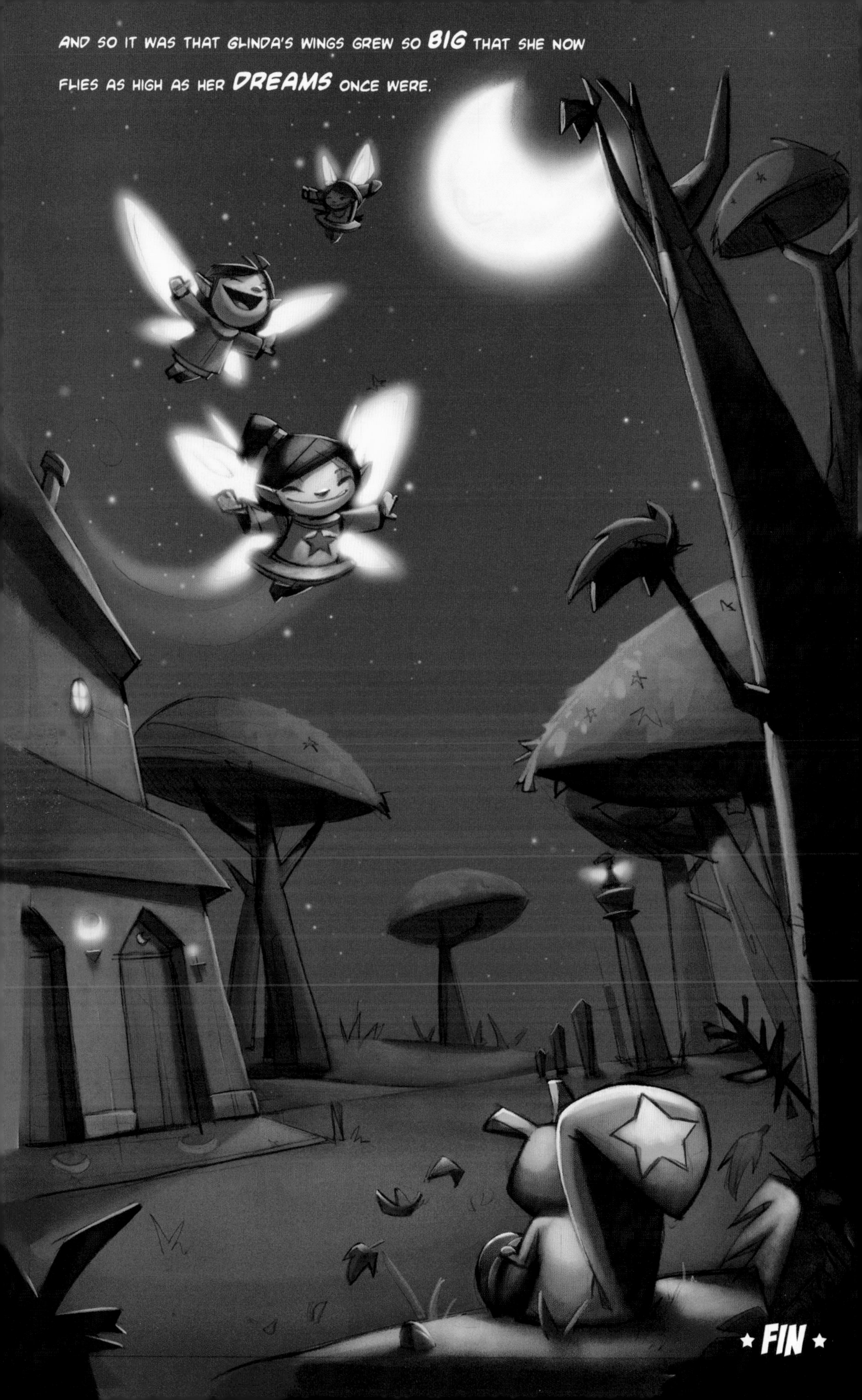
AND SO IT WAS THAT GLINDA'S WINGS GREW SO BIG THAT SHE NOW FLIES AS HIGH AS HER DREAMS ONCE WERE.
FIN

SKYBLUE

art·**KNESS**(www.kness.net)
story·**M.FORICHON**(matthieu.forichon.free.fr)
translation·**CLAIRE DE MASSÉ**
covercolor·**MADE**(www.m4de.com)

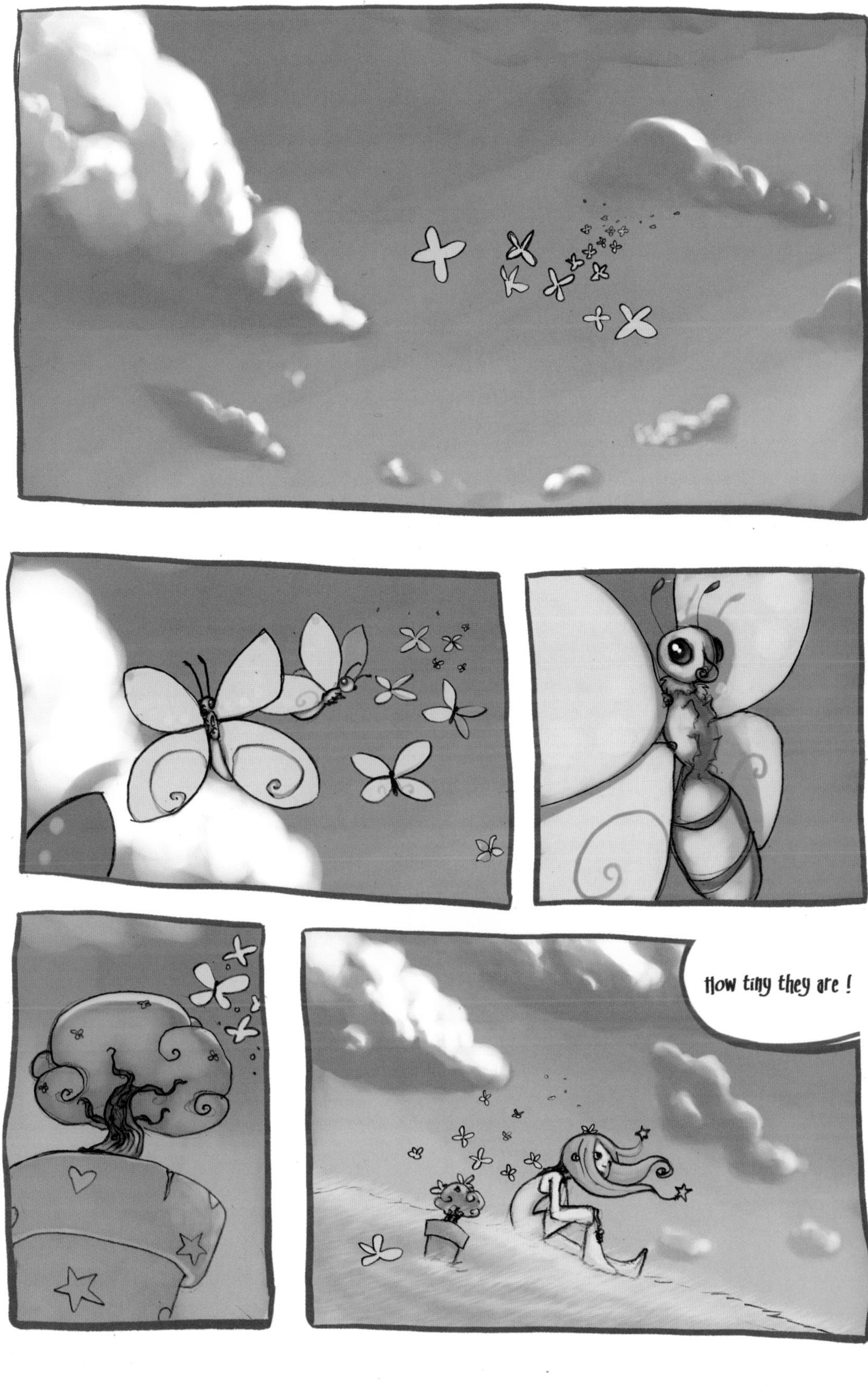
How tiny they are !

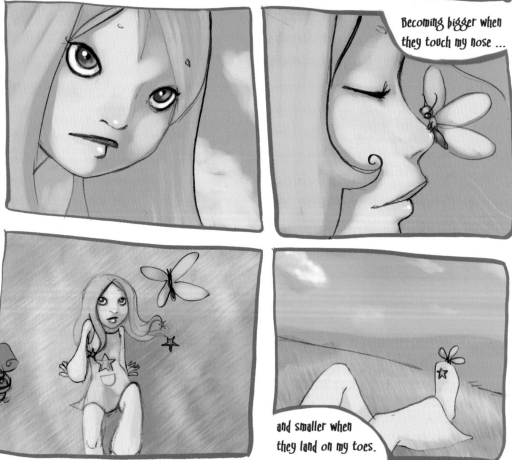

Becoming bigger when they touch my nose ...

and smaller when they land on my toes.

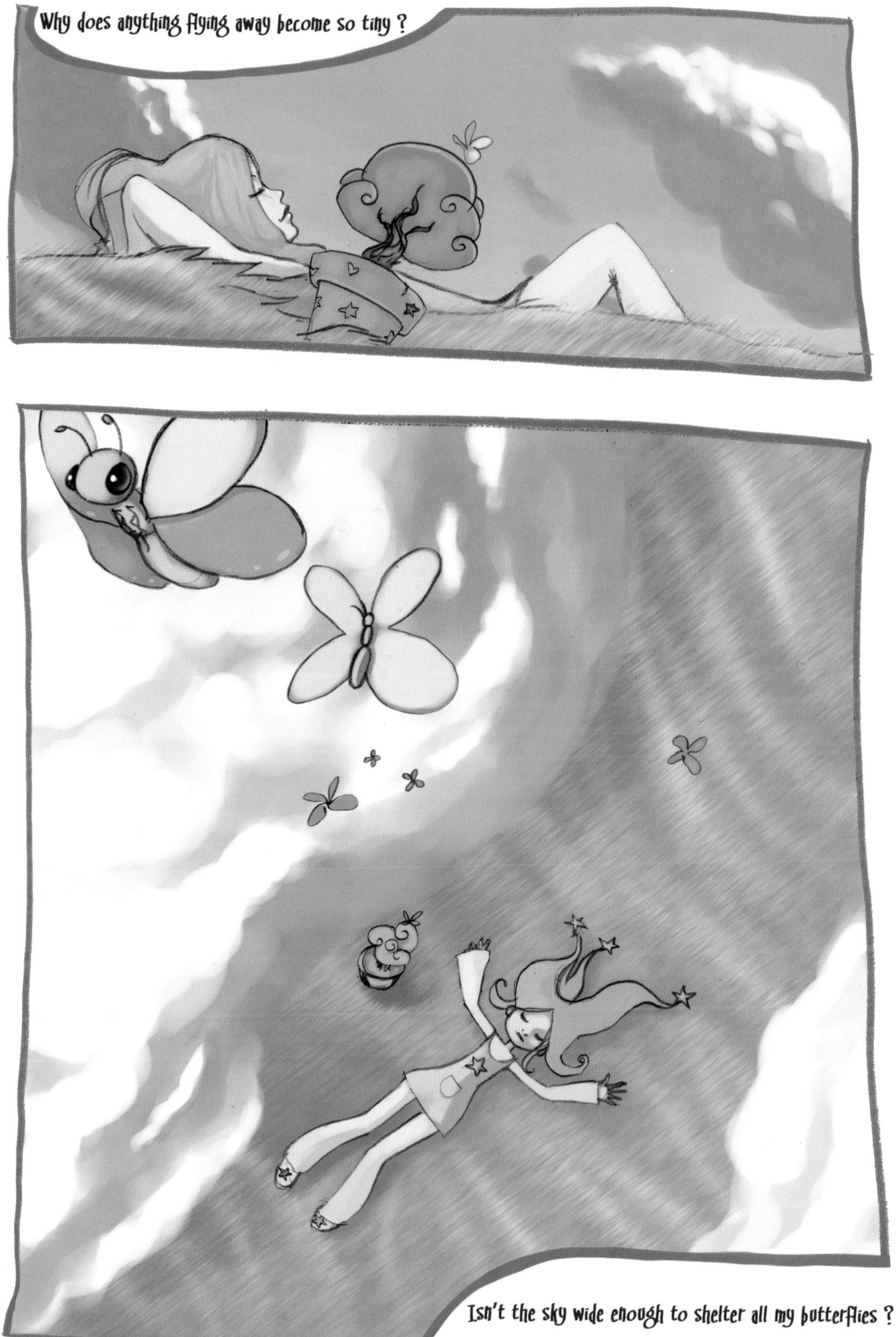
Why does anything flying away become so tiny ?
Isn't the sky wide enough to shelter all my butterflies ?

If they remained the same size as on my nose ...

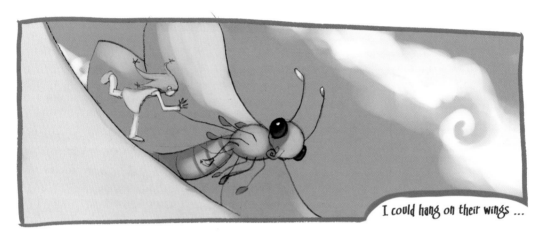

I could hang on their wings ...

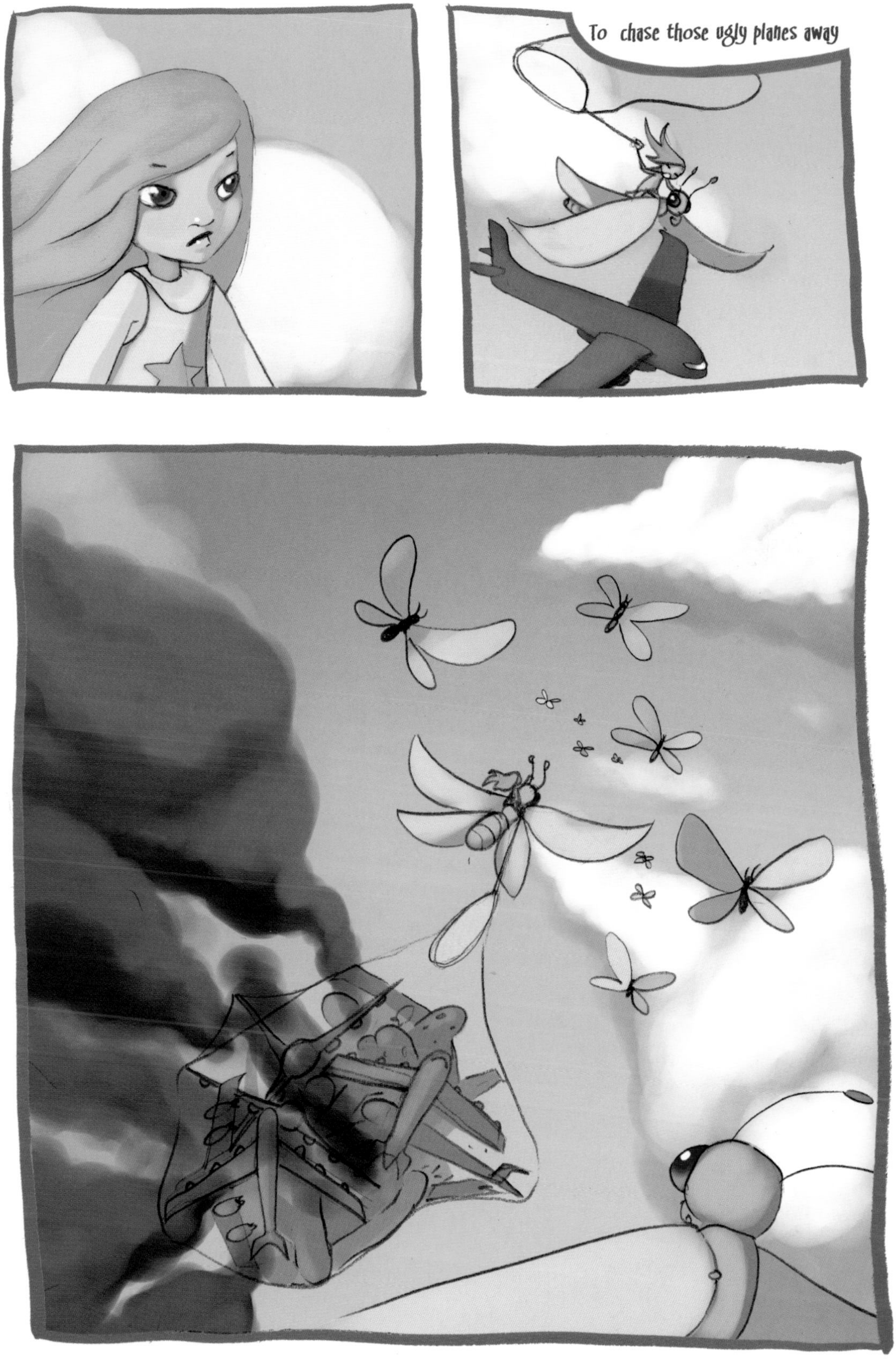
To chase those ugly planes away

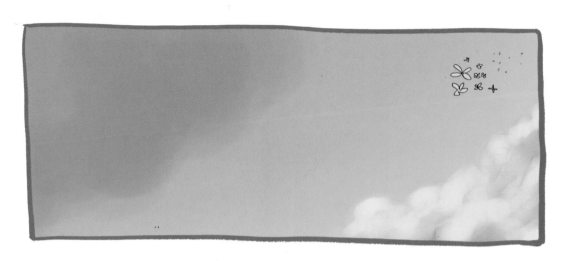

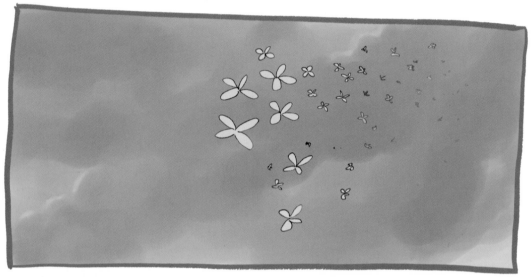

And see my parents again.

In my pockets,

I would bring pieces of clouds back

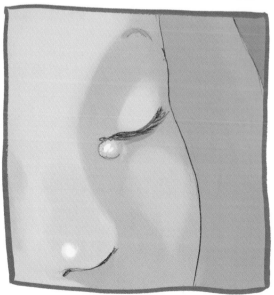

To dry our tears.

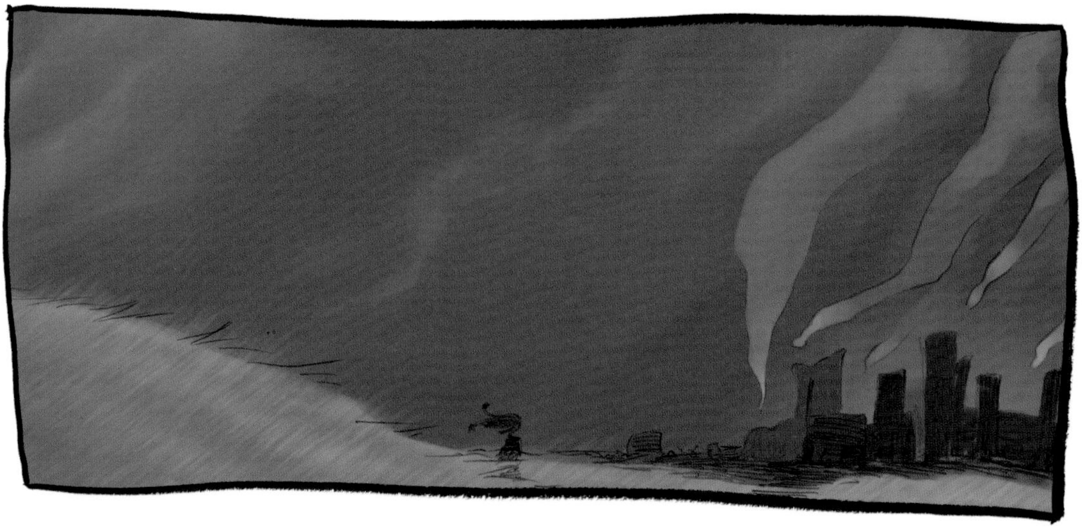

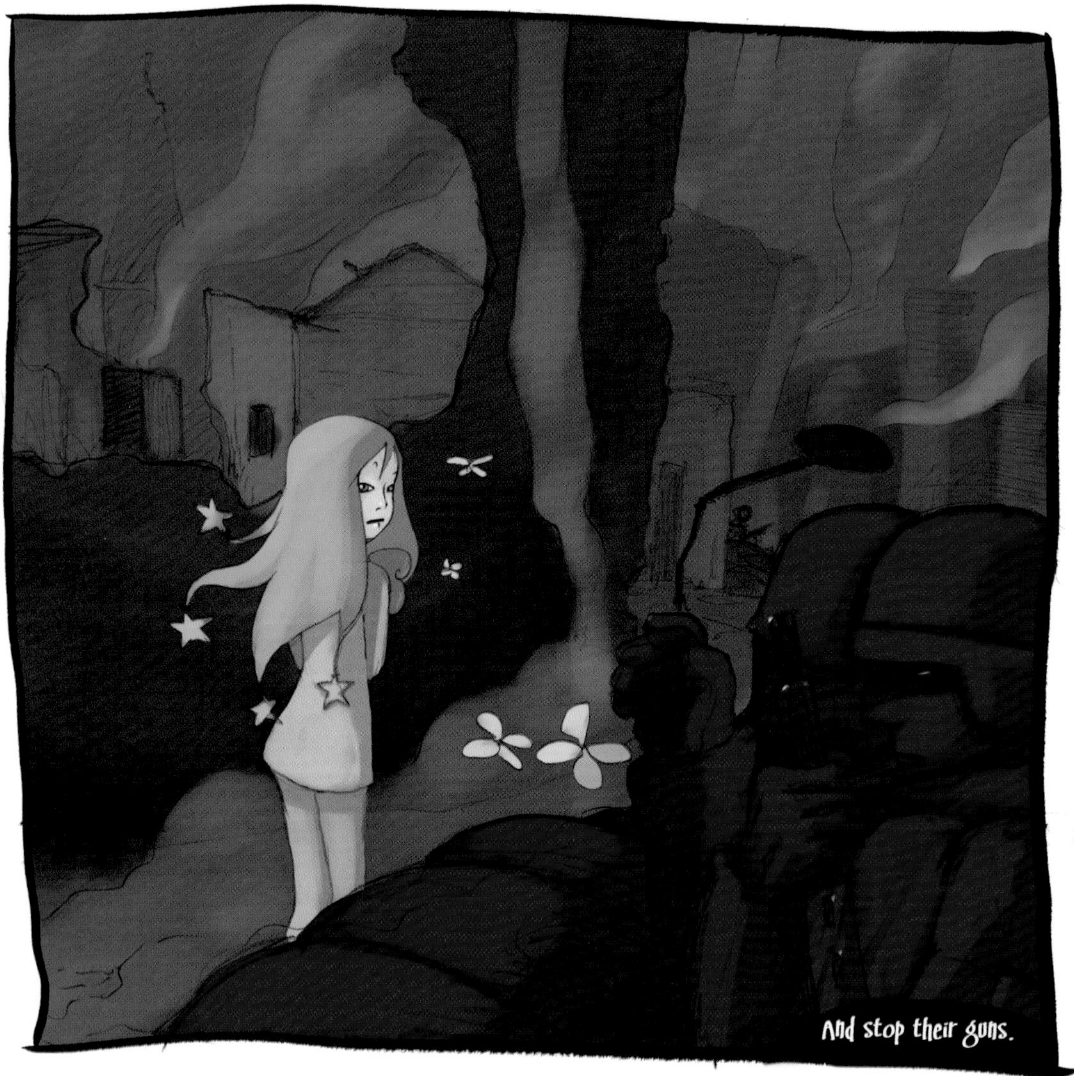
And stop their guns.

BÉISBOL

THE STORY OF FRANCISCO SANCHEZ

STORY AND ART
RICHARD POSE

COLORS
ISRAEL SANCHEZ

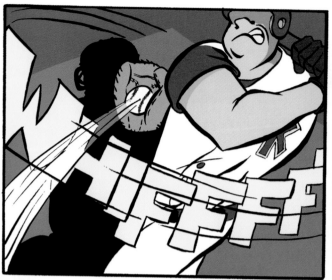

I CAN'T BELIEVE I'M ACTUALLY HERE...

...THE BIG LEAGUES

KING-FISH

I USED TO DREAM ABOUT THIS DAY...

BIG LEAGUE HITTERS...

POP UP.

BIG LEAGUE COACHES...

...NOW ALL I DREAM ABOUT ARE MY FRIENDS, MY FAMILY, AND MY COUNTRY...

BIG LEAGUE HOT DOGS...

AND...

BUM!

YOU SUCK!

MY GRAND BOOO HITS BETTER...

GOOD FER NOTHIN'.

BIG LEAGUE FANS!

...I WISH HE WERE HERE RIGHT NOW...

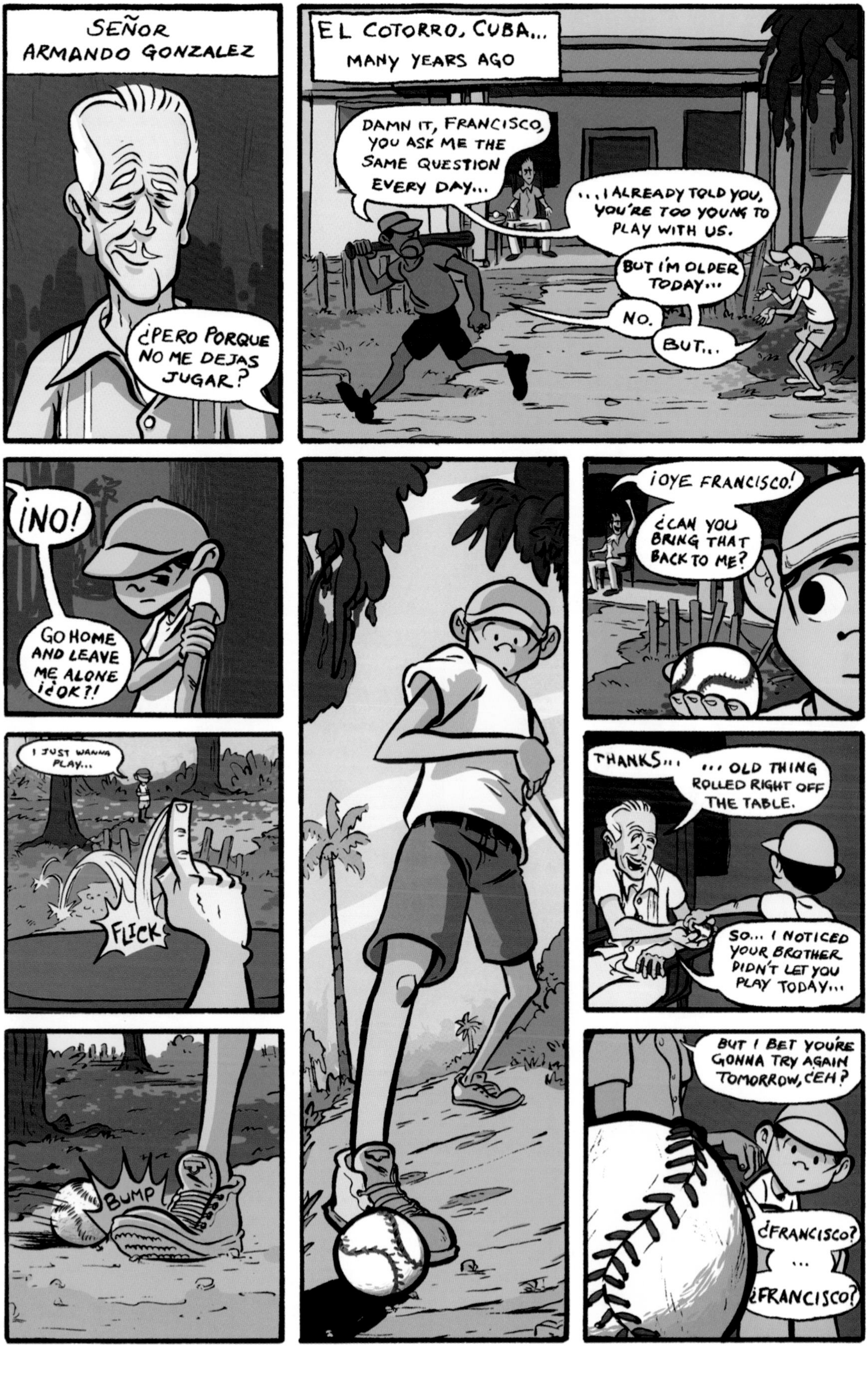
SEÑOR ARMANDO GONZALEZ
¿PERO PORQUE NO ME DEJAS JUGAR?
EL COTORRO, CUBA... MANY YEARS AGO
DAMN IT, FRANCISCO, YOU ASK ME THE SAME QUESTION EVERY DAY...
...I ALREADY TOLD YOU, YOU'RE TOO YOUNG TO PLAY WITH US.
BUT I'M OLDER TODAY...
NO.
BUT...
¡NO!
GO HOME AND LEAVE ME ALONE ¿OK?!
I JUST WANNA PLAY...
FLICK
BUMP
¡OYE FRANCISCO!
¿CAN YOU BRING THAT BACK TO ME?
THANKS...
...OLD THING ROLLED RIGHT OFF THE TABLE.
SO... I NOTICED YOUR BROTHER DIDN'T LET YOU PLAY TODAY...
BUT I BET YOU'RE GONNA TRY AGAIN TOMORROW, ¿EH?
¿FRANCISCO?
...
¿FRANCISCO?

414

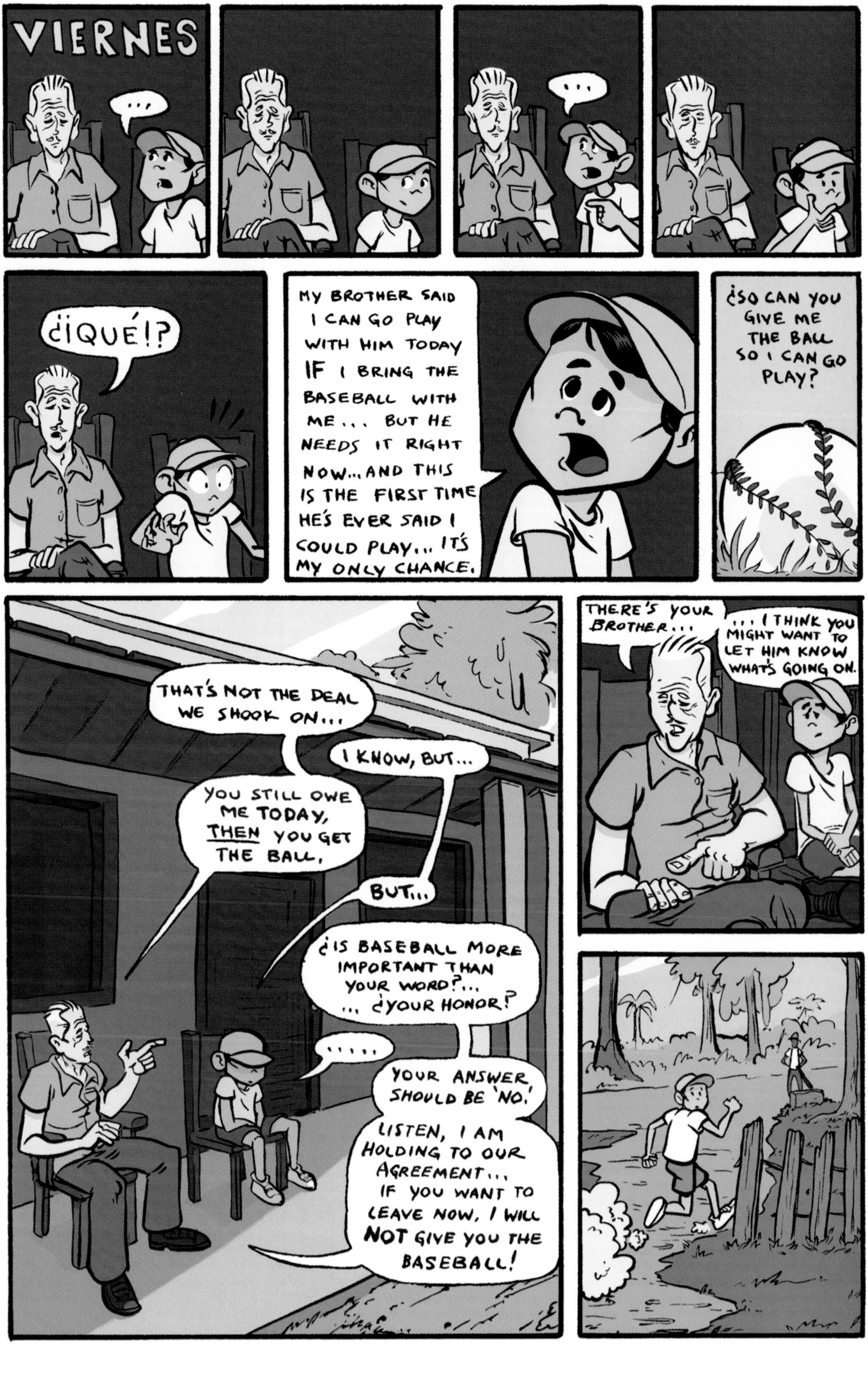
VIERNES
...
...
¿QUÉ!?
MY BROTHER SAID I CAN GO PLAY WITH HIM TODAY IF I BRING THE BASEBALL WITH ME... BUT HE NEEDS IT RIGHT NOW... AND THIS IS THE FIRST TIME HE'S EVER SAID I COULD PLAY... IT'S MY ONLY CHANCE.
¿SO CAN YOU GIVE ME THE BALL SO I CAN GO PLAY?
THAT'S NOT THE DEAL WE SHOOK ON...
I KNOW, BUT...
YOU STILL OWE ME TODAY, THEN YOU GET THE BALL.
BUT...
¿IS BASEBALL MORE IMPORTANT THAN YOUR WORD?... ...¿YOUR HONOR?
.....
YOUR ANSWER SHOULD BE 'NO.'
LISTEN, I AM HOLDING TO OUR AGREEMENT... IF YOU WANT TO LEAVE NOW, I WILL NOT GIVE YOU THE BASEBALL!
THERE'S YOUR BROTHER...
...I THINK YOU MIGHT WANT TO LET HIM KNOW WHAT'S GOING ON.

¿OH, SO YOU WANT TO SIT THERE ALL ANGRY AND POUTY?

¿YOU DON'T THINK THERE WILL BE ANOTHER DAY TO PLAY BASEBALL?

FINE THEN... I LIKE YOU BETTER WHEN YOU ARE QUIET ANYWAYS.

¡¡ALL I WANTED TO DO WAS PLAY!! ... ¡¡BUT YOU WOULDN'T LET ME!!

WITH THIS BASEBALL, YOU'LL HAVE THE FREEDOM TO DECIDE WHERE AND WHEN YOU WANT TO PLAY....

NOW, YOU CAN BE AS ANGRY AS YOU WANT, BUT I WILL KEEP MY WORD WITH YOU....

...IN A FEW HOURS I WILL HAND YOU THIS BASEBALL.

UNTIL THEN, WE CAN SIT IN SILENCE IF YOU WISH.

I'M SORRY SEÑOR GONZALEZ...

I DIDN'T MEAN TO YELL, BUT IT'S JUST. WELL, I LOVE BASEBALL SO MUCH.

YOU WOULDN'T UNDERSTAND, I MEAN ... YOU DON'T EVEN LIKE BASEBALL.

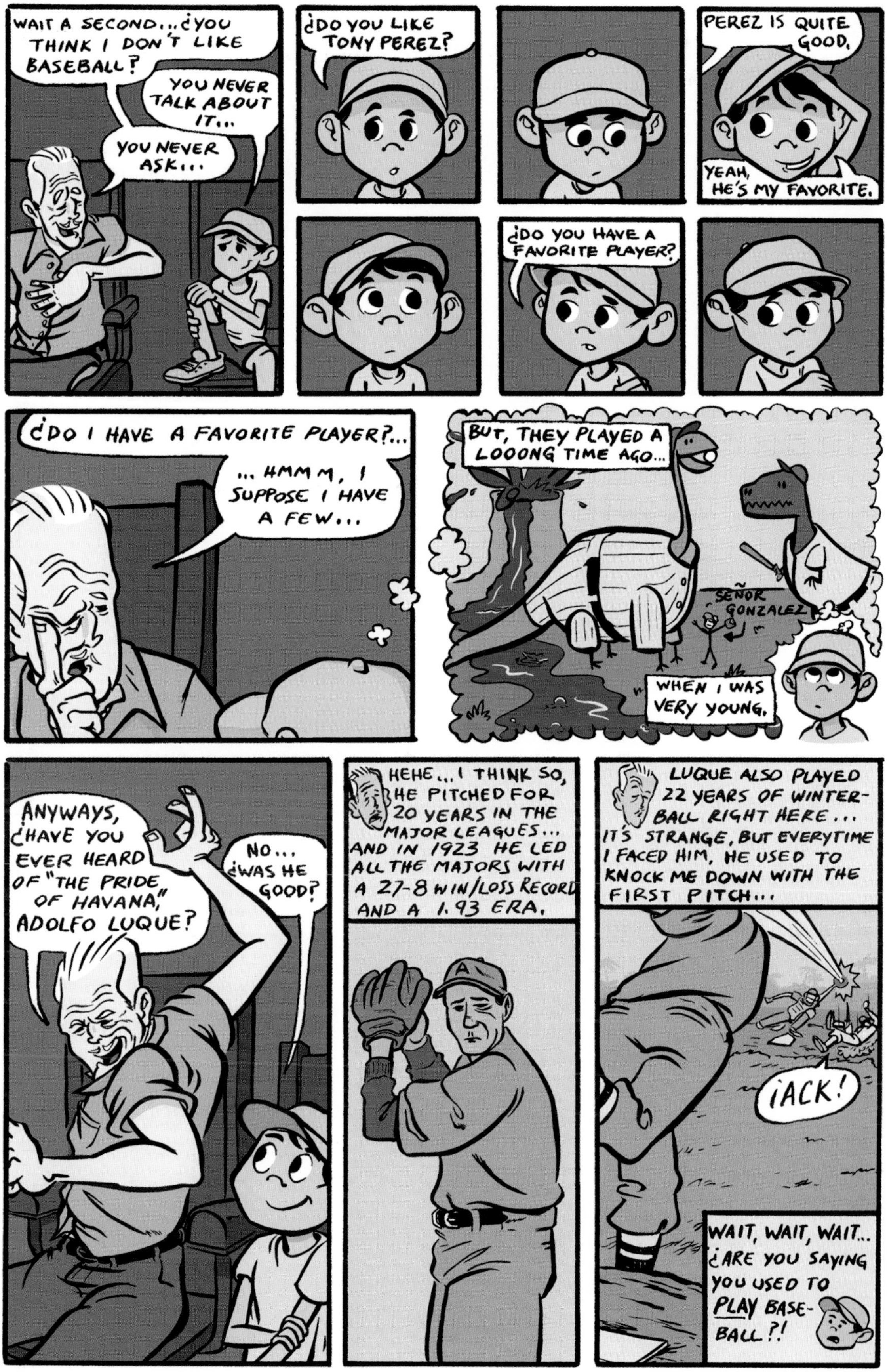
WAIT A SECOND... ¿YOU THINK I DON'T LIKE BASEBALL?
YOU NEVER TALK ABOUT IT...
YOU NEVER ASK...
¿DO YOU LIKE TONY PEREZ?
PEREZ IS QUITE GOOD.
YEAH, HE'S MY FAVORITE.
¿DO YOU HAVE A FAVORITE PLAYER?
¿DO I HAVE A FAVORITE PLAYER?...
... HMMM, I SUPPOSE I HAVE A FEW...
BUT, THEY PLAYED A LOOONG TIME AGO...
SEÑOR GONZALEZ
WHEN I WAS VERY YOUNG.
ANYWAYS, ¿HAVE YOU EVER HEARD OF "THE PRIDE OF HAVANA," ADOLFO LUQUE?
NO... ¿WAS HE GOOD?
HEHE... I THINK SO, HE PITCHED FOR 20 YEARS IN THE MAJOR LEAGUES... AND IN 1923 HE LED ALL THE MAJORS WITH A 27-8 WIN/LOSS RECORD AND A 1.93 ERA.
LUQUE ALSO PLAYED 22 YEARS OF WINTER-BALL RIGHT HERE... IT'S STRANGE, BUT EVERYTIME I FACED HIM, HE USED TO KNOCK ME DOWN WITH THE FIRST PITCH...
¡ACK!
WAIT, WAIT, WAIT... ¿ARE YOU SAYING YOU USED TO PLAY BASE-BALL?!

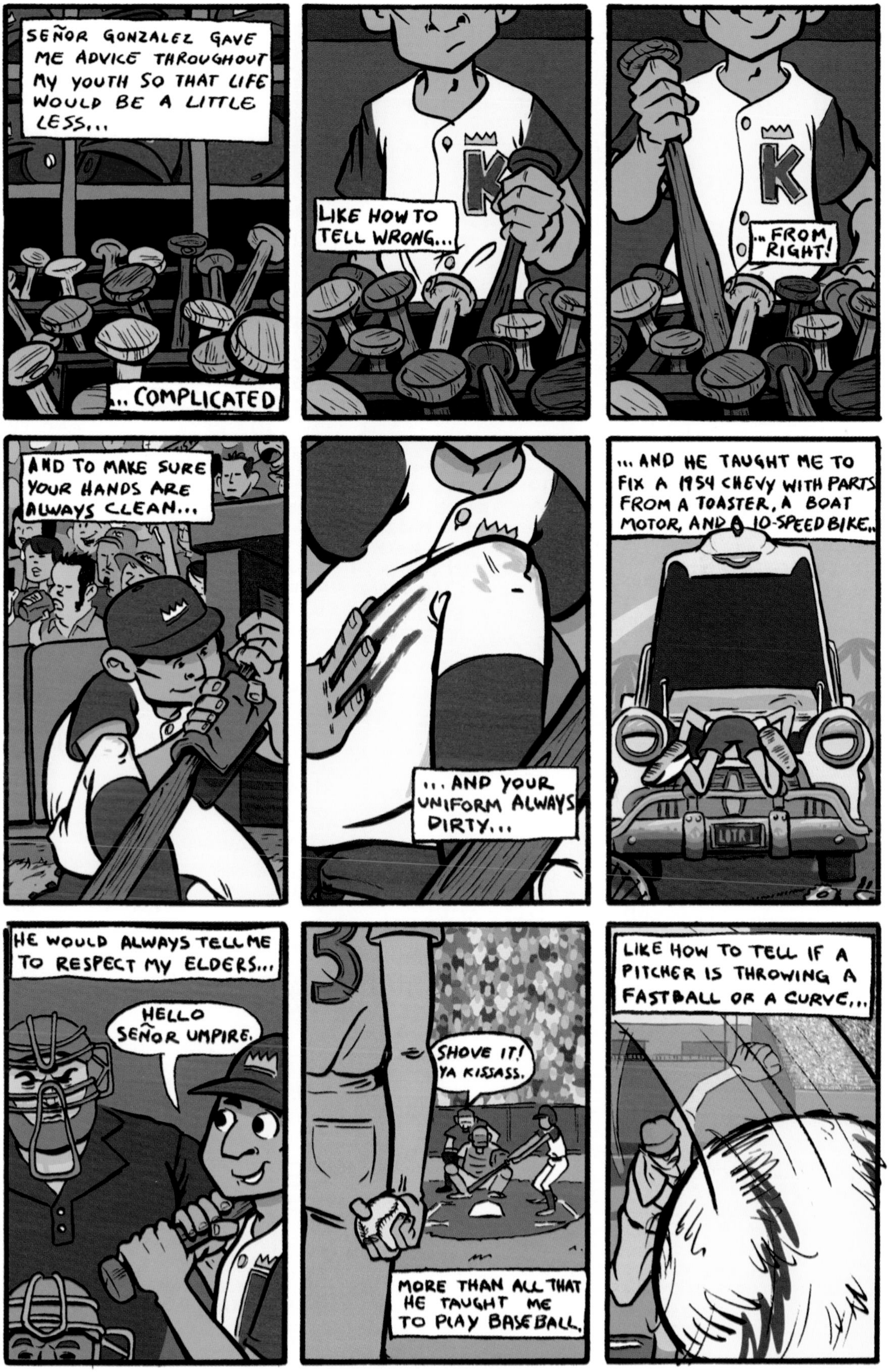
SEÑOR GONZALEZ GAVE ME ADVICE THROUGHOUT MY YOUTH SO THAT LIFE WOULD BE A LITTLE LESS...
...COMPLICATED
LIKE HOW TO TELL WRONG...
...FROM RIGHT!
AND TO MAKE SURE YOUR HANDS ARE ALWAYS CLEAN...
...AND YOUR UNIFORM ALWAYS DIRTY...
...AND HE TAUGHT ME TO FIX A 1954 CHEVY WITH PARTS FROM A TOASTER, A BOAT MOTOR, AND A 10-SPEED BIKE...
HE WOULD ALWAYS TELL ME TO RESPECT MY ELDERS...
HELLO SEÑOR UMPIRE.
SHOVE IT! YA KISSASS.
MORE THAN ALL THAT HE TAUGHT ME TO PLAY BASEBALL.
LIKE HOW TO TELL IF A PITCHER IS THROWING A FASTBALL OR A CURVE...

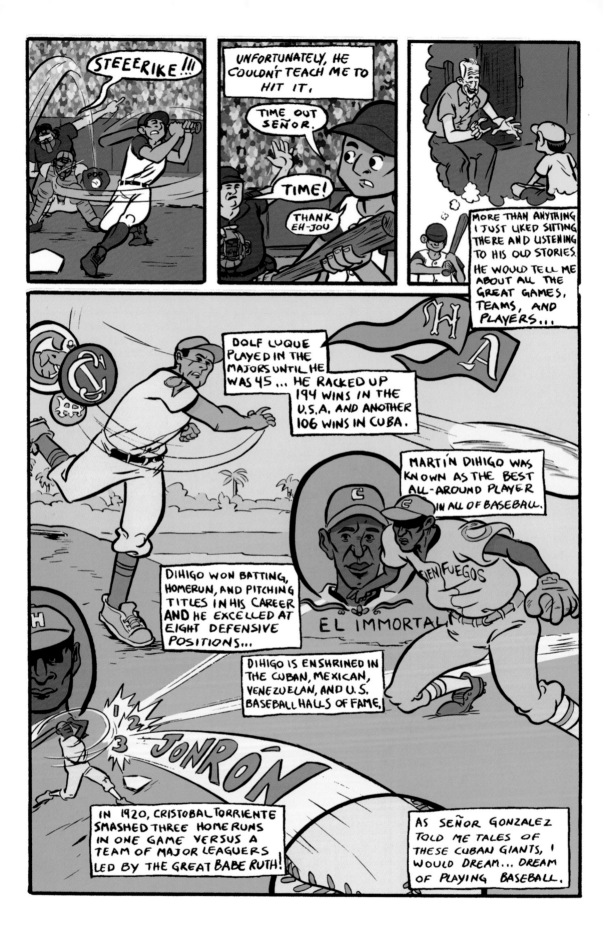

AT AGE 19, I FOUND MYSELF PLAYING FOR THE POPULAR IDUSTRIALES BÉISBOL CLUB.

F. SANCHEZ
2ᴰᴬB

I WAS ECSTATIC TO BE PLAYING PROFESSIONAL BASEBALL...

AND I DIDN'T WASTE MY OPPORTUNITY.

EACH NIGHT I WOULD RACE BACK AND GIVE SEÑOR GONZALEZ A RECAP OF THE GAME...

I COULDN'T BE HAPPIER... LIFE COULDN'T BE BETTER...

...¿OR COULD IT?

DON'T GET ME WRONG, I WAS VERY HAPPY IN CUBA, BUT...

...AS A BALLPLAYER, ONE ALWAYS WONDERS HOW HE WOULD PERFORM IN THE BIG LEAGUES...

... I SHOULD HAVE KEPT THAT THOUGHT TO MYSELF.

OYE CHEO... ¿YOU EVER WONDER ABOUT PLAYING IN THE UNITED STATES?

I HAD A DREAM LAST NIGHT, I WAS FACING ROGER CLEMENS...

NO COMPAÑERO...

I DON'T THINK OF THOSE THINGS...

EXCUSE ME FOR A MINUTE...

¿HELLO?

I HAVE SOME INFORMATION FOR YOU...

THE NEXT DAY, I FOUND MY LOCKER EMPTIED OUT...

I WAS KICKED OFF THE TEAM...

...AND BANNED FROM BASEBALL.

LIFE HAD SUDDENLY TURNED INTO A NIGHTMARE...

EVERYWHERE I WENT, GOVERNMENT AGENTS FOLLOWED ME...

FOR WEEKS I FOUND MYSELF UNABLE TO SLEEP... UNWILLING TO DREAM...

IT WAS RIDICULOUS, ALL I WANTED TO DO WAS PLAY BASEBALL, AND NOW THE GOVERNMENT WOULDN'T LET ME...

ONE RESTLESS NIGHT I FOUND MYSELF WANDERING THE STREETS OF HAVANA...

UNTIL....

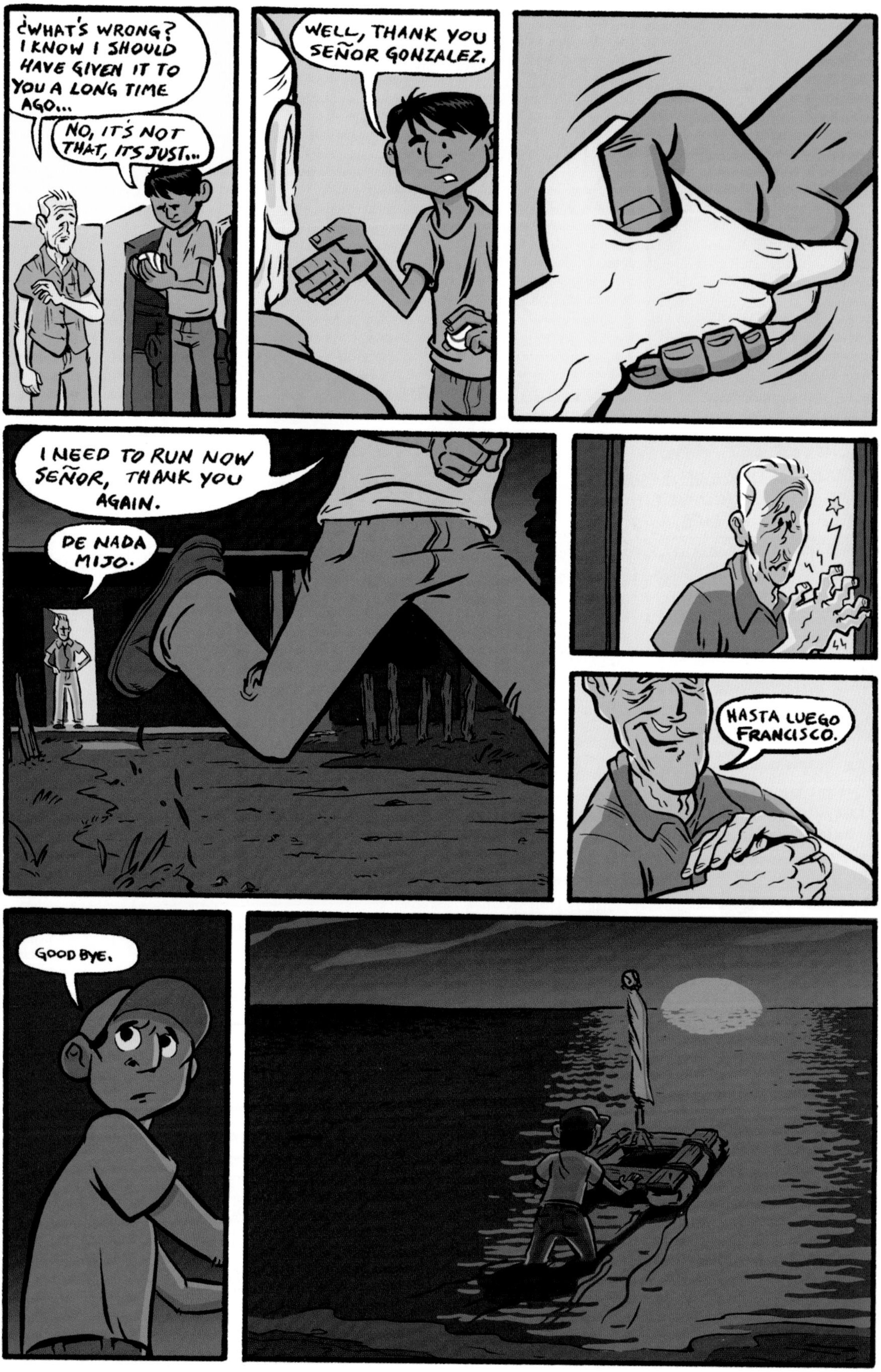
¿WHAT'S WRONG? I KNOW I SHOULD HAVE GIVEN IT TO YOU A LONG TIME AGO...
NO, IT'S NOT THAT, IT'S JUST...
WELL, THANK YOU SEÑOR GONZALEZ.
I NEED TO RUN NOW SEÑOR, THANK YOU AGAIN.
DE NADA MIJO.
HASTA LUEGO FRANCISCO.
GOOD BYE.

salmoning

by vera brosgol

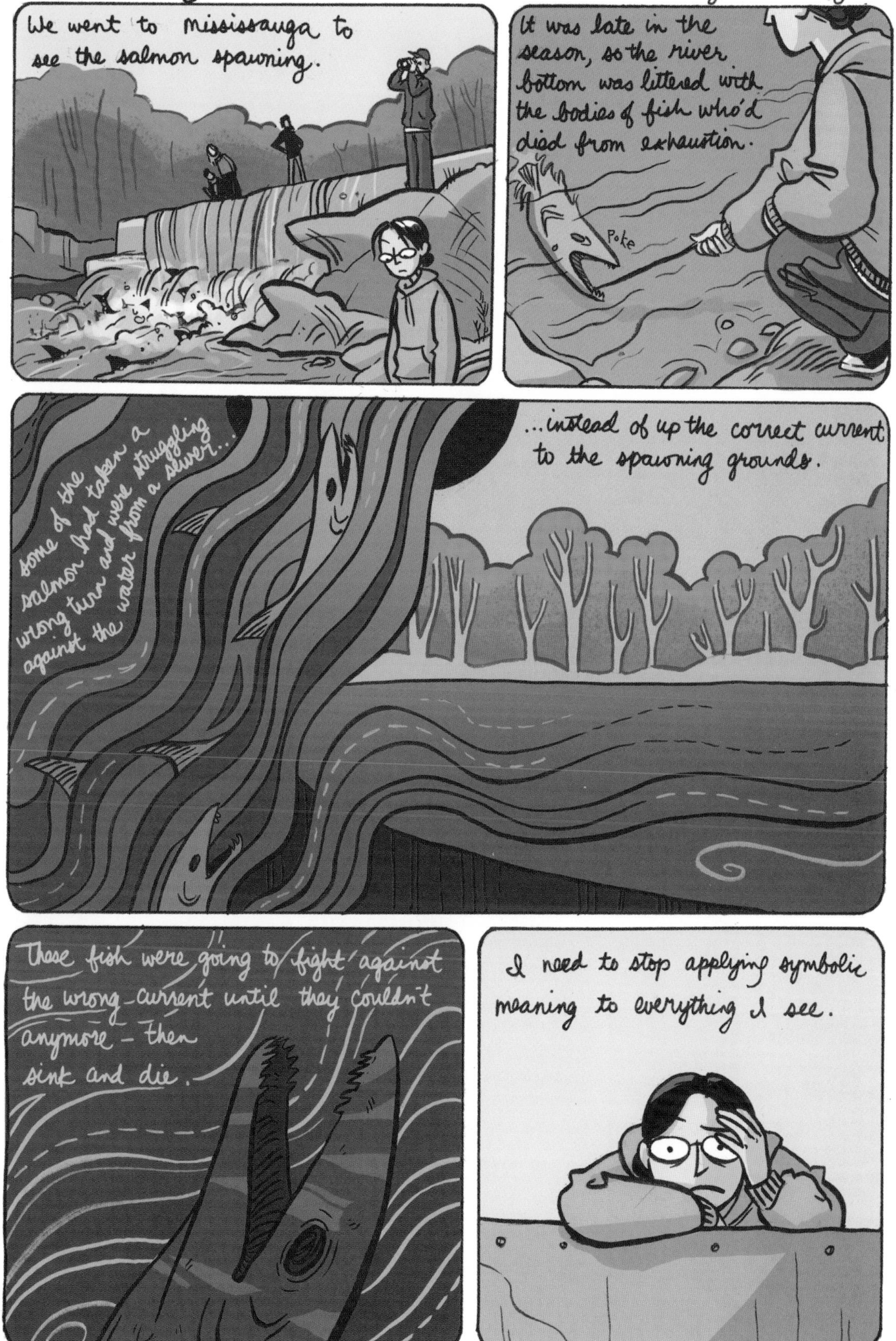

We went to mississauga to see the salmon spawning.
It was late in the season, so the river bottom was littered with the bodies of fish who'd died from exhaustion.
Poke
some of the salmon had taken a wrong turn and were struggling against the water from a sewer...
...instead of up the correct current to the spawning grounds.
These fish were going to fight against the wrong current until they couldn't anymore – then sink and die.
I need to stop applying symbolic meaning to everything I see.

FLIGHT: VOLUME TWO CONTRIBUTORS

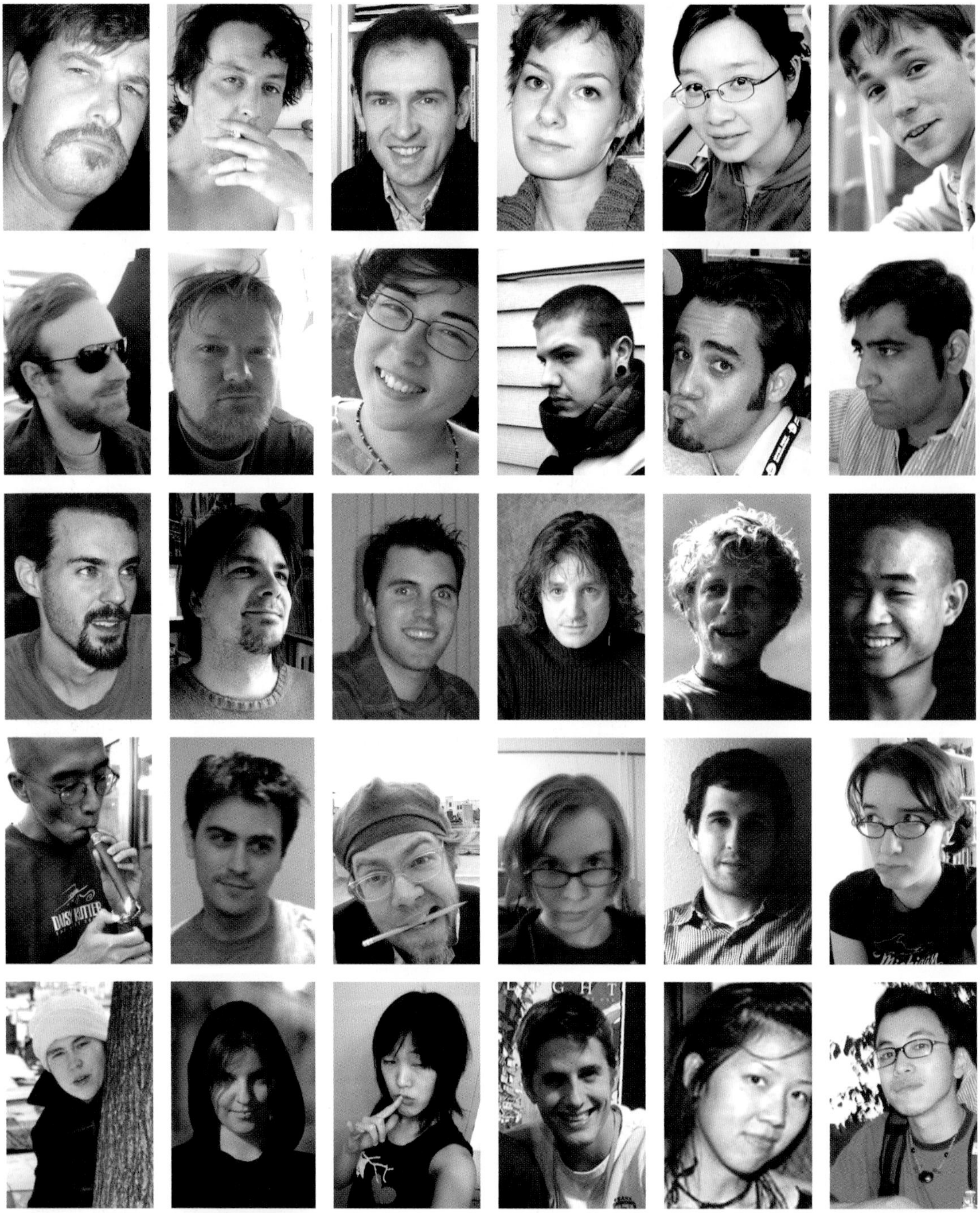
DAISY KUTTER

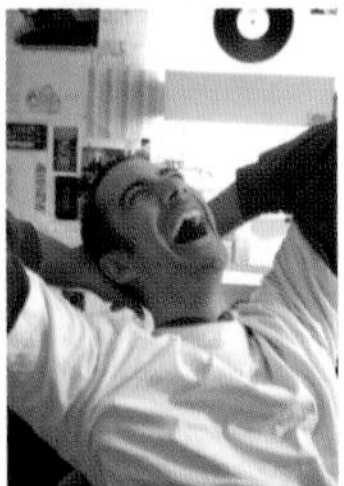

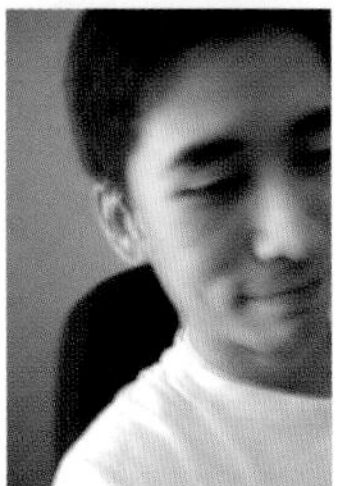

From left to right:

Top Row: Doug TenNapel, Rodolphe Guenoden, Herval, Hope Larson, Clio Chiang, Ben Hatke **2nd Row:** Michel Gagné, Doug Holgate, Amy Kim Ganter, Matthew Woodson, Richard Pose, Neil Babra **3rd Row:** Phil Craven, Bannister, Rad Sechrist, Jeff Smith, Giuseppe Ferrario, Sonny Liew **4th Row:** Kean Soo, Don Hertzfeldt, Ryan Sias, Becky Cloonan, Jake Parker, Vera Brosgol **5th Row:** Johane Matte, Kness, Jen Wang, Chris Appelhans, Catia Chien, Khang Le **Bottom Row:** Justin Ridge, Kazu Kibuishi, Joana Carneiro

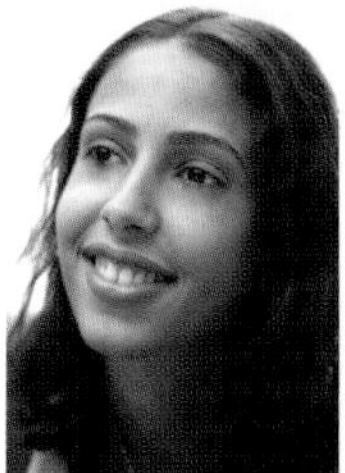

Born in 1980, **Amy Kim Ganter** has worked in the past as a freelance animator and illustrator. She is now working on a graphic novel with Tokyopop called *Sorcerers and Secretaries* and is also the creator of the epic fantasy comic *Reman Mythology,* currently being serialized on the Web. She enjoys mint green tea and staring into space. www.felaxx.com

Bannister was born in 1973 and lives as an illustrator/cartoonist/Flash animator near the French Alps with his girlfriend. His first book, *Félicité Bonaventure,* was published in France in 2004. He is currently working on various projects both in France and overseas, and hopes his drawings will one day help him to buy a house. www.bannister.fr

At the time of this writing, **Becky Cloonan** is perhaps best known for her artwork on *Demo.* In a few years, who really knows what people will remember her for? "More comics," she hopes. www.estrigious.com/becky/

Ben Hatke is a grizzled, crotchety chicken farmer living in Virginia with his charming wife and two children. He is a freelance illustrator and has worked on various comics and children's books, including the recent *Angel in the Waters.* www.househatke.com www.zitaspacegirl.com

Catia Chien is a concept artist, children's book illustrator, and gallery artist. She loves good stories and also finds time to doodle T-shirt designs, create vintage boxes, and occasionally sews one-of-a-kind scary plush toys for some of her not so lucky friends. www.catiachien.com

Chris Appelhans (cover illustration) currently works as a visual development artist on the film *Monster House* at Sony Imageworks. He is also the creator of the comic strip *Frank and Frank.* www.froghatstudios.com

Clio Chiang is on the way to finishing her time in the Capilano College Animation program and hopes to enter the work force soon afterward. She is currently obsessed with turning animals into construction vehicles and making goldfish bounce. www.cliochiang.com

Don Hertzfeldt is an Academy Award nominee whose animated films include *The Meaning of Life, Rejected, Billy's Balloon, Lily and Jim, Genre,* and *Ah, L'Amour.* www.bitterfilms.com

Doug Holgate is a freelance illustrator and cartoonist who is currently working on a series of children's books, as well as *Heidi Hyperwarp* for Image Comics, a graphic novel due out later in 2005. He lives in Melbourne, Australia and his palatial grounds are open to the public, 9–5 Monday through Friday. www.f1-comics.com

Doug TenNapel's comic work includes *GEAR, Creature Tech, Tommysaurus Rex,* and *Earthboy Jacobus.* He based "Solomon Fix" on the fancy Englishmen he worked with while creating *Earthworm Jim.* He lives in Glendale with his tolerant wife, pert daughter, noble son, and soon-to-arrive baby. www.tennapel.com

Giuseppe Ferrario lives in Milano, Italy, and has worked as a freelance illustrator and cartoonist for the past fourteen years, working with such characters as Bugs Bunny, Fred Flintstone, Geronimo Stilton, Mickey Mouse, and Scooby Doo. In 2002, he established Studio EFFIGIE, a cartoon and graphics studio, and is currently developing a TV series with a French broadcaster. www.giuseppeferrario.com

Born in 1966 in Rouen, France, and entirely self-taught, **Herval** has worked in the past for advertising agencies as a graphic designer and artistic director. Currently a freelance artist and illustrator, his published work includes a collection of short stories, BD Clip; an all-ages graphic novel, *Captain Pirate;* and a collection of pin-ups called Drôles de Pin-up. mapage.noos.fr/herval/

Hope Larson graduated from the School of the Art Institute of Chicago in 2004 and promptly immigrated to Canada, where she now lives with her husband and two cats. One half of the Secret Friend Society, she is currently hard at work finishing up her first graphic novel, *Salamander Dream.* www.hopelarson.com www.secretfriendsociety.com

Jake Parker dropped out of school to pursue a career in the animation industry, and he now works as an art director for Reel FX Creative Studios. He lives in Dallas with his wife, Alison, and two children, Tate and Lucy. His free time is spent working on projects like *Flight.* www.agent44.com

Jeff Smith is the author of the independent epic comic series *Bone.* Jeff currently resides in Columbus, Ohio, with his wife and business partner, Vijaya. Upcoming projects include *Captain Marvel: Monster Society of Evil* for DC Comics and *BIG, BIG* for Cartoon Books. www.boneville.com

Jen Wang celebrates her twenty-first birthday on the eve of this book's publication. She resides in San Francisco where she studies political and social science by day and draws cartoons by night. She likes big cities, soy, biological mishaps, and stars. www.jenwang.net

Joana Carneiro is twenty-five years old and was born and raised in Rio de Janeiro, Brazil. She has studied graphic design and currently works as a concept artist and illustrator for SeagullsFly. Joana is also developing a children's book called *Perninhas de Plantas,* to be released in 2005. www.joanacarneiro.com

Johane Matte works in animation and video games, will gladly organize your wine and cheese parties, and will sometimes manage to continue drawing her comic *Horus.* www.qosmiq.com/rufftoon/

Justin Ridge was born in 1981, and after graduating from CSU Fullerton, he has worked at Nickelodeon Studios as a character designer on *Fatherhood* and is currently an assistant director for *Avatar: The Last Airbender.* He is also working on a top-secret film noir graphic novel and posts a lot of silly drawings on his website. www.justinridge.com

Kazu Kibuishi is the editor and art director of *Flight: Volume Two*. He recently completed his first graphic novel, *Daisy Kutter: The Last Train,* and is currently at work on his next book, which will be serialized in the pages of *Flight.* www.boltcity.com

Kean Soo has a degree in electrical engineering and couldn't be happier that he is wasting his education by drawing comics. He continues to document his life with his autobiographical *Exit Music* comics, and he is also the other half of the Secret Friend Society, where his first full-length comic *Jellaby* is being serialized on the web. www.keaner.net
www.secretfriendsociety.com

Khang Le is currently working as a freelance concept artist for video games and films. When he's not painting fantasy worlds or drawing his *Flight* comic, he is most likely eating a steaming bowl of noodles. www.khangle.net

Kness is a twenty-five-year-old self-taught freelance illustrator and colorist living in Paris, France. She secretly wants to be a gecko, but then that would mean she wouldn't be drawing anymore. www.kness.net

Matthew Woodson is a freelance illustator who lives in Chicago with his girlfriend and a menagerie of baneful animals. He is currently working on a project for Top Shelf and will eventually compile his own work for a short story collection, post-graduation from the School of the Art Intistute of Chicago, in early summer 2005.

Michel Gagné was born in Québec, Canada, and has had a highly successful career drawing characters and special effects for animated and live-action feature films such as *The Iron Giant* and *Osmosis Jones*. His independent short film, *Prelude to Eden,* is a favorite among animation students and teachers, and has played in festivals throughout the world. Michel and his wife created Gagné International Press in 1998, and he has been writing, illustrating, and publishing books and comics ever since. www.gagneint.com

Neil Babra, a native son of Pennsylvania, is reasonably well educated and hygienic, except for an occasional hermit beard. www.neilcomics.com

Phil Craven is twenty-seven and hails from the state of Georgia, where he went to grad school at the Savannah College of Art and Design. These days, Phil draws story-boards for DreamWorks Animation. He maintains a keen interest in soccer and cereal. www.bluepillow.net

Rad Sechrist is a twenty-four-year-old freelance illustrator living in LA with his wife, Mandy. Along with working on *Flight,* Rad also does a webcomic called *Beneath the Leaves* on his website. www.radsechrist.com

Richard Pose graduated from CSU Fullerton and is one of the cocreators of the self-published comic *Smoke.* He is twenty-six and loves baseball—especially his Los Angeles Angels. www.richardpose.com

Rodolphe Guenoden studied animation at the Gobelins in Paris, and has worked for fifteen years in the animation industry as a 2D animator and storyboard artist on such films as *Fievel Goes West, Prince of Egypt, Road to El Dorado,* and *Sinbad.* Rodolphe lives in Los Angeles with his wife, their kids, and a cat. He loves drawing women and has always wanted to draw comics. www.rodguen.com

Ryan Sias draws storyboards by day and comics by night. He has worked on the Oscar-winning documentary *Bowling for Columbine* and Twentieth Century–Fox's *Robots.* Ryan is currently working on various children's books and his all-ages graphic novel, *Silent Kimbly.* www.ryansias.com / www.silentkimbly.com

Sonny Liew has worked on computer games and drawn comics like the Xeric-winning *Malinky Robot* and DC Vertigo's *My Faith in Frankie.* He lives in Singapore, where he sleeps with the fishes. www.sonnyliew.com

Vera Brosgol is in her final year of animation at Sheridan College and has worked as an artist on Oni's *Hopeless Savages.* She never had a piece of fresh fruit until she was twenty, and it was a lime. She still takes the existence of peaches on hearsay. www.verabee.com

----

Israel Sanchez (colorist, "Beisbol") studied art at Cal State Fullerton. He now lives in La Habra, California, where he trains for regional foosball competitions. www.israelsanchez.com

Paulo Visgueiro (colorist, "La Sonadora") is a designer and illustrator, currently working as an art director in his hometown of Rio de Janeiro, Brazil. www.visgueiro.com

Steve Hamaker (colorist, "Sirius and Betelgeuse") was a toy designer when he met Jeff Smith in 1998. After working on the Bone toys with Cartoon Books, Steve is currently coloring the 1,300 pages of *Bone* for Scholastic, in addition to an upcoming *Shazam* miniseries for DC comics. He self-published a comic book called *Fish N Chips,* and loves his job!

Vasilis Lolos (cowriter, "Heads Up") was born in 1981 in Athens, Greece. After switching schools several times, he solemnly devoted his life to comics. Vasilis's graphic novel, *Generator,* was published in 2004, and he is currently working on his first international book.

Aris (writer, "Impossible"), born in Toulouse, entered the comics field through several art studios. With Garrigue he created Le Studio, an association that published the annual magazine *Azimuts.* At the Salon de Colomiers, Aris met Christophe Gibelin, with whom he started the series "Le Vieux Ferrand" in 2000.